THE NEW WEBSTER'S VEST POCKET DICTIONARY

THE NEW WEBSTER'S DICTIONARY

Editors

Donald O. Bolander, M.A., Litt.D.
Valerie Law Stodden, M.Ed.

LEXICON PUBLICATIONS, INC.

ABBREVIATIONS USED IN THIS DICTIONARY

a. adjective
abbr. abbreviation
adv. adverb
art. article
aux. auxiliary
cap. capital
char. characterized
coll. colloquial
compar. comparative
conj. conjunction
constr. construction
def. definite
esp. especially
etc. et cetera
fig. figurative, figuratively
indef. indefinite
inf. informally
int. interrogative
interj. interjection
milit. military
mus. music
myth. mythology
n. noun
part. participle
photog. photography
pl. plural
pp. past participle
pt. past tense
poss. possessive case
prep. preposition
pron. pronoun
rel. religious

sing. singular
sl. slang
superl. superlative
sym. symbol
U.S. United States
usu. usually
v. verb
v.i. verb intransitive
v.t. verb transitive

A

a, *indef. art.* one; each.

aard·vark, *n.* burrowing African mammal that eats ants.

A·B., Bachelor of Arts.

a·back, *adv.* backward. **taken aback,** suddenly disconcerted.

ab·a·cus, *n. pl.,* **ab·a·cus·es, ab·a·ci.** frame with beads on wires used for calculating.

a·ban·don, *v.* give up completely; forsake; surrender; desert. *n.* **a·ban·don·er,** *n.* **a·ban·don·ment,** *n.*

a·base, *v.* **a·based, a·bas·ing.** humiliate; humble. **a·base·ment,** *n.*

a·bash, *v.* confuse; make embarrassed. **a·bash·ment,** *n.*

a·bate, *v.* **a·bat·ed, a·bat·ing.** lessen; diminish. **a·bate·ment,** *n.*

ab·bey, *n. pl.,* **ab·beys.** monastery or convent. **ab·bess,** *n. fem.* **ab·bot,** *n. mas.*

ab·bre·vi·a·tion, *n.* shortened form. **ab·bre·vi·ate,** *v.* shorten.

ab·di·cate, *v.* **-cat·ed, -cat·ing.** renounce or give up. **ab·di·ca·tion,** *n.*

ab·do·men, *n.* part of the body between the thorax and pelvis. **ab·dom·i·nal,** *a.*

ab·duct, *v.* kidnap. **ab·duc·tion,** *n.* **ab·duc·tor,** *n.*

ab·er·ra·tion, *n.* deviation from normal. **ab·er·rant,** *a.*

a·bet, *v.* **a·bet·ted, a·bet·ting. a·bet·tor,** *n.* incite or favor.

a·bey·ance, *n.* temporary inactivity.

ab·hor, *v.* **ab·horred, ab·hor·ring.** detest. **ab·hor·rence,** *n.* **ab·hor·rer,** *n.* **ab·hor·rent,** *a.*

a·bide, *v.i.,* **a·bode** or **a·bid·ed, a·bid·ing.** dwell; reside. *vt.* await; remain. **a·bid·ance,** *n.*

a·bil·i·ty, *n. pl.,* **-ties.** competence; capability.

ab·ject, *a.* humiliating; disheartening. **ab·jec·tion,** *n.* **ab·ject·ly,** *adv.*

ab·jure, *v.* **ab·jured, ab·jur·ing.** renounce or repudiate; retract. **ab·jur·ra·tion,** *n.* **ab·jur·er,** *n.*

a·ble, *a.* competent; qualified; skilled; talented. **a·bly,** *adv.*

ab·ne·gate, *v.* **-gat·ed, -gat·ing.** deny; renounce; reject.

ab·nor·mal, *a.* not normal; unnatural. **ab·nor·mal·ly,** *adv.* **ab·nor·mal·i·ty,** *n. pl.,* **-ties.**

a·board, *adv., prep.* on board.

a·bode, *n.* home; residence.

a·bol·ish, *v.* do away with; void. **a·bol·ish·a·ble,** *a.* **a·bol·ish·er,** *n.* **a·bol·ish·ment,** *n.* **ab·o·li·tion,** *n.* **ab·o·li·tion·ist,** *n.*

A-bomb, *n.* atomic bomb.

a·bom·i·nate, *v.,* **-nat·ed, -nat·ing.** abhor. **a·bom·i·na·tion,** *n.*

ab·o·rig·ine, *n.* earliest inhabitants of a region.

a·bor·tion, *n.* spontaneous or induced termination of pregnancy.

a·bound, *v.* to be in great plenty; to be very prevalent.

a·bout, *prep.* in regard to; concerning; *adv.* approximately.

a·bove, *prep.* over; higher than. *adv.* overhead. *a.* preceding.

a·brade, *v.,* **a·brad·ed, a·brad·ing.** rub off or wear down by friction; irritate. **a·bra·sive,** *a., n.* **a·bra·sion,** *n.*

a·breast, *adv., a.* side by side.

a·bridge, *v.,* **a·bridged, a·bridg·ing.** shorten; condense; diminish. **a·bridg·a·ble,** *a.* **a·bridg·ment,** *n.*

a·broad, *adv.* in a foreign country; out of doors.

ab·ro·gate, *v.,* **-gat·ed, -gat·ing.** repeal; cancel; annul.

ab·rupt, *a.* sudden; brusque; disconnected; steep; precipitous.

ab·scess, *n.* collection of pus in body tissue. **ab·scessed,** *a.*

ab·scond, *v.* depart in a secret manner; flee from the law.

ab·sent, *a.* not present; not existing; away. **ab·sence,** *n.*

ab·so·lute, *a.* perfect; pure; complete; unrestricted; ultimate. **ab·so·lute·ly,** *adv.* **ab·so·lut·ism,** *n.*

ab·solve, *v.,* **ab·solved, ab·solv·ing.** acquit; forgive; remit; set free. **ab·solv·a·ble,** *a.* **ab·solv·er,** *n.* **ab·so·lu·tion,** *n.*

ab·sorb, *v.* suck up; to take in. **ab·sorb·en·cy,** *n.* **ab·sorb·ent,** *a.* **ab·sorp·tion,** *n.*

ab·stain, *v.* refrain from doing voluntarily. **ab·sten·tion,** *n.* **ab·sti·nence,** *n.* **ab·sti·nent,** *a.*

ab·stract, *v.* summarize. *a.* not concrete; theoretical. *n.* summary. **ab·strac·tion,** *n.*

ab·struce, *a.* difficult to understand.

ab·surd, *a.* ridiculous; foolish. **ab·surd·i·ty,** *n. pl.,* **-ties.**

a·bun·dance, *n.* great quantity.

a·bun·dant, *a.* plentiful.

a·buse, *v.,* **a·bused, a·bus·ing.** misuse; use wrongly. *n.* misuse; insulting language. **a·bu·sive,** *a.*

a·but, *v.,* **a·but·ted, a·but·ting.** to border on; be adjacent to.

a·byss, *n.* bottomless pit.

ac·a·dem·ic, *a.* pertaining to schools; theoretical; scholastic. **ac·a·dem·i·cal·ly,** *adv.*

a·cad·e·my, *n. pl.,* **-mies.** private or military school; association of scholars, artists, etc.

ac·cede, *v.,* **ac·ced·ed, ac·ced·ing.** agree; assent; attain.

ac·cel·er·ate, *v.,* **-at·ed, -at·ing.** increase speed; go faster. **-er·a·tion,** *n.* **-er·a·tor,** *n.*

ac·cent, *n.* stress; stress mark; distinctive pronunciation. *v.* emphasize; accentuate.

ac·cen·tu·ate, *v.,* **-at·ed, -at·ing.** mark or pronounce with an accent; emphasize. **-a·tion,** *n.*

ac·cept, *v.* to take or receive; assent or agree to; accept. **ac·cept·ance,** *n.* **ac·cept·a·ble,** *a.*

ac·cer·bate, *v.,* **-bated, -bat·ing.** to make sour or bitter; to exasperate. **ac·cer·bi·ty,** *n., pl.* **-ties.**

ac·cess, *n.* way of approach.

ac·ces·si·ble, *a.* easy of access. **-si·bil·i·ty,** *n.*

ac·ces·so·ry, *a.* subordinate part; added part. *n. pl.,* **-ries.** one who aids an unlawful act; accompaniment.

ac·ci·dent, *n.* chance; unfortunate happening; unexpected happening. **ac·ci·den·tal,** *a.*

ac·claim, *v.* salute with words; applaud; *n.* approval.

ac·cla·ma·tion, *n.* loud applause; oral vote showing approval.

ac·cli·mate, *v.,* **-mat·ed, -mat·ing.** adapt to a new place or situation. **ac·cli·ma·tion,** *n.*

ac·co·lade, *n.* an honor; praise.

ac·com·mo·date, *v.t.,* **-dat·ed, -dat·ing.** adapt; adjust; oblige; make room for. *v.i.* agree, **ac·com·mo·da·tion,** *n.*

ac·com·pa·ny, *v.,* **-nied, -ny·ing.** to go with; play a musical part with. **ac·com·pa·ni·ment,** *n.* **ac·com·pa·nist,** *n.*

ac·com·plice, *n.* one who helps in a crime.

ac·com·plish, *v.* bring to pass; finish; complete; **-plish·ment,** *n.*

ac·cord, *n.* agreement; harmony, *v.t.* allow; agree, *v.i.* be in harmony. **-cor·dance,** *n.* **-cord·ing,** *a.*

ac·cost *v.* to boldly approach.

ac·count, *n.* narrative of events; explanatory statement; business record or statement. *v.i.* to furnish explanations.

ac·count·a·ble, *a.* responsible.

ac·cre·tion, *n.* growth in size.

ac·crue, *v.* result or addition by growth. **ac·cru·al,** *n.*

ac·cu·mu·late, *v.* **-lat·ed, -lat·ing.** gather or heap up; collect. **ac·cum·u·la·tion,** *n.*

ac·cu·ra·cy, *n.* correctness.

ac·cu·rate, *a.* correct; exact. **-rate·ly,** *adv.* **-rate·ness,** *n.*

ac·cuse, *v.,* **ac·cused, ac·cus·ing.** to charge or blame. **ac·cu·sa·tion,** *n.* **ac·cus·ing·ly,** *adv.*

ac·cus·tom, *v.* to familiarize by use or custom; habituate.

a·ce·tic, *a.* pertaining to vinegar.

ace·tone, *n.* volatile, liquid.

a·cet·y·lene, *n.* colorless gas used in metal welding and cutting.

ache, *n.* pain. *v.,* **ached, ach·ing.** suffer from pain; have pain.

a·chieve, *v.,* **a·chieved, a·chiev·ing.** succeed; accomplish.

ac·id, *a.* sour. *n.* compound that combines with a base to form salts. **a·cid·i·ty,** *n. sl.* LSD.

ac·knowl·edge, *v.,* **-edged, -edg·ing.** admit to; recognize; thank. **ac·knowl·edg·ment,** *n.*

ac·me, *n.* highest point.

ac·ne, *n.* pimples; blackheads.

ac·o·lyte, *n.* altar boy; attendant.

a·cous·tics, *n.* science of sound.

ac·quaint, *v.* to make familiar.

ac·quaint·ance, *n.* person known slightly.

ac·qui·esce, *v.* **-esced, -esc·ing.** to consent without protest. **ac·qui·es·cent,** *a.*

ac·quire, *v.* **ac·quired, ac·quir·ing.** to get, gain or secure. **ac·qui·si·tion,** *n.* **ac·quis·i·tive,** *a.*

ac·quit, *v.* **ac·quit·ted, ac·quit·ting.** declare not guilty; release from obligation. **ac·quit·tal,** *n.*

a·cre, *n.* unit of land measure, 43,560 sq. ft. **a·cre·age,** *n.*

ac·rid, *a.* sharp; bitter; irritating. **a·crid·i·ty,** *n.* **ac·ri·mo·ny,** *n.* **ac·ri·mo·ni·ous,** *a.*

ac·ro·bat, *n.* skilled performer on a trapeze, etc. **ac·ro·bat·ic,** *a.* **-bat·ics,** *n. pl.*

ac·ro·pho·bi·a, *n.* fear of high places.

a·cross, *prep.* from side to side: on the other side of.

act, *v.* a thing done; do; behave; to perform; pretend. *n.* deed; a law. **act·ing,** *a.*

ac·tion, *n.* doing something; deed; battle; lawsuit; behavior.

ac·ti·vate, *v.,* **-vat·ed, -vat·ing.** to make active; to start. **ac·ti·va·tion,** *n.* **ac·ti·va·tor,** *n.*

ac·tive, *a.* functioning; lively; busy. **ac·tive·ly,** *adv.* **ac·tive·ness,** *n.* **ac·tiv·i·ty,** *n.* .

ac·tiv·ism, *n.* act or policy of taking positive direct action. **ac·tiv·ist**, *n.* zealous worker.

ac·tu·al, *a.* real; present; existing, **ac·tu·al·ly**, *adv.*

ac·tu·ar·y, *n. pl.*, **-ies.** person who figures insurance rates, risks.

ac·tu·ate, *v.*, **-ated**, **-ating.** put into action. . **ac·tu·a·tion**, *n.*

a·cu·i·ty, *n.* acuteness.

a·cu·men, *n.* keen insight.

a·cute, *a.* keen; crucial; sharp; intense. **a·cute·ly**, *adv.* **a·cute·ness**, *n.*

A·D., in the year of the Lord.

ad·age, *n.* proverb.

ad·a·mant, *a.* unyielding; firm. **ad·a·mant·ly**, *adv.*

a·dapt, *v.* make fit; adjust. **a·dap·tive**, *a.* **ad·ap·ta·tion**, *n.*

add, *v.* join; combine; find the sum of. **add·a·ble, add·i·ble**, *a.*

ad·den·dum, *n. pl.*, things added; appendix.

ad·dict, *v.* habituate. *n.* a slave to a practice or habit. **ad·dic·tion**, *n.* **ad·dic·ted**, *a.*

ad·di·tion, *n.* process of adding; increase. **ad·di·tion·al**, *a.* **ad·di·tion·al·ly**, *adv.*

ad·di·tive, *a.* thing added.

ad·dress, *v.* speak to; *n.* speech; person's name and location.

ad·e·noid, *n.* mass of tissue in the throat.

a·dept, *n.* expert. *a.* skilled.

ad·e·quate, *a.* sufficient. **ad·e·quate·ly**, *adv.* **ad·e·qua·cy**, *n.*

ad·here, *v.*, **-hered, -hering.** cling; hold closely to. **ad·her·ence**, *n.* **ad·her·ent**, *a.*

ad·he·sive, *a.* sticky; *n.* glue-like substance. **ad·he·sive·ness**, *n.*

ad·ja·cent, *a.* close or next to.

ad·jec·tive, *n.* word that modifies a noun. **ad·jec·ti·val**, *a.*

ad·join, *v.* be next to.

ad·journ, *v.* postpone, end a meeting. **ad·journ·ment**, *n.*

ad·judge, *v.* **ad·judged, ad·judg·ing.** decree or condemn by law.

ad·junct, *n.* something added.

ad·just, *v.* fix; settle; adapt. **ad·just·ment**, *n.*

ad·lib, *v.* make up or improvise.

ad·min·is·ter, *v.* manage; direct; dispense.

ad·min·is·tra·tion, *n.* management; executive body. **ad·min·is·tra·tive**, *a.*

ad·mire, *v.*, **ad·mired, ad·mir·ing.** look up to, approve. **ad·mi·ra·ble**, *adj. n.* **ad·mir·ra·tion**, *n.*

ad·mis·si·ble, *a.* permitted.

ad·mis·sion, *n.* entrance fee; confession; accept as true.

ad·mit, *v.*, **ad·mit·ted, ad·mit·ting.** allow to enter; confess; permit. **ad·mit·tance**, *n.*

ad·mon·ish, *v.* reprove; advise against. **ad·mo·ni·tion**, *n.*

a·do·be, *n.* sun-dried brick.

ad·o·les·cence, *n.* period of youthful growth. **ad·o·les·cent**, *a.*

a·dopt, *v.* take as one's own; accept. **a·dop·tion**, *n.*

a·dore, *v.*, **a·dored, a·dor·ing.** worship; love reflect. **ad·o·ra·tion**, *n.*

a·dorn, *v.* decorate; add beauty.

a·dren·a·line, *n.* hormone heart stimulant.

a·droit, *a.* skillful.

ad·u·late, *v.*, **-lated, -lating.** flatter, praise excessively. **ad·u·la·tion**, *n.*

a·dult, *a.* mature. *n.* full-grown person. **a·dult·hood**, *n.*

a·dul·ter·y, *n.* sexual intercourse, with other than lawful mate. **a·dul·ter·ous**, *a.*

ad·vance, *v.*, **ad·vanced, ad·vanc·ing.** move forward; make progress; rise in rank. *a.* placed before. *n.* moving forward.

ad·van·tage, *n.* favorable condition; benefit. **ad·van·ta·geous**, *a.*

ad·ven·ture, *n.* exciting, unusual, or bold experience. *v.*, **-tured, -turing. ad·ven·tur·er**, *n.* **ad·ven·tur·ess**, *n. fem.* **ad·ven·tur·ous**, *a.*

ad·verb, *n.* word which modifies a verb, adjective, or adverb. **ad·ver·bi·al**, *a.*

ad·ver·sar·y, *n. pl.*, **-ies**, opponent; enemy; foe.

ad·verse, *a.* opposing; unfriendly; hostile. **ad·verse·ly**, *adv.*

ad·ver·si·ty, *n. pl.* **-ties**, distress; misfortune.

ad·ver·tise, *v.*, **-tised, -tis·ing.** give public notice of. **ad·ver·tise·ment**, *n.* **ad·ver·tis·ing**, *n.*

ad·vice, *n.* counsel; give opinion.

ad·vise, *v.*, **ad·vised, ad·vis·ing.** give advice. counsel; inform. **ad·vis·a·ble**.

ad·vo·cate, *n.* one who pleads a case. *v.*, **-cat·ed, -cat·ing.** speak in favor of; recommend.

ae·gis, *n.* protection; patronage.

aer·ate, *v.*, **-at·ed, -at·ing.** expose to air. **aer·a·tion**, *n.*

aer·i·al, *a.* pertaining to air or aircraft. *n.* antenna.

aer·o·naut·ics, *n. pl.* science of aircraft design and air flight. **aer·o·naut·ic**, *a.*

aer·o·space, *n.* atmosphere; science of missiles, rockets, etc.

aes·thete, *n.* lover of beauty.

aes·thet·ic, *a.* pertaining to taste or to beauty. **aes·thet·i·cal·ly**, *adv.*

a·far, *adv.* from a distance.

af·fa·ble, *a.* pleasant, courteous.

af·fair, *n.* matters of interest; event; happening; romance.

af·fect, *v.* have an effect on; influence; pretend. **af·fect·ing**, *n.*

af·fec·ta·tion, *n.* pretense.

af·fec·tion, *n.* fondness; love.

af·fec·tion·ate, *a.* loving; tender. **af·fec·tion·ate·ly**, *adv.*

af·fi·da·vit, *n.* written sworn statement.

af·fil·i·ate, *v.*, **-at·ed**, **-at·ing**. associate. *n.* affiliated member. **af·fil·i·a·tion**, *n.*

af·fin·i·ty, *n. pl.*, **-ties**. natural attraction; relation; similarity.

af·firm, *v.* declare to be true; assert; confirm, **af·fir·ma·tion**, *n.*

af·firm·a·tive, *n.* assent or agreement. *a.* affirming.

af·fix, *v.* append; attach; fasten.

af·flict, *v.* cause pain to; distress. **af·flic·tion**, *n.*

af·flu·ence, *n.* abundant supply; wealthy; **af·flu·ent**, *a.*

af·ford, *v.* able to bear the expense; yield; supply; spare.

af·front, *v.* offend; insult; show disrespect; *n.* insult.

a·flame, *a.*, *adv.* on fire.

a·float, *a.*, *adv.* floating.

a·foot, *a.*, *adv.* on foot; walking.

a·fraid, *a.* fearful.

a·fresh, *adv.* anew; again.

af·ter, *a.* later; subsequent. *conj.* later than. *adv.* afterward. *prep.* behind; in pursuit of.

af·ter·birth, *n.* placenta.

af·ter·burn·er, *n.*, jet engine device to increase thrust.

af·ter·noon, *n.* part of day between noon and evening.

a·gain, *adv.* once more; besides.

a·gainst, *prep.* in opposition to; in contact with; in defense from.

a·gape, *a.*, *adv.* openmouthed.

age, *n.* years a person has lived; state of being old; historical period. *v.*, **aged**, **aging** or **age·ing**, grow old.

a·gen·cy, *n. pl.*, **-cies**. action; means; office or business.

a·gen·da, *n.* things to be done.

a·gent, *n.* active power; one who acts for another; thing that causes.

ag·glom·er·ate, *v.*, **-at·ed**, **-at·ing**. mass or collect together. *a.* massed together. **ag·glom·er·a·tion**, *n.*

ag·gran·dize, *v.*, **-dized**, **-diz·ing**. increase; make greater. **ag·gran·dize·ment**, *n.*

ag·gra·vate, *v.*, **-vat·ed**, **-vat·ing**. make worse; irritate, provoke. **ag·gra·va·tion**, *n.*

ag·gre·gate, *v.*, **-gat·ed**, **-gat·ing**. gather together. *n.* mass, or group. *a.* total. **ag·gre·ga·tive**, *a.*

ag·gres·sion, *n.* attack or act of hostility; unprovoked attack.

ag·gress, *v.* commit aggression. **ag·gress·ive**, *a.* **ag·gress·or**, *n.*

ag·grieve, *v.*, **-grieved**, **-griev·ing**. injure unjustly; cause grief.

ag·ile, *a.* nimble; quick; active.

a·gil·i·ty, *n.* nimbleness.

ag·i·tate, *v.*, **-tat·ed**, **-tat·ing**. disturb, excite, argue; shake or move violently; debate. **ag·i·ta·tion**, *n.*

ag·nos·tic, *n.* person who disclaims God. **ag·nos·ti·cism**, *n.*

ag·o·nize, *v.*, **-nized**, **-niz·ing**, feel pain, strive painfully. **ag·o·ny**, *n. pl.*

a·grar·i·an, *a.* relating to land and its use; or farmers' interests.

a·gree, *v.*, **a·greed**, **a·gree·ing**. consent; be in harmony; get along with. **a·gree·ment**, *n.*

a·gree·a·ble, *a.* pleasing; willing to agree. **a·gree·a·ble·ness**, *n.*

ag·ri·cul·ture, *n.* farming; cultivation of land, **ag·ri·cul·tur·al**, *a.* **ag·ri·cul·tur·ist**, *n.*

a·gron·o·my, *n.* agriculture. **a·gron·o·mist**, *n.*

a·ground, *a.*, *adv.* run ashore.

a·head, *adv.* in front; before.

aid, *v.* give help. *n.* assistance.

ail, *v.* be in pain, ill health, or trouble; sick.

ail·ment, *n.* disease or illness.

aim, *v.* point or direct, *n.* act of aiming; purpose, intention. **aim·less**, *a.*

air, *n.* gases surrounding the earth; atmosphere; melody; manner. **airs**, unnatural manner. *v.* put out in air; ventilate. **air·less**, *a.*

air·borne, *a.* in the air.

air·con·di·tion, *v.* control the temperature, etc. of air indoors. **air·con·di·tioned**, *a.* **air con·di·tion·er**, *n.* **air con·di·tion·ing**, *n.*

air·craft, *n. pl.*, **air·craft**. any machine or craft for flying.

air·frame, *n.* structural part of airplane, missle, etc.

air·lift, *v.* transport by air.

air·line, *n.* aerial transportation company.

air·plane, *n.* power-driven aircraft.

air·sick·ness, *n.* nausea caused by flying. **air·sick,** *a.*

air·tight, *a.* no air can get in; no weak points.

air·wor·thy, *a.* safe or fit for service in the air. **air·worthi·ness,** *n.*

air·y, *a.,* **-ier, -iest.** like air; breezy. **air·i·ness,** *n.* **air·i·ly,** *adv.*

aisle, *n.* passageway between rows of seats.

a·jar, *a., adv.* partly opened.

a·kin, *a.* alike; similar; related by blood.

al·a·bas·ter, *n.* white marblelike mineral.

a·lac·ri·ty, *n.* liveliness; cheerful willingness; briskness.

a·larm, *n.* fear or fright; sound or device to warn; *v.* disturb with terror. **a·larm·ing,** *a.* **a·larm·ing·ly,** *adv.*

a·las, exclamation of grief, pity, or dread.

al·ba·tross, *n.* web-footed sea bird.

al·be·it, *conj.* although.

al·bi·no, *n. pl.,* **-nos.** person or animal who lacks pigmentation or color. **al·bin·ic,** *a.*

al·bu·men, *n.* white of an egg.

al·bu·min, *n.* water-soluble protein. **al·bu·mi·nouse,** *a.*

al·che·my, *n.* medieval chemistry.

al·co·hol, *n.* intoxicating ingredient of liquor. **al·co·hol·ic,** *a.*

al·cove, *n.* small room or recess.

ale, *n.* a bitter beer.

a·lert, *a.* watchful; wide awake, lively. *n.* signal of danger. *v.* warn. **a·lert·ness,** *n.*

al·fal·fa, *n.* plant grown as animal forage.

al·ga, *n. pl.,* **al·gae.** water plant lacking stems, roots, or leaves.

al·ge·bra, *n.* mathematics using signs and letters; problem solving by equations. **al·ge·bra·ic,** *a.* **al·ge·bra·i·cal,** *a.*

a·li·as, *n. pl.,* **a·li·as·es.** assumed name.

al·i·bi, *n.* fact showing innocence; excuse.

al·ien, *a.* foreign; strange; different in nature. *n.* foreigner. **al·ien·a·ble.**

al·ien·ate, *v.,* **-at·ed, -at·ing.** turn away, estrange. **al·ien·a·tion,** *n.*

a·light, *v.,* **a·light·ed** or **a·lit, a·light·ing.** get off; get down; settle; happen upon.

a·lign, *v.* bring into line; adjust; join; ally oneself. **a·lign·ment,** *n.*

a·like, *a.* similar. *adv.* equally; the same as.

al·i·ment, *n.* food; nourishment. *n.*

al·i·mo·ny, *n.* money paid for the support of former spouse.

a·line *v.,* align; line up.

a·live, *a.* living; aware; active; sensitive to.

al·ka·li, *n. pl.,* **-lies,** or **-lis.** any salt or mixture which neutralizes acids. **al·ka·line,** *a.*

al·ka·lize, *v.,* **-lized, -liz·ing.** make alkaline.

all, *a.* every one of; the whole of; any; everything; total. *adv.* completely.

all·a·round, *a.* versatile.

al·lay, *v.,* **al·layed, al·lay·ing.** quieten; relieve. lessen.

al·le·ga·tion, *n.* assertion without proof.

al·lege, *v.,* **al·leged, al·leg·ing.** assert, esp. without proof, state positively.

al·leged, *a.* declared to be true. **al·leg·ed·ly,** *adv.*

al·legiance, *n.* loyalty; devotion.

al·le·go·ry, *n. pl.,* **-ries.** symbolic story. **al·le·gor·i·cal,** *a. adv.*

al·le·gro, *a.* quick, lively.

al·ler·gy, *n. pl.,* **-gies.** sensitivity to pollen, foods, dust.

al·le·vi·ate, *v.,* **-at·ed, -at·ing.** make easier to endure. **al·le·vi·a·tion,** *n.* **al·le·vi·a·tor,** *n.* **al·le·vi·a·tive,** *a.*

al·ley, *n. pl.,* **al·leys.** a narrow backstreet; a bowling lane.

al·li·ance, *n.* union of interests; compact; association.

al·li·ga·tor, *n.* american reptile like a crocodile.

al·lo·cate, *v.,* **-cat·ed, -cat·ing.** assign or allot; apportion. **al·lo·ca·tion,** *n.*

al·lot, *v.,* **al·lot·ted, al·lot·ting.** divide and distribute; assign; set apart. **al·lot·ment,** *n.*

al·low, *v.* grant; admit; let have; permit.

al·low·able, *a.* not forbidden; permitted.

al·low·ance, *n.* portion or amount; permission; money; *v.,* **-anced, -anc·ing.** put on an allowance.

al·loy, *n.* metal mixture.

al·lude, *v.,* **al·lud·ed, al·lud·ing.** refer to indirectly.

al·lure, *v.,* **al·lured, al·lur·ing.** tempt; entice. *n.* fascinate charm; appeal.

al·lu·sion, *n.* indirect casual reference; **al·lu·sive,** *a.* **al·lu·sive·ly,** *adv.* **al·lu·sive·ness,** *n.*

al·lu·vi·um, *n. pl.,* **-vi·ums, -vi·a.** sand, mud, etc. deposited by flowing water.

al·ly, *v.t.,* **al·lied, al·ly·ing.** unite; connect; bind together; *vi.* form an alliance. **al·lied,** *a.*

al·ly, *n. pl.,* **al·lies.** confederate; supporter; friend; helper.

Al·ma Ma·ter, Al·ma Ma·ter, *n.* a person's school, college, or university.

al·ma·nac, *n.* publication containing statistical and astronomical annual information.

al·might·y, *a.* all-powerful.

al·mond, *n.* the nut or seed of the almond tree.

al·most, *adv.* nearly.

alms, *n. pl.*, charity; gifts.

a·loft, *adv.* high above.

a·lone, *a.* apart from; solitary. *adv.* only; solely; without help.

a·long, *adv.* lengthwise; in company; onward; *prep.* in accord with.

a·loof, *adv.* withdrawn; at a distance. *a.* uninvolved; reserved. **a·loof·ly**, *adv.* **a·loof·ness**, *n.*

a·loud, *adv.* not whispered; loud enough to be heard.

al·pac·a, *n.*, a variety of lliama; its silky wool.

al·pha·bet, *n.* letters of a written language. *a.* **al·pha·bet·i·cal**, *a.* **al·pha·bet·ize**, *v.*

al·read·y, *adv.* previously; so soon; before this time.

al·so, *adv.* in addition; likewise; too.

al·tar, *n.* sacred table or stand in a church.

al·ter, *v.* change; modify. **al·ter·a·ble**, *a.* **al·ter·a·bly**, *adv.* **al·ter·a·tion**, *n.*

al·ter·cate, *v.* quarrel; dispute angrily. **al·ter·ca·tion**, *n.* dispute; fight.

al·ter e·go, *n.* second self.

al·ter·nate, *v.*, **-nat·ed**, **-nat·ing**. occur or do by turns; interchange. *n.* substitute. *a.* occurring in turn or as every other one. **al·ter·nate·ly**, *adv.*

al·ter·na·tive, *n.* choice between two or more things; one of things to be chosen.

al·though, *conj.* even though.

al·tim·e·ter, *n.* instrument for measuring altitude for aircraft.

al·ti·tude, *n.* height.

al·to, *n.* contralto, lowest female voice.

al·to·geth·er, *adv.* wholly; entirely; completely. *n.* whole.

al·tru·ism, *n.* unselfish devotion. **al·tru·is·tic**, *a.*

a·lu·mi·num, *n.* a light, ductible, tarnish resisting metal.

a·lum·nus, *n. pl.*, **-ni**. graduate of a college or university. **a·lum·na**, *n. fem. pl.* **-nae**.

al·ways, *adv.* all the time; perpetually; forever.

a·m, A·M., midnight to before noon.

a·mal·gam, *n.* alloy of mercury with another metal; mixture.

a·mal·gam·ate, *v.*, **-at·ed**, **-at·ing**. combine; alloy with. **a·mal·gam·a·tion**, *n.*

a·mass, *v.* accumulate; collect.

am·a·teur, *n.* non-professional. **am·a·teur·ish**, *a.*

am·a·to·ry, *a.* of love.

a·maze, *v.* **a·mazed**, **a·maz·ing**. astound; astonish, surprise greatly. *adv.* **a·maze·ment**, *n.* **a·maz·ing**, *a.*

am·a·zon, *n.* big, strong woman.

am·bas·sa·dor, *n.* highest rank representative from one government to another.

am·ber, *n.* yellowish fossil resin; color of or made of amber.

am·bi·dex·trous, *a.* ability to use both hands equally well.

am·big·u·ous, *a.* obscure; indefinite. **am·bi·gu·i·ty**, *n.*

am·bi·tion, *n.* strong; desire; thing desired; aspiration. **am·bi·tious**, *a.*

am·biv·a·lence, *n.* condition of having contradictory feelings. **am·biv·a·lent**, *a.*

am·ble, *v.*, **am·bled**, **am·bling**. walk slowly and easily. *n.* gentle pace. **am·bler**, *n.*

am·bu·la·to·ry, *a.* able to walk; movable.

am·bu·late, *v.*, **-lat·ed**, **-lat·ing**. walk; move. **am·bu·lant**, *a.*

am·bus·cade, *n.* ambush.

am·bush, *n.* surprise attack; position of lying in wait. *v.* attack from ambush; to waylay. **am·bush·er**, *n.*

a·me·ba, *n.* amoeba.

a·mel·io·rate, *v.*, **-rat·ed**, **-rat·ing**. improve. **a·mel·io·ra·tion**, *n.* **a·mel·io·ra·tive**, *a.*

a·men, *interj.* be it so.

a·me·na·ble, *a.* open to suggestion. **a·me·na·bil·i·ty**, *n.* **a·me·na·bly**, *adv.*

a·mend, *v.* change; make better; revise; correct. **a·mend·a·ble**, *a.* **a·mend·ment**, *n.*

a·mends, *n. pl.* reparation.

a·men·i·ty, *n.* agreeableness. *pl.* socially pleasing acts.

A·mer·i·can, *a.* of America; native or citizen of America esp. of the U·S.

am·e·thyst, *n.* purple or violet quartz used for jewelry.

a·mi·a·ble, *a.* agreeable; pleasing; friendly. **a·mi·a·bil·i·ty**, *n.*

am·i·ca·ble, *a.* friendly; peaceable. **am·i·ca·bil·i·ty**, *n.*

a·mid, *prep.* in the midst or middle of; among. Also **amidst**.

a·mid·ships, *adv.* in or toward the middle of a ship.

a·mi·go, *n.*, a friend.

a·mi·no ac·id, *n.* basic building block of protein.

a·miss, *adv.*, *a.* faulty; wrong.

am·mo·nia, *n.* gas of nitrogen and hydrogen. **am·mon·ic**, *a.*

am·mu·ni·tion, *n.* projectiles for guns or other weapons.

am·ne·sia, *n.* loss of memory. **am·ne·sic,** *a.*

am·nes·ty, *n. pl.,* **-ties.** general pardon for past offenses. *v.,* **-tied, -ty·ing.**

a·moe·ba, *n. pl.,* **a·moe·bae, a·moe·bas.** microscopic, one-celled animal.

a·mong, *prep.* by; within or into the midst or number of.

a·mongst, *prep.* among.

a·mor·al, *a.* non-moral.

am·o·rous, *a.* loving; in love.

a·mor·phous, *a.* formless.

am·or·tize, *v.,* **-tized, -tiz·ing.** to set aside money for future payment. **am·or·ti·za·tion,** *n.*

a·mount, *n.* sum value. *v.* total; be equal to.

am·pere, *n.* unit measuring electric current.

am·phib·i·an, *a. n.* plant or animal living in water; seaplane.

am·phib·i·ous, *a.* able to live on land or water.

am·phi·the·a·ter, *n.* circular or oval arena.

am·ple, *a.,* **am·pler, am·plest,** large; abundant. **am·ply** *adv.*

am·pli·fy, *v.,* **-fied, -fy·ing,** increase; elaborate; expand. **am·pli·fi·ca·tion,** *n.* **am·pli·fi·er,** *n.*

am·pli·tude, *n.* abundance; fullness; extent; greatness.

am·pu·tate, *v.,* **-tat·ed, -tat·ing.** cut off. **am·pu·ta·tion,** *n.* **am·pu·tee,** *n.*

a·muck, *adv.* murderous frenzy.

am·u·let, *n.* charm against evil.

a·muse, *v.,* **a·mused, a·mus·ing.** cause to smile; entertain; divert. **a·mus·ing,** *a.* **a·muse·ment,** *n.*

an, *a, indef. art.* one; each.

a·nach·ro·nism, *n.* placing persons or events out of proper time. **a·nach·ro·nis·tic,** *a.*

an·a·con·da, *n.* large boa snake.

an·a·gram, *n.* word formed from another by transposing the letters.

a·nal, *a.* of or near the anus.

an·al·ge·sic, *a. n.* drug or other agent to remove pain.

a·nal·o·gize, *v.,* **-gized, -giz·ing.** explain by analogy.

an·a·logue, an·a·log, *n.,* a thing or part that is analogous.

a·nal·o·gy, *n. pl.,* similarity; likeness. **a·nal·o·gous,** *a.*

an·a·lyze, *v.,* **-lyzed, -lyz·ing.** determine or separate into important parts; examine critically. **an·a·ly·za·tion,** *n.* **a·nal·y·sis,** *n. pl.,* **-ses. an·a·lyst,** *n.* **an·a·lyt·ic,** *a.*

an·ar·chism, *n.* lawlessness; non-belief in government. **an·ar·chist,** *n.*

an·ar·chy, *n.* absence of government and law. **an·ar·chic** *a.*

a·nath·e·ma, *n. pl.,* anything which is hated or avoided; thing detested and condemned. **a·nath·e·ma·tize,** *v.,* **-ized, -iz·ing.**

a·nat·o·my, *n. pl.,* **-mies.** structure of an animal or plant or the study thereof.

an·ces·tor, *n.* forefather; precursor. **an·ces·tress,** *n. fem.* **an·ces·tral,** *a.* **an·ces·try,** *n. pl.,* **-tries.** lineage.

an·chor, *n.* iron weight which holds a ship in place. *v.* hold fast. **at an·chor,** anchored. **an·chor·age,** *n.*

an·cho·vy, *n. pl.,* **-vies.** small fish of the herring family.

an·cient, *a.* existing or occurring in times long past; old. *n.* very old person. **an·cient·ly,** *adv.*

an·cil·lary, *a.* subordinate; assisting. **and,** *conj.* also; as well as.

an·drog·y·nous, *a.* hermaphroditic.

an·ec·dote, *n.* short account of interesting event. **an·ec·do·tal,** *a.*

a·ne·mi·a, *n.* deficiency of red corpuscles. **a·ne·mic,** *a.*

an·e·mom·e·ter, *n.* instrument for measuring wind velocity.

an·es·the·sia, *n.* entire or partial loss of feeling, pain, etc.

an·es·thet·ic, *n.* substance causing anesthesia. **an·es·the·tist,** *n.* **an·es·the·tize,** *v.,* **-tized, -tizing.**

a·new, *adv.* again; once more.

an·gel, *n.* messenger or attendant of God. **an·gel·ic,** *a.*

an·ger, *n.* ire; wrath; fury, *v.* excite to anger.

an·gi·na pec·to·ris, *n.* serious heart disease causing sharp chest pains.

an·gle, *n.* space between two lines or surfaces that meet. *v.* **an·gled, an·gling.** bend in angles; fish with hook and line; scheme to get. **an·gled,** *a.* an·gler, *n.*

An·gli·cize, *v.,* **-cized, -ciz·ing.** to make or become English. **An·gli·ci·za·tion,** *n.*

an·gling, *n.* rod fishing.

An·glo-Sax·on, *n.* early settler in Britain. Member of the English race; old English.

An·go·ra, *n.* variety of long-haired goat or cat; long-haired goat wool.

an·gry, *a.* displaying or feeling anger; raging, **an·gri·ly,** *adv.*

an·guish, *n.* extreme pain, grief or distress. *v.* cause distress; suffer intensely.

an·gu·lar, *a.* having angles; sharp-cornered; bony; stiff and awkward. **an·gu·lar·i·ty,** *n.*

an·hy·drous, *a.* without water.

an·i·mal, *n.* any living thing that is not a plant; beast; brute.

an·i·mate, *v.,* **-mat·ed, -mat·ing.** make lively or gay; stimulate. **an·i·ma·tion,** *n.*

-ties. an·i·mos·i·ty, *n. pl.,* **-ties.** bitter feeling; enmity; hatred.

an·i·mus, *n.* ill will, violent hatred.

an·ise, *n.* plant with seeds used for flavoring.

an·kle, *n.* joint that connects the foot and leg.

an·nals, *n. pl.* chronological historical records; history.

an·neal, *v.* temper or toughen by heating (glass, metals, etc.).

an·nex, *v.* add to; unite; attach. *n.* addition. **an·nex·a·tion,** *n.*

an·ni·hi·late, *v.,* **-lat·ed, -lat·ing.** destroy. **an·ni·hi·la·tion,** *n.*

an·ni·ver·sa·ry, *n. pl.,* **-ries.** yearly return of a date of some event (birthday, etc.).

an·no·tate, *v.,* **-tat·ed, -tat·ing.** to make or provide explanatory notes. **an·no·ta·tion,** *n.*

an·nounce, *v.* **an·nounced, an·nounc·ing.** give notice; make known. **an·nounce·ment,** *n.*

an·noy, *v.* bother; pester; irritate. **-noy·ance,** *n.* **-noy·ing,** *a.*

an·nu·al, *a.* yearly. *n.* plant living one year or season.

an·nu·i·ty, *n.* yearly payment of money.

an·nul, *v.,* **an·nulled, an·nul·ling.** make void. **an·nul·ment,** *n.*

an·ode, *n.* positive electrode.

an·nun·ci·ate, *v.,* **-ated, -at·ing.** announce. **an·nun·ci·a·tion,** *n.*

a·noint, *v.* put oil or ointment on; consecrate. **a·noint·ment,** *n.*

a·nom·a·ly, *n.* something abnormal; irregularity. **a·nom·a·lism,** *v.* **a·nom·a·lous,** *a.*

a·non, *adv.,* at another time; soon.

a·non·y·mous, *a.* of unacknowledged or unknown authorship; nameless. **an·o·nym·i·ty,** *n.* **a·non·y·mous·ly,** *adv.*

an·oth·er, *a.* an additional one more; different; any other.

an·swer, *v.* reply to; respond. *n.* reply; response; solution. **an·swer·a·ble,** *a.*

ant·ac·id, *n.* an alkali.

an·tag·o·nize, *v.,* **-nized, -niz·ing.** make an enemy of; oppose; provoke. **an·tag·o·nist,** *n.*

ant·arc·tic, *a.* of or near the south pole.

ant·eat·er, *n.* mammal with long nose that eats ants.

an·te·ced·ent, *n.* happening or coming before; previous thing.

an·te·date, *v.,* **-dat·ed, -dat·ing.** date before; to come before.

an·te·di·lu·vi·an, *a.* before the flood; very old; old fashioned.

an·te·lope, *n. pl.,* **-lopes, -lope.** a deerlike animal.

an·ten·na, *n. pl.,* **-nae, -nas.** feeler on head of an insect; radio or television aerial.

an·te·ri·or, *a.* toward the front; earlier; previous.

an·them, *n.* sacred or patriotic song; song of praise.

an·thol·o·gy, *n. pl.,* **-gies,** collection of poems or prose. **an·thol·o·gist,** *n.*

an·thra·cite, *n.* hard coal.

an·thrax, *n. pl.,* **an·thra·ces,** a cattle disease.

an·thro·poid, *a.* manlike; resembling man. *n.* manlike ape.

an·thro·pol·o·gy, *n.* study of man. **an·thro·pol·o·gist,** *n.*

an·ti-. *prefix.* against; opposed.

an·ti·bi·ot·ic, *n.* substance that inhibits or kills microorganisms.

an·ti·bod·y, *n. pl.,* **-bod·ies.** substance in the blood that destroys or weakens bacteria.

an·tic·i·pate, *v.,* **-pat·ed, -pat·ing.** look forward to; forsee; expect. **an·tic·i·pa·tion,** *n.*

an·ti·cli·max, *n.* abrupt descent from the important to the trivial; descent in importance.

an·ti·mis·sle, *a.* defense against rockets or ballistic missles.

an·ti·dote, *n.* medicine or remedy to counteract poison.

an·ti·his·ta·mine, *n.* chemical compound used for the treatment of allergies and colds.

an·tip·a·thy, *n. pl.,* **-thies.** intense or instinctive dislike; a feeling against. **an·ti·pa·thet·ic,** *a.*

an·tip·o·de, *n.* the direct opposite. **an·tip·o·dal,** *a.*

an·ti·quate, *v.,* **-quat·ed, -quat·ing.** make old fashioned or outdated. **an·ti·quat·ed,** *a.*

an·tique, *a.* ancient. *n.* thing very old; out-of-date. *v.* **an·tiqued, an·tiqu·ing. cause to appear antique.**

an·tiq·ui·ty, *n. pl.,* **-ties,** times long ago; early ages of history.

an·ti·Sem·i·tism, *n.* dislike, prejudice or hatred of Jews.

an·ti·sep·tic, *a.* preventing infection; *n.* substance that kills germs.

an·ti·so·cial, *a.* averse to social contact; harmful to public welfare.

an·tith·e·sis, *n. pl.*, direct opposite; contrast of ideas.

an·ti·tox·in, *n.* serum.

an·ti·trust, *a.* referring to rules against certain trade practices.

ant·ler, *n.* branched bonelike horn of a deer. **ant·lered**, *a.*

an·to·nym, *n.* word opposite in meaning to another word.

a·nus, *n.* an opening at the lower end of the digestive canal.

an·vil, *n.* iron or steel block on which metals are hammered.

anx·i·e·ty, *n. pl.*, **-ties.** state of being troubled; worried; uneasy.

anx·ious, *a.* troubled; worried.

an·y, *a., pron.* one; of many; some; every. *adv.* at all.

an·y·bod·y, *pron.* anyone.

an·y·how, *adv.* in any way; in any case.

an·y·one, *pron.* any person.

an·y·thing, *n., pron.* any thing. *adv.* at all.

an·y·way, *adv.* in any way whatever; in any case; carelessly.

an·y·where, *adv.* in at or to any place.

a·or·ta, *n. pl.*, **-tas, tae.** main artery from the heart.

a·part, *adv.* in pieces; in separate parts; not together.

a·part·heid, *n.,* racial segregation.

a·part·ment, *n.* room or rooms where people live.

ap·a·thy, *n. pl.*, **-thies.** indifference; no interest. **ap·a·thet·ic**, *a.*

ape, *n.* large tailless monkeys. *v.*, **aped, ap·ing.** to mimic or imitate.

ap·er·ture, *n.* opening; hole.

a·pex, *n. pl.*, **a·pex·es, a·pi·ces.** highest point; tip; climax.

a·pha·sia, *n.,* inability to use or understand words.

aph·o·rism, *n.* proverb; maxim.

aph·ro·dis·i·ac, *n.* exciting sexual desire; erotic.

a·pi·ar·y, *n. pl.*, **-ies.** place where bees are kept.

a·piece, *adv.* for each one.

a·plomb, *n.* self-possession.

ap·o·gee, *n.* furthermost point.

a·pol·o·gize, *v.*, **-gized, -giz·ing.** make an apology.

a·pol·o·gy, *n. pl.*, **-gies.** words expressing regret; words in defense of; poor substitute.

ap·o·plec·tic, *a.* of apoplexy. *n.* person who has apoplexy.

ap·o·plex·y, *n.* paralysis or loss of powers caused by a stroke.

a·pos·ta·tize, *v.*, **-tized, -tiz·ing.** To forsake principles, faith, or political party. **a·pos·tate,** *n.*

a·pos·tle, *n.* disciple; missionary.

a·pos·tro·phe, *n.* sign (') used to show the omission of a letter in a word, or the possessive case.

ap·pall, ap·pal, *v.*, **ap·palled, ap·pal·ling.** fill with dismay.

ap·pa·ra·tus, *n. pl.*, **-tus, -tus·es.** machinery or tool.

ap·par·el, *n.* clothing; dress.

ap·par·ent, *a.* evident; plain to see; easy to see.

ap·pa·ri·tion, *n.* ghost; phantom.

ap·peal, *v.* ask or call for help; be attractive to. *n.* call for sympathy; request for help; *Law:* request to be heard by a higher court. **ap·peal·a·ble**, *a.* **ap·peal·er**, *n.*

ap·pear, *v.* come before; come in sight; perform publicly; seem. **ap·pear·ance**, *n.* act of appearing.

ap·pease, *v.* **-peased, -peas·ing.** make calm; quiet; assuage; satisfy. **ap·pease·ment**, *n.* **ap·peas·er**, *n.*

ap·pel·lant, *n.* one who appeals.

ap·pel·la·tion, *n.* name; title.

ap·pend, *v.* attach; add.

ap·pen·dage, *n.* thing attached.

ap·pen·dec·to·my, *n.* removal of the appendix by surgery.

ap·pen·di·ci·tis, *n.* inflammation of the vermiform appendix.

ap·pen·dix, *n. pl.*, **dix·es, di·ces,** part added to end of a book; vermiform appendix.

ap·per·tain, *v.* pertain; relate.

ap·pe·tite, *n.* desire for food; desire to satisfy.

ap·pe·tiz·ing, *a.* exciting or stimulating the appetite.

ap·plaud, *v.* show approval by clapping the hands or shouting; praise. **ap·plause**, *n.*

ap·pli·ance, *n.,* small machine or tool.

ap·pli·cant, *n.* person who applies for something.

ap·pli·ca·tion, *n.* act of applying thing applied; request; close study; use.

ap·ply, *v.*, **ap·plied, ap·ply·ing.** put to practical use, work hard; make a request. **ap·pli·ca·ble**, *a.*

ap·point, *v.* assign; choose; designate. **ap·point·ee**, *n.* **ap·poin·tive**, *a.* **ap·point·ment**, *n.*

ap·por·tion, *v.* divide in fair shares. **ap·por·tion·ment**, *n.*

ap·pose, v., **ap·posed**, **ap·pos·ing**. place side by side; put one thing next to another. **ap·po·si·tion**, n. **ap·pos·i·tive**, a., n.

ap·praise, v., **ap·praised**, **ap·prais·ing**. estimate the value, amount, etc. **ap·prais·al**, n.

ap·pre·ci·ate, v., **-at·ed**, **-at·ing**. be grateful for; regard highly; value properly; rise in value. **ap·pre·ci·a·tion**, n.

ap·pre·hend, v. arrest; understand. **ap·pre·hen·si·ble**, a. **ap·pre·hen·sion**, n. **ap·pre·hen·sive**, a.

ap·pren·tice, n. person learning a trade or art. v., **-ticed**, **-tic·ing**. become or take as an apprentice.

ap·prise, **ap·prize**, v., **ap·prised** or **ap·prized**, **ap·pris·ing** or **ap·priz·ing**. inform; notify.

ap·proach, v. come near. n. act of drawing near; way to come. **ap·proach·a·ble**, a.

ap·pro·ba·tion, n. approval.

ap·pro·pri·ate, v., **-at·ed**, **-at·ing**. take for oneself; set apart; provide. a. suitable. **ap·pro·pri·ate·ly**, adv. **ap·pro·pri·a·tion**, n. **ap·pro·pri·a·tive**, a.

ap·prov·al, n. official permission; consent; sanction.

ap·prove, v., **ap·proved**, **ap·prov·ing**. think or speak well of; commend; give permission to.

ap·prox·i·mate, a. nearly correct; v. come near to; estimate. **ap·prox·i·ma·tion**, n.

a·pron, n. garment worn over the front to protect clothes.

ap·ro·pos, adv. fittingly; suitable.

apt, a. fit; quick to learn; suitable. **apt·ly**, adv.

ap·ti·tude, n. natural ability; capacity; readiness in learning.

a·quar·i·um, n. pl., **-i·ums**, **-i·a**. glass fish tank or bowl.

a·quat·ic, a. growing or living in water. n. water-growing plant. pl. water sports.

aq·ue·duct, n. pipe or channel for carrying water.

a·que·ous, a. of or like water.

aq·ui·line, a. curved like an eagle's beak; hooked.

Ar·ab, n. native of Arabia, or a member of a Semitic people. **A·ra·bi·an**, a. breed of horse. **Ar·a·bic**, a., n.

Ar·a·bic nu·mer·als, n. figures 1 through 9 and 0.

ar·a·ble, a. fit for plowing.

ar·bi·ter, **ar·bi·tra·tor**, n. person chosen to decide a dispute.

ar·bi·trar·y, a. based on one's own will or desires; capricious. **ar·bi·trar·i·ly**, adv. **ar·bi·trar·i·ness**, n.

ar·bi·trate, v., **-trat·ed**, **-trat·ing**. act or submit to arbitration. **ar·bi·tra·tion**, n. settlement of a dispute by decision of somebody chosen.

ar·bor, n. tree-shaded place.

ar·bor·re·tum, n. pl., **-tums**, **-ta**. botanical garden.

arc, n. any part of a circle or curved line. v., **arced** or **arcked**, **arc·ing** or **arck·ing**.

arch, n. curved covering, or structure. v. form an arch.

arch-, prefix. chief; principal.

ar·chae·ol·o·gy, n. study of ancient peoples their remains, tools, customs, etc.

ar·cha·ic, a. out of date.

arch·bish·op, n. bishop of the highest rank.

arch·er·y, n. shooting with a bow and arrow. **arch·er**, n.

ar·che·type, n. original model or first pattern.

ar·chi·pel·a·go, n. pl., **-goes**, **-gos**. group of many islands.

ar·chi·tect, n. person who designs buildings.

ar·chi·tec·ture, n. science of design and construction of buildings. **ar·chi·tec·tur·al**, a.

ar·chive, n. public records; their location. **ar·chi·val**, a.

arch·way, n., an arch covering a passageway.

arc·tic, a. of or near the North Pole; cold, frigid.

ar·dent, a. passionate; fervent; eager; hot. **ar·dent·ly**, adv.

ar·dor, n. fervor; zeal.

ar·du·ous, a. difficult; steep.

ar·e·a., n. region; scope, as given in square units; range.

a·re·na, n. space where contests, games, etc. take place.

ar·gon, n. inert gas.

ar·got, n. jargon; slang.

ar·gue, v., **ar·gued**, **ar·gu·ing**. to discuss or offer reasons for or against; dispute. **ar·gu·a·ble**, a. **ar·gu·ment**, n. **ar·gu·men·ta·tive**, a.

a·ri·a., n. song or melody for a single voice.

ar·id, a. dry; barren; unimaginative. **a·rid·i·ty**, n.

a·rise, v., **a·rose**, **a·ris·en**, **a·ris·ing**. get up; come up; to rise.

a·ris·toc·ra·cy, n. pl., **-cies**. ruling body; nobility or upper class. **a·ris·to·crat**, n. **a·ris·to·crat·ic**, a.

a·rith·me·tic, n. computation by numbers. **a·rith·met·i·cal**, a. **a·rith·me·ti·cian**, n.

arm, *n.* part of body between shoulder and hand; anything that resembles an arm; weapon. *v.* supply with weapons. **arm·er,** *n.*

ar·ma·da, *n.* fleet of warships; fleet of airplanes.

ar·ma·dil·lo, *n. pl.,* **ar·ma·dil·los.** burrowing mammal covered with a shell of bony plates.

ar·ma·ment, *n.* war equipment and supplies; armed forces.

arm·ful, *n. pl.,* **arm·fuls,** as much as both arms can hold.

ar·mi·stice, *n.* truce.

ar·mor, *n.* defensive or protective covering. **ar·mored,** *a.*

ar·mor·y, *n. pl.,* place to store weapons.

arm·pit, *n.* hollow under the arm at the shoulder.

ar·my, *n. pl.,* **ar·mies,** military land force; large number.

a·ro·ma, *n.* fragrance, **ar·o·mat·ic,** *a.*

a·round, *adv., prep.* in a circle; closely surrounding; on all sides; somewhere near.

a·rouse, *v.,* **a·roused, a·rous·ing.** stir into action; awaken.

ar·range, *v.,* **ar·ranged, ar·rang·ing,** place in proper order; adapt; make plans. **ar·rang·er,** *n.* **ar·range·ment,** *n.*

ar·ray, *n.* clothes. *v.* arrange in order; adorn or dress.

ar·rest, *v.* stop; seize by legal authority. *n.* seizure.

ar·rive, *v.,* **ar·rived, ar·riv·ing.** reach a place; get to a destination. **ar·riv·al,** *n.*

ar·ro·gant, *a.* insolently proud; overbearing.

ar·ro·gate, *v.,* **-gat·ed, -gat·ing.** take or claim without right.

ar·row, *n.* pointed shaft for shooting from a bow.

ar·se·nal, *n.* a grayish-white element; a poison.

ar·se·nic, *n.* a poison.

ar·son, *n.* crime of intentionally burning property.

art, *n.* appealing, attractive object; any of the fine arts, esp. painting, drawing, sculpture; skill.

ar·ter·y, *n. pl.,* **ar·ter·ies,** vessels or tubes conveying blood from the heart. **ar·te·ri·al,** *a.*

ar·thri·tis, *n.* inflammation of the joints, **ar·thrit·ic,** *a.*

ar·ti·cle, *n.* single item; a literary composition; clause in a contract; part of speech: *a, an,* or *the.*

ar·tic·u·late, *v.,* **-lat·ed, -lat·ing.** speak clearly, distinctly; unite by joints. *a.* spoken distinctly. **ar·tic·u·la·tion,** *n.*

ar·ti·fi·cial, *a.* man-made; not natural; false; affected. **ar·ti·fi·cial·ness,** *n.*

ar·til·ler·y, *n.* mounted guns.

art·ist, *n.* person skilled in the arts, esp. the fine arts.

ar·tis·tic, *a.* of art or artists. **ar·tis·ti·cal·ly,** *adv.*

as, *adv.* to the same degree or extent; for example. *conj.* when; while. *prep.* like. *pron.* that.

as·bes·tos, as·bes·tus, *n.* fibrous mineral used to make fire-proof cloth or insulation.

as·cend, *v.* climb, rise, go up. **as·cend·an·cy, as·cend·en·cy,** *n.* **as·cend·ant, as·cend·ent,** *a.* **as·cen·sion,** *n.*

as·cent, *n.* upward movement; act of rising; an upward slope.

as·cer·tain, *v.* determine; find out; make certain.

as·cet·ic, *n.* person who practices unusual self-denial. *a.* very self-denying. **as·cet·i·cism,** *n.*

as·cribe, *v.,* **as·cribed, as·crib·ing.** attribute; assign.

a·sex·u·al, *a.* having no sex.

a·shamed, *a.* feeling shame.

a·side, *adv.* on or to one side; away.

as·i·nine, *a.* stupid; silly.

ask, *v.* request; question; inquire about; invite.

a·skance, *adv.* sideways; with suspicion.

a·skew, *adv., a.* awry; twisted.

a·sleep, *a., adv.* sleeping; numb.

asp, *n.* small poisonous snake.

as·par·a·gus, *n.* plant grown for its edible shoots,

as·pect, *n.* look; appearance; expression.

as·per·i·ty, *n. pl.,* **-ties.** roughness; or harshness; severity.

as·perse, *v.,* **as·persed, as·pers·ing.** slander. **as·per·sion,** *n.*

as·phalt, *n.* black substance used for pavements, roofs.

as·phyx·i·ate, *v.,* **-at·ed, -at·ing.** suffocate. **as·phyx·i·a·tion,** *n.*

as·pi·ra·tion, *n.* ardent desire.

as·pire, *v.,* **as·pired, as·pir·ing.** desire; have an ambition for. **as·pir·ant,** *n.*

as·pi·rin, *n.* drug used for colds, to relieve pain and reduce fever.

ass, *n.* donkey; stupid person.

as·sail, *v.* set upon; attack. **as·sail·a·ble,** *a.* **as·sail·ant,** *n.*

as·sas·sin, *n.* murderer.

as·sas·si·nate, *v.,* **-nat·ed, -nat·ing.** kill; murder. **as·sas·si·na·tion,** *n.* **as·sas·si·na·tor,** *n.*

as·sault, *n., v.* attack; onslaught.

as·say, *v.* analyze ore. **as·say·er,** *n.*

as·sem·ble, *v.,* **-bled, -bling.** bring or come together; fit together. **as·sem·blage,** *n.* **as·sem·bly,** *n. pl.,* **-blies.**

as·sent, *n.* consent. *v.* concur.

as·sert, *v.* state positively; **as·ser·tion,** *n.* **as·ser·tive,** *a.*

as·sess, *v.* tax; fine; evaluate. **as·sess·ment,** *n.* **as·ses·sor,** *n.*

as·set, *n.* something having value; property.

as·sid·u·ous, *a.* devoted; diligent. **as·si·du·i·ty,** *n.*

as·sign, *v.* apportion; set; appoint; refer. **as·sign·ment,** *n.*

as·sig·na·tion, *n.* appointment for a meeting; assignment of a property right.

as·sim·i·late, *v.,* **-lat·ed, -lat·ing.** absorb; digest; be ascribed; be like.

as·sist, *v., n.* aid; help. **as·sist·ance,** *n.* **as·sist·ant,** *a.*

as·so·ci·ate, *v.,* **-at·ed, -at·ing.** join; connect mentally; combine with. *a.* combined. *n.* ally; partner. **as·so·ci·a·tion,** *n.*

as·so·nance, *n.* resemblance in sound. **as·so·nant,** *a.*

as·sort *v.* sort out; classify. *a.* **as·sort·ed,** selected kinds; varied. *n.* **as·sort·ment.**

as·suage, *v.,* **as·suaged, as·suag·ing.** make less; moderate.

as·sume, *v.,* **as·sumed, as·sum·ing.** undertake; take for granted; put on; appropriate; suppose. **as·sump·tion,** *n.*

as·sure, *v.,* **as·sured, as·sur·ing.** make sure or certain; make confident. **as·sur·ance,** *n.*

as·ter·isk, *n.* star shaped mark (*).

a·stern, *adv.* at or toward the stern of a ship.

asth·ma, *n.* chronic disease causing difficult breathing. **asth·mat·ic,** *a.*

as·ton·ish, *v.* amaze; surprise greatly. **as·ton·ish·ment,** *n.*

as·tound, *v.* astonish; amaze.

a·stray, *adv., a.* out of the right way or path.

a·stride, *a., adv., prep.* with one leg on each side.

as·trin·gent, *a.,* something causing shrinking or contracting.

as·trol·o·gy, *n.* supposed science of the effect of celestial bodies on human affairs. **as·trol·o·ger,** *n.*

as·tro·naut, *n.* crew member of space ship.

as·tron·o·my, *n.* science of celestial bodies. **as·tron·o·mer,** *n.*

as·tute, *a.* sagacious; shrewd.

a·sun·der, *adv., a.* apart.

a·sy·lum, *n.* place of refuge; institution for the insane, blind, etc.

at, *prep.* showing position, state or location; in; on; by; near.

a·the·ism, *n.* nonbelief in God. godless living. **a·the·ist,** *n.*

ath·lete, *n.* person trained in sports of agility, speed, skill and strength. **ath·let·ic,** *a.*

ath·lete's foot, *n.* fungus disease of the feet.

a·thwart, *adv., prep.* across; in opposition to; against.

at·las, *n. pl.,* **at·las·es.** book of maps.

at·mos·phere. *n.* gases surrounding the earth; aura. **at·mos·pher·ic,** *a.*

at·oll, *n.* coral island enclosing a central lagoon.

at·om, *n.* smallest particle of a chemical element. **a·tom·ic,** *a.*

a·tom·ic pile, *n.* nuclear reactor.

at·om·ize, *v.,* **-ized, -iz·ing.** reduce to atoms; a fine spray. **at·om·iz·er,** *n.*

a·tone, *v.,* **a·toned, a·ton·ing.** make amends. **a·tone·ment,** *n.*

a·tro·cious, *a.* wicked; cruel; abominable; very bad. **a·troc·i·ty,** *n. pl.,* **a·troc·i·ties.**

a·tro·phy, *n. pl.,* **-phies.** wasting away or shriveling up. *v.,* **phied, -phy·ing.** **a·troph·ic,** *a.*

at·tach, *v.* fasten; join; affix. **at·tach·ment,** *n.*

at·tack, *v.* assault; assail; use force; invade.

at·tain, *v.* achieve; acquire; gain; reach. **at·tain·ment,** *n.*

at·tempt, *v.* make an effort; try. *n.* endeavor; putting forth effort.

at·tend, *v.* accompany; be present at; pay attention to; wait on; **at·tend·ance,** *n.* **at·tend·ant,** *n.*

at·ten·tion, *n.* paying heed; care; readiness. **at·ten·tive,** *a.*

at·test, *v.* give proof or evidence of; declare to be true. **at·tes·ta·tion,** *n.*

at·tire, *v.,* **at·tired, at·tir·ing.** dress; array. *n.* clothing.

at·ti·tude, *n.* manner of a person; position or posture.

at·tor·ney, *n. pl.,* **-neys.** authorized agent; lawyer.

at·tract, *v.* draw toward; entice; be pleasing to. **at·trac·tion,** *n.* **at·trac·tor,** *n.* **at·trac·tive,** *a.*

at·trib·ute, *v.,* **-but·ed, -but·ing.** ascribe; impute. *n.* characteristic of; a quality of. **at·tri·bu·tion,** *n.* **at·trib·u·tive,** *a.*

at·tri·tion, *n.* wearing away or down.

au·burn, *a., n.* reddish-brown.

auc·tion, *n.* public sale of items to the highest bidder. *v.* sell by auction.

au·da·cious, *a.* daring; bold; impudent. **au·dac·i·ty,** *n.*

au·di·ble, *a.* capable of being heard. **au·di·bly,** *adv.*

au·di·ence, *n.* people gathered together to see or hear; formal interview.

au·dit, *n.* official examination of accounts. *v.* make an audit of. **au·dit·or,** *n.*

au·di·tion, *n.* hearing; trial performance. *v.* give an audition.

au·di·to·ri·um, *n.* building or room used for public gatherings.

au·di·to·ry, *a.* of hearing.

aug·ment, *v.* increase; enlarge. **aug·men·ta·tion,** *n.*

aunt, *n.* sister of a person's father or mother; uncle's wife.

au·ra, *n. pl.,* **au·ras, au·rae.** subtle quality or atmosphere surrounding a person or thing.

au·re·o·my·cin, *n.* drug used to check or kill viruses and bacteria.

au·ri·cle, *n.* external ear; chamber of the heart.

au·ro·ra bo·re·a·lis *n.* polar lights in the sky. **au·ro·ral,** *a.*

aus·pice, *n. pl.,* **aus·pic·es.** omen. *pl.* patronage.

aus·pi·cious, *a.* propitious; favorable; fortunate.

aus·tere, *a.* harsh; stern; severe; strict. **aus·ter·i·ty,** *n.*

au·then·tic, *a.* genuine; reliable.

au·then·ti·cate, *v.,* **-cat·ed, -cat·ing.** prove authentic. **au·then·ti·ca·tion,** *n.* **au·then·tic·i·ty,** *n.*

au·thor, *n.* person who writes books, etc. originator or creator.

au·thor·i·ta·tive, *a.* having authority; dictatorial; commanding.

au·thor·i·ty, *n. pl.,* **-ties.** legal power to enforce; person exercising power; reference source or expert.

au·thor·ize, *v.,* **-ized, -iz·ing.** give power or right to; sanction; empower. **au·thor·i·za·tion,** *n.*

au·to·bi·og·ra·phy, *n. pl.,* **-phies.** story of a person's life written by himself. **au·to·bi·og·ra·pher,** *n.*

au·to·clave, *n.* vessel used for sterilizing or cooking.

au·to·crat, *n.* ruler with absolute power. **au·toc·ra·cy,** *n.* **au·to·crat·ic,** *a.*

au·to·graph, *n.* signature. *v.* writing one's signature.

au·to·mat·ic, *a.* involuntary or reflexive; self-regulating; acting by itself.

au·to·ma·tion, *n.* method of making a machine operate more automatically by controls.

au·to·mo·bile, *n.* car that has its own engine. **au·to·mo·tive,** *a.*

au·ton·o·mous, *a.* self-governing; independent. **au·ton·o·mous·ly,** *ad.* **au·ton·o·my,** *n.*

au·top·sy, *n.* medical examination of a body to determine cause of death.

au·tumn, *n.* season between summer and winter.

aux·il·ia·ry, *a.* helping; assistant. *n. pl.,* **aux·il·la·ries,** aid; helping group.

a·vail, *v.* assist; benefit; help; be of use; make use of.

a·vail·a·ble, *a.* can be used or had. **a·vail·a·bil·i·ty,** *n.*

av·a·lanche, *n.* large mass of snow, rock, or dirt sliding down a mountain.

a·vant-garde, *n.* people with the latest inventive ideas.

av·a·rice, *n.* greedy desire for money. **av·a·ri·cious,** *a.*

a·venge, *v.,* **a·venged, a·veng·ing.** get revenge. **a·veng·er,** *n.*

av·e·nue, *n.* wide street; way or means of access.

a·ver, *v.,* **a·verred, a·ver·ring.** state to be true; affirm.

av·er·age, *n.* arithmetic mean; typical example. *v.,* **-aged, -ag·ing.** find the average of; have as an average. *a.* usual; ordinary.

a·verse, *a.* opposed; unwilling. **a·verse·ly,** *adv.* **a·ver·sion,** *n.*

a·vert, *v.* turn away; prevent.

a·vi·ar·y, *n.* place where birds are kept.

a·vi·a·tion, *n.* science of airplanes. **a·vi·a·tor,** *n.* **a·vi·a·trix,** *n.*

av·id, *a.* eager; greedy.

av·o·ca·do, *n. pl.,* **-dos.** tropical fruit; alligator pear.

av·o·ca·tion, *n.* hobby; minor job.

a·void, *v.* shun; keep away from; annul. **a·void·a·ble,** *a.*

av·oir·du·pois, *n.* weight system in which 1 lb. contains 16 oz. *col.* a person's weight.

a·vow, *v.* declare openly; admit. **a·vow·al,** *n.* **a·vowed,** *a.*

a·wait, *v.* wait for; expect.

a·wake, *a.* not sleeping; alert. *v.* **a·woke, a·wak·ing; a·waked; a·wak·ing.**

a·ward, v. grant; give as a prize. n. judgment; prize.

a·ware, a. cognizant; knowing; conscious. **a·ware·ness,** n.

a·way, adv. at a distance; apart. a. not present; afar; gone.

awe, n. reverential fear. v., **awed, aw·ing.** fill with awe.

aw·ful, a. dreadful; terrible; objectionable. **aw·ful·ly,** adv.

a·while, adv. for some time.

awk·ward, a. clumsy; not skillful; inconvenient; embarrassing. **awk·ward·ly,** adv. **awk·ward·ness,** n.

a·wry, a., adv. crooked; wrong.

ax, axe, n. pl., **ax·es.** bladed tool for chopping, etc.

ax·i·om, n. self-evident truth. **ax·i·o·mat·ic,** a.

ax·is, n. pl., **ax·es.** imaginary or real line about which a body revolves or seems to resolve; an alliance.

ax·le, n. shaft on which or with which wheels rotate. **ax·i·al,** a.

az·ure, a. sky blue. n. blue color; a blue pigment.

B

bab·ble, v., **-bled, -bling.** make indistinct sounds; speak foolishly; murmur; tell secrets. n. senseless prattle. **bab·bler,** n.

ba·boon, n. large fierce monkey; stupid or uncouth person.

ba·bush·ka, n. head scarf.

ba·by, n. pl., **ba·bies.** very young child; infant; youngest of family. a. v., **ba·bied, ba·by·ing.** pamper. **ba·by·hood,** n. **ba·by·ish,** a.

bac·ca·lau·re·ate, n. bachelor's degree; commencement speech.

bac·cha·nal, n. drunken orgy; reveler. **bac·cha·na·li·an,** a.

bach·e·lor, n. unmarried man; college degree. **bach·e·lor·hood,** n.

ba·cil·lus, n. pl., **ba·cil·li.** bacteria. **ba·cil·la·ry,** a.

back, n. part of body opposite the front; rear. v. move backward; support. a. the rear; in a backward direction. adv. to or toward the rear. **back·er,** n. **back·ing,** n.

back·bone, n. spine; fortitude.

back·drop, n. curtain at back of a stage; background.

back·fire, n. premature explosion in a car engine; unexpected adverse result. v., **-fired, -fir·ing.**

back·ground, n. back part of picture or scene; past happenings, conditions, events or experiences.

back·hand, n. stroke made with hand turned outward; handwriting that slopes to the left. **back·hand·ed,** a.

back·side, n. back part of anything; posterior; rump.

back·slide, v., **-slid; -slid or -slid·den; -slid·ing.** slide back into wrong doing; turn away from religion. **back·slid·er,** n.

back·stage, adv. in the dressing rooms, rear of the stage.

back·track, v. go back over one's steps; retreat; withdraw.

back·ward, adv. toward the back, rear, or past; with the back first. a. in reverse; retarded; shy. **back·ward·ness,** n.

back·woods n. pl. uncleared areas far away from towns.

ba·con, n. salted and smoked back and sides of a hog.

bac·te·ri·a, n. pl. microscopic organism causing disease, fermentation or putrefaction. **bac·te·ri·al,** a. **bac·te·ri·al·ly,** adv.

bac·te·ri·ol·o·gy, n. study of bacteria. **bac·te·ri·ol·o·gist,** n.

bad, a. **worse, worst.** not good; evil; rotten; defective; harmful. n. that which is bad. **bad·ly,** adv. **bad·ness,** n.

badge, n. emblem; symbol.

badg·er, n. burrowing mammal related to the weasel. v. harass; pester; tease annoy.

bad·i·nage, n. banter, joking.

baf·fle, v., **-fled, -fling.** bewilder; perplex; hinder; thwart. **baf·fler,** n. **baf·fling,** a.

bag, n. container made of paper, leather, cloth, etc.; sack; valise; purse. v. **bagged, bag·ging.** hang loosely; put into a bag; to kill or catch. **bag·gy,** a.

bag·gage, n. suitcases; luggage.

bag·ni·o, n. pl., **-los.** brothel.

bag·pipe, n. musical instrument made of a leather bag and pipes. **bag·pip·er,** n.

bail, v. empty a (boat) of water, free from arrest by providing bail. n. amount guaranteed for a prisoner's release.

bail·iff, n. sheriff's assistant court officer; estate overseer.

bait, n. thing used to lure or entice. v. lure; annoy; torment.

bake, v., **baked, bak·ing.** cook by dry heat; dry or harden by heat. **bak·er,** n.

bak·er's doz·en, n. thirteen.

bak·er·y, n. pl., **-les.** place for baking bread and cakes.

bal·a·lai·ka, *n.* guitar-like Russian musical instrument.

bal·ance, *n.* device for weighing; equilibrium; equality; mental stability; difference between accounts debits and credits. *v.,* **-anced, -anc·ing.** weigh; adjust evenly; offset; total or settle. **bal·ance·a·ble,** *a.*

bal·co·ny, *n. pl.,* **-nies.** projecting platform or gallery inside or outside a building.

bald, *a.* having little or no hair on the head. bare; plain. **bald·ly,** *adv.* **bald·ness,** *n.*

bal·der·dash, *n.* nonsense.

bale, *n.* bundle. *v.,* **baled, bal·ing.** make into bales.

bale·ful, *a.,* harmful; evil. **bale·ful·ly.**

balk, *n.* check or thwart; *v.* hinder; stop and refuse to go on. **balk·y,** *a.*

ball, *n.* spherical; round body used in games; dance. *v.* to form into a ball.

bal·lad, *n.* simple song; narrative poem.

bal·last, *n.* heavy material carried in a ship to steady it; rock or gravel for a road bed. *v.* weigh down.

bal·le·ri·na, *n.* female ballet dancer.

bal·let, *n.* elaborate dance; the dancers.

bal·lis·tics, *n. pl.* science of projectiles in flight. **bal·lis·tic,** *a.* **bal·lis·ti·cian,** *n.*

bal·loon, *n.* bag filled with a gas lighter than air causing it to rise and float. *v.* expand.

bal·lot, *n.* paper used to vote; number of votes cast.

ball·room, *n.* large room for dancing or meetings.

balm, *n.* fragment ointment.

balm·y, *a.,* **-i·er, -i·est.** mild; soothing. *col.* crazy. **balm·i·ly,** *adv.* **balm·i·ness,** *n.*

ba·lo·ney, *n.* bologna sausage; *col.* nonsense.

bal·sa, *n.* light wood; the tree.

bal·sam, *n.* ointment; plant or tree that yields a balm.

bal·us·ter, *n.* pillarlike support for a railing or balustrade.

bam·bi·no, *n.* baby; small child.

bam·boo, *n.* hollow stemmed woody plant; its stems.

ban, *v.,* **banned, ban·ning.** prohibit; forbid. *n.* prohibition by authority.

ba·nal, *a.* common; trite; insipid. **ba·nal·i·ty,** *n.*

ba·nan·a, *n.* curved, pulpy tropical fruit.

band, *n.* group of musicians; strip; range of radio frequencies. *v.* tie or fetter with a band; unite.

band·age, *n.* strip of cloth used to dress (cover) wounds. *v.,* **-aged, -ag·ing.** dress wounds.

ban·dit, *n. pl.,* **-dits, -dit·ti.** robber; highwayman. **ban·dit·ry,** *n.*

bane, *n.* cause of death or harm; curse. **bane·ful,** *a.*

bang, *v.* beat noisily; slam. *n.* loud, sudden sound.

ban·ish, *v.* exile; drive away. **ban·ish·er,** *n.* **ban·ish·ment,** *n.*

ban·is·ter, *n.* handrail; baluster.

ban·jo, *n.* stringed, guitar class musical instrument having a body like a tambourine.

bank, *n.* mound; pile; heap; tier; row; institution for the deposit, keeping and lending of money. *v.* embank; to cover (a fire). **bank·a·ble,** *a.* **bank·er,** *n.* **bank·ing,** *n.*

bank·rupt, *a.* unable to pay one's debts; legally so adjudged. *v.* make bankrupt. **bank·rupt·cy,** *n. pl.,* **-cies.**

ban·ner, *n.* flag.

ban·quet, *n.* formal dinner. *v.* to feast. **ban·quet·er,** *n.*

ban·tam, *n.* small chicken-like fowl; small fighting person. *a.* small; light.

ban·ter, *n.* raillery; joking.

bap·tism, *n.* ritual of a Christian church of immersing in or sprinkling on water; first experience. **bap·tis·mal,** *a.* **bap·tist,** *n.*

bap·tize, *v.,* **-tized, -tiz·ing.** administer baptism; christen.

bar, *n.* long piece of wood or metal; obstruction; the legal profession; counter where drinks are served; band or stripe. *v.,* **barred, bar·ring.** prevent; exclude. *prep.* except.

barb, *n.* sharp point as on a spear; critical remark. **barbed,** *a.*

bar·bar·i·an, *n.* non-civilized person; savage.

bar·bar·ic, *a.* uncivilized; rough; rude; crudely splendid.

bar·ba·rous, *a.* rude and ignorant; barbaric; savagely cruel. **bar·barism,** *n.* **bar·bar·i·ty,** *n. pl.,* **-ties.**

bar·be·cue, *n.* food or meat roasted or baked over an open fire; the food so prepared. *v.,* **-cued, -cu·ing.**

barbed wire, *n.* wire having sharp points. Also **barb·wire.**

bar·ber, *n.* one who cuts and dresses hair. **bar·ber·shop,** *n.*

bar·bi·tu·rate, *n.* drug used as a sedative or hypnotic.

bare, *a.,* **bar·er, bar·est.** without covering; naked; plain; empty. *v.* reveal; uncover.

bare·ly, *adv.* scarcely; openly; plainly; nakedly.

bar·gain, *n.* an agreement; thing offered or bought at a low price. *v.* make a bargain. **bar·gain·er,** *n.*

barge, *n.* flat-bottomed boat; large boat for excursions, etc.; boat for commanding officer.

bar·i·tone, *n.* male voice between bass and tenor; brass instrument.

bark, *n.* covering of trees; cry of a dog; type of ship. *v.* scrape or rub off; make a barking sound.

bar·ley, *n. pl.,* **-leys.** cereal grain.

bar mitz·vah, *n.* ceremony recognizing a Jewish boy as an adult at age 13.

barn, *n.* farm building used for storage; *col.* big place.

bar·na·cle, *n.* crustacean.

ba·rom·et·er, *n.* instrument for measuring atmospheric pressure. **bar·o·met·ric,** *a.*

bar·on, *n.* lowest-ranking nobleman.

ba·roque, *a.* ornate; grotesque; tasteless; odd.

bar·rack, *n. usu. pl.* building for housing soldiers.

bar·ra·cu·da, *n. pl.,* **-da,-das.** large voracious fish.

bar·rage, *n.* barrier of artillery fire to stop the enemy.

bar·rel, *n.* cylindrical container with bulging sides; firing tube of a gun.

bar·ren, *a.* not producing; unfruitful; sterile. **bar·ren·ness,** *n.*

bar·rette, *n.* clasp for holding girl's or women's hair.

bar·ri·cade, *n.* barrier; blockade.

bar·ri·er, *n.* anything that stops or stands in the way.

bar·row, *n.* wheelbarrow.

bar·ten·der, *n.* person who serves alcoholic drinks.

bar·ter, *v.* trade by exchanging goods without money. **bar·ter·er,** *n.*

ba·salt, *n.* volcanic rock.

base, *n.* bottom of anything; fundamental principle or element; center of authority; military station; baseball goal. *v.,* **based, bas·ing.** make or form a base for. *a.,* **bas·er, bas·est.** morally low; mean. **ba·sal,** *a.*

base·ball, *n.* game with four bases played with bat and ball by two teams; the ball used.

base·born, *a.* of humble birth.

base·less, *a.* groundless.

base·ment, *n.* story of a building partly or wholly below ground.

bash·ful, *a.* shy; timid. **bash·ful·ly,** *adv.* **bash·ful·ness,** *n.*

ba·sic, *a.* forming the basis; fundamental. **ba·si·cal·ly,** *adv.*

ba·sil, *n.* aromatic plant or herb.

ba·sin, *n.* round, shallow bowl for holding liquids; reservoir; tract of land drained by a river; roundish valley.

ba·sis, *n. pl.,* **ba·ses.** main part; fundamental principle; foundation.

bask·et, *n.* container made of straw, twigs or thin strips of wood, etc. **bas·ket·ry,** *n.*

bass, *n.* lowest male voice; such a singer; lowest part; deeptoned instrument. *a.* low; deep. **bass,** *n.* a type of fish.

bas·set, *n.* dog with short legs and a long body.

bas·si·net, *n.* basket-like infant's bed or baby carriage.

bas·soon, *n.* deep-toned woodwind instrument.

bas·tard, *n.* illegitimate child. *a.* illegitimate; inferior; spurious; not genuine. **bas·tard·ize,** *v.*

baste, *v.,* **bast·ed, bast·ing.** sew with long stitches; drip or pour fat or liquid upon while cooking.

bas·tion, *n.* defense fortification.

batch, *n.* quantity of a thing made, handled or processed at once.

bath, *n. pl.,* **baths.** a washing of the body; bathtub or room.

bathe, *v.,* **bathed, bath·ing.** wash; take or give a bath; swim. **bath·er,** *n.*

bat·on, *n.* staff; wand.

bat·tal·ion, *n.* army tactical unit; large group or force.

bat·ter, *v.* beat with repeated blows; wear out; *n.* mixture of ingredients used in cookery.

bat·ter·y, *n.* cells that produce electric current; unlawful beating; pieces of artillery used together.

bat·tle, *n.* combat; fight. *v.,* **-tled, -tling.** join in battle.

bau·ble, *n.* showy trifle.

bawd·y, *a.,* **-i·er, -i·est.** obscene; lewd. **bawd,** *n.*

bawl, *v.* cry out; weep loudly.

bay, *n.* space between pillars or columns; projecting space with a window; gulf; reddish-brown horse; deep bark; stand made when cornered and forced to fight. *v.* bark at; hold at bay.

bay·o·net, *n.* sword for stabbing fixed to a gun.

bay·ou, *n.* marshy inlet or outlet of a lake, river, etc.

ba·zaar, *n.* street full of small shops; sale for charity.

ba·zoo·ka, *n.* portable rocket gun used against tanks.

be, *v.* pres. sing. **am, are, is;** pres. pl. **are;** past sing. **was, were, was;** past pl. **were;** pp. **been;** ppr. **being.** exist; live; take place; remain; continue.

beach, *n.* flat, sandy shore.

bea·con, *n.* a fire or light used as a guiding signal.

bead, *n.* small, perforated object threaded on string; a drop or bubble. *v.* **bead·ed.**

beak, *n.* bird's bill; a spout. **beaked,** *a.*

beak·er, *n.* open-mouthed vessel of glass, etc. with spout.

beam, *n.* long, heavy piece of timber, iron, etc.; horizontal main support of a building; width of a ship; ray of light; guiding radio signal. *v.* shine.

bean, *n.* edible seed contained in a pod; any bean-shaped seed.

bear, *n. pl.,* **bears, bear.** large four-legged animal with coarse hair; gruff person. *v.* **bore.** carry; bring; endure; give birth or produce. **bear·a·ble,** *a.* **bear·a·bly,** *adv.* **bear·er,** *n.* **bear·ing,** *n.* **bear·ish,** *a.*

beard, *n.* hair that grows on a man's face; hairs on plant heads. **beard·ed,** *a.* **beard·less,** *a.*

bear·ing, *n.* anyone or thing that carries; manner of sitting, walking, etc.; relationship; relative direction; part of a machine on which another part turns.

beast, *n.* four-footed animal; a coarse or brutal man. **beast·li·ness,** *n.* **beast·ly.**

beat, *v.,* **beat·en, beat·ing.** strike repeatedly; whip; overcome; mix by stirring. *n.* rhythmical blow; musical accent; police patrol area. **beat·er,** *n.*

beat·en, *v.,* whipped; thrashed; much traveled path; shaped by hammer blows; defeated; exhausted.

be·at·i·tude, *n.* blessing; bliss; great happiness.

beau·ty, *n. pl.,* **-ties.** loveliness; good looks; pleasing, attractive person or thing. **beau·te·ous,** *a.* **beau·ti·ful,** *a.* **beau·ti·ful·ly,** *adv.* **beau·ti·fy,** *v.*

bea·ver, *n.* amphibious dam-building rodent having soft brown fur and a broad flat tail.

be·cause, *conj.* for the reason of; on account of.

beck·on, *v.* signal a person by a motion of hand or head.

be·come, *v.,* **be·came, be·come, be·com·ing.** come; grow to be; be suitable for.

be·com·ing. *a.* attractive; appropriate.

bed, *n.* anything on which to sleep or rest; plot of ground in which plants are grown; solid base or foundation. **bed·ding,** *n.* blankets, etc.

be·dev·il, *v.,* **-iled, -il·ing.** torment; confuse; bewitch.

bed·lam, *n.* uproar and confusion; mad house.

be·drag·gle, *v.,* **-gled, -gling.** make limp and soiled with dirt.

bed·rid·den, *a.* confined to bed for a long time by illness.

bed·stead, *n.* framework that supports a bed.

bee, *n.* an insect that produces honey and wax.

beef, *n. pl.,* **beefs, beeves.** meat from cattle (steer, bull, cow). *col.* complaint.

bee·hive, *n.* house for bees; a busy active place.

beer, *n.* alcoholic beverage made of barley and hops. **beer·y,** *a.*

beet, *n.* red fleshy edible root; white sugar beet.

bee·tle, *n.* insects with hard outer wing coverings.

be·fall, *v.,* **be·fell, be·fall·en, be·fall·ing.** happen; happen to.

be·fit, *v.,* **be·fit·ted, be·fit·ting.** suitable to or for. **be·fit·ting,** *a.*

be·fore, *adv. prep.* in front of; previously; ahead of; earlier than; rather than; sooner than; in the presence of.

be·fore·hand, *adv.* in advance.

be·friend, *v.* make friends with; assist; aid; help.

beg, *v.,* **begged, beg·ging.** ask for charity; ask for help; beseech. **beg·gar,** *n.* **beg·gar·ly,** *a.*

be·gin, *v.* **be·gan, be·gun, be·gin·ning.** do the first part; start; originate. **be·gin·ner,** *n.* **be·gin·ning,** *n.*

be·grudge, *v.* be envious of somebody; be reluctant to give something.

be·guile, *v.,* **be·guiled, be·guil·ing.** cheat; deceive; charm; amuse; while away (time).

be·half, *n.* in the interest of.

be·have, *v.,* **be·haved, be·hav·ing.** do what is right; act properly, **be·hav·ior,** *n.*

be·head, *v.* decapitate.

be·hind, *prep.* at the back of; in support of; remaining after; later than.*adv.* not on time; backward; slow.

be·hold, *v.* look at; see. **-hold·er,** *n.*

beige, *n.* grayish tan.

be·ing, *n.* existence; life; living creature.

be·la·bor, v. beat; abuse; ridicule.

be·lat·ed, a. delayed; too late.

be·lea·guer, v. besiege; surround.

bel·fry, n. pl., **-fries**. bell tower.

be·lie, v. lie about; misrepresent; prove to be false.

be·lief, n. thing believed; trust; confidence; have faith.

be·lieve, v., **-lieved, -liev·ing**. accept as true; have faith; suppose. **be·liev·a·ble**, a.

bell, n. hollow metal object, which gives a ringing sound when struck.

bell·boy, n. one who carries luggage, runs errands, etc. in a hotel or club.

bel·li·cose, a. eager to fight.

bel·lig·er·ence, n. warfare; antagonism. **bel·lig·er·en·cy**, n. **bel·lig·er·ent**, a.

bel·low, n., v. roar; shout loudly.

bel·lows, n. instrument which produces a strong current of air (for a fire, organ, etc.).

bel·ly, n. pl., **-lies**. abdomen. v., **-lied, -ly·ing**. swell out; bulge.

be·long, v. have a proper place; be a member of. **be·long·ings**, n. pl. possessions.

be·loved, a. dearly loved. n. one greatly loved.

be·low, prep. lower than; beneath. adv. in a lower place.

belt, n. band or strip worn around the waist; strip. v. strike with a belt or fist. **belt·ed**, a.

be·mire, v. **-mired, -mir·ing**. sink in mud; make dirty.

be·moan, v. bewail; lament.

be·muse, v., **be·mused, be·mus·ing**. bewilder. **be·mused**, a.

bench, n. long seat; a court of justice.

bend, v., **bent, bend·ing**. make curved or crooked; flex; stoop; bow. n. bending; curve. **bend·er**, n.

be·neath, adv. below; underneath; unworthy. prep. under; below.

ben·e·dic·tion, n. closing prayer.

ben·e·fac·tion, n. a doing good benefit. **ben·e·fac·tor**, n.

ben·ef·i·cence, n. doing good.

ben·e·fi·cial, a. helpful; good; fit. **ben·e·fi·cial·ly**, adv.

ben·e·fi·ci·ar·y, n. pl., **-ar·ies**. one who receives benefits from insurance, a will, etc.; one who receives a benefit.

ben·e·fit, n. advantage; anything for the good of; v. **-fit·ed, -fit·ing**. do good to; receive good.

be·nev·o·lence, n. good will; kindness. **be·nev·o·lent**, a.

be·nign, a. kindly; gentle; not malignant. **be·nig·ni·ty**, n. pl., **-ties. be·nign·ly**, adv.

be·nig·nant, a. kindly; benign. **be·nig·nan·cy**, n. pl., **-cies**.

bent, a. not straight; determined. n. strongly inclined.

ben·ny, n. Benzadrine pill.

be·queath, v. give or leave by will; hand down to posterity.

be·quest, n. legacy; bequeathed.

be·rate, v. **be·rat·ed, be·rat·ing**. scold sharply; reprimand.

be·reave, v., **be·reaved** or **be·reft, be·reav·ing**. loss of someone loved; deprive ruthlessly; make desolate. **be·reave·ment**, n.

be·ret, n. soft, cloth cap without visor.

ber·i·ber·i, n. nerve disease caused by lack of vitamin B_1.

ber·ry, n. pl., **ber·ries**. small, juicy fruit, with many seeds.

ber·serk, a. adv. in a frenzy.

berth, n. ships place at a wharf or at anchor; sleeping place on a ship, train, etc.

be·seech, v., **-sought** or **seeched, -seech·ing**. beg earnestly for; implore.

be·set, v., **-set, -set·ting**. hem in; attack or surround on all sides. **be·set·ting**, a.

be·side, prep. near; by the side of; in comparison with; in addition to; apart from.

be·sides, adv. moreover. prep. in addition; except.

be·siege, v., **-sieged, -sieg·ing**. lay seige to; crowd around.

be·smirch, v. sully; soil.

be·speak, v. **-spoke, -spoke** or **-spok·en, -speak·ing**. order or engage in advance.

best, a., superl. of good. above all others in worth; largest; adv. in the highest degree; most. n. utmost state of excellence. v. defeat; outstrip.

bes·tial, a. like a beast, brutish, savage, vile. **bes·tial·ly**, adv. **bes·tial·i·ty**, n. pl., **-ties. be·stir**, v. stir into action; exert.

be·stir, v. stir into action.

be·stow, v. present; to apply; devote.

bet, n. wager; stake; pledge. v., **bet or bet·ted, bet·ting**. wager.

be·ta, n. second letter of Greek alphabet.

be·tray, v. help the enemy by treachery; seduce; disclose. **be·tray·al**, n.

be·troth, v. **be·troth·al**, to promise in marriage. n. **be·trothed**, a.

bet·ter, a., compar. of good. more excellent; greater; larger; improved in health. adv., compar. of well. in a more suitable manner. usu. pl. one's superiors. v. surpass, to outdo.

bet·ter·ment, *n.* improvement.

be·tween, *prep.* space or interval or space which separates; shared by; involving both of. *adv.* in the intermediate space, function, position, etc.

bev·er·age, *n.* drink; liquid.

bev·y, *n. pl.,* **bev·ies.** flock of birds, esp. quail; group, esp. women.

be·ware, *v.* be careful of; be on one's guard.

be·wil·der, *v.* perplex; confuse. **be·wil·der·ment,** *n.*

be·witch, *v.* cast a spell over; charm; fascinate. **be·witch·er·y,** *n.* **be·witch·ing,** *a.*

be·yond, *adv.* farther away. *prep.* later than; out of reach of; over and above.

bi·as, *n.* slanting line across a fabric; partiality; prejudice. *a.* diagonal. *adv.* obliquely. *v.,* **bi·ased, bi·as·ing, bi·assed, bi·as·sing;** to prejudice.

bib, *n.* apronlike cloth under a child's chin to protect clothes; front upper part of apron or overalls.

Bi·ble, *n.* sacred book of Christianity; Old Testament and New Testament; any religious holy book. **Bib·li·cal,** *a.* **Bib·li·cal·ly,** *adv.*

bib·li·og·ra·phy, *n. pl.,* **-phies,** list of books, materials, articles, etc. **bib·li·og·ra·pher,** *n.*

bi·cen·ten·ni·al, *n.* two-hundredth year anniversary.

bi·ceps, *n. pl.* upper arm muscles.

bick·er, *v.* squabble; argue.

bi·cy·cle, *n.* two-wheeled vehicle. *v.,* **-cled, -cling.** ride on a bicycle. **bi·cy·clist,** *n.*

bid, *v.,* **bid** or **bade, bid, bid·den, bid·ding.** to offer a price; to order; ask; tell. *n.* offer of a price; amount of a bid. **bid·da·ble.** *a.* **bid·der,** *n.*

bide, *v.,* **bid·ed, bid·ing.** abide.

bi·en·ni·al, *a.* happening every two years; *n.* plant that lives two years. **bi·en·ni·al·ly,** *adv.*

bier, *n.* portable platform for a coffin.

big, *a.,* **big·ger, big·gest.** of great size, extent, or capacity. large. *adv.* pompously.

big·a·my, *n. pl.,* **big·a·mies.** act of marrying second person while still married. **big·a·mist,** *n.* **big·a·mous,** *a.*

big·ot, *n.* narrow-minded, intolerant person. **big·ot·ed,** *a.* **big·ot·ry,** *n. pl.,* **-ries.**

bike, *n., v. inf.* bicycle; motorcycle.

bi·ki·ni *n.* very brief two piece bathing suit.

bi·lat·er·al, *a.* having two sides.

bile, *n.* bitter liquid secreted by the liver; bad temper; anger. **bil·i·ary,** *a.* **bil·ious,** *a.*

bi·lev·el *a.* having two ground floor levels.

bilge, *n.* lowest part of a ship's hull. *inf.* worthless remarks.

bilk, *v.* to cheat or swindle.

bill, *n.* statement of money due; a list; a poster or handbill; piece of paper money; draft of a proposed law; bird's beak. *v.* to list.

bill·board, *n.* a flat surface on which signs are posted.

bil·let, *n.* lodgings for a soldier. *v.* assign to quarters.

bill·fold, *n.* wallet.

bil·liards, *n. pl.* game played on a cloth-covered table with hard balls and a cue.

bil·lion, *n.* a thousand million. **bil·lionth,** *a.,* *n.* **bil·lion·aire,** *n.*

bil·low, *n.* large wave. **bil·low·y,** *a.,* **-i·er, -i·est.** *v.* bulge.

bil·ly goat, *n.* male goat.

bi·month·ly, *a.* advance every two months; twice a month. *n. pl.,* **-lies.** bimonthly publication.

bin, *n.* box or enclosed space used for storing things.

bi·na·ry, *a.* involving two.

bind, *v.* **bound; binding;** tie; hold; restrain; confine; fasten together sheets of a book in a cover; to obligate. **bind·er,** *n.* **bind·ing,** *a., n.*

bind·er·y, *n. pl.,* **-er·ies.** place that binds books.

binge, *n. inf.* unrestrained spree.

bin·go, *n.* gambling game like lotto.

bi·noc·u·lar, *n. usu. pl.* field or opera glasses. *a.* using both eyes at the same time.

bi·og·ra·phy, *n. pl.,* **-phies.** written history of a person's life. **bi·og·ra·pher,** *n.* **bi·o·graph·i·cal, bi·o·graph·ic,** *a.*

bi·ol·o·gy, *n.* science of plant and animal life. **bi·o·log·i·cal,** *a.* **bi·o·log·ist,** *n.*

bi·op·sy, *n. pl.,* **bi·op·sies.** removal of living tissue from a body for examination.

bi·par·ti·san, *a.* representing two parties.

bi·ped, *n.* a two-footed animal **bi·ped·al,** *a.*

birch, *n.* tree of smooth whitish bark and hard wood.

bird, *n.* any warm-blooded, two-legged, egg-laying vertebrate having feathers and wings.

bird·ie, *n.* golf score of one stroke under par for a hole.

birth, *n.* act of being born or coming into life; descent; lineage; origin.

birth·day, *n.* day or anniversary of birth or origin.

birth·mark, *n.* blemish on a person's body at birth.

bis·cuit, *n.* unleavened bread baked in flat pieces. *Brit.* cracker.

bi·sect, v. cut into two. **bi·sec·tion,** n.

bi·sex·u·al, a. pert. to both sexes.

bish·op, n. high-ranking churchman who oversees a diocese; a chess piece. **bish·op·ric,** n.

bi·son, n. American buffalo.

bisque, n. thick, creamy soup.

bis·tro, n. pl., **bis·tros.** small bar or eating place.

bit, n. small piece or quantity; small part in a play; cutting or drilling part of a tool; metal mouthpiece on a bridle.

bitch, n. female dog; spiteful woman. v. sl. complain.

bite, v., **bit, bit. bit·ten, bit·ing.** cut or seize with the teeth; to sting; take a bait. n. morsel of food; wound. **bit·ing,** a. **bit·ing·ly,** adv.

bit·ter, a. having a sharp taste; acrid; sorrowful; harsh. **bit·ter·ish,** a. **bit·ter·ness,** n.

bit·tern, n. wading bird of the heron family.

bit·tu·mi·nous coal, n. tar-yielding coal; soft coal.

bi·valve, n. mollusk, having shell of hinged valves, as the oyster, clam, etc.

biv·ou·ac, n. temporary encampment without housing. v., **-acked, -ack·ing.**

bi·zarre, a. odd; queer; strange. **bi·zarre·ness,** n.

blab, v., **blabbed, blab·bing.** give out (secrets); chatter.

black, a. color opposite white; very dark; sad; evil. n. black pigment; negro. v. to blacken. **black·ly,** adv.

black·ber·ry, n. pl., **-ries.** edible dark fruit from certain bushes and vines.

black·bird, n. black bird of the thrush family.

black·board, n. dark smooth surface used for writing on with chalk.

black·en, v. darken; slander.

black·guard, n. villain.

black·head, n. acne blemish.

black·heart·ed, a. wicked.

black·jack, n. pirate's flag; card game; small club.

black mag·ic, n. sorcery.

black·mail, n. extortion by intimidation. v. coerce by threats.

black·out, n. period of darkness; temporary loss of consciousness or electricity.

black·smith, n. crafter of horse shoes; metalworker.

blad·der, n. sac which collects urine.

blade, n. a leaf; broad, flat surface or bone; cutting part of a tool; dashing young man.

blame, v., **blamed, blam·ing.** to hold responsible; find fault with. n. criticism. **blame·ful,** a. **blame·less,** a.

blame·wor·thy, a. being at fault. **blame·wor·thi·ness,** n.

blanch, v. make white; scald.

bland, a. smooth; not irritating. **bland·ly,** adv. **bland·ness,** n.

blan·dish, v. coax; flatter.

blank, a. void of marks; empty. n. empty space; printed form. **blank·ly,** adv. **blank·ness,** n.

blan·ket, n. cloth cover. a. wide range of coverage.

blare, v., **blared, blar·ing.** sound loudly. n. loud noise.

blar·ney, n. excessive flattery.

bla·se, a. dulled taste; indifferent.

blas·pheme, v. with irreverence. **blas·phem·ous,** a. **blas·phem·y,** n. pl., **-phem·ies.**

blast, n. violent gust of air; explosive. sl. good time v. destroy; detonate. **blast·ed,** a.

bla·tant, a. clamorous; offensively obvious. **bla·tan·cy,** n.

blath·er, v. to talk foolishly. n. silly talk.

blaze, n. intense fire; outburst; splendor. v., **blazed, blaz·ing.** burn brilliantly; glow; mark.

bla·zon, n. a coat of arms; showy display. v. adorn.

bleach, v. make white. n. agent used for bleaching.

bleach·ers, n. pl. tiered seats for spectators.

bleak, a. unsheltered; harsh; gloomy. **bleak·ly,** adv. **bleak·ness,** n.

bleat, v. cry of a sheep; whine. n. the cry.

bleed, v., **bled, bleed·ing.** lose blood; emit blood.

blem·ish, v. impair; mar; sully. n. deformity; imperfection.

blend, v., **blend·ed** or **blent, blend·ing.** mix; merge together. n. combination mixture. **blend·er,** n.

bless, v., **blessed** or **blest, bles·sing.** consecrate; give happiness; make holy. **bless·ed,** a. **bless·ed·ness,** n. **bles·sing,** n.

blight, n. destructive plant disease v. ruin; wither.

blimp, n. small dirigible.

blind, a. sightless v. to make blind; dazzle. n. thing to obstruct sight or light. **blind·ness,** n. **blind·ing,** a. **blind·ly,** adv.

blind·fold, v. to cover the eyes. n. cloth placed over the eyes. **blind·fold·ed,** a.

blink, v. wink quickly; flash; n. act of blinking.

bliss, n. supreme happiness or joy. **bliss·ful,** a.

blis·ter, n. watery-filled bulge under the skin. v. raise a blister.

blis·ter·y, a. **blithe,** a. merryglad. **blithe·ly,** adv.

bliz·zard, n. severe snowstorm.

bloat, v. swell; to puff up.

bloc, n. group united to further its common cause.

block, n. solid mass; a city square; hindrance; obsruction. v. impede; mold. **block·age,** n. **block·er,** n.

block·ade, n. barrier to obstruct passage. v., **-ad·ed, -ad·ing.** prevent passage.

blond, blonde, a. of a light color of hair. n. person with light colored hair.

blood, n. red fluid that circulates in the body; kinship.

blood·hound, n. large keen-scented dog; inf. relentless tracker.

blood·shed, n. slaughter.

blood·shot, a. red eyes due to dilated blood vessels.

blood·y, a., **-i·er, -i·est.** like blood; containing blood; blood-thirsty. v., **blood·ied, bloody·y·ing.** stain with blood. **blood·i·ness,** n.

bloom, n. flower; state of freshness or vigor. v. blossom; flourish with health. **bloom·ing,** a.

bloop·er, n. stupid or funny mistake.

blos·som, n. bloom. v. thrive.

blot, n. spot; erasure. v., **blot·ted, blot·ting.** obscure; absorb with blotting paper. **blot·ter,** n.

blotch, n. blemish; imperfection; cause a mark. **blotch·y,** a.

blouse, n. loose, shirt-like garment.

blow, v., **blew, blown, blow·ing.** move; send forth wind or air; to sound when blown into; boast; strike; burst. n. gale; blast; stroke. **blow·er,** n.

blow·up, n. outburst; inf. explosion of anger; enlargement.

blub·ber, n. whale fat. v. weep loudly. **blub·ber·y,** a.

bludg·eon, n. short stick used as weapon. v. attack; hit.

blue, a., **blu·er, blue·est.** sky colored; sad; depressed. n. blue v., **blued, blu·ing.** dye. pl., depressed feeling; jazz music. **blue·ness,** n.

blue·bell, n. pl., **-ries.** shrub bearing bluish, edible berries.

blue·bird, n. small, blue American songbird.

blue jay, n. American bird with a blue crest and back.

bluejeans, n. denim pants

blue print, n. photographic reproduction in white on blue background.

blues, n. pl. melancholy slow jazz; mental depression.

bluff, a. rough; plain; abrupt. n. broad, steep bank; false pretense. v. mislead; threaten.

blun·der, v. flounder; stumble. n. foolish mistake. **blun·der·er,** n.

blunt, a. dull; abrupt; slow to perceive; to make dull. v. **blunt·ness,** n.

blur, v., **blurred, blur·ring.** obscure; blemish. n. smear; stain; blot. **blur·ry,** a.

blurb, n. advertisement.

blurt, v. utter impulsively.

blush, v. redden, as from shame. n. rosy tint of the face. **blush·ful,** a. **blush·ing·ly,** adv.

blus·ter, v. blow, as wind; be loud or swaggering. n. loud talk. **blus·ter·ous,** a.

boar, n. male swine; wild hog.

board, n. flat piece of wood; meals provided for pay; body of directors. v. close with boards; to go onto a ship, etc. **board·er,** n.

boast, v. brag; be vainly proud. n. boastful talk. **boast·ful,** a. **boast·ful·ness,** n.

boat, n. small open waterborne vessel.

boat-swain, n. ship's officer in charge of rigging anchors, etc.

bob, v., **bobbed, bob·bing.** move quickly up and down; cut hair short; short hair cut.

bob·cat, n. wildcat; lynx.

bob·o·link, n. American songbird.

bob·sled, n. short racing sled. v. to coast or ride.

bob·white, n. quail; partridge.

bode, v., **bod·ed, bod·ing.** v. portend; foreshadow.

bod·ice, n. upper part of woman's dress; vest.

bod·y, n. physical organism; torso; corpse; mass; principal part; group of people; substance. v., **bod·ied, bod·y·ing.** embody. **bod·ied,** a. **bod·i·ly,** a., adv.

bod·y·guard, n. person with duty of protecting another from harm.

bog, n. quagmire; swamp. v., **bogged, bog·ging.** to become stuck. **bog·gy,** a.

bogey, n. a bogy; golf, one stroke above par.

bog·gle, v. exhibit shyness; to be startled; to work clumsily.

bo·gus, a. counterfeit; spurious.

bo·gy, goblin; spirit.

boil, v. generate bubbles through heat; be agitated by; seethe; cook by boiling. n. state of boiling; inflamed suppurating sore. **boil·er,** n.

bois·ter·ous, a. rowdy; noisy; stormy. **bois·ter·ous·ly,** adv. **bois·ter·ous·ness,** n.

bold, a. daring; forward; venturesome; lacking restraint; striking to the eye. **bold·ly,** adv. **bold·ness,** n.

bo·lo·gna, n. lunchmeat made of beef, veal, and pork.

bol·ster, n. long narrow pillow. v. maintain. **bol·ster·er,** n.

bolt, n. stroke of lightning; metal rod or pin; sliding bar for fastening a door; roll of material. v. fasten with a bolt; swallow hurriedly; spring away suddenly.

bomb, n. explosive projectile or device; v. attack with bombs.

bom·bard, v. shoot shells at; drop bombs on. **bom·bar·dier,** n. **bom·bard·ment,** n.

bom·bast, n. pretentious speech. **bom·bas·tic,** a.

bo·nan·za, n. rich vein of ore; source of wealth.

bon·bon, n. small piece of candy.

bond, n. anything that ties or binds; obligation; interest-bearing certificate. v. secure; put under a legal bond. **bond·ed,** a.

bond·age, n. slavery; serfdom.

bone, n. hard material forming the skeleton. v., **boned, bon·ing.** remove bones from. sl., to study.

bon·fire, n. fire outdoors.

bon·net, n. covering for the head.

bo·nus, n. pl., **bo·nus·es.** amount paid over what is required; a premium.

bon·sai, n. art of dwarfing trees; such tree or shrub.

bon·y, a., **-i·er, -i·est.** of bone; having bones.

boo, interj., n. profound sound of disapproval or to frighten. v., **booed, boo·ing.** cry "boo".

boo-boo, n. inf. mistake.

boo·by, n. pl., **-bles.** foolish person.

boo·by trap, n. camouflaged mine or other trap.

book, n. printed work on papers bound together. v. record; reserve space. **book·bind·er,** n. **book·ish,** a.

book·keep·ing, n. work of recording business transactions. **book·keep·er,** n.

book·let, n. small book.

boom, n. deep hollow noise; vigorous growth; a spar. v. make a deep sound; flourish.

boom·er·ang, n. curved stick that returns to thrower. v. recoil.

boon, n. great benefit; blessing.

boor, n. rude or unmannerly person. **boor·ish,** a.

boost, v. push up; promote or aid. n. push from behind; increase in power. **booster,** n.

boot, n. protective covering for foot; tire patch; kick. v. put on boots; kick.

booth, n. a stall; seating compartment; small enclosure.

boot·leg, v., **-legged, -leg·ging.** sell things illegally, esp. liquor. a. surreptitious. **boot·leg·ger,** n.

boo·ty, n. pl., **-ties.** spoils of war.

booze, n. hard liquor v. drink alcohol excessively. **booz·er,** n. **booz·y,** a., **-i·er, -i·est.**

bor·der, n. rim; edge; margin; frontier. v. be adjacent; form a border. **bor·dered,** a.

bore, v., **bored, bor·ing.** make a hole by drilling; weary by dullness. n. monotonous tiresome person or thing; hollow part of a tube. **bore·dom,** n.

borne, a. be brought into life.

bor·ough, n. self-governing incorporated town.

bor·row, v. to take or obtain, with the intention of returning; appropriate. **bor·row·er,** n.

bos·om, n. the breast, a. intimate.

boss, n. employer; authority figure; v. manage; domineer; conrol.

boss·y, a., **-i·er, -i·est.** inf. domineering. **boss·i·ness,** n.

bot·a·ny, n. science of plants. **bo·tan·ic, bo·tan·i·cal,** a. **bot·a·nist,** n. mess.

botch, n. mess; poorly done work. v. perform in a clumsy manner. **botch·y,** a., **-i·er, -i·est.**

both, a., pron. the two together. conj. together; equally.

both·er, n. worry; fuss. v. bewilder; perplex; trouble. **both·er·some,** a.

bot·tle, n. container for holding liquids. v., **-tled, -tling.** put into bottles. **bot·tler,** n.

bot·tom, n. lowest position; base; foundation. a. undermost.

bot·u·lism, n. food poisoning.

bou·doir, n. woman's bedroom.

bough, n. tree branch.

bought, pt. and pp. of **buy.**

bouil·la·baisse, n. fish chowder.

bouil·lon, n. clear soup.

boul·der, n. large round rock.

boul·e·vard, n. broad street.

bounce, *v.,* **bounced, bounc·ing.** strike a surface and cause to rebound. *n.* bound; a sudden leap. **bounc·er,** *n.* **bounc·ing,** *a.*

bound, *n. usu. pl.* boundary; jump. *v.* abut; set restraints; confine; leap. *a.* tied; under obligation; destined.

bound·a·ry, *n. pl.,* **-ries.** limits; border.

boun·te·ous, *a.* generous; plentiful. **boun·te·ous·ness,** *n.*

boun·ty, *n. pl.,* **-ties.** generosity; reward; premium.

bou·quet, *n.* bunch of flowers; fragrant smell.

bour·bon, *n.* whiskey.

bour·geois, *n. pl.,* **-geois.** middle class person. *a.* middle-class.

bout, *n.* contest; match.

bou·tique, *n.* small shop.

bo·vine, *a.* cowlike; slows; dull. *n.* cow or ox.

bow, *n.* weapon for shooting arrows; implement with horsehairs for playing stringed instrument; decorative knot. *v.* bend ; play with a bow.

bow, *v.* bend, as in respect; stoop; yield. *n.* bodily inclination; forward part of a ship.

bow·el, *n. usu. pl.* intestines; inner part.

bowl, *n.* round, deep dish. *v.* roll the ball in bowling. **bowl·er,** *n.*

bow·leg, *n.* leg curved outward. **bow·leg·ged,** *a.*

bowl·ing, *n.* game in which a heavy ball is rolled at a group of pins. *v.* act of rolling ball to pins.

box, *n.* container; carton; receptacle; compartment. *v.* enclose, as in a case; fight with the fists. **box·er,** *n.* **box·ing,** *n.*

box·car, *n.* roofed freight car.

boy, *n.* male child; son. **boy·hood,** *n.* **boy·ish,** *a.* **boy·ish·ness,** *n.*

boy·cott, *v.* refuse to buy, sell, or work with. *n.* concerted refusal to deal with, etc.

bra, *n.* brassiere.

brace, *a* a pair *n.* support; prop; clasp. *v.,* **braced, brac·ing** tie; bind; strengthen; acquire vigor. **brac·er,** *n.* **brac·ing,** *n.*

brace·let, *n.* ornamental chain or band for the wrist or ankle; **brace·let·ed,** *a.*

brack·et, *n.* projecting support, for a shelf, etc.; one of two marks. *v.* support with or enclose in brackets.

brack·ish, *a.* somewhat salty.

brad, *n.* thin wire nail.

brag, *v.,* **bragged, brag·ging.** boast, *n.* boastful talk.

brag·gart, *n.* arrogant boaster; bragger.

braid, *v.* interweave; plait. *n.* braided thing. **braid·ing,** *n.*

Braille, *n.* printing for the blind, using raised dots to represent letters.

brain, *n.* cranial nerve tissue. *a. pl.* intellectual power. *v.* beat severely about the head.

brain·y, *a.,* **-i·er, -i·est.** having intelligence; intellectual.

braise, *v.,* **braised, brais·ing.** saute meat or vegetables in fat, then simmer.

brake, *n.* device for stopping. *v.,* **braked, brak·ing.** stop; slow down.

bram·ble, *n.* prickly shrub or vine; its berry. **bram·bly,** *a.*

bran, *n.* outer husk of a grain.

branch, *n.* limb; natural plant subdivision. *v.* separate into branches. **branch·ed,** *a.*

brand, *n.* mark put on cattle with hot instrument; trademark; class of goods; *v.* burn a mark upon; mark indelibly.

bran·dish, *v.* wave; flourish.

bran·dy, *n. pl.,* **bran·dies.** liquor distilled from wine or fermented juice. *v.,* **bran·died, bran·dy·ing. bran·died,** *a.*

brash, *a.* rash; impudent.

brass, *n.* soft yellow metal; musical instruments; military officers. *a.* made of brass.

bras·siere, *n.* woman's undergarment worn to protect and support the breasts.

brass·y, *a.,* **-i·er, -i·est.** shamelessly bold; harsh; impudent.

brat, *n.* ill-mannered, annoying child.

brat·wurst, *n.* highly seasoned sausage.

bra·va·do, *n.* feigned confidence; swaggering.

brave, *a.* courageous; without fear. *v.* **braved, brav·ing.** defy, face with courage. **brav·er·y,** *n.* Indian warrior.

bra·vo, *interj.* well done!

bra·vu·ra, *n.* show of daring; brilliant technique.

brawl, *v.* to quarrel or fight noisily. *n.* noisy fight. **brawl·er,** *n.*

brawn, *n.* full, strong muscles. **brawn·y,** *a.,* **-i·er, -i·est.**

bray, *v.* the cry of a donkey.

bra·zen, *a.* made of brass; impudent. *v.* behave shamelessly.

bra·zier, *n.* metal pan to hold charcoal.

breach, *n.* break; violation of law; gap. *v.* make an opening in; break.

bread, *n.* baked food made from flour, milk, etc.; sustenance. *v.* cover with bread crumbs.

breadth, *n.* width.

break, *v.,* **broke, bro·ken, break·ing.** shatter; violate; annul; smash; ruin financially;

tame. *n.* breaking; interruption; gap; rupture. **break·a·ble,** *a.* **break·age,** *n.*

break·er, *n.* person or thing that breaks; large wave.

break·fast, *n.* morning meal. *v.* eat breakfast.

break·wa·ter, *n.* barrier serving to break the force of waves.

breast, *n.* milk-secreting gland; upper part of chest.

breast·bone, *n.* sternum.

breath, *n.* air taken into the lungs; life.

breathe, *v.,* **breathed, breathing.** inhale and exhale air; blow gently; utter softly; live. **breath·er,** *n.* take arest. **breath·ing,** *n.*

breech, *n.* lower part of anything.

breed, *v.,* **bred, breed·ing.** engender; produce (offspring); raise; foster. *n.* lineage; variety. **breed·er,** *n.*

breeze, *n.* gentle wind. *v.* blow lightly; hurry. **breez·y,** *a.,* **-i·er, -i·est. breez·i·ness,** *n.*

breth·ren, *n. pl.* of brother; sect member.

brev·i·ty, *n.* shortness; conciseness; briefness.

brew, *v.* prepare by steeping; plot. *n.* liquid which is brewed. **brew·er,** *n.* **brew·er·y,** *n. pl.,* **-ies.**

bribe, *n.* price, gift, reward, etc., to corrupt. *v.,* **bribed, brib·ing.** give a bribe. **brib·a·ble,** *a.* **-er·y,** *n. pl.,* **-ies.**

brick, *n.* hardened clay block for building. *v.* lay with brick.

bride, *n.* woman just married, or about to be. **brid·al,** *a.*

bride·groom, *n.* man just married, or about to be.

brides·maid, *n.* woman attendant of a bride.

bridge, *n.* structure built over a river, road, etc.; link; bony part of nose; mounting for artificial teeth; card game. *v.* connect.

bri·dle, *n.* headgear of a horse. *v.,* **bri·dled, bri·dling.** restrain; curb.

brief, *a.* terse; abrupt; short; *n.* summary. *v.* coach; instruct. **brief·ly,** *adv.* **brief·ing,** *n.*

bri·er, *n.* plant bearing thorns.

brig, *n.* confinement area on a ship; two-masted ship.

bri·gade, *n.* large body of troops.

brig·and, *n.* a bandit.

bright, *a.* reflecting light; shining; clever. **bright·ness,** *n.*

bright·en, *v.* make bright, shiny.

bril·liance, *n.* mental keenness; great brightness; splendor. **bril·lian·cy,** *n.* **bril·liant,** *a.*

brim, *n.* upper edge, as a glass; projecting edge, as of a hat. *v.,* **brimmed, brim·ming.** to be filled.

brim·stone, *n.* sulfur.

brin·dled, *a.* having dark streaks; flecked.

brine, *n.* salt water, **brin·y,** *a.*

bring, *v.,* **brought, bring·ing.** fetch; induce; convey; lead; carry.

brink, *n.* rim of a steep place.

bri·quette, bri·quet, *n.* compacted brick of coal dust or coke for fuel.

brisk, *a.* tangy; alert; sharp, quick. **brisk·ly,** *adv.* **brisk·ness,** *n.*

bris·ket, *n.* breast of an animal; cut of meat.

bris·tle, *n.* short, coarse hair, *v.,* **bris·tled, bris·tling.** erect the hairs. **bris·tly,** *a.*

brit·tle, *a.* hard, but breaking easily; fragile.

broach, *v.* mention a subject for the first time.

broad, *a.* wide; spacious; of great breadth; blunt.

broad·cast, *v.,* **-cast** or **cast·ed, -cast·ing.** send out by radio or television; scatter widely. *n.* medium of transmission.

broad·mind·ed, *a.* tolerant.

broad·side, *n.* simultaneous attack. *adv.* directly in the side.

bro·cade, *n.* fabric woven in a raised pattern. *v.,* **-cad·ed, -cad·ing.** weave a design into.

broc·co·li, *n.* green vegetable with edible shoots.

bro·chure, *n.* booklet.

bro·gan, *n.* heavy work shoe.

broil, *v.* cook by direct heat or fire; grill.

bro·ken, *a.* in pieces; fractured; ruptured; tamed.

bro·ker, *n.* agent who buys and sells, on commission. **bro·ker·age,** *n.*

bron·chus, *n.* main branch of the windpipe.

bron·chi·tis, *n.* inflammation of the bronchial tubes.

bronze, *n.* copper and tin alloy; brown, yellowish color. *v.,* **bronzed, bronz·ing.** give appearance of bronze.

brooch, *n.* ornament held by pin or clasp.

brood, *n.* family of young birds; family's offspring. *v.* worry about something; incubate; hatch.

brook, *n.* small stream; creek.

broom, *n.* sweeping implement. *v.* sweep.

broth, *n.* thin soup or stock from cooking.

broth·el, *n.* house of prostitution; whorehouse.

broth·er, *n. pl.,* **broth·ers, broth·ren.** male of the same parents; kinsman; monk. **broth·er·hood,** *n.*

broth·er-in-law, *n. pl.,* **broth·ers-in-law.** brother of one's spouse; one's sister's husband.

brow, *n.* forehead; steep edge.

brow·beat, *v.*, **-beat**, **-beat·en**, **-beat·ing.** bully; intimidate.

brown, *a.* coffee-colored. *n.* dark color. *v.* make brown; cook in fat.

browse, *v.*, **browsed**, **brows·ing.** nibble; graze; examine casually.

bruise, *v.*, **bruised**, **bruis·ing.** injury without skin breakage; contuse; crush. *n.* bruised area of tissue.

bru·net, *a.* black or dark-brown haired. *n.* person with dark complexion, hair, and eyes.

brunt, *n.* principal stress, force, or shock.

brush, *n.* bristled device for cleaning, etc.; brushing; thick growth of bushes. *v.* apply with a brush; sweep, rub, polish.

brusque, **brusk**, *a.* abrupt; blunt.

bru·tal, *a.* inhuman; savage; cruel. **bru·tal·i·ty**, *n.*

bru·tal·ize, *v.*, **-ized**, **-iz·ing.** treat brutally or inhumanly.

brute, *a.* resembling a beast. *n.* savage creature. **brut·ish**, *a.*

bub·ble, *n.* globule of liquid inflated with air or gas; delusive scheme. *v.*, **-bled**, **-bling.** cause to bubble.

buck, *n.* male deer, goat, antelope, etc. (sl.) one dollar. *v.* rear upward; to throw by rearing and humping; *inf.* to oppose..

buck·et, *n.* pail; vessel. *v.*, **-et·ed**, **-et·ing.** lift or carry in pails.

buck·le, *n.* fastening clasp for two loose ends. *v.*, **-led**, **-ling.** clasp with a buckle; warp.

buck·shot, *n.* leaden pellet.

bu·col·ic, *a.* pastoral; rustic; rural.

bud, *n.* undeveloped plant shoot or blossom. *v.*, **bud·ded**, **-ding.** cause to bud; start to grow.

bud·dy, **bud·die**, *n. pl.*, **-dies.** pal.

budge, *v.* move slightly; shift.

budg·et, *n. v.* estimate of income and expense. **budg·et·ar·y**, *a.*

buff, *n.* tan color. *v.* polish. **buff·er**, *n.*

buf·fa·lo, *n.* wild ox; bison.

buf·fet, *n.* blow. *v.*, **-fet·ed**, **-fet·ing.** strike; contend against.

buf·fet, *n.* sideboard for china, linen, etc.; counter for serving refreshments.

buf·foon, *n.* clown; jester. **-er·y**, *n. pl.*, **-ies.**

bug, *n.* insect; hobbyist; *inf.* disease-producing germ; concealed microphone; defect. *v.*, **bugged**, **bug·ging.** *inf.* plant a listening device; annoy. **bug·gy**, *a.*, **-gi·er**, **-gi·est.**

bug·bear, *n.* imaginary goblin; needless fear.

bug·gy, *n. pl.*, **-gies.** light horse carriage; baby carriage.

bu·gle *n.* horn-like instrument; mint plant. *v.*, **-gled**, **-gling.** sound a bugle. **bu·gler**, *n.*

build, *v.*, **built**, **build·ing.** construct create; establish. *n.* general figure. **build·er**, *n.*

build·ing, *n.* structure. *v.* constructing.

bulb, *n.* underground bud; round part of electric light. **bul·bous**, *a.*

bulge, *n.* outward swelling; protrusion. *v.*, **bulged**, **bulg·ing**; **bulg·y**. *a.* protrude.

bu·lim·ia, *n.* disease causing insatiable appetite for food.

bulk, *n.* large mass; magnitude; trunk; volume. *v.* increase in size. **bulk·y**, *a.*, **-i·er**, **-i·est.**

bull, *n.* adult male bovine animal. (sl.) talk idly.

bul·let, *n.* small projectile shot from rifles or pistols.

bul·le·tin, *n.* short news statement; announcement.

bul·lion, *n.* gold or silver in the mass before coinage or other use.

bull's-eye, *n.* central mark on a target; direct hit.

bul·ly, *n. pl.*, **-lies.** person who browbeats others smaller than himself. *v.*, **-lied**, **-ly·ing.** threaten; frighten.

bul·rush, *n.* marsh plant.

bul·wark, *n.* defensive wall. *v.* fortify.

bum, *n.* tramp; vagrant. *v.* live idly. *a.*, **bum·mer**, **bum·mest.** *inf.* poor quality; worthless; inferior.

bum·ble·bee, *n.* large, hairy bee.

bump, *v.* strike against; collide with. *n.* jolt; lump; swelling. **bump·y**, *a.*, **-i·er**, **-i·est.**

bump·er, *n.* shock-absorbing device. *a.* unusually abundant.

bump·tious, *a.* arrogant; forward.

bun, *n.* type of bread or roll; coil of hair.

bunch, *n.* cluster; tuft; group. *v.* gather in. **bunch·y**, *a.*, **-i·er**, **-i·est.**

bun·dle, *n.* things fastened together; package. *v.*, **-dled**, **-dling.** tie into a bundle.

bun·ga·low, *n.* one-storied house.

bun·gle, *n.* mistake. *v.*, **-gled**, **-gling. bun·gler**, *n.* perform clumsily.

bun·ion,, *n.* inflamed knob on the side of the big toe.

bunk, *n.* shelf-like bed. *v. inf.* occupy a bed.

bun·ny, *n. pl.*, **-nies.** small rabbit.

bunt·ing, *n.* material used for flags; blanket for babies; type of small bird.

bu·oy, *n.* floating marine marker. *v.* keep from sinking.

buoy·an·cy, *n.* ability to float or rise; vivacity. **buoy·ant**, *a.* **buoy·ant·ly**, *adv.*

bur·den, *n.* load; responsibility; anything carried; sorrow; *v.* load; oppress. **bur·den·some,** *a.*

bu·reau, *n. pl.,* **bu·reaus, bu·reaux.** chest of drawers; administrative agency or department.

bu·reauc·ra·cy, *n. pl.,* **-cies.** government characterized by inflexible routine; body of government officials. **bu·reau·crat,** *n.*

bur·geon, *n.* bud. *v.* bloom.

bur·glar·ize, *v.,* **-ized, -iz·ing.** steal after breaking and entering. **bur·glar,** *n.* **bur·gla·ry,** *n. pl.,* **-ries.**

bur·i·al, *n.* act of interment.

burl, *n.* knot in wool; knot in tree trunk.

bur·lap, *n.* coarse material made of jute, hemp, etc.

bur·lesque, *n.* mockery by caricature; bawdy humor. *a.* comical. *v.,* **-lesqued, -les·quing.** caricature. **-les·quer,** *n.*

bur·ly, *a.,* **-li·er, -li·est.** heavily built; rough.

burn, *v.,* **burned** or **burnt, -ing.** to consume fuel; be or set on fire; glow as fire; injure by heat; scorch. *n.* injury or mark caused by burning; sunburn. **-a·ble,** *a.* **-ing.** *a.* **-er,** *n.*

bur·nish, *n.* gloss. *v.* make shiny. **bur·nish·er,** *n.*

burr, bur, *n.* prickly seedcase; rough edge; whir.

bur·ro, *n. pl.,* **-ros.** donkey.

bur·row, *n.* groundhole made by animal. *v.* dig; delve; search.

burst, *v.,* **burst, -ing.** break apart; explode; emerge suddenly. *n.* explosion; spurt. **-er,** *n.*

bur·y, *v.,* **-ied, -y·ing.** inter; cover over.

bus, *n. pl.,* **bus·es, bus·ses.** motor coach for public transportation. *v.,* **bused** or **bussed, bus·ing** or **bus·sing.** travel by bus.

bush, *n.* low shrub; woodland; uncleared country. **bush·y,** *a.,* **-i·er, -i·est.**

bush·el, *n.* unit of dry measure equal to 4 pecks or 32 quarts; container of this capacity.

busi·ness, *n.* commerce; trade; occupation; task; firm; factory; concern; responsibility.

bust, *n.* woman's bosom; sculpture representing the head, shoulders, and chest. *v.* hit; strike; demote.

bus·tle, *v.,* **-tled, -tling.** move or act with noisy activity. *n.* commotion; pad beneath skirt of a dress. **-tling,** *a.*

bus·y *a.,* **-i·er, -i·est.** not idle; industrious. *v.,* **-ied, -y·ing.** be occupied. **-i·ly,** *adv.*

but, *conj.* except; save; on the contrary; only or merely. *prep.* except.

butch·er, *n.* one who prepares meat for market; ruthless murder. *v.* slaughter.

but·ler, *n.* head manservant.

butt, *n.* target of ridicule; thick or blunt end; stump. *v.* joint at the end; ram with head; abut.

butte, *n.* isolated hill with steep sides.

but·ter, *n.* solidified fat from milk. *v.* spread or cover. **but·ter·y,** *a.*

but·ter·fly, *n. pl.,* **-flies.** insect with colored wings.

but·ter·scotch, *n.* hard candy made of butter and brown sugar.

but·tocks, *n. pl.* rump.

but·ton, *n.* knob or disk for fastening. *v.* close with buttons.

but·tress, *n.* projecting structure; prop. *v.* bolster; reinforce.

bux·om, *a.* full-bosomed.

buy, *v.,* **bought, buy·ing.** purchase. *n.* something purchased. **-a·ble,** *a.* **buy·er,** *n.*

buzz, *v.* hum like bees; gossip; murmur; signal on a buzzer. *n.* humming sound. **buzz·er,** *n.*

buz·zard, *n.* bird of prey; rapacious person.

by, *prep.* close at hand; not later than: through the means of; in relation to. *adv.* near to something; past.

by·gone, *a.* in the past; former. *n. pl.* that which is past.

by·law, *n.* standing rule of an organization.

by·pass, *n.* detour; deflected route; shunt. *v.* circumvent.

by·product, *n.* secondary or incidental product.

by·stand·er, *n.* spectator.

by·word, *n.* proverbial saying.

C

cab, *n.* vehicle for hire; closed shelter on truck or train for driver and operating controls.

ca·bal, *n.* clique united for intrigue. *v.,* **-balled, -ball·ing.** plot.

cab·a·ret, *n.* restaurant with entertainment and dancing.

cab·bage, *n.* vegetable with short stem and edible head.

cab·in, *n.* simple crude house; compartment in a plane or ship.

cab·i·net, *n.* cupboard with shelves and doors. *(often cap.)* group of government officials.

ca·ble, *n.* strong wire or chain, often several wires twisted together; stranded conductor;

cablegram. *v.*, **-bled, -bling.** send a cablegram.

ca·ble·gram, *n.* message sent by submarine cable.

ca·boose, *n.* end car of a freight train, for the crew.

cache, *n.* storing place, esp. for provisions; hidden material. *v.* **cached, cach·ing.** to hide.

ca·chet, *n.* a seal esp. of official approval; a distinguishing mark.

cack·le, *v.*, **-led, -ling.** make a sharp, broken cry. *n.* sharp cry of a hen. **cack·ler,** *n.*

ca·coph·o·ny *n. pl.*, **-nies.** discordant sound.

cac·tus, *n. pl.*, **-tus·es, -ti.** spiny flowering plant of arid regions.

cad, *n.* contemptible, ungentlemanly person. **cad·dish,** *a.*

ca·dav·er, *n.* corpse. **-ous,** *a.*

cad·die, cad·dy, *n.* small box; person who carries a golfer's clubs. *v.*, **-died, -dying.** work as a caddy.

ca·dence, *n.* rhythmic sequence of language sounds; beat of any rhythmical movement.

ca·det, *n.* student in military academy.

ca·dre, *n.* group of personnel capable of training others; framework.

ca·fé, ca·fe, *n.* small restaurant; tavern.

caf·e·te·ri·a, *n.* restaurant where customers serve themselves.

caf·feine, *n.* bitter stimulating compound found in coffee, tea, etc.

cage, *n.* enclosure with bars. *v.*, **caged, cag·ing.** imprison.

cagey, *a.* wary of being deceived; shrewd; cautious.

ca·hoots, *n. pl.* (slang) partnership; league.

ca·jole, *v.*, **-joled, -jol·ing.** persuade by deliberate flattery. **-jol·er·y,** *n. pl.*, **-ies.**

cake, *n.* sweet batter of flour and eggs which is baked; block of compacted matter. *v.*, **caked, cak·ing.** form into a mass.

cal·a·boose, *n. inf.* jail; lockup.

ca·lam·i·ty, *n. pl.*, **-ties.** diaster; grievous affliction; mishap. *a.*

cal·ci·fy, *v.*, **-fied. -fy·ing.** harden by deposit of calcium salts. **-fi·ca·tion,** *n.*

cal·ci·um, *n.* silver white alkaline element in bones, teeth, chalk, etc.

cal·cu·late, *v.*, **-lat·ed, -lat·ing.** determine by mathematical process; compute; estimate; rely. **-lat·ed,** *a.* **-la·tion,** *n.* **-la·tor,** *n.* machine for mathematical computations.

cal·cu·lat·ing, *a.* scheming.

cal·cu·lus, *n. pl.*, **-li, -lus·es.** method of calculation in higher mathematics.

cal·dron, *n.* cauldron, large kettle or boiler.

cal·en·dar, *n.* chronological list, system of reckoning time.

calf, *n. pl.*, **calves.** young cow, elephant, seal, etc.; back part of the leg below the knee.

cal·i·ber, cal·i·bre, *n.* diameter of a circular section, as a bullet; degree of quality or importance.

cal·i·brate, *v.*, **-brat·ed, -brat·ing.** determine the caliber of. **cal·i·bra·tion,** *n.*

cal·i·co, *n. pl.*, **-coes, -cos.** printed cotton cloth; spotted animal.

ca·liph, ca·lif, *n.* Islamic religious and civil leader. **ca·liph·ate, cal·if·ate,** *n.*

cal·is·then·ics, *n.* systematic exercises without apparatus.

call, *v.* shout; request to come; telephone; name; summon; halt. *n.* animal cry; telephone communication; short visit; request.

call·ing, *n.* vocation; inner impulse.

cal·li·o·pe, *n.* organ-like musical instrument which plays whistle sounds.

cal·lous, *a.* hardened; feeling no emotion. **-loused,** *a.*

cal·low, *a.* lacking adult sophistication; inexperienced.

cal·lus, *n. pl.*, **cal·lus·es.** thickened, hard portion of skin.

calm, *n.* absence of wind. *a.* still; tranquil; serene. *v.* quiet.

cal·o·rie, *n. pl.*, **-ries.** unit of heat; measure of food energy.

cal·um·ny, *n. pl.*, **-nies.** slander. **-ni·ate,** *v.*, **-at·ed, -at·ing. -ni·a·tion,** *n.*

ca·lyp·so, *n. pl.*, **ca·lyp·sos.** improvised ballad; rhythmic music of the West Indies.

ca·lyx, *n. pl.*, **ca·lyx·es, cal·y·ces.** external part of a flower; sepals.

cam, *n.* device for transmitting irregular rotary motion.

cam·el, *n.* one or two-humped animal used for burden bearing.

cam·e·o, *n.* precious gem carved with a raised design.

cam·er·a, *n.* device for taking photographs.

cam·ou·flage, *n.* disguise or plan used as a false front; behavior intended to deceive. *v.*, **-flaged, -flag·ing.** disguise or hide.

camp, *n.* temporary lodging or shelter. *v.* set up or stay in shelters. **camp·er,** *n.*

cam·paign, *n.* military operation; organized activity for a special purpose. *v.* engage in or conduct a campaign. **-er,** *n.*

cam·pus, *n. pl.*, **cam·pus·es.** grounds of a college.

can, *aux. v.,* know how to; be able to.

can, *n.* cylindrical metal container. *v.,* **canned, can·ning.** preserve by sealing in a can or jar.

ca·nal, *n.* artificial waterway; anatomical passage.

ca·nard, *n.* false story; hoax; rumor.

ca·nar·y, *n.* small singing finch often kept as a pet; sweet wine.

ca·nas·ta, *n.* card game using two decks and jokers.

can·cel, *v.,* **-celed, -cel·ing** or **-celled, -cel·ling.** annul; call off; delete; offset. **can·cel·la·tion,** *n.*

can·cer, *n.* malignant growth or tumor.

can·de·la·brum, *n. pl.,* **-bra, -brums.** branched candlestick.

can·did, *a.* outspoken; honest.

can·di·date, *n.* one running for office. **can·di·da·cy,** *n. pl.,* **-cies.**

can·dle, *n.* piece of wax enclosing a wick, burned for light. *v.* examine eggs put up to light.

can·dor, *n.* frankness; fairness.

can·dy, *n. pl.,* **-dies.** confection made from sugar syrup. *v.* coat with sugar; sweeten. **can·died,** *a.*

cane, *n.* hollow or pithy stem; certain grasses or reeds; walking stick; flogging rod. *v.,* **caned, can·ing.** flog; make cane.

ca·nine, *a.* relating to dogs. *n.* dog.

can·is·ter, *n.* small container for tea, coffee, etc.

can·ker, *n.* ulcerous sore.

can·na·bis, *n.* marijuana plant.

can·ni·bal, *n.* person who eats human flesh. **-ism,** *n.*

can·ni·bal·ize, *v.,* **-ized, iz·ing.** to strip (old or worn equipment) of parts for use in other units.

can·non, *n. pl.,* **can·nons,** or **can·non.** heavy mounted gun.

can·ny, *a.,* **-i·er, -i·est.** shrewd; cautious. **-ni·ly,** *adv.*

ca·noe, *n.* long narrow boat, propelled by paddles. *v.,* **ca·noed, -noe·ing.** transport by canoe.

can·on, *n.* church law; official list; accepted rule.

can·on·ize, *v.,* **-ized, -iz·ing.** raise to sainthood; glorify. **-i·za·tion,** *n.*

can·o·py, *n. pl.,* **-pies.** covering or protection.

cant, *n.* hypocritical talk; slanting position. *v.* tilt; tip.

can·ta·loup, can·ta·loupe, can·ta·lope, *n.* muskmelon.

can·tan·ker·ous, *a.* ill-natured.

can·teen, *n.* military store; flask for carrying water.

can·ter, *n.* an easy gallop. *v.* ride at a moderate gait.

can·tor, *n.* official who leads religious singing.

can·vas, *n.* strong cloth, used for sails, tents, etc.; thing made of or on canvas.

can·vass, *v.* solicit information; examine in detail. *n.* act of asking. **can·vass·er,** *n.*

can·yon, *n.* deep valley with steep slopes, usu. with stream.

cap, *n.* brimless head covering; small, tight-fitting lid. *v.,* **capped, cap·ping.** cover with a cap.

ca·pa·ble, *a.* able; efficient. **ca·pa·bly,** *adv.* **ca·pa·bil·i·ty,** *n. pl.,* **-ties.**

ca·pac·i·ty, *n. pl.,* **-ties.** power of receiving or containing; volume; ability; position.

cape, *n.* point or extension of land into water; sleeveless outer garment fastened at neck.

ca·per, *n.* frolicsome leap; shrub; prank. *v.* prance.

cap·il·lar·y, *a.* having a small walled tube. *n. pl.,* **-lar·ies.** minute blood vessels.

cap·i·tal, *a.* punishable by death; chief in importance; *n.* capital letter; capital city; accumulated goods; possessions.

cap·i·tal·ism, *n.* economic system of free enterprise. **-is·tic,** *a.* **-ist,** *n.*

cap·i·tal·ize, *v.,* **-ized, -iz·ing.** put in capital letters; convert into capital; supply capital.

cap·i·tol, *n.* statehouse.

ca·pit·u·late, *v.,* **-lat·ed, -lat·ing.** surrender; acquiesce.

ca·price, *n.* sudden change of mind; whim. **-pri·cious,** *a.* **-pri·cious·ness,** *n.*

cap·size, *v.,* **-sized, -siz·ing.** cause to overturn.

cap·sule, *n.* closed receptacle; gelatinous case enclosing medicine; spaceship cabin. *a.* extremely brief; very compact. **cap·su·lar,** *a.*

cap·tain, *n.* leader; officer; commander. *v.* to lead.

cap·tion, *n.* heading; text below a picture.

cap·ti·vate, *v.,* **-vat·ed, -vat·ing.** enthrall; charm. **-ti·va·tion,** *n.*

cap·tive, *a.* held prisoner; confined. *n.* prisoner. **cap·tiv·i·ty,** *n. pl.,* **-ties.**

cap·ture, *v.,* **-tured, -tur·ing.** to take by force; seize. **cap·tur·er,** *n.*

car, *n.* automobile; vehicle moved on wheels.

ca·rafe, *n.* wide-based bottle for water or wine.

car·a·mel, *n.* burnt sugar; firm chewy candy usually in blocks.

car·at, *n.* unit of weight for gemstones.

car·a·van, *n.* group of travelers or vehicles.

car·a·way, *n.* herb having seeds used for flavoring.

car·bo·hy·drate, *n.* organic compound important as food.

car·bon, *n.* nonmetallic element; paper for duplicating printed material.

car·bo·nate, *n.* carbonic acid salt. **car·bo·na·tion**, *n.*

car·bon di·ox·ide, *n.* colorless, odorless, incombustible gas.

car·bon mon·ox·ide, *n.* odorless, lethal, poisonous gas.

car·bun·cle, *n.* painful swelling and inflammation of tissue.

car·bu·re·tor, *n.* device supplying engine with fuel and air mixture.

car·cass, car·case, *n.* dead animal body.

car·ci·no·ma, *n. pl.,* **-mas, -ma·ta**, malignant tumor; cancer.

card, *n.* thin pasteboard; greeting card; playing card; *pl.* game using cards.

card·board, *n.* stiff pasteboard.

car·di·ac, *a.* pertaining to the heart.

car·di·gan, *n.* knitted sweater.

car·di·nal, *n.* N. American red finch; deep red color; Catholic dignitary. *a.* of prime importance.

care, *v.,* **cared, car·ing.** to feel interest; be concerned. *n.* worry; anxiety; concern; caution; **care·free**, *a.* **care·ful**, *a.* **care·less**, *a.*

ca·reer, *n.* one's life's work; progress; course.

ca·ress, *n.* tender touch or embrace. *v.* touch or stroke gently.

care·tak·er, *n.* one in charge of a thing, place, or person.

car·go, *n. pl.,* **-goes** or **-gos.** freight on a ship, plane, etc.

car·i·bou, *n. pl.,* **-bous** or **bou.** large N. American reindeer.

car·i·ca·ture, *n.* exaggerated picture; *v.,* **-tured, -tur·ing.** make a distorted character of.

car·ies, *n.* decay, esp. bone or tooth.

car·il·lon, *n.* set of fixed bells.

car·nage, *n.* slaughter; massacre.

car·nal, *a.* worldly; temporal; sensual **car·nal·i·ty**, *n.*

car·na·tion, *n.* cultivated, double-flowered pinks.

car·ni·val, *n.* revelry; traveling amusement show.

car·niv·o·rous, *a.* flesh-eating.

car·ol, *n.* song of religious joy *v.,* **-oled, -ol·ing.** to sing; warble.

ca·rouse, *n.* drunken spree *v.,* **-roused, -rous·ing. ca·rous·er**, *n.*

carp, *n. pl.,* **carp, carps.** a freshwater fish *v.* find fault.

car·pen·ter, *n.* person who builds with wood. **car·pen·try**, *n.*

car·pet, *n.* heavy fabric floor covering. *v.* to cover with a carpet. **car·pet·ing**, *n.*

car·riage, *n.* conveyance; horse-drawn wheeled vehicle; posture.

car·ri·er, *n.* one who conveys for hire.

car·ri·on, *n.* dead, decaying flesh.

car·rot, *n.* plant with long, edible root. **car·rot·y**, *a.*

car·rou·sel, *n.* a merry-go-round.

car·ry, *v.,* **-ried. -ry·ing.** bear; take from one place to another; convey, stock merchandise.

cart, *n.* two-wheeled vehicle used for hauling. *v.* convey in a cart. **car·ter**, *n.* **cart·age**, *n.*

car·tel, *n.* international syndicate or combine.

car·ti·lage, *n.* flexible tissue of the skeleton.

car·tog·ra·phy, *n.* the making of maps. **car·tog·ra·pher**, *n.*

car·ton, *n.* cardboard box.

car·toon, *n.* caricature; satirical drawing; comic strip. **car·toon·ist**, *n.*

car·tridge, *n.* cylindrical case holding a bullet and charge of powder for a firearm.

carve, *v.,* **carved, carv·ing.** fashion or shape by cutting; decorate by cutting; cut meat. **carv·ing**, *n.*

cas·cade, *n.* waterfall. *v.,* **-cad·ed, -cad·ing.** to fall in folds; rippling fall of lace, etc.

case, *n.* instance; condition; suit; receptacle; object of investigation. *v.,* **cased, cas·ing.** enclose.

cash, *n.* money on hand. *v.* pay or obtain cash for.

cash·ew, *n.* tropical American tree; its edible nut.

cash·ier, *n.* person who collects money. *v.,* dismiss with disgrace.

cash·mere, *n.* fabric made of fine wool from undercoat of goats.

cas·ing, *n.* protective covering; door or window framework.

ca·si·no, *n. pl.,* **-nos.** building for gambling, amusements, etc.

cask, *n.* barrellike container.

cas·ket, *n.* coffin; small box.

cas·se·role, *n.* covered baking dish; food cooked in a casserole.

cas·sette, *n.* encased audio or video tape cartridge.

cas·sock, *n.* long, close-fitting garment worn by clergymen.

cast, *v.,* **cast, cast·ing.** throw; direct; discard; deposit, as a vote; assign (a part); mold. *n.* actors in a play; reproduction; act of casting.

cas·ta·nets, *n.* pair of shells or hard wood struck together as rhythmic instrument.

caste, *n.* social group; class distinction.

cast·er, *n.* a small wheel mounted on a swivel.

cas·ti·gate, *v.,* **-gat·ed, -gat·ing.** punish in order to correct; criticize. **cas·ti·ga·tion,** *n.* **cas·ti·ga·tor,** *n.*

cast iron, *a.* iron alloy. **cast-iron,** *a.* of cast iron; rigid; hardy.

cas·tle, *n.* fortified building; massive house; *chess.* rook.

cast·off, *a.* thrown away. *n.* thing or person discarded.

cas·tor, *n.* oil used in medicine and as a lubricant.

cas·trate, *v.,* **-trat·ed, -trat·ing.** remove the testicles. **cas·tra·tion,** *n.*

cas·u·al, *a.* accidental; occasional; informal. **cas·u·al·ly,** *adv.*

cas·u·al·ty, *n. pl.,* **-ties.** disaster or accident; person injured or killed.

cat, *n.* small, domesticated mammal kept as a pet; lions, tigers, etc.

cat·a·clysm, *n.* violent upheaval. **cat·a·clys·mal,** *a.*

cat·a·comb, *n. usu. pl.* underground place of burial.

cat·a·log; cat·a·logue, *n.* list arranged according to a system; register. *v.,* **-loged, -log·ing,** or **-logued, -logu·ing.** list.

cat·a·lyst, *n.* agent initiating a chemical reaction.

cat·a·ma·ran, *n.* a raft; any craft with twin parallel hulls.

cat·a·pult, *n.* device for launching missiles. *v.,* to hurl.

cat·a·ract, *n.* waterfall; clouding of the eye lens; steep rapids.

cat·as·tro·phe, *n.* momentous tragic event. **cat·as·troph·ic,** *a.*

catch, *v.,* **caught, catch·ing.** entrap; detect; snatch; seize; get. *n.* anything that catches; act of catching; that which is caught; hidden condition. **catch·er.** *n.*

catch·ing, *a.* infectious; alluring.

catch·y, *a.* **-i·er, -i·est.** tricky; pleasing.

cat·e·chism, *n.* religious instruction book. **cat·e·chis·mal,** *a.*

cat·e·gor·i·cal, *a.* positive; absolute. **cat·e·gor·i·cal·ly.** *adv.*

cat·e·go·ry, *n. pl.,* **-ries.** class; classificatory division.

cat·e·gor·ize, *v.,* **-rized, -riz·ing.** group or classify.

ca·ter, *v.* give special attention; to provide food service. **ca·ter·er,** *n.*

cat·er·pil·lar, *n.* larva of butterfly, moth, etc.; endless moving track; tractor.

ca·thar·sis, *n. pl.,* **-ses.** purification. **ca·thar·tic,** *a., n.*

ca·the·dral, *n.* principal church of a diocese.

cath·e·ter, *n.* hollow tube to drain bodily fluids.

cath·o·lic, *a.* universal; comprehensive; (*cap.*) Roman Catholic. *n.* **Ca·thol·i·cism,** *n.*

cat·nap, *n.* short snooze. *v.,* **-napped, -nap·ping.** doze.

cat·nip, *n.* mint plant attractive to felines.

cat·sup, *n.* ketchup.

cat·tail, *n.* reedy marsh plant.

cat·tle, *n.* bovine animals; cows, etc. **cat·tle·man,** *n. pl.,* **-men.**

cat·ty, *a.,* **-ti·er, -ti·est.** spiteful; **cat·ti·ness,** *n.* malicious.

cau·cus, *n. pl.,* **-cus·es.** political party meeting to nominate candidates, elect delegates, etc. *v.,* **-cused, -cus·ing.**

cau·li·flow·er, *n.* vegetable with large, fleshy, edible white head.

caulk, calk, *v.* make watertight by filling seams.

cau·sal·i·ty, *n. pl.,* **-ties.** the relation of cause and effect.

cause, *n.* that from which something results; motive; grounds; reason. *v.,* **caused, caus·ing.** to bring about.

cause·way, *n.* raised, paved road; highway.

caus·tic, *a.* capable of destroying living tissue; sarcastic. *n.* caustic substance.

cau·ter·ize, *v.,* **-ized, -iz·ing.** burn for curative purposes.

cau·tion, *n.* prudence; carefulness. *v.* warn. **cau·tious,** *a.*

cav·al·cade, *n.* procession.

cav·a·lier, *n.* mounted soldier; courtly gentleman. *a.* gallant; haughty.

cav·al·ry, *n. pl.,* **-ries.** troops on horseback. **cav·al·ry·man,** *n. pl.,* **-men.**

cave, *n.* underground cavity. *v.,* **caved, cav·ing.** fall in.

cav·ern, *n.* large underground chamber. **cav·ern·ous,** *a.*

cav·i·ar, cav·i·are, *n.* fish roe used as an appetizer.

cav·il, *v.,* **-iled, -il·ing.** find trivial, annoying objections; quibble.

cav·i·ty, *n. pl.,* **-ties.** any hollow place.

ca·vort, *v.* bound about; caper.

cay·enne, *n.* hot, red pepper.

cease, *v.,* **ceased, ceas·ing.** discontinue; come to an end; stop. **cease·less,** *a.*

cease-fire, *n.* military order to suspend firing.

ce·dar, *n.* coniferous tree.

cede, *v.,* **ced·ed, ced·ing.** resign or surrender to another.

ceil·ing, *n.* overhead interior lining of a room; upper limit.

cel·e·brate, *v.,* **-brat·ed, -brat·ing.** observe in a special way; praise; honor; solemnize. **-bra·tion,** *n.*

cel·e·brat·ed, *a.* renowned.

ce·leb·ri·ty, *n. pl.,* **-ties.** famous or renowned person.

ce·ler·i·ty, *n.* swiftness; speed.

cel·er·y, *n.* plant with edible leafstalks.

ce·les·tial, *a.* heavenly; divine.

cel·i·ba·cy, *n.* state of not being married. **cel·i·bate,** *n.*

cell, *n.* small room in a prison, convent, etc.; small compartment; basic unit of all living matter; device which generates electricity. **cel·lu·lar,** *a.*

cel·lar, *n.* basement; wine stock.

cel·lo, 'cel·lo, *n. pl.,* **-los.** baritone violin. **cel·list,** *n.*

cel·lo·phane, *n.* thin transparent, viscose material.

cel·lu·lose, *n.* chief constituent of cell walls of plants.

ce·ment, *n.* mixture of lime and silica, used to make floors, sidewalks, etc.; glue. *v.* unite by cement.

cem·e·ter·y, *n. pl.,* **-ies.** graveyard; burial ground.

cen·sor, *n.* moral supervisor; official who examines books, magazines, etc., and removes objectionble material. *v.* prohibit; suppress. **-ship.** *n.*

cen·sure, *n.* expression of disapproval; *v.,* **-sured, -sur·ing.** criticize. **-sur·a·ble,** *a.*

cen·sus, *n. pl.,* **cen·sus·es.** official enumeration of inhabitants.

cent, *n.* hundredth part of U·S. dollar or other monetary unit.

cen·ten·ni·al, *a.* pertaining to 100 years; lasting 100 years. *n.* 100th anniversary; celebration of 100 years.

cen·ter, *n.* middle point; axis; core. *v.* place in a center.

cen·ti·grade, *a.* of a thermometer with a freezing point of water as 0° and the boiling point as 100°.

cen·ti·me·ter, *n.* one-hundredth part of a meter.

cen·tral, *a.* in, at, near, or forming the center; principal.

cen·tral·ize, *v.,* **-ized, -iz·ing.** draw to or toward a center; bring under one's control.

cen·trif·u·gal, *a.* moving or directed away from the center.

cen·tu·ry, *n. pl.,* **cen·tu·ries.** period of a one-hundred years.

ce·ram·ics, *n.* art of making earthenware products; earthenware articles. **-ic,** *a.*

ce·re·al, *n.* plants yielding edible grain; the grain, wheat, oats, barley, rice, etc.

ce·re·bral, *a.* relating to the brain; intellectual.

cer·e·mo·ny, *n. pl.,* **-nies.** formalities observed on special occasions; ritual. **cer·e·mo·ni·ous,** *a.*

ce·rise, *n.,* a moderate red.

cer·tain, *a.* sure; true; fixed; dependable; destined. **-ly,** *adv.* **-ty,** *n. pl.,* **-ties..**

cer·tif·i·cate, *n.* document attesting truth of something.

cer·ti·fy, *v.,* **-fied, -fy·ing.** guarantee as certain; assure. **-fi·a·ble,** *a.* **-fi·ca·tion,** *n.*

ces·sa·tion, *n.* ceasing; pause.

ces·sion, *n.* act of ceding.

chafe, *v.,* **chafed, chaf·ing.** make warm or sore by rubbing; irritate; fret.

chaff, *n.* grain debris separated by thrashing. *v.* tease; ridicule.

cha·grin, *n.* disappointment; feeling of vexation; humiliation. *v.* **-grined, -grin·ing.** mortify.

chain, *n.* fetter; series of connected links. *v.* fasten.

chair, *n.* seat with legs and back.

chair·man, *n. pl.,* **-men.** presiding officer of an organization.

chaise longue, *n.* long chair or couch for reclining.

chal·et, *n.* Swiss dwelling.

chal·ice, *n.* drinking cup.

chalk, *n.* limestone; marking material. **chalk·y,** *a.*

chal·lenge, *n.* dare; protest. *v.,* **chal·lenged, chal·leng·ing.** call to account; object to.

cham·ber, *n.* room; compartment in revolver cylinder; enclosed space.

cham·bray, *n.* lightweight fabric; cambric.

cha·me·le·on, *n.* lizard able to change skin color.

cham·ois, *n.,* goatlike antelope; soft pliable leather.

cham·pagne, *n.* sparkling wine.

cham·pi·on, n. militant advocate; defender; winner.

chance, n. luck; fate; risk. v., happen.

chan·cel·lor, n. high ranking administrative official.

chan·de·lier, n. suspended, branched lighting fixture.

change, v., **changed, changing.** alter in condition; substitute. n. low value coins; money owed from a payment.

chan·nel, n. waterway; frequency band; bed of a stream.

chant, v. sing. n. simple melody.

cha·os, n. complete confusion or disorder. **cha·ot·ic,** a.

chap, v., **chapped, chapping.** split; roughen the skin. n. chapped in the skin; fellow.

chap·el, n. private place for worship and prayer.

chap·er·on, chap·er·one, n. one accompanying a single person or group of young unmarried people.

chap·lain, n. ecclesiastic appointed to an institution, military, etc.

chap·ter, n. main division of a book; branch of a society.

char, v., **charred, charring.** burn to a charcoal; scorch.

char·ac·ter, n. symbol; distinguishing feature; moral excellence; peculiar person; actor's part.

char·ac·ter·is·tic, a. typical. n. distinguishing quality.

char·ac·ter·ize, v., **-ized, -iz·ing.** portray. **-i·za·tion,** n. **-iz·er,** n.

cha·rade, n. parlor game using pantomime. transparent pretense.

char·coal, n. porous carbon; charcoal pencil drawing.

chard, n. beet with large leaves and edible stalk.

charge, v., **charged, charg·ing.** fill; impose a responsibility; impose a price; accuse; defer payment; attack. n. store of force; obligation; command; ward.

char·i·ot, n. ancient two-wheeled horse-drawn vehicle. **char·i·ot·eer,** n.

cha·ris·ma, n., personal magic of leadership; magnetic charm.

char·i·ta·ble, a. benevolent.

char·i·ty, n. pl., **-ties.** good will; relief for the poor; lenient judgment.

char·la·tan, n. quack.

charm, n. incantation; amulet; trait of allurement. v. enchant; soothe by attraction; compel. **-er,** n.

chart, n. diagram or table; marine map. v. plan; map out.

char·ter, n. written contract; constitution. v. rent.

char·treuse, n. light yellow green; a liqueur.

chase, v., **chased, chas·ing.** pursue; put to flight. n. pursuit. **chas·er,** n.

chasm, n. deep gap in the earth.

chas·sis, n. frame of a vehicle.

chaste, a. virtuous; pure. **-ly,** adv. **chas·ti·ty,** n.

chas·tise, v., **-tised, -tis·ing.** inflict corporal punishment on; scold. **chas·tise·ment,** n.

chat, v., **-ted, -ting.** talk informally. n. friendly talk.

chat·tel, n. personal property.

chat·ter, v. talk rapidly; jabber. n. foolish talk.

chauf·feur, n. paid driver of a vehicle. v. act as a chauffeur.

chau·vin·ist, n. blind enthusiasm for a cause, country, sex, etc. **-ism,** n.

cheap, a. priced low; of small value; stingy. adv. at a low price or cost. **cheap·ly,** adv.

cheap·en, v. make or become cheap or cheaper.

cheat, v., deceive; beguile; defraud. n. swindle; fraud.

check, n. stop; restraint; order directing bank to pay money; bill; mark put against items on a list; pattern in squares. v. stop; restrain; investigate; verify; designate by a check.

check·mate, n. position of a king in chess where escape is impossible; defeat. v., **-mat·ed, -mat·ing.** put in check.

cheek, n. fleshy sides of face.

cheek·y a., **-i·er, -i·est.** saucy; impudent. **cheek·i·ly,** adv.

cheer, n. joy; shout of encouragement. v. instill with hope; comfort; rejoice.

cheer·ful, a. gay; pleasant.

cheese, n. curd of milk used as food.

chee·tah, n. cat like the leopard.

chef, n. skilled cook.

chem·i·cal, n. substance produced by or used in a chemical process. a. of chemistry. **chem·i·cal·ly,** adv.

chem·ise, n. loose straight-hanging dress or undergarment.

chem·is·try, n. science dealing with composition and structure of substances.

cher·ish, v. to hold dear; nurture.

cher·ry, n. pl., **-ries.** small, red, pitted fruit; the tree itself.

cher·ub, n. pl., **cher·ubs, cher·u·bim.** winged child-like angel; **che·ru·bic,** a. innocent child.

chess, *n.* game played by two on a checkerboard with 16 pieces. **chess·man,** *n. pl.,* **-men.**

chest, *n.* trunk of the body; storage container with lid.

chew, *v.* grind with the teeth. *n.* something for chewing.

chic, *a.* modish; attractive.

chi·can·er·y, *n. pl.,* **-ies.** trickery.

Chi·ca·no, *n. pl.,* **-nos.** American of Mexican descent.

chick, *n.* young of any bird.

chick·en, *n.* common domestic fowl; its meat; coward.

chic·o·ry, *n. pl.,* **-ries.** plant used for salads, and as a coffee substitute.

chide, *v.,* **chid·ed** or **chid, chid·ed** or **chid·den, chid·ing.** scold; reprove mildly.

chief, *a.* highest in rank; leading. *n.* leader. **chief·ly,** *adv.*

chief·tain, *n.* head of a tribe.

chif·fon, *n.* light, delicate material.

child, *n. pl.,* **chil·dren.** very young person; descendant. **-hood,** *n.* **-ish,** *a.* **-like,** *a.*

chil·i, chil·li, chil·e, *n. pl.,* **-ies, -lies, -es.** hot pepper.

chill, *n.* coldness; sensation of cold with shivering. *v.* put on ice; make cold. *a.*

chime, *n.* tuned set of bells. *v.* sound harmoniously.

chim·ney, *n.* passage for smoke from a fire or furnace; glass tube for lamp.

chim·pan·zee, *n.* small intelligent anthropoid ape.

chin, *n.* lower extremity of face.

chi·na, *n.* ceramic ware.

chin·chil·la, *n.* S. American rodent; its soft fur.

chink, *n.* crack; fissure.

chip, *v.,* cutting off or breaking off in small pieces. *n.* fragment; token for money; dried dung.

chip·munk, *n.* terrestrial squirrel.

chi·rop·o·dist, *n.* foot doctor. **chi·rop·o·dy,** *n.*

chi·ro·prac·tic, *n.* therapeutic treatment based on adjustment of body structure. **-tor,** *n.*

chirp, *v.* utter short, sharp sounds, as by birds.

chis·el, *n.* metal tool for shaping wood, stone, etc. *v.,* **-led, -lled, -ling, -lling.** cut with a chisel; cheat. **chis·el·er,** *n.*

chit·chat, *n.* light conversation.

chiv·al·ry, *n. pl.,* **-ries.** knightlike qualities, i·e., valor, etc. **-ric,** *a.* **-rous,** *a.*

chive, *n.* herb used for flavoring.

chlo·rine, *n.* chemical element used as bleaching and disinfecting agent.

chlo·ro·phyll, *n.* green coloring matter in plants.

choc·o·late, *n.* ground cacao beans; beverage or candy made with chocolate.

choice, *n.* selection; option. *a.* excellent. **-ly,** *adv.*

choir, *n.* company of singers.

choke, *v.,* **choked, choking.** suffocate; obstruct. *n.* something that chokes; engine valve.

chol·er·a, *n.* acute disorder of digestive tract.

chol·er·ic, *a.* irate; angry.

cho·les·ter·ol, *n.* fatty substance in animal tissue.

choose, *v.,* **chose, chosen, choosing.** select; make a choice; prefer; select.

chop, *v.,* **chopped, chopping.** cut with a quick, heavy blow; mince. *n.* downward blow; cut of meat.

chop·py, *a.,* **-pier, -piest.** jerky; forming short irregular waves. **-pi·ness,** *n.*

cho·ral, *a.* sung by a chorus. *n.* sacred tune.

cho·rale, *n.* hymn; psalm.

chord, *n.* combination of tones. **-al,** *a.*

cho·re·og·ra·phy, *n.* art of arranging dances. **-pher,** *n.*

chor·tle, *v.,* **-tled, -tling.** laugh or chant exultantly. *n.*

cho·rus, *n. pl.,* **-rus·es.** organized singing group; recurring part of song; refrain. *v.,* **-rused, -rusing.**

chos·en, *a.* selected for favor or by preference.

chow·der, *n.* soup or stew made of fish or clams.

Christ, *n.* Jesus the Messiah.

chris·ten, *v.* baptize; name; dedicate. **-ing** *n.*

Chris·ten·dom, *n.* Christian lands; collectively, all Christians.

Chris·ti·an·i·ty, *n. pl.,* **-ties.** religion derived from Christ. **Chris·tian,** *n., a.*

Christ·mas, *n.* Christian feast on Dec. 25; Christ's birthday.

chro·mat·ic, *a.* pertaining to color; *mus.* of semitones.

chrome, *n.* chromium.

chro·mi·um, *n.* hard, lustrous element used in alloys.

chro·mo·some, *n.* cell bodies that contain the genes.

chron·ic, *a.* long-lasting; frequently recurring; habitual. **-i·cal·ly,** *adv.*

chron·i·cle, *n.* history; narrative; in the order of occurrence. *v.,* **-cled, -cling. chron·i·cler,** *n.*

chron·o·log·i·cal, *a.* arranged in the order of time.

chro·nom·e·ter, *n.* timepiece designed for great accuracy.

chrys·a·lis, *n.* pupa of a butterfly.

chry·san·the·mum, *n.* daisylike plant with colorful flowers.

chub·by, *a.*, **-bier**, **-biest**. round and plump. **-bi·ness**, *n.*

chuck, *v.* give a light pat; tap; throw. *n.* cut of beef; a clamp.

chuck·le, *v.*, **-led**, **-ling**. laugh in a soft, amused manner. *n.*

chum, *n.* pal; close friend.

chum·my, *a.*, **-mier**, **-miest**. intimate; sociable. **-mi·ly**, *adv.*

chump, *n.* blockhead; fool.

chunk, *n.* thick lump. **-y**, *a.*

church, *n.* building for public worship; body of believers.

churl·ish, *a.* surly; ill-mannered.

churn, *n.* butter-making vessel. *v.* agitate.

chute, *n.* waterfall; tube for conveying things.

chutz·pah or **chutz·pa**, *n.* supreme self-confidence; gall.

ci·der, *n.* apple juice.

ci·gar, *n.* roll of tobacco leaves for smoking.

cig·a·rette, **cig·a·ret**, *n.* finely cut tobacco wrapped in paper for smoking.

cil·i·a, *n. pl.*, of **cilium**. short hairs; eyelashes.

cinch, *n.* girth for a saddle; sure thing; tight grip. *v.* to gird.

cinc·ture, *n.* girdle; *v.* encompass.

cin·der, *n.* burned-out coal, wood; etc.; slag.

cin·e·ma, *n. pl.*, **-mas**. motion pictures; movie theater.

cin·na·mon, *n.* spice from tree bark from E. Indies.

ci·pher, *n.* zero; code; key to a code. *v.* calculate; write in code.

cir·ca, *adv.*, *prep.* about.

cir·cle, *n.* closed plane curve having every point equally distant from center; cycle; realm of influence; orb. *v.*, **-cled**, **-cling**. enclose; revolve. **cir·cler**, *n.*

cir·cuit, *n.* roundabout journey; path of an electric current; regular tour; theater chain. *v.* make a circuit.

cir·cu·lar, *a.* round; indirect. *n.* leaflet for distribution. **cir·cu·lar·i·ty**, *n.*

cir·cu·late, *v.*, **-lated**, **-lating**. move in a circle; move through the body as blood; spread; distribute. **-la·tion**, *n.*

cir·cum·cise, *v.*, **-cised**, **-cising**. remove the foreskin of the penis. **-ci·sion**, *n.*

cir·cum·fer·ence, *n.* outer boundary of a circle; distance around.

cir·cum·lo·cu·tion, *n.* roundabout way of speaking.

cir·cum·scribe, *v.*, **-scribed**, **-scribing**. encircle; draw a line around; limit.

cir·cum·spect, *a.*, cautious; watchful; prudent.

cir·cum·stance, *n.* existing fact, condition or event; a detail; *pl.*, financial condition. **-stan·tial**, *a.*

cir·cum·vent, *v.* outwit; entrap.

cir·cus, *n. pl.*, **-cus·es**. traveling company of performers; entertainment arena.

cir·rho·sis, *n.* liver disease.

cir·rus, *n. pl.*, **cir·ri**. fleecy cloud; filament; tendril.

cis·tern, *n.* reservoir; vessel.

cit·a·del, *n.* fortress.

cite, *v.*, **cited**, **citing**. summon; quote; refer to. **ci·ta·tion**, *n.*

cit·i·zen, *n.* member of a nation; inhabitant of town or city;

cit·rus, *n. pl.*, **-rus**, **-rus·es**. genus of trees and shrubs grown for edible fruit, limes, oranges, etc.

cit·y, *n. pl.*, **cit·ies**. large, important town; incorporated municipality.

civ·ic, *a.* of a city or citizen.

civ·il, *a.* municipal; pertaining to citizens; polite. **civ·il·ly**, *adv.*

ci·vil·ian, *n.* non-military person. *a.* of civilians.

ci·vil·i·ty, *n. pl.*, **-ties**. politeness; courtesy; attention.

civ·i·li·za·tion, *n.* advanced state of society; culture of a specific group.

civ·i·lize, *v.*, **-lized**, **-lizing**. change from savage existence; refine.

civ·il war, *n.* war between people of the same country.

civ·et, *n.* long-bodied African cat; musky substance from cat, used for perfume.

clad, *a.*, clothed; covered.

claim, *v.* assert; require as due. *n.* demand; just title to a thing; thing claimed. **-a·ble**, *a.* **-ant**, *n.*

clair·voy·ance, *n.* power to see beyond the range of vision; intuitive knowledge. **clair·voy·ant**, *a.*

clam, *n.* edible mollusc.

clam·my, *a.*, **-mier**, **-miest**. sticky; moist. **-mi·ness**, *n.*

clam·or, *n.* noisy shouting. *v.* make a din. **-or·ous**, *a.*

clamp, *n.* device that presses two objects together. *v.* fasten with clamps.

clan, *n.* group with common ancestor. **-nish,** *a.*

clan·des·tine, *a.* secret; underhand.

clang, *n.* loud, ringing, metallic sound. *v.* make a clang.

clap, *v.,* **clapped** or **clapt, clap·ping.** strike noisily together; applaud. *n.* hard slap or sound.

claret, *n.* dry red table wine.

clar·i·fy, *v.,* **-fied. -fying.** make intelligible; become clear. **-fi·ca·tion,** *n.*

clar·i·net, *n.* tubular woodwind instrument with single reed.

clar·i·ty, *n.* clearness.

clash, *v.* conflict; disagree. *n.* loud sound; collision.

clasp, *n.* device for fastening objects together; grasp. *v.* fasten; embrace.

class, *n.* group of same level; caste; biological subdivision; style. *v.* classify. **class·a·ble,** *a.*

clas·sic, *a.,* standard of excellence; Greek or Roman style traditional. *n.* author, artist, or production of first rank.

clas·si·cal, *a.* classic; serious music.

clas·si·fy, *v.,* **-fied, -fying.** assign to groups; arrange in classes; **-fi·ca·tion, -fied,** *a.*

clat·ter, *v.,* make a rattling sound. *n.*

clause, *n.* section of a discourse; group of words with subject and predicate.

claus·tro·pho·bia, *n.* abnormal fear of being in closed or narrow places.

clav·i·cle, *n.* shoulder bone.

claw, *n.* sharp curved nail on foot of a bird or animal. *v.* scratch; tear.

clay, *n.* earthy, plastic material.

clean, *a.* pure; free from filth; innocent; complete. *v.* get rid of dirt. *adv.* **clean·er,** *n.* **clean·li·ness,** *n.* **clean·ly,** *a.*

cleanse, *v.,* **cleansed, cleansing.** make clean; purify.

clear, *a.* transparent; luminous; clean; distinct; evident; open; free. *v.* explain; pass; gain. **clear·ly,** *adv.* **clear·ness,** *n.*

clear·ance, *n.* clear space.

clear·ing, *n.* area of land cleared of wood.

cleat, *n.* something used to provide a grip or traction.

cleave, *v.,* **cleft, cleaved, clove; cleft, cleaved, cloven; cleaving.** part by a cutting blow; split; adhere firmly; cling.

clef, *n.* musical symbol that indicates pitch.

cleft, *n.* crack; fissure. *a.* split.

clem·en·cy, *n.* mercy; leniency; mild weather. **clem·ent,** *a.*

clench, *v.* hold tightly; clutch.

clep·to·ma·ni·an. abnormal, persistent impulse to steal.

cler·gy, *n. pl.,* **-gies.** ministers, priests, rabbis, etc., collectively.

cler·i·cal, *a.* relating to the clergy, relating to office clerks or their work.

clerk, *n.* general office worker; salesperson; minor official. *v.* do clerical work.

clev·er, *a.* resourceful; dexterous; ingenious. **-ness,** *n.*

click, *n.* slight, sharp noise. *v.* make a click.

cli·ent, *n.* person engaging a professional service; customer.

cliff, *n.* high steep face of rock; precipice.

cli·mate, *n.* weather conditions of a region. **cli·mat·ic,** *a.*

cli·max, *n.* highest point; culmination. *v.* arrive at a climax.

climb, *v.* rise; ascend by grasping. *n.* act of climbing. **-ber,** *n.* **-a·ble,** *a.*

clinch, *v.* secure; fasten; settle.

cling, *v.,* **clung, cling·ing.** adhere; stick; hold fast. **-er** *n.*

clin·ic, *n.* place to treat non-resident patients. **-i·cal,** *a.*

clip, *v.,* **ped, -ping.** cut; shear; trim, curtail. *n.* sharp blow; metal clasp.

clique, *n.* exclusive group of people. **cliqu·ish,** *a.*

cloak,*n.* loose outer garment; disguise; pretext. *v.* cover with a cloak; disguise; hide.

clock, *n.* instrument for measuring time. *v.* time with a timing device.

clod, *n.* lump or mass; oaf.

clog, *v.,* **-ged, -ging.** obstruct; stick together *n.* impediment; shoe with a thick sole.

clois·ter, *n.* covered walk; monastery; convent. *v.* confine in a cloister. **clois·tral,** *a.*

clone, *n.* copy of an organism generated by its cells.

close, *v.* **closed, clos·ing.** suspend; terminate; shut; finish. *n.* conclusion.

close, *a.* shut; confined; compact; near; nearly equal. *adv.* near. **-ness,** *n.*

clos·et, *n.* small storage room, *v.*

clot, *n.* mass; lump. *v.,* **-ted, -ting.** coagulate.

cloth, *n. pl.,* **cloths.** fabric formed by weaving.

clothe, *v.,* **clothed** or **clad, cloth·ing.** dress; attire. **cloth·ing,** *n.*

clothes, *n. pl.,* garments.

cloud, *n.* visible mass of water particles in the air; thing that darkens or threatens. *v.* grow cloudy; taint; make dark. **-y,** *a.* **-i·ness,** *n.*

clove *n.* aromatic spice or oil; small bulb.

clo·ver, *n.* three-leaved herb.

clown, *n.* circus comic performer; buffoon. *v.* act comically. **-ish**, *a.*

cloy, *v.* satiate.

club, *n.* heavy bat; used as a weapon; *pl.* playing card suit; social association. *v.* beat with a cudgel.

clue, *n.* anything that guides in the solution of a problem or mystery.

clum·sy, *a.*, **-sier**, **-siest**. awkward; unweildy. **-si·ness**, *n.*

clus·ter, *n.* bunch of the same kind. *v.* collect in groups.

clutch, *v.* hold tightly; snatch. *n.* grip; critical situation; *usu. pl.* power; device for engaging and disengaging machinery.

clut·ter, *n.* confusion; disorder; litter. *v.* to litter.

coach, *n.* enclosed vehicle, as a bus; private tutor; athletic trainer. *v.* instruct as a coach.

co·ag·u·late, *v.*, **-lated**, **-lat·ing**. congeal; clot; curdle. **-la·tion**, *n.*

coal, *n.* carbonized matter used for fuel; an ember.

co·a·lesce, *v.*, **-lesced**, **-lescing**. fuse; unit. **-les·cence**, *n.*

co·a·li·tion, *n.* union into one mass or body; alliance.

coarse, *a.*, **coars·er**, **coars·est**. rough; base. **coars·en**, *v.*

coast, *n.* seashore. *v.* slide or ride down a hill. **coast·er**, *n.*

coat, *n.* outer garment with sleeves; layer; animal fur, etc.*v.* cover or provide with a coat. **coat·ing**, *n.*

coax, *v.* influence by persuasion.

co·balt, *n.* a silver-white metallic element.

cob·ble, *v.*, **-bled**, **-bling**. put together coarsely; make or repair, as shoes. **cob·bler**, *n.*

co·bra, *n.* poisonous snake.

co·caine, *n.* additive drug used as an anesthetic and narcotic.

cock, *n.* adult male bird; faucet. *v.* raise the hammer of a gun; tilt up.

cock·a·too, *n. pl.*, **-toos**. noisy, showy crested parrot.

cock·le, *n.* edible mollusk.

cock·roach, *n.* nocturnal insect.

cock·tail, *n.* iced drink with liquor mixed; appetizer.

cock·y, *a.*, **-i·er**, **-i·est**. *inf.* pert; conceited. **-i·ness**, *n.*

co·coa, *n.* powdered chocolate.

co·co·nut, **co·coa·nut**, *n.* hard-shelled palm tree fruit with white edible meat and milk.

co·coon, *n.* silken envelope of insect larvae.

cod, *n.* large soft-finned food fish. Also **cod·fish**.

cod·dle, *v.*, **-dled**, **-dling**. pamper; boil gently.

code, *n.* system of laws and regulations; system of signals; cipher. *v.*, **cod·ed**, **cod·ing**. enter in a code.

cod·i·fy, *v.*, **-fied**, **-fy·ing** arrange in systematic form. reduce (laws, etc.) to a code.

co·ed, *n.* female college student.

co·ed·u·ca·tion, *n.* education of both sexes in same institution.

co·erce, *v.*, **-erced**, **-erc·ing**. bring about by force; compel. **-er·cion**, *n.* **-er·cive**, *a.*

cof·fee, *n.* drink made from ground, roasted coffee beans.

cof·fer, *n.* chest, box, esp. for valuables.

cof·fin, *n.* casket; box for a corpse.

cog, *n.* tooth on rim of a wheel.

co·gent, *a.* having power to compel; convincing. **-gen·cy**, *n.*

cog·i·tate, *v.*, **-tat·ed**, **-tat·ing**. ponder; think over intently.

cog·nac, *n. French brandy.*

cog·ni·zance, *n.* knowledge, awareness; heed. **-zant**, *a.*

co·here, *v.*, **co·hered**, **co·her·ing**. hold or stick together firmly.

co·her·ent, *a.* holding together; logically consistent. **-ence**, *n.*

co·hort, *n.* accomplice.

coif·fure, *n.* hair style.

coil, *n.* ring or series of spiral loops. *v.* wind in spirals.

coin, *n.* metal money. *v.* to mint; invent. **coin·age**, *n.*

co·in·cide, *v.*, **-cid·ed**, **-cid·ing**. occupying same place or time; correspond. **-ci·dence**, *n.* **-ci·den·tal**, *a.*

co·i·tus, *n.* sexual intercourse. **co·i·tal**, *a.*

coke, *n.* lumps of fuel from heated coal. *sl.*, cocaine.

col·an·der, *n.* draining strainer.

cold, *a.*, chilly; lacking warmth; *n.* low temperature; cold weather; bodily disorder. **cold·ness**, *n.*

cole·slaw, *n.* sliced raw cabbage salad.

col·ic, *n.* sharp abdominal pain. **col·ick·y**, *a.*

col·i·se·um, *n.* large stadium.

col·lab·o·rate, *v.*, **-rat·ed**, **-rat·ing**. work with others; assist the enemy. **-ra·tion**, *n.*

col·lapse, *v.*, break down; fall in or down. **-lapsed**, **-lap·sing**. *n.* act of disintegrating; failure. **col·lap·si·ble**, *a.*

col·lar, *n.* anything worn or placed around the neck.

col·late, *v.*, **-lat·ed**, **-lat·ing**. to compare carefully; to put together in sequence. **col·la·tion**, *n.*

col·lat·er·al, *a.* situated at the side; additional. *n.* property pledged as security.

col·league, *n.* associate.

col·lect, *v.*, accumulate; receive payment for. **col·lec·tion**, *n.*

col·lege, *n.* institution of higher learning. **col·le·gi·ate**, *a.*

col·lide, *v.*, **-lid·ed**, **-lid·ing**. clash; crash together. **-li·sion**, *n.*

col·lo·qui·al, *a.* informal conversation or word usage. **-al·ly**, *adv.* **-al·ism**, *n.*

col·lu·sion, *n.* secret cooperation for fraud.

co·logne, *n.* perfumed liquid.

co·lon, *n.* portion of large intestine; punctuation mark (:).

colo·nel, *n.* commissioned army officer.

col·on·nade, *n.* series of columns supporting a roof or arches.

col·o·ny, *n. pl.*, **-nies.** group of people in new territory with ties to former state; the new territory; localized body of organisms. *a.* **-nist**, *n.* **-ni·za·tion**, *n.*

col·or *n.* pigment; dye; hue. *pl.* flag. *v.* tint; blush; distort. **-ed**, *a.* **-ful**, *a.* **-ing**, *n.*

co·los·sal, *a.* gigantic; huge.

col·umn, *n.* pillar; upright shaft; newspaper section. vertical section of printed page. **-ist**, *n.*

co·ma, *n. pl.*, state of unconsciousness. **-tose**, *a.*

comb, *n.* toothed implement to arrange or wear in hair; crest on head of fowl. *v.* comb hair; search.

com·bat, *v.*, **-bat·ed**, **-bat·ing** or **-bat·ted**, **-bat·ting**. fight. *n.* conflict. **-ant**, *a.*

com·bi·na·tion, *n.* things brought together; sequence of numbers.

com·bine, *v.*, **-bined**, **-bin·ing**. unify; blend; bring together. *n.* business group; harvesting machine.

com·bus·ti·ble, *a.* inflammable.

com·bus·tion, *n.* act or process of burning.

come, *v.*, **came**, **come**, **com·ing**. move toward something; arrive; appear; occur.

co·me·di·an, *n.* comedy actor. **co·me·di·enne**, *n. fem.*

com·e·dy, *n. pl.*, **-dies.** humorous drama; light play.

come·ly, *a.* pleasing appearance.

com·et, *n.* celestial body orbiting the sun.

com·fort, *v.*, give strength or hope to. *n.* cheer; consolation. **-a·ble**, *a.*

com·ic, *a.* funny; humorous. *n.* comedian. **com·i·cal**, *a.*

com·ma, *n. pl.*, **-mas.** punctuation mark (,).

com·mand, *v.* order with authority. *n.* directive; ability to control. **-mand·er**, *n.*

com·man·deer, *v.* to seize for military or other public use.

com·mand·ment, *n.* mandate; precept from God.

com·mem·o·rate, *v.*, **-rat·ed**, **-rat·ing**. to honor the memory of. **com·mem·o·ra·tion**, *n.*

com·mence, *v.*, **-menced**, **-menc·ing**. begin; start; enter upon.

com·mence·ment, *n.* beginning; college graduation ceremony.

com·mend, *v.* mention as worthy; praise; **-men·da·tion**, *n.*

com·ment, *v.*, remark; explanation. *n.* explanatory note.

com·men·tar·y, *n. pl.*, **-ies.** series of explanatory notes. *n.* **-ta·tor.**

com·merce, *n.* trade; business.

com·mer·cial, *n.* radio or television ad. *a.* of commerce; engaged in business.

com·mis·er·ate, *v.* feel sorry for; condole.

com·mis·sar·y, *n. pl.*, **-ies.** store supplying provisions.

com·mis·sion, *n.* authority; military rank; group charged to act; agents fee. *v.* authorize; order. **-mis·sioned**, *a.* **-mis·sion·er**, *n.*

com·mit, *v.*, **-mit·ted**, **-mit·ting**. entrust; institutionalize, consign; perform. **-mit·ment**, *n.*

com·mit·tee, *n.* group delegated to consider or act on something.

com·mo·di·ous, *a.* spacious; roomy.

com·mod·i·ty, *n. pl.*, **-ties.** agricultural or mining product; article exchanged in commerce.

com·mon, *a.* ordinary; public; shared; familiar; coarse.

com·mon·law *n.* law based on custom, usage, and court decisions.

com·mon·place, *n.* unremarkable thing. *a.* ordinary.

com·mon·wealth, *n.* self-governing nation; democracy.

com·mo·tion, *n.* tumult; unrest.

com·mune, *v.*, **-muned**, **-mun·ing**. talk together; partake of Eucharist. *n.* community based on common needs.

com·mu·ni·cate, *v.*, **-cat·ed**, **-cat·ing**. transmit; make known. impart; convey; share. **-ca·ble**, *a.* **-ca·tion**, *n.*

com·mun·ion, *n.* participation; fellowship; the Eucharist.

com·mun·ism, *n.* social system based on common ownership of property. **-mun·ist**, *n.*

com·mu·ni·ty, *n. pl.*, **-ties**. social group whose members reside in the same locality.

com·mute, *v.*, **-mut·ed**, **-mut·ing**. exchange; travel back and forth regularly; reduce (punishment, etc.) to one less severe. **-mut·er**, *n.*

com·pact, *n.* contract; agreement; face powder case. *a.* solid; dense.

com·pan·ion, *n.* one in the company of another; mate for a thing.

com·pa·ny, *n. pl.*, **-nies**. assembled group; visitors; business association.

com·pare, *v.*, **-pared**, **-par·ing**. represent as similar; note similarities and differences. **pa·ra·ble**, *a.* **-par·i·son**, *n.* **-parable**, **-par·ative**, *a.*

com·part·ment, *n.* part or space marked or partitioned off.

com·pass, *n.* device for determining directions; instrument for drawing circle.

com·pas·sion, *n.* mercy; empathy; pity. **-sion·ate**, *a.*

com·pat·i·ble, *a.* harmonious.

com·pa·tri·ot, *n.* fellow countryman; colleague.

com·pel, *v.*, **-pelled**, **-pel·ling**. drive or urge with force; oblige.

com·pen·sate, *v.*, **-sat·ed**, **-sat·ing**. pay for; offset; recompense. **-pen·sa·tion**, *n.*

com·pete, *v.*, **-pet·ed**, **-pet·ing**. contend; **-pet·i·tor**, *n.*

com·pe·tence, *n.* sufficiency.

com·pe·tent, *a.* well-qualified; sufficient.

com·pe·ti·tion, *n.* contest; rivalry; skill. **-pet·i·tive**, *a.*

com·pile, *v.*, **-piled**, **-pil·ing**. collect into a volume; gather together. **-pi·la·tion**, *n.*

com·pla·cence, *n.* self-satisfaction; pleased. **-cent**, *a.*

com·plain, *v.* express discontent or pain; find fault; charge formally. **-plaint**, *n.*

com·ple·ment, *n.* that which makes whole, completes, or makes perfect; full quantity.

com·plete, *a.* entire; concluded; thorough; finished. *v.*, **-plet·ed**, **-plet·ing**. make perfect; finish. achieve fully. **-ple·tion**, *n.*

com·plex, *a.* complicated; intricate; composed of interconnected parts. *n.* a complex whole or system. *n.* **-i·ty**, *n. pl.*, **-ties**.

com·plex·ion, *n.* color or appearance of the skin; appearance; aspect.

com·pli·cate, *v.*, **-cat·ed**, **-cat·ing**. make complex, intricate or involved. **-cat·ed**, difficult. *a.* **-ca·tion**, *n.*

com·pli·ment, *n.* expression of admiration or esteem; *pl.* regards. *v.* praise.

com·pli·men·ta·ry, *a.* conveying a compliment; free.

com·ply, *v.*, **-plied**, **-ply·ing**. act in accordance with; fulfill; conform. **-pli·ance**, *n.* **-pli·ant**, *a.*

com·po·nent, *n.* part; ingredient.

com·port, *v.* accord; suit; behave.

com·pose, *v.*, **-posed**, **-pos·ing**. fashion; create; write; calm. **-po·si·tion**, *n.*

com·pos·ite, *a.* made up of distinct parts. *n.* something made of different parts.

com·po·sure, *n.* self-possession; calmness.

com·pote, *n.* fruits cooked in syrup; glass dish with stem for fruit, candy, etc.

com·pound, *v.* put together; combine. *a.* composite. *n.* thing formed by a union of parts.

com·pre·hend, *v.* grasp mentally; embrace; understand. **-hen·sion**, *n.* **-hen·sive**, *a.*

com·press, *v.* force into less space; press together; condense. *n.* folded pad or cloth. **-pres·sion**, *n.*

com·prise, *v.*, **-prised**, **-pris·ing**. contain; to consist of.

com·pro·mise, *n.* settlement by mutual concessions. *v.*, **-mised**, **-mis·ing**. settle by a compromise; endanger reputation.

comp·trol·ler, *n.* controller.

com·pul·sion, *n.* act of compelling; an irresistable impulse. **-sive**, *a.* **-so·ry**, *a.*

com·punc·tion, *n.* uneasiness of conscience; contrition; remorse.

com·pute, *v.*, **-put·ed**, **-put·ing**. calculate. **-pu·ta·tion**, *n.*

com·pu·ter, *n.* programmable electronic device that processes data.

com·rade, *n.* associate.

con, *adv.* in opposition.

con·cave, *a.* curved inward.

con·ceal, *v.* hide from sight.

con·cede, *v.*, **-ced·ed**, **-ced·ing**. admit as true; yield.

con·ceit, *n.* exaggerated opinion of one's self.

con·ceit·ed, *a.* vain.

con·ceive, *v.*, **-ceived**, **-ceiv·ing**. to form; understand; become pregnant; think. **-ceiv·a·ble**, *a.*

con·cen·trate, *v.*, **-tra·ted**, **-trat·ing**. gather into a group; intensify; focus; strengthen. **-tra·tion**, *n.*

con·cept, *n.* notion; thought; idea. **con·cep·tu·al**, *a.*

con·cep·tion, *n.* act of conceiving; beginning; idea; design.

con·cern, v. relate to; affect. interest. n. solicitude; care; anxiety; business firm. -**cerned,** a.

con·cern·ing, prep. regarding.

con·cert, n. musical performance; in agreement.

con·ces·sion, n. act of yielding; something conceded.

conch, n. pl. large spiral-shaped mollusk.

con·cil·i·ate, v., -**at·ed,** -**at·ing.** placate; reconcile; gain the favor of; -**i·a·tion,** n.

con·cise, a. brief; succinct.

con·clave, n. private meeting; secret assembly.

con·clude, v., -**clud·ed,** -**clud·ing.** finish; form an opinion. -**clu·sion,** n.

con·coct, v., combine ingredients; devise; plot. -**coc·tion,** n.

con·cord, n. state of harmony.

con·course, n. assemblage; boulevard; open gathering space.

con·crete, a. tangible, actual; specific. n. hard building material.

con·cu·bine, n. mistress; secondary wife.

con·cur, v., -**curred,** -**cur·ring.** agree; coincide. -**rence,** accord. n. -**rent,** a.

con·cus·sion, n. shock or brain injury caused by a blow or collision. -**sive,** a.

con·demn, v. declare guilty or wrong; convict; sentence. -**dem·na·tion,** n. censure.

con·dense, v., -**densed,** -**dens·ing.** compact; abridge; concentrate; compress. -**den·sa·tion,** n.

con·de·scend, v. humble oneself; patronize. -**scen·sion,** n.

con·di·ment, n. seasoning.

con·di·tion, n. existing state; stipulation; prerequisite; qualification. v. make conditional; modify; put in proper state. -**al,** a.

con·do·lence, n. sympathy.

con·do·min·i·um, n. individually owned apartment unit.

con·done, v., -**doned,** -**don·ing.** pardon; overlook. -**do·na·tion,** n.

con·dor, n. large American vulture.

con·du·cive, a. furthering; contributing; helpful.

con·duct, v. escort; guide; lead; direct; behave. n. management; behavior. -**duc·tor,** n.

con·duit, n. pipe; tube.

cone, n. figure with a circular base, tapering to a point.

con·fec·tion, n. candy or sweet. -**tion·a·ry,** a.

con·fed·er·a·cy, n. pl., -**cies.** league; alliance; conspiracy; southern states during U·S. Civil War.

con·fed·er·ate, a. united with. n. accomplice; ally. -**a·tion,** n.

con·fer, v., -**ferred,** -**fer·ring.** bestow; grant publicly; consult. -**fer·ral,** n. -**fer·ence,** n.

con·fess, v. admit; acknowledge; avow. -**fes·sion,** n. -**fes·sion·al,** n. -**fes·sor,** n.

con·fet·ti, n. pl. bits of colored paper made for throwing at parties, carnivals, etc.

con·fide, v., -**fid·ed,** -**fid·ing.** show confidence and trust by imparting secrets.

con·fi·dence, n. faith; trust; assurance; a secret; self-reliance. -**fi·dent,** a.

con·fi·den·tial, a. private; intimate; secret.

con·fig·u·ra·tion, n. external arrangement by parts; form.

con·fine, n. usu. pl. border; boundary. v., -**fined,** -**fin·ing.** to enclose; limit or restrict; imprison. -**fined,** a. -**fine·ment,** n.

con·firm, v. make firm; approve; verify; admit to church membership. -**fir·ma·tion,** n.

con·fis·cate, v., -**cat·ed,** -**cat·ing.** to seize; appropriate. -**ca·tion,** n.

con·fla·gra·tion, n. large disastrous fire.

con·flict, n. battle; controversy. v. clash; oppose.

con·form, v. act in accord; become similar in form. -**i·ty,** n. pl., -**ties.**

con·found, v. perplex; confuse.

con·front, v. face in challenge; bring face to face. -**fron·ta·tion,** n.

con·fuse, v., -**fused,** -**fus·ing.** perplex; disconcert. adv. -**fu·sion,** n.

con·fute, v., -**fut·ed,** -**fut·ing.** prove false or wrong.

con·geal, v. coagulate; freeze.

con·gen·ial, a. compatible; agreeable; suited in spirit, etc.

con·gen·i·tal, a. existing at or from birth but not hereditary.

con·gest, v. clog; overcrowd. -**ges·tion,** n. -**ges·tive,** a.

con·glom·er·ate, n. a. composite mass or mixture. -**a·tion,** n.

con·grat·u·late, v., -**lat·ed,** -**lat·ing.** express pleasure or joy on a happy occasion. -**la·tion,** n. usu. pl.

con·gre·gate, v., -**gat·ed,** -**gat·ing.** come together or collect in a group; assemble. -**ga·tion,** n.

con·gress, n. an assembly of representatives; (cap) U·S. Senate and House. -**gres·sion·al,** a. -**gress·man,** n. pl., -**men.**

con·gru·ent, *a.* agreeing; corresponding; having same size and shape.

co·ni·fer, *n.* evergreen tree bearing cones.

con·jec·ture, *n.* form opinion with insufficient proof. *v.,* **-tured, -tur·ing.** guess. **-tur·al,** *a.*

con·ju·gal, *a,* of marriage.

con·ju·gate, *v.,* **-gat·ed, -gat·ing.** inflect (a verb); couple.

con·junc·tion, *n.* combination; word serving to link words.

con·jure, *v.,* **-jured, -jur·ing.** entreat solemnly; affect magically. **-jur·er, -jur·or,** *n.*

con·nect, *v.* unite; fasten together; join. **-nec·tion,** *n.*

con·nive, *v.,* **-nived, -niv·ing.** cooperate secretly.

con·nois·seur, *n.* person competent to judge in matters of taste or fine arts.

con·note, *v.,* **-not·ed, -not·ing.** signify (ideas, etc.) in addition to primary meaning; imply. **-no·ta·tion,** *n.*

con·quer, *v.* gain by force of arms; win; be victorious. **-or,** *n.* **-quest,** *n.*

con·science, *n.* sense of moral goodness; faculty which decides right and wrong.

con·sci·en·tious, *a.* scrupulous; meticulous; painstaking.

con·scious, *a.* aware; perceiving; mentally aware; purposeful; intentional. **-ness,** *n.*

con·se·crate, *v.,* **-crat·ed, -crat·ing.** declare sacred; hallow. **-cra·tive,** *a.* **-cra·tion,** *n.*

con·sec·u·tive, *a.* following in order. successive. **-tive·ly,** *adv.*

con·sen·sus, *n.* majority opinion; general agreement.

con·sent, *v.* give approval. *n.* agreement; acquiescence.

con·se·quence, *n.* effect or result. **-quent,** *a.* **-quent·ly,** *adv.*

con·se·quent, *a.* effect or result; resulting. **-quent·ly,** *adv.*

con·serv·a·tive, *n.* traditional; cautious; moderate. *n.*

con·serv·a·to·ry, *n. pl.,* **-rie.** greenhouse; fine arts school.

con·serve, *v.,* **-served, -serv·ing.** keep safe or sound; preserve. **-ser·va·tion,** *n.*

con·sid·er, *v.* think about with care; suppose; esteem; take into account; judge to be. **-ate,** *a.* **-a·tion,** *n.* **-ing,** *prep.*

con·sid·er·a·ble, *a.* important; much; large. **-ably,** *adv.*

con·sign, *v.* to hand over, deliver, transfer, set apart, transmit.

con·sist, *v.* be composed, made up or formed of.

con·sist·en·cy, *n. pl.,* **-cies.** coherence; density of a liquid; harmony; conformity. **-ent,** *a.*

con·sole, *v.,* **-soled, -sol·ing.** comfort; solace. *n.* cabinet. **-sol·a·ble,** *a.* **-so·la·tion,** *n.*

con·sol·i·date, *v.,* **-dat·ed, -dat·ing.** unite; strengthen; combine. **-da·tion,** *n.*

con·som·me, *n.* clear soup made from meat stock.

con·so·nant, *n.* any alphabet letter except a, e, i, o, u. *a.* in agreement.

con·sort, *n.* spouse; associate; ship that travels with another. *v.* keep company.

con·spic·u·ous, *a.* easy to be seen; visable; striking.

con·spire, *v.,* **-spired, -spir·ing.** plot; agree secretly. **-spir·a·cy,** *n. pl.,* **-cies. -spir·a·tor,** *n., a.*

con·sta·ble, *n.* police officer. **-stab·u·lar·y,** *n. pl.,* **-ies.**

con·stant, *a.* invariable; continuing; regular; faithful. *n.* anything regular; fixed value number. **-stan·cy,** *n.* **-stant·ly,** *adv.*

con·stel·la·tion, *n.* groups of stars with names.

con·ster·na·tion, *n.* dismay.

con·sti·pa·tion, *n.* difficult bowel evacuation. **-sti·pate,** *v.*

con·stit·u·ent, *a.* component. *n.* essential part; voter.

con·sti·tute, *v.* form; appoint; create; set up.

con·sti·tu·tion, *n.* make up or composition; fundamental principles of government; body physique. **-tion·al,** *n.*

con·strain, *v.* restrict; confine. **-straint,** *n.*

con·struct, *v.* make; build. **-struc·tive,** *a.* **-struc·tion,** *n.*

con·strue, *v.,* **-strued, -stru·ing.** interpret; infer; explain.

con·sul, *n.* government's representative residing in a foreign city. **-su·late,** *n.*

con·sult, *v.,* ask advice of; consider; counsel together. **-ant,** *a.* **-sul·ta·tion,** *n.*

con·sume, *v.,* **-sumed, -sum·ing.** destroy; expend; use up; eat. **-sum·er,** *n.* **-sump·tion,** *n.*

con·sum·mate, *v.,* **-mat·ed, -mat·ing.** finish; achieve; *a.* perfect. **-ma·tion,** *n.*

con·tact, *n.* touch; union of surfaces; association. *v.* get in touch with.

con·ta·gion, *n.* transmission of disease. **-gious,** *a.*

con·tain, *v.* keep within limits; hold or have within. **-tain·er,** *n.*

con·tam·i·nate, *v.,* **-nat·ed, -nat·ing.** defile; infect; taint; pollute. **-na·tion,** *n.*

con·tem·plate, v., **-plat·ed**, **-plat·ing**. consider; gaze at; meditate. **-pla·tion**, n. **-pla·tive**, a.

con·tem·po·rar·y, a. occurring at the same time; modern. n. pl., **-rar·ies**. people living at the same time.

con·tempt, n. disdain; scorn; willful disobedience; disrespect. **-tempt·i·ble**, a. **-temp·tu·ous**, a.

con·tend, v. struggle; strive; argue; maintain.

con·tent, a. happy; pleased; n. usu. pl. subject matter; capacity; substance. **-tent·ed**, a.

con·test, v. dispute; challenge; vie. n. competition; rivalry. **-ant**, n.

con·text, n. parts of passage near word or phrase that help explain its meaning.

con·ti·nent, n. large land areas of the earth, as Africa. a. self-restrained. **-nen·tal**, a. n.

con·tin·gent, a. possible; unpredictable; conditional. n. people drawn from a group. **-gen·cy**, n. pl., **-cies**.

con·tin·ue, v., **-ued**, **-u·ing**. maintain; endure; stay; persist; start again. **-u·al**, a. **-u·a·tion**, n. **-u·ous**, a.

con·tort, v. twist or bend out of shape. **-tor·tion**, n.

con·tour, n. outline of a figure, land, etc.; shape; form.

con·tra·band, n. unlawful trade; smuggled goods.

con·tra·cep·tive, a. preventing pregnancy. n. contraceptive agent or device. **-cep·tion**, n.

con·tract, v. shorten; catch; shrink; make an agreement. n. legal agreement. **-trac·tion**, n. **-trac·tor**, n.

con·tra·dict, v. assert to be the contrary or opposite of. **-dic·tion**, n. **-dic·to·ry**, a.

con·tral·to, n. pl., **-tos** or **-ti**. lowest female singing voice.

con·trap·tion, n. inf. contrivance; gadget; device.

con·tra·ry, a. opposite; unfavorable perverse; stubborn. n. pl., **-ries**. the opposite.

con·trast, v. compare by pointing out noticeable differences; n. difference.

con·trib·ute, v., **-ut·ed**, **-ut·ing**. donate; submit for publication; give; **-tri·bu·tion**, n.

con·trite, a. deeply repentant. **-ly**, adv. **-tri·tion**, n.

con·trive, v., **-trived**, **-triv·ing**. devise; scheme. **-triv·ance**, n.

con·trol, v., **-trolled**, **-trol·ling**. regulate; rule. dominate. n. power to command; restraint; reserve.

con·trol·ler, n. person in charge of finances, as in a business; comptroller; person or device which controls.

con·tro·ver·sy, n. pl., **-sies**. dispute; strife; quarrel. **-ver·sial**, a.

con·tuse, v., **-tused**, **-tus·ing**. bruise. **-tu·sion**, n.

con·va·lesce, v., **-lesced**, **-lesc·ing**. regain health. **-les·cence**, n. **-les·cent**, a., n.

con·vec·tion, n. transference of heat by circulation of a fluid.

con·vene, v., **-vened**, **-ven·ing**. summon; assemble. **-ven·er**, n.

con·ven·ient, a. suitable to the needs or purpose; handy; near. **-ience**, n..

con·vent, n. building for nuns.

con·ven·tion, n. assembly; customary practice. **-tion·al**, a.

con·verge, v., **-verged**, **-verg·ing**. move to a point; meet. **-ver·gence**, n. **-ver·gent**, a.

con·ver·sant, a. knowledgeable; experienced; familiar.

con·ver·sa·tion, n. informal talk; verbal exchange. **-tion·al**, a.

con·verse, v., **-versed**, **-vers·ing**. talk. n. conversation; opposite or contrary.

con·vert, v. change from one form, belief, etc., to another. n. one converted. **-ver·sion**, n.

con·vert·i·ble, n. car with a top that can be lowered.

con·vex, a. curving outward.

con·vey, v. transport; communicate; transmit. **-ance**, n.

con·vict, v. prove guilty. n. one serving a prison sentence.

con·vic·tion, n. act or state of being convicted; strong belief.

con·vince, v., **-vinced**, **-vinc·ing**. persuade by argument; prove. **-vinc·ing**, a.

con·viv·i·al, a. festive.

con·vo·ca·tion, n. assembly.

con·voy, v. accompany. n. protecting escort; group of vehicles traveling together.

con·vulse, v., **-vulsed**, **-vuls·ing**. shake violently; agitate. **-vul·sion**, n. **-vul·sive**, a.

cook, v. prepare food by use of heat. n. chef.

cook·ie, **cook·y**, n. pl., **cookies**. small, flat, sweet cake.

cool, a. moderately cold; calm; unfriendly. v. lose heat. **-ness**, n **-er**, n.

coop, n. small cage for poultry. v. confine.

co·op·er·ate, v., **-at·ed**, **-at·ing**. work or act with others. **-a·tion**, n. **-a·tive**, a.

co·or·di·nate, *v.*, **-nat·ed**, **-nat·ing**. adjust; function harmoniously. *a.* equal in rank. **-na·tion**, *n.*

cop, *v.*, **copped**, **cop·ping**. *inf.* capture; steal. *n.* policeman.

co·pa·cet·ic, *a.* very satisfactory.

cope, *v.*, **coped**, **cop·ing**. deal with problems; priest's cape.

co·pi·ous, *a.* abundant; plentiful; wordy. **-ness**, *n.*

cop·per, *n.* malleable, reddish metallic element. **-per·y**, *a.*

cop·u·late, *v.*, **-lat·ed**, **-lat·ing**. engage in sexual intercourse. **-la·tion**, *n.*

cop·y, *n. pl.*, **cop·ies**. imitation or reproduction of an original work. *v.*, **-ied**, **-y·ing**. duplicate; imitate.

cop·y·right, *n.* author's sole right of property to his literary or artistic work.

co·quette, *n.* flirtatious girl.

cor·al, *n.* hard, stony skeletons of marine life forming reefs; red hue.

cord, *n.* heavy string or rope; unit of cut wood 128 cu. ft²; a bond; fabric rib. **-ed**, *a.*

cor·date, *a.* heart-shaped.

cor·dial, *a.* friendly; warm. **-i·ty**, *n.* liqueur.

cor·do·van, *a.* fine-grained, colored leather.

cor·du·roy, *n.* heavy cotton fabric with ribs. *a.*

core, *n.* central or important part. *v.*, **cored**, **cor·ing**.

cork, *n.* bark of an oak tree; stopper. *v.* plug with a cork.

cork·screw, *n.* device to pull corks from bottles. *a.* spiral.

corn, *n.* tall cereal plant grown for its edible kernels; local hardening of the skin, esp. on a toe.

cor·ner *n.* point where converging lines or surfaces meet; monopoly; angle. *v.* force into an awkward position.

cor·net, *n.* valved brass wind instrument.

cor·nice, *n.* ornamental projecting piece forming top of building.

cor·nu·co·pi·a, *n.* horn-shaped container overflowing with flowers and fruit, symbolizing plenty.

cor·ol·lar·y, *n. pl.*, **-ies**. inference; result.

co·ro·na, *n. pl.*, **-nas**, **-nae**. colored circle of light; crown.

cor·o·nar·y, *a.* pertaining to the arteries supplying blood to the heart; resembling a crown. *n.* coronary disease.

cor·o·na·tion, *n.* act of crowning a sovereign.

cor·o·ner, *n.* public officer who investigates unnatural deaths.

cor·po·ral, *a.* of the body.

cor·po·ral, *n.* lowest ranking noncommissioned officer.

cor·po·rate, *a.* formed into association with rights and liabilities endowed by law. **-ra·tive**, *a.*

cor·po·ra·tion, *n.* group of people, by law, operating as a single person in business.

corps, *n. pl.*, **corps**. organized group (military, diplomatic).

corpse, *n.* dead body.

cor·pu·lent, *a.* stout; obese. **-lence**, **-pu·len·cy**, *n.*

cor·pus·cle, *n.* small particle; esp. of blood. **-cu·lar**, *a.*

cor·ral, *n.* enclosure for livestock. *v.*, **-ralled**, **-ral·ling**. drive into a pen; round up.

cor·rect, *v.* make right; mark errors; scold. *a.* proper; conforming; accurate. **-rec·tion**, *n.*

cor·re·late, *v.*, **-lat·ed**, **-lat·ing**. place in or bring into mutual or reciprocal relation. **-la·tion**, *n.*

cor·re·spond, *v.* be in agreement or conformity; exchange letters. **-spond·ing**, *a.* **-spond·ence**, *n.* **-ent**, *a.*, *n.*

cor·ri·dor, *n.* hall; passageway.

cor·rob·o·rate, *v.*, **-rat·ed**, **-rat·ing**. support with evidence; confirm. **-ra·tion**, *n.*

cor·rode, *v.*, **-rod·ed**, **-rod·ing**. eat or wear away gradually. **-ro·sion**, *n.* **-ro·sive**, *a.*

cor·ru·gate, *v.*, **-gat·ed**, **-gat·ing**. fold into ridges and grooves. **-ga·tion**, *n.*

cor·rupt, *v.* spoil morally; bribe. *a.* **-rup·tion**, *n.* degenerate; depraved.

cor·sage, *n.* small flower bouquet worn by a woman; dress bodice.

cor·set, *n.* undergarment worn for shape or support.

cos·met·ic, *a.* beautifying. *n.* any beautifying preparation.

cos·mic, *a.* relating to the universe; vast.

cos·mo·pol·i·tan, *a.* worldwide scope. *n.* person who feels at home anywhere.

cos·mos, *n.* the universe as an orderly, harmonious system.

cost, *n.* price paid to acquire; a loss or penalty; expenditure.

cost·ly, *a.*, **-li·er**, **-li·est**. expensive; costing much. **-li·ness**, *n.*

cos·tume, *n.* fashion belonging to another period or place; outer clothes for some occasion.

cot, *n.* light collapsible bed.

co·til·lion, *n.* intricate dance; formal ball.

cot·tage, *n.* small house.

cot·ton, *n.* soft white fiber of the cotton plant; fabric thread or cloth made of cotton. *a.* of cotton. **-ton·y,** *a.*

couch, *n.* article of furniture for reclining; sofa.

cough, *n.* noisy expulsion of air from the lungs. *v.* expel air from the lungs.

could, past form of **can.**

coun·cil, *n.* advisory or legislative body; meeting. **-or, -man,** *n.*

coun·sel, *n.* adviser; advice; lawyer. *v.,* **-seled, -sel·ing,** advise; consult. **-sel·ing,** *n.* **-se·lor,** *n.*

count, *v.* tally; say numbers in order; have importance; rely on; include. *n.* act of counting; allegation; tally; score; nobleman. **-a·ble,** *a.*

coun·te·nance, *n.* face; facial expression. *v.,* **-nanced, -nanc·ing.** give; support; approve.

count·er, *n.* level surface for serving food; scorekeeper; token. *a. adv.* in contrary manner. *v.* oppose.

coun·ter·act, *v.* make ineffective; neutralize; oppose. **-ac·tive,** *a.*

coun·ter·feit, *a.* not genuine; pretended; forged. *n.* imitation; forgery. *v.* copy with intent to deceive. **-er,** *n.*

coun·ter·part, *n.* duplicate; complement; equivalent.

coun·ter·sign, *n.* signature added to another signature for confirmation; secret signal. *v.* ratify.

count·ess, *n.* a count's wife.

count·less, *a.* innumerable.

coun·tri·fied, *a.* rustic; rural.

coun·try, *n. pl.,* **-tries.** land; nation; territory; farm areas. *a.* rural.

coun·ty, *n. pl.,* **-ties.** territorial division of a state.

coup, *n.* successful stroke.

coupe, *n.* closed, two-door automobile.

cou·ple, *n.* two persons paired together; pair; two. *inf.* few. *v.,* **-pled, -pling.** link; bond; join.

cou·pon, *n.* ticket redeemable for something of value; order form.

cour·age, *n.* fearlessness; valor; bravery. **cou·ra·geous,** *a.*

cour·i·er, *n.* messenger.

course, *n.* progress; channel of movement; direction taken; mode of conduct; educational program; part of a meal.

court, *n.* uncovered space surrounded by walls; sovereign and his retinue; judicial room, building, or body. *v.* seek affection of.

cour·te·ous, *a.,* polite; gracious.

cour·te·sy, *n. pl.,* **-sies.** politeness; considerate act.

court·ly, *a.,* **-li·er, -li·est.** dignified; elegant. **-li·ness,** *n.*

court-mar·tial, *n. pl.,* **courts-mar·tial.** trial in a military court. *v.,* **-mar·tialed, -mar·tial·ing.** try by court-martial.

court·ship, *n.* act or process of wooing.

cous·in, *n.* son or daughter of one's uncle or aunt.

cou·ture, *n.* business of designing, making, and selling exclusive women's clothes.

cove, *n.* small sheltered inlet.

cov·e·nant, *n.* agreement; pact.

cov·er, *v.* put something over protect; hide; overlay. *n.* that which protects; lid; top. **-ered,** *a.*

cov·ert, *a.* sheltered; hidden. **cov·ert·ly,** *adv.* **-ness,** *n.*

cov·et, *v.* desire eagerly.

cov·et·ous, *a.* inordinately or wrongly desirous. **-ous·ness,** *n.*

cow, *n. pl.,* **cows.** mature female bovine animal; any bovine animal. *v.* make afraid.

cow·ard, *n.* one easily intimidated; lacking courage. **-ard·ice,** *a.*

cow·er, *v.* crouch in fear.

cowl, *n.* monk's cloak; automobile hood. **-ed,** *a.*

coy, *a.* bashful; demure. **-ly,** *adv.* **-ness,** *n.*

coy·o·te, *n.* Amer. prairie wolf.

co·zy, *a.,* **-zi·er, -zi·est.** snug; **-zi·ness** *n.*

crab, *n.* hardshelled marine crustacean; ill-tempered person. *v.,* **crabbed, -bing.** complain. **-by,** *a.*

crab ap·ple, *n.* small, apple.

crack, *v.* break; snap; fail; open; make an explosive noise. *n.* flaw; sharp noise.

crack·er, *n.* thin crisp wafer.

crack·le, *v.,* **-led, -ling.** make small sharp noises; change by forming network of tiny cracks; sparkle. *n.*

cra·dle, *n.* rocking baby bed; framework. *v.,* **-dled, -dling.** put in cradle; protect lovingly; rear.

craft, *n.* skill or art; trade; small boat; guile.

crafts·man, *n. pl.,* **-men,** artisan. **-ship,** *n.* highly skilled.

craft·y, *a.,* **-i·er, -i·est.** cunning; sly. **-i·ness,** *n.*

crag, *n.* steep, rugged rock or cliff. **-ged,** *a.* **-gy,** *a.*

cram, *v.,* **crammed, -ming.** pack tight; sate; stuff; study hastily for a test.

cramp, v. confine. n. painful muscle contraction; pl. abdominal spasm and pain.

cran·ber·ry, n. pl., **-ries.** shrub with a red sour, edible fruit.

crane, n. large wading bird; machine for lifting heavy weights. v., **craned, cran·ing.** stretch one's neck.

cra·ni·um, n. skull; brain enclosure.

crank, n. arm at right angle to shaft of machine which imparts circular motion; inf. grouch. v. start with a crank.

crank·y, a., **-i·er, -i·est.** crotchety; irritable. **-i·ness,** n.

crash, v. smash, collapse. n. go to pieces with loud noise; sudden failure.

crass, a. insensitive. **-ness,** n.

crate, n. slatted, ventilated box. v. encase in framework.

cra·ter, n. bowl-shaped cavity; pit. **-tered,** a.

cra·vat, n. necktie; scarf.

crave, v., **craved, crav·ing.** desire strongly; beg. **crav·ing,** n.

cra·ven, a. cowardly. n. coward. **cra·ven·ly,** adv.

crawl, v. move slowly; creep along the ground on hands and knees. n. slow creeping movement; swim stroke. **-y,** a.

cray·fish, n. pl., **-fish·es, -fish.** small lobster-like crustacean.

cray·on, n. stick of colored wax, chalk, or charcoal for writing or drawing.

cra·zy, a., **-zi·er, -zi·est.** inf. insane; mentally unbalanced; erratic.

creak, v. harsh, squeaking sound, as a door. n.

cream, n. fatty part of milk; emulsified preparation; cosmetic. **-y,** a., **-i·er, -i·est.**

crease, n. ridge made by folding. v., **creased, creas·ing.** make a crease; wrinkle.

cre·ate, v., **-at·ed, -at·ing.** originate; cause; produce. **-a·tion,** n. **cre·a·tive,** a. **-a·tor,** n.

crea·ture, n. animal; person.

cre·den·tial, n. qualification; basis for confidence; pl. documents conferring acceptance.

cred·it, v., believe; ascribe. n. favorable bank account balance; positive ledger entry; financial reputation; esteem; academic unit, honor. **-it·a·ble,** a. **-i·tor,** n.

cre·do, n. pl., **-dos.** creed.

cred·u·lous, a. gullible.

creed, n. statement of belief.

creek, n. small natural stream.

creep, v., **crept, creep·ing.** move along the ground; go slowly. n. slang. annoying person. **-y,** a.

cre·mate, v., **-mat·ed, -mat·ing.** burn to ashes. **-ma·tion,** n.

crêpe, n. thin, crinkled fabric; thin pancake with filling.

cres·cent, n. first or last stage of moon; something shaped in a curve.

crest, n. head; top; emblem.

cre·vasse, n. deep fissure.

crev·ice, n. narrow crack.

crew, n. group associated with joint work.

crib, n. baby's bed; pen; stall.

crick·et, n. chirping insect; outdoor game.

crime, n. unlawful act; sin.

crim·i·nal, a. related to crime. n. unlawful person.

crimp, v. make wavy; inhibit.

crim·son, a., n. deep red color.

cringe, v., **cringed, cring·ing.** draw back when afraid; cower.

crin·kle, v., **-kled, -kling.** make wrinkly; rustle. **-kly,** a., **-i·er, -i·est.**

crip·ple, n. disabled or lame animal or person. v., **-pled, pling.** disable.

cri·sis, n. pl., **cri·ses.** turning point; troubled time.

crisp, a. easily broken; brisk, sharp; tidy. **-ness,** n.

cri·te·ri·on, n. pl., **-ri·a, -ri·ons.** standard rule by which to judge.

crit·ic, n. person who judges.

crit·i·cal, a. tending to find fault; decisive; important.

crit·i·cize, v., **-cized, -ciz·ing.** analyze; find fault. **-cism,** n.

croak, v. make froglike noise; grumble. sl. die. n. hoarse sound.

cro·chet, v., **-cheted, -chet·ing.** do needlework with a hook.

crock·er·y, n. earthenware.

croc·o·dile, n. reptile with massive jaws similar to an alligator.

crook, n. curve. inf. criminal; thief. **-ed,** a.

croon, v. sing softly.

crop, n. cultivated produce; harvest yield; whip; bird gullet. v., **cropped, -ping.** trim; appear unexpectedly.

cro·quet, n. lawn game played by driving wooden balls through hoops with mallets.

cro·quette, n. fried ball of minced meat or fish.

cross, n. figure formed by two intersecting lines; hybrid. a. ill-humored. v. to lie or pass across; intersect; contradict; obstruct; interbreed; betray. **-ly,** adv. **-ing,** n.

cross·ex·am·ine, v., **-ined, -in·ing.** examine by questions.

crotch, *n.* angle formed by parting of two legs, branches, or members.

crouch, *v.* bend or stoop down.

crou·ton, *n.* small piece of toast.

crow, *n.* glossy, black bird; rooster's cry. *v.* shrill; exult gloatingly.

crow·bar, *n.* wedge-shaped metal bar, used as a lever.

crowd, *n.* throng. *v.* press close; force; jostle.

crown, *n.* royal headdress; acme; head; exalting attribute; top. *v.* enthrone; adorn.

cru·cial, *a.* important; decisive.

cru·ci·ble, *n.* container capable of withstanding immense heat; severe test.

cru·ci·fix, *n.* representation of Christ on the cross; any cross.

cru·ci·fy, *v.*, **-fied, -fying.** put to death on a cross; torture. **-fix·ion,** *n.*

crude, *a.*, **crud·er, crud·est.** unaltered; immature; lacking culture.

cru·el, *a.* disposed to inflict pain; merciless. **-ty,** *n.*

cruise, *v.*, **cruised, crus·ing.** sail to and fro or from place to place. **cruis·er,** *n.*

crumb, *n.* small fragment.

crum·ble, *v.*, **-bled, -bling.** break into small pieces. **crum·bly,** *a.*, **-bli·er, -bli·est.**

crum·ple, *v.*, **-pled, -pling.** press out of shape; collapse. **-ply,** *a.*

crunch, *v.* chew with crushing noise. *n.* act or sound of grinding. **crunch·y,** *a.*, **-i·er, -i·est.**

cru·sade, *n.* zealous campaign to improve conditions or promote a cause. *v.*, **-sad·ed, -sad·ing. -sad·er,** *n.*

crush, *v.* squeeze by pressure; oppress; subdue. *n.* crowd; *inf.* infatuation. **-crush·ing,** *a.*

crust, *n.* hard exterior of bread or pie. *v.* form a hard surface layer. **crus·tal,** *a.*

crus·ta·cean, *n.* hard-shelled aquatic anthropods.

crust·y, *a.*, **-i·er, -i·est.** having crust; irascible. **crust·i·ness,** *n.*

crutch, *n.* forked support; prop.

cry, *v.*, **cried, cry·ing.** weep; lament; shout; beg. *n. pl.*, **cries. -ing,** *a.*

crypt, *n.* underground burial vault.

cryp·tic, *a.* secret meaning; occult and curt.

crys·tal, *n.* transparent quartz; glass with high degree of brilliance. *a.*

crys·tal·lize, *v.*, **-lized, -liz·ing.** form crystals; to give definite form. **-li·za·tion,** *n.*

cub, *n.* young carnivorous mammal, as bear, fox.

cube, *n.* solid with six equal squared sides; third power of a number. *v.*, **cubed, cub·ing. cu·bic,** *a.*

cuck·oo, *n. pl.*, **-oos.** European bird, noted for its call; fool.

cu·cum·ber, *n.* edible fruit of vine from gourd family.

cud·dle, *v.*, **-dled, -dling.** hug tenderly; snuggle; nestle. **-dle·some,** *a.* **-dly,** *a.*

cudg·el *n.* short heavy club. *v.*, **-eled, -eling.** beat.

cue, *n.* suggestive hint or signal; queue; rod for playing pool.

cuff, *n.* something encircling the wrist; trouser hem; slap. *v.*, strike with the hand or fist.

cui·sine, *n.* style of cooking.

cu·li·nar·y, *a.* of the kitchen.

cull, *v.* choose; reject as inferior.

cul·mi·nate, *v.*, **-nat·ed, -nat·ing.** bring to a head; climax; finish. **-na·tion,** *n.*

cul·prit, *n.* person accused of a crime; guilty one.

cult *n.* formal religious veneration; ritualistic sect. **-cul·tic,** *a.*

cul·ti·vate, *v.*, **-vat·ed, -vat·ing.** prepare land for crops; till; foster growth of; refine. **-va·tion,** *n.*

cul·ture, *n.* civilization characteristics; refinement; tillage, growth of bacteria. *v.*, **-tured, -tur·ing.** develop; grow in a medium. **-tur·al,** *a.*

cul·vert, *n.* drain; conduit.

cum·ber, *v.* hinder; hamper; overload. **-some,** *a.*

cu·mu·late, *v.*, **-lat·ed, -lat·ing.** heap; build up; amass. **-la·tion,** *n.*

cun·ning, *n.* craftiness; skill. *a.* scheming, plotting.

cup, *n.* drinking vessel with handle; eight ounces. *v.* **cupped, -ping.** *a.*

cup·cake, *n.* small cake.

cup·ful, *n. pl.*, **-fuls.** amount that a cup holds; eight ounces.

cu·pid·i·ty, *n.* avarice; greed.

cu·po·la, *n.* rounded roof or ceiling; small dome. **-laed,** *a.*

cur, *n.* mongrel dog.

cur·a·tor, *n.* person in charge of museum or library. **-to·ri·al,** *a.* **-ship,** *n.*

curb, *n.* restraint; raised edge along a street. *v.* check; restrain.

curd, *n.* (often pl·) thick part of coagulated milk.

cur·dle, *v.*, **-dled, -dling.** coagulate; go sour.

cure, *v.*, **cured, cur·ing.** free from disease; process for preservation. *n.* remedy.

cur·few, *n.* regulation to be inside at certain hour.

cu·ri·o, *n. pl.*, any rare or unusual article.

cu·ri·os·i·ty, *n. pl.*, **-ties**. desire to know; inquisitiveness. **-ous**, *a.*

curl, *v.* form ringlets, as the hair; coil. *n.* ringlet; coil. **-y**, *a.*

cur·rant, *n.* small acidic fruit grown on shrubs.

cur·ren·cy, *n. pl.*, **-cies**. medium of exchange; money.

cur·rent, *a.* most recent; prevailing. *n.* that which flows.

cur·ric·u·lum, *n. pl.*, **-lums, -la**. school courses of study.

cur·ry, *n. pl.*, **-ries**. spicy condiment. *v.*, **-ried, -ry·ing**. rub and clean a horse.

curse, *v.*, **cursed** or **curst** or **curs·ing**. swear profanely, express a wish of evil against; *n.* imprecation; torment.

cur·so·ry, *a.* superficially done.

curt, *a.* rudely abrupt; terse. **-ly**, *adv.* **-ness**, *n.*

cur·tail, *v.* diminish; reduce; shorten. **-ment**, *n.*

cur·tain, *n.* hanging fabric window or theater screen. *v.*

curve, *n.* continuously bending line with no angles. *v.*, **curved, curv·ing**. form or bend in a curve. *a.* **curved**.

cush·ion, *n.* baglike case; pillow; something to absorb shock. *v.* provide with a cushion.

cus·tard, *n.* baked, sweetened mixture of milk and eggs.

cus·to·di·an, *n.* caretaker.

cus·to·dy, *n. pl.*, **-dies**. guardianship; keeping; imprisonment.

cus·tom, *n.* usual or habitual practice; convention; duty or tax. *a.* made specially for. **-ar·y**, *a.*

cus·tom·er, *n.* one who buys.

cut, *v.*, **cut, -ting**. divide; sever; shorten; carve; gash; detach mow; intersect. *n.* cutting; wound; share reduction. *a.* diluted. **-ting**, *a., n.*

cute, *a.*, **cut·er, cut·est**. pretty; attractive. **-ness**, *n.*

cu·ti·cle, *n.* non-living skin around the nails; epidermis.

cut·ler·y, *n.* knives, scissors and other cutting instruments.

cut·let, *n.* small slice of meat for broiling or frying.

cut-rate, *a.* sold or selling at a reduced price or rate.

cy·a·nide, *n.* a poison.

cy·cle, *n.* period of time when events repeat themselves; bicycle, tricycle, etc. *v.*, **-cled, -cling**. pass in cycles; ride a cycle. **-clic**, *a.* **-cli·cal·ly**, *adv.* **-clist**, *n.*

cy·clone, *n.* violent storm with rotating wind; tornado.

cy·clo·tron, *n.* accelerator which propels charged particles at high speeds.

cyl·in·der, *n.* figure having curved sides and parallel round bases. **-dric, -dri·cal**, *a.*,

cym·bal, *n.* flat, brass musical instrument. **-ist**, *n.*

cyn·ic, *n.* a faultfinder; person who denies others' goodness and motives. **-i·cism**, *n.* **-i·cal**, *a.*

cy·press, *n.* evergreen with a hard durable wood.

cyst, *n.* abnormal sac in body tissue containing fluid. **cys·tic**, *a.*

czar, *n.* Russian emperor; autocratic ruler; despot.

cza·ri·na, *n.* wife of a czar.

D

dab, *v.*, **dabbed, -bing**. touch lightly. *n.* poke; pat. **-ber**, *n.*

dab·ble, *v.*, **-bled, -bling**. spatter; half-hearted attempt. **-bler**, *n.*

daft, *a.* foolish; mad.

dag·ger, *n.* short, sharp-pointed weapon for stabbing.

dai·ly, *a.* occurring each day. *adv.* every day.

dain·ty, *a.*, **-ti·er, -ti·est**. tasty; delicately; lovely. **dain·ti·ly**, *adv.* **-ti·ness**, *n.*

dair·y, *n. pl.*, **-ies**. place for production of milk and butter.

da·is, *n.* raised platform.

dale, *n.* valley; a vale.

dal·ly, *v.*, **-lied, -ly·ing**. waste time; play amorously. **-li·ance**, *n.*

dam, *n.* barrier preventing the flow of a liquid; *v.* **dammed, -ming**.

dam·age, *n.* loss or harm from injury to a person, property, etc. *v.* **-aged, -aging**. injure. **-age·a·ble**, *a.*

damn, *v.* condemn. **damned. dam·na·ble**, *a.* *adv.* **dam·na·tion**, *n.*

damp, *a.* moist; humid. **-en**, *v.*

dance, *v.*, **danced, danc·ing**. move rhythmically. **dan·cer**, *n.*

dan·druff, *n.* scales on the scalp.

dan·ger, *n.* exposure to harm, risk, evil, or loss. *a.* **-ous·ly**, *adv.* **-ous·ness**, *n.*

dan·gle, *v.*, **-gled, -gling**. hang loosely; swing. **-gler**, *n.*

dank, *a.* unpleasantly moist; humid. **-ly**, *adv.* **-ness**, *n.*

dap·per, *a.* neat and trim in appearance; alert and lively.

dap·ple *n.* spotted coloring. *v.*, **-pled, -pling. -pled**, *a.*

dare, *v.*, **dared, daring.** be bold; challenge; have the necessary courage. **dar·ing**, *n.* **dar·ing·ly**, *adv.*

dark, *a.* without light.

dark·en, *v.* make dark; dim; tarnish. **-ish**, *a.* **-ly**, *adv.* **-ness**, *n.*

dar·ling, *n.* a much loved person; favorite. **-ly**, *adv.* **-ness**, *n.*

darn, *v.* mend with stiches.

dart, *n.* small missile; sudden pain; stitched garment fold. *v.*, throw suddenly; move rapidly.

dash, *v.* strike violently. *n.* punctuation mark (-); small quantity.

dash·board, *n.* instrument panel.

das·tard, *n.* sneaky, malicious coward. **-li·ness**, *n.* **-ly**, *a.*

date, *n.* time an event occurs; appointment; social engagement; edible fruit of palm. *v.* **dat·ed, dating.** determine or mark date of; originate. **-dat·a·ble**, *a.*

daub, *v.* smear. **-er**, *n.*

daugh·ter, *n.* human female offspring. **-ter·ly**, *a.*

daugh·ter-in-law, *n. pl.*, **daugh·ters-in-law.** son's wife.

daunt·less, *a.* bold; fearless. *adv.* **-ness**, *n.*

daw·dle, *v.*, **-dled, -dling.** spend time idly; linger. **-dler**, *n.*

dawn, *v.* grow light; begin to appear. *n.* daybreak; start.

day, *n.* time between sunrise and sunset; period of 24 hours.

day·break, *n.* dawn.

day·dream, *n.* reverie; pleasant vision. **-er**, *n.*

daze, *v.*, **dazed, daz·ing.** stun or stupefy. *n.* state of being stunned. **daz·ed·ly**, *adv.*

daz·zle, *v.*, **-zled, -zling.** overpower with bright light; excite admiration. **-zler**, *n.* **-zling·ly**, *adv.*

dea·con, *n.* church official. **-ry**, *n.* **-ship**, *n.* *fem.* **dea·con·ess.**

dead, *a.* without life, lacking vitality; without motion, etc.; complete; exact; nonresiliant; without current; obsolete.

dead-end, *a.* closed at one end.

dead·ly, *a.*, **-lier, -liest.** causing or tending to cause death; fatal. **-li·ness**, *n.*

deaf, *a.* unable to hear. **-ly**, *adv.* **-ness**, *n.*

deaf-mute, *n.* a person unable to hear or speak.

deal, *n.* amount; an agreement; hand of cards; *v.* distribute; trade with; **dealt, -er**, *n.*

dean, *n.* college or church administrative head. **-ship**, *n.*

dear, *a.* beloved; precious; expensive. **-ly**, *adv.* **-ness**, *n.*

death, *n.* act or fact of ending life. **-less**, *a.* **-ly**, *a.*, *adv.*

de·ba·cle, *n.* rout; ludicrous collapse or failure.

de·bar, *v.*, **de·barred, -ring.** to prevent. **-ment**, *n.*

de·bate, *n. v.*, **-bat·ing.** a discussion; contend with words. **-bat·a·ble**, *a.* **-bat·er**, *n.*

de·bauch, *v.* lead morally astray; corrupt. **-er**, *n.* **-ment**, *n.* **-er·y**, *n. pl.*, **-ies.**

de·bil·i·tate, *v.*, **-tat·ed, -tat·ing.** make weak; weaken. **-ta·tion**, *n.*

de·bil·i·ty, *n. pl.*, **-ties.** weakness; infirmity.

deb·it, *n.* amount owed; debt. *v.*

deb·o·nair, deb·o·naire, *a.* friendly; genial; jaunty; sprightly.

de·bris, *n.* ruins; rubble.

debt, *n.* thing or amount owed.

debt·or, *n.* one who owes.

de·but, dé·but, *n.* first public appearance. **deb·u·tante**, *n.*

de·cade, *n.* period of ten years.

dec·a·dent, *a.* decaying; deteriorating. *n.* **-dent·ly**, *adv.*

de·cal, *n.* special picture or design made to be transferable.

de·cant·er, *n.* ornamental bottle for serving wine, water, etc.

de·cay, *v.* decompose; deteriorate.

de·cease, *v.* die; expire. **-ceased**, *a.*, *n.*

de·ceit, *n.* fraud; dishonest action; trick. **-ful**, *a.* **-ful·ly**, *adv.*

de·ceive, *v.*, **-ceived, -ceiv·ing.** mislead; trick; beguile.

De·cem·ber, *n.* twelfth month.

de·cen·cy, *n. pl.*, **-cies.** propriety. **-cent**, *a.* **-cent·ly**, *adv.*

de·cep·tion, *n.* fraud; trick. **-tive**, *a.* **-tive·ly**, *adv.*

de·cide, *v.*, **-cid·ed, -cid·ing.** arrive at a solution; settle. **-ci·sion**, *n.*

de·cid·ed, *a.* unquestionable; resolute. **-ed·ly**, *adv.*

dec·i·mal, *a.* pertaining to tenths.

de·ci·pher, *v.* decode; interpret.

de·ci·sive, *a.* **-ly**, *adv.* resolute; conclusive. **-ness**, *n.*

deck, v. array. n. ship platform or floor; tier; pack of playing cards.

de·clare, v., **-clared, -clar·ing.** make known; state explicitly. **dec·la·ra·tion,** n.

de·cline, v., **-clined, -clin·ing.** withhold consent; refuse; slope downward.

de·com·pose, v., **-posed, -pos·ing.** break down; rot. **-po·si·tion,** n.

dec·o·rate, v., **-rated, -rating.** adorn; honor. **-ra·tion,** n. **-ra·tive,** a. **-ra·tor,** n.

de·coy, n. thing or person used to lure into a snare.

de·crease, v., **-creased, -creas·ing.** get or make smaller or less. **-creas·ing·ly,** adv.

de·cree, n. official order. v., **-creed, -cree·ing.**

de·crep·it, a. weakened by infirmities or age; broken down.

de·cry, v., **-cried, -cry·ing.** belittle; speak out against.

de·duce, v., **-duced, -duc·ing.** infer; figure out by logic.

de·duct, v. subtract; take away. **-i·ble,** a. **-duc·tion,** n.

deed, n. an exploit; thing done.

deem, v. believe; think.

deep, a. extending far down; profound; abstruse. **-en,** v.

de·face, v., **-faced, -fac·ing.** to disfigure; mar.

de·fame, v., **-famed, -fam·ing.** slander; disgrace. **def·a·ma·tion,** n.

de·fault, n. failure to complete an obligation. v. **-fault·er,** n.

de·feat, v. beat; overcome. n.

de·fect, n. imperfection; fault. v. desert. **-fec·tion,** n. **-fec·tor,** n. **-fec·tive,** a.

de·fend, v. protect; hold off.

de·fend·ant, n. person charged in a legal suit.

de·fense, de·fence, n. protection; justification. **-fen·sive,** a. **-fen·sive·ly,** adv.

de·fer, v., **-ferred, -fer·ring.** delay; yield. **-fer·ment,** n.

def·er·ence, n. submission or yielding; regard; respect.

de·fi·ance, n. a challenge; resistance. **-fi·ant,** a. **-fi·ant·ly,** adv.

de·fi·cient, a. lacking. **-cien·cy,** n. pl., **-cies. -cient·ly,** adv.

def·i·cit, n. amount one is short.

de·file, v., **-filed, -fil·ing.** sully; besmirch.

de·fine, v., **-fined, -fin·ing.** demarcate; explain the meaning; characterize. **def·i·ni·tion,** n.

def·i·nite, a. unambiguous; clearly defined. **-ly,** adv.

de·fin·i·tive, a. ultimate; conclusive; final. **-ly,** adv.

de·flate, v., **-flat·ed, -flat·ing.** release gas or air from; reduce in size or importance. **-fla·tion,** n. **-fla·tion·ary,** a.

de·flect, v. bend or turn aside.

de·form, v. disfigure; change the shape of; make ugly. n. **-formed,** a. **-form·i·ty,** n. pl., **-ties.**

de·fraud, v. cheat; trick.

de·fray, v. pay; expend.

deft, a. skillful. **-ly,** adv. **-ness,** n.

de·funct, a. dead; extinct.

de·fy, v., **-fied, -fy·ing.** challenge; resist. **-fi·er,** n.

de·gen·er·ate, v., **-ated, -ating.** deteriorate; decline physically.

de·grade, v., **-grad·ed, -grad·ing.** reduce; to lower in rank. **deg·ra·da·tion,** n.

de·gree, n. step in a scale, order, etc.; extent; title.

de·hy·drate, v., **-drat·ed, -drat·ing.** remove water from; lose water. **-dra·tion,** n.

de·i·fy, v., **-fied, -fy·ing.** make a god of; glorify.

deign, v. condescend.

de·i·ty, n. pl., **-ties.** divinity; god.

de·ject·ed, a. depressed; sad. **-ject·ed·ly,** adv. **-jec·tion,** n.

de·lay, v. put off; postpone.

de·lec·ta·ble, a. very pleasing.

del·e·gate, v., **-gat·ed, -gat·ing.** entrust or assign to another. n. representative. **-ga·tion,** n.

de·lete, v., **-let·ed, -let·ing.** take out; remove. **-le·tion,** n.

de·lib·er·ate, v., **-at·ed, -at·ing.** ponder. a. carefully considered or done. **-ly,** adv.

del·i·ca·cy, n. pl., **-cies.** fine texture, etc.; luxurious treat.

del·i·ca·tes·sen, n. store selling ready-to-eat foods.

de·li·cious, a. extremely pleasing to the taste or smell.

de·light, v. to give joy. n. **-ed,** a. **-ed·ly,** adv. **-ful,** a. **-ful·ly,** adv. **ful·ness,** n.

de·lin·e·ate, v., **-at·ed, -at·ing.** trace the outline of; depict. **-a·tion,** n. **-a·tor,** n.

de·lin·quent, a. neglectful; guilty of an offense. n. **-quen·cy,** n. pl., **-cies.**

de·lir·i·um, n. pl., **-iums, -i·a.** mental disorder characterized by confusion and delusions. **-ous,** a. **-ous·ly,** adv.

de·liv·er, v. hand over; convey; rescue; aid in birth. **-a·ble,** a. **-er,** n. **-ance,** n. **-y,** n.

del·ta, n. alluvial deposit at the mouth of a river.

de·lude, *v.,* **-lud·ed, -lud·ing.** deceive; trick; mislead. **-lu·sive,** *a.* **-lu·sion,** *n.*

del·uge, *n.* great flood. *v.,* **-uged, -ug·ing.** overwhelm; inundate.

de·luxe, *a., adv.* of superior quality; elegant.

delve, *v.,* **delved, delv·ing.** search thoroughly; dig.

dem·a·gogue, dem·a·gog, *n.* one who gains power by appealing to emotion, prejudice, etc. **-gogu·er·y,** *n.* **-gog·ic,** *a.*

de·mand, *v.* ask for urgently or with authority.

de·mar·ca·tion, de·mar·ka·tion. *n.* separation; boundary.

de·mean, *v.* degrade; debase.

de·mean·or, *n.* behavior; conduct.

de·ment·ed, *a.* mentally deranged.

de·mer·it, *n.* fault; poor conduct mark.

demi·tasse, *n.* small cup of black coffee; the cup itself.

de·mise, *n.* termination; death; transfer.

de·moc·ra·cy, *n. pl.,* **-cies.** government by the people. **dem·o·crat,** *n.* **dem·o·crat·ic,** *a.* **dem·o·crat·i·cal·ly,** *adv.*

de·mol·ish, *v.* raze; smash; destroy; pull down. **dem·o·li·tion,** *n.*

de·mon, *n.* evil spirit. **-ic,** *a.*

dem·on·strate, *v.,* **-strat·ed, -strat·ing.** show by reasoning; explain with examples, charts, etc. **-stra·tion,** *n.* **-stra·tive,** *a.* **-stra·tor,** *n.*

de·mor·al·ize, *v.,* **-ized, -iz·ing.** deprive of spirit; discourage.

de·mote, *v.,* **-mot·ed, -mot·ing.** reduce in grade or rank. **-mo·tion,** *n.*

de·mur, *v.* **-murred, -mur·ring.** object; take exception.

den, *n.* animal lair; cavern; comfortable room.

den·im, *n.* heavy cotton fabric.

de·nom·i·na·tion, *n.* general name for a class of things; religious sect. **-al,** *a.*

de·nom·i·na·tor, *n.* the lower part of a fraction.

de·note, *v.,* **-not·ed, -not·ing.** signify; mean; indicate.

de·nounce, *v.,* **-nounced, -noun·cing.** accuse publicly; condemn. **-ment,** *n.* **-nun·ci·a·tion,** *n.*

dense, *a.,* **den·ser, den·sest.** compact; thick-headed; thick. **-ly,** *adv.* **den·si·ty,** *n. pl.,* **-ties.**

dent, *n.* a hollow or depression. *v.* make an impression in.

den·tal, *a.* of or for the teeth.

den·tist, *n.* a doctor specializing in care of the teeth.

den·ture, *n.* false teeth.

de·nude, *v.,* **-nud·ed, -nud·ing.** strip of covering.

de·nun·ci·ate, *v.,* **-at·ed, -at·ing.** to denounce, accuse publicly. **-a·to·ry,** *a.*

de·ny, *v.,* **-nied, -ny·ing.** declare untrue; refuse. **denial,** *n.*

de·o·dor·ant, *n.* preparation for destroying odors. *a.* **-ize,** *v.,* **-ized, -iz·ing.**

de·part, *v.* leave. **-par·ture,** *n.*

de·part·ment, *n.* functional division; a major section. **de·part·men·tal,** *a.*

de·pend, *v.* to rely on for support; to be contingent; to trust. **-ence, -ance,** *n.* **-en·cy, -an·cy,** *n. pl.,* **-cies. -ent, -ant,** *n.*

de·pict, *v.* to portray; picture in words; describe. **-pic·tion,** *n.*

de·plete, *v.,* **-plet·ed, -plet·ing.** use up; reduce. **-ple·tion,** *n.*

de·plore, *v.,* **-plored, -plor·ing.** be sorry about; regret deeply. **-plor·a·ble,** *a.* **-plor·a·bly,** *adv.*

de·port, *v.* expel from a country. **-por·ta·tion,** *n.*

de·port·ment, *n.* behavior.

de·pose, *v.,* **-posed, -pos·ing.** remove from high office; testify under oath.

de·pos·it, *v.* give as a pledge; entrust; put down. *n.* something laid down or placed for safekeeping. **-i·tor,** *n.*

de·pot, *n.* station; warehouse.

de·prave, *v.,* **-praved, -prav·ing.** prevent; corrupt. **-praved,** *a.* **-prav·i·ty,** *n.*

de·pre·ci·ate, *v.,* **-ated, -ating.** reduce in value; disparage. **-a·tion,** *n.* **-a·to·ry,** *a.*

de·press, *v.* lower; make gloomy. **-pres·sant,** *n.* **-pressed,** *a.*

de·pres·sion, *n.* dejection of emotional spirits; a hollow; decline in business.

de·prive, *v.,* **-prived, -priv·ing.** take something away from. **dep·ri·va·tion,** *n.*

depth, *n.* distance inward, downward, or backward; deepness; abstruseness.

dep·u·ty, *n. pl.,* **-ties.** person appointed to act for another.

de·range, *v.* **-ranged, -rang·ing.** upset the order of; **-ranged,** *a.* **-range·ment,** *n.*

der·e·lict, *a.* abandoned; negligent; delinquent. *n.* destitute person. **-lic·tion,** *n.*

de·ride, *v.,* **-rid·ed, -rid·ing.** ridicule; mock. **-ri·sion,** *n.* **-ri·sive,** *a.*

de·rive, *v.,* **-rived, -riv·ing.** receive; trace from a source; deduce. **-riv·a·ble,** *a.* **der·i·va·tion,** *n.* **-riv·a·tive,** *a.*

der·ma·tol·o·gy, *n.* a branch of science dealing with the skin.

de·rog·a·to·ry, *a.* degrading; disparaging. -**to·ri·ly**, *adv.*

der·rick, *n.* device for lifting heavy weights.

de·scend, *v.* go from a higher to a lower place. -**ent**, -**ant**, *a.*

de·scend·ant, *n.* offspring.

de·scribe, *v.*, -**scribed**, -**scrib·ing**. tell or write about. -**scrib·a·ble**, *a.* -**scrip·tion**, *n.* -**scrip·tive**, *a.* -**scrip·tive·ly**, *adv.*

des·e·crate, *v.* violate; profane.

de·seg·re·gate, *v.*, -**gated**, -**gat·ing**. eliminate racial segregation. -**ga·tion**, *n.*

de·sert, *v.* abandon; forsake; leave one's post.

des·ert, *n.* dry, barren sandy region; wild and uninhabited.

de·serve, *v.*, -**served**, -**serv·ing**. merit; to be worthy. -**serv·ing**, *a.*

de·sign, *v.* plan; create; devise; scheme. *n.* -**er**, *n.*

des·ig·nate, *v.*, -**nat·ed**, -**nat·ing**. appoint; indicate. -**na·tion**, *n.*

de·sire, *v.*, -**sired**, -**sir·ing**. crave; wish for; want. -**sir·a·ble**, *a.*

de·sist, *v.* cease; stop.

desk, *n.* writing table.

des·o·late, *v.*, -**lat·ed**, -**lat·ing**. devastate. *a.* lonely; deserted. -**la·tion**, *n.*

de·spair, *v.* loss of hope. -**ing**, *a.*

des·per·ate, *a.* frantic; reckless; dangerous. -**ate·ly**, *adv.* -**a·tion**, *n.*

des·pi·ca·ble, *a.* contemptible. -**bly**, *adv.*

de·spise, *v.*, -**spis·ing**. scorn; contempt; disdain.

de·spite, *prep.* notwithstanding.

de·spoil, *v.* rob; plunder.

de·spond, *v.* become disheartened. -**en·cy**, *n.* -**ent**, *a.*

des·pot, *n.* absolute ruler; autocrat. -**ic**, *a.* -**ism**, *n.*

des·sert, *n.* last course of a meal.

des·ti·na·tion, *n.* predetermined end of a journey.

des·tine, *v.* -**tined**, -**tin·ing**. intend for; predetermine.

des·ti·ny, *n. pl.*, -**nies**. predetermined course of events; one's lot or fortune; fate.

des·ti·tute, *a.* lacking possessions and resources; poverty. -**tu·tion**, *n.*

de·stroy, *v.* ruin; demolish.

de·struc·tion, *n.* act of destroying; demolition. -**struct·i·ble**, *a.*

de·tach, *v.* separate and remove; disengage. -**a·ble**, *a.* -**tached**, *a.*

de·tail, *v.* enumerate. *n.* small part of a design or structure. -**tailed**, *a.*

de·tain, *v.* keep from proceeding; delay; restrain.

de·tect, *v.* discover. -**a·ble**, *a.*

dé·tente, *n.* lessening of tension.

de·ter, *v.*, -**terred**, -**ter·ring**. discourage or restrain. -**rent**, *n.*

de·ter·gent, *n.* cleansing agent.

de·te·ri·o·rate, *v.*, -**rated**, -**rating**. make or become worse. -**ra·tion**, *n.*

de·ter·mine, *v.*, -**mined**, -**min·ing**. settle, establish; resolve; regulate; decide. -**mi·na·tion**, *n.*

de·ter·mined, *a.* resolute; firm.

de·test, *v.* hate; abhor. -**a·ble**, *a.*

de·tour, *n.* a roundabout way. *v.*

de·tract, *v.* take away; withdraw. -**trac·tion**, *n.* -**trac·tor**, *n.*

det·ri·ment, *n.* loss, injury or damage. -**men·tal**, *a.*

de·val·u·ate, *v.*, -**ated**, -**ating**. lessen the value of. -**a·tion**, *n.*

dev·as·tate, *v.*, -**tated**, -**tating**. waste; bring to ruin. -**ta·tion**, *n.* -**ta·ting**, *a.*

de·vel·op, *v.* make visible; make better, stronger, etc.; bring out possibilities; evolve. -**ment**, *n.*

de·vi·ate, *v.*, -**ated**, -**ating**. depart from norm; turn aside. -**ant**, -**a·tion**, *n.* eccentric person.

de·vice, *n.* invention for a specific purpose; a scheme; strategem.

dev·il, *n.* evil spirit; demon; reckless or mischievous person. -**ish**, *a.*

de·vi·ous, *a.* indirect; roundabout.

de·vise, *v.*, -**vised**, -**vis·ing**. to plan; invent; plot.

de·void, *a.* empty; lacking.

de·vote, *v.*, -**voted**, -**vot·ing**. give one's time or attention to; dedicate.

de·vot·ed, *a.* dedicated; ardent; loving. -**ly**, *adv.*

de·vo·tion, *n.* dedication; religious fervor; ardent love. -**al**, *a.*, *n.*

de·vour, *v.* eat ravenously; engulf.

de·vout, *a.* religious; earnest. -**ly**, *adv.* -**ness**, *n.*

dew, *n.* condensed moisture deposited on cool surfaces at night.

dex·ter·ous, *a.* competent with the hands; mentally adroit. -**i·ty**, *n.*

di·a·be·tes, *n.* disease marked by excessive sugar in the blood, or a heavy urine discharge. -**bet·ic**, *a.*, *n.*

di·a·bol·ic, *a.* fiendish. -**i·cal**. -**i·cal·ly**, *adv.*

di·ag·nose, *v.*, -**nosed**, -**nos·ing**. determine a condition by studying signs and symptoms.

-no·sis, *n. pl.*, **-ses. -nos·tic**, *a.* **-nos·ti·cian**, *n.*

di·ag·o·nal, *a.* extending from one corner to the opposite in a 4-sided figure. **-ly**, *adv.*

di·a·gram, *n.* a drawing; chart; outline. *v.* **-gramed, -graming** or **-grammed, -gram·ming.**

di·al, *n.* any face with graduations on which a pointer moves to indicate a measurement; a rotatable plate or knob. *v.*, **di·aled, di·al·ing.** measure or turn with a dial; telephone.

di·a·lect, *n.* local characteristics of speech. **-lec·tal**, *a.*

di·a·logue, *n.* discussion between two or more persons.

di·am·e·ter, *n.* straight line passing from one side to the other through the center of a circle; the length of such a line. **di·a·met·ric**, *a.* **di·a·met·ri·cal·ly**, *adv.*

dia·mond, *n.* crystallized carbon; precious gem; baseball playing field.

di·a·per, *n.* absorbent cloth drawn between infant's legs and fastened at waist; fabric with repetitious geometric design. *v.*

di·a·phragm, *n.* separating membrane or device; vibrating disk.

di·ar·rhe·a, *n.* abnormally frequent and fluid discharge of the bowels.

di·a·ry, *n. pl.*, **-ries.** daily record; journal. **di·a·rist**, *n.*

di·a·tribe, *n.* violent attack in speech or writing; ironical criticism.

dice, *n. pl.*, *sing.* **die.** small cubes. *v.*, **-diced, -dicing.** cut into small cubes.

dic·tate, *v.*, **-tat·ed, -tat·ing.** give orders; read aloud for transcription. *n.* authoritative rule.

dic·ta·tor, *n.* ruler with absolute power. **-tor·ship**, *n.* **-to·ri·al**, *a.*

dic·tion, *n.* enunciation; choice of words.

dic·tion·ar·y, *n. pl.*, **-ar·ies.** reference book listing alphabetically arranged words of a language and their meanings.

did, *v.* past tense of **do.**

die, *v.*, **died, dy·ing.** stop living. *n.* tool for molding, stamping, cutting, etc.

di·et, *n.* customary nourishment; prescribed food for a special purpose such as weight loss. *v.* eat according to a diet. **di·e·tar·y**, *a. n. pl.*, **-tar·ies. di·e·ti·cian**, *n.*

dif·fer, *v.* be unlike; disagree.

dif·fer·ence, *n.* unlikeness between two or more people or things; discord; dispute; subtraction remainder.

dif·fer·ent, *a.* unlike; other; separate. **-ly**, *adv.*

dif·fi·cult, *a.* hard to do, manage, understand, or please. **-cul·ty**, *n. pl.*, **-ties.**

dif·fuse, *v.* **-fused, -fusing.** pour out and spread; scatter. *a.* widely spread. **-ly**, *adv.* **-fu·sion**, *n.* **-fu·sive·ly**, *adv.*

dig, *v.*, **dug, dig·ging.** turn up soil with a spade, trowel, etc.; delve into. **-ger**, *n.* **-gings**, *n. pl.*

di·gest, *v.* convert food to absorbable form; assimilate mentally. *n.* information or book condensation. **-i·ble**, *a.* **-i·bil·i·ty**, *n.* **di·ges·tion**, *n.*

dig·it, *n.* finger; toe; any figure between 0 and 9.

dig·ni·fy, *v.*, **-fied, -fy·ing.** give distinction or honor to. **-fied**, *a.*

dig·ni·ty, *n. pl.*, **-ties.** noble manner; worthiness; esteem; self-respect.

di·gress, *v.* depart temporarily from the main purpose or subject. **-gres·sion**, *n.* **-gres·sive**, *a.* **-gres·sive·ly**, *adv.*

dike, *n.* dam made to control water; levee.

di·lap·i·dat·ed, *a.* ruined; decayed; run-down. **-da·tion**, *n.*

di·late, *v.*, **-lat·ed, -lat·ing.** make wider or larger. *adv.* **-la·tion**, *n.* **-dil·a·ta·tion**, *n.*

di·lem·ma, *n.* difficult choice.

dil·et·tante, *n.* an admirer of the arts; person with superficial interest in art or science.

dil·i·gence, *n.* constant and earnest effort. **-gent**, *a.* **-gent·ly**, *adv.*

dill, *n.* aromatic herb used to flavor pickles.

di·lute, *v.*, **-lut·ed, -lut·ing.** weaken by mixing with water or other liquid. *n.* **-lu·tion**, *n.*

dim, *a.*, **-mer, -mest.** not bright; obscure. *v.*, **dimmed, -ming. -ly**, *adv.* **-ness**, *n.*

di·men·sion, *n.* magnitude in length, breadth, thickness, or time; extent; size. **-less**, *a.*

di·min·ish, *v.* to make smaller in size; dwindle; taper. **-a·ble**, *a.*

di·min·u·tive, *a.* extremely small; tiny. **-ly**, *adv.* **-ness**, *n.*

dim·ple, *n.* small natural indentation in the human body.

din, *n.* loud noise.

dine, *v.*, **dined, din·ing.** eat dinner.

di·nette, *n.* alcove for eating; table and chairs set.

din·ghy, *n.* ship's small boat; rubber raft.

din·gy, *a.*, **-gi·er, -gi·est.** dirty-colored; not bright. **-gi·ness**, *n.*

din·ner, *n.* principal meal of the day.

di·no·saur, *n.* extinct reptile.

di·o·cese, *n.* district of a bishop's jurisdiction. **di·oc·e·san**, *a.*

dip, *v.,* **dipped, dip·ping.** immerse momentarily into a liquid.

diph·the·ri·a, *n.* contagious bacterial disease of the air passages.

diph·thong, *n.* complex vowel sound, gliding of one vowel sound into another.

di·plo·ma, *n.* document conferring power, privilege, honor, esp. a graduation certificate.

di·plo·ma·cy, *n. pl.,* **-cies.** art of conducting negotiation; tact. **dip·lo·mat,** *n.* **dip·lo·mat·ic,** *a.* **dip·lo·mat·i·cal·ly,** *adv.*

dire, *a.,* **dir·er, dir·est.** dreadful; dismal; awful. **-ly,** *adv.* **-ness,** *n.*

di·rect, *a.* straightest course; frank. *v.* guide; order; command. **-ness,** *n.* **-ly,** *adv.* **di·rec·tor,** *n.*

di·rec·tion, *n.* guidance; supervision; trend; course along which a thing moves. **-al,** *a.*

dirt, *n.* filthy substance; obscenity; dust; loose soil. **-y,** *a., v.*

dis·a·ble, *v.,* **-bled, -bling.** to make unable or crippled. **-bil·i·ty,** *n. pl.,* **-ties.**

dis·ad·van·tage, *n.* loss; handicap; unfavorable condition. *v.,* **-taged, -taging. -ta·geous,** *a.*

dis·a·gree, *v.,* **-greed, -greeing.** differ in opinion. **-ment,** *n.*

dis·a·gree·a·ble, *a.* offensive.

dis·ap·pear, *v.* pass from view; vanish. **-ance,** *n.*

dis·ap·point, *v.* fail to fulfill expectations or wishes. **-ment,** *n.*

dis·ap·prove, *v.,* **-proved, -proving.** not approve or withhold approval; censure. **-prov·al,** *n.* **-prov·ing·ly,** *adv.*

dis·arm, *v.* deprive of weapons; divest of hostility.

dis·ar·ray, *n.* confusion; disorder.

dis·as·ter, *n.* sudden great misfortune. **-trous,** *a.* **trous·ly,** *adv.*

dis·a·vow, *v.* deny knowledge or responsibility. **-al,** *n.*

dis·band, *v.* disperse; break up.

dis·bar, *v.,* **-barred, -bar·ring.** expel from the legal profession or from a specific court.

dis·burse, *v.,* **-bursed, -bursing.** pay out. **-ment,** *n.* **-burs·er,** *n.*

disc, *n., v.* see disk.

dis·card, *v.* get rid of; reject.

dis·cern, *v.* recognize differences; see clearly. **-i·ble,** *a.* **-i·bly,** *adv.* **-ing,** *a.* **-ment,** *n.*

dis·charge, *v.,* **-charged, charg·ing.** unload; release; relieve or free.

dis·ci·ple, *n.* follower; pupil.

dis·ci·pline, *n.* order; punishment; field of study. *v.,* **-plined, -plining.** punish. **-pli·nar·y,** *a.*

dis·claim, *v.* refuse to acknowledge; disavow. **-er,** *n.*

dis·close, *v.,* **-closed, -closing.** make known; reveal. **-clo·sure,** *n.*

dis·col·or, *v.* change or spoil the color; stain. **-a·tion,** *n.*

dis·com·fort, *n.* physical uneasiness.

dis·con·cert, *v.* throw into mental confusion. **-ing,** *a.* **-ed,** *a.*

dis·con·nect, *v.* break the connection of. **-nec·tion,** *n.* **-nect·ed,** *a.*

dis·con·so·late, *a.* hopelessly sad. **-ly,** *adv.*

dis·con·tent, *n.* uneasiness; dissatisfaction. **-ed,** *a.* **-ed·ly,** *adv.*

dis·con·tin·ue, *v.,* **-ued, -u·ing.** cease; give up; terminate. **-u·ance,** *n.* **-u·a·tion,** *n.* **u·ous,** *a.*

dis·cord, *n.* disagreement; noise.

dis·count, *n.* reduction in regular price.

dis·cour·age, *v.,* **-aged, -ag·ing.** dissuade; dishearten. **-ment,** *n.*

dis·cour·te·ous, *a.* ill-mannered; impolite; rude. **-ly,** *adv.*

dis·cov·er, *v.* expose; display; find. **-y,** *n. pl.,* **-ies.**

dis·cred·it, *v.* cast doubt on.

dis·creet, *a.* cautious; prudent. **-creet·ly,** *adv.* **-cre·tion,** *n.*

dis·crep·an·cy, *n. pl.,* **-cies.** inconsistency; lack of agreement.

dis·crim·i·nate, *v.,* **-nated, nat·ing.** differentiate; distinguish. **-na·tion,** *n.*

dis·cuss, *v.* consider and talk over. **-cus·sion,** *n.*

dis·dain, *v.* hold in contempt; scorn. *n.* **-ful,** *a.* **-ful·ly,** *adv.*

dis·ease, *n.* illness. **-eased,** *a.*

dis·en·chant, *v.* disillusion. **-ment,** *n.*

dis·fig·ure, *v.,* **-ured, -ur·ing.** mar the appearance; deface.

dis·grace, *n.* loss of reputation; dishonor. *v.,* **-graced, -grac·ing. dis·grace·ful,** *a.* **-ful·ly,** *adv.*

dis·guise, *v.,* **-guised, -guis·ing.** change in appearance to make unrecognizable. *n.* pretense.

dis·gust, *n.* loathing; repugnance. *v.* cause loathing. **-ed,** *a.* **-ing,** *a.*

dis·heart·en, *v.* discourage; cause to lose morale. **-en·ing,** *a.*

dis·hon·est, *a.* not honest; deceitful; untruthful. **-es·ty,** *n. pl.,* **-ties.**

dis·hon·or, *n.* shame; loss of respect; disgrace. *v.* **-a·ble,** *a.*

dis·il·lu·sion, *v.* free from illusion.

dis·in·fect, *v.* cleanse of or destroy disease germs. **-ant,** *n., a.*

dis·in·her·it, *v.* deprive of inheritance.

dis·in·te·grate, *v.,* **-grated, -grating.** reduce to fragments, particles, or parts. **-gra·tion,** *n.*

disk, disc, *n.* thin, round flat plate; phonograph record; plate for storing computer data.

dis·like, *n. v.* feeling of aversion.

dis·lo·cate, *v.,* **-cated, -cating.** put out of place; disrupt. **-ca·tion,** *n.*

dis·loy·al, *a.* faithless. **-ty,** *n.*

dis·mal, *a.* dreary; gloomy.

dis·man·tle, *v.,* **-tled, -tling.** take apart; pull down.

dis·may, *v.* fill with alarm.

dis·mem·ber, *v.* cut off or separate the members of.

dis·miss, *v.* send away; fire.

dis·o·bey, *v.* refuse to follow orders. **-be·di·ence,** *n.*

dis·or·der, *n.* confusion; irregularity; ailment. **-ly,** *a.* **-li·ness,** *n.*

dis·or·gan·ize, *v.* **-ized, -izing.** throw into confusion or disorder. **-i·za·tion,** *n.*

dis·ori·ent, *v.* cause to lose bearings; confuse. **-en·tate. -ta·tion,** *n.*

dis·own, *v.* refuse to acknowledge as one's own; renounce.

dis·par·age, *v.,* **-aged, ag·ing.** degrade; discredit. **-ag·ing·ly,** *adv.*

dis·par·i·ty, *n.* difference.

dis·patch, *v.* send out or off; kill. *n.* haste; a message.

dis·pel, *v.* **-pelled, -pelling.** scatter; disperse.

dis·pense, *v.,* **-pensed, -pensing.** deal out in portions; administer; exempt. **-pen·sa·tion,** *n.*

dis·perse, *v.,* **-persed, -pers·ing.** cause to break up; distribute; scatter.

dis·place, *v.,* **-placed, -placing.** remove from usual place; banish.

dis·play, *v.* put into view; exhibit.

dis·please, *v.,* **-pleased, -pleasing.** make unhappy. **-pleas·ure,** *n.*

dis·pose, *v.,* **-posed, -posing.** arrange; settle; throw away. **-pos·a·ble,** *a.* **-po·si·tion,** *n.*

dis·prove, *v.,* **-proved, -proving.** show to be false.

dis·pute, *v.,* **-puted, -puting.** quarrel; argue over. *n.* argument; quarrel.

dis·qual·i·fy, *v.,* **-fied, -fying.** make ineligible because of breaking rules. **-fi·ca·tion,** *n.*

dis·re·gard, *n.* lack of attention. *v.* pay no attention to.

dis·rep·u·ta·ble, *a.* disgraceful.

dis·re·spect, *n.* lack of respect. **-ful,** *a.*

dis·rupt, *v.* break apart; interrupt.

dis·sat·is·fy, *v.,* **-fied, -fy·ing.** fail to please. **-fac·tion,** *n.*

dis·sect, *v.* divide; cut apart.

dis·sent, *v.* differ in opinion. *n. a.* **-sen·sion,** *n.* **-sent·er,** *n.*

dis·ser·vice, *n.* ill service; injury.

dis·si·pate, *v.,* **-pated, -pating.** scatter; waste; vanish.

dis·solve, *v.,* **-solved, -solving.** to make a solution of; break up; dismiss; disappear gradually.

dis·so·nance, *n.* inharmonious harsh sounds; discord.

dis·suade, *v.,* **-suaded, -suad·ing.** persuade someone from doing something. **-sua·sion,** *n.*

dis·tance, *n.* space or length between two points; separation in time; remoteness.

dis·tant, *a.* far-off; away; cold.

dis·taste, *n.* dislike; aversion. **-ful,** *a.* **-ful·ly,** *adv.*

dis·till, *v.,* **-tilled, -till·ing.** condense; to vaporize and then fall in drops; drip; concentrate. **-er·y,** *n.*

dis·tinct, *a.* separate from others; unmistakable.

dis·tinc·tion, *n.* difference; honor.

dis·tin·guish, *v.* perceive the difference in; make famous; separate and classify. **-a·ble,** *a.*

dis·tin·guished, *a.* conspicuous; eminent; famous.

dis·tort, *v.* twist out of shape; misrepresent; pervert.

dis·tract, *v.* divert attention from. **-tract·ed,** *a.* **-trac·tion,** *n.*

dis·traught, *a.* troubled; agitated.

dis·tress, *n.* suffering; pain; sorrow; misery. *v.* **-ing,** *a.*

dis·trib·ute, *v.,* **-uted, -uting.** divide in shares; give out; apportion; scatter. **-tri·bu·tion,** *n.*

dis·trict, *n.* territorial division.

dis·trust, *n.* lack of confidence; suspicion. *v.*

dis·turb, *v.* destroy quiet; agitate; make uneasy. **-ance,** *n.*

dis·u·nite, *v.* **-nit·ed, -nit·ing.** divide; separate.

ditch, *n.* a trench; waterway.

di·ur·nal, *a.* pertaining to each day; daily.

di·van, *n.* sofa or couch.

dive, *v.,* **dived** or **dove, diving.** plunge head first into water; submerge; attack zestfully. **div·er,** *n.*

di·verge, *v.,* **-verged, -verg·ing.** branch off; differ; deviate. **-ver·gence,** *n.*

di·verse, *a.* unlike; different. **-ver·si·fy,** *v.,* **-fied, -fying. -ver·si·fied,** *a.*

di·vert, *v.* turn from one course or use to another; amuse. **-ver·sion,** *n.* **-ver·sion·ar·y,** *a.* **-ver·si·ty,** *n.*

di·vide, *v.,* **-vid·ed, -vid·ing.** separate into parts; classify; apportion. **-vis·i·ble,** *a.* **-vi·sion,** *n.* **-vi·sive,** *a.*

div·i·dend, *n.* number to be divided; a share of something; profit distribution. *n.*

di·vine, *a.* pertaining to God; *coll.* very pleasing, attractive. *v.,* **divined, divining.** infer; prophesy. **-vin·i·ty,** *n. pl.,* **-ties.**

di·vorce, *n.* legal dissolution of a marriage; any complete separation. *v.,* **-vorced, -vorc·ing.**

di·vulge, *v.,* **-vulged, -vulg·ing.** make public; disclose. **-vul·gence,** *n.*

diz·zy, *a.,* **-zi·er, -zi·est.** having whirling sensation in head; giddy; foolish. **-zi·ness,** *n.*

do, *v.,* **did, done, doing.** perform; accomplish; render; finish; tour; suit.

doc·ile, *a.* easy to teach; manage.

dock, *n.* loading or unloading platform; wharf; ship slip. *v.* guide into a slip; meet mechanically in space; cut short (a tail); deduct wages.

doc·tor, *n.* person licensed to practice medicine; a physician, dentist, or veterinarian; person holding highest university degree. *v.* repair; alter.

doc·trine, *n.* something that is taught; body of teachings; dogma. **doc·tri·nal,** *a.*

doc·u·ment, *n.* legal or official paper. *v.* support by documentary evidence.

doc·u·men·ta·ry, *a.* derived from documents, *n., pl.,* **-ries.** nonfiction films.

dodge, *v.,* **dodged, dodg·ing.** move back and forth or to and fro; avoid by evasion.

doe, *n. pl.,* **does, doe.** adult female of deer, goat, antelope, rabbit, and certain other animals.

doff, *v.* take off; remove.

dog, *n.* carnivorous domesticated mammal.

dog·ged, *a.* stubbornly determined. **-ly,** *adv.* **-ness,** *n.*

dog·ma, *n., pl.,* **-mas.** established opinion or belief; doctrine. **-mat·ic,** *a.* **-mat·i·cal·ly,** *adv.*

doi·ly, *n. pl.,* **-lies.** small lace or cloth decorative mat.

dole, *n.* that which is distributed; money, food, etc. given in charity; government grant for the needy. *v.,* **doled, dol·ing.**

doll, *n.* small-scale human figure used as a toy.

dol·lar, *n.* monetary unit of the U·S. equal to 100 cents.

dol·ly, *n. pl.,* **-lies.** low platform on wheels for transporting.

dol·or·ous, *a.* sorrowful; sad.

dolt, *n.* stupid person.

do·main, *n.* land owned or ruled; sphere of influence.

dome, *n.* large hemispherical roof. *v.,* **domed, dom·ing.**

do·mes·tic, *a.* relating to the home; tame. *n.* hired servant. **-ti·cal·ly,** *adv.*

do·mes·ti·cate, *v.,* **-cat·ed, -cat·ing.** accustom to the home; tame.

dom·i·cile, *n.* dwelling place; home.

dom·i·nate, *v.,* **-nat·ed, -nat·ing.** rule; control; have power over. **-nance,** *n.* **-nant,** *a.* **-na·tion,** *n.*

dom·i·neer, *v.* tyrannize; rule arbitrarily. **-ing,** *a.*

do·min·ion, *n.* power to rule; territory governed.

don, *v.,* **donned, don·ning.** put on clothing, etc.

do·nate, *v.,* **-nat·ed, -nat·ing.** contribute. **-na·tion,** *n.* **-nor,** *n.*

done, *a.* finished; completed.

doom, *n.* judgment; destiny. *v.* condemn; destine.

door, *n.* movable barrier by which passage is made into a room.

dope, *n.* narcotic preparation; stupid person; absorbent lubricant. *v.* **doped, dop·ing.** affect with drugs.

dor·mant, *a.* temporarily devoid of external activity; inactive; sleeping.

dor·mer, *n.* roof window; roofed structure with window.

dor·mi·to·ry, *n., pl.,* **-ties.** large sleeping room; residence hall.

dor·sal, *a.* of or near the back.

dose, *n.* amount of medicine, punishment, or radiation administered at one time. **dos·age,** *n.*

dos·sier, *n.* file of detailed papers.

dot, *n.* small speck or spot, *v.,* **-ted, -ting.** mark with dots.

dot·age, *n.* senility.

dou·ble, *a.* twofold; repeated; duplicate; a fold. *v.*, **-bled**, **-bling**. make twice as great; impersonate; fold.

doubt, *v.* be uncertain about. *n.* lack of confidence. **-ful**, *a.* **-less**, *adv.*, *a.*

dough, *n.* mixture of flour and other ingredients for baking, etc. *Inf.* money.

dough·nut, *n.* ring-shaped fried cake.

dour, *a.* sullen; harsh.

douse, *v.*, **doused**, **dous·ing**. plunge into water; drench.

dow·a·ger, *n.* widow holding property inherited from her deceased husband.

dow·dy, *a.*, **-di·er**, **-di·est**. shabby; unfashionable.

down, *adv.* from higher to lower. *prep.* in a descending direction on, over, or along. *a.* downward; depressed; dejected. *n.* soft fluffy feathers of birds.

down·cast, *a.* dejected.

down·fall, *n.* sudden fall, as from power.

down·grade, *v.*, **-grad·ed**, **-grad·ing**. reduce; minimize; depreciate. *n.* slope.

down·heart·ed, *a.* dejected; discouraged.

down·ward, *adv.* to a lower place. Also **down·wards**.

doze, *v.*, **dozed**, **doz·ing** sleep lightly or fitfully.

doz·en, *n. pl.*, **doz·ens**. group of twelve units or things.

drab, *a.*, **-ber**, **-best**. dull; cheerless. **-ly**, *adv.* **-ness**, *n.*

draft, *n.* act of pulling or drawing; a current of air; the selection of persons; team of animals; portion for drinking; written order for the payment of money; a sketch or drawing. **-y**, *a.*, **-i·er**, **-i·est**.

drag, *v.*, **dragged**, **drag·ging**. pull heavily along; pull by force; trawl; pass tediously.

drag·on, *n.* fabulous mythical monster.

drain, *v.* draw off gradually; empty; exhaust. *n.* burden; means by which anything is drained. **-age**, *n.*

dra·ma, *n.* a play; literary composition. **-mat·ic**, *a.* **-mat·i·cal·ly**, *adv.* **dram·a·tize**, *v.*, **-tized**, **-tiz·ing**. **dram·a·ti·za·tion**, *n.*

dra·mat·ics, *n. pl.* art of producing or performing plays; dramatic effect.

dram·a·tist, *n.* playwright.

drape, *v.*, **draped**, **drap·ing**. cover or hang in folds. *n.* loose hanging cloth. **dra·per·y**, *n. pl.*, **-per·ies**.

dras·tic, *a.* acting with force or violently; severe. **dras·ti·cal·ly**, *adv.*

draw, *v.*, **drew**, **drawn**, **draw·ing**. haul; attract; provoke; inhale; take money from a bank; take out a pistol, etc.; sketch. **-ing**, *n.*

draw·back, *n.* objectional feature.

draw·er, *n.* sliding storage compartment, as in a dresser.

drawl, *v.* speak slowly. *n.*

dread, *v.* anticipate with fear or uneasiness. *n.* apprehension; fear. **-ful**, *a.* **-ful·ly**, *adv.*

dream, *n.* series of mind images during sleep. *v.*, **dreamed** or **dreamt**, **dream·ing**. have a dream; fantasize. **-er**, *n.* **-y**, *a.*, **-i·er**, **-i·est**.

drear·y, *a.*, **-i·er**, **-i·est**. sad; dismal. **-i·ly**, *adv.*

dredge, *n.* contrivance for sucking up water-bed debris through a tube. *v.*, **dredged**, **dredg·ing**.

drench, *v.* soak; saturate.

dress, *v.*, **dressed** or **drest**, **dres·sing**. put clothes on; to trim. *n.* apparel.

dress·er, *n.* chest of drawers.

drib·ble, *v.*, **-bled**, **-bling**. trickle in drops; drool.

drift, *n.* a driving movement or force; deviation from a set course; something piled into masses by currents. *v.* be heaped up; move along aimlessly; accumulate in a mass.

drift·wood, *n.* wood drifted by the water; flotsam.

drill, *v.* bore with a drill; teach by repetition. *n.* tool for boring holes; instruction by repetition; military training.

drink, *v.*, **drank**, **drunk**, **drink·ing**. swallow liquid. *n.* beverage.

drip, *v.*, **dripped** or **dript**, **drip·ping**. to fall in drops. *n.* the falling of drops.

drive, *v.*, **drove**, **driv·en**, **driv·ing**. propel ahead; transport in a vehicle; move along. *n.* act of driving; any strong motivating force; organized effort; public road; animal collection.

driv·el, *v.*, **-eled**, **-el·ing**. to talk or act childishly or foolishly. *n.* saliva or mucous; silly talk.

driz·zle, *v.*, **-zled**, **-zling**. light rain; sprinkle.

droll, *a.* whimsical; comical. **-er·y**, *n. pl.*, **-er·ies**.

drom·e·dary, *n.* one-humped camel.

drone, *n.* male bee; a hum; pilotless airplane; one who lives off the labor of others. **droned**, **dron·ing**. talk in a monotonous tone.

droop, *v.* sink, bend, hang down. *a.*, **-i·er**, **-i·est**.

drop, *n.* a liquid globule; fall; small quantity. **dropped** or **dropt**, **drop·ping**.

drought, *n.* prolonged period of dryness; lacking rain.

drown, *v.* die or be killed by submersion in fluid.

drowse, *v.*, **drowsed, drows·ing.** be inactive; be sleepy. **drow·sy**, *a.*, **-si·er, -si·est. drow·si·ly**, *adv.* **drow·si·ness**, *n.*

drudg·er·y, *n. pl.*, **-er·ies.** distasteful, boring work; menial labor.

drug, *n.* any medicinal preparation; a narcotic. *v.*, **drugged, drug·ging.** administer drugs to; stupefy.

drum, *n.* percussion instrument; metal container. *v.*, **drummed, drum·ming.** beat or tap rhythmically on anything.

drum·stick, *n.* stick for beating a drum; poultry leg.

drunk, *a.*, intoxicated with or by liquor.

drunk·ard, *n.* an inebriate.

drunk·en, *a.* intoxicated. **-en·ly**, *adv.* **-en·ness**, *n.* **druth·ers**, *n. pl.* free choice; preference.

dry, *a.*, **dri·er, dri·est.** free from moisture; not moist; uninteresting; barren. *v.* **-ly**, *adv.* **-ness**, *n.*

du·al, *a.* consisting of two. **-i·ty**, *n.*

dub, *v.*, **dubbed, dub·bing.** beknight; dignify; nickname; add sound to film.

du·bi·ous, *a.* skeptical. **-ly**, *adv.*

duch·ess, *n.* wife or widow of a duke; woman ruling duchy.

duck, *v.* thrust under water quickly; avoid; dodge. *n.* swimming bird.

duct, *n.* bodily tube; pipe.

duc·tile, *a.* pliable; easily led.

dud, *n. pl.* clothes. *n.* failure. *a.* valueless.

dude, *n.* fastidious man; fop.

due, *a.* owed or payable as an obligation; lawful; attributable; fitting; adequate; expected. *n.*

du·el, *n.* two-person combat; any contest between two persons or parties. *v.*, **-eled, -el·ing. -el·ist**, *n.*

du·et, *n.* music composition for or by two performers.

duke, *n.* nobleman; ruler of a duchy.

dul·cet, *a.* luscious; sweet; melodious; soothing. **-ly**, *adv.*

dull, *a.* stupid; insensible; lacking sharpness; not bright; tedious. *v.* **dull·ness, dul·ness**, *n.*

du·ly, *adv.* properly; fitly.

dumb, *a.* devoid of speech. *Inf.* stupid.

dum·found, *v.* strike dumb with amazement. Also **dumb·found.**

dum·my, *n. pl.*, **-mies.** mute; stupid one; imitation model; exposed bridge hand.

dump, *v.* discard materials recklessly; unload in a heap. *n.* refuse area.

dump·ling, *n.* cooked mass of dough; baked fruit dessert.

dunce, *n.* dull-witted person.

dune, *n.* ridge of sand, piled up by wind.

dun·ga·ree, *n.* coarse, durable cotton; clothes made of this fabric.

dun·geon, *n.* dark underground prison or vault.

dupe, *n.* person easily tricked. *v.*, **duped,** **dup·ing.** deceive.

du·pli·cate, *v.*, **-cat·ed, -cat·ing.** copy exactly. *a.* double. **-ca·tion**, *n.* **-ca·tor**, *n.*

du·plic·i·ty, *n. pl.*, **-ties.** double-dealing; deception.

du·ra·ble, *a.* lasting; stable.

du·ra·tion, *n.* continuance in time; time a thing lasts.

du·ress, *n.* forcible restraint.

dur·ing, *prep.* throughout; in the course of.

dusk, *n.* dim stage at twilight. **-y**, *a.*, **-i·er, -i·est. -i·ly**, *adv.*

dust, *n.* fine dry powdery particles. *v.* free from dust; sprinkle particles on. **-y**, *a.*, **-i·er, -i·est.**

du·ty, *n. pl.*, **-ties.** obligation; respect; import tax. **-ti·ful**, *a.*

dwarf, *n.* smaller than normal size; stunted. *v.*, *a.*

dwell, *v.*, **dwelt** or **dwelled, -ing.** reside. **-ing**, *n.*

dwin·dle, *v.*, **-dled, -dling.** become steadily less.

dye, *n.* hue or color. *v.*, **dyed, dye·ing.** to color. **-ing**, *n.*

dy·nam·ic, *a.* active; forceful; any force. **-i·cal**, *a.*

dy·na·mite, *n.* a high explosive. *v.* shatter with dynamite.

dy·nas·ty, *n. pl.*, **-ties.** sequence of rulers of same family; period during which they rule.

dys·en·tery, *n.* diarrhea.

E

each, *a.* one of two or more; every. *pron.* each one. *adv.* apiece.

ea·ger, *a.* enthusiastic; keen in desire; impatient. **-ly**, *adv.* **-ness**, *n.*

ea·gle, *n.* large, strong bird of prey. **-glet**, *n.* young eagle.

ear, *n.* organ of hearing; ability to distinguish sounds; attention; spike of corn or other plant. **eared**, *a.*

ear·drum, *n.* tympanic membrane; middle ear.

earl, *n.* British nobleman, the third in rank. **-dom**, *n.*

ear·ly, *adv., a.,* **-li·er, -li·est.** near the beginning; before the usual time. **-li·ness**, *n.*

earn, *v.* gain in return for labor or service; get as one's desert or due. **-er**, *n.*

ear·nest, *a.* serious; grave; important. *n.* pledge. **-ly**, *adv.*

earn·ings, *n. pl.* money earned; wages; profit.

ear·ring, *n.* jewelry worn on the lobe of the ear.

ear·shot, *n.* range of hearing.

earth, *n. (often cap)* our planet; soil; dirt; ground.

earth·en·ware, *n.* pottery, dishes, etc., of baked clay.

earth·quake, *n.* vibration or movement of the earth's crust.

earth·y, *a.,* **-i·er, -i·est.** of earth; worldly; crude. **-i·ness**, *n.*

ease, *n.* comfort; facility. **eased, eas·ing.** alleviate; reduce; moderate; render less difficult; lessen tension, pain, etc.

ea·sel, *n.* supporting frame as for an artist's canvas.

eas·i·ly, *adv.* in an easy manner; without trouble. **-ness**, *n.*

east, *n.* direction of sunrise; areas lying east. *a., adv.* **-ern**, *a.*

east·ward, *a., adv.* toward the east. Also **east·wards**.

eas·y, *a.,* **-i·er, -i·est.** comfortable; free from worry or care; not difficult; lenient.

eas·y·go·ing, *a.* carefree; relaxed.

eat, *v.,* **ate, eat·en, eat·ing.** consume food; corrode; waste away. **-a·ble**, *a., n.*

eaves, *n. pl.* overhanging lower edge of a roof.

eaves·drop, *v.,* **-dropped, -drop·ping.** listen secretly. **-per**, *n.*

ebb, *n.* reflux of tidewater to the sea; decline. *v.* recede; weaken; decline.

eb·on·y, *n. pl.,* **-ies.** hard, heavy, black wood. *a.* black; dark.

ec·cen·tric, *a.* deviating from established pattern; odd; off center. *n.* **-i·ty**, *n. pl.,* **-ties.**

ec·cle·si·as·tic, *n.* of the church or clergy. *n.* clergyman. **-ti·cal**, *a.*

ech·o, *n. pl.,* **-oes.** repetition of sound. *v.,* **-oed, -o·ing.** imitate; repeat. **-o·er**, *n.*

eclat, *n.* brilliance; ostentatious display; acclaim.

eclec·tic, *a.* selecting from various systems, doctrines, or sources.

e·clipse, *n.* obscuring of the light of the sun or moon by intervention of the other. *v.,*

e·clipsed, e·clips·ing. outshine; obscure. **e·clip·tic**, *a.*

e·col·o·gy, *n.* study of organisms, their interrelationships, and their environment. **e·co·log·ic**, *a.* **e·col·o·gist**, *n.*

e·co·nom·i·cal, *a.* frugal; thrifty.

e·co·nom·ics, *n. pl.* science of the production, distribution, and consumption of wealth. **e·co·nom·ic**, *a.* **e·con·o·mist**, *n.*

e·con·o·mize, *v.,* **-mized, -miz·ing.** manage with thrift.

e·con·o·my, *n. pl.,* **-mies.** savings; production and distribution of a nation's goods and services.

ec·sta·sy, *n. pl.,* **-sies.** overpowering joy; rapture. **-stat·ic**, *a.*

ec·u·men·i·cal, *a.* universal; furthering Christian unity. **-ism**, *n.*

ec·ze·ma, *n.* skin inflammation marked by red, scaly lesions.

ed·dy, *n.* variable or contrary air or water current, esp. one whirling.

edge, *n.* cutting side of a blade; keenness; border; brink; advantage. *v.,* **edged, edg·ing.** advance slowly; put an edge on; move edgeways. **edged**, *a.*

edg·y, *a.* **-i·er, -i·est.** tense; irritable; nervous.

ed·i·ble, *a.* fit to be eaten. *n.*

e·dict, *n.* decree; proclamation.

ed·i·fice, *n.* large building.

ed·i·fy, *v.,* **-fied, -fy·ing.** instruct; spiritually enlighten. **-fi·ca·tion**, *n.*

ed·it, *v.* prepare for publication or presentation. **ed·i·tor**, *n.*

e·di·tion, *n.* form in which a text is published; specific special or daily publication.

ed·i·to·ri·al, *a.* of editors. *n.* article giving staff statement of opinion. **-ize**, *v.,* **-ized, -iz·ing.**

ed·u·cate, *v.,* **-cat·ed, -cat·ing.** provide schooling; develop mentally. **-ca·tion**, *n.*

eel, *n. pl.,* **eels, eel.** snakelike fish with slimy skin.

ee·rie, *a.,* **ee·ri·er, ee·ri·est.** scary; weird.

ef·face, *v.,* **-faced, -fac·ing.** wipe out; destroy; make inconspicuous. **-ment**, *n.*

ef·fect, *n.* result; outcome; influence; intent. *pl.* property. *v.* accomplish. **-fec·tive**, *a.* **-ly**.

ef·fem·i·nate, *a.* unmanly; having womanly characteristics.

ef·fer·vesce, *v.,* **-vesced, -vesc·ing.** to bubble; exhilarate. **-ves·cence**, *n.* **-ves·cent**, *a.*

ef·fi·ca·cious, *a.* effectual.

ef·fi·cient, *a.* productive without waste; competent. **-cien·cy**, *n. pl.,* **-cies.**

ef·fi·gy, n. pl., **-gies.** image, esp. a sculptured likeness; crude representation of.

ef·fort, n. exertion; attempt; endeavor. **-less,** a.

ef·fuse, v., **-fused, -fus·ing.** pour out; disseminate. **-fu·sion,** n. **-fu·sive,** a.

e·gal·i·tar·i·an·ism, n. a belief in human equality.

egg, n. female reproductive cell in a shell or membrane. v. incite, urge, or provoke.

e·go, n. pl., **e·gos.** the self of any person.

e·go·tism, n. self-conceit. **-tist,** n.

e·gre·gious, a. conspicuously bad; flagrant.

e·gress, n. act of going out; exit.

e·gret, n. heron; wading bird with white, flowing plumes.

ei·ther, a., pron. one or the other; each of the two. adv. too; also; likewise.

e·ject, v. drive out by force; expel. **e·jec·tion,** n. **e·jec·tor,** n.

e·lab·o·rate, v., **-rat·ed, -rat·ing.** develop with great detail. a. complicated; detailed. **-ra·tion,** n.

e·lapse, v., **-lapsed, -laps·ing.** (of time) slip by, or pass away.

e·las·tic, a. springy; flexible; adaptable. **-i·ty,** n.

e·late, v., **e·lat·ed, e·lat·ing.** fill with joy; make happy. **e·la·tion,** n.

el·bow, n. arm joint. v. jostle.

eld·er, a. of greater age; senior. n. one who is senior; church official.

el·der·ly, a. quite old.

eld·est, a. oldest; first-born.

e·lect, v. select by vote; choose. a. chosen. **e·lec·tion,** n. **e·lec·tive,** a., n. **e·lec·tor,** n.

e·lec·tor·ate, n. body of people entitled to vote.

e·lec·tric, a. of electricity; thrilling. Also **-tri·cal.**

e·lec·tri·cian, n. one who installs or works with electric devices.

e·lec·tric·i·ty, n. source of energy from particles of matter.

e·lec·tri·fy, v., **-fied, -fy·ing.** charge or equip with electricity; thrill or excite.

e·lec·tro·cute, v., **-cut·ed, -cut·ing.** kill by electric current. **-cu·tion,** n.

e·lec·trode, n. conductor used to transmit electrical current.

e·lec·tron·ics, n. pl. science of the behavior and movement of electrons. **-tron·ic,** a.

el·e·gant, a. tastefully fine; gracefully refined; superior in quality. **-gance, -gan·cy,** n.

el·e·gy, n. pl., **-gies.** mournful, melancholy poem. **-gize,** v.

el·e·ment, n. component part of a whole; natural habitat.

el·e·men·ta·ry, a. first principles; introductory; simple; rudiments; primary.

el·e·phant, n. large, thickset mammal with long trunk and ivory tusks. **-phan·tine,** a.

el·e·vate, v., **-vat·ed, -vat·ing.** raise; exalt; lift. **-va·tion,** n.

el·e·va·tor, n. cage and hoisting machinery for conveying things to different levels.

elf, n. pl., **elves.** small imaginary, mischievous fairy with magical powers. **-in,** a., n. **-ish,** a.

e·lic·it, v. draw or bring out.

el·i·gi·ble, a. qualified to be chosen; desirable. **-bil·i·ty,** n.

e·lim·i·nate, v., **-nat·ed, -nat·ing.** cast out; remove; omit; expel. **-na·tion,** n.

e·lite, n. **e·lit·ist,** n. finest group or part.

e·lix·ir, n. sweetened liquid containing medicinal agents.

elk, n. large deer.

el·lipse, n. oval; closed plane curve. **el·lip·ti·cal,** a.

el·o·cu·tion, n. art of effective public speaking. **-ist,** n.

e·lon·gate, v., **-gat·ed, -gat·ing.** lengthen; stretch out.

e·lope, v., **e·loped, e·lop·ing.** run away to be married; escape. **e·lope·ment,** n. **e·lop·er,** n.

el·o·quence, n. using language with fluency and force; persuasive discourse. **-quent,** a.

else, a. other than; in addition. adv. otherwise.

else·where, adv. in, at, or to some other place; somewhere else.

e·lu·ci·date, v., **-dat·ed, -dat·ing.** make clear or lucid; explain.

e·lude, v., **e·lud·ed, e·lud·ing.** escape by skill, alacrity, or trickery; baffle; evade. **e·lu·sive,** a.

e·ly·sian, a. blissful; delightful.

e·ma·ci·ate, v., **-at·ed, -at·ing.** lose flesh gradually; waste away physically. **-a·tion,** n.

em·a·nate, v., **-nat·ed, -nat·ing.** flow out; issue; originate.

e·man·ci·pate, v., **-pat·ed, -pat·ing.** release or free from bondage. **-pa·tion,** n.

em·balm, v. to treat (a dead body) in order to prevent rapid decay. **-er,** n.

em·bar·go, n. pl., **-goes.** stoppage of freight or commerce by government order.

em·bark, v. board a ship; start an enterprise.

em·bar·rass, v. to disconcert; make uncomfortable or self-conscious.

em·bas·sy, *n. pl.*, **-sies.** ambassador's official office or residence.

em·bel·ish, *v.* make beautiful.

em·ber, *n.* live coal; glowing piece of wood; smoldering ash.

em·bez·zle, *v.*, **-zled, -zling.** take entrusted property, such as money, dishonestly for one's own use. **-zler**, *n.*

em·blem, *n.* symbol; identifying badge or mark.

em·boss, *v.* to raise surface designs in relief.

em·brace, *v.*, **-braced, -brac·ing.** clasp in the arms; hug; accept; cherish; surround. *n.*

em·broi·der, *v.* decorate with needlework; embellish. **-der·y**, *n. pl.*, **-der·ies.**

em·bry·o, *n. pl.*, **-bry·os.** earliest stage of living being; undeveloped stage of anything.

em·er·ald, *n.* rich green gemstone. *a.* bright green color.

e·merge, *v.*, **-merged, -merg·ing.** come forth; rise into view. **e·mer·gence**, *n.*

e·mer·gen·cy, *n. pl.*, **-cies.** unforeseen circumstances calling for urgent action.

em·er·y, *n.* mineral used for grinding and polishing.

em·i·grate, *v.*, **-grat·ed, -grat·ing.** leave one country to settle in another. **-grant**, *n.* - **gra·tion**, *n.*

em·i·nent, *a.* conspicuous; lofty; prominent; noteworthy. **-nence**, *n.*

em·is·sar·y, *n. pl.*, **-sar·ies.** an agent sent on a mission.

e·mit, *v.*, **-ted, -ting.** to send forth or give out; utter; issue. **e·mis·sion**, *n.* **e·mit·ter**, *n.*

e·mo·tion, *n.* feelings of joy, hate, sorrow, fear, love, etc.

em·pa·thy, *n.* emotional or intellectual identification with another.

em·per·or, *n.* supreme monarch of an empire. **em·press**, *n. fem.*

em·pha·sis, *n. pl.*, **-ses.** force of expression; importance or significance; stress. **-phat·ic**, *a.*

em·phy·se·ma, *n.* disease char. by distention and weakness of lungs.

em·pire, *n.* supreme rule; government by emperor; extensive social or economic organization under the control of one person, family, or corporation.

em·ploy, *v.* use; devote; hire; keep occupied. **-ploy·ee**, **-ploy·e**, *n.* **-er**, *n.* **-ment**, *n.*

em·pow·er, *v.* to give power.

emp·ty, *a.* containing nothing; vacant; meaningless. *v.*, **-tied, -ty·ing.** to remove or discharge the contents. **-ti·ness**, *n.* **-ti·ly**, *adv.*

em·py·re·al, *a.* celestial; sublime.

em·u·late, *v.*, **-lat·ed, -lat·ing.** strive to equal or excel; imitate.

e·mul·sion, *n.* mixture of two liquids that do not dissolve in each other. **-sive**, *a.*

en·a·ble, *v.*, **-bled, -bling.** make possible; sanction.

en·act, *v.* make into a law; to ordain; act the part of.

e·nam·el, *n.* glassy substance; glossy paint or varnish; hard covering of a tooth. *v.*, **-eled, -el·ing.** *n.*

en·am·or, *v.* inflame with love; charm; captivate. **-ored·ness**, *n.*

en·case, *v.*, **-cased, -cas·ing.** enclose in a case.

en·chant, *v.* cast a spell over; charm. **-ing**, *a.* **-ment**, *n.* **-ress**, *n.*

en·cir·cle, *v.*, **-cled, -cling.** surround; make a circle around.

en·close, *v.*, **-closed, -clos·ing.** surround; close in. **-clo·sure**, *n.*

en·com·pass, *v.* enclose; envelop; include. **-ment**, *n.*

en·core, *n.* demand for additional performance, song, etc.

en·coun·ter, *v.* meet face to face; meet unexpectedly; engage in conflict. *n.*

en·cour·age, *v.*, **-aged, -ag·ing.** inspire with courage, hope, etc.; hearten. **-ag·ing**, *a.*

en·croach, *v.* trespass gradually; intrude. **-ment**, *n.*

en·cum·ber, *v.* hinder; burden.

en·cy·clo·pe·di·a, *n.* book or books containing information on all subjects. Also **en·cy·clo·pae·di·a**.

end, *n.* conclusion; death; result; remnant; extremity; purpose; bounds. *v.* terminate; conclude. **-ing**, *n.*

en·dan·ger, *v.* imperil.

en·dear, *v.* make beloved.

en·deav·or, *n.* attempt. *v.* make an effort; try.

en·dorse, *v.*, **-dorsed, -dors·ing.** sign one's name on the back (of a check); publicly express approval. **-ment**, *n.*

en·dow, *v.* furnish with an income; enrich.

en·dure, *v.*, **-dured, -dur·ing.** withstand hardship, suffering, etc.; tolerate; last. - **dur·ance**, *n.* **-dur·ing**, *a.*

en·e·my, *n. pl.*, **-mies.** foe; adversary; antagonistic one.

en·er·gy, *n. pl.*, **-gies.** capacity for being active; natural power. **-get·ic**, *a.*

en·er·vate, *v.* **-vat·ed, -vat·ing.** cause to lose vigor; weaken.

en·force, *v.*, **-forced, -forc·ing.** give force to; impose by force; compel. **-forc·er**, *n.*

en·gage, v., **-gaged, -gag·ing.** hire; betroth; attract; do battle with; bind to something; participate; mesh. **-gaged**, a. **-gage·ment**, n. **-gag·ing**, a.

en·gen·der, v. beget; originate.

en·gine, n. machine that uses energy to develop mechanical power; locomotive.

en·gi·neer, n. one who practices engineering.

en·gi·neer·ing, n. practical application of math, science, physics, etc.

Eng·lish, a. of England or the English language; n. English language or people.

en·grave, v., **-graved, -grav·ing.** etch designs or letters on a hard substance. **-grav·er**, n. **-grav·ing**, n.

en·gross, v. absorb; occupy wholly. **-ing**, a.

en·gulf, v. swallow up; overwhelm; submerge. **-ment**, n.

en·hance, v., **-hanced, -hanc·ing.** make greater; increase the value.

e·nig·ma, n. riddle; puzzling. **en·ig·mat·ic, en·ig·mat·i·cal**, a.

en·join, v. command; prohibit.

en·joy, v. receive pleasure from; have and use with satisfaction; have the benefit of. **-ment**, n.

en·large, v., **-larged, -larg·ing.** make bigger; expand. **en·larg·er**, n. **en·large·ment**, n.

en·light·en, v. give knowledge to; instruct; shed light on.

en·list, v. join the mlitary; obtain the help of. **-ment**, n.

en·liv·en, v. add spirit to.

en·mi·ty, n. pl., **-ties.** hostility.

en·no·ble, v., **-bled, -bling.** dignify; elevate.

en·nui, n. feeling of weariness; boredom.

e·nor·mi·ty, n. pl., **-ties.** something outrageous or heinous, as an offense.

e·nor·mous, a. immense; huge.

e·nough, a., n. adequate; sufficient. adv. sufficiently.

en·rage, v., **-raged, -rag·ing.** make furious; infuriate.

en·rich, v. make rich; supply riches; improve the quality of.

en·roll, v. register; enlist; record; roll or wrap up. **-ment**, n.

en·sconce, v., **-sconced, -sconc·ing.** to cover or shelter; to settle securely.

en·sem·ble, n. complete outfit; group of musicians, etc.

en·shrine, v., **-shrined, -shrin·ing.** place in a shrine; cherish.

en·sign, n. flag or banner; milit. lowest commissioned officer in the navy.

en·slave, v., **-slaved, -slav·ing.** make a slave of; subjugate.

en·sue, v., **-sued, -su·ing.** follow in order; follow as a consequence; result.

en·tail, v. limit an inheritance; bring on by necessity.

en·tan·gle, v., **-gled, -gling.** make tangled; complicate; to involve.

en·ter, v. come or go into; begin; join; set down in a record; register; pierce.

en·ter·prise, n. a project undertaken; business firm; initiative. **-pris·ing**, a.

en·ter·tain, v. treat hospitably; harbor; amuse; take into consideration. **-er**, n. **-ment**, n.

en·thrall, v., **-thralled, -thrall·ing.** charm; captivate.

en·thu·si·asm, n. absorbing, active or lively interest. **-ast**, n.

en·tice, v., **-ticed, -tic·ing.** tempt; lure; allure. **-ment**, n.

en·tire, a. whole; full; intact; complete. **-ly**, adv. **-ty**, n.

en·ti·tle, v., **-tled, -tling.** give a legal right; give a name or title to; designate. **-ment**, n.

en·ti·ty, n. pl., **-ties.** being; existence; thing that has definite existence in reality or the mind.

en·tou·rage, n. one's attendants or associates; retinue.

en·trance, n. act of entering; admission; doorway or passage. Also **en·trance·way.**

en·trance, v., **-tranced, -tranc·ing.** fill with delight; enrapture.

en·treat, v. ask earnestly; plead; beg. **-y**, n.

en·trée, en·tree n. main course of a meal; right of entry.

en·trench, v. dig a defensive trench around; establish in a strong position. **-ment**, n.

en·trust, v. trust to the care of; commit in trust.

en·try, n. pl., **-tries.** act of entering; vestibule; door; person or item entered in a contest.

e·nu·mer·ate, v. **-at·ed, -at·ing.** list or name one by one; count. **-a·tion**, n.

e·nun·ci·ate, v., **-at·ed, -at·ing.** pronounce; state definitely.

en·vel·op, v., **-oped, oping.** enclose completely.

en·ve·lope, n. wrapper; flat (letter) container.

en·vi·ron·ment, n. factors and conditions influencing an organism; surroundings.

en·voy, n. diplomatic agent.

en·vy, n. pl., **-vies.** desire for another's possessions, looks, popularity, etc., jealousness.*v.*, **-vied, -vy·ing,** to feel envy toward. **-vi·er,** *n.* **-vi·ous,** *a.*

en·zyme, *n.* organic catalyst in metabolism.

e·phem·er·al, *a.* transitory; short-lived.

ep·ic, *a.* heroic; majestic. *n.* narrative poem relating heroic events.

ep·i·cure, *n.* person who enjoys and has discriminating taste in wine and food.

ep·i·dem·ic, *a.* affecting many; contagious. *n.* outbreak which spreads rapidly.

ep·i·der·mis, *n.* outermost layer of the skin.

ep·i·lep·sy, *n.* nervous disorder characterized by convulsive seizures. **-tic,** *a.*, *n.*

ep·i·logue, ep·i·log, *n.* concluding section of a piece of literature.

ep·i·sode, *n.* an incident; one of the parts of a serial book or play.

e·pis·tle, *n.* a letter or communication.

ep·i·taph, *n.* commemorative inscription on a tomb or monument.

ep·i·tome, *n.* summary; ideal example; embodiment. **-mize,** *v.*

ep·och, *n.* particular or distinctive period of time. **-al,** *a.*

e·qua·ble, *a.* fair; even; uniform; steady. **-bil·i·ty,** *n.*

e·qual, *a.* alike in quantity, value, ability, etc.; like; uniform; identical; impartial; even. *n.* one who or that which is equal. *v.*, **e·qualed, e·qual·ling. -ly,** *adv.* **-ity,** *n. pl.,* **-ties.**

e·qual·ize, *v.*, **-ized, -iz·ing.** balance; make equal. **-iz·er,** *n.*

e·qua·nim·i·ty, *n.* composure.

e·quate, *v.*, **e·quat·ed, e·quat·ing.** to state, show, or represent as equivalent; make equal. **e·qua·tion,** *n.*

e·qua·tor, *n.* imaginary great circle dividing the earth into N. and S. hemispheres.

e·ques·tri·an, *a.* pertaining to horses or horsemanship. *n.* rider on horseback. **-enne,** *n. fem.*

e·qui·lib·ri·um, *n. pl.,* **-ums, -a.** equal balance between forces.

e·qui·nox, *n.* time when day and night are of equal length.

e·quip, *v.*, **-e·quipped, e·quip·ping.** provide with material for; to furnish. **-per,** *n.* **-ment,** *n.*

eq·ui·ta·ble, *a.* just; fair; reasonable. **-eq·ui·ty,** *n. pl.,* **-ties.**

e·quiv·a·lent, *a.* equal in force, amount, or value. *n.*

e·quiv·o·cal, *a.* having two meanings; suspicious; ambiguous. **-cate,** *v.*

e·ra, *n.* period of time or history marked by special events.

e·rad·i·cate, *v.*, **-cat·ed, -cat·ing.** do away with; exterminate. **-ca·tion,** *n.*

e·rase, *v.*, **-e·rased, e·ras·ing.** rub out; delete. **e·ras·er,** *n.*

e·rect, *v.* set in a vertical position; build; establish. *a.* upright. **e·rec·tive,** *a.* **e·rec·tion,** *n.*

e·rode, *v.*, **e·rod·ed, e·rod·ing.** to eat out or slowly wear away. **e·ro·sion,** *n.*

e·rot·ic, *a.* relating to sexual love or desire; increasing sexual desire. **-i·cism,** *n.*

err, *v.* make a mistake; sin; go astray. **-ing·ly,** *adv.*

er·rand, *n.* trip to convey a message or to do something.

er·rant, *a.* traveling; erring; straying. **-ly,** *adv.*

er·rat·ic, *a.* wandering; deviating; queer; inconsistent.

er·ro·ne·ous, *a.* wrong; mistaken.

er·ror, *n.* mistake; inaccuracy.

er·satz, *n.* a substitute or synthetic.

erst·while, *a.* previous; former.

er·u·dite, *a.* learned or scholarly. **-di·tion,** *n.*

e·rupt, *v.* burst forth; force out; release suddenly; explode. **e·rup·tion,** *n.*

es·ca·la·tor, *n.* moving staircase.

es·ca·pade, *n.* reckless or mischievous adventure; prank.

es·cape, *v.*, **-caped, -cap·ing.** get free or away; avoid capture; fade away; slip away. *n.* act of escaping; leakage; means of escaping; avoidance of reality.

es·chew, *v.* abstain; shun; avoid.

es·cort, *n.* woman's date; person or group accompanying others for protection. *v.* accompany.

es·crow, *n.* deed, bond, money, etc. held in custody until fulfillment of some condition.

e·soph·a·gus, *n. pl.,* **-gi.** muscular (food) tube between pharynx and stomach.

es·o·ter·ic, *a.* understood by or meant for only a select few; confidential.

es·pe·cial, *a.* special; distinctive; peculiar. **es·pe·cial·ly,** *adv.*

es·pi·o·nage, *n.* system or practice of spying.

es·pouse, *v.*, **-poused, -pous·ing.** marry; support a cause. **es·pous·al,** *n.*

es·prit, *n.* vivacious cleverness or wit.

es·py, *v.*, **-pied, -py·ing.** catch sight of; discover; spy.

es·say, *n.* short, literary piece, *v.* attempt; try.

es·sence, *n.* intrinsic nature of elements; extract; perfume.

es·sen·tial, *a.* important; basic; indispensable. *n.* basic; necessary.

es·tab·lish, v. institute; prove; found. **-ment,** n.

es·tate, n. landed property with a large house; property; possessions; condition.

es·teem, v. respect; consider; believe. n. high regard.

es·thet·ic, a. aesthetic.

es·ti·ma·ble, a. worthy of esteem; able to be estimated.

es·ti·mate, v., **-mat·ed, -mat·ing.** calculate approximately; judge. n. **-ma·tor,** n. - **ma·tion,** n., *approximate judgment of value, amount, etc.*

es·trange, v., **-tranged, -trang·ing.** turn away in feeling or affection; to remove or keep away.

es·tro·gen, n. hormone producing female characteristics.

es·tu·ar·y, n. pl., **-ies.** wide mouth of a river; sea inlet.

et cet·er·a, n. and so forth; and so on. *Abbr.* etc.

etch, v. engrave by the corrosive action of an acid on metal, etc.; to depict or impress distinctly. **-ing,** n.

e·ter·nal, a. without beginning or end; unchanging; everlasting. **-ly,** adv.

e·ter·ni·ty, n. pl., **-ties.** time without beginning or end; immortality.

e·ther, n. liquid used as anesthetic or solvent.

e·the·re·al, a. delicate; airy; light; heavenly.

eth·ics, n. pl. principles of moral conduct; the study of morals, the good, the right. **-i·cal,** a.

eth·nic, a. of races; of groups sharing common language or customs. Also **eth·ni·cal.**

et·i·quette, n. conventional code of social behavior.

é·tude, n. musical composition.

et·y·mol·o·gy, n. pl., **-gies.** history of the origin of words. **-gist,** n.

eu·lo·gize, v., **-gized, -giz·ing.** to praise highly; extol. **-gy,** n. pl., **-gies.**

eu·nuch, n. castrated man.

eu·phe·mism, n. agreeable expression substituted for an offensive one. **-mist,** n.

eu·pho·ny, n. agreeableness of sound. **eu·phon·ic,** a.

eu·pho·ri·a, n. feeling or state of well-being. **eu·phor·ic,** a.

eu·tha·na·sia, n. mercy killing.

e·vac·u·ate, v., **-at·ed, -at·ing.** leave; empty; vacate; withdraw from. **-a·tion,** n.

e·vade, v., **e·vad·ed, e·vad·ing.** avoid, escape from; elude.

e·val·u·ate, v., **-at·ed, -at·ing.** ascertain the value or amount of; appraise. **-a·tion,** n.

e·van·gel·i·cal, a. of the Gospel; of salvation by faith in Christ.

e·van·ge·list, n. Gospel writer; preacher of the Gospel; revivalist. **-lism,** n.

e·vap·o·rate, v., **-rat·ed, -rat·ing.** turn or change to vapor; vanish; disappear. **-ra·tion,** n.

e·va·sion, n. act of avoiding; subterfuge. **-sive,** a.

eve, n. evening; night before; period preceding an event.

e·ven, a. level; smooth; flat; uniform; balanced; exact; a number divisible by two. v. make even. **-ly,** adv.

eve·ning, n. time from late day to early night. a.

e·vent, n. anything (esp. important) that happens; occurrence. **-ful,** a.

e·ven·tu·al, a. occurring later.

e·ven·tu·al·i·ty, n. pl., **-ties.** contingent or possible event.

ev·er, adv. at any time; always; continually; in any way.

ev·er·y, a. each; all possible.

e·vict, v. expel from property legally. **e·vic·tion,** n.

ev·i·dence, n. proof; testimony. v., **-denced, -denc·ing.** prove; indicate.

ev·i·dent, a. plain or clear.

e·vil, a. morally wrong; wicked; depraved. adv. badly; ill. **-do·er,** n.

e·voke, v., **e·voked, e·vok·ing.** to call up; summon.

ev·o·lu·tion, n. process of change; development.

e·volve, v., **e·volved, e·volv·ing.** develop gradually.

ewe, n. adult female sheep.

ex·ac·er·bate, v., **-bat·ed, -bat·ing.** make more violent, bitter, or severe; aggravate.

ex·act, v. extort; demand. a. strictly accurate; factual. **-ing,** a.

ex·ag·ger·ate, v., **-at·ed, -at·ing.** enlarge; overstate. **-a·tion,** n.

ex·alt, v. elevate in rank, honor, etc.; dignify; praise; extol. **-al·ter,** n. **-al·ta·tion,** n.

ex·am·ine, v., **-ined, -in·ing.** inspect closely; investigate; question. **-i·na·tion,** n. **-in·er,** n.

ex·am·ple, n. sample; model.

ex·as·per·ate, v., **-at·ed, -at·ing.** irritate; annoy; anger. **-a·tion,** n.

ex·ca·vate, v., **-vat·ed, -vat·ing.** dig or hollow out; unearth. **-va·tion,** n.

ex·ceed, v. go beyond; surpass.

ex·ceed·ing, a. extraordinary; excessive. **-ly,** adv.

ex·cel, v., **-celled, -cel·ling.** surpass; outdo; be superior to.

ex·cel·lent, a. extremely good; exceptional; choice. **-lence,** n.

ex·cept, v. exclude; object. prep. other than. conj. unless. **ex·cep·tion,** n.

ex·cep·tion·al, a. rare; superior; not ordinary.

ex·cerpt, v. extract a passage from a book. n. an extract.

ex·cess, n. superfluity; amount by which one thing exceeds another. **ex·ces·sive,** a.

ex·change, v., **-changed, -chang·ing.** trade; transfer. n. act of exchanging; place of exchanging.

ex·cise, n. internal tax. v. remove by cutting out.

ex·cite, v., **-cit·ed, -cit·ing.** stir into action; stimulate. **-cit·a·ble,** a. **-cite·ment,** n. **-cit·ing,** a.

ex·claim, v. cry out; speak suddenly. **-cla·ma·tion,** n.

ex·clude, v., **-clud·ed, -clud·ing.** shut or keep out; expel. **-clu·sion,** n. **-clu·sive,** a.

ex·com·mu·ni·cate, v., **-cat·ed, -cat·ing.** expel from church membership. **-ca·tion,** n.

ex·co·ri·ate, v. denounce harshly.

ex·cre·ment, n. waste matter from the bowels; feces.

ex·cur·sion, n. short journey; trip; trip made at reduced fares.

ex·cuse, v., **-cused, -cus·ing.** remove blame from; justify; pardon; dispense with. n. reason; explanation.

ex·e·cute, v., **-cut·ed, -cut·ing.** legally put to death; perform or do; put into effect. **-cu·tion,** n.

ex·ec·u·tive, a. suited for managing or executing. n. person or body charged with administrative work. **-ly,** adv.

ex·ec·u·tor, n. law. person appointed to carry out a will.

ex·em·pla·ry, a. worthy of imitation; commendable.

ex·empt., v., release from; grant immunity to. a. not included; excused. **-emp·tion,** n.

ex·er·cise, n. bodily exertion; maneuver; performance; something done as practice or training. v., **-cised, -cis·ing.** put through exercises; use.

ex·ert, v. put forth; strive in action. **ex·er·tion,** n.

ex·hale, v., **-haled, -hal·ing.** breathe out; emit.

ex·haust, v. use up; completely drain of resources; wear out; discharge contents. **-haus·tion,** n. **-haus·tive,** a.

ex·hib·it, v. expose to view; place on display. n. thing exhibited. **-i·tor,** n. **ex·hi·bi·tion,** n.

ex·hil·a·rate, v., **-rat·ed, -rat·ing.** make cheerful; invigorate.

ex·hort, v. arouse; appeal strongly. **-hor·ta·tion,** n.

ex·hume, v., **-humed, hum·ing.** bring back from neglect or obscurity; disinter a dead body.

ex·i·gent, a. urgent; demanding.

ex·ile, n. banishment from one's country; person exiled. v., **-iled, -il·ing.** banish.

ex·ist, v. to have being; to have life. **-ence,** n.

ex·it, n. way out of. v. to leave.

ex·o·dus, n. mass departure.

ex·on·er·ate, v. **-at·ed, -at·ing.** relieve of responsibility; clear from blame.

ex·or·bi·tant, a. excessive.

ex·o·tic, a. of foreign origin; not native; strikingly different; unusual.

ex·pand, v. spread out or unfold; amplify; swell; increase; enlarge. **-pan·sion,** n. **-pan·sive,** a.

ex·panse, n. extensive stretch of anything.

ex·pect, v. look for; anticipate; regard as likely to occur; suppose. **-an·cy,** n. pl., **-cies.** **-ant,** a. **-ant·ly,** adv. **-ex·pec·ta·tion,** n.

ex·pe·di·en·cy, n. advantageous rather than what is necessarily right; politic; sense of self interest. **-ent,** a., n.

ex·pe·dite, v., **-dit·ed, -dit·ing.** carry out rapidly; speed up the progress of; dispatch. **-dit·er,** n.

ex·pe·di·tion, n. excursion or trip made for some specific purpose; persons engaged in it.

ex·pel, v., **-pelled, -pel·ling.** drive or force out; cut off from membership; oust.

ex·pend, v. to pay out; consume by use. **-i·ture,** n.

ex·pense, n. cost or charge; pl. charges incurred.

ex·pen·sive, a. costly; high-priced.

ex·pe·ri·ence, n. instance of personally undergoing something; knowledge or wisdom gained from what one has undergone. v., **-enced, -enc·ing.** have experience of; meet with; undergo.

ex·per·i·ment, n. test or trial. v. to try out; test. **-men·tal,** a.

ex·pert, *a.* experienced; skillful. *n.* knowledgeable person. **-ly**, *adv.*

ex·per·tise, *n.* specialized knowledge or skill in a field.

ex·pire, *v.*, **-pired**, **-pir·ing.** exhale; die; conclude.

ex·plain, *v.* make understandable; elucidate; give the meaning of or for. **-pla·na·tion**, *n.*

ex·ple·tive, *n.* word or phrase used as a filler; obscene or profane exclamation.

ex·plic·it, *a.* clearly, precisely expressed; definite. **-ly**, *adv.*

ex·plode, *v.*, **-ex·plod·ed**, **ex·plod·ing.** blow up; burst; discredit. **-plo·sion**, *n.*

ex·ploit, *n.* notable deed; heroic act. *v.* use for one's advantage. **-ploi·ta·tion**, *n.* **-ploit·er**, *n.*

ex·plore, *v.* search through; travel for purpose of discovery; investigate. **-plo·ra·tion**, **-plor·er**, *n.*

ex·po·nent, *n.* one who explains or expounds; one who or that which stands as a symbol.

ex·port, *v.* send for sale or use in foreign countries. *n.* item exported. *a.* of goods exported. **por·ta·tion**, *n.*

ex·pose, *v.*, **-posed**, **-pos·ing.** leave unprotected; uncover; reveal; display. **-po·sure**, *n.*

ex·po·si·tion, *n.* exhibition; laying open; detailed explanation.

ex·pound, *v.* explain in detail; defend with argument.

ex·press, *v.* put into words; state feelings; symbolize; send rapidly. *n.* vehicle, agency, or method of sending goods quickly. *adv.* **-er**, *-r*.

ex·pres·sion, *n.* act or manner of putting into words; utterance; showing of feelings, as by the face. **-sive**, *a.*

ex·pul·sion, *n.* act of forcing or driving out; expelling. **-sive**, *a.*

ex·qui·site, *a.* exceptional beauty, charm, or quality. **-ly**, *adv.*

ex·tant, *a.* in existence.

ex·tem·po·ra·ne·ous, *a.* without notes; on the spur of the moment; impromptu.

ex·tend, *v.* stretch out; proffer; prolong; lengthen. **ex·ten·sion**, *n.*

ex·ten·sive, *a.* broad in scope or area. **-ly**, *adv.*

ex·tent, *n.* space or degree to which a thing extends; scope; magnitude.

ex·te·ri·or, *a.* external; outside; outer. *n.* outer surface or part.

ex·ter·mi·nate, *v.*, **-nat·ed**, **-nat·ing.** destroy totally. **-na·tion**, *n.*

ex·ter·nal, *a.* on the outside, exterior.

ex·tinct, *a.* no longer existing. **-tinc·tion**, *n.*

ex·tin·guish, *v.* put out (a fire, etc.).

ex·tol, *v.*, **-tolled**, **-toll·ing.** praise highly; glorify.

ex·tort, *v.* obtain from a person by force or intimidation. **-tor·tion**, *n.*

ex·tra, *a.* more than what is usual or necessary; additional. *n.* something additional. *adv.* in excess of the usual.

ex·tract, *v.* pull out forcibly; withdraw; take out; to separate or obtain. *n.* something extracted; passage selected from a book. **-trac·tion**, *n.*

ex·tra·or·di·nar·y, *a.* beyond the usual; exceptional; remarkable.

ex·trav·a·gant, *a.* going beyond reason in spending money; wasteful. **-gance**, *n.*

ex·trav·a·gan·za, *n.* lavish or spectacular show; loose-structured musical or literary fantasy.

ex·treme, *a.* utmost in degree; going to great lengths; farthest from. *n.* highest degree; maximum; excessive length. **-ly**, *adv.*

ex·trem·i·ty, *n. pl.*, **-ties.** extreme or terminal point or part; body limb, as a hand.

ex·tri·cate, *v.*, **-cat·ed**, **-cat·ing.** disengage; disentangle; free.

ex·tro·vert, *n.* one who is outgoing; one concerned with what is external. **-ver·sion**, *n.*

ex·u·ber·ant, *a.* high-spirited; vigorous; growing profusely; effusive. **-ance**, *n.*

ex·ude, *v.*, **-ud·ed**, **-ud·ing.** ooze; discharge slowly.

ex·ult, *v.* rejoice exceedingly; be highly elated. **-ult·ant**, *a.*, **-ul·ta·tion**, *n.*

eye, *n.* organ of sight; *v.*, **eyed**, **ey·ing** or **eye·ing.** view; watch closely; look at.

eye·sight, *n.* power of seeing.

eye·sore, *n.* something unpleasant to look at.

eye·tooth, *n. pl.*, **-teeth.** upper canine tooth.

eye·wit·ness, *n.* one who observes an act and can report on it.

F

fa·ble, *n.* brief moral tale; a myth; fictitious narrative.

fab·ric, *n.* cloth; framework.

fab·ri·cate, *v.*, **-cat·ed**, **-cat·ing.** make; create; invent, esp. to deceive.

fab·u·lous, *a.* wonderful; fictitious.

fa·cade, *n.* face of a building; superficial appearance.

face, *n.* front of the head; appearance; presence; dignity. *v.*, **faced**, **fac·ing.** turn face toward; confront. **fa·cial**, *a.*

fac·et, *n.* small plane surface; definable aspects to a whole.

fa·ce·tious, *a.* humorous.

fac·ile, *a.* easily accomplished; moving or acting with ease.

fa·cil·i·tate, *v.v.,* **-tat·ed, -tat·ing.** make easier.

fa·cil·i·ty, *n. pl.,* **-ties.** ease; aptitude; skill; something built for a particular purpose.

fac·sim·i·le, *n.* exact copy.

fact, *n.* happening; actuality; truth; reality.

fac·tion, *n.* group within a main group; clique.

fac·ti·tious, *a.* not natural or genuine; artificial.

fac·tor, *n.* causal element; agent; ingredient.

fac·to·ry, *n. pl.,* **-ries.** building used for manufacturing.

fac·tu·al, *a.* actual; correct.

fac·ul·ty, *n.* innate ability; teaching staff.

fad, *n.* passing fashion; craze.

fade, *v.,* **fad·ed, fad·ing.** lose color or strength; disappear gradually.

Fahr·en·heit, *a.* of a thermometer on which the boiling point of water is 212°, the freezing point is 32°.

fail, *v.* default; weaken; not succeed; become bankrupt; abandon; miss; get low grade; disappoint. **-ure,** *n.*

faint, *v.* lose consciousness. *n. a.* cowardly; dizzy; barely perceptible. **-ness,** *n.*

fair, *a.* beautiful; clear and sunny; blond; impartial; moderately good size; mediocre. **-ly,** *adv. n.* exposition, carnival.

fair·y, *n. pl.,* **-ies.** tiny mythical being with human form and superhuman powers.

faith, *n.* loyalty; belief in God; trust; belief without proof.

faith·ful, *a.* loyal; steadfast; exact. **-ful·ly,** *adv.*

fake, *v.,* **faked, fak·ing.** pretend; counterfeit; specious. *n., a.*

fal·con, *n.* hawk trained to hunt.

fall, *v.,* **fell, fall·en, fall·ing.** drop down suddenly; descend freely; stumble; occur. *n.* a dropping; slope; autumn; decline; overthrow.

fal·la·cy, *n.* false idea; illogical reasoning. **-la·cious,** *a.*

fal·li·ble, *a.* liable to error.

fall·out, *n.* radioactive materials from an atomic explosion; descent of such particles.

fal·low, *a.* land plowed but unseeded; uncultivated.

false, *a.* not true or correct; treacherous; not genuine. **false, false·ly,** *adv.* **fal·si·fy,** *v.,* **-fied, -fy·ing, fal·si·ty,** *n.*

false·hood, *n.* a lie.

fal·ter, *v.* walk unsteadily; stumble; stammer; waver.

fame, *n.* widespread renown; public reputation.

fa·mil·iar, *a.* well-known; forward; informal; friendly; intimate. **-i·ar·i·ty,** *n.,* **-iar·ize,** *v.*

fam·i·ly, *n. pl.,* **-lies.** group with common ancestry; household; group of related things.

fam·ine, *n.* extreme scarcity of food; starvation.

fam·ish, *v.* make or be very hungry.

fa·mous, *a.* widely known.

fan, *n.* implement for producing air currents; admirer; avid supporter. *v.,* **fanned, fan·ning.** move air with a fan; stir up; spread out.

fa·na·tic, *n.* unreasonably enthusiastic. Also **-i·cal,** *a.,* **-i·cism,** *n.*

fan·ci·er, *n.* one having a special liking or interest.

fan·cy, *n. pl.,* **-cies.** imagination; a whim; a fondness; a notion. **fan·ci·ful,** *a.* Also *a.,* **-ci·er, -ci·est.** ornamental; extra fine. *v.,* **-cied, -cy·ing.** imagine; like.

fan·fare, *n.* flourish of trumpets; showy outward display.

fang, *n.* long sharp tooth.

fan·tas·tic, *a.* unreal; outstanding; eccentric; unbelievable.

fan·ta·sy, *n. pl.,* **-sies.** a creation of the imagination; whim.

far, *a., adv.* **far·ther** or **fur·ther, far·thest** or **fur·thest.** at or to a great distance; a long way off; to a great degree.

far·a·way, *a.* distant; dreamy.

farce, *n.* satirical comedy with absurd plot; absurd pretense. **far·ci·cal,** *a.*

fare, *v.,* **fared, far·ing.** to go or get on. *n.* price of transportation; food; paying customer.

fare·well, *interj.* good-bye. *n., a.* parting; leave taking.

far-fetched, *a.* improbable.

farm, *n.* land for raising crops or livestock. *v.* cultivate (land). **-er,** *n.,* **-ing,** *n.*

far-off, *a.* remote; distant.

far-sight·ed, *a.* seeing far objects best; planning wisely.

fas·ci·nate, *v.,* **-nat·ed, -nat·ing.** attract; enchant; captivate.

fas·cism, *n.* militaristic political regime advocating nationalism. **-cist,** *n.*

fash·ion, *n.* prevailing style or custom; manner or mode. *v.* form or make.

fash·ion·a·ble, *a.* stylish.

fast, *a.* rapid; fixed; tightly shut; lasting; staunch. *adv.* rapidly; deeply. *v.* abstain from food. *n.*

fas·ten, *v.* to secure; to attach.

fas·tid·i·ous, *a.* hard to please; very critical.

fat, *a.*, **-ter**, **-test**. plump; oily, greasy; rich. *n.* oily animal tissue; best part; excess matter.

fa·tal, *a.* causing death; mortal.

fa·tal·ism, *n.* acceptance of events as being inevitable. **-ist**, *n.*

fa·tal·i·ty, *n. pl.*, **-ties**. death from an accident; fate; deadliness.

fate, *n.* destiny; fortune; end; outcome; death; ruin. **-ful**, *a.*

fa·ther, *n.* male parent; a priest; provider; originator or founder. *v.* beget. **-hood**, *n.*

fa·ther-in-law, *n. pl.*, **fa·thers-in-law**. father of one's husband or wife.

fath·om, *n. pl.*, **-oms**, **om**. nautical depth of six feet. *v.* to comprehend; penetrate.

fa·tigue, *n.* weariness; menial work. *v.* to tire or weary.

fat·u·ous, *a.* inanely foolish; silly.

fau·cet, *n.* fixture with a valve to control flow of liquid from a pipe.

fault, *n.* defect; error; cause for blame; character weakness; fracture in earth's crust. *v.* err; fracture; find fault with. **-y**, **-i·er**, **-i·est**, *a.*, **-less**, *a.*

fau·na, *n. pl.*, **-nas**, **-nae**. the animals of a given region.

faux pas, *n.* social error in manners or conduct.

fa·vor, *n.* kind act; approval; token of good will; partiality. *v.* resemble. **-vor·a·ble**, *a.*, **-vored**, *a.*

fa·vor·ite, *n.*, *a.* best-liked; preferred (one). **-it·ism**, *n.*

fawn, *n.* young deer. *v.* grovel.

faze, *v.*, **fazed**, **faz·ing**. disturb.

fear, *n.* anxiety caused by expectation of evil, danger; awe; dread. *v.* to feel fear. **-ful**, *a.* afraid. **-less**, *a.* bold. **-some**, *a.* frightening.

fea·si·ble, *a.* possible; reasonable; likely. **-bil·i·ty**, *n.*

feast, *n.* large meal; banquet. *v.* have a feast; delight.

feat, *n.* act of courage, skill.

feath·er, *n.* plumage covering a bird's body. **-ered**, **-er·y**, *a.*

fea·ture, *n.* facial part; characteristic; detail; special attraction. *v.*, **-tured**, **-tur·ing**.

Feb·ru·ar·y, *n.* second month.

fe·ces, *n. pl.* excrement.

fe·cund, *a.* capable of producing.

fed·er·al, *a.* of a union of states under a central government.

fed·er·a·tion, *n.* act of forming a union. **-er·ate**, *v.*

fee, *n.* payment for services.

fee·ble, *a.* weak. **-bly**, *adv.*

feed, *v.*, **fed**, **feed·ing**. eat; give food to; satisfy; support; carry material forward for processing. *n.* meal; fodder.

feel, *v.*, **felt**, **feel·ing**. touch; perceive; search; be aware of; believe; appear. *n.* sense of touch; sensation.

feel·ing, *a.* sensitive. *n.* sense of touch; sensation; emotion; opinion; awareness; perception.

feign, *v.* pretend; imagine.

feint, *n.* a deceiving movement meant to distract.

fe·lic·i·tate, *v.*, **-tat·ed**, **-tat·ing**. congratulate. **-ta·tion**, *n.*

fe·lic·i·tous, *a.* appropriate.

fe·lic·i·ty, *n.* happiness; aptness.

fe·line, *n.*, a cat; *a.* sly.

fell, *v.* to knock or cut down.

fel·low, *n.* man or boy; peer; comrade; scholarship student. *a.* associate. **-ship**, *n.*

fel·on, *n.* criminal.

fel·o·ny, *n.* serious crime.

felt, *n.* cloth made of wool, fur, and other pressed fibers.

fe·male, *a.*, *n.* of the sex that produces offspring; girl or woman.

fem·i·nine, *a.* womanly; like a woman. **-nin·i·ty**, *n.*

fem·i·nism, *n.* theory of equality of the sexes.

fe·mur, *n.* thighbone.

fen, *n.* watery lowland.

fence, *n.* barrier of posts, wire, etc.; *inf.* person who receives stolen goods. *v.* enclose with a fence; fight with swords. **fenc·ing**, *n.*

fend, *v.* ward off; repel; manage alone.

fen·der, *n.* protective device.

fer·ment, *v.* agitate; excite; undergo chemical decomposition. **-men·ta·tion**, *n.*

fern, *n.* flowerless plant with spores and feathery leaves.

fe·ro·cious, *a.* fierce; cruel; savage. **-ci·ty**, *n.*

fer·ret, *n.* kind of polecat; persistent searcher. *v.* search out.

fer·ric, *a.* relating to iron.

fer·ry, *v.* carry across water by boat; transport. *n.* a ferryboat.

fer·tile, *a.* producing plentifully; able to produce; inventive. **-til·i·ty,** *n.*

fer·ti·lize, *v.* make productive.

fer·ti·liz·er, *n.* substance used to enrich soil; manure.

fer·vor, *n.* intense feeling; enthusiasm; zeal. **-vent, -vid,** *a.*

fes·ter, *v.* form pus; suppurate; decay; rankle.

fes·ti·val, *n.* celebration; cultural or festive event.

fes·tive, *a.* joyous; gay. **fes·tiv·i·ty,** *n. pl.,* **-ties.**

fetch, *v.* go and bring back.

fetch·ing, *a.* pleasing; charming; attractive.

fete, *n.* lavish party; celebration. *v.* honor with a fete.

fet·id, *a.* stinking; malodorous.

fet·ish, *n.* object thought magical; object of irrational devotion.

fet·ter, *n.* foot shackle; restraint. *v.* confine; restrain.

fe·tus, *n.* unborn vertebrate.

feud, *v., n.* prolonged quarrel.

feu·dal·ism, *n.* medieval European social system. **feu·dal,** *a.*

fe·ver, *n.* high body temperature; intense excitement. **-ish,** *a.*

few, *a.* consisting of a small number; not many. *n.*

fi·an·ce, *n.* man engaged to be married. **fi·an·cee,** *fem.*

fi·as·co, *n. pl.,* **-cos, coes.** ignominious failure.

fib, *n.* trivial falsehood. *v.,* **fibbed, fib·bing.**

fi·ber, fi·bre, *n.* threadlike piece; filament; cellulose (plant fiber that stimulates peristalsis); strong character. **-brous,** *a.*

fi·ber·glass, *n.* material made of fine, flexible glass filaments.

fick·le, *a.* inconstant.

fic·tion, *n.* anything made up; imaginative narrative literature. **-ti·tious,** *a.*

fid·dle, *v., n.* (to play) a violin. *v.* to fidget; spend time aimlessly. **-dler,** *n.*

fi·del·i·ty, *n.* faithfulness.

fidg·et, *v.* act nervously. **-et·y,** *a.*

fi·du·ci·ar·y, *a.* of a confidence; holding in trust.

field, *n.* open land; sphere of interest; expanse; all entrants in a contest. *v.* give impromptu answer; put into a field.

fiend, *n.* demon; addict. **-ish,** *a.* fanatic; cruel person.

fierce, *a.* savage; hostile; intense; pugnacious. **-ly,** *adv.*

fier·y, *a.* burning; flammable; hot; feverish; red.

fifth, *a., n.* following fourth; one of five equal parts.

fif·ty, *a.* five times ten. **-ti·eth,** *a.,* **-ties,** *n. pl.*

fig, *n.* edible oblong-shaped fruit.

fight, *n., v.,* **fought, fight·ing.** battle; struggle; contest. **-er,** *n.*

fig·ment, *n.* imagined thing.

fig·ur·a·tive, *a.* metaphorical, not literal; emblematic.

fig·ure, *n.* shape; person; likeness of a person or thing; emblem; numeral; diagram; personage. *v.* compute; portray; consider; be conspicuous.

fig·ure·head, *n.* leader with little or no real power.

fig·ur·ine, *n.* small statue.

fil·a·ment, *n.* fine thread; thin, flexible, threadlike part.

filch, *v.* steal furtively; pilfer.

file, *n.* ridged tool for cutting, smoothing; cabinet or folder for storage of papers or other materials; vertical row. *v.* reduce; rub smooth; arrange; move in a file; apply for.

fi·let, *n.* boneless slice of meat or fish. Also **fil·let.** *v.*

fil·i·bus·ter, *v., n.* delay legislation by obstructive tactics, esp. by long speeches.

fil·i·gree, *n.* lacy ornamental work of fine wire.

fill, *v.* make or become full; plug; occupy; satisfy; complete. *n.* anything that fills.

fill·ing, *n.* anything which is used to fill.

fil·ly, *n. pl.,* **-lies.** young female colt or horse.

film, *n.* thin layer; haze; thin sheet; flexible cellulose material used in photography; motion picture. *v.* to make a motion picture.

fil·ter, *n.* device for straining out impurities or collecting solids from liquids; device which selects or blocks the flow of energy, as light, electricity, sound, etc. *v.* to pass through a filter.

filth, *n.* foul matter; corruption. **-y,** *a.,* **-i·er, -i·est, -i·ness,** *n.*

fi·na·gle, *v.,* **-gled, -gling.** obtain by deception. **-gler,** *n.*

fi·nal, *a.* the end; last; conclusive. **-ist, -i·ty,** *n.* last exam. **-ly,** *adv.*

fi·na·le, *n.* last part of a musical work or any performance.

fi·nance, *n.* money management; *pl.* funds. *v.,* **-nanced, -nanc·ing.** to conduct or manage finances; provide money for. **fi·nan·cial,** *a.* **fin·an·cier,** *n.*

finch, *n.* small songbird.

find, *v.*, **found**, **find·ing**. come upon by chance; locate by search; discover; recover; judge. *n.*

fine, *a.* **fin·er**, **fin·est**. excellent; sharp; delicate; elegant. *n.* payment exacted as penalty. *v.* impose a fine.

fin·er·y, *n.* fine or showy dress.

fi·nesse, *n.* delicacy of execution; skillful handling of a situation.

fin·ger, *n.* a digit of the hand, usu. excluding thumb. *v.* touch or handle with the fingers; steal.

fin·ger·print, *n.* impression of the fingertip; markings for identification.

fin·ish, *v.* end; complete; use up; terminate; prepare the surface of. *n.* the conclusion; surface appearance.

fi·nite, *a.* having distinct limits.

fink, *n.* informer; strikebreaker.

fir, *n.* evergreen tree; the wood.

fire, *n.* heat and light of combustion; enthusiasm; discharge of firearms. *v.*, **fired**, **fir·ing**. add fuel to; to discharge (a gun), (from a job). **on fire**, burning; ardent.

fire·arm, *n.* gun that fires a projectile.

fire·crack·er, *n.* paper cylinder containing explosive.

fire·man, *n.* one who fights or tends fires; fire fighter.

fire·works, *n. pl.* devices for displays of brilliant lighting effects or loud nosies.

firm, *n.* business company. *a.* vigorous; definite; hard; solid; stiff; fixed; steady. *v.* make or become firm. **-ly**, *adv.*, **-ness**, *n.*

fir·ma·ment, *n.* sky; heavens.

first, *a.* before any others; earliest. *n.* ordinal of one; something that is first. *adv.* sooner.

first aid, *n.* emergency care for injuries, illness.

first-hand, *a.*, *adv.* from the original source.

fis·cal, *a.* pertaining to finances.

fish, *n. pl.*, **fish**, **fish·es**. cold-blooded, aquatic animal (usu·) with scales, fins, and gills. *v.* catch fish; seek to obtain information indirectly. **-er·man**, **-er·y**, *n.*

fish·y, *a.* of fish; suspicious.

fis·sion, *n.* splitting into parts.

fis·sure, *n.* narrow opening.

fist, *n.* hand clenched tightly.

fist·i·cuff, *n. pl.* combat with the fists; a cuff with the fist.

fit, *n.* convulsion; outburst. *a.*, **-ter**, **-test**. suitable; competent; proper. *v.*, **fit·ted** or **fit**, **fit·ting**. be suitable; to put into place; to outfit; prepare; accommodate; adjust.

fit·ful, *a.* irregular; convulsive.

fit·ting, *n.* clothes try-on; *pl.* furnishings, fixtures. *a.* appropriate.

fix, *v.* make fast, firm, or stable; determine; repair; prepare; attach; establish; cure; spay. *inf.* influence by bribery. *n.* a predicament; calculated position. **fixed**, *a.*

fix·a·tion, *n.* morbid preoccupation; arrested development.

fix·a·tive, *n.* something that sets or stabilizes.

fix·ture, *n.* permanently attached part.

fiz·zle, *v.*, **-zled**, **-zling**. hiss; sputter; fail. *n.* fiasco; failure.

fjord, *n.* narrow inlet of the sea.

flab·by, *a.*, **-bi·er**, **-bi·est**. limp; feeble; flaccid.

flac·cid, *a.* flabby; lacking vigor.

flag, *n.* cloth used as a symbol or signal. *v.*, **flagged**, **flag·ging**. signal.

flag·on, *n.* container for liquids.

fla·grant, *a.* notorious; glaring.

flair, *n.* natural skill; talent.

flak, *n.* antiaircraft fire; dissension.

flake, *n.* a scale; a small, flat loose bit; chip. *v.*, **flaked**, **flak·ing**. form into flakes. **flak·y**, *a.*

flam·boy·ant, *a.* showy; ornate.

flame, *v.*, *n.* (send out) tongues of fire; blaze; glow. **flam·ing**, *a.*

flam·ma·ble, *a.* easily ignited.

flank, *n.* side. *v.* be at or pass around the side of; border.

flap, *v.*, **flapped**, **flap·ping**. swing or sway loosely, esp. with noise. *n.* broad piece; uproar.

flare, *v.*, **flared**, **flar·ing**. blaze up; burst out; spread outward. *n.* blaze of fire or light used to signal; a sudden burst.

flash, *n.* sudden brief outburst of flame, light; an instant. *v.* burst suddenly into light, etc. **flash·y**, *a.*, **-i·er**, **-i·est**. sparkling; gaudy; showy.

flash·back, *n.* representation in a novel or motion picture of some event occurring at a previous time.

flash·light, *n.* hand-held battery operated electric torch.

flask, *n.* bottle, usu. for liquor.

flat, *a.* level; broad and thin; dull; tasteless; prostrate; fixed; deflated. *mus.* below pitch. *adv.* in a flat position; positively. Also **flat·ly**. *n.* flat part; deflated tire; apartment; *mus.* note ¹/₂ step below another.

flat·ten, *v.* make or become flat.

flat·ter, *v.* compliment or praise insincerely; display to advantage. **-ter·y**, *n.*

flaunt, *v.* display ostentatiously.

fla·vor, *n.* taste. *v.* give flavor to.

fla·vor·ing, *n.* something that gives or adds to the flavor.

flaw, *n.* imperfection; hidden defect; blemish. *v.* produce a flaw in.

flax, *n.* plant grown for seeds and fiber (for linen).

flay, *v.* to skin; excoriate verbally.

flea, *n.* small, wingless, leaping, blood-sucking insect.

fleck, *n.* a spot; flake; particle.

fledg·ling, *n.* young, newly-feathered bird; inexperienced person.

flee, *v.,* **fled, flee·ing.** run away, as from danger.

fleece, *n.* sheep's wool. *v.* to shear; swindle. **fleec·y,** *a.* fluffy.

fleet, *a.* nimble; swift. *n.* group of ships, vehicles, airplanes, etc.

fleet·ing, *a.* passing swiftly.

flesh, *n.* soft body tissue; skin; mankind; fruit or vegetable pulp.

flex, *v.* bend; contract.

flex·i·ble, *a.* easily bent; adaptable; willing to yield.

flick·er, *v.* burn or shine unsteadily. *n.* flutter.

fli·er, *n.* aviator.

flight, *n.* act, manner, or power of flying; swift movement; to flee; series of stairs.

flim·sy, *a.,* **-si·er, -si·est.** limp; of inferior materials; of small worth.

flinch, *v.* shrink from pain, danger; wince.

fling, *v.,* **flung, fling·ing.** throw with force; discard; move hastily. *n.* brief, wild time.

flint, *n.* spark-producing quartz.

flip, *v.,* **flipped, flip·ping.** toss with a sudden movement; turn over; throw; flick; leaf.

flip·pant, *a.* disrespectful; pert.

flirt, *v.* to trifle in love; to toy with an idea. **flir·ta·tion,** *n.*

flit, *v.,* **-ted, -ting.** move swiftly and lightly; dart.

float, *v.* rest or move gently on the surface of liquid or in air; move or drift freely. *n.* something that floats; decorated parade vehicle.

flock, *n.* group of birds or animals of one kind; crowd of people; church congregation.

floe, *n.* mass of floating ice.

flog, *v.,* **flogged, flog·ging.** beat hard with a whip or stick.

flood, *n.* rising and overflowing of water, esp. over land; superabundance. *v.*

floor, *n.* bottom surface of a room; story of a building; the right to speak. *v.* knock down.

flop, *v.,* **flopped, -ping.** fall or plump down suddenly, heavily, or clumsily; to fail. **-py,** *a.*

flo·ra, *n. pl.,* **-ras, rae.** plants of a particular region or period.

flo·ral, *a.* of flowers.

flor·id, *a.* very showy; ruddy.

flo·rist, *n.* one who grows or sells flowers or plants.

flo·til·la, *n.* small fleet of ships.

flot·sam, *n.* floating cargo or wreckage from a ship.

flounce, *v.,* **flounced, flounc·ing.** move with exaggerated jerky motions. *n.* a ruffle.

floun·der, *v.* struggle for footing. *n.* marine food fish.

flour, *n.* finely ground meal of grain; fine soft powder.

flour·ish, *v.* thrive; brandish; succeed. *n.* ostentatious display.

flout, *v.* mock; scorn; scoff.

flow, *v.* move in a stream; circulate. *n.*

flow·er, *n.* a blossom; plant in bloom; best part. *v.* to blossom.

flu, *n. inf.* influenza.

flub, *v.,* **flubbed, -bing.** *inf.* to botch or blunder.

fluc·tu·ate, *v.,* **-at·ed, -at·ing.** ebb and flow in waves; swing.

flue, *n.* duct or passage.

flu·ent, *a.* able to speak and write easily. **-en·cy,** *n.*

fluff, *n.* light, downy particles. *v.* make or become fluffy. **-y,** *a.*

flu·id, *a.* capable of flowing; tending to change; of a smooth, easy style. *n.* substance that flows.

fluke, *n.* accidental luck.

flunk, *v. inf.* fail a course, exam, or grade.

flu·o·res·cent, *a.* tubular electric bulb with cool light.

fluor·i·da·tion, *n.* addition of fluoride to drinking water.

fluor·o·scope, *n.* type of X-ray machine.

flur·ry, *n. pl.,* **-ries.** gust of wind; light snowfall; sudden commotion.

flush, *v.* wash out; to redden; fly out suddenly. *n.* blush; surge. *a.* even; level; sated; affluent; red; lusty.

flus·ter, *v.* discompose; upset.

flute, *n.* woodwind instrument with finger holes or keys.

flut·ter, *v.* wave or flap rapidly; to beat fast and irregularly. *n.* quick, irregular motions.

flux, *n.* constant change; flow. *v.* become fluid; fuse.

fly, *n. pl.,* **flies.** winged insect; flap covering a fastener, etc. *v.,* **flew, flown, fly·ing.** move through the air on wings; soar; move or pass quickly; vanish; flee; transport by aircraft.

fly·wheel, *n.* wheel that equalizes speed of a machine.

foal, *n.* young horse.

foam, *n.* frothy mass of bubbles formed on liquids. **-y,** *a.*

fo·cus, *n. pl.,* **-cus·es, fo·ci.** point at which rays of light meet; lens adjustment to get a clear image; center of attraction or activity. *v.,* **-cused** or **-cussed, -cus·ing, -cus·sing.** adjust for vision; concentrate.

fod·der, *n.* livestock feed.

foe, *n.* an enemy; adversary.

fog, *n.* dense mist; fine spray; haze; mental confusion. *v.,* **fogged, fog·ging.**

fo·gy, fo·gey, *n. pl.,* **-gies, -geys.** old-fashioned person.

foi·ble, *n.* minor character flaw.

foil, *n.* thin sheet of metal; one serving as contrast to another; fencing sword. *v.* frustrate; prevent.

foist, *v.* impose by fraud.

fold, *v.* double over itself; clasp; enwrap; embrace; collapse. *n.* a pen for or a group of sheep; pleat.

fold·er, *n.* printed circular; holder for loose papers.

fol·de·rol, *n.* useless trifle; nonsense.

fo·li·age, *n.* leaves of plants.

folk, *n. pl.,* **folk** or **folks.** people in general. *a.* of common people. **folks,** *n. pl.* relatives.

folk·lore, *n.* traditional beliefs, customs, legends of a people.

fol·li·cle, *n.* small cavity, sac, or gland; dry seed capsule.

fol·low, *v.* go or come after; obey; imitate; go along; result from; take up, pursue; understand. **-er,** *n.*

fol·low·ing, *n.* group of adherents. *a.* succeeding.

fol·ly, *n. pl.,* **-lies.** foolishness.

fo·ment, *v.* treat with moist heat; to incite.

fond, *a.* loving; affectionate. **-ly,** *adv.*

fon·dle, *v.,* **-dled, -dling.** caress.

font, *n.* baptismal receptacle; source.

food, *n.* sustenance for plant and animal growth; nourishment.

fool, *n.* silly person; dupe; clown. *v.* jest; trick; fritter.

fool·har·dy, *a.* recklessly bold.

fool·ish, *a.* silly; unwise; absurd.

fool·proof, *a.* never failing.

foot, *n. pl.,* **feet.** bottom of the leg; measure of 12 inches; bottom; base.

foot·hold, *n.* footing.

foot·ing, *n.* secure position; base or basis; foundation.

foot·note, *n.* note or comment at the bottom of a page.

foot·print, *n.* mark left by a foot.

foot·step, *n.* a step of the foot; sound of a step; a footprint.

fop, *n.* vain man; dandy.

for, *prep.* with the purpose of; in consideration of; appropriate to; in favor of; in place of; in the interest of; as far or as long as; meant to be used with. *conj.* since; because.

for·age, *n.* food for horses, cattle. *v.* search for food; raid.

for·ay, *n., v.* raid; plunder.

for·bear, *v.,* **-bore, -borne, -bear·ing.** refrain from; withhold; abstain; be patient.

for·bid, *v.,* **-bade** or **-bad, -bid·den, -bid·ding.** prohibit; hinder; bar. **-bid·den,** *a.* threatening; disagreeable.

force, *n.* strength; violence; group combined for joint action. *v.,* **forced, forc·ing.** compel; coerce; break into. **force·ful,** *a.*

for·ceps, *n.* instrument for seizing and holding objects.

for·ci·ble, *a.* done or taken by force; effective; convincing.

ford, *n.* a shallow place where a river may be crossed by wading. *v.*

fore, *a., n.* front; forward.

fore·arm, *n.* arm between elbow and wrist. *v.* to arm beforehand.

fore·bode, for·bode, *v.* foretell; portend; warn; predict. **-bod·ing,** *n., a.*

fore·cast, *v.* predict; foretell. *n.* prediction.

fore·close, *v.* deprive a mortgagor of right to redeem his property.

fore·fa·ther, *n.* an ancestor.

fore·fin·ger, *n.* finger that is next to the thumb.

fore·go, *v.,* **-went, -gone, -going.** to go before; precede. **-go·ing, -gone,** *a.*

fore·ground, *n.* the front part of a scene.

fore·head, *n.* part of the face above the eyes; any front.

for·eign, *a.* of another country; alien; not native. **-er,** *n.*

fore·man, *n. pl.,* **-men.** supervisor of workers; jury head.

fore·most, *a., adv.* first in place, etc.

fore·noon, *n.* period of daylight before noon.

fo·ren·sic, *a.* for public discussion; argumentative.

fore·run·ner, *n.* one sent ahead; omen; harbinger; ancestor.

fore·see, *v.,* **-saw, -seen, -see·ing.** anticipate; know in advance.

fore·sight, *n.* provision for the future; insight; prudence.

fore·skin, *n.* fold of skin over the glans of the penis.

for·est, *n.* dense growth of trees.

fore·stall, *v.* prevent by measures taken in advance.

for·est·ry, *n.* science of managing forests; study of timber.

fore·tell, *v.,* **-told, -tell·ing.** predict; forecast; prophesy.

for·ev·er, *adv.* eternally; continually; for a limitless time.

fore·word, *n.* preface.

for·feit, *v.* lose the right to by some fault, offense, or crime. **-fei·ture,** *n.* penalty.

forge, *n.* furnace or shop to heat metal for shaping. *v.* form by heating and hammering; imitate with intent to defraud; counterfeit; move forward slowly. **for·ger·y,** *n.*

for·get, *v.,* **-got, -got·ten** or **-got, -get·ting.** lose remembrance; omit; neglect. **-ful,** *a.*

for·give, *v.,* **-gave, -given, -giv·ing.** cease to feel resentment; pardon; excuse. **-give·ness,** *n.,* **-giv·ing,** *a.*

for·go, *v.,* **-went, -gone, -go·ing.** abstain from; do without.

fork, *n.* pronged instrument; point of branching. *v.* use a fork; branch.

for·lorn, *a.* abandoned; bereft; forsaken; desolate; sad.

form, *n.* shape; mold; style; a body; document to be filled in; manner of behavior. *v.* give shape to; to assume form; fashion; organize.

for·mal, *a.* customary; conventional; marked by ceremony. **-i·ty,** *n. pl.,* **-ties.**

for·mat, *n.* general plan or arrangement; shape; makeup.

for·ma·tion, *n.* development; structure; shape. **form·a·tive,** *a.*

for·mer, *a.* coming before in time; first mentioned. **-ly,** *adv.*

for·mi·da·ble, *a.* arousing fear; alarming size, strength, etc.

for·mu·la, *n. pl.,* **-las, -lae.** rule; recipe; prescription; algebraic expression; concept. **-late,** *v.*

for·ni·ca·tion, *n.* voluntary sexual intercourse between unmarried persons. **-cate,** *v.*

for·sake, *v.,* **-sook, -sak·en, -sak·ing.** desert; abandon.

fort, *n.* fortified place.

forth, *adv.* forward; onward or outward; onward in time.

forth·com·ing, *a.* soon to appear; approaching.

forth·right, *a.* direct; frank.

forth·with, *adv.* immediately.

for·ti·fi·ca·tion, *n.* the act of fortifying; a fort; strengthening.

for·ti·fy, *v.,* **-fied, -fy·ing.** to strengthen; encourage.

for·ti·tude, *n.* courage; grit; pluck.

fort·night, *n.* two weeks.

for·tress, *n.* stronghold.

for·tu·i·tous, *a.* accidental; lucky; fortunate.

for·tu·nate, *a.* having good fortune; lucky. *n.* **-ness.** *adv.* **-ly.**

for·tune, *n.* great wealth; luck; chance; success; fate.

for·ty, *n. pl.,* **-ties.** four times ten. **-ti·eth,** *n., a.*

fo·rum, *n.* public discussion or opinion; court or tribunal.

for·ward, *adv.* toward; onward; ahead. Also **forwards.** *a.* in the front; precocious; brash. *v.* send on; promote; dispatch; transmit.

fos·sil, *n.* remains or traces of previous animal or plant life found in earth's crust.

fos·ter, *v.* nurture; encourage.

foul, *a.* offensive; loathsome; dirty; stormy; entangled; treacherous; unlawful. *n.* an act contrary to rules. *v.*

found, *v.,* pt. and pp. of **find;** set up or establish. **-er,** *n.*

foun·da·tion, *n.* establishment; lowest part of a building; base; support; corset; endowed institution.

found·er, *v.* become disabled; collapse; sink; fail.

found·ling, *n.* abandoned child.

found·ry, *n. pl.,* **-ries.** place for production of metal castings.

fount, *n.* fountain; source.

foun·tain, *n.* spring of water; a jet of water; source.

four·score, *a.* four times twenty; eighty.

fourth estate, *n.* the public press.

fowl, *n.* a bird, esp. domestic.

fox, *n. pl.,* **fox·es.** wild member of dog family. *v.* outwit, deceive. **foxy,** *a.* cunning; crafty.

foy·er, *n.* vestibule.

fra·cas, *n.* noisy fight; brawl.

frac·tion, *n.* part of a whole; portion; fragment.

frac·tious, *a.* quarrelsome.

frac·ture, n. a break; rupture.

frag·ile, a. delicate; brittle.

frag·ment, n. a part broken off.

fra·grance, n. sweet or pleasing scent. **fra·grant**, a.

frail, a. weak; delicate; easily broken. **frail·ty**, n. pl., **-ties.**

frame, n. structure; enclosing border; physique; mood. v. surround; plan; formulate; devise falsely; shape.

frame·work, n. structure of parts fitted and united together.

fran·chise, n. right to vote; privilege to sell products.

frank, a. candid; outspoken. v. send a letter free. **frank·ly**, adv. **frank·ness**, n.

frank·furt·er, n. small sausage made of beef and pork.

fran·tic, a. wild with excitement, fear, pain, etc. **-ti·cal·ly**, adv.

frap·pé, n. frozen drink; milk shake.

fra·ter·nal, a. brotherly.

fra·ter·ni·ty, n. pl., **-ties.** group of persons with common purpose; men's school social club.

frat·er·nize, v. associate in a friendly way; mingle.

fraud, n. deceit, trickery; an imposter; deception. **-u·lent**, a.

fraught, a. attended (with); full of.

fray, v. to wear or ravel. n. quarrel; brawl; fight.

freak, n. abnormal person or thing. a. odd; unusual; irregular.

freck·le, n. small brownish-yellow spot on the skin, esp. on the face.

free, a., **fre·er**, **fre·est.** having liberty; independent; unleashed; open; copious; clear; acquitted; without charge; loose. v. make free. **-dom,** n.

free-for-all, n. fight; brawl.

free·way, n. toll-free, controlled access expressway.

freeze, v., **froze**, **fro·zen**, **freez·ing.** to harden into ice; become extremely cold; become rigid; fix rents, wages, etc. at a certain stage or level.

freight, n. things being transported; cost of the transportation; train for freight.

freight·er, n. cargo ship.

French, a. relating to the people or language of France.

fre·net·ic, a. frantic; frenzied.

fren·zy, n. pl., **-zies.** temporary madness; wild excitement.

fre·quen·cy, n. pl., **-cies.** habitual occurrence; repetition rate; times an event occurs.

fre·quent, a. happening often; regular. v. visit habitually.

fres·co, n. pl., **-coes, -cos.** painting on moist plaster.

fresh, a. not stale, smoked, frozen, etc.; new; not worn; vigorous; pure or cool. **fresh·en,** v.

fresh·man, n. pl., **-men.** first-year college student; novice.

fret, v. worry; vex. **-ful**, a.

fri·a·ble, a. easily crumbled.

fric·as·see, n. stewed meat.

fric·tion, n. rubbing together of two surfaces; conflict; tension.

friend, n. person known and liked by another. **-ship,** n. **-ly,** a., **-li·er, -li·est.** helpful; favorable.

frieze, n. ornamental, usu. sculptured band around a room, building, etc.

fright, n. sudden, extreme fear.

fright·en, v. scare; terrify; drive away by scaring.

fright·ful, a. terrifying; fearful.

frig·id, a. intensely cold.

frill, n. ruffle; not essential.

fringe, n. ornamental border of threads. a. something extra to.

frisk, v. gambol; frolic. inf. search by feeling over clothing.

frisk·y, a., **-i·er, -i·est.** lively.

frit·ter, v. waste away little by little. n. small fried cake.

friv·o·lous, a. not serious; unimportant; self-indulgent.

frock, n. gown or dress; loose outer garment.

frog, n. web-footed, tailless amphibian; corded dress loop.

frol·ic, n. merry prank. v. play happily; romp. **-some**, a.

from, prep. starting at; going between; out of; not like; a place away; because of.

frond, n. large leaf, esp. of a palm or fern.

front, n. forehead; forward part or surface; line of battle; appearance; vanguard; movement to achieve a common goal. a. of or at the front. v. face, confront. **fron·tal,** a.

front·age, n. front of a building or lot.

fron·tier, n. a country's border; outermost limits; new, unexplored area. **-tiers·man**, n. pl., **-men.**

frost, n. freezing temperature; minute ice crystals. v. cover with frost or icing.

frost·bite, n. bodily injury due to severe cold. **-bit·ten**, a.

frost·ing, *n.* icing; dull finish.

froth, *n.* bubbles; foam.

fro·ward, *a.* perverse; willfully disobedient.

frown, *v.* wrinkle the brow to show displeasure; scowl. *n.* stern look.

frow·zy, *a.,* **-zi·er, -zi·est.** slovenly; unkempt; untidy.

fru·gal, *a.* thrifty; prudent.

fruit, *n.* any plant product; sweet, edible, pulpy plant parts; anything produced. **fruit·ful,** *a.* abundant. **fruit·less,** *a.* unproductive; futile.

fru·i·tion, *n.* fulfillment; attainment; fruit of one's labor.

frus·trate, *v.,* **-trat·ed, -trat·ing.** defeat; discourage; nullify; thwart. **-tra·tion,** *n.*

fry, *v.,* **fried, fry·ing.** cook over heat in fat.

fuch·sia, *n.* flowering plant.

fudge, *v.* exceed bounds; cheat; falsify. *n.* a soft, creamy candy.

fu·el, *n.* combustible matter burned for heat or power. *v.* stimulate; incite.

fu·ga·cious, *a.* lasting a short time.

fu·gi·tive, *a.* running away; elusive; transient. *n.* a runaway; escapee.

ful·crum, *n., pl.,* **-crums, -cra.** support on which a lever rests or turns; a prop.

ful·fill, ful·fil, *v.,* **-filled, -fil·ing.** accomplish; perform; satisfy. **-fill·ment, -fil·ment,** *n.*

full, *a.* filled; complete; entire; satisfied; maximum. *adv.* exactly; very. *n.* utmost extent. **full·ness,** *n.,* **ful·ly,** *adv.*

full-fledged, *a.* fully developed; of full rank or status.

ful·mi·nate, *v.* explode; denounce vehemently; condemn.

ful·some, *a.* offensive to good taste; disgusting.

fum·ble, *v.* grope or handle clumsily; drop a ball. *n.* act of fumbling.

fume, *n.* odorous smoke, gas, or vapor; irritable mood. *v.* emit fumes; feel anger.

fu·mi·gate, *v.* expose to fumes, esp. for disinfecting pests.

fun, *n.* that which is enjoyable, amusing, mirthful. *a.*

func·tion, *n.* occupation; normal activity; social occasion. *v.* perform specified activity. **-tion·al,** *a.*

fund, *n.* a stock of money. *pl.* money. *v.* provide money for.

fun·da·men·tal, *a.* primary; basic. *n.* basic principle.

fu·ner·al, *n.* burial ceremony.

fu·ne·re·al, *a.* gloomy; sad.

fun·gus, *n. pl.,* **-gi, -guses.** any of nongreen lower plants such as mushrooms, mold, mildew, etc.

fun·nel, *n.* cone-shaped tube for directing downward liquid flow; flue. *v.,* **-neled, -nel·ing.**

fun·ny, *a.,* **-ni·er, -ni·est.** amusing; provoking mirth; queer.

fur, *n.* soft, thick, hairy coat of a mammal; dressed pelt. **fur·ry,** *a.*

fur·bish, *v.* polish; renovate.

fu·ri·ous, *a.* full of anger.

furl, *v.* wrap or roll.

fur·long, *n.* one-eighth of a mile; 220 yards.

fur·lough, *n.* leave of absence, esp. one granted to a soldier.

fur·nace, *n.* enclosed structure for generating heat.

fur·nish, *v.* supply with something needed; give; equip; outfit.

fur·nish·ings, *n. pl.* furniture; articles of dress.

fur·ni·ture, *n.* movable articles in a room; fittings; accessories.

fu·ror, *n.* outburst of rage, excitement, etc·; vogue.

fur·row, *n.* narrow trench made by a plow; wrinkle. *v.* make or become grooved.

fur·ther, *adv.* to a greater extent; moreover. *a.* additional; farther. *v.* advance; promote.

fur·ther·more, *adv.* besides.

fur·thest, *a., adv.* most distant.

fur·tive, *a.* taken or done stealthily; surreptitious.

fu·ry, *n. pl.,* **-ries.** intense rage; violent anger.

fuse, *n.* safety device in an electric circuit; cord used to ignite an explosive. *v.* melt or blend together.

fu·se·lage, *n.* airplane body.

fu·sion, *n.* state of being melted or blended together.

fuss, *n.* restless activity; excessive anxiety over trifles. *v.* make much ado about trifles.

fuss·y, *a.,* **-i·er, -i·est.** anxious; elaborate.

fus·ty, *a.* moldy; conservative.

fu·tile, *a.* having no results; useless; trivial. **-til·i·ty,** *n.*

fu·ture, *n.* any time or state that is to come; what will happen.

fuzz, *n.* loose, light, fluffy matter. **fuzz·y,** *a.* covered with fuzz; indistinct; not clear.

G

ga·ble, *n.* triangular wall enclosed by sloping ends of a ridged roof.

gad, v., **-ded, -ding.** wander restlessly; roam. **-a·bout,** n.

gad·fly, n. large stinging fly; annoying person.

gaff, n. strong hook with a handle for landing large fish.

gag, v., **gagged, gag·ging.** stop up mouth to prevent speech; cause to vomit; choke; obstruct. n. something thrust into mouth; inf. joke; hoax.

gai·e·ty, n. merrymaking; cheerfulness; finery.

gai·ly, adv. cheerfully.

gain, v. win; earn; achieve; increase; profit; make progress. n. increase or profit.

gain·say, v., **-said, -say·ing.** contradict; deny; dispute.

gait, n. manner of moving; pattern of stepping.

ga·la, a. festive. n. festive occasion; celebration.

gal·ax·y, n. pl., **-ies.** system of stars; group of celebrities.

gale, n. strong wind.

gall, n. bile; rancor; bitterness of spirit; impudence; plant tumor. v. chafe; irritate.

gal·lant, a. brave; spirited; noble; showy; chivalrous. **-ry,** n. man attentive to women.

gal·ler·y, n. pl., **-ies.** body of spectators; long covered walkway used for displays; balcony; colonnade.

gal·ley, n. early oar- and sail-propelled ship; ship's kitchen.

gal·li·vant, v. gad about, usu. with opposite sex; look for pleasure.

gal·lon, n. four quarts.

gal·lop, v., n. ride a horse at full speed.

gal·lows, n. wooden frame for hanging condemned persons.

ga·losh, n. usu. pl. overshoe worn in storms and slush.

gal·va·nize, v., **-nized, -niz·ing.** stimulate by or as by electric current; coat metal with zinc.

gam·bit, n. stratagem to gain an initial advantage, as in chess.

gam·ble, v., **-bled, -bling.** play game of chance for stakes; bet; risk. n. risky undertaking.

gam·bol, v., n. frolic; skip.

game, n. amusement; diversion; play; trick; wild animals hunted for sport or profit; a. lame. v. play games of chance.

gam·ut, n. whole scale or range of a series.

gan·der, n. male goose; inf. glance; look.

gang, n. a band or group of persons.

gan·gling, a. awkwardly tall and slender; spindling; lanky.

gang·plank, n. movable bridge for getting on and off a ship; ramp.

gan·grene, n. the dying of tissue from lack of blood.

gang·ster, n. member of a criminal gang; racketeer.

gap, n. opening; cleft; mountain pass; break; separation; blank.

gape, v. open mouth wide; stare open-mouthed; yawn.

ga·rage, n. building for sheltering, repairing motor vehicles.

garb, n. style of dress; attire.

gar·bage, n. food waste; worthless goods; refuse.

gar·ble, v., **-bled, -bling.** distort; jumble the meaning.

gar·con, n. waiter; young man.

gar·den, n. plot of ground for growing vegetables, flowers.

gar·gan·tu·an, a. gigantic; huge.

gar·gle, n., v. wash or rinse the mouth or throat.

gar·ish, a. excessively bright; loud; flashy; glaring.

gar·land, n. wreath or rope of leaves, twigs, flowers.

gar·ment, n. article of clothing.

gar·ner, v. gather into; earn; collect; store. n.

gar·net, n. deep red gem; hue.

gar·nish, v. embellish; decorate. n. decoration.

gar·ri·son, n. troops stationed in a fort; military post.

gar·ru·lous, a. very talkative.

gar·ter, n. band or strap to hold up a stocking.

gas, n. vapor-like state of matter; gasoline. v. overcome with gas. **-e·ous,** a.

gash, n., v. a deep, long cut; slash.

gas·ket, n. ring used to make a joint leakproof.

gas·o·line, n. liquid fuel or solvent made from petroleum.

gasp, v. inhale suddenly; choke; pant.

gas·tric, a. of the stomach.

gas·tron·o·my, n. art or science of good eating.

gate, n. movable barrier in a fence or wall; entrance passageway; total of paid admissions.

gath·er, v. collect; harvest; pick; pucker material; grow; increase. n. a fold in cloth.

gauche, a. awkward; clumsy.

gaud·y, a., **-i·er, -i·est.** garish.

gauge, n. standard or scale of measure; dimensions; tool for measuring. v., **gauged, gaug·ing.** to measure; estimate; judge.

gaunt, *a.* haggard; thin.

gaunt·let, *n.* protective glove; combat challenge; ordeal.

gauze, *n.* thin transparent fabric of meshlike weave; surgical dressing. **gauz·y,** *a.*

gav·el, *n.* small mallet used by presiding officer.

gawk, *v.* stare or gape stupidly.

gawk·y, *a.,* **-i·er, -i·est.** awkward; clumsy; ungainly.

gay, *a.* cheerfully lively; merry; brilliantly colored. *inf.* homosexual.

gaze, *v.,* **gazed, gaz·ing.** look steadily or intently. *n.*

ga·zelle, *n.* small antelope.

ga·zette, *n.* newspaper; journal.

gaz·et·teer, *n.* geographical dictionary; a journalist.

gear, *n.* clothing; toothed wheel; paraphernalia; equipment. *v.* connect by gearing; adjust.

gel·a·tin, *n.* glutinous substance obtained from animal tissues. **ge·lat·i·nous,** *a.*

geld, *v.,* **geld·ed** or **gelt, geld·ing.** castrate, esp. animals. **-ing,** *n.*

gem, *n.* precious or semiprecious stone; jewel.

gen·der, *n.* classification of words as masculine, feminine, neuter; *inf.* sex.

gene, *n.* chemical unit of a chromosome that transmits an inherited characteristic.

ge·ne·al·o·gy, *n.* study of family history; pedigree; lineage.

gen·er·al, *a.* of the whole; usual; not specific or special; indefinite; military officer; not local.

gen·er·al·i·ty, *n.* indefinite or vague statement. **-ize,** *v.*

gen·er·ate, *v.* cause to be; bring into existence; produce. **-a·tive,** *a.*

gen·er·a·tion, *n.* people born and living at same time; span between parents and children; producing.

gen·er·a·tor, *n.* machine for converting mechanical into electrical energy; dynamo.

ge·ner·ic, *a.* referring to a genus or class; not registered as a trademark; not specific.

gen·er·ous, *a.* unselfish; ample; abundant; noble. **-os·i·ty,** *n.*

gen·e·sis, *n.* origin; (*cap.*) first book of Old Testament.

ge·net·ics, *n. pl.* science of heredity of organisms. **-ic,** *a.*

gen·ial, *a.* kindly; gracious.

gen·i·tals, *n. pl.* sexual organs.

gen·ius, *n.* (person with) extraordinary intellectual power; creative ability; person with high I.Q.; penchant.

gen·o·cide, *n.* deliberate extermination of a people.

gen·teel, *a.* aristocratic; polite.

gen·tile, *a., n.* non-Jewish (person), esp. a Christian.

gen·til·i·ty, *n.* refinement; elegance; good family line.

gen·tle, *a.* kind; mild; docile; delicate; gradual. **-tly,** *adv.*

gen·tle·man, *n. pl.,* **-men.** man of good breeding; courteous person; valet.

gen·u·ine, *a.* authentic; sincere.

ge·nus, *n.* kind; category; class.

ge·og·ra·phy, *n.* science of the surface and natural elements of the earth. **-gra·phic, -graph·i·cal,** *a.* **-gra·pher,** *n.*

ge·ol·o·gy, *n.* science of history and structure of the earth, its changes, etc. **-o·log·ic, -o·log·i·cal,** *a.* **-ol·o·gist,** *n.*

ge·om·e·try, *n.* branch of mathematics dealing with measurement and properties of angles, solids, etc. **-o·met·ric,** *a.*

ge·o·phys·ics, *n. pl.* science dealing with weather, earthquakes, winds, etc. and their effects on the earth. **-o·phys·i·cal,** *a.*

ger·i·at·rics, *n. pl.* area of medicine dealing with diseases and problems of the aged. **-i·at·ric,** *a.*

germ, *n.* disease-producing microorganism; microbe; seed.

ger·mane, *a.* pertinent; appropriate; relevant.

ger·mi·nate, *v.* begin or cause to develop; sprout; evolve. **-na·tion,** *n.*

ger·und, *n.* *-ing* verb form used as a noun.

ges·ta·tion, *n.* period of pregnancy; conception and development, esp. in the mind.

ges·tic·u·late, *v.* express by gestures, with or without speech.

ges·ture, *n.* motion or action of limbs or body expressive of an idea or emotion. *v.*

get, *v.,* **got, got** or **gotten, getting.** earn; catch; understand; gain; obtain; come to have; achieve power over.

gey·ser, *n.* spring spurting hot water and steam.

ghast·ly, *a.,* **-li·er, -li·est.** frightful; dreadful; terrifying; horrible.

gher·kin, *n.* small immature cucumber used for pickles.

ghet·to, *n.* city quarter populated by a minority group.

ghost, *n.* disembodied soul of a dead person; spirit; demon; iota; shadow. **ghost·ly,** *a.*

ghoul, *n.* evil demon who robs graves and feeds on corpses.

GI, *n.* U·S. serviceman, esp. an enlisted man. Also **G.I.**

gi·ant, *n.*, *a.* person or thing of great size or strength; huge.

gib·ber·ish, *n.* rapid, unintelligible language.

gib·bon, *n.* small, tailless ape.

gib·bous, *a.* humpbacked; convex; protuberant; swollen on one side.

gibe, jibe, *v.*, *n.* taunt; scoff.

gib·let, *n. usu. pl.* edible viscera of a fowl.

gid·dy, *a.* frivolous; silly; dizzy; flighty. -**di·ness,** *n.*

gift, *n.* a present; natural quality; talent; aptitude.

gi·gan·tic, *a.* colossal; huge.

gig·gle, *v.* laugh in a silly, undignified way; titter.

gig·o·lo, *n. pl.*, **-los.** man supported by a woman; male escort.

gild, *v.* cover with gold; embellish. **gilt,** *a.*

gill, *n.* breathing organ of fish.

gim·mick, *n.* crafty device; gadget; scheme; trick.

gin, *n.* machine for separating cotton from its seeds; alcoholic liquor; card game.

gin·ger, *n.* spice from pungent, aromatic root of ginger plant.

gin·ger·bread, *n.* cake flavored with ginger; gaudy ornament.

gin·ger·ly, *adv.* cautiously. *a.* wary; careful.

ging·ham, *n.* cotton fabric usually striped or checked.

gi·raffe, *n.* long-necked spotted African animal; tallest ruminant quadruped.

gir·an·dole, *n.* radiating composition; branched candle holder.

gird, *v.* encircle with a belt or girdle; *fig.* equip oneself for action.

gird·er, *n.* a main horizontal supporting beam.

gir·dle, *n.* that which encircles; sash; light corset.

girl, *n.* female child. **-ish,** *a.*

girth, *n.* strap passed under horse's belly; circumference.

gist, *n.* main point; essence.

give, *v.*, **gave, giv·en, giv·ing.** place into another's grasp; donate; trade; permit; perform; sacrifice; bestow; administer; transfer; proffer; allot; produce; yield.

giv·en, *a.* bestowed; stated; inclined; fixed.

gla·cier, *n.* large ice and snow mass. **-cial,** *a.*

glad, *a.* happy; pleased. **-ly,** *adv.*, **-ness,** *n.*, **-den,** *v.*

glade, *n.* open space in a forest.

glad·i·o·lus, *n.* plant with sword-like leaves and spikes of variously colored flowers.

glam·our, glam·or, *n.* alluring charm; fascination. **-ous,** *a.*

glance, *v.* look quickly; strike and glide off. *n.* hasty look.

gland, *n.* organ that secretes substances for the body to use or throw off. **glan·du·lar,** *a.*

glare, *v.*, **glared, glar·ing.** shine with a strong, dazzling light; stare piercingly, *n.* dazzling light; fierce look; garishness.

glar·ing, *a.* too bright; flagrant; obvious.

glass, *n.* hard, brittle, transparent substance; thing made of glass; optical lenses; *pl.* spectacles.

glass·y, *a.*, **-i·er,** **-i·est.** smooth; transparent; expressionless.

glau·co·ma, *n.* disease of the eye.

glaze, *v.*, *n.* (cover with) a smooth, glossy coating; furnish or coat with glass.

gla·zier, *n.* one who fits windows, etc., with glass.

gleam, *n.* flash of light; faint light. *v.* shine softly.

glean, *v.* gather slowly and arduously; ascertain.

glee, *n.* joy; hilarity. **-ful,** *a.*

glen, *n.* secluded narrow valley.

glib, *a.* fluent; nonchalant; slick.

glide, *v.* move smoothly and easily. *n.*

glim·mer, *v.* shine faintly. *n.* a faint, unsteady light.

glimpse, *n.* a hurried or quick look. *v.* get a quick sight of.

glint, *n.*, *v.* flash; gleam; glitter.

glis·ten, *v.*, *n.* shine with a sparkling light.

glitch, *n.* unwanted electrical surge; malfunction.

glit·ter, *v.*, *n.* (shine with) brilliant sparkling light.

gloat, *v.* contemplate with (usually evil) satisfaction.

globe, *n.* the earth; spherical body; an orb. **glob·al,** *a.*

glob·ule, *n.* a small spherical body.

gloom, *n.* darkness; overcast; despondency. -**y,** *a.*

glo·ry, *n.* praise; blessings of heaven; renown; magnificence. *v.* rejoice; exult. **-ri·fy,** *v.*, -**ri·ous,** *a.*

gloss, *n.* luster; sheen; deceptive appearance; brief margin explanation. **-y,** *a.*, *v.* pass over lightly; scan.

glos·sa·ry, *n.* specialized dictionary; list of specialized terms at back of a book.

glot·tis, *n.* opening between vocal chords and larynx.

glove, *n.* covering for the hand.

glow, *v.* emit bright light and heat without flame. *n.* warm color or emotion.

glow·er, *v.* stare with anger; frown.

glue, *v., n.* (join with) strong adhesive material.

glum, *a.* dreary; morose.

glut, *v.* feed or fill to excess; oversupply; satiate. *n.*

glut·ton, *n.* one who overindulges in something, esp. eating. **-ton·y,** *n.*

gnash, *v.* to grind the teeth together, esp. in rage or pain.

gnat, *n.* small biting fly.

gnaw, *v.* wear away or remove by persistent biting; to torment; corrode; consume.

gnome, *n.* folklore dwarf.

gnu, *n.* African antelope.

go, *v.,* **went, gone, go·ing.** move; proceed; depart; suit or fit; result; be or become; extend; lead; pass; happen; follow. *n. act of going; inf.* success; energy; an attempt.

goad, *n.* animal prod; motive. *v.* incite; spur.

goal, *n.* aim or objective; intention; terminal point in a sport.

goat, *n.* agile, hollow-horned sheeplike mammal.

goat·ee, *n.* small, pointed beard on a man's chin.

gob·ble, *v.* swallow food hastily; gulp. *n.* noise made by a male turkey.

gob·let, *n.* drinking glass with a foot and stem.

gob·lin, *n.* evil or mischievous sprite.

God, *n.* supreme Being, creator and ruler of the universe.

god, *n.* person, spirit, or object worshipped; powerful ruler. **-dess,** *n. fem.*

god·ly, *a.,* **-lier.** divine; pious.

god·par·ent, *n.* sponsor of a child at its baptism. **god·fa·ther, god·moth·er,** *n.*

god·send, *n.* unexpected or needed thing which arrives at opportune time.

gog·gle, *n.* bulge-eyed stare. *pl.* protective spectacles.

go·ing, *n.* departure; progression. *a.* living; prevailing.

goi·ter, *n.* thyroid gland enlargement.

gold, *n.* precious, yellow metallic element; bright yellow color. **-en,** *a.* made of or colored like gold.

golf, *n.* game played with clubs and a small ball on a grassy course with 9 or 18 holes.

go·nad, *n.* primary sex gland; an ovary or testis.

gon·do·la, *n.* long, narrow boat used on Venetian canals. **gon·do·lier,** *n.* boatman.

gong, *n.* disc producing a resounding tone when hit.

gon·or·rhe·a, *n.* venereal disease of the genital tract.

good, *n. pl.* possessions. *a.,* **bet·ter, best.** efficient; beneficial; unspoiled; valid; healthy; sound; worthy; happy; pious; of favorable quality; proper; genuine; pleasant; ample. **-ness,** *n.*

good-by, good-bye, *a. int.* farewell; parting expression.

good-heart·ed, *a.* charitable; kind; generous.

good·ly, *a.,* **-li·er, -li·est.** pleasing; large; considerable.

goose, *n. pl.,* **geese.** large, web-footed, long-necked water fowl; simpleton.

gore, *n.* blood that is shed; triangle of cloth. *v.* pierce or wound with a horn or tusk.

gorge, *n.* narrow cleft. *v.* stuff with food; glut.

gor·geous, *a.* magnificent; colorful; resplendent.

gosh, *interj.* expression of surprise; mild oath.

gos·ling, *n.* young goose; dolt.

gos·pel, *n.* doctrine taught by Christ and his apostles.

gos·sa·mer, *n.* cobweb film floating in air; any fine, filmy substance or fabric. *a.* filmy.

gos·sip, *n.* rumors; idle talk, esp. about the affairs of others.

gouge, *n.* chisel; groove. *v.* make grooves; *fig.* extort.

gou·lash, *n.* beef stew with vegetables; jumble.

gourd, *n.* fruit of melons, pumpkins, squash, etc.

gour·mand, *n.* one who enjoys good eating and drinking.

gour·met, *n.* excellent judge and savorer of food and drink; epicure.

gout, *n.* disease characterized by inflamed and swollen joints.

gov·ern, *v.* exercise authority; control; influence; restrain.

gov·ern·ess, *n.* woman teacher hired to instruct children usually in their own home.

gov·ern·ment, *n.* political rule and authority; governing organization; system by which power is vested and exercised.

gov·er·nor, *n.* one who rules; head of a state in U.S.

gown, *n.* woman's dress; official robe; coverall.

grab, *v.* seize suddenly; grasp; snatch.

grace, *n.* unmerited divine help; privilege; elegance of form; mercy; pardon; payment delay; titles; short prayer. *v.* adorn; honor; dignify. **-ful,** *a.*

gra·cious, *a.* kind; courteous; pleasing; merciful.

gra·da·tion, *n.* succession by gradual steps; advance by degree.

grade, *n.* stage in any series; one year of school; a mark rating a pupil's work; elevation; slope. *v.* arrange in stages or series; level off; rank.

grad·u·al, *a.* proceeding by steps or degrees. **-al·ly,** *adv.*

grad·u·ate, *v.* grant or receive a degree or diploma; mark with degrees for measuring; pass to a higher stage. *n.* one who has received an academic degree. **-a·tion,** *n.*

graf·fi·to, *n. pl.,* **-ti,** inscription scrawled on open surface.

graft, *n.* plant shoot inserted in another plant or tree to grow there; transplanted body tissue; dishonest gain by public officials or others. *v.* transplant by grafting.

grail, *n. (cap.)* Christ's Last Supper cup; object of quest.

grain, *n.* seeds of cereal grasses; particle; minute portion; pattern of fibers in wood.

gram, *n.* basic unit of weight of the metric system, about .035 oz.

gram·mar, *n.* study of word forms and the rules of a language. **-mat·i·cal,** *a.*

gra·na·ry, *n. pl.,* **-ries.** storehouse for grain; chief source.

grand, *a.* foremost; highest in rank; comprehensive; definitive; main; lofty; lavish; fine; stately.

grand·child, *n.* a son's or daughter's child.

gran·dil·o·quence, *n.* lofty speech; bombast.

gran·di·ose, *a.* impressive; imposing; splendid.

grand ju·ry, *n.* jury that hears evidence of alleged violations and has power to indict for trial by a petty jury.

grand·par·ent, *n.* parent of one's mother or father.

grand·stand, *n.* elevated seats for spectators.

grange, *n.* farm, with its house and outbuildings.

gran·ite, *n.* hard igneous rock; unyielding endurance.

grant, *v.* consent; allow; give; bestow; admit. *n.* act of granting; thing granted.

gran·u·late, *v.* form into grains.

gran·ule, *n.* small particle. **gran·u·lar,** *a.*

grape, *n.* edible, pulpy, smooth-skinned berry or fruit which grows in clusters on vines.

grape·fruit, *n.* large, round, yellow citrus fruit with highly-flavored juicy, acid pulp.

graph, *n.* diagram of a system of connections or interrelations between two or more things.

graph·ic, *a.* lifelike; vividly described; pertaining to graphs, writing, etc. **-ic·ly,** *adv.*

graph·ite, *n.* soft carbon used in lead pencils and as a lubricant.

grap·nel, *n.* device with hooks or clamps for seizing or holding objects; anchor.

grap·ple, *n.* grapnel; grip. *v.* seize; hand-to-hand struggle.

grasp, *v.* seize and hold; clutch; comprehend. *n.* handle; embrace; grip; mastery.

grasp·ing, *a.* greedy; covetous.

grass, *n.* herbage for grazing animals; plant with long, narrow leaves; lawn; *inf.* marijuana. **-y,** *n.*

grass·hop·per, *n.* leaping insect.

grate, *n.* metal bar framework. *v.* reduce into particles by rubbing; scrape with a harsh noise; irritate.

grate·ful, *a.* thankful; appreciative.

grat·i·fy, *v.* give pleasure to; satisfy; indulge. **-fi·ca·tion,** *n.*

grat·ing, *n.* partition of bars.

gra·tis, *a., adv.* free of cost.

grat·i·tude, *n.* gratefulness.

gra·tu·i·tous, *a.* free; without obligation; unwarranted.

gra·tu·i·ty, *n. pl.,* **-ties.** gift; tip.

grave, *n.* burial place; tomb. *a.* solemn; serious; weighty.

grav·el, *n.* mix of small stones and pebbles for roads, etc.

grave·yard, *n.* cemetery; storage place for worn-out things.

grav·i·tate, *v.* move toward some attractive influence.

grav·i·ta·tion, *n.* natural force of attraction of particles or bodies to each other.

grav·i·ty, *n. pl.,* **-ties.** seriousness; earth's attraction.

gra·vy, *n.* sauce of meat juices; *inf.* unearned gain.

gray, grey, *a.* color between white and black; dismal; hoary.

graze, *v.* feed on growing grass; munch; touch lightly in passing; abrade.

grease, *n.* melted animal fat; oily matter; lubricant. *v.* smear with grease. **greas·y,** *a.*

great, *a.* large; ample; predominant; numerous; grand; main.

greed, *n.* excessive desire for possessions; avarice. **greed·y,** *a.*

green, *a.* grass color; covered with grass; unripe; inexperienced; fresh; unseasoned.

green·er·y, *n.* vegetation; foliage.

greet, *v.* meet; salute; address.

greet·ing, *n.* salutation at meeting; friendly message.

gre·gar·i·ous, *a.* sociable.

gre·nade, *n.* small explosive shell or missile.

grid, *n.* grating of crossed bars.

grid·dle, *n.* flat rimless metal surface or pan for frying.

grid·i·ron, *n.* football field; grate.

grief, *n.* deep sadness; distress.

griev·ance, *n.* complaint; wrong.

grieve, *v.* cause to suffer; distress; mourn.

griev·ous, *a.* causing grief or sorrow; sorrowful; atrocious.

grif·fin, grif·fon, *n.* mythical monster, part eagle, part lion.

grill, *v.* broil on a grate; *inf.* torment; question relentlessly. *n.* cooking grate.

grim, *a.* stern; unrelenting.

grim·ace, *n.* facial distortion expressing pain, disgust, etc.

grime, *n.* ingrained dirt; soot; soil. **grim·y,** *a.*

grin, *v., n.* (give a) broad smile.

grind, *v.,* **ground, grinding,** to wear smooth, sharpen, or reduce to powder or particles by friction; whet; rub harshly; oppress.

grind·stone, *n.* revolving stone disc for sharpening tools.

grip, *n.* strong grasp; handle; handclasp; control; small valise. *v.* take firm hold.

gris·ly, *a.* frightful; gruesome.

grist, *n.* ground grain.

gris·tle, *n.* cartilage.

grit, *n.* fine, hard particles; courage; firmness of character. *v.* grate; grind. **grit·ty,** *a.*

griz·zled, griz·zly, *a.* gray-haired.

groan, *v.* utter a low sound of grief, pain, disapproval. *n.* a low, mournful sound; moan.

gro·cer·y, *n. pl.,* **-ies.** retail food store. *pl.* foodstuffs.

groin, *n.* fold where thigh joins the abdomen.

groom, *n.* bridegroom; male servant; horse or stable aide. *v.* make clean, neat; polish; prepare for a specific purpose.

groove, *n.* narrow channel; rut; depression; fixed routine.

grope, *v.* feel about blindly; feel one's way.

gross, *a.* total before deductions; bulky; earthy; vulgar; flagrant; enormous. *n.* twelve dozen.

gro·tesque, *a.* distorted; awkward; unnatural; bizarre.

grot·to, *n. pl.,* **-toes, -tos.** small cave.

grouch, *v. inf.* show discontent. *n.* grumbler; irritable person. **grouch·y,** *a.*

ground, *n. sometimes pl.* land; earth; basis; support; dregs. *v.* restrict to the ground; give reason for; connect to a ground.

ground hog, *n.* woodchuck.

ground·work, *n.* foundation, base, or basis.

group, *n.* assemblage of persons or things. *v.* arrange in order; form a group.

grouse, *v. inf.* grumble. *n.* a game bird; complaint.

grove, *n.* small wood of trees.

grov·el, *v.,* **-eled, -el·ing.** humble oneself; wallow; crawl.

grow, *v.,* **grew, grown, grow·ing.** develop to maturity; survive; arise; increase gradually.

growl, *v.* utter a deep guttural sound of anger or hostility.

grown-up, *n.* an adult. **grown-up,** *a.* reaching the age of maturity.

growth, *n.* act of growing; increase in size or mental development; vegetation.

grub, *v.,* **grubbed, grub·bing.** dig up; drudge. *n.* insect larva.

grub·by, *a.,* **-bi·er, -bi·est.** dirty; slovenly; contemptible.

grudge, *v.* permit with reluctance. *n.* ill will; resentment; envy.

gru·el·ing, *a.* exhausting.

grue·some, *a.* horrible; frightening; repulsive; grisly.

gruff, *a.* surly; harsh; terse.

grum·ble, *v.* complain ill-humoredly; growl.

grump·y, *a.* irritable; cross.

grunt, *v.* utter a deep guttural sound, like a hog.

guar·an·tee, *n., v.* pledge or warranty of quality or that obligations will be met. Also **guar·an·ty.**

guard, *v.* protect; watch; take precautions. *n.* sentry.

guard·i·an, *n.* one who guards or protects any person or thing. *a.* protecting.

gu·ber·na·to·ri·al, *a.* of or pertaining to a governor.

gud·geon, *n.* pivot; journal; dupe. *v.* cheat.

guer·ril·la, *n.* soldier of an independent group who harass and attack the enemy.

guess, *v.* deduce; estimate; suppose or believe. *n.* conjecture.

guest, *n.* person shown hospitality at home or place of business.

guf·faw, *n.* loud, coarse, sudden burst of laughter.

guide, *v.* lead, direct; steer; pilot. *n.* person or thing that guides. **guid·ance**, *n.*

guile, *n.* treachery; deceit.

guil·lo·tine, *n.* machine for beheading persons.

guilt, *n.* fact of having done wrong; remorse for an offense.

guilt·y, *a.*, **-i·er**, **-i·est**. judged responsible for an offense; blameworthy.

guin·ea pig, *n.* small rodent used in experiments or as a pet.

guise, *n.* outward appearance; pretense; costume; semblance.

gui·tar, *n.* musical instrument with violinlike body and (usu.) 6 strings which are plucked.

gulch, *n.* deep narrow ravine.

gulf, *n.* portion of ocean partly enclosed by land; any wide separation, as in education, etc.

gull, *n.* sea bird; person easily deceived. *v.* to cheat, deceive.

gul·let, *n.* esophagus; throat.

gul·li·ble, *a.* easily deceived.

gul·ly, *n. pl.*, **-lies**. ravine; ditch.

gulp, *v.* swallow greedily or quickly; gasp. *n.* large swallow.

gum, *n.* fleshy tissue surrounding teeth; sticky substance; chewing gum.

gum·bo, *n.* soup thickened with okra; heavy sticky mud.

gun, *n.* portable firearm. *v.* shoot; hunt with a gun.

gun·ny, *n.* strong coarse cloth made of jute.

gun·pow·der, *n.* explosive mixture for projectiles, fireworks.

gun·smith, *n.* one who designs, makes, repairs small firearms.

gun·wale, **gun·nel**, *n.* upper edge of a boat's or ship's side.

gup·py, *n.* small tropical fish.

gur·gle, *v.* (utter) a bubbling sound; irregular, noisy current.

gur·ney, *n.* wheeled cot or stretcher.

gush, *v.* issue copiously; make effusive display.

gust, *n.* strong blast of wind.

gus·ta·tory, *a.* of taste or tasting.

gut, *n.* alimentary canal; cord made of intestine, *pl. inf.* courage. *v.* destroy the inside of; eviscerate.

gut·ter, *n.* trough or channel for carrying off water or fluid.

gut·tur·al, *a.* pertaining to the throat; harsh; rasping.

guy, *n.* guiding rope. *inf.* fellow.

guz·zle, *v.* drink greedily.

gym, *n. inf.* gymnasium.

gym·na·si·um, *n.* place for physical education activities.

gym·nas·tics, *n. pl.* athletic exercises. **-nas·tic**, *a.* **-nast**, *n.*

gy·ne·col·o·gy, *n.* medical science dealing with functions and diseases of women.

gyp, *n.*, *v. inf.* cheat; swindle.

gyp·sum, *n.* chalky mineral.

gyp·sy, *n. pl.*, **-sies**. wanderer.

gy·rate, *v.* rotate; whirl.

gy·ro·scope, *n.* rotating wheel mounted to spin freely to maintain equilibrium or determine direction.

H

ha, **hah**, *interj.* exclamation of surprise, wonder, joy, etc.

hab·it, *n.* acquired repetitive behavior pattern; custom; costume.

hab·it·a·ble, *a.* suitable to live in.

hab·i·tat, *n.* natural abode or locality of a plant or animal.

hab·i·ta·tion, *n.* residence.

ha·bit·u·al, *a.* usual; customary; regular. **-u·al·ly**, *adv.*

ha·bit·u·ate, *v.*, **-at·ed**, **-at·ing**. accustom; familiarize.

hack, *v.* cut with blows; chop; emit short coughs. *n.* short, broken cough; worn-out horse; rough cut; *inf.* taxi.

hack·neyed, *a.* trite; stale.

had, *v.* pt. and pp. of **have**.

hag, *n.* ugly old woman; witch.

hag·gard, *a.* appearing emaciated or worn; gaunt.

hag·gle, *v.*, **-gled**, **-gling**. bargain with; wrangle; dispute over terms. **-gler**, *n.*

hail, *v.* salute; greet; acclaim; call out to. *n.* greeting; precipitation of small snow or ice pellets.

hail·stone, *n.* pellet of hail.

hair, *n.* threadlike outgrowth from the skin; mass of such fibers, as on the head; trifle. *a.* of or for hair. **hair·y**, *a.*, **-i·er**, **-i·est**.

hair·breadth, *n.* very small distance. *a.* very narrow. Also **hair's·breadth**.

hale, *v.*, **haled**, **hal·ing**. haul; compel. *a.*, **hal·er**, **hal·est**. free from disease; robust.

half, *n. pl.*, **halves**. one of two equal parts; partner; semester. *a.* being one of the half parts; partial. *adv.* partially; to the extent of half; in part.

half-heart·ed, *a.* lacking spirit or enthusiasm. **-ly,** *adv.*

half·way, *a.* midway between two points; partial.

half-wit, *n.* imbecile; feebleminded person. **-wit·ted,** *a.*

hal·i·but, *n. pl.,* **-but, -buts.** large edible flatfish.

hal·i·to·sis, *n.* bad breath.

hall, *n.* large room for public assembly; auditorium; vestibule; passageway.

hal·le·lu·jah, *interj.* Praise ye the Lord!

hal·low, *v.* consecrate; venerate.

hal·lu·ci·na·tion, *n.* apparent perception; illusion. **-to·ry,** *a.*

hal·lu·cin·o·gen, *n.* substance that causes hallucinations.

hall·way, *n.* corridor; vestibule.

ha·lo, *n. pl.,* **-los, -loes.** circle of light; aura of glory.

halt, *n.* stop. *v.* stop; restrain; hesitate; terminate; discontinue; end; waver. **-ing,** *a.,* **-ing·ly,** *adv.*

hal·ter, *n.* noosed rope for fastening horses, etc.; woman's backless sports waist.

halve, *v.,* **halved, halv·ing.** divide into two equal parts.

ham, *n.* meat of a hog's thigh. **ham·my,** *a. inf.* overacted.

ham·burg·er, *n.* ground beef; patty; (bun) sandwich.

ham·let, *n.* small village.

ham·mer, *n.* tool for pounding or striking. *v.* beat, drive, or form with a hammer; pound.

ham·mock, *n.* hanging canvas or netted cord bed.

ham·per, *v.* disrupt; encumber; impede. *n.* kind of large basket.

hand, *n.* end part of the arm; person employed in manual labor; applause. *a.* by, using, or for the hand. *v.* grasp, touch, or guide with the hands; pass; provide. **-ful,** *n. pl.,* **-fuls. -i·ly,** *adv.*

hand·bag, *n.* pocketbook; purse.

hand·book, *n.* guidebook.

hand·cuff, *n. usu. pl.* metal shackle with lock. *v.* put handcuffs on; manacle.

hand·i·cap, *n.* disadvantage or advantage; physical disability. *v.,* **-capped, -cap·ping.**

hand·i·craft, *n.* occupation requiring manual skill; articles so fashioned.

hand·i·work, *n.* work done or things made by the hands.

hand·ker·chief, *n.* square of cloth for wiping face, nose, etc.

han·dle, *n.* part intended to be grasped by the hand. *v.,* **-dled, -dling.** touch or use the hands on; manage; deal with; deal or trade in. **-dler,** *n.*

hand·some, *a.,* **-som·er, -som·est.** goodlooking; generous.

hand·y,, *a.,* **-i·er, -i·est.** convenient; nearby; skillful with the hands; deft; dextrous.

hand·y·man, *n. pl.,* **-men.** one who does odd jobs.

hang, *v.,* **hung** or **hanged.** fasten from above; dangle; suspend by the neck until dead; droop; attach to walls; hold fast. **-ing,** *a.,* *n.*

hang·ar, *n.* airplane shelter.

hang·er-on, *n. pl.,* **-ers-on.** follower.

hank, *n.* coil; loop; skein.

hank·er, *v.* long for. **-er·ing,** *n.*

hap·haz·ard, *a.* marked by lack of order; aimless. **-ly,** *adv.*

hap·less, *a.* luckless. **-ly,** *adv.*

hap·pen, *v.* take place; occur; come to pass by chance; have the fortune to do.

hap·pen·ing, *n.* occurrence.

hap·py, *a.,* **-pi·er, -pi·est.** joyful; pleased; glad; content. **-pi·ness,** *n.*

ha·rangue, *n.* loud speech; tirade; bombast. *v.,* **-rangued, -rangu·ing.**

har·ass, *v.* annoy by persistent efforts; torment. **-ment,** *n.*

har·bor, *n.* port; refuge. *v.* shelter; conceal; entertain within the mind.

hard, *a.* solid; firm; difficult; factual; unfeeling; tough; strenuous; severe. *adv.* firmly; tightly; strenuously; harshly. **-ness,** *n.*

hard-core, *a.* unyielding; resistant; enduring.

hard·en, *v.* make or become hard; be stubborn. **-er,** *n.*

hard-heart·ed, *a.* unfeeling.

hard·ly, *adv.* scarcely; barely; unlikely; harshly.

hard·ship, *n.* difficult condition; something hard to bear.

hard·ware, *n.* metal articles.

har·dy, *a.,* **-di·er, -di·est.** robust; vigorous; bold. **-di·ly,** *adv.*

hare, *n.* rabbit.

har·em, *n.* area for women in Oriental house; the women.

hark, *v.* listen; pay attention.

har·le·quin, *n.* comedy character with mask; variegated material or color; buffoon.

har·lot, *n.* prostitute. **-ry,** *n.*

harm, *n.* injury; damage. *v.* to damage or hurt. **-ful,** *a.* **-ful·ness,** *n.* **-less,** *a.*

har·mon·i·ca, *n.* mouth organ.

har·mo·nize, *v.,* **-nized, -niz·ing.** sing or play in harmony.

har·mo·ny, *n. pl.,* **-nies.** accord; agreement; tranquility. **-ni·ous,** *a.*

har·ness, *n.* working gear of a horse. *v.* put a harness on; yoke; utilize.

harp, *n.* musical instrument with strings. *v. inf.* tiresomely dwell on a subject. **-ist,** *n.*

har·poon, *n.* barbed spear used to kill whales. *v.* to harpoon something.

har·row, *n.* spiked implement for leveling plowed soil. *v.* cultivate; vex; harass.

har·row·ing, *a.* distressing.

har·ry, *v.,* **-ried, -ry·ing.** raid; pillage; harass; torment; worry.

harsh, *a.* having rough surface; unpleasant; severe. **-ness,** *n.*

har·vest, *n.* gathering of any crop; season gathered; ripe crop; quantity reaped; reward of effort. *v.* reap. **-ves·ter,** *n.*

has, *v.* third person, pres. sing., of **have.**

hash, *n.* chopped food; restatement; jumble. *v.* mince; confuse; review.

hasp, *n.* clasp; fastening device.

has·sle, *n. inf.* heated argument; fight. *v.,* **-sled, -sling.** vex.

has·sock, *n.* footstool; cushion.

haste, *n.* swiftness; rashness.

has·ten, *v.* hurry; accelerate.

hast·y, *a.,* **-i·er, -i·est.** speedy; hurried; eager; rash. **-i·ly,** *adv.* **-i·ness,** *n.*

hat, *n.* head covering.

hatch, *n.* cover for or a hatchway. *v.* emerge from the egg; devise; concoct; originate.

hatch·et, *n.* small ax.

hatch·way, *n.* opening in a ship's deck or in a floor, roof, etc.

hate, *v.,* **hat·ed, hat·ing.** feel enmity; dislike greatly; detest. *n.* intense aversion. **hat·er,** *n.,* **-ful,** *a.*

ha·tred, *n.* great animosity.

haugh·ty, *a.,* **-ti·er, -ti·est.** proud; arrogant; disdainful. **-ti·ly,** *adv.,* **-ti·ness,** *n.*

haul, *v.* pull; transport; drag. *n.* pulling; thing hauled; distance hauled. **-age,** *n.*

haunch, *n.* hip; hindquarter.

haunt, *v.* frequent; linger; appear as a ghost. *n.* place one frequents. **-ed,** *a.*

haut·bois or **haut·boy,** *n.* oboe.

hau·teur, *n.* haughty manner.

have, *v.,* **have, has;** had; **hav·ing.** possess; be impelled; experience; conduct; contain; obtain; accept; beget; bring about or cause to do; allow.

ha·ven, *n.* port; refuge; harbor.

hav·er·sack, *n.* bag worn over the shoulder for provisions.

hav·oc, *n.* devastation; disorder.

hawk, *n.* bird of prey; swindler; militant. *v.* sell; cough; clear the throat. **-ish,** *a.*

haw·ser, *n.* rope used in towing, mooring, or securing a ship.

hay, *n.* cut and dried grass; fodder herbage.

haz·ard, *n.* risk; danger; chance; obstacle (water, etc.) on a golf course. *v.* risk. **-ous,** *a.*

haze, *n.* mist, smoke, or dusty vapor; mental vagueness. *v.*

ha·zel, *n.* tree producing edible nuts. *a.* reddish-brown color.

ha·zy, *a.,* **-zi·er, -zi·est.** misty; clouded; vague. **-zi·ness,** *n.*

he, *pron.,* sing. nom. **he,** poss. **his,** obj. **him;** intens. and refl. **himself;** *pl.* nom. **they,** poss. **their** or **theirs,** obj. **them.** male in question or mentioned; anyone.

head, *n.* upper part of the body; mind; director or chief; crisis; top part. *v.* lead; surpass. *a.* chief; principal. **head·ship,** *n.*

head·ache, *n.* pain in the head; *inf.* annoying problem.

head·ing, *n.* title; caption.

head·land, *n.* promontory.

head·line, *n.* title line over a page or newspaper article.

head·long, *adv.* headfirst; hastily. *a.* hasty; precipitate.

head·most, *a.* foremost; leading.

head·quar·ters, *n. pl.* main office; administrative center.

head·stone, *n.* grave stone.

head·strong, *a.* obstinate; willful.

head·way, *n.* advance; progress.

head·y, *a.,* **-i·er, -i·est.** rashly impetuous; intoxicating. **-i·ness,** *n.*

heal, *v.* make whole; cure; restore to health; mend. **-er,** *n.*

health, *n.* condition of the body; well-being; physical or mental vigor. **-ful,** *a.* **-y,** *a.,* **-i·er, -i·est. -i·ness,** *n.*

heap, *n.* pile; lot. *v.* cast in a heap; pile in great quantity.

hear, *v.,* **heard, -ing.** perceive by the ear; heed; learn. **-er,** *n.,* **-ing,** *n.*

heark·en, *v.* listen; give heed.

hear·say, *n.* rumor; gossip.

hearse, *n.* funeral vehicle.

heart, *n.* organ that circulates blood; seat of emotion and passions; core; most essential part.

heart·ache, *n.* grief; anguish.

heart·break, *n.* overwhelming sorrow; disappointment. **-ing,** *a.*

heart·en, *v.* encourage; cheer.

heart·felt, *a.* deeply felt; earnest.

hearth, *n.* floor or front of a fireplace; fireside; home.

heart·less, *a.* cruel; merciless.

heart·rend·ing, *a.* grievous.

heart·sick, *a.* depressed; grieved.

heart·y, *a.,* **-i·er, -i·est.** sincere; jovial; healthy; substantial. **heart·i·ness,** *n.*

heat, *n.* warmth; ardor; stress; single course in a race; spicy flavor; pressure; animal sexual excitement (esp. female). *v.* make warm; become excited. **-ed,** *a.,* **-er,** *n.*

heath, *n.* open wasteland.

hea·then, *a., n.* pagan; irreligious.

heave, *v.,* **heaved** or **hove, heav·ing.** raise with effort; breathe with effort; retch; cast; hurl. *n.* rhythmical rise and fall.

heav·en, *n.* firmament; sky; happy state; *rel.* God's home; abode of the blessed after death. **-ly,** *a.*

heav·y, *a.,* **-i·er, -i·est.** of great weight, force, or intensity; hard to lift; serious, difficult. **-i·ly,** *adv.,* **-i·ness,** *n.*

heavy-duty, *a.* sturdy for long use.

heav·y-hand·ed, *a.* clumsy; harsh.

heav·y-heart·ed, *a.* sorrowful.

heck·le, *v.,* **-led, -ling.** harass by interrupting; badger.

hec·tic, *a.* great excitement; turmoil. **-ti·cal·ly,** *adv.*

hedge, *n.* boundary of shrubbery; barrier; protection against loss. *v.,* **hedged, hedg·ing.** hinder; avoid a direct statement. **hedg·er,** *n.*

he·do·nism, *n.* doctrine that pleasure is chief good in life.

heed, *v.* listen to with care; mind. *n.* care; attention.

heel, *v.* tilt; list; tip; follow closely. *n.* part of foot or shoe; end bread crust; despicable one.

heft, *n.* weight; bulk; importance. **-y,** *a.,* **-i·er, -i·est.** *v.* hoist.

heif·er, *n.* young female cow.

height, *n.* state of being tall; elevation; summit; zenith; altitude.

height·en, *v.* raise higher; augment; elevate.

hei·nous, *a.* abominable.

heir, *n.* one who inherits. **heir·ess,** *n. fem.*

heir·loom, *n.* possession passed from generation to generation.

hel·i·cop·ter, *n.* aircraft held in the air by propellors rotating on a vertical axis.

he·li·um, *n.* gaseous element.

he·lix, *n. pl.,* **hel·i·ces, he·lix·es.** spiral object or part.

hell, *n.* place of punishment for wicked after death; evil place; torment. **-ish,** *a.*

hel·lion, *n.* mischievous person.

hel·lo, *interj.* greeting.

helm, *n.* steering apparatus of a ship; head. **helms·man,** *n.* one who steers a vessel.

hel·met, *n.* protective head covering.

help, *v.* assist; aid; remedy; promote; benefit. *n.* aid; relief; hired servants. **-er,** *n.,* **-ful,** *a.*

help·ing, *n.* single portion of food; act of one who helps.

help·less, *a.* defenseless; weak; dependant. **-less·ness,** *n.*

hem, *n.* edge or border. *v.,* **hemmed, -ming.** surround; confine; fold over and sew down the edge.

hem·i·sphere, *n.* half of a sphere or the terrestrial globe. **-spher·ic, -spher·i·cal,** *a.*

hem·lock, *n.* evergreen tree; poisonous herb.

hem·or·rhage, *n.* copious discharge of blood. *v.,* **-rhaged, -rhag·ing.** bleed heavily.

hem·or·rhoid, *n. usu. pl.* dilation of a blood vein at the anus; a pile.

hemp, *n.* tall herb producing hashish and fibers for making rope or coarse fabrics.

hen, *n.* female fowl or bird.

hence, *adv.* from this place or time; therefore; thus; away.

hence·forth, *adv.* from this time forward. Also **hence·for·ward.**

hench·man, *n.* trusted follower or attendant.

hep·a·ti·tis, *n.* inflammation of the liver; liver disease.

her, *pron.* obj. and poss. case of **she.**

her·ald, *n.* bearer of messages; harbinger; announcer; forerunner. *v.* proclaim. **he·ral·dic,** *a.*

herb, *n.* plant used in medicines, scents, or seasonings. **her·ba·ceous,** *a.* **her·bage,** *n.*

her·biv·o·rous, *a.* plant-eating animal.

her·cu·lean, *a.* very great in strength, courage, size, or difficulty.

herd, *n.* group of animals traveling or feeding together. *v.* assemble together. **-er,** *n.* **herds·man,** *n.*

here, *adv.* in this place; now; at this point; present state. *n.* this place.

here·af·ter, *adv.* after this. *n.* life after death; future.

he·red·i·ty, n. pl., **-ties.** qualities genetically passed between generations; inheritance; tradition. **-tar·y,** a.

here·in, adv. in this place.

her·e·sy, n. pl., **-sies.** belief contrary to accepted doctrine. **-tic,** n. **he·ret·i·cal,** a. **he·ret·i·cal·ly,** adv.

here·to·fore, adv. until now.

her·i·tage, n. legacy; inherited property; birthright.

her·met·ic, a. airtight. Also **her·met·i·cal, her·met·i·cal·ly,** adv.

her·mit, n. recluse.

her·ni·a, n. rupture.

he·ro, n. pl., **he·roes.** courageous, valorous man. **-ic,** a., **her·o·ine,** n. fem., **her·o·ism,** n.

he·ro·ics, n. melodramatic talk or action meant to seem important.

her·o·in, n. addictive narcotic.

her·on, n. wading bird.

hers, pron. poss. case of **she.**

her·self, pron. form of **her.**

hes·i·tate, v., **-tat·ed, -tat·ing.** pause; doubt; stammer. **-i·tant,** a., **-tan·cy,** n. pl., **-cies. -ta·tion,** n.

het·er·o·ge·ne·ous, a. having dissimilar elements; mixed.

hew, v., **hewed, hewed** or **hewn, -ing.** chop; adhere. **-er,** n.

hex·a·gon, n. six-sided figure. **-ag·o·nal,** a.

hey, interj. exclamation to call attention or express surprise.

hey·day, n. prime period of vigor.

hi·ber·nate, v., **-nat·ed, -nat·ing.** pass the winter in a dormant state. **-na·tion,** n.

hic·cup, n. spasmodic intake of breath. v., **-cuped** or **-cupped, -cup·ing** or **-cup·ping.** Also **hic·cough.**

hide, v., **hid, hid·den** or **hid, hid·ing.** secrete; shield; conceal. n. animal pelt. **hid·er,** n.

hid·e·ous, a. extremely ugly; offensive; shocking. **-ness,** n.

hie, v., **hied, hie·ing** or **hy·ing.** to hasten; speed.

hi·er·ar·chy, n. pl., **-chies.** arrangement according to rank; authoritative body.

hi·er·o·glyph·ic, n. system of writing using pictographic inscriptions. Also **hi·er·o·glyph.**

high, a. lofty; elevated; tall; shrill; noble; serious. adv. at or to a high place. n. elevated region; sky.

high·fa·lu·tin, a. pompous.

high·flown, a. extravant in aims.

high-hat, a. inf. snobbish. v., **-hat·ted, -hat·ting.** snub.

high·light, v. to emphasize. n. best part; striking part.

high·ten·sion, a. high voltage.

high·way, n. public road.

hi·jack, high·jack, v. steal or commandeer an airplane, ship, etc·; to steal goods from smugglers, etc.

hike, v., **hiked, hik·ing.** to march, walk, tramp; raise with a jerk. n. march. **hik·er,** n.

hi·lar·i·ous, a. very funny; boisterous gaiety. **-i·ty,** n.

hill, n. conspicuous elevation of land; mound. **-y,** a., **-i·er, -i·est.**

hill·ock, n. small hill.

hilt, n. handle of a sword, dagger, tool, etc.

him, pron. obj. case of **he.**

him·self, pron. reflexive or emphatic form of **he.**

hind, a., **-er, -most** or **-er·most.** in the rear or back.

hin·der, v. impede; hamper; thwart. **-er,** n. **hin·drance,** n.

hind·sight, n. perception or understanding after the fact.

hinge, n. joint on which one thing turns on another. v., **hinged, hing·ing.** depend.

hint, n. suggestion; clue; trace. v. allude indirectly. **-er,** n.

hip, n. haunch; hip joint.

hip·po·pot·a·mus, n. pl., **-mus·es, -mi.** herbivorous African aquatic mammal.

hire, v. engage the services of for pay; employ. n. wages.

hire·ling, n. mercenary.

hir·sute, a. hairy; roughly hairy.

his, pron. of or belonging to him.

hiss, v. make condemning sound; make sibilant (s) sound. n.

his·to·ry, n. pl., **-ries.** record of past events; account. **-to·ri·an,** n. **his·tor·ic, his·tor·i·cal,** a.

his·tri·on·ic, a. theatrical; affected. Also **-i·cal. -i·cal·ly,** adv.

hit, v., **hit, hit·ting.** strike a blow; come into collision; find by chance; occur; reach; affect severely. n. impact; athletic stroke; blow; success.

hitch, v. fasten by a knot or hook; fasten onto; jerk. n. catch; hindrance.

hitch·hike, v., **-hiked, -hik·ing.** travel by obtaining free rides.

hith·er, adv. to this place.

hith·er·to, adv. up to this time.

hive, n. shelter for a colony of bees; pl. itchy skin eruptions.

hoard, *n.* articles preserved for future use; cache. *v.* lay away. **-ing,** *n.*

hoarse, a. (voice) sounding husky or harsh. **-ness,** *n.*

hoax, *n.* trick; dupe. *v.* play a trick on. **hoax·er,** *n.*

hob·ble, *v.,* **-bled, -bl·ing.** limp; cripple; impede. *n.* limp; fetter.

hob·by, *n. pl.,* **-bies.** activity carried on for pleasure; pastime.

hob·nob, *v.,* **-nobbed, -nob·bing.** associate familiarly.

ho·bo, *n. pl.,* **-boes, -bos.** tramp.

hock, *n.* tarsal joint. *v. inf.* pawn something.

hock·ey, *n.* team game played on ice or a field.

hod, *n.* trough for carrying mortar and bricks; coal bucket.

hodge·podge, *n.* jumble; mess.

hoe, *n.* tool used for loosening earth and weeding. *v.,* **hoed, hoe·ing.**

hog, *n.* swine. *v.,* **hogged, hog·ging.** be gluttonous; take more than one's share. **hog·gish,** *a.*

hoi pol·loi, *n.* common people.

hoist, *v.* to raise or lift. *n.* apparatus for hoisting.

hold, *v.,* **held, hold·ing.** have in the hand; keep in a certain position; contain; keep; possess; arrest; delay; constrain; support; reserve; comport; harbor; esteem; halt; adhere. *n.* interior of a ship. **hold·er,** *n.*

hold·ing, *n.* tenure of land; *often pl.* property.

hole, *n.* hollow place; cavity; opening; burrow; fault; gap. *v.,* **holed, hol·ing, hole·y,** *a.*

hol·i·day, *n.* day of rest; holy day; *pl.* vacation.

ho·li·ness,, *n.* being holy.

hol·ler, *v. inf.* cry out; shout. *n.* complaint.

hol·low, *a.* not solid; sunken; deep or low; muffled; false; meaningless. *n.* cavity. **-ness,** *n.*

hol·ly, *n. pl.,* **-lies.** trees or shrubs having red berries.

hol·o·caust, *n.* great destruction, usu. by fire, war, etc.; a sacrifice consumed by fire.

hol·ster, *n.* leather case for a pistol or revolver.

ho·ly, *a.,* **-li·er, -li·est.** consecrated to God; sacred; saintly.

hom·age, *n.* deference; respect.

home, *n.* dwelling; residence; house; habitat; headquarters. *a.* domestic; being the headquarters. *adv.* **-less,** *a.*

home·less, *n.* (*pl·*) group of people who live in streets or public shelters.

home·ly, *a.,* **-li·er, -li·est.** unattractive; plain; simple.

home·made, *a.* made at home.

home run, *n. baseball.* scoring run making circuit of all bases.

home·sick, *a.* ill or depressed by longing for home. **-ness,** *n.*

home·spun, *a.* plain. *n.* loosely woven homemade fabric.

home·ward, *a., adv.* toward home. Also **home·wards.**

home·y, hom·y, *a.,* **-i·er, -i·est.** *inf.* cozy; homelike.

hom·i·cide, *n.* killing of one human being by another; the killer. **-ci·dal,** *a.*

hom·i·ly, *n. pl.,* **-lies.** religious discourse; sermon; moralizing talk.

hom·i·ny, *n.* edible hulled corn, boiled.

ho·mo·gen·e·ous, *a.* uniform in structure; essentially alike.

ho·mog·e·nize, *v.,* **-nized, -niz·ing.** make homogeneous; blend into a mixture.

hom·o·nym, *n.* one of two or more words pronounced alike but different in meaning.

Ho·mo sa·pi·ens, *n.* modern man.

ho·mo·sex·u·al, *n.* one who has sexual feelings for persons of the same sex.

hone, *n.* whetstone used for sharpening instruments. *v.,* **honed, hon·ing.** sharpen on a hone.

hon·est, *a.* without deceit or fraud; truthful; legitimate; upright; sincere. **hon·es·ty,** *n. pl.,* **-ties.**

hon·ey, *n. pl.,* **-eys.** sweet syrupy fluid made by bees; nectar; sweetheart. *v.,* **-eyed** or **-ied, ey·ing.** flatter.

hon·ey·comb, *n.* structure of wax cells formed by bees for storing honey. *v.* pierce with many holes; subvert; weaken.

hon·ey·moon, *n.* holiday spent by a newly married couple.

hon·ey·suck·le, *n.* upright or climbing shrub with varicolored flowers.

honk, *n.* cry of a goose; any similar sound.

hon·or, *n.* public esteem; good name; privilege; credit; fame; glory; sense of moral standards; (*usu. cap.*) title; *pl.* civilities. *v.* confer honor; fulfill; respect; salute.

hon·or·a·ble, *a.* worthy of honor; ethical. **-bly,** *adv.*

hon·or·ar·y, *a.* bestowed in honor (without prerequisites); voluntary.

hood, *n.* cowl; anything that resembles a hood. **-ed,** *a.*

hood·lum, *n.* thug; mobster.

hood·wink, v. deceive; cheat; impose upon. **-er**, n.

hoof, n. pl., **hoofs, hooves.** horny covering encasing the end of the foot of some mammals.

hook, n. curved piece of metal adapted to catch, hold, or pull something. v. fasten or catch with a hook; curve. **hooked**, a. addicted.

hoop, n. circular strip; ring; basketball rim. **hooped, hoop-like**, a.

hoot, v. shout, esp. in contempt; cry as an owl. n. **-ing·ly**, adv.

hop, v., **hopped, hop·ping.** leap on one foot; jump over n. dance; inf. short trip.

hope, n. feeling that one's wish will come true; thing hoped for. v., **hoped, hop·ing.** long for. **hop·er**, n., **hope·ful**, a., **hope·less**, a.

hop·per, n. funnel-shaped receptacle for storing things.

horde, n. mob; pack; throng.

ho·ri·zon, n. apparent junction of earth and sky; range of one's experience.

hor·i·zon·tal, a. parallel to the horizon or base line; level.

hor·mone, n. glandular substance carried to organs and tissues. **-mo·nal**, a.

horn, n. bone growth on animal heads; wind instrument. **horned**, a., **horn·y**, a., **-i·er**, **-i·est.**

hor·net, n. large social wasp.

ho·rol·o·gy, n. science of measuring time; art of making timepieces.

hor·o·scope, n. diagram of the zodiac used by astrologers.

hor·ren·dous, a. dreadful; horrible. **-ly**, adv.

hor·ri·ble, a. conducive to horror; terrible. **-bly**, adv.

hor·rid, a. hideous; offensive; repulsive. **-ness**, n.

hor·ri·fy, v., **-fied, -fy·ing.** cause to feel horror; appall. **-fi·ca·tion**, n.

hor·ror, n. powerful feeling of fear; abhorrence, dread; consternation.

hors d'oeuvre, n. appetizer.

horse, n. pl., **hors·es, horse.** large domesticated herbivorous quadruped; supporting frame.

horse·rad·ish, n. herb with pungent root, used as condiment.

horse·shoe, n. U-shaped iron plate attached to a horse's hoof; pl. form of quoits.

hor·ti·cul·ture, n. science of growing vegetables, flowers, etc. **-tur·ist**, n.

ho·san·na, interj. exclamation of praise, adoration to God.

hose, n. pl., **hose.** pl. stockings.

hose, n. pl., **hos·es.** flexible tube. v., **hosed, hos·ing.** spray.

ho·sier·y, n. stockings; socks.

hos·pice, n. lodging for travelers.

hos·pi·ta·ble, a. being gracious to guests; cordial. **-tal·i·ty**, n. pl., **-ties.**

hos·pi·tal, n. institution in which persons are given medical care. **-ize**, v., **-i·za·tion**, n.

host, n. one who receives and entertains guests; animal with parasite; multitude. **-ess**, n. fem.

hos·tage, n. person held as a pledge.

hos·tile, a. antagonistic; of an enemy or like an enemy; unfriendly; forbidding. **-ly**, adv., **-til·i·ty,**, n. pl., **-ties.**

hot, a., **-ter, -test.** having a high temperature; very warm; pungent; passionate, inflamed; violent; eager; inf. stolen.

hot-blood·ed, a. excitable.

ho·tel, n. a public house offering lodging, food, etc. for travelers or for long-term resident guests.

hot·house, n. greenhouse.

hound, n. hunting dog; any dog. v. pursue relentlessly.

hour, n. 60 minutes; particular time; customary time. **hour·ly**, a., adv.

house, n. pl., **hous·es.** building where people live; legislative body; business organization. v., **housed, hous·ing.** lodge.

hous·ing, n. shelter; lodging; houses publicly provided.

hov·el, n. shed; mean dwelling; hut. v., **-eled, -el·ing.**

hov·er, v. hang fluttering or suspended in the air; wait nearby; remain uncertain; waver. **-ing**, a.

how, adv. in what way or manner; to what extent; in what condition; why; what. **how·ev·er**, adv. notwithstanding; yet; no matter how; to whatever extent. conj. in whatever manner or degree.

howl, v. utter a loud, mournful cry, as a dog; wail. n. **-er**, n.

how·so·ev·er, adv. in whatever way; by whatever means.

hub, n. central part of a wheel; center of activity; core.

hub·bub, n. tumult; uproar.

hu·bris, a. wanton insolence; arrogance.

huck·ster, n. peddler; haggling merchant. v.

hud·dle, v., **-dled, -dling.** crowd together; hunch oneself up. n. crowd; heap.

hue, *n.* color; shade; tint.

huff, *n.* feeling of anger. *v.* puff; blow. **-y**, *a.*, **huf·fi·er**, **huf·fi·est**.

hug, *v.*, **hugged**, **hug·ging**. embrace; keep close to; squeeze. *n.*

huge, *a.*, **hug·er**, **hug·est**. very large in bulk, quantity, area, etc.; enormous. **-ly**, *adv.* **-ness**, *n.*

hulk, *n.* unwieldy ship; deserted ship or wreck; clumsy or bulky thing or person. **-ing**, *a.*

hull, *n.* husk or outer shell of a seed or fruit; frame or body of a ship.

hum, *v.*, **hummed**, **-ming**. make a low droning sound; sing with lips closed. *n.* indistinct murmuring sound. **-mer**, *n.*

hu·man, *a.* of mankind or man. *n.* human being. **-ness**, *n.*

hu·mane, *a.* kind; tender; merciful. **-ly**, *adv.* **-ness**, *n.*

hu·man·i·tar·i·an, *a.* philanthropic. *n.* one who promotes the interests of all mankind.

hu·man·i·ty, *n. pl.*, **-ties**. mankind; quality of being human; branch of learning dealing with human thought and relations.

hum·ble, *a.*, **-bler**, **-blest**. modest; low in station; not proud. *v.*, **-bled**, **-bling**. abase. **-ble·ness**, *n.* **-bly**, *adv.*

hum·bug, *n.* hoax, fraud. *v.*, **-bugged**, **-bug·ging**. deceive; dupe. **-ger·y**, *n.*

hum·drum, *a.* dull; monotonous; boring.

hu·mid, *a.* full of water vapor; moist or damp. **-ly**, *adv.*

hu·mid·i·fy, *v.*, **-fied**, **-fy·ing**. make humid. **-fier**, *n.*

hu·mid·i·ty, *n.* dampness; moisture.

hu·mil·i·ate, *v.*, **-ated**, **-at·ing**. hurt a person's pride; mortify. **-ing**, *a.* **-a·tion**, *n.*

hu·mil·i·ty, *n.* quality of being humble.

hu·mor, *n.* quality of being funny; quality for perceiving the amusing; temperament. *v.* to indulge someone. **-ist**, *n.* **-ous**, *a.*

hump, *n.* rounded protuberance. *v. inf.* exert vigorously. **humped**, *a.* **-y**.

hu·mus, *n.* decayed plant and animal matter in soil.

hunch, *v.* assume crooked position; thrust forward; jostle; shove. *n.* push; lump; intuitive feeling.

hunch·back, *n.* deformed, curved back; humpback. **-backed**, *a.*

hun·ger, *n.* need for food; craving; eager desire. *v.* feel hunger. **-gry**, *a.*, **-gri·er**, **-gri·est**. **-gri·ness**, *n.*

hunk, *n. inf.* large piece; lump.

hunt, *v.* chase or search for; seek; pursue. *n.* chase; search. **-er**, *n.* **-ing**, *n.*

hur·dle, *n.* barrier to be jumped over; obstacle. *v.*, **-dled**, **-dling**. jump over, as in racing; overcome; surmount.

hurl, *v.* throw or fling forcefully; pitch. **-er**, *n.*

hur·rah, *int.* exclamation of joy, applause, etc. *n.* fanfare. *v.* cheer. Also **hur·ray**.

hur·ri·cane, *n.* violent tropical cyclone.

hur·ry, *v.*, **-ried**, **-ry·ing**. drive or impel to greater speed; go with haste; prod; expedite. *n.* urgency. **-ried**, *a.* **-ried·ly**, *adv.*

hurt, *v.*, **-ing**. inflict or feel pain; harm; damage; offend; hamper. *n.* anguish.

hur·tle, *v.*, **-tled**, **-tling**. move swiftly; hurl.

hus·band, *n.* married man. *v.* manage economically.

hush, *v.* silence; calm. *n.* silence; quiet.

husk, *n.* outer covering of fruits or seeds. *v.* strip off the husk. **-er**, *n.*

husk·y, *a.*, **-i·er**, **-i·est**. hoarse; robust; burly. **-i·ness**, *n.*

hus·sy, *n. pl.*, **huss·ies**. brazen woman or girl.

hus·tle, *v.*, **-tled**, **-tling**. shove; jostle; force hurriedly; work or move. *n.* hustling. **-tler**, *n.*

hut, *n.* small humble dwelling.

hutch, *n.* storage chest; low cupboard; animal coop; shack.

hy·a·cinth, *n.* bulbous spring plant with bell-shaped flowers.

hy·brid, *n.* offspring of genetically different species or parents. **-ism**, *n.*

hy·drant, *n.* upright discharge pipe with valves and water outlet.

hy·drau·lic, *a.* pertaining to or operated by water or other liquid. **-li·cal·ly**, *adv.*

hy·dro·e·lec·tric, *a.* pertaining to production of electricity by moving water.

hy·dro·gen, *n.* colorless, inflammable gas; lightest known element.

hy·dro·gen bomb, *n.* bomb using the fusion of hydrogen isotopes to produce a powerful explosion. Also **H-bomb**.

hy·dro·pho·bi·a, *n.* morbid fear of water; rabies.

hy·dro·phone, *n.* device for locating sources of sound under water.

hy·drous, *a.* containing water.

hy·e·na, *n.* nocturnal African and Asiatic animal, about size of a dog. Also **hy·ae·na**.

hy·giene, *n.* study of health; principles of health and cleanliness practices. **-gi·en·ic**, *a.* **-gi·en·i·cal·ly**, *adv.* **-gien·ist**, *n.*

hymn, *n.* song in praise of God.

hym·nal, *n.* book of hymns. Also **hymn·book**.

hy·per·crit·i·cal, *a.* overcritical.

hy·per·sen·si·tive, *a.* abnormally sensitive. **-tiv·i·ty,** *n.*

hy·per·ten·sion, *n.* high blood pressure.

hy·phen, *n.* short line (-) used to divide words. **-ate,** *v.*

hyp·no·sis, *n. pl.,* **-ses.** artificially induced sleepy state marked by susceptibility to suggestion. **-not·ic,** *a.* **-tize,** *v.*

hy·po·chon·dri·a, *n.* abnormal preoccupation with one's health; having imagined illnesses.

hy·poc·ri·sy, *n. pl.,* **-sies.** act of feigning feelings or beliefs; pretense of piety. **hyp·o·crite,** *n.*

hy·po·der·mic, *a.* pertaining to the injection of medical remedies under the skin.

hy·pos·ta·tize, *v.* to treat or regard as a reality.

hy·pot·e·nuse, *n.* side of a right triangle opposite the right angle.

hy·poth·e·sis, *n. pl.,* **-ses.** unproved theory; assumption; temporary explanation. **-e·size,** *v.,* **-sized, -siz·ing, -po·thet·i·cal,** *a.*

hys·ter·ec·to·my, *n.* removal of the uterus.

hys·te·ri·a, *n.* emotional frenzy. **-ter·ic,** *a.* **ter·i·cal,** *a.*

hys·ter·ics, *n. pl.* fit of hysteria.

I

I, *pron.* pron. by which a speaker or writer denotes himself.

i·bis, *n. pl.,* **i·bis·es, i·bis.** large heron-like wading bird.

ice, *n.* frozen water; state of coldness; sherbet. *v.,* **iced, ic·ing.** frost.

ice·berg, *n.* large floating mass of ice from a glacier.

ice cream, *n.* frozen dessert food made of buttercream.

i·ci·cle, *n.* hanging mass of ice.

ic·ing, *n.* cake frosting.

i·con, *n.* religious image.

i·con·o·clast, *n.* one who attacks established beliefs; destroyer of images. **-clasm,** *n.*

i·cy, *a.,* **i·ci·er, i·ci·est.** of ice; slippery; cold; unfriendly.

i·de·a, *n.* thought; notion; belief; scheme; plan.

i·de·al, *a.* achieving a standard of perfection. *n.* conception or standard of perfection; model person or thing; principle; goal. **-ism,** *n.* **-ist,** *n.*

i·de·al·ize, *v.,* **-ized, -iz·ing.** regard as ideal; make ideal. **-i·za·tion,** *n.*

i·den·ti·cal, *a.* exactly the same. **-ly,** *adv.* **-ness,** *a.*

i·den·ti·fy, *v.,* **-fied, -fy·ing.** recognize; connect closely; prove. **-fi·ca·tion,** *n.*

i·den·ti·ty, *n. pl.,* **-ties.** sameness; individuality.

i·de·ol·o·gy, *n. pl.,* **-gies.** system of ideas; doctrine.

id·i·om, *n.* expression peculiar to a people or language; dialect. **-o·mat·ic,** *a.*

id·i·o·syn·cra·sy, *n. pl.,* **-sies.** quirk; peculiarity.

id·i·ot, *n.* foolish or mentally retarded person. **-ot·ic,** *a.* **-i·o·cy,** *n. pl.,* **-cies.**

i·dle, *a.,* **-dler, -dlest.** doing nothing; useless; unemployed; futile; unfounded. *v.,* **-dled, -dling.** spend time inactively. **-ness,** *n.* **id·ly,** *adv.*

i·dol, *n.* false god; object or person worshiped.

i·dol·a·try, *n. pl.,* **-tries.** worship of idols. **a·ter,** *n.* **-a·trous,** *a.*

i·dol·ize, *v.,* **-ized, -iz·ing.** regard with adoration.

if, *conj.* in case that; even though; whether; supposition.

ig·nite, *v.,* **-nit·ed, -nit·ing.** set on fire; get excited; incite. **-ni·tion,** *n.*

ig·no·ble, *a.* mean; base.

ig·no·min·y, *n. pl.,* **-ies.** public disgrace; shame; dishonor.

ig·no·ra·mus, *n.* ignorant person.

ig·no·rant, *a.* lacking knowledge or experience; uninformed. **-rant·ly,** *adv.* **-rance,** *n.*

ig·nore, *v.,* **-nored, -nor·ing.** refuse to notice; disregard.

ilk, *n.* kind; sort.

ill, *a.* sick; evil; unfortunate; bad; adverse. **-ness,** *n.*

ill-ad·vised, *a.* imprudent; unwise.

il·le·gal, *a.* not legal; unlawful.

il·leg·i·ble, *a.* hard or impossible to read. **-bly,** *adv.*

il·le·git·i·mate, *a.* born out of wedlock; unlawful. **-ma·cy,** *n. pl.,* **-cies.**

il·lic·it, *a.* unlawful.

il·lit·er·ate, *a. n.* unable to read or write; uneducated; ignorant. **-a·cy,** *n. pl.,* **-cies.**

il·log·i·cal, *a.* contrary to logic or reason. **-ic,** *n.*

il·lu·mi·nate, *v.,* **-nat·ed, -nat·ing.** light up; make clear; enlighten; animate; decorate. **na·tion,** *n.*

il·lu·sion, *n.* false impression or belief; hallucination.

il·lu·so·ry, *a.* deceptive.

il·lus·trate, *v.,* **-trat·ed, -trat·ing.** make clear by examples; furnish with drawings or pictures. **-tra·tion,** *n.*

il·lus·tri·ous, *a.* distinguished.

im·age, *n.* likeness of a person or thing; mirror likeness; mental picture. -ag·er, *n.*

im·ag·i·nar·y, *a.* fancied.

im·ag·i·na·tion, *n.* act of forming mental images; resourcefulness. -tive, *a.*

im·ag·ine, *v.,* -ined, -in·ing. conceive; guess; visualize.

im·be·cile, *n.* mentally retarded person. *a.* retarded; foolish.

im·bibe, *v.,* -bibed, -bib·ing. drink; absorb. -bib·er, *n.*

im·bro·glio, *n.* confusing situation; disagreement.

im·brue, *v.* -brued, -bruins. wet; soak (usu· with blood.

im·bue, *v.,* -bued, -bu·ing. soak with color; permeate; impregnate feelings, etc.

im·i·tate, *v.,* -tat·ed, -tat·ing. copy; mimic.

im·i·ta·tion, *n.* act of imitating; a copy; counterfeit.

im·mac·u·late, *a.* spotless; innocent; perfect; pure.

im·ma·nent, *a.* inherent.

im·ma·te·ri·al, *a.* not pertinent.

im·ma·ture, *a.* not mature, ripe, developed. -tu·ri·ty, *n.*

im·meas·ur·a·ble, *a.* limitless.

im·me·di·ate, *a.* instant; without delay; nearest to; present time.

im·me·mo·ri·al, *a.* going back beyond memory or record.

im·mense, *a.* vast; very large; huge. -men·si·ty, *n.*

im·merse, *v.,* -mersed, -mers·ing. plunge or dip into, as in a fluid; to involve deeply. -mer·sion, *n.*

im·mi·grate, *v.,* -grat·ed, -grat·ing. move to a country to settle there. -grant, *n.* -gra·tion, *n.*

im·mi·nent, *a.* impending.

im·mo·bile, *a.* stationary.

im·mod·er·ate, *a.* not moderate; excessive; extreme.

im·mod·est, *a.* not modest; indecent; shameless; impudent.

im·mor·al, *a.* not moral; wicked.

im·mor·tal, *a.* lasting forever; enduring. -i·ty, *n.*

im·mov·a·ble, *a.* stationary.

im·mune, *a.* exempt; not susceptible. -mu·ni·ty, *n. pl.,* -ties.

im·mu·ta·ble, *a.* unchangeable; unalterable. -bil·i·ty, *n.*

imp, *n.* mischievous child.

im·pact, *n.* collision; force of a collision; shock; impinging.

im·pair, *v.* make worse; damage; weaken. -ment, *n.*

im·part, *v.* make known; tell.

im·par·tial, *a.* not partial; fair.

im·pas·sioned, *a.* filled with zeal.

im·pas·sive, *a.* without emotion.

im·pa·tient, *a.* anxious; intolerant. -tience, *n.*

im·peach, *v.* challenge; discredit; accuse an official of misconduct. -a·ble, *a.,* -ment, *n.*

im·pec·ca·ble, *a.* faultless.

im·pede, *v.,* -ped·ed, -ped·ing. obstruct; hinder; delay.

im·ped·i·ment, *n.* hindrance; physical defect, esp. a speech defect.

im·pel, *v.,* -pelled, -pel·ling. drive or urge forward; propel.

im·pend·ing, *a.* about to happen.

im·per·a·tive, *a.* urgent; obligatory; commanding; compelling.

im·per·fect, *a.* having defects.

im·per·fec·tion, *n.* defectiveness; shortcoming; blemish.

im·pe·ri·al, *a.* of an empire; majestic; of superior quality.

im·per·il, *v.,* -iled, -il·ing. endanger; put in peril. -ment, *n.*

im·pe·ri·ous, *a.* domineering.

im·per·ish·a·ble, *a.* indestructible; not subject to death or decay.

im·per·ma·nent, *a.* not lasting; temporary. -nence, *n.*

im·per·me·a·ble, *a.* not permitting (fluid) passage; impervious.

im·per·son·al, *a.* not personal; without personal reference or connection. -al·ly, *adv.*

im·per·son·ate, *v.,* -at·ed, -at·ing. pretend to be or assume the appearance, etc., of someone; mimic. -a·tion, *n.*

im·per·ti·nent, *a.* rude; insolent; irrelevant.

im·per·vi·ous, *a.* incapable of being passed through; not affected by.

im·pe·ti·go, *n.* contagious skin disease marked by pustules.

im·pet·u·ous, *a.* impulsive; rash; moving with great force; rushing.

im·pe·tus, *n. pl.,* -tus·es. force of motion; stimulus; incentive.

im·pinge, *v.* strike; hit; make inroads; encroach. -ment, *n.*

im·pi·ous, *a.* not reverent. -e·ty, *n. pl.,* -ties.

im·plac·a·ble, *n.* not to be pacified or appeased; stubborn.

im·plant, v. fix firmly; embed; plant deeply; instill. n. organ or device inserted in body.

im·plan·ta·tion, n.

im·plau·si·ble, a. provoking disbelief.

im·ple·ment, n. tool; utensil; means to an end. v. provide means for accomplishing.

im·pli·cate, v., **-cat·ed, -cat·ing.** involve in a matter; imply.

im·pli·ca·tion, n. act of implying; something implied.

im·plic·it, a. suggested though not clearly expressed; implied; inherent; absolute.

im·plode, v. burst inward.

im·plore, v., **-plied, -ply·ing.** entreat; beg; beseech.

im·ply, v. **-plied, ply·ing.** hint; signify; suggest.

im·po·lite, a. discourteous; rude.

im·po·li·tic, a. unwise; injudicious.

im·pon·der·a·ble, a. that cannot be measured or explained.

im·port, v. bring in (goods) from a foreign country; signify. n. thing imported; meaning.

im·por·tance, n. significance; consequence. **-tant**, a.

im·por·tune, v., **-tuned, -tun·ing.** bother with demands; annoy; trouble.

im·pose, v., **-posed, pos·ing.** act by authority; force on; foist. **-im·po·si·tion**, n.

im·pos·ing, a. impressive in size, dignity. **-ly**, adv.

im·pos·si·ble, a. incapable of occurring. **-bil·i·ty**, n. pl., **-ties. -bly**, adv.

im·pos·tor, n. one who deceives under an assumed character or name of another; pretender.

im·po·tent, a. lacking strength; ineffective; helpless; lacking sexual power. **-tence, -ten·cy**, n.

im·pound, v. seize and retain; confine.

im·pov·er·ish, v. reduce to poverty; deprive of resources.

im·prac·ti·ca·ble, a. not practicable; unsuitable.

im·prac·ti·cal, a. not practical.

im·pre·cate, v. pray for; invoke (evil).

im·pre·cise, a. not definite.

im·preg·na·ble, a. not able to be captured or entered; firm.

im·preg·nate, v., **-nat·ed, -nat·ing.** make pregnant; fill or saturate; imbue; fertilize.

im·pre·sa·ri·o, n. pl., **-ri·os.** organizer of an opera or concert company.

im·pre·scrip·ti·ble, a. inviolable.

im·press, v. stamp or imprint; affect deeply; urge; influence. **-pres·sion**, n.

im·pri·ma·tur, n. permission to publish or print a book, etc.

im·print, v. mark; impress; fix.

im·pris·on, v. incarcerate.

im·prob·a·ble, a. not likely.

im·promp·tu, a., adv. offhand; without preparation.

im·prop·er, a. not suitable.

im·pro·pri·e·ty, n. indecorous remark or action; improper use of a word.

im·prove, v., **-proved, -prov·ing.** make better. **-ment**, n.

im·prov·i·dent, a. lacking foresight.

im·pro·vise, v., **-vised, -vis·ing.** extemporize; prepare hastily or offhand. **im·pro·vi·sa·tion**, n.

im·pru·dent, a. indiscreet; rash.

im·pu·dent, a. disrespectful.

im·pugn, v. attack by argument or criticism.

im·pulse, n. a force, esp. one that occurs for a short time and produces motion; a sudden mental urge to act.

im·pu·ni·ty, n. exemption from punishment.

im·pure, a. foul; unclean; not morally pure; corrupt. **-ly**, adv. **-pu·ri·ty**, n. pl., **-ties.**

im·pute, v., **-put·ed, -put·ing.** attribute; ascribe.

in, prep. inclusion within space, time, place, situation, action, etc.; during; comprising, action, manner, relation, etc. adv. into; within; on the inside. n. those who are in power.

in·a·bil·i·ty, n. lack of power, means, capability, or ability.

in ab·sen·ti·a, adv. during one's absence; although not present.

in·ac·ces·si·ble, a. impossible to reach.

in·ac·cu·ra·cy, n. error; mistake. **-rate**, a.

in·ac·tive, a. inert; idle; sluggish.

in·ad·e·quate, a. not adequate; insufficient; lacking.

in·ad·mis·si·ble, a. not allowed.

in·ad·vert·ent, a. unintentional.

in·ad·vis·a·ble, a. unwise; not prudent.

in·al·ien·a·ble, a. not capable of being taken away or transferred.

in·am·o·ra·ta, n. sweetheart; mistress.

in·ane, a. empty; foolish; silly.

in·an·i·mate, a. without life; dull.

in·an·i·ty, n. pl., **-ties.** emptiness; silliness.

in·ap·pre·ci·a·ble, a. negligible.

in·ap·pro·pri·ate, a. unsuitable.

in·ar·tic·u·late, a. mute; not able to speak effectively.

in·as·much as, *conj.* insofar as; seeing that; since; because.

in·au·gu·rate, *v.*, **-rat·ed**, **-rat·ing**. install or induct into office; begin. **-ra·tion**, *n.*

in·aus·pi·cious, *a.* unfavorable; unlucky.

in·born, *a.* innate; hereditary.

in·cal·cu·la·ble, *a.* beyond calculation; uncertain.

in·can·des·cent, *a.* glowing or white with heat; bright; brilliant. **-cence**, *n.*

in·ca·pa·ble, *a.* not capable; unable; lacking ability. **-bly**, *adv.*

in·ca·pac·i·tate, *v.*, **-tat·ed**, **-tat·ing**. make unfit; disable.

in·car·cer·ate, *v.* imprison; jail; confine.

in·car·nate, *v.*, **-nat·ed**, **-nat·ing**. invest with a bodily form; personify. **-na·tion**, *n.*

in·cen·di·ar·y, *a.* setting on fire; tending to promote strife, sedition, etc.; inflammatory.

in·cense, *n.* substance burned for its sweet odor. *v.*, **-censed**, **-cens·ing**. make or be angry.

in·cen·tive, *n.* motive; stimulus.

in·cep·tion, *n.* beginning; start.

in·ces·sant, *a.* continuous.

in·cest, *n.* sexual intercourse between close blood relations. **-ces·tu·ous**, *a.*

inch, *n.* measure, one-twelfth of a foot. *v.* move by small degrees.

in·cho·ate, *a.* just begun; not yet formed.

in·ci·dence, *n.* extent or range of occurrence.

in·ci·dent, *n.* occurrence; happening; event.

in·ci·den·tal, *a.* occurring with; accidental; casual. *n. pl.*, minor expenses. **-ly**, *adv.*

in·cin·er·ate, *v.*, **-at·ed**, **-at·ing**. burn; cremate. **-a·tor**, *n.*

in·cip·i·ent, *a.* in the beginning stage; beginning to exist.

in·ci·sion, *n.* cut; gash; slit.

in·ci·sive, *a.* cutting; sharp; acute.

in·cite, *v.*, **-cit·ed**, **-cit·ing**. move to action; stir up; urge on.

in·clem·ent, *a.* severe; rough.

in·cli·na·tion, *n.* leaning; slope; liking.

in·cline, *v.*, **-clined**, **-clin·ing**. cause to lean or bend; slant; tend. *n.* slope; grade. **-cli·na·tion**, *n.* **-clined**, *a.*

in·clude, *v.*, **-clud·ed**, **-clud·ing**. put within limits; contain; categorize. **-clu·sion**, *n.* **-clu·sive**, *a.*

in·cog·ni·to, *a.* having a concealed identity; disguised. *adv.*

in·co·her·ent, *a.* illogical; confused.

in·come, *n.* money received from labor, investments, etc.

in·com·pa·ra·ble, *a.* unequaled.

in·com·pat·i·ble, *a.* not harmonious.

in·com·pe·tent, *a.* unable; inadequate; not legally qualified.

in·com·plete, *a.* not finished.

in·com·pre·hen·si·ble, *a.* not understandable.

in·con·ceiv·a·ble, *a.* unimaginable; unthinkable; incredible.

in·con·clu·sive, *a.* leading to no result.

in·con·gru·ous, *a.* out of place; inappropriate; unsuitable.

in·con·se·quen·tial, *a.* of no consequence; trivial; irrelevant.

in·con·sid·er·ate, *a.* thoughtless.

in·con·sis·tent, *a.* not consistent; lacking agreement.

in·con·spic·u·ous, *a.* not conspicuous or prominent.

in·con·ti·nent, *a.* unrestrained; unable to hold.

in·con·ven·ience, *n.* troublesome; a bother; discomfort *v.*, **-ienced**, **-ienc·ing**. **-ient**, *a.*

in·cor·po·rate, *v.*, **-rat·ed**, **-rat·ing**. form a corporation; combine or merge. **-ra·tion**, *n.*

in·cor·rect, *a.* not correct; inaccurate; faulty; improper. **-ly**, *adv.*

in·cor·ri·gi·ble, *a.* not capable of being reformed or improved.

in·crease, *v.*, **-creased**, **-creas·ing**. make greater; grow; add to. *n.* growth or augmentation. **-creas·a·ble**, *a.*

in·cred·i·ble, *a.* unbelievable.

in·cred·u·lous, *a.* skeptical.

in·cre·ment, *n.* increase; gain.

in·crim·i·nate, *v.*, **-nat·ed**, **-nat·ing**. accuse; implicate.

in·cu·ba·tor, *n.* temperature-controlled apparatus for artificially hatching eggs or for premature babies.

in·cul·cate, *v.* teach by repetition.

in·cum·bent, *a.* lying or resting upon; obligatory; holder of an office.

in·cur, *v.*, **-curred**, **-cur·ring**. become liable or subject to.

in·cur·a·ble, *a.* not curable.

in·debt·ed, *a.* beholden. **-ness**, *n.*

in·de·cent, *a.* offensive; obscene. **-cen·cy**, *n. pl.*, **-cies**.

in·de·ci·sion, *n.* irresolution.

in·deed, *adv.* in fact; in truth; truly. *int.* expression of surprise.

in·de·fat·i·ga·ble, *a.* untiring.

in·def·i·nite, *a.* not definite; without fixed limit; not clearly defined; not precise. **-ly**, *adv.*

in·de·fen·si·ble, *a.* not justified.

in·del·i·ble, *a.* incapable of being destroyed or obliterated. **-bly**, *adv.*

in·del·i·cate, *a.* coarse; immodest.

in·dem·ni·fy, *v.,* **-fied, -fy·ing.** insure; repay. **-ni·ty,** *n.*

in·de·pend·ent, *a.* free from influence or bias of others; not relying on others. **-ence,** *n.*

in·de·scrib·a·ble, *a.* surpassing description; not describable.

in·de·struct·i·ble, *a.* incapable of being destroyed. **-bly,** *adv.*

in·dex, *n. pl.,* **-dex·es, -di·ces.** alphabetical list, facilitating reference; forefinger; sign or indication.

in·di·cate, *v.,* **-cat·ed, -cat·ing.** point out; show; signify. **-ca·tion,** *n.* **-dic·a·tive,** *a.*

in·dict, *v.* accuse or charge with a crime; implicate. **-ment,** *n.*

in·dif·fer·ent, *a.* without interest or concern; neutral. **-ence,** *n.*

in·dig·e·nous, *a.* native; innate.

in·di·gent, *a., n.* needy; poor; destitute. **-gence,** *n.*

in·di·ges·tion, *n.* difficulty in digesting food; stomach disorder.

in·dig·nant, *a.* showing displeasure at what seems unjust or unworthy. **-ly,** *adv.* **-na·tion,** *n.*

in·dig·ni·ty, *n. pl.,* **-ties.** humiliating affront, insult, or injury.

in·di·rect, *a.* roundabout.

in·dis·creet, *a.* unwise; not prudent; lacking judgment. **-cre·tion,** *n.*

in·dis·crim·i·nate, *a.* random; promiscuous. **-nat·ing,** *a.*

in·dis·pen·sa·ble, *a.* absolutely necessary or requisite.

in·dis·posed, *a.* mildly ill; averse; unwilling. **-po·si·tion,** *n.*

in·dis·tinct, *a.* obscure; fuzzy.

in·di·vid·u·al, *a.* single; separate; peculiar to a person or thing; unique. *n.* single person or thing; particular person. **-i·ty,** *n. pl.,* **-ties.**

in·di·vis·i·ble, *a.* that cannot be divided.

in·doc·tri·nate, *v.,* **-nat·ed, -nat·ing.** instruct; teach; inculcate; imbue. **-na·tion,** *n.*

in·do·lent, *a.* lazy; idle.

in·dom·i·ta·ble, *a.* unyielding.

in·du·bi·ta·ble, *a.* unquestionable.

in·duce, *v.,* **-duced, -duc·ing.** persuade; bring on; produce; cause. **-ment,** *n.*

in·duct, *v.* lead or bring in. **-duct·ee,** *n.* **in·duc·tion,** *n.* **-duc·tive,** *a.*

in·duc·tile, *a.* not pliant.

in·dulge, *v.,* **-dulged, -dulg·ing.** gratify; yield; humor. **-dul·gence,** *n.*

in·du·rate, *v.* harden; make callous.

in·dus·tri·al, *a.* of industry.

in·dus·tri·ous, *a.* hardworking; zealous; diligent. **-ly,** *adv.*

in·dus·try, *n. pl.,* **-tries.** trade; manufacturing; business; diligence in work.

in·e·bri·ate, *v.,* **-at·ed, -at·ing.** intoxicate; exhilarate. *n.* drunkard. **-a·tion,** *n.*

in·ed·u·ca·ble, *a.* incapable of learning.

in·ef·fa·ble, *a.* too overwhelming to describe; unutterable.

in·ef·fec·tive, *a.* not effective; inefficient. **-ness,** *n.* **-tual,** *a.*

in·el·i·gi·ble, *a.* not eligible; not qualified. **-bil·i·ty,** *n.*

in·ept, *a.* not apt, fitted or suitable; inappropriate. **-i·tude,** *n.*

in·ert, *a.* having no power to move or act; inactive; sluggish.

in·er·tia, *n.* inert condition; inactivity; property of matter by which it retains its state of rest or of motion. **-tial,** *a.*

in·es·cap·a·ble, *a.* inevitable.

in·es·ti·ma·ble, *a.* too great to be measured.

in·ev·i·ta·ble, *a.* sure to happen; unavoidable.

in·ex·o·ra·ble, *a.* unalterable.

in·ex·pert, *a.* not skilled.

in·ex·pli·ca·ble, *a.* incapable of being explained or understood.

in·ex·tri·ca·ble, *a.* that cannot escape; unsolvable.

in·fal·li·ble, *a.* never wrong; reliable.

in·fa·my, *n. pl.,* **-mies.** shameful notoriety; wickedness. **-mous,** *a.*

in·fant, *n.* baby. *a.* in the earliest stage of progress. **in·fan·cy,** *n. pl.,* **-cies.**

in·fan·tile, *a.* childish; immature.

in·fan·try, *n. pl.,* **-tries.** foot soldiers.

in·fat·u·ate, *v.,* **-at·ed, -at·ing.** inspire with or possess foolish passion. **-a·tion,** *n.*

in·fect, *v.* contaminate with disease; contaminate morally; taint. **-fec·tion,** *n.* **-fec·tious,** *a.*

in·fer, *v.,* **-ferred, -fer·ring.** derive or conclude by reasoning; imply. **-ence,** *n.*

in·fe·ri·or, *a.* lower in place or position; of poor quality. **-i·ty,** *n.*

in·fer·nal, *a.* hellish; diabolical.

in·fer·tile, *a.* barren; sterile.

in·fest, *v.* overrun; swarm; be parasitic. **-fes·ta·tion,** *n.*

in·fi·del, *n.* disbeliever; atheist.

in·fi·del·i·ty, *n. pl.,* **-ties.** disloyalty; unfaithfulness.

in·fil·trate, *v.,* **-trat·ed, -trat·ing.** permeate; filter into.

in·fi·nite, *a.* endlessly great.

in·fin·i·tes·i·mal, *a.* infinitely small; close to zero.

in·fin·i·tive, *n.* verb form which expresses meaning without specifying person or number.

in·fin·i·ty, *n.* boundlessness.

in·firm, *a.* feeble; weak; vacillating. **-ness,** *n.*

in·fir·ma·ry, *n. pl.,* **-ries.** small hospital; place for the sick.

in·fir·mi·ty, *n. pl.,* **-ties.** physical weakness or ailment.

in·flame, *v.,* **-flamed, -flam·ing.** set afire; excite; kindle; cause redness and swelling. **-flam·ma·tion,** *n.*

in·flam·ma·ble, *a.* easily burned or angered.

in·flate, *v.,* **-flat·ed, -flat·ing.** distend; swell; elate; raise. **-fla·tion,** *n.*

in·flect, *v.* modulate, as the voice; to bend; decline or conjugate. **-flec·tion,** *n.*

in·flict, *v.* strike; afflict; cause to suffer from; impose. **-flic·tion,** *n.* **in·flic·tive,** *a.*

in·flu·ence, *v.,* **-enced, -enc·ing.** sway; affect; exert power. *n.*

in·flu·en·za, *n.* highly contagious virus disease. Also **flu.**

in·flux, *n.* act of flowing in.

in·form, *v.* impart knowledge. **in·formed,** *a.* **in·for·mer,** *n.*

in·for·mal, *a.* unofficial; casual; familiar use. **-mal·ly,** *adv.*

in·for·ma·tion, *n.* news; facts; data; knowledge. **-tive,** *a.*

in·fra·red, *a.* heat rays beyond red of the visible spectrum.

in·fre·quent, *a.* not often; rare.

in·fringe, *v.,* **-fringed, -fring·ing.** violate; encroach. **-ment,** *n.*

in·fu·ri·ate, *v.,* **-at·ed, -at·ing.** anger; enrage. **-a·tion,** *n.*

in·fuse, *v.,* **-fused, -fus·ing.** inspire; pour into; instill. **-fu·sive,** *a.* **-fu·sion,** *n.*

in·gen·ious, *a.* clever; inventive; resourceful. **in·ge·nu·i·ty,** *n.*

in·gé·nue, *n.* naive, innocent, unworldly girl.

in·gest, *v.* swallow; absorb.

in·got, *n.* mass of cast metal.

in·grain. *v.* fix deeply and firmly; infuse. **-grained,** *a.*

in·gra·ti·ate, *v.* to establish (oneself) in the favor or good graces of others.

in·grat·i·tude, *n.* lack of gratitude; unthankfulness.

in·gre·di·ent, *n.* one of the substances in a mixture.

in·gress, *n.* act of entering; entrance.

in·hab·it, *v.* live in; occupy; dwell. **-ed,** *a.* **-ant,** *n.*

in·hale, *v.,* **-haled, -hal·ing.** draw in by breathing.

in·her·ent, *a.* existing in something as an inseparable element or attribute.

in·her·it, *v.* to receive anything by heredity; receive a legacy. **-ance,** *n.*

in·hib·it, *v.* restrain; hinder; forbid; arrest. **-hi·bi·tion,** *n.*

in·hos·pi·ta·ble, *a.* not offering protection; barren; forbidding.

in·hu·man, *a.* not human; brutal; cruel; savage.

in·im·i·ta·ble, *a.* unmatched.

in·iq·ui·ty, *n. pl.,* **-ties.** gross injustice; sin; wickedness.

in·i·tial, *a.* of the beginning. *n.* first letter of a word or name. *v.* **-tialed, -tial·ing.** mark with one's initials. **-tial·ly,** *adv.*

in·i·ti·ate, *v.,* **-at·ed, -at·ing.** originate; begin; admit to membership; introduce. **-a·tion,** *n.* **-a·tor,** *n.*

in·i·ti·a·tive, *n.* introductory act; enterprise; referendum.

in·ject, *v.* force a fluid into; interject. **-jec·tion,** *n.*

in·ju·di·cious, *a.* indiscreet; unwise.

in·junc·tion, *n.* act of ordering or directing; writ; admonition.

in·jure, *v.,* **-jured, -jur·ing.** wrong; impair; do harm to; hurt; offend. **-ju·ry,** *n. pl.,* **-ries. -ju·rious,** *a.*

in·jus·tice, *n.* wrong; unjust act.

ink·ling, *n.* hint; suggestion.

in·laid, *a.* set in pieces to form surface decoration.

in·let, *n.* narrow water passage or entrance.

in·mate, *n.* person confined; occupant of hospital, prison, etc.

inn, *n.* public house; tavern.

in·nate, *a.* inborn; native; congenital; hereditary.

in·ner, *a.* interior; private.

in·ner·vate, *v.,* **-vat·ed, -vat·ing.** to stimulate.

in·no·cent, *a.* free from sin, guilt, etc.; blameless; candid; ignorant; unaware. **-cence,** *n.*

in·noc·u·ous, *a.* inoffensive; harmless; insipid.

in·no·vate, *v.,* **-vat·ed, -vat·ing.** something new. **-va·tion,** *n.* **-va·tive,** *a.*

in·nu·en·do, *n. pl.,* **-dos, -does.** insinuation; hint; allusion.

in·nu·mer·a·ble, *a.* countless.

in·oc·u·late, v., **-lat·ed, -lat·ing.** vaccinate; introduce something into. **-la·tion,** n. **-la·tor,** n.

in·op·er·a·ble, a. not suitable for surgery.

in·op·por·tune, a. inconvenient, unreasonable.

in·or·gan·ic, a. of matter not animal or plant; mineral.

in·pa·tient, n. person who gets housing and food as well as treatment at a hospital.

in·put, n. anything put in, as power into a machine; data put into the computer.

in·quest, n. legal or judicial inquiry or investigation.

in·quire, v., **-quired, -quir·ing.** ask for information; investigate. **-quir·y,** n. pl., **-ies.**

in·qui·si·tion, n. act of inquiring or investigating.

in·quis·i·tive, a. desirous of knowledge; unduly curious.

in·road, n. usu. pl. encroachment; raid; invasion.

in·sane, a. not sane; mad; senseless. **-san·i·ty,** n. pl., **-ties.**

in·sa·tia·ble, a. incapable of being satisfied; quenchless.

in·scribe, v., **-scribed, -scrib·ing.** write or engrave; enroll. **-scrip·tion,** n.

in·scru·ta·ble, a. hard to grasp; mysterious.

in·sect, n. small arthropod having three pairs of legs and usually wings.

in·se·cure, a. prone to fear or doubt; anxious; shaky.

in·sen·sate, a. lacking sensation, feeling, understanding, or judgment.

in·sen·si·ble, a. unconscious; unfeeling; apathetic.

in·sep·a·ra·ble, a. incapable of being separated. **-bly,** adv.

in·sert, v. put or set in; interpolate. n. something inserted. **-ser·tion,** n.

in·side, n. inner side or surface; interior. a. within; internal. adv. on the inside. prep. within.

in·sid·i·ous, a. treacherous.

in·sight, n. mental vision or discernment; perception.

in·sig·ni·a, n. pl. badges of office, honor, etc.; emblems.

in·sig·nif·i·cant, a. unimportant; trifling. **-cance,** n.

in·sin·u·ate, v., **-at·ed, -at·ing.** hint or suggest slyly; imply. **-a·tion,** n.

in·sip·id, a. tasteless; dull; flat.

in·sist, v. demand emphatically and firmly; assert. **-ence,** n. **-ent,** a.

in·so·lent, a. disrespectful; rude. **-lence,** n.

in·sol·u·ble, a. incapable of being dissolved or solved. n.

in·som·ni·a, n. abnormal inability to sleep. **-ac,** n., a.

in·spect, v. examine carefully. **-spec·tion,** n. **-spec·tor,** n.

in·spire, v., **-spired, -spir·ing.** arouse or affect with a feeling or thought; influence; impel; inhale. **-spi·ra·tion,** n.

in·spis·sate, v. make thick or thicker.

in·sta·ble, a. unstable.

in·stall, v. position for use; induct into an office. **-stal·la·tion,** n.

in·stall·ment, n. any of the divisions of a debt, story, etc.

in·stance, n. example; a case.

in·stant, a. immediate; urgent. n. very short space of time; a moment.

in·stan·ta·ne·ous, a. occurring or completed within an instant.

in·stead, adv. in the place of; in lieu of.

in·step, n. arched middle part of the human foot.

in·sti·gate, v., **-gat·ed, -gat·ing.** incite; foment. **-ga·tion,** n.

in·still, v., **in·stilled, in·still·ing.** introduce drop by drop; impart gradually. **-stil·la·tion,** n.

in·stinct, n. innate, inborn impulse; natural aptitude. **-stinc·tive,** a. Also **-stinc·tu·al.**

in·sti·tute, v., **-tut·ed, -tut·ing.** establish; inaugurate; begin. n. society for carrying on a particular work. **-tu·tion,** n.

in·struct, v. teach; inform; order. **-struc·tion,** n. **-struc·tor,** n.

in·stru·ment, n. tool; means; utensil; implement; musical device. **-men·tal,** a.

in·suf·fer·a·ble, a. intolerable; unendurable; unending.

in·suf·fi·cient, a. not sufficient; inadequate. **-cien·cy,** n.

in·su·late, v., **-lat·ed, -lat·ing.** cover or surround to prevent the passage of electricity, heat, etc.; isolate. **-la·tion,** n.

in·su·lin, n. pancreatic hormone used for treating diabetes.

in·sult, n. affront; rude action or speech. v. treat insolently or rudely.

in·sure, v., **-sured, -sur·ing.** make sure; guarantee against risk or loss. **-sur·ance,** n.

in·sur·gen·cy, n. state of revolt against a government.

in·sur·rec·tion, n. revolt.

in·tact, a. unimpaired; unaltered; uninjured; whole.

in·tan·gi·ble, *a.* impalpable; abstract.

in·te·ger, *n.* whole number 0, 1, 2, etc., as distinguished from a fraction.

in·te·gral, *a.* whole; necessary; constituent part. **-ly**, *adv.*

in·te·grate, *v.*, **-grat·ed**, **-grat·ing**. bring into a whole; make available equally to all; unite. **-gra·tion**, *n.*

in·teg·ri·ty, *n.* honesty; soundness; unimpaired condition.

in·teg·u·ment, *n.* skin; shell; rind, etc.

in·tel·lect, *n.* power to know or understand; mental capacity; intelligence. **-lec·tu·al**, *a.*

in·tel·li·gence, *n.* ability to understand and reason; intellectual power; information; shrewdness. **-gent**, *a.*

in·tel·li·gi·ble, *a.* comprehensible; capable of being understood.

in·tem·per·ance, *n.* immoderation; excessive drinking.

in·tend, *v.* design, mean or plan. **-er**, *n.* **-ed**, *a.*

in·tense, *a.* very great or strong; existing in extreme degree; considerable. **-ten·sive**, *a.* **-ten·si·ty**, *n.*

in·ten·si·fy, *v.*, **-fied**, **-fy·ing**. make intense; strengthen; sharpen.

in·tent, *a.* concentrated; engrossed; earnest. *n.* design; purpose; significance.

in·ten·tion, *n.* purpose; end; design; import. **-al**, *a.*

in·ter, *v.*, **in·terred**, **in·ter·ring**. bury. **-ment**, *n.*

in·ter·act, *v.* act on one another. **-ac·tion**, *n.*

in·ter·breed, *v.*, **-bred**, **-breed·ing**. crossbreed.

in·ter·cede, *v.*, **-ced·ed**, **-ced·ing**. interpose or plead on behalf of. **-ces·sion**, *n.*

in·ter·cept, *v.* take or seize while on the way; stop or check. **-cep·tion**, *n.* **-cep·tive**, *a.*

in·ter·change, *v.*, **-changed**, **-chang·ing**. to change one for another; transpose; exchange reciprocally. *n.* exchange; alternate succession; highway intersection.

in·ter·con·ti·nen·tal, *a.* between continents.

in·ter·cos·tal, *a.* between the ribs.

in·ter·course, *n.* dealings or communications between persons or nations; copulation.

in·ter·est, *n.* attention or curiosity; ownership share; benefit; money paid for the use of money. **-ed**, *a.* **-ing**, *a.*

in·ter·face, *n.* surface forming common boundary.

in·ter·fere, *v.*, **-fered**, **-fer·ing**. meddle. **-ference**, *n.*

in·ter·ga·lac·tic, *a.* between galaxies.

in·ter·im, *n.* intervening time; interval. *a.* temporary.

in·te·ri·or, *a.* being within; situated inland; internal. *n.* inside part of a building or room.

in·ter·ject, *v.* throw in abruptly; interpose.

in·ter·jec·tion, *n.* act of interjecting; exclamation of emotion or passion.

in·ter·lock, *v.* lock on with another; to fit together.

in·ter·lop·er, *n.* intruder.

in·ter·mar·ry, *v.*, **-mar·ried**, **-mar·ry·ing**. marry between different races, religions, etc., or within the limits of the family. **-riage**, *n.*

in·ter·me·di·ate, *a.* situated between two points. *v.*, **-at·ed**, **-at·ing**. intervene; mediate.

in·ter·mi·na·ble, *a.* endless.

in·ter·mis·sion, *n.* space of time between periods of action; interruption; pause.

in·ter·mit, *v.*, **-mit·ted**, **-mit·ting**. stop for a time. **-mit·tent**, *a.* alternately starting and stopping.

in·tern, *n.* medical graduate in a hospital acting as assistant; person in training but not yet hired as a regular employee. *v.* confine or hold within an area. **-ship**, *n.*

in·ter·nal, *a.* of the inside; situated in the interior; inner. **-ly**, *adv.*

in·ter·na·tion·al, *a.* between or among nations; pertaining to different nations. **-ize**, *v.*, **-ized**, **-iz·ing**.

in·ter·plan·e·tar·y, *a.* situated within the solar system.

in·ter·play, *n.* reciprocal play.

in·ter·po·late, *v.*, **-lat·ed**, **-lat·ing**. alter by insertion of new or spurious material. **-la·tion**, *n.*

in·ter·pose, *v.*, **-posed**, **-pos·ing**. place between; intervene; come between. **-po·si·tion**, *n.*

in·ter·pret, *v.* explain; translate; construe. **-pre·ta·tion**, *n.*

in·ter·ro·gate, *v.*, **-gat·ed**, **-gat·ing**. examine by questions; ask questions. **-ga·tion**, *n.*

in·ter·rupt, *v.* break in; break off; hinder. **-rup·tion**, *n.* **-rup·tive**, *a.*

in·ter·sect, *v.* cut into; divide by passing through; cross. **-sec·tion**, *n.*

in·ter·sperse, *v.*, **-spersed**, **-spers·ing**. scatter; diversify. **-sper·sion**, *n.*

in·ter·state, *a.* between states.

in·ter·val, *n.* intervening period of time; space between things.

in·ter·vene, *v.*, **-vened**, **-ven·ing**. come between; interpose. **-ven·tion**, *n.*

in·ter·view, *n.* face-to-face meeting for a talk or evaluation, or to secure information; the conversation. *v.* **-er,** *n.*

in·tes·tate, *a.* without a will.

in·tes·tine, *n. often pl.* part of alimentary canal from stomach to anus. **-ti·nal,** *a.*

in·ti·mate, *a.* private; personal; familiar. *v.,* **-mat·ed, -mat·ing.** hint; suggest. **-ma·tion.** *n.,* a hint; suggestion. *n.* confidant.

in·tim·i·date, *v.,* **-dat·ed, -dat·ing.** make timid; frighten. **-da·tor,** *n.*

in·to, *prep.* to the inside of; to change to.

in·tol·er·a·ble, *a.* unendurable.

in·tol·er·ant, *a.* bigoted; prejudiced. **-ance,** *n.*

in·to·na·tion, *n.* change in pitch of the voice, esp. the pitch pattern of a sentence.

in·tox·i·cate, *v.,* **-cat·ed, -cat·ing.** make drunk or to drug; excite mentally. **-ca·tion,** *n.*

in·trac·ta·ble, *a.* obstinate.

in·tra·mu·ral, *a.* within the walls or limits of an institution.

in·tran·si·gent, *a.* uncompromising.

in·tran·si·tive, *a.* of a verb having no direct object.

in·tra·per·son·al, *a.* within mind or self.

in·tra·state, *a.* within a state.

in·tra·ve·nous, *a.* within a vein or injection into a vein.

in·trep·id, *a.* fearless

in·tri·cate, *a.* entangled; complicated. **-ca·cy,** *n. pl.,* **-cies. -ly,** *adv.*

in·trigue, *v.,* **-trigued, -tri·guing.** arouse the curiosity of; plot; scheme. *n.* machination; plot; secret love affair. **-tri·guing,** *a.*

in·trin·sic, *a.* inherent; essential.

in·tro·duce, *v.,* **-duced, -duc·ing.** make acquainted; present; bring to notice; bring forward; insert. **-duc·tion,** *n.*

in·tro·spec·tion, *n.* self-examination.

in·tro·vert, *v.* direct the mind inward. *n.* one concerned chiefly with his own thoughts. **-vert·ed,** *a.*

in·trude, *v.,* **-trud·ed, -trud·ing.** to thrust oneself in uninvited. **-trud·er,** *n.*

in·tu·i·tion, *n.* perception without reasoning; insight. **-tive,** *a.*

in·ure, *v.,* **-ured, -ur·ing.** become used to pain, etc.; harden.

in·vade, *v.,* **-vad·ed, -vad·ing.** enter with force; intrude upon. **-va·sion,** *n.* **-vad·er,** *n.*

in·va·lid, *n.* disabled person; sickly one.

in·val·id, *a.* not valid.

in·val·u·a·ble, *a.* priceless.

in·var·i·a·ble, *a.* constant.

in·vent, *v.* originate; contrive; fabricate. **-ven·tion,** *n.*

in·ven·to·ry, *n. pl.,* **-ries.** list of assets; stock.

in·verse, *a.* opposite in order.

in·vert, *v.* turn upside down; reverse position. **-ver·sion,** *n.*

in·ver·te·brate, *a.* having no spinal column. *n.* animal having no backbone.

in·vest, *v.* clothe; install; envelop; besiege; infuse; put (money) into, for a profit. **-ves·tor,** *n.* **-ment,** *n.*

in·ves·ti·gate, *v.,* **-gat·ed, -gat·ing.** inquire into; examine; observe. **-ga·tion,** *n.*

in·ves·ti·ture, *n.* act of establishing in office; clothing.

in·vet·er·ate, *a.* confirmed; established; habitual.

in·vid·i·ous, *a.* envious; obnoxious.

in·vig·or·ate, *v.,* **-at·ed, -at·ing.** fill with life and energy.

in·vin·ci·ble, *a.* unconquerable.

in·vi·o·la·ble, *a.* unassailable; sacred.

in·vis·i·ble, *a.* imperceptible.

in·vite, *v.,* **-vit·ed, -vit·ing.** ask to come or go somewhere; request the presence of; allure. **in·vi·ta·tion,** *n.*

in·voice, *n.* itemized list of items sold to purchaser; bill.

in·voke, *v.,* **-voked, -vok·ing.** call upon in prayer; appeal to.

in·vol·un·tar·y, *a.* not voluntary

in·volve, *v.,* **-volved, -volv·ing.** include as necessary; affect; bring into; entangle. **-ment,** *n.*

in·vul·ner·a·ble, *a.* immune to attack.

in·ward, *adv.* toward the inside; in the mind. *a.* internal; located inside. Also **in·wards.**

i·o·dine, *n.* nonmetallic element used as an antiseptic.

i·on, *n.* electrically charged atom.

i·o·ta, *n., a.* jot; very tiny amount.

i·rate, *a.* enraged; angry.

ire, *n.* anger; wrath.

ir·i·des·cent, *a.* play of colors producing rainbow effect.

i·ris, *n. pl.,* **-ris·es, i·ris·es.** colored portion of the eye; plant having showy flowers.

irk, *v.* annoy; irritate. **-some,** *a.*

i·ron, *n.* metallic element; something hard; appliance for pressing cloth. *pl.* fetters. *a.* of iron. *v.* press clothing.

i·ron·clad, *a.* covered with iron; rigid or strict.

i·ron·y, *n. pl.,* **-nies.** figure of speech in which the literal meaning is the opposite of the intended meaning. **i·ron·ic,** *a.* Also **i·ron·i·cal.**

ir·ra·di·ate, *v.,* **-at·ed, -at·ing.** illuminate; heal by radiation. **-a·tion,** *n.*

ir·ra·tion·al, *a.* without reason; illogical. **-al·i·ty,** *n.*

ir·rec·on·cil·a·ble, *a.* not reconcilable; incompatible.

ir·re·deem·a·ble, *a.* not redeemable; inconvertible; hopeless.

ir·re·duc·i·ble, *a.* not reducible.

ir·ref·u·ta·ble, *a.* incapable of being proved wrong.

ir·reg·u·lar, *a.* not conforming; uneven shape; not in accordance with rules or customs. **-i·ty,** *n.*

ir·rel·e·vant, *a.* not relevant; not pertinent. **-vance,** *n.*

ir·re·me·di·a·ble, *a.* irreparable.

ir·re·mis·si·ble, *a.* not remissible; unpardonable.

ir·rep·a·ra·ble, *a.* not reparable.

ir·re·place·a·ble, *a.* cannot be replaced.

ir·re·press·i·ble, *a.* incapable of being repressed or held back.

ir·re·proach·a·ble, *a.* innocent; faultless; blameless.

ir·re·sist·i·ble, *a.* not resistible; tempting; not opposable.

ir·res·o·lute, *a.* uncertain.

ir·re·spec·tive, *a.* without regard to something.

ir·re·spon·si·ble, *a.* unreliable.

ir·rev·er·ence, *n.* lack of reverence or respect; irreverent conduct, words, etc. **-ent,** *a.*

ir·rev·o·ca·ble, *a.* irreversible.

ir·ri·gate, *v.,* **-gat·ed, -gat·ing.** water by artificial means; flush with a liquid. **-ga·tion,** *n.*

ir·ri·ta·ble, *a.* readily excited to impatience or anger.

ir·ri·tate, *v.,* **-tat·ed, -tat·ing.** make impatient or angry; provoke; vex. **-ta·tion,** *n.*

is, *v.* third person pres. sing. of the verb **be.**

is·land, *n.* land, smaller than a continent, surrounded by water.

i·so·late, *v.,* **-lat·ed, -lat·ing.** place apart; separate; detach. **-la·tion,** *n.*

i·sos·ce·les, *a.* triangle having two equal sides.

is·sue, *n.* offspring; matter in dispute; quantity printed at one time. *v.,* **-sued, -su·ing.** give forth; distribute; publish; emit.

isth·mus, *n.* strip of land connecting two larger bodies of land.

it, *pron.* third person sing. neuter pron. corresponding to **he** and **she.**

i·tal·ic, *n. usu. pl.* printing in which the letters slope to the right.

i·tal·i·cize, *v.,* **-cized, -ciz·ing.** use italics; underscore with a single line.

itch, *v.* have an irritation of the skin which causes a desire to scratch. *n.* itching; desire to get or do something. **itch·y,** *a.*

i·tem, *n.* separate article or particular; single detail of any list.

i·tem·ize, *v.,* **-ized, -iz·ing.** state or list by items.

i·tin·er·ant, *a.* traveling from place to place. *n.* traveler.

i·tin·er·ar·y, *n. pl.,* **-ies.** travel route; account of a journey.

its, *pron., a.* poss. case of **it.**

it·self, *pron.* reflexive or emphatic form of **it.**

i·vo·ry, *n. pl.,* **-ries.** hard white substance from the tusks of elephants, walrus, etc. *a.* of ivory.

J

jab, *v.,* **jabbed, jab·bing.** poke or thrust sharply. *n.* a poke.

jab·ber, *v.* talk rapidly, indistinctly, foolishly. *n.* chatter.

jack, *n.* mechanical device for raising weights; playing card; electric plug-in receptacle, *v.* raise or move as with a jack.

jack·ass, *n.* male donkey; fool.

jack·et, *n.* short protective outer garment; coat; outer casing.

jack·knife, *n. pl.,* **-knives.** large pocketknife; type of dive. *v.,* **-knifed, -knif·ing.** bend in the middle like a jackknife.

jack·pot, *n.* the stakes which accumulate during poker game; highest price; unexpected reward.

jade, *n.* hard green gemstone. **jad·ed,** *a.* worn out; bored; sated.

jag·uar, *n.* large, ferocious black-spotted feline.

jail, *n.* prison. *v.* imprison.

jai·a·lai, *n.* court game similar to handball.

ja·lop·y, *n. pl.,* **-ies.** *inf.* old, dilapidated car.

jal·ou·sie, *n.* window blind with adjustable slats.

jam, *v.,* **jammed, jam·ming.** squeeze tightly between bodies or surfaces; fill or block up; render unworkable by wedging. *n.* act of jamming; crowded mass that obstructs; fruit preserve; *inf.* predicament.

jamb, *n.* side piece of a doorway, window, or opening.

jam·bo·ree, *n.* boy scout rally; *inf.* noisy merry making; carousal.

jan·gle, *v.,* **-gled, -gling.** *n.* to sound harshly or discordantly; quarrel.

jan·i·tor, *n.* caretaker of a building; doorkeeper.

Jan·u·ar·y, *n.* first month of the year.

jar, *n.* broad-mouthed vessel. *v.* **jarred, jar·ring.** make a harsh sound; jolt; shake. *n.* harsh, grating sound; jolt.

jar·di·niere, *n.* ornamental flower stand.

jar·gon, *n.* unintelligible talk; language of a class, trade, or profession.

jaun·dice, *n.* disease causing yellow skin; affect with prejudice, envy. *v.* distorted views.

jaunt, *v.*, *n.* (make) a short pleasure trip or journey.

jaun·ty, *a.*, **-ti·er, -ti·est.** easy and sprightly; smartly trim, as dress.

jave·lin, *n.* light wooden spear.

jaw, *n.* one of two bones that form framework of the mouth. *v.* scold; gossip.

jazz, *n.* dance music with syncopated rhythms.

jazz·y, *a.*, **-i·er, -i·est.** *inf.* lively; gaudy; flashy.

jeal·ous·y, *n. pl.*, **-ies.** envious resentment; suspicious uneasiness. **jeal·ous**, *a.*

jean, *n. pl.* clothes made of denim, usu. for work clothes or casual wear.

jeep, *n.* small military or all-purpose motor vehicle.

jeer, *v.*, *n.* ridicule; deride.

Je·ho·vah, *n.* God.

je·june, *a.* not nutritious; dull; unsatisfying.

jel·ly, *n. pl.*, **-lies.** soft gelatinous food preparation of pectin, boiled fruit juice and sugar.

jel·ly·fish, *n. pl.*, **-fish, -fish·es.** gelatinous sea animal with long, trailing tentacles.

jeop·ar·dy, *n.* hazard or risk of loss or harm; danger. **-dize**, *v.*, **-dized, -diz·ing.**

jerk, *v.*, *n.* (give a) quick sharp pull, or twitch; spasm. **-y**, *a.*, **-i·er, -i·est.** *n. inf.* a fool.

jer·sey, *n.* soft, elastic knitted fabric; close-fitting garment.

jest, *n.* joke; jeer; banter.

Je·sus, *n.* founder of Christian religion.

jet, *n.* a shooting forth; spout in a stream; jet engine; jet plane. *v.*, **jet·ted, jet·ting.**

jet·sam, *n.* goods thrown overboard to lighten a vessel.

jet·ti·son, *v.* to throw overboard.

jet·ty, *n. pl.*, **-ties.** protective pier extending into the water.

Jew, *n.* believer in Judaism; Hebrew; Israelite.

jew·el, *n.* gem; precious possession; person of great worth.

jew·el·er, *n.* one who designs, repairs, or deals in jewelry.

jew·el·ry, *n.* articles for personal adornment.

jib, *n.* triangular sail in front of the foremast; arm of a crane.

jig, *n.* lively dance; device for holding or guiding a tool. *v.*, **jigged, jig·ging.**

jig·gle, *v.*, **-gled, -gling.** move with short, quick jerks.

jig saw, *n.* narrow saw for curved or irregular cuts.

jilt, *v.* discard or cast off (a lover) unfeelingly.

jim·my, *n. pl.*, **-mies.** short crowbar. *v.*, **-mied, -my·ing.**

jin·gle, *v.*, *n.*, **-gled, gling.** (make) a tinkling or clinking sound. *n.* short, catchy tune.

jinx, *n. inf.* anything that brings bad luck.

jit·ney, *n.* small bus with regular schedule.

jit·ter, *v. inf.* behave nervously. **jit·ters**, *n. pl. inf.* nervousness. **jit·ter·y**, *a.*

job, *n.* piece of work; the object worked on; task. *v.*, **jobbed, job·bing.** work by the piece; buy and sell by the lot; let out work. **job·ber**, *n.*

job lot, *n.* miscellaneous goods sold by a jobber.

jock·ey, *n. pl.*, **-eys.** race-horse rider. *v.*, **-eyed, -ey·ing.** maneuver for advantage; trick; cheat.

jo·cose, *a.* joking; playful or jesting.

joc·u·lar, *a.* joking; merry. **-i·ty**, *n.*

joc·und, *a.* cheerful; merry.

jodh·purs, *n. pl.* riding breeches.

jog, *v.*, **jogged, -ging.** shake with a push; trot at a slow, steady pace. **-ger**, *n.*

join, *v.* connect; bring or put together; become a member. *n.*

joint, *n.* connection allowing movement; the joining of two or more bones; *inf.* disreputable place. *a.* shared by two or more. *v.* unite by a joint. **-ed**, *a.* **-ly**, *adv.*

joist, *n.* horizontal timber supports for floor or ceiling.

joke, *n.* thing said or done to cause laughter; or done in fun or to tease. *v.* jok·er, *n.*

jol·ly, *a.*, **-li·er, -li·est.** merry; jovial; joyous.

jolt, *v.* jar, disturb composure. *n.* jarring blow; shock.

josh, *v. inf.* banter, tease.

jos·tle, *v.*, **-tled, -tling.** bump; push; shove; elbow.

jot, *n.* a tiny amount. *v.*, **-ted, -ting.** write down hurriedly.

jour·nal, *n.* a diary; a record of occurrences or transactions; newspaper or magazine.

jour·nal·ism, *n.* occupation of writing for or conducting a periodical. **-ist**, *n.*

jour·ney, *n.* a trip. *v.* to travel.

jour·ney·man, *n. pl.*, **-men.** one who has served his apprenticeship and works for another.

jo·vi·al, *a.* jolly; merry; good-humored.

jowl, *n.* the under jaw; the cheek; fold of skin under the jaw.

joy, *n.* happiness; pleasure; delight. **-ful, -ous,** *a.*

ju·bi·la·tion, *n.* a rejoicing; exaltation. **-lant,** *a.*

ju·bi·lee, *n.* celebration of the 25th, 50th, 60th, or 75th anniversary; a commemoration or festivity.

Ju·da·ism, *n.* Jewish religion.

judge, *v.* **judged, judg·ing.** hear and decide, as a court case; form an opinion; pass judgment. *n.* one who judges; court official.

judg·ment, *n.* act of judging; decision; verdict; good sense; discernment.

ju·di·cial, *a.* relating to courts of law, justice or judges.

ju·di·ci·ar·y, *a.* judicial; *n.* court system; judges.

ju·di·cious, *a.* showing sound judgment; discreet; prudent.

ju·do, *n.* method of self-defense; jujitsu.

jug, *n.* vessel for holding liquids, usu. with handle and spout.

jug·ger·naut, *n.* object that crushes whatever is in its path. *n. cap.* Hindu divinity.

jug·gle, *v.* perform feats of manual or bodily dexterity. *n.* act of juggling; deception.

jug·u·lar, *a.* the throat or neck; large veins of the neck.

juice, *n.* liquid or moisture from plants or animals. **juic·y,** *a.*

ju·jit·su, *n.* style of Japanese defense; judo.

Ju·ly, *n.* seventh month.

jum·ble, *v., n.* (mix) in a disorderly mass.

jum·bo, *a.* very large.

jump, *v.* spring into the air; bypass; move suddenly; leap over. *n.*

jump·er, *n.* one who jumps; a sleeveless dress.

jump·y, *a.* nervous, excited.

junc·tion, *n.* act or place of joining or meeting.

junc·ture, *n.* point of union; connection; point of time.

June, *n.* sixth month.

jun·gle, *n.* tropical forest.

jun·ior, *a.* lower in rank or younger in standing; third year of four year school.

ju·ni·per, *n.* evergreen tree or shrub with purple berries.

junk, *n.* discarded articles; scrap; Oriental ship.

jun·ket, *n.* custardlike pudding; pleasure trip (usu·) made at public expense.

jun·ta, *n.* a meeting; council.

ju·ris·dic·tion, *n.* power, range, or area of authority or control.

ju·ris·pru·dence, *n.* science or philosophy of law; body of laws or court decisions.

ju·rist, *n.* one versed in law; judge; lawyer.

ju·ror, *n.* member of a jury.

ju·ry, *n. pl.,* **-ries.** group selected to give a verdict.

just, *a.* reasonable; righteous; deserved; fair; proper; legal. *adv.* exactly; barely.

jus·tice, *n.* righteousness; equitableness; lawfulness; a judge.

jus·ti·fy, *v.,* **-fied, -fy·ing.** show to be just, right, warranted; absolve. **-fi·ca·tion,** *n.* **-fi·a·ble,** *a.*

jut, *v.* extend beyond the main body; project or protrude out.

jute, *n.* strong fiber used for bags, cordage, etc.

ju·ve·nile, *a.* young; immature. *n.* young person; youth.

jux·ta·pose, *v.* place side by side.

K

ka·bob, *n.* cubes of meat cooked on a skewer.

ka·lei·do·scope, *n.* tube that shows various colors and symmetrical forms by means of bits of glass and mirrors.

kan·ga·roo, *n. pl.,* **-roos, roo.** herbivorous, pouched, leaping Australian marsupial.

ka·put, *a. slang.* destroyed; useless; done for.

kar·at, *n.* measure of fineness of gold or weight of gems.

ka·ra·te, *n.* Japanese method of combat and self-defense.

kay·ak, kai·ak, *n.* Eskimo canoe.

keel, *n.* center piece stretching along bottom of a ship from stern to stern.

keen, *a.* sharp, mentally acute or perceptive; intense; enthusiastic. **-ly,** *adv.*

keep, *v.* **kept, keep·ing.** retain; save; reserve; tend; fulfill; protect; hold in custody; continue. *n.* food and shelter; care.

keep·ing, *n.* just conformity; custody or care.

keg, *n.* small barrel or cask.

kelp, *n.* large, brown seaweed.

ken·nel, *n.* dog shelter; place where dogs are bred, boarded, or held.

ker·chief, *n.* cloth head covering; handkerchief.

ker·nel, *n.* inner softer part of a nutshell, seed, fruit stone; central part; nucleus; core.

ker·o·sene, *n.* distilled oil for heating, lighting, etc.

ket·tle, *n.* metallic vessel used for boiling liquids, in cooking foods, etc.

ket·tle·drum, *n.* drum of brass or copper, with a skin head that can be tuned.

key, *n.* instrument for fastening or opening a lock; essential person or thing; a means of explaining, understanding, or solving; part pressed in operating a piano, typewriter, etc.; musical tone. *a.* chief; major; fundamental.

key·board, *n.* row of keys on a piano, typewriter, etc.

key·note, *n.* note on which a system of tones is founded; fundamental idea; main policy speech.

key·stone, *n.* stone at summit of an arch which locks the whole; something on which other things depend.

khak·i, *n., a.* (cloth of) yellowish-brown color; military uniform.

kick, *v.* strike with the foot; recoil; *inf.* thrill.

kick·off, *n.* kicking the ball to begin play in football; commencement of something.

kid, *n.* young goat, or its skin; *inf.* child. *v. inf.* tease; banter.

kid·nap, *v.* abduct a person or child, usu. for ransom.

kid·ney, *n.* bean-shaped organ which excretes urine.

kill, *v.* deprive of life; destroy; defeat; put an end to.

kiln, *n.* oven used to bake, dry, or burn, esp. brick or ceramics.

kil·o·cy·cle, *n.* unit equal to 1000 cycles per second.

kil·o·gram, *n.* weight equal to 1000 grams.

kil·o·me·ter, *n.* metric unit of length equal to 1000 meters.

kil·o·watt, *n.* unit of energy equal to 1000 watts of electric power.

kilt, *n.* knee-length pleated skirt, usu. tartan, worn esp. by men in Scotland.

ki·mo·no, *n.* loose Japanese robe with wide sleeves and broad sash; loose dressing gown.

kin, *n.* one's relatives.

kind, *n.* variety, sort; species; category; the same way. *a.* good; sympathetic; considerate. **-ly,** *a., adv.* **-ness,** *n.*

kin·der·gar·ten, *n.* school for young pre-school children.

kind·heart·ed, *a.* kindly.

kin·dle, *v.* set on fire; excite; arouse; provoke.

kin·dling, *n.* material for lighting a fire.

kin·dred, *n.* relatives. *a.* related; similar.

ki·net·ic, *a.* of the motion between bodies and forces; lively; dynamic.

king, *n.* male ruler of a nation; playing card; chess piece.

king·dom, *n.* realm of a king, queen; realm or sphere of influence or control.

kink, *n.* twist or tight curl; whim; mental quirk. **kink·y,** *a.*

kin·ship, *n.* family relationship; affinity.

kins·man, *n. pl.,* **-men.** male relative; person of the same race.

ki·osk, *n.* open pavilion.

kiss, *v.* touch with the lips in greeting or affection.

kit, *n.* set of tools, supplies, for a special purpose; case containing these items.

kitch·en, *n.* room with cooking facilities.

kite, *n.* light paper-covered frame to fly in the wind; hawk.

kit·ten, *n.* young cat. Also **kit·ty.**

kit·ty, *n.* stakes in a card game.

klep·to·ma·ni·a, *n.* neurotic impulse to steal.

knack, *n.* special skill; aptitude.

knap·sack, *n.* supply case carried on the back of travelers.

knave, *n.* dishonest, unprincipled person; rogue.

knead, *v.* work, press, and squeeze dough into a mixture.

knee, *n.* joint between the thigh and lower part of the leg.

kneel, *v.,* **knelt** or **kneeled,** **-ing.** fall or rest on the knees.

knell, *n.* funeral bell.

knick·knack, *n.* a pleasing trifle; a trinket; trivial article.

knife, *n. pl.,* **knives.** cutting implement with thin blade and handle. *v.* slash or stab with a knife.

knight, *n.* medieval mounted soldier; *Br.* man holding honorary title *Sir;* chess piece.

knit, *v.,* **knit·ted** or **knit,** **knit·ting.** weave; form fabric by interlacing yarn; join closely. *n.* a knitted fabric. **-ting,** *n.*

knob, *n.* rounded handle; lump.

knock, *v.* strike a blow; to rap; make a pounding noise; *inf.* criticize. *n.* a rap.

knoll, *n.* small round hill; mound.

knot, *n.* interlacement of rope, cord, etc.; cluster of persons or things; lump in wood where a branch has grown; a nautical mile per hour. *v.,* **-ted,** **-ting.** to tie a knot or become entangled.

knot·ty, *a.* full of knots; involved, intricate, as a problem.

know, *v.,* **knew, known, know·ing.** perceive or understand as fact or truth; to be aware of, familiar with, skilled in.

know·ing, *a.* shrewd; astute.

knowl·edge, *n.* facts, truths, principles gained by experience, study or investigation.

knowl·edge·a·ble, *a.* wise.

knuck·le, *n.* joint of a finger. *v.* yield; submit; apply oneself earnestly.

ko·a·la, *n.* Australian tree marsupial.

Ko·ran, *n.* sacred scriptures of Islam.

ko·sher, *a.* fit, lawful, ritually permitted according to Jewish dietary laws.

ku·chen, *n.* sweet dough coffee cake.

kum·quat, *n.* small yellow-orange citrus fruit.

L

la·bel, *n.* paper slip or other material on an object to indicate contents, brand, destination, owner, etc. *v.,* **-beled, -bel·ing.**

la·bi·al, *a.* of the lips.

la·bor, *n.* work; expenditure of effort; human activity that provides goods and services; persons engaged in work; task; process of childbirth. *v.* work; toil; move with effort. **-er,** *n.*

lab·o·ra·to·ry, *n. pl.,* **-ries.** building or room with apparatus for scientific investigation.

la·bored, *a.* laboriously formed; not easy or natural.

la·bo·ri·ous, *a.* requiring much labor.

lab·y·rinth, *n.* maze.

lace, *n.* string used for drawing two edges together; delicate fabric. *v.* intertwine. **laced,** *a.* **lac·ing,** *n.* **lac·y,** *a.*

lac·er·ate, *v.,* **-at·ed, -at·ing.** tear roughly; mangle. **-a·tion,** *n.*

lack, *n.* deficiency of something desired or needed. *v.* be deficient in.

lack·a·dai·si·cal, *a.* spiritless.

lack·ey, *n.* manservant; servile follower; footman; toady.

lack·lus·ter, *a.* dull.

la·con·ic, *a.* brief; concise.

lac·quer, *n.* varnish producing a hard, glossy surface. *v.* coat with lacquer.

lac·tic, *a.* of or from milk.

lad, *n.* young man; boy; youth.

lad·der, *n.* frame of wood, metal, with cross-pieces forming steps for climbing.

lade, *v.,* **lad·ed, lad·en** or **lad·ed, lad·ing.** to burden or load; to fill abundantly.

la·dle, *n.* deep-bowled long-handled spoon; dipper. *v.* **-dled, -dling.**

la·dy, *n.* polite term for any woman; noblewoman.

lag, *v.,* **lagged, lag·ging.** fall behind; linger; loiter. *n.* a falling behind; retardation.

lag·gard, *a.* backwards; dilatory; slow. *n.* one who lags.

la·gniappe, *n.* small gift from a merchant.

la·goon, *n.* shallow body of water near a larger one. Also **la·gune.**

la·i·cal, *a.* lay; secular. *n.* layman.

laid, pt. and pp. of **lay.**

lain, pp. of **lie.**

lair, *n.* den of a wild beast.

la·i·ty, *n. pl.,* **-ties.** church members not part of clergy.

lake, *n.* sizable body of standing water; surrounded by water.

lam, *v.,* **lammed, lam·ming.** *inf.* flee hastily; beat. *n. inf.* escape.

lamb, *n.* young sheep; its meat; innocent person.

lam·baste, *v.,* **-bast·ed, -bast·ing.** *inf.* beat severely.

lame, *a.,* **lam·er, lam·est.** crippled, esp. in the legs or feet; disabled. *v.,* **lamed, lam·ing.** make lame or defective. **lame·ly,** *adv.*

la·mé, *n.* fabric of interwoven metallic and other threads.

la·ment, *v.* mourn; regret; wail. *n.* elegy. **lam·en·ta·tion,** *n.*

lam·i·nate, *v.,* **-nat·ed, -nat·ing.** split into thin layers; construct by placing layer upon layer. **-na·tion,** *n.*

lamp, *n.* device, usu. decorative, for providing artificial light.

lam·poon, *n.* malicious satire.

lam·prey, *n. pl.,* **-preys.** eellike animal with sucking mouth.

lance, *n.* sharp-pointed shaft. *v.,* **lanced, lanc·ing.** make an incision in; hurl.

land, *n.* solid, exposed part of the earth's surface; soil; a region or country. *v.* bring, bring down or come to land; disembark; gain. **-ed, -ing,** *n.*

land·locked, *a.* enclosed by land; cut off from the sea.

land·lord, *n.* owner who leases land, etc., to others; innkeeper.

land·mark, *n.* conspicuous object that serves as a guide or distinguishes a locality.

land·scape, *n.* natural scenery; picture of natural scenery; amount one sees in one look. *v.,* **-scaped, -scap·ing.** improve the landscape. **-scap·er,** *n.*

land·slide, *n.* sliding of soil or rock down a slope; overwhelming victory.

lane, *n.* narrow way or passage; fixed route.

lan·guage, *a.* drooping; listless; lacking in spirit or vigor.

lan·guish, v. be or become weak, feeble, or spiritless; pine with desire for. **-ing,** a.

lan·guor, n. lassitude; weakness; apathy; weariness.

lank, a. meagerly slim; lean; gaunt. **-ness,** n.

lank·y, a., **-i·er, -i·est.** ungracefully thin and tall.

lan·o·lin, n. fatty substance extracted from wool.

lan·tern, n. transparent protective case for enclosing a light.

lap, v., **lapped, lap·ping.** fold; wrap; overlap; lick or take up with the tongue. n. part from the waist to the knees when sitting; amount by which an object overlaps; racecourse circuit; a complete turn; segment.

la·pel, n. front facings of a garment that are turned back.

lap·i·dary, n. one who works with precious stones.

lapse, n. trivial error; passage of time; slipping downward; discontinuance. v., **lapsed, laps·ing.** to err; slip into ruin.

lar·ce·ny, n. pl., **-nies.** theft; wrongful taking. **lar·ce·nous,** a.

lard, n. rendered fat of hogs. v. dress for cooking; garnish.

lar·der, n. a pantry.

large, a., **larg·er, larg·est.** of great size in amount, number, or extent.

large·ly, adv. to a great extent; mainly; extensively.

lar·gess, lar·gesse, n. generous gifts.

lar·i·at, n. lasso; long light rope.

lark, n. singing bird; frolic; prank.

lar·va, n. pl., **-vae.** second stage in the life cycle of an insect. **-val,** a.

lar·yn·gi·tis, n. inflammation of the larynx.

lar·ynx, n. pl., **-es** or **la·ryn·ges.** upper part of the trachea containing vocal cords. **la·ryn·ge·al,** a.

la·sag·na, n. broad, flat noodles; Italian dish with noodles, tomato, cheese and beef.

las·civ·i·ous, a. lustful; lewd. **-ly,** adv.

la·ser, n. device emitting an intense, direct light beam.

lash, n. whip; assail with words. v. whip; goad; move violently; bind. **-ing, -er,** n.

lass, n. girl; young woman.

las·si·tude, n. weariness; fatigue; listlessness.

las·so, n. pl., **-sos** or **-soes.** lariat; long rope with a running noose. v. catch with a lasso.

last, a. occurring or coming latest, after all the others; utmost. adv. finally. v. endure; continue.

last·ing, a. enduring.

last·ly, adv. finally; in conclusion.

latch, n. fastening for a door or gate. v. secure.

late, a., **lat·er** or **lat·ter, lat·est** or **last.** after the usual time; far advanced; dead; recent. **-ly,** adv. recently. **-ness,** n. **lat·er,** a. adv.

la·tent, a. hidden; dormant. **la·ten·cy,** n.

lat·er·al, a. of or toward a side. **-ly,** adv.

la·tex, n. pl., **-es** or **lat·i·ces.** milky juice of certain plants, source of chicle and rubber.

lath, n. thin, narrow supporting board. **-er, -ing,** n.

lathe, n. machine for holding and shaping wood, metal, etc.

lath·er, n. foam or froth made from water and soap or profuse sweat, as on a horse. v. **-y,** a.

lat·i·tude, n. distance from the equator measured in degrees; freedom from restrictions.

la·trine, n. toilet.

lat·ter, a. second of two; later.

lat·tice, n. crossed strips with spaces between. **-ticed,** a.

laud·a·ble, a. praiseworthy; commendable. **-to·ry,** a.

laugh, v. express amusement, etc., with an explosive voice sound. n. act or sound of laughing. **-a·ble,** a. **-ter,** n.

launch, v. propel; hurl; catapult; send off; set afloat; initiate. n. type of motorboat.

laun·der, v. wash and iron clothes. **-er,** fem. **dress,** n.

laun·dry, n. pl., **-dries.** place for laundering; articles of clothes to be washed.

lau·rel, n. small evergreen tree with flowers; pl. honor for achievement.

la·va, n. molten or fluid rock.

la·va·liere, n. pendant on chain worn as necklace.

lav·a·to·ry, n. pl., **-ries.** room with a sink and often with a toilet; basin for washing.

lav·en·der, n. mint yielding flowers for sachet and a fragrant oil. a. pale, delicate purple.

lav·ish, a. profuse; extravagant. v. bestow or expend in great abundance. **-ness,** n.

law, n. body of regulations, customs, or practices; litigation; injunction; legal profession; governing rules or authority.

law·a·bid·ing, a. obedient to the law.

law·ful, a. not contrary to law.

law·less, a. contrary to law; not controlled by law. **-ness,** n.

lawn, n. closely mown grass around a house.

law·suit, n. a suit at law; prosecution in a court of justice.

law·yer, *n.* attorney-at-law.

lax, *a.* loose or slack; negligent; not strict. **-i·ty,** *n.*

lax·a·tive, *a., n.* mild purgative to loosen the bowels.

lay, *v.,* **laid, lay·ing.** place or put in a position of rest; set; calm; bury; impute; bet; present; impose.

lay, *v.* past tense of **lie.**

lay·er, *n.* thickness; stratum.

lay·ette, *n.* clothing, toilet articles, etc., for a newborn child.

lay·man, *n. pl.,* **-men.** one not a clergyman or member of a profession.

lay·out, *n.* plan; arrangement.

la·zy, *a.,* **-zi·er, -zi·est.** disinclined to work; slow; idle; indolent; sluggish. **-zi·ly,** *adv.* **-zi·ness,** *n.*

lead, *n.* malleable metallic element; marking part of pencil; bullets; shot; graphite.

lead, *v.,* **led, lead·ing.** show the way; command; induce; direct. *n.* vanguard; initiative; example; star drama role; guidance.

lead·en, *a.* made of lead; inertly heavy; oppressive; gloomy.

lead·er, *n.* one who leads; musical conductor; principal editorial article.

lead·ing, *a.* guiding; foremost.

leaf, *n. pl.,* **leaves.** lateral outgrowth of a stem; page of a book; movable table top. *v.* produce leaves; turn pages. **-less,** *a.*

leaf·let, *n.* printed folder or pamphlet.

leaf·y, *a.,* **-i·er, -i·est.** abounding in leaves.

league, *n.* association of persons, groups, etc., for promotion of a common purpose. *v.,* **leagued, lea·guing.** unite in a league.

leak, *n.* unintended hole, crack, etc., by which water, air, etc., enters or escapes. *v.* act of leaking; become known despite concealment; divulge. **-age,** *n.* **-y,** *a.,* **-i·er, -i·est.**

lean, *v.,* **leaned** or **leant, lean·ing.** incline; slope; slant; tend toward; rely. *a.* spare; scrawny; lanky; containing little fat. **-ness,** *n.* fat-free meat.

lean·ing, *n.* tendency; penchant.

leap, *v.,* **leaped** or **leapt, leap·ing.** spring; jump over. *n.* bound; jump. **-er,** *n.*

learn, *v.,* **learned** or **learnt, learn·ing.** acquire knowledge, skill, etc.; become informed. **-er,** *n.*

learn·ed, *a.* having much knowledge; scholarly. **-ly,** *adv.* **-ness,** *n.*

lease, *n.* contract or the period of time for rental. *v.,* **leased, leas·ing.** give a lease.

leash, *n.* line for leading a dog; restraint.

least, *a.* slightest; smallest in size, etc. *n.* smallest. *adv.* to the lowest degree.

leath·er, *n.* tanned animal skin. *a.* of leather. **-y,** *a.*

leave, *v.,* **left, leav·ing.** go away; deliver; quit; allow to remain; bequeath. *n.* liberty granted to act; permission; departure. **leav·er,** *n.*

leav·en, *n.* yeast; fermentation agent; modifying agent.

leaves, *n.* plural of **leaf.**

lech·ery, *n.* inordinate sexual indulgence.

lec·tern, *n.* church reading desk.

lec·ture, *n.* discourse delivered, esp. for instruction; reprimand. *v.,* **-tured, -tur·ing.** deliver a lecture. **-tur·er,** *n.*

ledge, *n.* projecting rock ridge; flat rock shelf.

ledg·er, *n.* account book.

lee, *n.* shelter; the side turned away from the wind. *a.*

leech, *n.* flat, freshwater, bloodsucking worm; parasite; hanger-on. *v.*

leer, *n.* a side glance, esp. sly, malicious, or lascivious. *v.* to leer. **-ing·ly,** *adv.*

leer·y, *a. inf.* wary, suspicious.

lee·way, *n.* degree of freedom or variation; tolerance.

left, *a.* side turned toward the west when one faces north; side of body which contains heart. *n.* left side; persons holding radical views. *adv.* on or to the left side. **-ist,** *n., a.*

leg, *n.* limb which supports and moves the body; something resembling a leg; stage of a trip. *v.,* **legged, leg·ging.**

leg·a·cy, *n.* gift by will; heritage.

le·gal, *a.* pertaining to or permitted by law; lawful. **-ly,** *adv.*

le·gal·i·ty, *n. pl.,* **-ties.** lawfulness.

le·gal·ize, *v.,* **-ized, -iz·ing.** make legal; sanction. **-i·za·tion,** *n.*

le·ga·tion, *n.* body of diplomats on a mission.

leg·end, *n.* story handed down by tradition; popular myth; person of renown; caption. **-ar·y,** *a.*

leg·er·de·main, *n.* sleight of hand.

leg·i·ble, *a.* easily read or deciphered. **-bil·i·ty,** *n.*

le·gion, *n.* large military force; multitude. *a.* innumerable. **-naire,** *n.*

leg·is·late, *v.,* **-lat·ed, -lat·ing.** make or enact laws. **-la·tive,** *a.* **-la·tor,** *n.* **-la·tion,** *n.*

leg·is·la·ture, *n.* body of persons with authority to make laws.

le·git·i·mate, *a.* lawful; born of parents legally married. *v.,* **-mat·ed, -mat·ing. -ma·cy,** *n.*

le·git·i·mize, v., **-mized, -miz·ing.** make legitimate.

lei·sure, n. time free from work or duty; unoccupied time. a. free.

lei·sure·ly, a., adv. unhurried; deliberate.

lem·on, n. tart yellow citrus fruit; dud. a. light yellow color.

lend, v., **lent, lend·ing.** give for temporary use; adapt; accommodate. **-er,** n.

length, n. linear measure from end to end; extent; duration in time; distance. **-en,** v. **-wise,** adv., a.

length·y, a., **-i·er, -i·est.** extended; long. **-i·ness,** n.

le·ni·ent, a. mild; merciful; indulgent. **-ence, -en·cy,** n.

lens, n. pl., **lenses.** curved piece, usu. glass, used for changing the direction of light rays; eye part.

leo·pard, n. large, ferocious, carnivorous spotted cat.

lep·er, n. person affected with leprosy; outcast.

lep·ro·sy, n. chronic bacterial disease. **-rous,** a.

les·bi·an, n. female homosexual.

le·sion, n. injury; wound.

less, a. fewer; slighter; lower in importance. n. smaller amount. adv. to a smaller degree. prep. minus. **-er,** a.

less·en, v. decrease.

les·son, n. something to be learned; piece of instruction; teaching; reprimand.

lest, conj. for fear that.

let, v., **let, let·ting.** permit; allow; suffer; make; rent.

le·thal, a. deadly; fatal.

leth·ar·gy, n. pl., **-gies.** sluggish inactivity; drowsy dullness. **le·thar·gic, le·thar·gi·cal,** a.

let·ter, n. symbol representing a speech sound; alphabet unit; strict meaning; written message; pl. learning; literature. v. inscribe. **-tered,** a. **-ter·er,** n. **-ter·ing,** n.

let·ter·head, n. printed heading on stationery, esp. business.

let·tuce, n. vegetable having edible leaves; salad green.

leu·ke·mi·a, n. cancer affecting white blood cells.

lev·ee, n. embankment; quay; reception.

lev·el, n. device for determining the horizontal plane; elevation; flat surface; status. a. having an even surface. v., **-eled, -el·ing.** make flat or even; equalize; raze. **-er,** n. **-ly,** adv.

lev·er, n. bar used for lifting or prying by applied force.

lev·er·age, n. action of a lever.

lev·i·tate, v., **-tat·ed, -tat·ing.** rise or float in the air. **-ta·tion,** n.

lev·i·ty, n. frivolity; lightness.

lev·y, n. pl., **-ies.** raising or collecting. v., **-ied, -y·ing.** impose, as an assessment; enlist.

lewd, a. indecent; obscene; salacious; unchaste. **-ly,** adv. **-ness,** n.

lex·i·con, n. dictionary.

li·a·bil·i·ty, n. pl., **-ties.** debt; disability; drawback.

li·a·ble, a. obligated; likely to incur; susceptible.

li·ai·son, n. contact; intercommunication; illicit affair.

li·ar, n. one who lies.

li·ba·tion, n. sacrificial pouring of a liquid; act of drinking; beverage.

li·bel, n. defamatory writing or representation. v., **-beled, -bel·ing. -er,** n. **-ous,** a.

lib·er·al, a. generous; tolerant; broadminded; ample; loose; favoring reforms. **-ism,** n. **-i·ty,** n. pl., **-ties,** n.

lib·er·al·ize, v., **-ized, -iz·ing.** make or become liberal.

lib·er·ate, v., **-at·ed, -at·ing.** set free. **-a·tion,** n. **-a·tor,** n.

lib·er·ty, n. pl., **-ties.** freedom; independence; immunity; privilege; sailor's leave.

li·bi·do, n. sexual drive.

li·brar·y, n. pl., **-ies.** place with literary material to use but not to buy; collection of books. **-i·an,** n.

li·bret·to, n. pl., **-tos, ti.** words of an opera; opera text.

lice, n. plural of **louse.**

li·cense, n. formal permission; official permit; freedom of action, etc.; licentiousness. v., **-censed, -cens·ing.** authorize. **li·cen·see,** n.

li·cen·tious, a. unrestrained by law; lascivious; lewd.

lick, v. pass the tongue over; inf. beat; defeat. n.

lic·o·rice, li·quo·rice, n. sweet-tasting plant extract; candy.

lid, n. container cover.

lie, v., **lay, lain, ly·ing.** recline; extend; remain; be placed.

lie, v., **lied, ly·ing.** speak falsely. n. intentional untruth.

lien, n. legal claim.

lieu, n. place; stead. **in lieu of,** in place of.

lieu·ten·ant, *n.* one empowered to act for higher officer; commissioned military officer.

life, *n. pl.,* **lives.** quality of being alive; period during which thing exists; person's history; vitality; prison sentence; course of living.

life·guard, *n.* one employed to protect bathers.

life·less, *a.* dead; dull; inanimate.

life·long, *a.* lasting or continuing through life.

life-size, *a.* natural size. Also **life-sized.**

life·time, *n.* period of time that anything lives.

lift, *v.* raise; elevate; rescind; plagiarize; transport; elate. *n.* act of lifting. **-er,** *n.*

lig·a·ment, *n.* band of fibrous tissue connecting bones or holding organs in place.

lig·a·ture, *n.* anything that binds; thread, wire, etc., as for tying blood vessels. *v.,* **-tured, -tur·ing.** bind.

light, *n.* radiant energy; illuminating source; dawn; aspect. *a.* pale, whitish; not heavy; trifling. *adv.* lightly. *v.,* **-ed** or **lit, -ing.** kindle; land. **-er,** *n., a.* **-ness,** *n.*

light·en, *v.* grow brighter; illumine; make less heavy; lessen.

light-head·ed, *a.* dizzy; delirious.

light-heart·ed, *a.* cheerful; optimistic; gay.

light·ly, *adv.* nimbly; frivolously; gently; easily.

light·ning, *n.* discharge of atmospheric electricity resulting in a flash of light. *v.,* **-ninged, -ning.**

light·ning rod, *n.* metallic rod to deflect lightning from structures.

light-year, *n.* distance traversed by light in a vacuum in one year.

lig·nite, *n.* brownish-black coal.

like, *a.* similar; resembling. *prep.* in the manner of. *v.,* **liked, lik·ing.** find agreeable; regard with favor. *n. usu. pl.* liking. **lik·a·ble, like·a·ble,** *a.*

like·ly, *a.,* **-li·er, -li·est.** credible; probable; seemingly. *adv.* probably. **-li·hood,** *n.*

lik·en, *v.* compare; represent.

like·ness, *n.* resemblance, portrait; appearance; copy.

like·wise, *adv.* in like manner; also; similarly.

li·lac, *n.* shrub with large clusters of fragrant purple flowers. *a.* lavender color.

lilt, *n.* springing step; rhythmical swing; sprightly tune. **-ing,** *a.*

lil·y, *n. pl.,* **-ies.** plant with showy funnel-shaped flowers.

limb, *n.* appendage, as a leg; branch of a tree.

lim·ber, *a.* flexible; supple.

lime, *n.* calcium oxide; green tart citrus fruit. **lim·y,** *a.*

lime·light, *n.* spotlight; center of public attention.

lim·er·ick, *n.* amusing verse consisting of five lines.

lime·stone, *n.* rock chiefly of calcium carbonate.

lim·it, *n.* final or furthest point; boundary; restraint; prescribed amount. *v.* restrict. **-i·ta·tion,** **-it·ed,** *a.*

limn, *v.* draw; paint; describe.

lim·ou·sine, *n.* luxurious (usu. chauffeur-driven) automobile.

limp, *v.* walk lamely. *n.* act of limping. *a.* slack; drooping; exhausted; spiritless. **-ness,** *n.*

lim·pid, *a.* transparent; clear.

line, *n.* a mark or stroke; thread; cord; piping; written note; route; course of conduct; limit; genealogy; transportation company; contour; business and associated merchandise. *v.,* **lined, lin·ing.** mark with a line or lines; form a line; cover the inner surface.

lin·e·age, *n.* line of family descent; roots; race.

lin·e·al, *a.* hereditary.

lin·e·ar, *a.* of a line or lines; straight; measurement in one dimension only. **-ly,** *adv.* **-ity,** *n.*

line-up, line·up, *n.* formation of persons or things into a line for a particular purpose.

linger, *v.* tarry; loiter; saunter; procrastinate. **-er,** *n.*

lin·ge·rie, *n.* women's underwear.

lin·go, *n. pl.,* **-goes.** language characteristic of a special group; strange talk; jargon.

lin·gui·ne, *n. pl.* thin, flat pasta.

lin·guist, *n.* language specialist. **lin·guis·tics,** *n. pl.*

lin·i·ment, *n.* preparation for rubbing on the skin.

link, *n.* single ring of a chain; anything that connects. *v.* join; connect. **linked,** *a.* **-er,** *n.*

li·no·le·um, *n.* floor covering.

lin·seed, *n.* flaxseed.

lint, *n.* material for dressing wounds; fuzz or fabric ravelings. **-y,** *a.,* **-i·er, -i·est.**

li·on, *n.* large, tawny carnivorous cat. **-ness,** *n. fem.* **-like,** *a.*

lip, *n.* either of two fleshy parts that are margins of the mouth; edge of a vessel.

lip·py, *a.,* **-pi·er, -pi·est.** *inf.* insolent.

lip·stick, *n.* waxy colored stick for coloring the lips.

liq·ue·fy, *v.,* **-fied, -fy·ing.** convert to a liquid. **-fi·er,** *n.*

li·queur, *n*. strong, sweet liquor.

liq·uid, *a*. able to flow freely; unconstrained; capable of being converted to cash. *n*. fluid substance.

liq·ui·date, *v*., **-dat·ed**, **-dat·ing**. settle an account; do away with. **-da·tion**, *n*. **-da·tor**, *n*.

liq·uor, *n*. distilled alcoholic beverage; liquid substance.

lisp, *v*. pronounce imperfectly *(s* and *z* as *th)*. *n*. lisping.

lis·some, *a*. lithe; nimble.

list, *n*. series of names, words, etc.; roll; catalog. *v*. make a list; register; tilt. **-ed**, *a*. **-ing**, *n*.

lis·ten, *v*. give heed. **-er**, *n*.

list·less, *a*. lacking interest; languid; spiritless.

lit·er·al, *a*. exact; factual; verbatim; plain. **-ly**, *adv*.

lit·er·ar·y, *a*. pertaining to literature; well-read; bookish. **-i·ly**, *adv*.

lit·er·ate, *a*. able to read and write; educated; lucid. **-a·cy**, *n*.

lit·er·a·tim, *a*. or *adv*. letter for letter; literally.

lit·er·a·ture, *n*. writings of prose or verse; accumulated works of one subject, country, period, etc.

lithe, *a*. pliant; limber; flexible; graceful.

li·thol·o·gy, *n*. study of rocks.

lit·i·gate, *v*., **-gat·ed**, **-gat·ing**. to contest at law. **-ga·tion**, *n*.

lit·ter, *n*. scattered rubbish; young born at one birth; stretcher. *v*. to strew; scatter.

lit·tle, *a*., **lit·tler** or **less** or **less·er**; **lit·tlest** or **least**. small; short; brief; trivial. *n*. short time; small amount. *adv*., **less**, **least**. in a small degree; slightly; rarely.

lit·ur·gy, *n*. *pl*., **-gies**. ritual of worship; church rites.

live, *v*., **lived**, **liv·ing**. have life; subsist; dwell; have great experiences; reside; pass or spend. **liv·er**, *n*. **liv·ing**, *a*., *n*.

live, *a*. being alive; full of life; vivid; glowing; afire; unexploded; current.

live·li·hood, *n*. means of supporting life.

live·ly, *a*., **-li·er**, **-li·est**. active; stimulating; sprightly; animated; spirited. **-li·ness**, *n*.

liv·en, *v*. enliven; cheer.

liv·er, *n*. glandular organ having many functions.

live·stock, *n*. domestic animals.

liv·id, *a*. having a dull bluish or leaden color, as a bruise.

liz·ard, *n*. four-legged reptile.

lla·ma, *n*. camel-like So. Amer. ruminant with no hump.

lo, *int*. look; see; behold.

load, *n*. burden; cargo; quantity carried. *v*. place on or in; burden; weight dice; charge a gun. **-ed**, *a*. **-er**, *n*.

loaf, *n*. *pl*., **loaves**. molded mass of bread or other food. *v*. idle time away. **-er**, *n*.

loam, *n*. rich soil. **-y**, *a*.

loan, *n*. money lent at interest; anything lent. *v*. lend.

loath, **loth**, *a*. reluctant.

loathe, *v*., **loathed**, **loath·ing**. detest. **loath·ing**, *n*. **loath·some**, *a*.

lob·by, *n*. *pl*., **-bies**. entrance hall; waiting room; corridor; anteroom; influencing group. *v*. try to influence public officials. **-ist**, *n*.

lobe, *n*. curved or rounded projection; lower part of the external ear. **lobed**, *a*.

lob·ster, *n*. edible marine crustacean having two claws.

lo·cal, *a*. of a particular place or part. **-i·ty**, *n·pl*., **-ties**. a place.

lo·cale, *n*. site; scene.

lo·cate, *v*., **-cat·ed**, **-cat·ing**. discover; ascertain the whereabouts of; establish; settle; station. **-ca·tion**, *n*.

lock, *n*. device for fastening or securing something. *v*. fasten; secure by a lock; interlace; join. **-er**, *n*.

lock·et, *n*. case with memento worn on chain.

lo·co·mo·tive, *a*., *n*. self-propelling train engine; ability to move independently.

lo·cus, *n*. *pl*., **loci**. place; locality; site.

lo·cust, *n*. destructive migratory grasshopper.

lo·cu·tion, *n*. regional expressions; phraseology.

lode, *n*. ore deposit; vein.

lodge, *v*., **lodged**, **lodg·ing**. shelter; dwell; come to a rest; file (a complaint); be fixed in a position. *n*. hotel; seasonal residence; fraternal group, its building. **lodg·er**, *n*. **lodg·ing**, *n*.

lo·ess, *n*. wind-deposited loam.

loft, *n*. hayloft; gallery; attic.

loft·y, *a*., **-i·er**, **-i·est**. extremely high; esoteric; haughty; supercilious.

log, *n*. length of unshaped timber; record. *v*. record. **-ger**, *n*.

log·a·rithm, *n*. exponential power of a number.

loge, *n*. booth; theater box.

log·ic, *n*. science of formal reasoning; sound sense; convincing force. **log·i·cian**, *n*. **-i·cal**, *a*.

lo·go, *n*. identifying picture; motto.

loin, *n. usu. pl.* part between the lower ribs and the hipbone; cut of animal meat from this area.

loi·ter, *v.* linger idly; dawdle; lag. **-er,** *n.*

loll, *v.* lounge; droop; dangle.

lone, *a.* solitary; isolated.

lone·ly, *a.,* **-li·er, -li·est.** deserted; solitary; desolate; lonesome. **-li·ness,** *n.*

lone·some, *a.* lonely; sad.

long, *a.* great in distance, length, duration, or extent; having many items. *adv.* for a great extent of space or time. *v.* strongly desire.

lon·gev·i·ty, *n.* long life.

long·ing, *n.* yearning; craving.

lon·gi·tude, *n.* distance east or west of the prime meridian.

long·shore·man, *n. pl.,* **-men.** wharf laborer.

long-suf·fer·ing, *a.* long and patient endurance.

look, *v.* fix the eyes on something; examine; see; seem; seek; seem to the mind. *n.* glance; aspect. *usu. pl.* outward appearance.

look·out, *n.* watch kept; person keeping such a watch; view.

loom, *n.* machine for weaving. *v.* appear indistinctly or in enlarged form.

loon, *n.* fish-eating diving bird.

loon·y, *a.,* **-i·er, -i·est.** crazy; foolish. **-i·ness,** *n.*

loop, *n.* doubling of a portion of a cord, etc., upon itself, leaving an opening; anything similar to a loop. *v.* form loops; encircle; fasten.

loop·hole, *n.* small opening; outlet for escape or evasion.

loose, *a.,* **loos·er, loos·est.** free; slack; not tight; lax; not firmly fixed; lewd; unchaste. *v.,* **loosed, loos·ing.** untie; detach; discharge; relax; release. **loosely,** *adv.* **loos·en,** *v.*

loot, *n.* spoils; *inf.* money. *v.* plunder. **loot·er,** *n.*

lop, *v.,* **lopped, lop·ping.** remove; cut off; trim.

lope, *v.,* **loped, loping.** move with a long easy stride. *n.* act or the gait of loping.

lop·sid·ed, *a.* inclining to one side; lacking symmetry.

lo·qua·cious, *a.* talkative.

lord, *n.* ruler, governor, etc.; *(cap·)* God. *v.* domineer. **-ly,** *a.,* **-li·er, -li·est.**

lore, *n.* body of knowledge.

lose, *v.,* **lost, los·ing.** mislay; suffer the loss of; cease to have; fail to get; fail to win. **los·er,** *n.* **los·ing,** *a., n.*

loss, *n.* that which is lost; deprivation of; detriment.

lost, *a.* no longer possessed, retained, or to be found; having gone astray; that which one has failed to win; wasted.

lot, *n.* objects drawn to decide a question, etc.; drawing of such objects; decision so made; allotted share. *v.,* **lot·ted, lot·ting.** cast or draw lots for; allot; apportion.

Lo·thar·io, *n. pl.,* **-ios.** man who seduces women.

lo·tion, *n.* liquid preparation for the skin.

lot·ter·y, *n. pl.,* **-ies.** scheme for raising money by sale of numbered tickets with prizes to be awarded by chance.

loud, *a.* strongly audible sounds; clamorous; noisy. **-ly,** *adv.* **-ness,** *n.*

loud·speak·er, *n.* device for amplifying speech, music, etc.

lounge, *v.,* **lounged, loung·ing.** loll; recline or pass time indolently. *n.* kind of sofa; place for lounging. **loung·er,** *n.*

louse, *n. pl.,* **lice.** wingless, parasitic bloodsucking insect; *inf.* contemptible person.

lout, *n.* stupid person.

lou·ver, *n.* slanted strips or slats covering an opening so as to admit air but exclude rain.

love, *n.* strong or passionate affection; devotion; object of love. *v.,* **loved, lov·ing.** feeling deep affection for; be in love; caress. **love·less,** *a.* **lov·a·ble, love·a·ble,** *a.* **lov·er,** *n.*

love·ly, *a.,* **-li·er, -li·est.** charming; beautiful. **-li·ness,** *n.*

lov·ing, *a.* affectionate; fond. **-ness,** *n.*

low, *a.* not high; not far above ground, base, etc.; lying below the general level; humble; vulgar; depressed; near depletion. *adv.* in or to a low position. *n.* that which is low. **-ness,** *n.*

low·er, *v.* reduce in amount, price, force, etc.; to bring down in rank; let down; humble.

low·er·ing, *a.* dark and threatening, as the sky; frowning or sullen, as the face.

low·ly, *a.,* **-li·er, -li·est.** low; humble; meek. *adv.* in a low position. **-li·ness,** *n.*

loy·al, *a.* faithful to. **-ist,** *n.* **-ty,** *n. pl.,* **-ties.**

loz·enge, *n.* medicated candy.

lu·au, *n.* Hawaiian feast.

lub·ber, *n.* clumsy individual; unskilled seaman.

lu·bri·cate, v., **-cat·ed, -cat·ing.** apply oil or grease; make slippery. **-cant**, n. **-ca·tion**, n.

lu·cid, a. clear, intelligible; shining or bright; sane. **-i·ty**, n.

luck, n. chance; fate; good fortune; success. **-i·ness**, n.

luck·y, a., **-i·er, -i·est.** having good luck; fortunate; bringing good luck.

lu·cra·tive, a. profitable. **-ness**, n.

lu·di·crous, a. absurdly comical; ridiculous.

lug, v., **lugged, lug·ging.** drag; pull along or carry.

lug·gage, n. baggage; suitcases.

lu·gu·bri·ous, a. mournful; dismal.

luke·warm, a. tepid; indifferent.

lull, v. soothe; subside; become calm. n. a temporary stillness.

lull·a·by, n. pl., **-bies.** song to lull babies; cradle song.

lum·ber, v. move clumsily; encumber. n. sawed timber or logs. **-ing**, n., a.

lu·mi·nar·y, n. pl., **-ies.** person of eminence; source of light.

lu·mi·nous, a. radiating or reflecting light; intelligible; lighted; shining. **-nos·i·ty**, n.

lump, n. shapeless mass; aggregation; swelling. v. unite into one mass; make into a lump. **-y**, a., **-i·er, -i·est. -i·ness**, n.

lu·na·cy, n. pl., **-cies.** intermittent insanity; extreme foolishness.

lu·nar, a. of the moon.

lu·na·tic, n. insane person. a. mad.

lunch, n. light midday meal.

lung, n. saclike respiratory organ in the thorax.

lunge, n. a thrust; sudden forward movement. v. to thrust; move with a lunge.

lure, n. anything that attracts or entices; decoy; bait. v., **lured, lur·ing.** attract.

lu·rid, a. sensational; shining with an unnatural glare.

lurk, v. be about furtively; skulk.

lus·cious, a. tasty; seductive.

lush, a. having luxuriant foliage; opulent; plentiful; savory. **-ness**, n.

lust, n. sexual appetite; lasciviousness. v. desire; crave. **-ful**, a.

lus·ter, n. sheen; radiance; glory. **-trous**, a.

lus·ty, a., **-i·er, -i·est.** robust; vigorous; hearty. **-i·ness**, n.

Lu·ther·an, n. Protestant following doctrine of Martin Luther.

lux·u·ri·ant, a. abundant; productive; lush; profuse. **-ance**, n.

lux·u·ri·ous, a. opulent; voluptuous; abundant.

lux·u·ry, n. pl., **-ries.** nonessential, usu. costly; indulgence in sumptuous living.

lymph, n. yellowish bodily fluid. **lym·phat·ic**, a.

lynch, v. put to death without authority, esp. by hanging. **-er**, n. **-ing**, n.

lynx, n. pl., **lynx, lynx·es.** wildcat.

lyr·ic, a. songlike; having a light, flexible quality; expressing personal feelings. n. lyric poem; usu. pl. text of a song. **-i·cal**, a. **-i·cist**, n.

M

ma·ca·bre, a. gruesome; of death; grisly.

mac·ad·am, n. road made of small broken stones.

mac·a·ro·ni, n. flour dough in form of hollow tubes.

ma·caw, n. large showy parrot.

mace, n. medieval spiked weapon; ornamental staff; spice.

Mace, n. Trademark. a chemical spray which renders a person docile on contact.

mac·er·ate, v. make or become soft.

ma·chet·e, n. large heavy knife.

mach·i·nate, v. contrive or devise with evil purpose. **-na·tion**, n.

ma·chine, n. apparatus used to perform work; group controlling political activity; vehicle, conveyance. v. make or prepare by machine.

ma·chin·er·y, n. machines; mechanical apparatus; the parts of a machine.

ma·chin·ist, n. one who operates machinery or machine tools.

mack·er·el, n. abundant food fish.

mack·i·naw, n. short woolen coat of blanketlike material.

mack·in·tosh, mac·in·tosh, n. rubberized, waterproof raincoat; the fabric.

mac·ro·cosm, n. the great world, or universe.

mad, a., **-der, -dest.** insane; foolish; frenzied; furious; rabid; angry. **-ly**, adv. **-ness**, n. **-den**, v.

mad·am, n. polite term of address for any woman.

mad·ame, n. French title of respect for a married woman.

mad·cap, a. impulsive; reckless.

mad·e·moi·selle, n. French title of respect for a girl or unmarried woman.

mad·house, n. place of commotion and confusion; insane asylum.

mad·man, n. lunatic.

Ma·don·na, *n.* the Virgin Mary.

mad·ri·gal, *n.* short love poem for music.

maes·tro, *n.* master in an art.

mael·strom, *n.* violent whirlpool; turmoil.

mag·a·zine, *n.* periodical publication; storage room for military supplies; supply chamber.

ma·gen·ta, *n.* purplish-red color.

mag·got, *n.* legless, wormlike fly larva.

mag·ic, *n.* creation of illusions; sleight of hand; performance of tricks; sorcery. **-i·cal,** *a.* **-i·cal·ly,** *adv.*

ma·gi·cian, *n.* one skilled in magic; conjurer.

mag·is·trate, *n.* local civil officer who administers the law.

mag·nan·i·mous, *a.* generous; not vindictive; high-minded.

mag·nate, *n.* person of influence, dominance, esp. in business.

mag·ne·sia, *n.* white substance used as an antacid and laxative.

mag·ne·si·um, *n.* metallic element usd in alloys.

mag·net, *n.* body that attracts iron; person or thing that attracts. **-ic,** *a.* **-ism,** *n.* **-ize,** *v.*

mag·nif·i·cent, *a.* extraordinarily fine or superb; splendid. **-cence,** *n.*

mag·ni·fy, *v.,* **-fied, -fy·ing.** increase the apparent size; enlarge. **-fi·ca·tion,** *n.*

mag·ni·tude, *n.* size; extent; great amount; importance; number.

ma·hog·a·ny, *n.* reddish-brown hard wood of a tropical tree.

maid, *n.* female servant; young unmarried woman; spinster.

maid·en, *n.* girl; young unmarried woman. *a.* unmarried; virgin; made, appearing, etc., for the first time.

mail, *n.* letters, packages, etc., sent through the postal system; armor made of metal mesh. *v.* send by mail. **-box,** *n.* **-man,** *n.*

maim, *v.* mutilate; cripple.

main, *a.* principal; chief; utmost. *n.* principal part; water pipe or duct. **-ly,** *adv.*

main·land, *n.* principal part of a continent.

main·spring, *n.* principal spring in a mechanism; chief motive.

main·tain, *v.* preserve; support; sustain; keep in condition; continue; assert. **-te·nance,** *n.*

maize, *n.* Indian corn; yellow.

ma·jes·ty, *n.* regal; lofty. (*usu. cap·*) title of royalty. **ma·jes·tic,** *a.*

ma·jor, *n.* one of superior rank; academic field of study; military officer. *v.* pursue a principal field of study. *a.* greater; serious; *mus.* half step higher than the minor.

ma·jor·i·ty, *n. pl.,* **-ties.** greater part or number; more than half; full legal age.

make, *v.,* **made, mak·ing.** bring into existence; produce; form; manufacture; cause; establish; gain; compel; create; fashion; construct; enact; do; perform. *n.* style, form; manner of construction. **mak·er,** *n.*

make·shift, *n.,* *a.* temporary expedient or substitute.

make·up, *n.* cosmetics; physical or mental constitution.

mal·ad·just·ment, *n.* faulty adjustment. **-just·ed,** *a.*

mal·a·dy, *n. pl.,* **-dies.** ailment.

mal·aise, *n.* feeling of inner disorder.

mal·a·prop·ism, *n.* humorous misuse of a word.

ma·lar·i·a, *n.* disease with chills and fever, transmitted by mosquitoes.

mal·con·tent, *a.,* *n.* dissatisfied person.

mal de mer, *n.* seasickness.

male, *a.* of the sex which produces sperm; masculine. *n.* a male human being or animal.

male·dic·tion, *n.* a curse; slander.

male·fac·tor, *n.* an offender or criminal. **-tion,** *n.*

mal·ev·o·lent, *a.* having ill will; malicious. **-lence,** *n.*

mal·fea·sance, *n.* illegal, wrongful conduct, esp. in public office.

mal·for·ma·tion, *n.* faulty structure. **-formed,** *a.*

mal·ice, *n.* desire to inflict injury; ill will. **ma·li·cious,** *a.*

ma·lign, *v.* defame; speak ill of. *a.* evil; harmful.

ma·lig·nant, *a.* injurious; malevolent; tending to cause death, as a tumor. **-nancy,** *n.*

ma·lin·ger, *v.* feign illness or injury to avoid duty or work.

mall, *n.* landscaped public area for walking; enclosed shopping area.

mal·lard, *n.* wild duck.

mal·le·a·ble, *a.* capable of being shaped by hammering or by pressure; adaptable; tractable.

mal·let, *n.* hammer with non-metallic head.

mal·nu·tri·tion, *n.* imperfect, insufficient nourishment.

mal·oc·clu·sion, *n.* faulty bite.

mal·o·dor, *n.* bad odor; stench. **-ous,** *a.*

mal·prac·tice, *n.* improper, negligent performance of public or professional duty.

malt, *n.* grain, usu. barley, used in brewing and distilling.

mam·mal, *n.* vertebrate animal whose young feed on milk from the mother's breast.

mam·moth, *n.* large extinct elephant. *a.* huge; gigantic.

man, *n. pl.,* **men.** human being, esp. a male adult; the human race; game piece. *v.* furnish with men.

man·a·cle, *n. often pl.* shackles; handcuffs; restraints.

man·age, *v.* control; direct; manipulate; contrive; carry on. **-a·ble,** *a.* **-ag·er, -age·ment,** *n.*

man·date, *n.* command; policy direction; authorization dictated by electorate; territory controlled by another nation. **-da·to·ry,** *a.*

man·da·to·ry, *a.* obligatory.

mane, *n.* long neck hair of some animals, as the horse.

ma·nege, *n.* art of horsemanship.

ma·neu·ver, *n.* regulated movement; tactical exercise; clever action; scheme *v.* perform military exercises; handle skillfully; scheme; manipulate.

man·ga·nese, *n.* metallic element used as an alloy.

mange, *n.* skin disease.

man·ger, *n.* feedbox, trough for livestock fodder.

man·gle, *v.* destroy, slash, or badly damage. *n.* machine to press cloth using heated rollers.

man·go, *n.* edible tropical fruit.

man·gy, *a.,* **-gi·er, -gi·est.** having mange; squalid; shabby; seedy.

man·han·dle, *v.* handle roughly; move by men, not machines.

man·hole, *n.* circular hole for entering a sewer, drain, etc.

man·hood, *n.* state of being an adult male; manly qualities; men collectively.

ma·ni·a, *n.* great excitement or enthusiasm; craze. **man·ic,** *a.*

ma·ni·ac, *n.* raving lunatic; madman.

man·i·cure, *n.* care of the nails and hands. *v.* trim or care for.

man·i·fest, *a.* clearly evident; obvious. *v.* make clear; reveal; prove. *n.* itemized shipping document. **-fes·ta·tion,** *n.*

man·i·fes·to, *n.* public declaration of policy, views, etc.

man·i·fold, *a.* having many different parts, forms, etc. *n.* exhaust pipe or system.

ma·nip·u·late, *v.* work, control, handle, or use with skill; change or falsify. **-la·tion,** *n.* **-la·tive,** *a.*

man·kind, *n.* all human beings; the human race.

man·ly, *a.,* **-li·er, -li·est.** qualities appropriate to a man; brave; resolute. **-li·ness,** *n.*

man·na, *n.* food from heaven; thing needed and unexpectedly received.

man·ne·quin, *n.* life-sized figure of the human body; fashion model.

man·ner, *n.* way or method of doing something; customary behavior; *pl.* polite social behavior.

man·ner·ly, *a., adv.* polite.

man·or, *n.* landed estate; mansion.

man·pow·er, *n.* power by human strength; collective strength.

manse, *n.* clergyman's residence.

man·sion, *n.* large residence.

man·slaugh·ter, *n.* unlawful, unintended killing of a person.

man·tel, *n.* shelf above a fireplace; ornamental work surrounding it.

man·tle, *n.* loose, sleeveless cloak. *v.* cover; envelop.

man·u·al, *a.* made, done, worked, or used by the hands. *n.* book of instructions.

man·u·fac·ture, *n.* producing goods by manual labor or machinery. *v.* make by hand or machinery; make up excuses, etc.

ma·nure, *n.* animal waste used to fertilize soil.

man·u·script, *n.* handwritten or typewritten work.

man·y, *a.,* **more, most.** numerous; large, indefinite number. *n., pron.* a large number.

map, *n.* representation of the earth's surface. *v.* make a map; plan in detail.

ma·ple, *n.* genus of shade tree important for lumber, syrup.

ma·ra·ca, *n.* gourd-shaped rattle.

mar, *v.,* **marred, mar·ring.** injure; blemish; damage; spoil.

mar·a·schi·no, *n.* sweet liqueur; preserved cherries.

mar·a·thon, *n.* long-distance foot race (usu. 26 miles); endurance contest.

ma·raud, *v.* raid or roam for plunder. **-er,** *n.*

mar·ble, *n.* hard limestone; little glass, etc., ball used in a child's game. *a.* hard or veined like marble.

march, *v.* move with steady stride; proceed; advance. *n.* measured, uniform walk; progress; marching music; organized walk on a public issue.

mare, *n.* female horse.

mar·ga·rine, *n.* vegetable oil buttery spread or cooking fat.

mar·gin, n. border; edge; limit; difference between cost and selling price; amount more than what is needed; security money deposited against loss. **-gi·nal,** a.

ma·ri·a·chi, n. Mexican street band.

mar·i·gold, n. garden plant grown for showy flowers.

ma·ri·jua·na, n. narcotic from dried leaves of hemp plant.

ma·rim·ba, n. kind of xylophone.

ma·ri·na, n. small boat basin where moorings, supplies, and services are available.

mar·i·nate, v. soak in seasoned pickling sauce before cooking.

ma·rine, a. of the sea; nautical; maritime. n. member of U·S. Marine Corps; country's naval shipping.

mar·i·ner, n. seaman; sailor.

mar·i·on·ette, n. jointed, stringed puppet or doll.

mar·i·tal, a. of marriage; conjugal.

mar·i·time, a. on or near the sea; of sea navigation, shipping.

mar·jo·ram, n. aromatic herb used for cooking.

mark, n. spot, scratch, stain; a symbol or sign, as a punctuation mark; brand or label to show ownership or maker; a grade or rating; object serving as a guide. v. make marks on; to characterize; grade or rate; take note; write, record. **marked,** a. **mark·ed·ly,** adv. **mark·er,** n.

mar·ket, n. trade in goods, services; store selling provisions; those buying. v. to buy or sell; to offer for sale; buy provisions. **-a·ble,** a.

mark·ing, n. often pl. characteristic arrangement of marks, as on fur, feathers.

mar·lin, n. oceanic sport fish.

mar·ma·lade, n. preserve made with oranges or other fruit.

ma·roon, v. abandon; leave isolated. n. dark red.

mar·quee, n. rooflike projection over an entrance.

mar·quis, n. British nobleman above an earl.

mar·riage, n. wedlock; wedding; any close union.

mar·row, n. tissue in bone cavities; essential or best part.

mar·ry, v., **-ried, -ry·ing.** join as husband or wife; wed; join closely.

marsh, n. swamp; morass; bog.

mar·shal, n. high military officer; sheriff-like official; person in charge of ceremonies, etc. v., **-shaled, -shal·ing.** direct; arrange; lead.

marsh·mal·low, n. soft, spongy confection.

mar·su·pi·al, n. animal with a pouch for carrying young.

mar·tial, a. military; militaristic.

mar·tial art, n. Oriental self-defense technique; judo; karate.

mar·tyr, n. one tortured or killed because of his faith or beliefs; person suffering misery a long time. v. make a martyr of.

mar·vel, n. wonderful, astonishing thing; prodigy; miracle. v. be amazed, wonder.

mas·car·a, n. cosmetic for coloring eyelashes.

mas·cot, n. thing or animal thought to bring good luck.

mas·cu·line, a. of the male sex; having male qualities, vigor, strength, etc. **-lin·i·ty,** n.

mash, n. any soft, pulpy mass. v. reduce to a mash.

mask, n. face covering worn for disguise, protection. v. disguise; conceal.

mas·och·ism, n. pleasure, esp. sexual, from emotional or physical pain. **-ist,** n. **-is·tic,** a.

ma·son, n. person who works with stone, brick, etc.

ma·son·ry, n. stone or brick work.

mas·quer·ade, n. ball or party with costumed, masked guests; disguise; pretense. v. disguise oneself; act under a pretense.

mass, n. body of indefinite size or shape; large number or quantity; bulk; majority; cap. communion service. a. of a large number. v. form into a mass.

mas·sa·cre, n. slaughter; indiscriminate killing. v., **-cred, -cring.**

mas·sage, v. rub, knead, tap a body for remedial or hygienic purposes. n.

mas·seur, n. man who gives massage. **-seuse,** n. fem.

mas·sive, a. bulky; heavy; large scale; imposing.

mass-pro·duce, v. quantity production, esp. by machine. **mass pro·duc·tion,** n.

mast, n. long upright pole (on a ship) used for support; derrick pole; any large, upright pole.

mas·ter, n. male teacher; college degree; ruler; employer; skilled craftsperson. v. overcome; become proficient. a. dominant; skilled; proficient; superlative. **-y,** n.

mas·ter·ful, a. authoritative; skillful; competent.

mas·ter·piece, n. supreme artistic achievement.

mas·ti·cate, v. chew; grind.

mas·tiff, n. large, powerful dog with hanging lips.

mas·to·don, n. extinct animal resembling elephant; giant.

mas·toid, a., n. (of) the projection of the temporal bone behind the ear.

mas·tur·ba·tion, n. self-manipulation of one's genital organs. **-bate,** v.

mat, n. woven or plaited fabric, or rubber, etc., to lie on, cover a floor, table, etc. v. tangle; cover.

mat, a. cardboard or cloth border. v. frame a picture.

mat·a·dor, n. bullfighter.

match, n. person, thing that closely equals another; a contest; marriage; tipped wood or cardboard ignited by friction. v. be equal to; correspond to; pair; place in competition.

mate, n. one of a pair; companion; officer on a ship; spouse. v. join as a pair; couple in marriage or sexual union.

ma·te·ri·al, a. of matter; physical; of the body. n. what a thing is made of; cloth or fabric; data that may be used; supplies, tools, etc., needed for use.

ma·te·ri·al·ize, v. become fact; appear suddenly or unexpectedly. **-i·za·tion,** n.

ma·ter·nal, a. motherly.

ma·ter·ni·ty, n. motherhood. a. for or of pregnant women.

math·e·mat·ics, n. pl. science dealing with forms, quantities, magnitudes, etc., by the use of numbers and symbols.

mat·i·nee, n. daytime performance; afternoon show.

ma·tri·arch, n. woman who heads or rules her family or tribe.

ma·tric·u·late, v. enroll as a member, esp. in a college.

mat·ri·mo·ny, n. rite of marriage; married state.

ma·trix, n. pl., **-tri·ces, -trix·es.** that within which something originates, takes form, etc.; die or mold.

ma·tron, n. dignified married woman or widow; female institutional supervisor.

mat·ter, n. substance of which physical objects are composed; constituent material; subject being considered; trouble. v. be of importance.

mat·ting, n. woven fabric of hemp, straw, etc., for mats, floor covering, etc.; dull finish.

mat·tress, n. cloth casing filled with resilient material, used as or on a bed.

ma·ture, a. full grown; fully developed; ripe. v. make, become mature; become due. **ma·tu·ri·ty,** n.

ma·tu·ti·nal, a. occurring in the morning; early.

maud·lin, a. foolishly, tearfully sentimental.

maul, mall, n. large heavy hammer. v. maltreat; bruise; beat.

maun·der, v. act aimlessly; talk ramblingly.

mau·so·le·um, n. imposing tomb; stone building or entombment.

mauve, n. delicate purple.

mav·er·ick, n. unbranded animal; political nonconformist.

maw, n. stomach, throat, gullet.

max·il·la, n. upper jaw.

max·im, n. established principle; general truth; proverbial saying.

max·i·mum, n., a. greatest quantity, value, degree; upper limit.

may, v. pt. **might.** permission, likelihood or possibility, wish, contingency.

may·be, adv. perhaps.

may·hem, n. maiming a person; deliberate destruction or violence.

may·on·naise, n. salad dressing made of egg yolks, oil, etc.

may·or, n. chief executive of a city or other municipality.

maze, n. confusing intricate network of passages.

me, pron. objective case of **I.**

mead·ow, n. tract of grass land; pasture.

mea·ger, a. thin; scanty; lacking in quality or quantity.

meal, n. food prepared, served, eaten at one time; ground grain.

mean, v., **meant, mean·ing.** intend; signify; denote; to be significant. a. inferior; shabby; ill-tempered; humble; contemptible; base; stingy; unkind; halfway between extremes; intermediate. n. simple average. pl. that used to accomplish an end; income.

me·an·der, v. to wind or turn; wander aimlessly; ramble.

mean·ing, n. what is intended or signified; import. **-ful, -less,** a. **-ful·ly,** adv.

mean·time, n., adv. during the intervening time; at the same time.

mea·sles, n. acute infectious disease marked by red spots.

meas·ure, n. extent; dimensions; capacity; standard or instrument of measurement; course of action; section of notes in music, poetry. v. determine or estimate extent, dimensions, capacity; proportion; compare;

be of a specified measurement. **-ure·ment,** *n.* **-ur·a·ble,** *a.*

meat, *n.* animal flesh used as food; edible inner part; substance or essence. **-y,** *a.*

me·chan·ic, *n.* worker skilled in using tools or in operation, repair of machinery.

me·chan·i·cal, *a.* of or produced by tools, machinery; automatic.

me·chan·ics, *n.* study of motion of material bodies and the action of forces on bodies.

mech·an·ism, *n.* working parts of a machine system whose parts work together.

mech·a·nize, *v.* make mechanical; introduce machinery into.

med·al, *n.* inscribed piece of metal for awarding to a person or commemorating an event.

me·dal·lion, *n.* large medal; oval or round design; thin cut of meat.

med·dle, *v.* interfere.

me·di·an, *a.* situated in or having the value of the middle; intermediate.

me·di·ate, *v.* act as an agent in a dispute. **-a·tion,** *n.* **-a·tor,** *n.*

Med·ic·aid, *n.* government sponsored medical program for the poor.

med·i·cal, *a.* connected with the study or practice of medicine.

Med·i·care, *n.* government sponsored medical program for the aged.

med·i·cate, *v.* treat with medicine; add medicine to. **-ca·tion,** *n.*

me·dic·i·nal, *a.* of medicine; curative; healing; relieving.

med·i·cine, *n.* substance to treat disease, relieve pain; science of preventing and curing disease.

me·di·e·val, *a.* of the Middle Ages (A·D. 500 to 1500).

me·di·o·cre, *a.* average or below; ordinary. **-oc·ri·ty,** *n.*

med·i·tate, *v.* ponder; reflect; think deeply; plan. **-ta·tion,** *n.*

me·di·um, *n. pl.,* **-a.** thing placed or ranked in the middle; communication channel; environment; nutritive substance; means of effecting something; artist's material. *a.* intermediate.

med·ley, *n.* mixture; musical composition; jumble.

meek, *a.* patient and mild; submissive.

meet, *v.,* **met, meet·ing.** come upon; be present at the place of arrival of; find; join; settle; encounter; face directly; oppose; satisfy. *n.* sports gathering.

meet·ing, *n.* a coming together; gathering; intersection.

meg·a·phone, *n.* funnel-shaped device to intensify or direct the voice.

meg·a·ton, *n.* explosive force equal to a million tons of TNT.

mel·an·chol·y, *n., a.* state of sadness, dejection.

mé·lange, *n.* mixture; medley.

me·lee, *n.* confused struggle.

mel·lif·lu·ous, *a.* sounding sweet and smooth.

mel·low, *a.* soft and sweet; full flavored; rich, soft, and pure; gentle and understanding.

mel·o·dra·ma, *n.* sentimental, extravagantly theatrical drama. **-mat·ic,** *a.*

mel·o·dy, *n.* pleasing series of sounds. **me·lod·ic,** *a.*

mel·on, *n.* fruit of a gourd plant.

melt, *v.* change from a solid to a liquid or flowing state by heat; merge or blend; soften.

melt·down, *n.* dangerous situation in which radiation is released from a nuclear reactor if the fuel rods melt.

mem·ber, *n.* a limb or other body part; person belonging to an organization.

mem·ber·ship, *n.* state of being a member; the number of members.

mem·brane, *n.* thin layer of tissue that covers or lines an organ or part.

me·men·to, *n. pl.,* **-tos, toes.** souvenir to remind.

mem·o, *n. inf.* memorandum.

mem·oir, *n.* record of events; biography.

mem·o·ra·bil·ia, *n.* things worthy of remembrance.

mem·o·ra·ble, *a.* worth remembering; notable.

mem·o·ran·dum, *n. pl.,* **-dums, -da.** short note; brief record.

me·mo·ri·al, *n.* anything to help preserve the memory of a person or event. *a.* **-ize,** *v.*

mem·o·rize, *v.* commit to memory; learn by heart.

mem·o·ry, *n. pl.,* **-ries.** process of retaining and recalling what has been learned; total of things remembered; commemoration.

men·ace, *v.* threaten. *n.* a threat.

me·nag·er·ie, *n.* collection of animals, esp. for exhibition.

mend, *v.* repair; reform; restore; improve; correct; cure.

me·ni·al, *a.* servile; low; humble. *n.* domestic servant.

men·o·pause, *n.* permanent cessation of menstruation.

men·stru·a·tion, *n.* monthly flow of blood and mucus from uterus. **-ate,** *v.* **-al,** *a.*

men·tal, *a.* of or in the mind; mentally ill. **-ly,** *adv.*

men·tal·i·ty, *n.* mental capacity.

men·thol, *n.* crystalline substance with the odor and coolness of peppermint.

men·tion, *n.* reference to. *v.* cite; call attention to.

men·tor, *n.* wise loyal adviser.

men·u, *n.* list of foods.

mer·can·tile, *a.* of merchants, trade, business, commerce.

mer·ce·nar·y, *a.* greedy. *n.* soldier hired into foreign army for pay.

mer·cer·ize, *v.* treat thread for luster, strength, etc.

mer·chan·dise, *v.* buy and sell goods, etc. *n.* things bought and sold.

mer·chant, *n.* retail dealer; storekeeper; trader.

mer·cu·ri·al, *a.* of mercury; fickle; inconstant.

mer·cu·ry, *n.* heavy, silver-white, liquid metallic element used in scientific instruments and for industrial purposes.

mer·cy, *n.* (act of) kindness; clemency; compassion. **-ci·ful, -ci·less,** *a.*

mere, *a.* nothing more or other than. **-ly,** *adv.*

merge, *v.* blend; mingle; combine; unite.

merg·er, *n.* combination of companies into one; merging of anything.

me·rid·i·an, *n.* great circle of the earth passing through the poles; highest point of course of heavenly body.

me·ringue, *n.* beaten egg whites and sugar used as pie covering.

mer·it, *n.* excellence; worth; something deserving. *v.* deserve. **-i·to·ri·ous,** *a.*

mer·maid, *n.* imaginary sea creature, half woman, half fish.

mer·ry, *a.,* **-ri·er, -ri·est.** full of fun. **-ri·ly,** *adv.* **-ri·ment,** *n.*

mer·ry-go-round, *n.* revolving circular platform with wooden animals and seats; carousel; whirl.

me·sa, *n.* small, high plateau with steep sides, flat-topped.

mesh, *n.* net; network; web; snare. *v.* entangle; interlock.

mes·mer·ize, *v.* hypnotize; fascinate.

mes·quite, *n.* thorny tree or shrub with pods, used as fodder.

mess, *n.* confused mixture; untidy or dirty; communal meal. *v.* make untidy; bungle; putter. **-y,** *a.,* **-i·er, -i·est.**

mes·sage, *n.* communication; chief idea of a statement.

mes·sen·ger, *n.* one who carries a message or does an errand.

me·tab·o·lism, *n.* process of breaking down food for use in the living body.

met·al, *n.* opaque, ductile, solid chemical substance. **-lic,** *a.*

met·al·lur·gy, *n.* science and technology of metals.

met·a·mor·pho·sis, *n. pl.,* **-ses.** change of form, structure; any marked change or transformation.

met·a·phor, *n.* figure of speech; figurative language.

met·a·phys·ics, *n.* branch of philosophy concerned with study of the ultimate causes and reasons for things. **-i·cal,** *a.*

me·tas·ta·sis, *n. pl.,* **-ta·ses.** change of position, state, or form.

mete, *v.,* **met·ed, met·ing.** allot.

me·te·or, *n.* small, solid body entering earth's atmosphere at great speed with streak of light. **-ic,** *a.*

me·te·or·ite, *n.* meteor that reaches earth's crust as a mass of stone or metal.

me·te·or·ol·o·gy, *n.* science of weather, climate. **-o·gist,** *n.*

me·ter, me·tre, *n.* rhythm in music or verse; basic unit of length of metric system equal to 39·37 inches; instrument that measures. **met·ric,** *a.*

meth·a·done, *n.* synthetic, addictive narcotic drug.

meth·ane, *n.* colorless, odorless, flammable gas.

meth·od, *n.* mode or process of procedure; system of doing; orderly procedure. **meth·od·i·cal,** *a.*

me·tic·u·lous, *a.* exceedingly careful of details; scrupulous.

met·ric sys·tem, *n.* decimal system of weights and measures.

met·ro·nome, *n.* instrument that beats time as for music.

me·trop·o·lis, *n.* large city; chief city. **met·ro·pol·i·tan,** *a.*

met·tle, *n.* spirit, courage, ardor. **-some,** *a.* spirited.

mez·za·nine, *n.* low-ceilinged story between two main ones; lower theater balcony or first few rows of balcony seats.

mez·zo, *a. mus.* medium; moderate; half. *adv. mus.* moderately.

mi·ca, *n.* mineral that can be separated into thin, flexible sheets.

mi·crobe, *n.* microscopic organism, esp. a disease germ.

mi·cro·cir·cuit, *n.* miniature circuit for computers, space equipment, etc.

mi·cro·cosm, *n.* little world; community that is a world in itself.

mi·cro·dot, *n.* photographed reproduction of any document reduced to pinpoint size.

mi·cro·elec·tron·ics, *n.* study of miniaturization of electronic components.

mi·cro·fiche, *n.* reduced-sized document filed on microfilm for easier storage.

mi·cro·film, *n.* film on which documents, etc. are photographically greatly reduced in size.

mi·crom·e·ter, *n.* device for measuring minute distances.

mi·cro·phone, *n.* device that converts sound waves into an electrical signal.

mi·cro·scope, *n.* optical instrument for greatly enlarging objects, as microorganisms.

mi·cro·scop·ic, *a.* invisible except through a microscope.

mi·cro·wave oven, *n.* device where cooking is by penetration of electromagnetic waves into food.

mid, *a.* middle.

mid·day, *n.* noon.

mid·dle, *a.* equally distant from two points, times, etc.; medial; central; intermediate; medium. *n.* point halfway between two extremes; the waist.

mid·dle·man, *n.* person who buys from the producer and sells to the consumer or retailer; a go-between.

midg·et, *n.* very small person or thing. *a.* miniature.

mid·night, *n.* twelve o'clock at night.

mid·riff, *n.* mid-section between chest and waist.

mid·ship·man, *n. pl.,* **-men.** student naval officer.

midst, *n.* middle central part. *prep.* amidst.

mid·way, *a.* being in the middle. *adj.* halfway. *n.* part of a fair, amusement park, etc., where side shows, amusements, etc., are located.

mid·wife, *n. pl.,* **-wives.** woman who assists other women in childbirth.

mien, *n.* demeanor; aspect; appearance; bearing.

miff, *n. inf* trivial quarrel. *v.* offend.

might, *n.* ability; power; bodily strength. **-y,** *a.,* **-i·er, -i·est.** *v.* pt. of **may.**

mi·graine, *n.* severe recurring headache, usu. on one side.

mi·grate, *v.* move from one place to another. **mi·gra·tion,** *n.* **mi·gra·to·ry,** *a.*

mi·ka·do, *n.* emperor of Japan.

mil, *n.* ·001 of an inch.

mild, *a.* gentle in feeling or behavior; temperate; soft; malleable. **-ly,** *adv.*

mil·dew, *n.* fungi producing a whitish coating on damp cloth, paper, or living plants.

mile, *n.* unit of linear measure, 5,280 feet.

mile·age, *n.* distance in miles traveled in a given time; allowance for travelling expenses.

mile·stone, *n.* important point in progress, development.

mi·lieu, *n. pl.,* **-lieus.** environment; social setting.

mil·i·tant, *a.* combative; aggressive; fighting; warring.

mil·i·ta·rism, *n.* military spirit; preparedness for war. **-rist,** *n.* **-ris·tic,** *a.*

mil·i·tar·y, *n.* of soldiers, war. *n.* armed forces.

mi·li·tia, *n.* citizen's army.

milk, *n.* white fluid secreted by mammary glands of female mammals as nourishment for young. *v.* extract milk from. **-y,** *a.*

milk·sop, *n.* timid, unmasculine man; mollycoddle.

mill, *n.* building where grain is ground into flour; textile factory; machine for cutting, grinding, etc.; one-tenth of a cent. *v.* grind in a mill; form ridges; move slowly in a circle.

mil·len·ni·um, *n. pl.,* **-ni·a, -ni·ums.** a thousand years; period of peace, happiness for everyone.

mil·li·me·ter, *n.* ·001 of a meter.

mil·li·ner, *n.* designer, seller of women's hats. **-y,** *n.*

mil·lion, *n.* a thousand thousands. **mil·lionth,** *n., a.*

mil·lion·aire, *n.* person whose wealth is at least a million dollars.

mill·stone, *n.* stone for grinding grain; heavy burden.

mime, *n.* pantomime; actor. *v.* mimic.

mim·ic, *v.,* **-icked, -ick·ing.** imitate; mock. *n.* one who imitates. **-ry,** *n.*

mince, *v.* cut into very small pieces; pronounce with affectation; weaken; walk with affected daintiness.

mince·meat, *n.* chopped mixture of raisins, spices, suet, sometimes meat, used as pie filling.

mind, *n.* sanity; opinion; intention; disposition; intelligence; memory. *v.* give heed; be careful; obey; take care of; concerning; intend; object. **-ful,** *a.*

min·a·tory, *a.* threatening.

mine, *pron.* possessive of **I.** belonging to me. *n.* excavation from which mineral substances are taken; encased explosive; rich source of supply. *v.* dig; take. **min·er, min·ing,** *n.*

min·er·al, *a., n.* inorganic, naturally occurring substance, neither animal nor plant.

min·gle, *v.* mix together; combine; join with others.

min·i·a·ture, *n., a.* (reproduction) on a very small scale.

min·i·mize, *v.* make as small as possible; disparage.

min·i·mum, *a., n.* smallest or lowest amount, degree, quantity.

min·is·ter, *n.* person who conducts religious services; government official; diplomatic officer. *v.* administer; serve.

min·is·try, *n.* act of serving; office or function of a minister; the clergy; government department under a minister.

mink, *n.* semi-aquatic, slim, carnivorous weasel-like mammal; its valuable fur.

min·now, *n.* small fish.

mi·nor, *a.* inferior; not important; under legal age. *n.* secondary field of study; subordinate; person under legal age.

mi·nor·i·ty, *n.* racial, religious or political group smaller than the majority; state of being under legal age; smaller part or number.

mint, *n.* place where money is coined; a large amount; aromatic plant. *v.* coin; fabricate; invent. *a.* new; in unused condition.

min·u·et, *n.* graceful dance.

mi·nus, *prep.* less; without. *n.* minus sign; negative quantity. *a.* less; negative.

min·ute, *n.* 60th part of an hour; sixty seconds; moment. *pl.* official record of a meeting.

mi·nute, *a.,* **-nut·er, -nut·est.** infinitesimal; trifling; detailed.

mir·a·cle, *n.* a marvel; supernatural event. **mi·rac·u·lous,** *a.*

mi·rage, *n.* optical illusion; delusion.

mire, *n.* mud; marsh; bog. *v.* to cause or to sink in mire.

mir·ror, *n.* smooth surface that reflects images; looking glass.

mirth, *n.* merriment; gaiety. **-ful,** *a.* **-less,** *a.*

mis·ad·ven·ture, *n.* unlucky accident; mishap.

mis·an·thrope, *n.* one who hates or distrusts mankind.

mis·ap·ply, *v.* apply or use badly or improperly.

mis·ap·pre·hend, *v.* misunderstand. **-hen·sion,** *n.*

mis·be·have, *v.* behave improperly. **-ha·vior,** *n.*

mis·cal·cu·late, *v.* miscount; miscompute; judge erroneously. **-la·tion,** *n.*

mis·car·riage, *n.* premature expulsion of a nonviable fetus; failure to carry out what was intended or justified. **-ry,** *v.,* **-ried, -ry·ing.**

mis·ce·ge·na·tion, *n.* marriage or sexual relations between persons of different races.

mis·cel·la·ne·ous, *a.* various kinds; mixed. **-ny,** *n.*

mis·chance, *n.* bad luck; mishap.

mis·chief, *n.* playful tricks or behavior that annoys; trouble, harm, or damage. **mis·chie·vous,** *a.*

mis·con·ceive, *v.* interpret wrongly; misunderstand. **-cep·tion,** *n.*

mis·con·duct, *n.* mismanagement; malfeasance; improper conduct.

mis·con·strue, *v.* misinterpret.

mis·cre·ant, *n.* a criminal. *a.* villainous.

mis·deed, *n.* offense; evil act.

mis·de·mean·or, *n.* offense less serious than a felony.

mi·ser, *n.* hoarder of wealth; stingy person.

mis·er·a·ble, *a.* wretched; causing misery; inadequate; unhappy, sick. **-bly,** *adv.*

mis·er·y, *n.* distress because of pain, sorrow, poverty, etc.

mis·fea·sance, *n.* perform lawful action in illegal manner.

mis·fit, *n.* bad fit; person not suited to his position, associates, etc.

mis·for·tune, *n.* ill luck; adversity; mishap.

mis·giv·ing, *n. often pl.* feeling of doubt, apprehension.

mis·guide, *v.* guide wrongly.

mis·hap, *n.* unfortunate accident.

mis·judge, *v.* judge wrongly.

mis·lay, *v.,* **-laid, -lay·ing.** put in a place afterward forgotten; lay improperly (tile, etc.).

mis·lead, *v.,* **-led, -lead·ing.** lead astray; deceive. **-ing,** *a.*

mis·no·mer, *n.* misnaming person in legal document; wrong name.

mi·sog·y·ny, *n.* hatred, distrust of women. **-nist,** *n.*

mis·print, *v.* print incorrectly.

mis·rep·re·sent, *v.* represent badly; falsify; belie.

miss, *v.* fail to hit, reach, meet, catch, obtain, or perceive; regret, notice, feel the absence of; avoid. *n. cap.* title of unmarried female.

mis·sal, *n.* Roman Catholic prayer book for the mass.

mis·sile, *n.* weapon, projectile thrown or launched.

miss·ing, *a.* absent; lost.

mis·sion, *n.* group sent by church, government, etc., to perform a special duty; mission headquarters.

mis·sion·ar·y, *n.* one who tries to spread religious faith in unbelievers.

mis·sive, *n.* a letter; message.

mis·spell, *v.*, **-spelled** or **-spelt**. spell incorrectly. **-ing**, *n.*

mist, *n.* visible watery vapor; haze; film; thing which blurs vision. **-y**, *a.*

mis·take, *v.*, **-took, -tak·en, -tak·ing.** perceive wrongly; misjudge; misinterpret; miscalculate. *n.*

Mis·ter, *n.* title of respect for a man. Abbr. **Mr.**

mis·tle·toe, *n.* evergreen plant with white berries.

mis·treat, *v.* treat wrongly or improperly; abuse. **-ment**, *n.*

mis·tress, *n.* woman in charge; woman copulating unlawfully with a man.

mis·trust, *n.* lack of confidence; suspicion. *v.* suspect; doubt.

mis·un·der·stand, *v.*, **-stood, -stand·ing.** understand incorrectly; misinterpret; miscomprehend.

mis·use, *v.* use improperly; abuse; mistreat.

mite, *n.* a very small creature; small amount.

mi·ter, mi·tre, *n.* bishop's headdress; angled fitted joint.

mit·i·gate, *v.* become or make milder or less severe.

mitt, *n.* type of glove.

mit·ten, *n.* glove with a thumb but no separately divided fingers.

mix, *v.* blend into one mass; combine; confuse. *n.* combination of ingredients; state of confusion. **mixed**, *a.* **mix·ture**, *n.*

mne·mon·ic, *a.* technique for improving memory.

moan, *v.*, *n.* (utter) a low dull sound from grief, pain; lament; complain.

moat, *n.* deep broad ditch surrounding a fortified place.

mob, *n.* disorderly lawless crowd. *v.* overcrowd; to throng; attack by crowding.

mo·bile, *a.* easily moved; adaptable; movable. **-bil·i·ty**, *n.*

mo·bi·lize, *v.* make movable; make ready; organize.

moc·ca·sin, *n.* kind of soft shoe.

mock, *v.* mimic esp. in derision; deride; delude; defy; jeer; copy. *a.* false. **-er·y**, *n.*

mode, *n.* way of acting or doing; fashion; style; method.

mod·el, *n.* standard of excellence; representation in miniature; one who poses for artists, displays clothes; example; pattern; ideal. *v.* form; plan; display (wear).

mo·dem, *n.* acronym for MOdulator-DEModulator, a device that converts the form of data so that it can be transmitted by another medium.

mod·er·ate, *a.* temperate; mild; medium quality, etc. *n.* person with moderate views. *v.* make moderate; preside over (a meeting, etc.). **-ly**, *adv.* **-a·tion**, *n.* **-a·tor**, *n.*

mod·ern, *a.* of the present or recent times; latest trends. **-ize**, *v.*

mod·est, *a.* holding a moderate opinion of oneself; unpretentious; humble. **-es·ty**, *n.*

mod·i·fy, *v.* change; alter in some way. **-fi·ca·tion**, *n.*

mod·u·late, *v.* control, modify, vary, adapt. **-la·tion**, *n.*

mod·ule, *n.* unit of measurement; detachable section. **-u·lar**, *a.*

mo·gul, *n.* magnate; great personage.

mo·hair, *n.* cloth or fabric of Angora goat hair.

moist, *a.* slightly wet; damp.

mois·ten, *v.* make damp.

mois·ture, *n.* slight wetness.

mo·lar, *n.* tooth for grinding.

mo·las·ses, *n.* thick, dark syrup produced from refining of sugar.

mold, mould, *n.* rich, organic soil; form in which a thing is shaped; fungous growth. *v.* exert influence on; shape; fashion.

mold·ing, mould·ing, *n.* decorative edging; cornice.

mole, *n.* discolored spot on skin; burrowing insect-eating animal; *inf.* espionage agent.

mol·e·cule, *n.* smallest particle of an element with all the properties of that element.

mo·lest, *v.* annoy; make improper sexual advances.

mol·li·fy, *v.* soothe, pacify.

mol·lusk, mol·lusc, *n.* invertebrate animal with soft, unsegmented body and hard shell, as an oyster or clam.

molt, moult, *v.* shed feathers, skin, etc., prior to new growth.

mol·ten, *a.* liquefied by heat; melted; glowing.

mo·ment, *n.* indefinite brief period of time; instant; importance. **-men·tar·y**, *a.* **-men·tar·i·ly**, *adv.*

mo·men·tous, *a.* very important; consequential.

mo·men·tum, n. impetus of a moving object.

mon·arch, n. person reigning over a kingdom; large migratory butterfly.

mon·as·ter·y, n. residence for those, esp. monks, living under religious vows.

mo·nas·tic, a. of or like a monastery or its people. self-denying.

Mon·day, n. 2nd day of week.

mon·e·tar·y, a. of money or currency; pecuniary.

mon·ey, n. coin, paper used as medium of exchange; wealth.

mon·grel, n., a. (plant, animal) of mixed or cross breeding.

mon·i·tor, n. one who helps keep order; teacher's helper; receiver to check radio or TV transmission. v. listen to; watch or check.

monk, n. male member of religious order vowed to celibacy, poverty, etc.

mon·key, n. pl., **-keys.** any non-human primate; impish child. v. mimic; play idly.

mo·nog·a·my, n. practice or state of being married to only one person at a time.

mon·o·gram, n. initials of a person's name in a design.

mon·o·graph, n. scholarly article; learned treatise.

mon·o·lith, n. large single stone block; organized whole that acts as a single power force.

mon·o·logue, mon·o·log, n. long speech (esp. monopolizing conversation) by one person; play or skit for one person; soliloquy.

mo·nop·o·ly, n. exclusive control of a commodity or service in a given market. **-lize,** v.

mon·o·rail, n. railway with single rail with cars suspended from it or balanced on it.

mon·o·syl·la·ble, n. word of one syllable.

mon·o·the·ism, n. belief that there is only one God.

mon·o·tone, n. utterance or musical tone without change of key or pitch.

mo·not·o·ny, n. tiring repetition; sameness of tone. **-nous,** a.

mon·sieur, n. pl., **mes·sieurs.** French title for a man.

mon·soon, n. seasonal wind of Asia; rainy season.

mon·ster, n. malformed or huge person or thing; wicked person. **-stros·i·ty**, n. **-strous,** a.

mon·tage, n. composite picture from a number of different pictures.

month, n. one of twelve parts of a year.

month·ly, a., adv. done, happening, appearing, payable, etc., every month.

mon·u·ment, n. memorial marker, statue, building, etc.

mon·u·men·tal, a. massive.

mooch, v. (sl.) sponge; beg.

mood, n. particular state of mind; humor, temper, feeling.

mood·y, a., **-i·er, -i·est.** subject to having changing moods, as depression.

moon, n. heavenly body which revolves around any planet; earth's satellite. v. behave in an idle dreamy way. **-light,** n. **-lit,** a.

moor, n. open waste land. v. secure (a ship, etc.) by cables; anchors, etc.

moor·ing, n. usu. pl. lines, cables, etc.; place where ship is moored.

moose, n. pl., **moose.** largest animal of deer family.

moot, a. debatable; arguable.

mop, n. rags, yarn, or a sponge on a stick for cleaning floors. v.

mope, v. act gloomy, apathetic, listless.

moral, a. of or concerned with right and wrong; virtuous; ethical; righteous. n. ethical lesson. pl. ethics; principles. **-ly,** adv.

mo·rale, n. mental condition of courage, enthusiasm, confidence; esprit de corps.

mo·ral·i·ty, n. virtue; principles of right conduct.

mor·al·ize, v. explain in terms of right and wrong; improve the morals of.

mo·rass, n. marsh; swamp; bog; thing that creates difficulties.

mor·a·to·ri·um, n. pl., **-ums, -a.** authorized delay of activity; legal period of delay.

mo·ray, n. brightly colored eel.

mor·bid, a. diseased; gruesome; gloomy.

mor·dant, a. caustic; sarcastic.

more, a. greater; further; additional. n. greater quantity, amount, importance, etc. adv. in, to a greater extent or degree; moreover.

more·o·ver, adv. besides; also.

mo·res, n. pl. folkways; customs; conventions.

morgue, n. place where bodies of dead persons are kept until burial; newspaper reference department.

mor·i·bund, a. dying; deathlike.

morn·ing, n. day from midnight (or sunrise) to noon; dawn.

mo·ron, n. feebleminded adult; inf. stupid, foolish person. **-ic,** a.

mo·rose, a. gloomy; sullen.

mor·phine, n. habit-forming narcotic derived from opium.

mor·sel, *n.* small quantity of food; little piece of anything.

mor·tal, *a.* subject to death; fatal; pertaining to or causing death; tedious; prolonged; extreme. *n.* human being. **-ly,** *adv.*

mor·tal·i·ty, *n.* mortal nature of man; death rate; humanity; large scale deaths.

mor·tar, *n.* bowl in which substances are reduced to powder with pestle; cannon; cement mixture for binding together stones, bricks; plaster.

mort·gage, *n.* deed pledging property to creditor as security for payment of a loan. *v.* pledge.

mor·ti·cian, *n.* undertaker.

mor·ti·fy, *v.* humiliate; shame; control one's physical desires.

mor·tu·ar·y, *n.* funeral home.

mo·sa·ic, *n.* inlaid design of bits of colored glass, stones, etc.

mo·sey, *v. slang,* move leisurely; saunter.

mos·qui·to, *n.* small, flying, bloodsucking insect.

moss, *n.* small, green plant growing in velvety clusters on rocks, ground, etc.

most, *a.* greatest in amount, quantity, degree. *adv.* in or to the greatest, highest degree.

most·ly, *adv.* mainly; usually.

mote, *n.* speck, as of dust.

mo·tel, *n.* lodging place with accessible parking.

moth, *n.* nocturnal, winged butterfly-like insect.

moth·er, *n.* female parent. *a.* of, like a mother. *v.* nourish; care for. **-hood,** *n.* **-ly,** *a.*

moth·er-in-law, *n. pl.,* **moth·ers·in·law.** mother of one's spouse.

mo·tif, *n.* repeated theme, design; dominant idea.

mo·tile, *a.* capable of movement.

mo·tion, *n.* movement; proposal for action; activity; formal suggestion. *v.* gesture.

mo·ti·vate, *v.* impel; incite; induce. **-va·tion,** *n.*

mo·tive, *n.* some inner drive; incentive; goal.

mot·ley, *a.* of many colors; varied; of diverse elements.

mo·tor, *n.* anything which imparts motion; engine; thing that changes natural energy to mechanical energy. *a.* of or operated by a motor. *v.* travel by automobile. **-ist,** *n.*

mo·tor·cy·cle, *n.* two-wheeled vehicle propelled by an internal-combustion engine.

mot·tle, *v.* mark with streaks, blotches of colors. **-tled,** *a.*

mot·to, *n. pl.,* **-toes, -tos.** phrase; maxim expressing ideals or goals.

mound, *n.* heap of earth; small hill. *v.* heap up.

mount, *n.* mountain; frame; support; animal used for riding. *v.* increase; climb; raise; ascend; get up on; place on a support; start.

moun·tain, *n.* land mass rising conspicuously above adjacent land. **-ous,** *a.* **-eer,** *n.*

moun·te·bank, *n.* quack; charlatan.

mourn, *v.* grieve for; feel sorrow. **-er,** *n.* **-ful,** *a.*

mourn·ing, *n.* expression of grief; period of sadness.

mouse, *n. pl.,* **mice.** small rodent; *inf.* black eye; timid person.

mouth, *n.* facial opening for speaking and food; an opening. *v.* form words soundlessly.

mouth·piece, *n.* part held against, close to, or in the mouth; *inf.* spokesman, lawyer.

move, *v.* change position, place; shift; persuade; set in motion; rouse the emotions; change residence; take action; progress. *n.* act of moving. **mov·er,** *n.* **mov·ing,** *a.* **mov·a·ble,** *a.*

move·ment, *n.* act of moving; shift in position; organized action by group working toward some goal; trend; moving parts; *mus.* principal parts.

mow, *v.,* **mowed, mowed** or **mown, mow·ing.** cut down (grass, grain); kill.

much, *adv., a.,* **more, most.** (to a) great degree or extent; often; nearly. *n.* great quantity; something great.

mu·ci·lage, *n.* gummy adhesive substance; glue; paste.

muck, *n.* manure; dirt; filth.

mu·cous, *a.* of, containing, or secreting mucus.

mu·cus, *n.* secretion to moisten and protect mucous membranes.

mud, *n.* wet, soft earth. **-dy,** *a.*

mud·dle, *v.* mix up; confuse; make turbid; befog; bungle. *n.* mess; confusion.

muff, *n.* tubular cover to warm hands; fumble; bungling action.

muf·fin, *n.* quick bread baked in cup-shaped molds.

muf·fle, *v.* enfold or wrap; deaden the sound of; suppress.

muf·fler, *n.* neck scarf; device for deadening sound.

mug, *n.* drinking cup; *inf.* the face. *v. inf.* assault; grimace.

mug·gy, *a.* warm; damp; close.

mug·wump, *n.* person independant in politics.

mul·ber·ry, *n.* tree with edible purple fruit.

mulch, *n.* loose organic protective covering around plantings.

mulct, *v.* swindle; defraud. *n.* a fine.

mule, *n.* offspring of horse and donkey; *inf.* stubborn person.

mul·ish, *a.* obstinate.

mul·ti·far·i·ous, *a.* having many parts or elements.

mul·ti·ple, *a.* having many parts; manifold. *n.* number that is the product of any specified number by another number.

mul·ti·plic·i·ty, *n.* great number.

mul·ti·ply, *v.* increase; find the number by multiplication; propagate. **-pli·ca·tion,** *n.*

mul·ti·tude, *n.* a large number of persons or things.

mul·ti·tu·di·nous, *a.* many.

mum·ble, *v.* speak indistinctly.

mum·my, *n.* dead body preserved by embalming.

mumps, *n.* acute viral disease causing salivary gland swelling.

mun·dane, *a.* worldly; routine.

mu·nic·i·pal, *a.* of a town or city; internal affairs.

mu·nic·i·pal·i·ty, *n.* city or town with local self-government.

mu·nif·i·cent, *a.* very generous.

mu·ni·tions, *n.* war materials; ammunition.

mu·ral, *n.* large picture or painting on a wall.

mur·der, *n.* unlawful or premeditated killing of one human by another. **-ous,** *a.*

murk, mirk, *n.* darkness; gloom. **-y,** *a.,* **-i·er, -i·est.**

mur·mur, *n.* low, continuous, indistinct sound; mumbled complaint. *v.*

mus·cle, *n.* contractive tissue that produces bodily motion; muscular strength. *v.* force one's way. **-cu·lar,** *a.*

muse, *v.* ponder; meditate. *n.* deep meditation.

mu·se·um, *n.* building for exhibiting objects of art, history, science, etc.

mush, *n.* boiled cornmeal; any soft mass; *inf.* maudlin sentimentality.

mush·room, *n.* fleshy fungi with stalk and umbrella-like cap. *v.* grow or spread rapidly.

mu·sic, *n.* arrangement of sounds into pleasing patterns, with pitch, harmony, melody, rhythm. **-mu·si·cal,** *a.*

mu·si·cian, *n.* person skilled in music; composer; performer.

musk, *n.* strong-smelling secretion of male musk deer used in perfume.

musk·rat, *n. pl.,* **-rat, -rats.** large, aquatic rodent.

mus·lin, *n.* heavy cotton cloth.

mus·sel, *n.* edible bivalve marine mollusk.

must, *v.* obliged, bound, or required to; probability; certainty.

mus·tache, *n.* hair growing on human upper lip.

mus·tard, *n.* powdered seeds of mustard plant used as condiment or medicine.

mus·ter, *v.* gather; assemble; bring together. *n.* an assembling.

mus·ty, *a.* moldy smell or taste; trite; stale.

mu·ta·tion, *n.* basic alteration; change; individual or thing resulting from mutation.

mute, *a.* silent; dumb; incapable of speech. *n.* device to soften sound; *v.* tone down.

mu·ti·late, *v.* cut off or damage a part; cripple; maim.

mu·ti·ny, *n.* revolt against authority. *v.* disobey superiors; revolt.

mut·ter, *v.* speak in a low indistinct way; grumble.

mut·ton, *n.* edible flesh of grown sheep.

mu·tu·al, *a.* done by two or more; reciprocal; shared alike.

muz·zle, *n.* projecting mouth or nose of an animal; open end of a weapon; snout; mouth harness to prevent biting. *v.*

my, *pron.* possessive case of **I.**

my·o·pi·a, *n.* nearsightedness. **my·op·ic,** *a.*

myr·i·ad, *n.* large number.

myrrh, *n.* fragrant gum resin used as perfume base.

myr·tle, *n.* evergreen shrub.

my·self, *pron. pl.,* **our·selves.** intensive or reflexive form of **I.**

mys·ter·y, *n.* secret, unexplained, enigma; story of this kind. **-te·ri·ous,** *a.*

mys·tic, *a.* mysterious; occult; magical. *n.* one seeking truth beyond understanding. **mys·ti·cal,** *a.*

mys·ti·cism, *n.* a seeking to solve mysteries of existence by intuition and meditation.

mys·ti·fy, *v.* perplex; puzzle.

mys·tique, *n.* attitudes or feelings surrounding some person, activity, etc.

myth, *n.* fable; legend; fictitious story. **-ic, -i·cal,** *a.*

my·thol·o·gy, *n.* study of myths; myths collectively. **myth·o·log·i·cal,** *a.*

N

nab, *v.,* **nabbed, nab·bing.** *inf.* seize suddenly; arrest.

na·dir, *n.* lowest point of celestial sphere opposite the zenith.

nag, *v.,* **nagged, nag·ging.** harass; find fault; scold; badger; worry. *n.*

nail, *n.* piece of pointed metal for driving into wood for fastening; thin, horny substance on the end of a finger or toe. *v.*

na·ive, *a.* without common wisdom; inexperienced; simple; credulous. **-te,** *n.*

na·ked, *a.* not covered; bare; nude. **-ness,** *n.*

name, *n.* title; fame; family; reputation. *v.,* **named, nam·ing.** mention; appoint; specify. *a.* well-known.

name·ly, *adv.* that is to say.

nap, *v.,* **napped, nap·ping.** have a brief, light sleep. *n.* sleep; hairy surface on cloth. **napped,** *a.*

nape, *n.* back of the neck.

nap·kin, *n.* small cloth or paper used at meals.

nar·cis·sism, *n.* self-love.

nar·cot·ic, *n.* drug, often addictive, which relieves pain and induces sleep. *a.*

nar·rate, *v.,* **-rat·ed, -rat·ing.** tell; relate. **-ra·tor,** *n.* **-ra·tion,** *n.* **-ra·tive,** *n., a.*

nar·row, *a.* small in width; limited. *v.* limit; contract; decrease. **-ness,** *n.*

na·sal, *a.* of the nose.

nas·ty, *a.,* **-ti·er, -ti·est.** dirty; filthy; vile; harmful; indecent; mean. **-ti·ly,** *adv.* **-ti·ness,** *n.*

na·tal, *a.* of one's birth; native.

na·ta·tion, *n.* art of swimming.

na·tion, *n.* community of people with common territory, culture, political institutions, etc. **-al,** *a., n.*

na·tion·al·ism, *n.* patriotism; loyalty to the interests and independence of one's nation. **-ist,** *n.*

na·tion·al·i·ty, *n. pl.,* **-ties.** national status or quality; status of belonging to a nation; a national group.

na·tive, *a.* inborn; natural; belonging to an area by birth; indigenous. *n.* one born in an area or country.

na·tiv·i·ty, *n.* birth; *(cap·),* birth of Christ; Christmas.

nat·ty, *a.,* **-ti·er, -ti·est.** neatly dressed; smart. **-ti·ness,** *n.*

nat·u·ral, *a.* of nature; not artificial; inborn; normal. **-ral·ly,** *adv.* **nat·u·ral·ness,** *n.*

nat·u·ral·ize, *v.,* **-ized, -iz·ing.** confer citizenship upon an alien. **-i·za·tion,** *n.*

na·ture, *n.* essential traits; essence; inborn character, instincts; all phenomena of the physical universe.

naught, *n.* nothing; zero.

naugh·ty, *a.,* **-ti·er, -ti·est.** disobedient; ill-behaved; improper. **-ti·ness,** *n.*

nau·se·a, *n.* stomach upset; disgust. **-seous,** *a.*

nau·se·ate, *v.,* **-at·ed, -at·ing.** feel or cause nausea. **-at·ing,** *a.*

nau·ti·cal, *a.* of ships, sailors.

na·val, *a.* of, or for a navy, its ships, personnel, etc.

nave, *n.* main middle part, lengthwise, of a church.

na·vel, *n.* scar or depression in the middle of the abdomen.

nav·i·ga·ble, *a.* wide or deep enough for passage of ships; able to be steered, directed, navigated.

nav·i·gate, *v.,* **-gat·ed, -gat·ing.** steer or direct a ship or aircraft; travel on or over. **-ga·tion,** *n.* **-ga·tion·al,** *a.* **-ga·tor,** *n.*

na·vy, *n. pl.,* **-vies.** a fleet of ships; warships of a nation.

nay, *adv.* no. *n.* denial.

neap, *n.* either of two lowest monthly tides.

near, *a.* close; not far; direct; short; stingy. *adv.* almost; nearly. *prep.* close to. *v.* approach. **-ness,** *n.*

near·by, *a., adv.* close at hand.

near·sight·ed, *a.* better vision near than far; myopic. **-ness,** *n.*

neat, *a.* clean and orderly; tidy and precise. **-ly,** *adv.* **-ness,** *n.*

neb·u·la, *n. pl.,* **-las, lae.** vast cloudlike star or gas masses. **-lous,** *a.* confused; indistinct.

nec·es·sar·y, *a.* inevitable; inescapable; compulsory; essential. *n. pl.,* **-ies.** requisite.

ne·ces·si·tate, *v.,* **-tat·ed, -tat·ing.** make necessary or unavoidable.

neck, *n.* part connecting the head and body; narrow connecting or projecting part.

nec·tar, *n.* any delicious beverage; sweet fluid in flowers.

need, *n.* lack of something required; obligation; necessity; poverty. *v.* want; require.

nee·dle, *n.* slender, pointed instrument or leaf. *v.,* **-dled, -dling.** *inf.* tease. **-dler,** *n.*

need·less, *a.* unnecessary.

need·y, *a.,* **-i·er, -i·est.** poverty-stricken; poor; wanting.

ne·far·i·ous, *a.* wicked; evil.

ne·gate, *v.,* **-gat·ed, -gat·ing.** deny; nullify. **ne·ga·tion,** *n.*

neg·a·tive, *a.* expressing denial; lacking positive attributes; number less than zero. *n.* negative reply; refusal; *photog.* negative plate or film. *v.,* **-tived, -tiv·ing.** deny; veto; disprove; contradict. **-ness,** *n.*

ne·glect, *v.* disregard; be inattentive; fail to perform. *n.* **-ful,** *a.*

neg·li·gee, *n.* woman's dressing gown; informal attire.

neg·li·gent, *a.* careless; lax; inattentive. **-gence,** *n.*

neg·li·gi·ble, *a.* unimportant; inconsiderable.

ne·go·ti·ate, *v.,* **-at·ed, -at·ing.** discuss in order to reach an agreement; to settle or arrange for; transfer; surmount; cross. **-a·ble,** *a.* **-a·tion, -a·tor,** *n.*

ne·gri·tude, *n.* pride in being black.

Ne·gro, *n.* member of the black race.

neigh, *n.* the cry of a horse; whinny.

neigh·bor, *n.* one who lives near another. *a.* adjacent. *v.* be nearby. **-ing, -ly,** *a.* **-hood,** *n.*

nei·ther, *a., conj.* not either. *pron.* not the one or the other.

nem·a·tode, *n.* class of parasitic or free-living worms.

nem·e·sis, *n.* one inflicting punishment; thing that thwarts.

ne·o·lith·ic, *a.* of the later part of the stone age.

ne·on, *n.* colorless gaseous element. *a.*

neph·ew, *n.* son of one's brother, sister, sister-in-law or brother-in-law.

nep·o·tism, *n.* favoritism shown to relatives.

nerve, *n.* fiber which conveys sensation and originates motion through the body; courage; *inf.* impudence; brass.

nerv·ous, *a.* of nerves; easily agitated; timid; jumpy; tense.

nerv·y, *a.,* **-i·er, -i·est.** *inf.* arrogant; brash; bold. **-i·ness,** *n.*

nest, *n.* place used by a bird, insects, etc., for eggs; a place of rest. *v.* fit one within another.

nes·tle, *v.,* **-tled, -tling.** lie close and snug; cuddle.

net, *n.* meshed fabric; snare. *v.,* **net·ted, net·ting.** ensnare.

net, *a.* balance remaining after deductions (expenses, etc.); final result. *n.* a net amount, profits, weights, etc. *v.* to gain as a profit.

net·tle, *n.* weed with stinging hairs. *v.,* **-tled, -tling. irritate; annoy; to sting.**

net·work, *n.* system of interlocking wires, etc.; an interconnected system; chain of radio or T·V. stations; group of cooperating people.

neu·ral·gia, *n.* acute pain along the course of a nerve. **-gic,** *a.*

neu·ri·tis, *n.* inflammation of a nerve. **neu·rit·ic,** *a.*

neu·ro·sis, *n. pl.,* **-ses.** functional mental disorder, with anxiety, phobias, etc. **-rot·ic,** *a., n.*

neu·ter, *a.* neither male nor female; having no sex organs; spayed.

neu·tral, *a.* on neither side; indefinite; unaligned; no decided color. *n.* person or nation that remains neutral; disengaged gear. **-i·ty,** *n.*

neu·tral·ize, *v.,* **-ized, -iz·ing.** declare neutral; counteract effectiveness of, or active properties of. **-i·za·tion,** *n.*

neu·tron, *n.* fundamental particle in the nucleus of an atom.

nev·er, *adv.* not ever; at no time; not at all.

nev·er·the·less, *adv.* however; in spite of that; nonetheless.

new, *a.* recent; just made; different from former; novel; modern; fresh; original. *adv.* recently. , *n.*

new·el, *n.* post at top or bottom of stairs that supports handrail.

new·fan·gled, *a.* new; novel.

new·ly, *adv.* recently; afresh.

new·ly·wed, *n.* recently married person.

news, *n. pl.* current information; reports of recent happenings.

next, *a.* immediately or following; nearest. *prep.* beside; nearest to. *n.* one immediately following.

nib·ble, *v.,* **-bled, -bling.** eat with small bites; small gentle bites. *n.* small morsel. **-bler,** *n.*

nice, *a.,* **nic·er, nic·est.** pleasing; kind; delicate. **-ness,** *n.*

ni·ce·ty, *n. pl.,* **-ties.** subtle detail; fine distinction.

niche, *n.* recess or hollow, as in a wall; place or position where one is best fitted.

nick, *n.* small cut, chip, etc., on a surface. *v.* make a nick in.

nick·el, *n.* hard metallic, malleable element; five-cent coin.

nick·name, *n.* familiar form of a proper name; substitute or descriptive name. *v.,* **-named, -nam·ing.** give a substitute name.

nic·o·tine, nic·o·tin, *n.* poisonous alkaloid, derived from tobacco, used in insecticides.

niece, *n.* daughter of a brother or sister or of a brother-in-law or sister-in-law.

nig·gard·ly, *a.* stingy; miserly; scanty.

nigh, *v., adv. prep., a.*, **-er, -est.** near; close.

night, *n.* period of time from sunset to sunrise. *a.* of night.

night·in·gale, *n.* singing bird of the thrush family.

night·ly, *a.* occurring at night, or every night. *adv.* by night.

night·mare, *n.* frightening dream; terrifying experience. **-mar·ish**, *a.*

night·time, *n.* time between dusk and dawn.

nil, *n.* nothing.

nim·ble, *a.*, **-bler, -blest.** alert; quick; agile; quick-witted.

nine, *n.* number between eight and ten. *a.* one more than eight. **ninth**, *a., n.*

nine·teen, *n.* number which follows 18. *a.* one more than 18. **nine·teenth**, *a., n.*

nine·ty, *n. pl.*, **-ties.** number which follows 89. *a.* one more than 89. **-ti·eth**, *a., n.*

nin·ny, *n. pl.*, **-nies.** fool; dolt.

nip, *v.*, **nipped, nip·ping.** pinch, clip; destroy progress or maturing of; chill; sip. *n.* pinch; stinging quality; sip. **nip·per**, *n.*

nip·ple, *n.* protuberance on the breast; teat; thing resembling a nipple.

ni·tro·gen, *n.* gaseous chemical element, a component of all life.

ni·tro·glyc·er·in, *n.* flammable, explosive oil.

nit·wit, *n.* stupid person.

no, *adv.* nay; not at all. *n. pl.*, **noes, nos.** denial. *a.* not any.

no·bil·i·ty, *n. pl.*, **-ties.** aristocracy; noble birth or rank.

no·ble, *a.*, **-bler, -blest.** illustrious; famous; grand; lofty; of high rank, or title. *n.* **-man, -ness**, *adv.* **no·bly**, *adv.*

no·bod·y, *pron.* no one. *n. pl.*, **-ies.** person of no standing.

noc·tur·nal, *a.* occurring at night; active at night.

noc·u·ous, *a.* harmful.

nod, *v.*, **-ded, -ding.** let the head sink from drowsiness; bob the head; signify by a nod. *n.*

nod·ule, *n.* small knot or rounded lump. **-u·lar**, *a.*

no-fault, *a.* of insurance where the victim collects although blame is not established; of a divorce without blame being indicated.

noise, *n.* din; sound. *v.*

nois·y, *a.*, **-i·er, -i·est.** loud; boisterous; clamorous. **nois·i·ly**, *adv.*

no·mad, *n.* wanderer. *a.* wandering. **-ic**, *a.* **-ism**, *n.*

nom de plume, *n.* pen name; pseudonym.

no·men·cla·ture, *n.* name; designation; system of classifying.

nom·i·nal, *a.* something in name only; not in fact; small amount; of a noun.

nom·i·nate, *v.*, **-nat·ed, nat·ing.** name or appoint to an office; propose as a candidate. **-na·tion**, *n.* **-na·tor**, *n.*

nom·i·nee, *n.* person nominated.

non·cha·lant, *a.* coolly unconcerned; indifferent. **-lance**, *n.*

non·com·ba·tant, *n.* non-fighter; civilian.

non·com·mit·tal, *a.* not indicating point of view.

non·con·form·ist, *n.* one who does not conform to accepted customs or beliefs. **-i·ty**, *n.*

non·de·script, *a.* defying description; hard to classify.

none, *pron.* no one; not one; not any. *adv.* not at all. *n.* nothing.

non·en·ti·ty, *n. pl.*, **-ties.** nonexistent; insignificant person.

non·fea·sance, *n.* failure to act.

non·fer·rous, *a.* containing no iron.

non·flam·ma·ble, *a.* hard to ignite; slow burning.

no·non·sense, *a.* business-like; serious.

non·pa·reil, *n.* person or thing unequaled, unrivaled. *a.* without equal.

non·par·ti·san, *a.* not controlled by a single political party.

non·plus, *v.*, **-plused, -plus·ing.** completely perplex, bewilder.

non·prof·it, *a.* not conducted for purpose of making money.

non·sense, *n.* absurd words or actions; foolish behavior. **-sen·si·cal**, *a.*

non se·qui·tur, *n.* illogical inference; fallacy; statement that doesn't follow the train of thought.

non·vi·a·ble, *a.* not able to develop or function successfully.

noo·dle, *n.* dried egg dough, usu. shaped in ribbon-like strips.

nook, *n.* corner; recess; secluded spot.

noon, *n.* midday; twelve o'clock; highest point. **-time**, *n.*

no one, *pron.* nobody.

noose, *n.* loop with a slip knot; thing restricting freedom.

nor, *conj.* and not.

norm, *n.* standard of achievement or conduct; model.

nor·mal, *a.* usual; regular; average. *n.* standard. **-cy**, **-i·ty**, *n.* **-ly**, *adv.*

north, *a.*, *adv.* in, of, to, or toward the north. *n.* direction lying to the right of a person facing the sunset. **-ern**, *a.* **-ward**, *a.*, *adv.*

north·er, *n.* strong north wind; storm.

north·ern lights, *n. pl.* Aurora borealis.

nose, *n.* facial feature which contains the nostrils; snout; sense of smell. *v.*, **nosed**, **nos·ing.** pry; scent; nuzzle.

nos·tal·gia, *n.* longing for former times or things; homesickness. **-gic**, *a.*

nos·tril, *n.* opening of the nose.

nos·y, *a.*, **-i·er**, **-i·est.** *inf.* prying; inquisitive. **-i·ness**, *n.*

not, *adv.* in no way at all; to no degree; negative term.

no·ta·ble, *a.* worth of note; distinguished. *n.* famous person or thing. **-bly**, *adv.*

no·ta·rize, *v.*, **-rized**, **-riz·ing.** authenticate; certify. **no·ta·ry**, *n. pl.*, **-ries.** Also **no·ta·ry pub·lic.** official who attests to things.

no·ta·tion, *n.* brief note jotted down; note; system of signs or symbols (music, etc.). **-al**, *a.*

notch, *n.* V-shaped cut; deep pass; gap. *v.* cut a notch. **notched**, *a.*

note, *n.* *often pl.* brief record; memorandum; short statement or letter; *mus.* symbol; tone. *v.*, **not·ed**, **not·ing.** heed; observe; write down.

not·ed, *a.* notable; eminent.

note·wor·thy, *a.* outstanding.

noth·ing, *n.* no thing; not anything; nonentity; zero. *adv.* not at all.

no·tice, *n.* announcement; warning; attention; printed sign; brief review. *v.*, **-ticed**, **-tic·ing.** observe; pay attention to. **-a·ble**, *a.*

no·ti·fy, *v.*, **-fied**, **-fy·ing.** inform; give notice to. **-fi·ca·tion**, *n.*

no·tion, *n.* general concept; impression; theory; whim; *pl.* small useful articles; sundries.

no·to·ri·ous, *a.* widely known; unfavorably known. **-e·ty**, *n.*

not·with·stand·ing, *prep.* in spite of. *adv.* nevertheless; however. *conj.* although.

nou·gat, *n.* nut or fruit confection.

nought, *n.* nothing; zero.

noun, *n.* word that denotes a person, place, or thing.

nour·ish, *v.* feed; cause to grow; nurture; rear; support; maintain. **-ment**, *n.*

nou·veau riche, *n.* person newly rich.

nov·el, *n.* long, fictitious prose narrative. *a.* of a new kind; unusual; strange. **-ist**, *n.*

nov·el·ty, *n. pl.*, **-ties.** newness; something novel; innovation.

No·vem·ber, *n.* eleventh month.

nov·ice, *n.* beginner; amateur.

now, *adv.* at the present time; very recently or soon. *conj.* since. *n.* the present time.

no·where, *adv.* not in, at, or to any place. *n.* non-existent or remote place.

nox·ious, *a.* destructive to life; morally corrupting; distasteful; pernicious.

noz·zle, *n.* spout at the end for controlling something.

nu·ance, *n.* subtle distinction.

nu·bile, *a.* marriageable, esp. sexually mature.

nu·cle·ar, *a.* of a nucleus; of or using energy of atomic nucleli.

nu·cle·us, *n. pl.*, **-us·es**, **-i.** central part, esp. of living cells, atoms, etc.; core.

nude, *a.* naked; unclothed; bare. *n.* naked figure. **nu·di·ty**, *n.* **nud·ist**, *n.*

nudge, *n.* gentle push. *v.*, **nudged**, **nudg·ing.** jog.

nu·ga·to·ry, *a.* worthless; invalid.

nug·get, *n.* lump, esp. of gold.

nui·sance, *n.* annoying thing or person; pest.

null, *a.* invalid; insignificant.

nul·li·fy, *v.*, **-fied**, **-fy·ing.** make null; invalidate.

numb, *a.* with little or no sensation. *v.* deaden. **-ly**, *adv.* **-ness**, *n.* **-ing**, *a.*

num·ber, *n.* word or symbol used in counting, calculating, or to denote a total; group of persons or things; single performance; *pl.* numerical strength. *v.* total or count. **-less**, *a.*

nu·mer·al, *n.* figure or word denoting a number.

nu·mer·a·tor, *n.* term above the line in a fraction.

nu·mer·i·cal, *a.* in or by numbers.

nu·mer·ous, *a.* very many.

nu·mis·mat·ics, *n.* study of coins.

num·skull, *n.* dunce; moron.

nun, *n.* woman devoted to a religious life.

nup·tial, *a.* of marriage; of mating. *n. pl.* a wedding.

nurse, *n.* person trained to tend the sick; one who cares for young children, or the ill or aged. *v.*, **nursed**, **nurs·ing.** suckle; care for or try to cure.

nurs·er·y, *n. pl.*, **-ies.** child care center; room for babies; place where trees, plants, etc., are raised.

nur·ture, *n.* food; education; upbringing. *v.*-**tured**, **-tur·ing.** nourish; train; foster.

nut, kernel enclosed in a shell; bolt fastener.

nut·meg, *n.* aromatic seed used as a spice when grated.

nu·tri·ent, *a.* nourishing. *n.* anything which nourishes.

nu·tri·tion, *n.* process by which organisms absorb and utilize food in their systems.

nu·tri·tious, *a.* nourishing.

nut·ty, *a.,* **-ti·er, -ti·est.** containing nuts; tasting of nuts; *inf.* enthusiastic; crazy. **nut·ti·ness,** *n.*

nuz·zle, *v.,* **-zled, -zling.** push or rub with the nose; nestle; snuggle.

ny·lon, *n.* synthetic, tough, thermoplastic substance; *pl.* sheer hosiery.

nymph, *n. myth.* inferior divinity, conceived as a beautiful maiden; lovely, young maiden.

O

oaf, *n.* stupid, clumsy person.

oak, *n.* tree with hard, durable wood. *a.* of oak. **-en,** *a.*

oar, *n.* pole with a blade used to row a boat; paddle.

o·a·sis, *n. pl.,* **o·a·ses.** fertile place in the desert; refuge.

oat, *n. usu. pl.* grass cultivated for its edible cereal grain.

oath, *n. pl.,* **oaths.** declaration, by appeal to God, that one will speak the truth; a swear word.

ob·du·rate, *a.* hardhearted; unrepenting; stubborn.

o·be·di·ence, *n.* act of obeying; submission; compliance. **-ent,** *a.*

o·bei·sance, *n.* gesture of respect; deference; homage.

o·bese, *a.* very fat. **o·bes·i·ty,** *n.*

o·bey, *v.* be obedient; carry out orders. **-er,** *n.*

o·bit·u·ar·y, *n.* death notice. *a.* recording a death.

ob·ject, *n.* thing that can be seen, etc.; person or thing to which something is directed; purpose; goal. *v.* be adverse to; state disapproval of. **-tion,** *n.*

ob·jec·tive, *a.* dealing with the actual rather than thoughts or the mind; without bias. *n.* goal; purpose. **-tiv·i·ty,** *n.*

ob·jur·gate, *v.* denounce harshly; castigate.

ob·li·gate, *v.,* **-gat·ed, -gat·ing.** bind morally or legally. *a.* bound. **-ga·tion,** *n.* **-li·ga·to·ry,** *a.*

o·blige, *v.,* **-bliged, -blig·ing.** compel by moral, legal, or physical force; make indebted for favor done; do a favor for. **-blig·ing,** *a.*

ob·lique, *a.* slanting; inclined; indirect. **-ly,** *adv.*

ob·lit·er·ate, *v.,* **-at·ed, -at·ing.** erase; blot out; destroy any sign of. **-a·tion,** *n.*

ob·liv·i·on, *n.* getting or being forgotten. **-ous,** *a.* forgetful; unaware. **-ness,** *n.*

ob·long, *a.* longer in one direction. *n.* oblong figure, as a rectangle.

ob·nox·ious, *a.* odious; repugnant; offensive. **-ness,** *n.*

o·boe, *n.* double-reed woodwind instrument. **o·bo·ist,** *n.*

ob·scene, *a.* indecent; disgusting; lewd. **-scen·i·ty,** *n. pl.,* **-ties.**

ob·scure, *a.,* **-scur·er, -scur·est.** not clear; dim; ambiguous; not well-known. *v.,* **-scured, -scur·ing.** make dark or obscure; conceal; confuse. **-scu·ri·ty,** *n. pl.,* **-ties.**

ob·se·qui·ous, *a.* subservient; fawning.

ob·serv·ance, *n.* act of observing a law, custom, etc.; ceremony; rite; practice.

ob·ser·va·to·ry, *n. pl.,* **-ries.** building for making scientific observations, esp. astronomical.

ob·serve, *v.,* **-served, -serv·ing.** keep or adhere to (a law, etc.); notice or perceive; comment on. **-ser·vant,** *a., a.* **-ser·va·tion,** *n.* **-ser·ver,** *n.*

ob·sess, *v.* preoccupy the mind abnormally; trouble. **-ses·sive,** *a.* **-ses·sion,** *n.*

ob·so·les·cent, *a.* becoming obsolete, out-of-date. **-cence,** *n.*

ob·so·lete, *a.* no longer in use; out-of-date; outmoded.

ob·sta·cle, *n.* obstruction; impediment; hindrance.

ob·stet·rics, *n.* medical branch dealing with pregnancy, childbirth.

ob·sti·nate, *a.* stubborn. **-na·cy,** *n. pl.,* **-cies.**

ob·strep·er·ous, *a.* aggressively noisy; clamorous; unruly.

ob·struct, *v.* block; hinder; cut off; impede. **-struc·tion,** *n.*

ob·tain, *v.* get; acquire; prevail.

ob·tuse, *a.* not acute; blunt; more than 90° angle; dull.

ob·verse, *a.* turned toward or facing one; having base narrower than top.

ob·vi·ate, *v.,* **-at·ed, -at·ing.** prevent; make unnecessary.

ob·vi·ous, *a.* easy to see or understand; evident.

oc·ca·sion, *n.* special time or event; an opportunity; an occurrence. *v.* cause; bring about.

oc·ca·sion·al, *a.* happening now and then; infrequent; for use as the need arises.

oc·clude, *v.* obstruct; prevent; hinder.

oc·cult, *a.* secret; magic; supernatural. **-ism,** *n.*

oc·cu·pa·tion, *n.* one's trade, profession, etc.; military seizure of a country. **-al,** *a.*

oc·cu·py, *v.,* **-pied, -py·ing.** dwell in; to hold (a position, etc.); to busy oneself; take possession of; employ; fill; inhabit.

oc·cur, *v.,* **-curred, -cur·ring.** come to mind; take place; happen. **-rence,** *n.*

o·cean, *n.* great body of salt water. **o·ce·an·ic,** *a.*

ocher or **ochre,** *n.* reddish or yellow clay.

oc·ta·gon, *n.* eight-sided figure. **-tag·o·nal,** *a.*

oc·tave, *n. mus.* tone the eighth degree from a given tone.

oc·tet, *n.* group of eight.

Oc·to·ber, *n.* tenth month.

oc·to·pus, *n.* soft-bodied mollusk having eight arms with suckers.

oc·u·lar, *a.* of the eye.

odd, *a.* not divisible by two; only one of a pair; random; singular; strange. **-ly,** *adv.*

odd·i·ty, *n. pl.,* **-ties.** peculiarity.

odds, *n. pl.* probability; difference in favor of; disagreement.

o·di·ous, *a.* arousing hatred or loathing; disgusting. **-ly,** *adv.* **-ness,** *n.*

o·dom·e·ter, *n.* instrument for measuring miles.

o·dor, *n.* a smell, pleasant or unpleasant. **-dored,** *a.* **-less,** *a.* **-ous,** *a.*

of, *prep.* from; with; at; on; due to; composed of.

off, *adv.* keep away; away from. *a.* no longer operating; distant; not attached; in error. *prep.* away from; by means of.

off·beat, *a. inf.* unusual; eccentric; unconventional; mistaken.

of·fend, *v.* do wrong; make angry; affront; insult. **-er,** *n.*

of·fense, *n.* crime; sin; act of attacking. **-fen·sive,** *a.,* *n.*

of·fer, *v.* present for consideration; volunteer; bid. *n.* proposal; act of offering; thing offered. **-ing,** *n.*

off·hand, *a.,* *adv.* extemporaneously; without preparation.

of·fice, *n.* place where business is carried on; position of authority; rite; function.

of·fic·er, *n.* person holding position of authority in business, army, etc.

of·fi·cial, *a.* by or with the proper authority; legal. *n.* person holding office. **-ly,** *adv.*

of·fi·cious, *a.* meddlesome; offering unwanted advice.

off·set, *v.,* **-set, -set·ting.** balance or compensate. *n.* an offshoot; thing that compensates; printing method.

off·shoot, *n.* anything that branches from a main source.

off·spring, *n. pl.,* **-spring, -springs.** children; progeny.

of·ten, *adv.* frequently; repeatedly; many times.

o·gle, *v.,* **-gled, -gling.** look at boldly, desirously. **-gler,** *n.*

o·gre, *n.* legendary man-eating monster; hideous or cruel person.

oil, *n.* slippery, combustible liquid obtained from animals, vegetables, etc.; petroleum. *v.* lubricate with oil.

oil·y, *a.,* **-i·er, -i·est.** of or containing oil; greasy; unctuous.

oint·ment, *n.* unguent; salve.

O.K., *a.,* *adv.* all right; correct.

old, *a.,* **old·er** or **eld·er; old·est** or **eld·est.** having lived, existed for a long time; aged; of a certain age; of great age. *n.* time past; something old. **-en,** *a.*

old-fash·ioned, *a.* antiquated; out-of-date; conservative.

o·le·o·mar·ga·rine, *n.* butter-like table spread or cooking fat.

ol·ive, *n.* fruit of an evergreen tree, edible and valuable for its oil. *a.* of a drab, yellowish-green color.

om·buds·man, *n. pl.,* **-men.** official who investigates complaints of citizens against public officials.

om·e·let, om·e·lette, *n.* beaten eggs fried and folded in half.

o·men, *n.* sign; warning; augury. *v.* foretell; portend.

om·i·nous, *a.* threatening; sinister.

o·mis·sion, *n.* act of leaving out; something neglected.

o·mit, *v.,* **-ted, -ting.** neglect; fail to do; leave out.

om·ni·bus, *n. pl.,* **-bus·es.** bus. *a.* providing for many things at once.

om·ni·far·i·ous, *a.* of all varieties, types, or forms.

om·ni·po·tence, *n.* unlimited or infinite power or influence. **-tent,** *a.* **-tent·ly,** *adv.*

om·nis·cience, *n.* infinite understanding; knowing all things. **-cient,** *a.*

om·niv·or·ous, *a.* eating any sort of food; taking in all things indiscriminately. **-ni·vore**, *n.*

on, *prep.* upon; in contact with, covering; supported by; at the time of; directed toward; with respect to. *adv.* forward; continuously. *a.* in action; near.

once, *adv.* one time; at any time; formerly. *a.* former. *conj.* if ever. *n.* one time.

on·com·ing, *n.* approach. *a.* approaching.

one, *a.* being a single thing; united; being in accord. *n.* first cardinal number; single person or thing. *pron.* some; a certain person or thing.

on·er·ous, *a.* burdensome; oppressive. **-ly**, *adv.*

one·self, *pron.* a person's own self. Also **one's self.**

one-sid·ed, *a.* involving only one side; partial, unjust, unequal.

one-time, *a.* former.

one-track, *a. inf.* able to deal with only one thing at a time.

on·ion, *n.* edible bulb with a strong pungent odor and taste. **-y**, *a.*

on-line, *a.* designating equipment, etc., connected to and controlled by a computer that executes instructions.

on·look·er, *n.* passive spectator.

on·ly, *adv.* and no other; solely. *a.* alone of its kind. *conj.* but.

on·set, *n.* attack; beginning; commencement.

on·slaught, *n.* fierce attack.

on·to, *prep.* to a position on; upon.

o·nus, *n.* unpleasant task.

on·ward, *a., adv.* forward; advancing. Also **on·wards.**

ooze, *n.* soft mud or slime. *v.*, **oozed, ooz·ing.** flow or leak out slowly; seep; exude slowly. **ooz·i·ness**, *n.* **oo·zy**, *a.*, **-zi·er, -zi·est.**

o·pal, *n.* iridescent semiprecious gem.

o·paque, *a.* not letting light through; obscure; obtuse. **o·pac·i·ty**, *n. pl.*, **-ties.**

o·pen, *a.* not closed; not enclosed; accessible; liable; unfolded; vacant; responsive; unfilled; candid; spread out. *v.* make accessible or available; begin; disclose; expose. *n.* outdoors; golf tournament. **-er**, *n.* **-ly**, *adv.* **-ness**, *n.*

o·pen-hand·ed, *a.* generous.

o·pen·ing, *v.* making or becoming open. *n.* start; hole or gap; an opportunity.

o·pen-mind·ed, *a.* unprejudiced.

op·er·a, *n.* play set to music and sung, acted, etc., with orchestra. **op·er·at·ic**, *a.*

op·er·ate, *v.*, **-at·ed, -at·ing.** be in action; work, act, or function; perform surgery; control; effect. **-a·tion**, *n.* **-a·tive**, *a.. n.* **-a·tor**, *n.*

op·er·a·tion, *n.* act or method of operating; a procedure; military movement; plan, project, etc.; surgical procedure.

o·pi·ate, *n.* any medicine that contains opium; narcotic. *a.*

o·pin·ion, *n.* judgment; belief.

o·pin·ion·at·ed, *a.* unduly adhering to opinion; dogmatic.

o·pi·um, *n.* narcotic drug made from juice of opium poppy.

o·pos·sum, *n.* tree-dwelling nocturnal mammal that carries its young in a pouch.

op·po·nent, *n.* antagonist; rival; adversary. *a.* opposing.

op·por·tune, *a.* timed right; timely. **-ly**, *adv.*

op·por·tu·ni·ty, *n. pl.*, **-ties.** favorable combination of circumstances; a good chance or occasion.

op·pose, *v.*, **-posed, -pos·ing.** place against; resist; contend. **-pos·er**, *n.* **-po·si·tion**, *n.*

op·po·site, *a.* situated on opposed sides of; hostile; contrary. *n.* anything opposite. *adv.* on opposing sides. *prep.* across from.

op·press, *v.* weigh heavy on the mind; tyrannize. **-pres·sor**, *n.* **-pres·sion**, *n.* **-pres·sive**, *a.*

opt, *v.* to make a choice.

op·tic, *a.* of the eye or sight.

op·ti·cal, *a.* of sight; visual; for aiding vision. **-ly**, *adv.*

op·ti·cian, *n.* one who makes or deals with eyeglasses.

op·ti·mal, *a.* best; favorable.

op·ti·mism, *n.* tendency to take the most cheerful view. **-mist**, *n.*

op·ti·mum, *n.* best; most desirable.

op·tion, *n.* liberty of choosing; thing that can be chosen. **-al**, *a.* **-al·ly**, *adv.*

op·tom·e·try, *n.* profession of examining and measuring the eyes and prescribing of glasses. **-to·met·ric**, *a.* **-tom·e·trist**, *n.*

op·u·lent, *a.* wealthy; abundant; rich; profuse. **-lence**, *n.*

or, *conj.* used to connect alternative or synonomous terms.

or·a·cle, *n.* place of revelation; one who does such revealing; wise person. **o·rac·u·lar**, *a.*

o·ral, *a.* of the mouth; spoken; using speech. **-ly**, *adv.*

or·ange, *n.* round reddish-yellow edible citrus fruit. *a.* reddish-yellow.

o·rang·u·tan, *n.* herbivorous and arboreal ape with long arms and hairless face.

o·ra·tion, *n.* formal speech.

or·a·tor, *n.* eloquent public speaker. **-i·cal**, *a.*

orb, *n.* sphere; globe.

or·bit, *n.* path along which a heavenly body moves; range of influence. *v.* to circle around. **-al**, *a.*

or·chard, *n.* land area for the raising of fruit or nut trees.

or·ches·tra, *n.* group of musicians playing together; space where they sit; main floor theater seats. **-tral**, *a.*

or·chid, *n.* plant with bulbous roots and flowers with three petals, one lip-shaped. *a.* light purple.

or·dain, *v.* invest with holy orders; decree; order; enact.

or·deal, *n.* severe trial; painful test.

or·der, *n.* proper arrangement; group united in formal way; rank; level; category; rites; command; kind. *v.* regulate; direct to be made, supplied, etc.; issue orders. **-dered**, *a.*

or·der·ly, *a.* arranged in a pattern; well-behaved; tidy; methodical; peaceful. *adv.* in regular sequence. *n. pl.,* **-lies.** attendant. **-li·ness**, *n.*

or·di·nance, *n.* authoritative command; law; edict.

or·di·nar·i·ly, *adv.* usually.

or·di·nar·y, *a.* customary; usual; common; inferior.

ord·nance, *n.* artillery; cannon.

ore, *n.* substance from which minerals can be extracted; a native metal.

or·gan, *n.* large wind instrument of pipes, keyboards, etc.; differentiated animal or plant part having some specific function; a periodical.

or·gan·ic, *a.* of or derived from living organisms; of an organ; inherent; of carbon compounds. **-i·cal·ly**, *adv.*

or·gan·ism, *n.* living thing.

or·gan·ize, *v.,* **-ized, -iz·ing.** arrange orderly; establish; form an organization or group; unionize. **-i·za·tion**, *n.* **-iz·er**, *n.*

or·gy, *n. pl.,* **-gies.** drunken revelry; sexual indulgence.

o·ri·ent, *n.* east; (*cap·*) the Far East, Asia. *v.* adjust or adapt to a particular situation. **O·ri·en·tal**, *a.*

o·ri·en·tate, *v.,* **-tat·ed, -tat·ing.** orient; face east; adjust to a situation. **-ta·tion**, *n.*

or·i·fice, *n.* an opening or mouth.

or·i·ga·mi, *n.* art of paper-folding.

or·i·gin, *n.* beginning; ancestry.

o·rig·i·nal, *a.* first; earliest; inventive thought and imagination; new; novel. *n.* original work. **-i·ty**, *n.* **-ly**, *adv.*

o·rig·i·nate, *v.,* **-nat·ed, -nat·ing.** initiate; start; create; invent. **-na·tion**, *n.* **-na·tor**, *n.*

or·na·ment, *n.* adornment; decoration. *v.* to decorate. **-men·ta·tion**, *n.*

or·nate, *a.* adorned; excessively decorated. **-ness**, *n.*

or·ner·y, *a.* cantankerous; irritable.

or·ni·thol·o·gy, *n.* study of birds. **-gist**, *n.*

or·phan, *n.* child whose parents are dead; motherless animal. *v.* **-age**, *n.*

or·tho·don·tics, *n.* dentistry specializing in irregularities of teeth.

or·tho·dox, *a.* usual beliefs; established doctrine; conventional. **-dox·y**, *n.*

or·tho·pe·dics, *n.* study of bone diseases, deformities and their treatment.

os·cil·late, *v.,* **-lat·ed, -lat·ing.** swing back and forth; vibrate. **-la·tion**, **-la·tor**, *n.* **-la·to·ry**, *a.*

os·cu·late, *v.,* **-lat·ed, -lat·ing.** kiss. **-la·tion**, *n.*

os·mo·sis, *n.* tendency of a solvent to pass through a membrane; gradual absorption; diffusion. **os·mot·ic**, *a.*

os·si·fy, *v.,* **-fied, -fy·ing.** change or form into bone.

os·ten·si·ble, *a.* professed; seeming; apparent. **-bly**, *adv.*

os·ten·ta·tion, *n.* pretentious, showy display. **-tious**, *a.*

os·te·op·a·thy, *n.* medical system emphasizing manipulation of muscles.

os·tra·cize, *v.,* **-cized, -ciz·ing.** exile; banish; exclude. **-cism**, *n.*

os·trich, *n.* large flightless bird.

oth·er, *a.* being the remaining one; different, distinct, or additional. *pron.* other one; another. *adv.* otherwise.

oth·er·wise, *adv.* differently; in other respects. *a.* different.

o·ti·ose, *a.* idle; futile; useless.

ot·to·man, *n.* low upholstered chair or couch with no back.

ought, *aux. v.* to express a moral obligation, advisability, expectation, or desirability.

ounce, *n.* one-sixteenth of a pound; fluid ounce.

our, *pron.* a. belonging to, made or done by us; poss. case of **we.**

ours, *pron.* belonging to us; poss. form of **we.**

our·selves, *pron. pl.* reflexive or emphatic form of **we.**

oust, *v.* eject; drive out; expel; forcibly remove.

out, *adv.* away from; beyond control; to a conclusion; forth from; aloud. *prep.* out through. *int.* begone. *a.* external; outlying; away from; extinguished. *n.* escape; excuse; retired batter. *v.* come out; put out.

out·break, *n.* sudden manifestation; epidemic; revolt; riot.

out·burst, *n.* eruption; surge of activity; spurt.

out·cast, *n.* one who is rejected or cast out. *a.* rejected.

out·class, *v.* surpass; excel.

out·come, *n.* result; consequence.

out·cry, *n. pl.,* **-cries.** loud cry; objection or protest.

out·dated, *a.* obsolete.

out·distance, *v.* leave behind.

out·do, *v.,* **-did, -done, -do·ing.** excel; surpass.

out·doors, *adv.* outside; in the open air.

out·er, *a.* exterior; far removed.

out·er·most, *a.* located the farthest out.

out·face, *v.,* **-faced, -fac·ing.** defy; stare down.

out·fit, *n.* articles or equipment needed for an activity; ensemble of clothing; group of persons associated as a unit. *v.,* **-fit·ted, -fit·ting.** equip; supply. **-fit·ter,** *n.*

out·flank, *v.* to go around the flank of the enemy; thwart; outwit.

out·fox, *v.* outsmart.

out·go, *v.,* **-went, -gone, -go·ing.** excel; surpass. *n. pl.,* **-goes.** that which is paid out; expenditure. **-go·ing,** *a., n.*

out·grow, *v.,* **-grew, -grown, -grow·ing.** grow faster or larger than; grow too large for; lose or get rid of by becoming mature.

out·growth, *n.* offshoot; consequence; result.

out·ing, *n.* excursion; trip.

out·land·ish, *a.* odd; fantastic.

out·law, *n.* criminal. *v.* prohibit; make illegal; ban.

out·lay, *n.* disbursement; expenditure. *v.,* **-laid, -lay·ing.** spend (money).

out·let, *n.* opening by which anything is let out; vent; retail or wholesale market.

out·line, *n.* contour; profile; silhouette; *sometimes pl.* sketch of a plan. *v.,* **-lined, -lin·ing.** make the outline of; list the main ideas of.

out·live, *v.,* **-lived, -liv·ing.** live longer than.

out·look, *n.* mental attitude; prospect; place for looking out.

out·mod·ed, *a.* obsolete.

out·num·ber, *v.* exceed in number.

out-of-date, *a.* obsolete; dated.

out·post, *n.* military post or group away from the main group.

out·put, *n.* production; yield.

out·rage, *n.* vicious act; great insult; great anger. *v.,* **-raged, -rag·ing.** abuse; rape; insult. **-ra·geous,** *a.*

out·rank, *v.* exceed in rank.

out·right, *adv.* entirely; openly; at once. *a.* complete; downright; straightforward.

out·set, *n.* setting out; beginning; commencement.

out·shine, *v.,* **-shone, -shin·ing.** outdo; surpass.

out·side, *n.* outer part or surface; exterior. *a.* outer; slight possibility. *adv.* on or to the outside. *prep.* to or on the outer side of; beyond the limits of.

out·sid·er, *n.* one not a member of a particular group.

out·skirts, *n. pl.* outer areas.

out·smart, *v.* outwit; be clever.

out·spoken, *a.* unrestrained in speech; candid.

out·stand·ing, *a.* prominent; unsettling; projecting; unpaid.

out·strip, *v.* **stripped, strip·ping.** go faster than; get ahead of; excel; surpass.

out·ward, *a.* exterior; obvious; to or toward the outside; visible. Also **out·wards.**

out·wear, *v.,* **-wore, -worn, -wear·ing.** last longer than.

out·wit, *v.,* **-wit·ted, -wit·ting.** get the better of; trick.

o·val, *a.* having the form of an egg; elliptical. *n.*

o·va·ry, *n. pl.,* **-ries.** female reproductive gland.

o·va·tion, *n.* enthusiastic public acclaim or welcome.

ov·en, *n.* compartment for baking, roasting, heating, or drying.

o·ver, *prep.* in, at, or to a position; above; higher than; in preference to; upon; across. *adv.* above, across, or to the other side; again; more. *a.* upper; higher up; extra; completed or past.

o·ver·age, *n.* excess; surplus. *a.* too old for use.

o·ver·all, *a.* including everything. *adv.* generally.

o·ver·bear·ing, *a.* domineering; arrogant; overriding.

o·ver·blown, *a.* swollen; exaggerated; excessive; pompous.

o·ver·board, *adv.* over a ship's side; *inf.* to go to extremes.

o·ver·cast, *n., a.* cloudy; gloomy.

o·ver·charge, *v.,* **-charged, -charg·ing.** charge too high a price; to overload.

o·ver·coat, *n.* heavy topcoat.

o·ver·come, *v.,* **-came, -come, -com·ing.** defeat; conquer; win; master.

o·ver·do, *v.,* **-did, -done, -do·ing.** do to excess; exhaust.

o·ver·dose, *n.* dose to excess.

o·ver·due, *a.* past the time of payment, arrival, etc.; belated; delayed.

o·ver·es·ti·mate, *v.,* **-mat·ed, -mat·ing.** price or value too highly. **-ma·tion,** *n.*

o·ver·flow, *v.,* **-flowed, -flown, -flow·ing.** flow or spread across; flood. *n.* an overflowing; surplus; an outlet.

o·ver·flight, *n.* flight over an area, esp. for reconnisance, espionage.

o·ver·grow, *v.,* **-grew, -grown, -grow·ing.** overspread with growth; grow excessively. **-growth,** *n.*

o·ver·haul, *v.* make needed repairs. *n.* thorough repair.

o·ver·head, *adv.* aloft; above the head. *n.* regular business expenses.

o·ver·hear, *v.,* **-heard, -hear·ing.** hear something not intended for listener.

o·ver·joy, *v.* give great joy to; delight. **-joyed,** *a.*

o·ver·kill, *n.* oversupply of nuclear arms; excess of effort in achieving an end.

o·ver·lap, *v.,* **-lapped, -lap·ping.** extend over; lap over; coincide in part. *n.*

o·ver·lie, *v.* **-lay, -lain, -ly·ing.** to lie on or over.

o·ver·look, *v.* excuse; fail to notice; ignore; inspect. *n.* a height or the view from it.

o·ver·ly, *adv.* too much.

o·ver·night, *adv.* through or during the night; suddenly. *a.* done or lasting the night.

o·ver·pass, *n.* bridge over a road, railroad, etc.

o·ver·pow·er, *v.* vanquish; defeat; subdue. **-ing,** *a.*

o·ver·print, *v.* print over something previously printed.

o·ver·rate, *v.,* **-rat·ed, -rat·ing.** rate or estimate too highly.

o·ver·ride, *v.,* **-rode, -rid·den, -rid·ing.** ride over; nullify; overrule; trample.

o·ver·rule, *v.,* **-ruled, -rul·ing.** set aside; prevail over; rule against; reverse.

o·ver·run, *v.,* **-ran, -run, -run·ning.** swarm over; invade; grow rapidly over; exceed.

o·ver·see, *v.,* **-saw, -seen, -see·ing.** supervise; examine; manage. **-se·er,** *n.*

o·ver·shad·ow, *v.* cast a shadow over; be more important than by comparison.

o·ver·sight, *n.* careless mistake or omission.

o·ver·sleep, *v.,* **-slept, -sleep·ing.** sleep beyond intended time.

o·ver·state, *v.,* **-stat·ed, -stat·ing.** exaggerate (facts, etc.). **-ment,** *n.*

o·ver·step, *v.,* **-stepped, -step·ping.** go beyond the limits.

o·vert, *a.* open; not hidden. **-ly,** *adv.*

o·ver·take, *v.,* **-took, -tak·en, -tak·ing.** come upon or catch up with and often pass.

o·ver·tax, *v.* tax too heavily; make excessive demands on.

o·ver·throw, *v.,* **-threw, -thrown, -throw·ing.** throw or turn over; conquer; upset. *n.* defeat.

o·ver·time, *n.* time one works beyond normal hours; pay for overtime; extra sports period. *a., adv.* of, during, or for overtime.

o·ver·ture, *n.* musical introduction; proposal; opening; offer.

o·ver·turn, *v.* turn over; destroy; upset; capsize.

o·ver·view, *n.* a general survey.

o·ver·weight, *n.* surplus weight. *a.* above the allowed weight.

o·ver·whelm, *v.* overpower; crush.

o·ver·work, *v.,* **-worked, -work·ing.** work or use to excess; work too hard. *n.* excessive work.

o·ver·wrought, *a.* nervous or excited; adorned surface; too elaborate.

o·vi·form, *a.* egg shaped.

o·vum, *n. pl.,* **o·va.** mature female egg cell.

owe, *v.,* **owed, ow·ing.** be in debt to (for an amount or thing).

owl, *n.* large-headed, night bird of prey. **-ish,** *a.*

own, *a.* belonging to oneself. *v.* possess; confess; acknowledge; admit. **-er,** *n.*

ox, *n. pl.,* **ox·en.** bovine animal (buffalo, etc.); castrated bull.

ox·y·gen, *n.* colorless, odorless, tasteless gaseous element essential to life.

oys·ter, *n.* edible marine mollusk with irregular bivalve shell.

o·zone, *n.* form of oxygen; pure, refreshing air.

P

pab·u·lum, *n.* food; nourishment for the mind.

pace, *n.* single step; tempo; gait. *v.,* **paced, pac·ing.** regulate; walk to and fro; lead; precede. **pac·er,** *n.*

pace·mak·er, *n.* one who sets the pace; electronic device for regulating heartbeat.

pach·y·derm, *n.* any thick-skinned hoofed mammal, as the elephant.

pa·cif·ic, *a.* peaceful; calm.

pac·i·fism, *n.* opposition to force and war. **-fist,** *n.*

pac·i·fy, *v.,* **-fied, -fy·ing.** make peaceful; calm; soothe.

pack, *n.* bundle; container; package; a group of things or persons. *v.* put together; carry; send off; crowd; fill.

pack·et, *n.* small package; mail, cargo boat.

pact, *n.* treaty; agreement.

pad, *n.* cushion; tablet. *v.,* **-ded, -ding.** to stuff.

pad·dle, *n.* short oar with wide blade. *v.,* **-dled, -dling.** row (a canoe, etc.); spank. **-dler,** *n.*

pad·dock, *n.* enclosed area for exercising and saddling horses.

pad·lock, *n.* removable lock.

pa·dre, *n.* priest.

pa·gan, *n.* heathen. **-ism,** *n.*

page, *n.* leaf of a book, etc.; youthful messenger. *v.,* **paged, pag·ing.** summon by calling.

pag·eant, *n.* spectacular show.

pag·i·nate, *v.,* **-nat·ed, -nat·ing.** number the pages (of a book, etc.).

pa·go·da, *n.* Oriental temple.

pail, *n.* bucket.

pain, *n.* physical or emotional distress; localized suffering; hurting; *pl.* great care. *v.* cause distress. **-ful,** **-less,** *a.* **-less·ness,** *n.*

pains·tak·ing, *a.* diligent; very careful. **-ly,** *adv.*

paint, *v.* make pictures; apply paint. *n.* pigment; cosmetic. **-er,** *n.* **-ing,** *n.*

pair, *n. pl.,* **pairs, pair.** set of two; duo. *v.* match; mate.

pa·jam·as, *n. pl.* two-piece set of sleep apparel.

pal·ace, *n.* splendid house; sovereign residence.

pal·at·a·ble, *a.* savory, agreeable. **-bil·i·ty,** *n.* **-bly,** *adv.*

pal·ate, *n.* roof of the mouth; sense of taste.

pa·la·tial, *a.* magnificent; stately. **-ly,** *adv.*

pa·lav·er, *n.* idle talk; chatter; flattery. *v.* flatter; talk.

pale, *a.* pallid; light color; wan. *n. v., fence stake.* **paled, pal·ing.** turn or make pale. **-ly,** *adv.* **-ness,** *n.*

pa·le·on·tol·o·gy, *n.* study of fossils and ancient life. **-to·log·i·cal,** *a.* **-tol·o·gist,** *n.*

pal·ette, *n.* thin board on which to mix colors; the colors used.

pal·i·sade, *n.* fence for defense; line of steep cliffs. *v.,* **-saded, -sad·ing.**

pall, *v.* satiate; bore. *n.* large cloth coffin covering; dark, anything that darkens or causes gloom.

pall·bear·er, *n.* one who helps bear the coffin at a funeral.

pal·let, *n.* portable wooden storage platform; straw bed; wooden tool.

pal·li·ate, *v.* ease without curing; alleviate; excuse.

pal·lid, *a.* pale; faint in color.

pal·lor, *n.* paleness; lack of color.

palm, *n.* tropical tree with fan-shaped leaves; underside of hand. *v.* conceal in the hand.

palm·is·try, *n.* telling fortunes by lines of the hand. **-ist,** *n.*

pal·o·mi·no, *n.* golden-coated horse with white tail, mane.

pal·pa·ble, *a.* perceptible; tangible; obvious. **-bil·i·ty,** *n.* **-bly,** *adv.*

pal·pate, *v.,* **-pat·ed, -pat·ing.** examine by touching. **-pa·tion,** *n.*

pal·pi·tate, *v.,* **-tat·ed, -tat·ing.** beat rapidly; throb; quiver. **-ta·tion,** *n.*

pal·sy, *n.* muscle paralysis, sometimes with tremors.

pal·ter, *v.* act insincerely; quibble.

pal·try, *a.,* **-tri·er, -tri·est.** petty; worthless. **-tri·ness,** *n.*

pam·pas, *n. pl.* treeless plains.

pam·per, *v.* coddle; indulge.

pam·phlet, *n.* small unbound booklet; brochure.

pan, *n.* shallow cooking vessel. *v.,* **panned, pan·ning.** separate (gold, etc.) by washing; move camera to follow moving object; *inf.* criticize unfavorably.

pan·a·ce·a, *n.* cure-all. **-ce·an,** *a.*

pa·nache, *n.* carefree style; flamboyance.

pan·a·ma, *n.* lightweight hat made of leaves.

pan·cake, *n.* thin fried cake.

pan·chro·mat·ic, *a.* sensitive to light of all colors.

pan·cre·as, *n.* gland secreting digestive juices.

pan·dem·ic, *n.* disease widely spread.

pan·de·mo·ni·um, *n.* wild disorder or confusion; chaos.

pan·der, *n.* pimp; exploiter.

pane, *n.* single sheet of glass.

pan·e·gyr·ic, *n.* formal speech or letter of praise.

pan·el, *n.* section or part of a surface; board for controls; group of selected persons. **-ist,** *n. v.,* **-eled, -el·ing.** provide with panels.

pang, *n.* sharp brief pain; sudden feeling of mental anguish.

pan·han·dle, *n.* handle of a pan; narrow extension of land. *v.*, **-dled, -dling.** *inf.* to beg.

pan·ic, *n.* hysterical fear; *inf.* comical person or thing.

pan·o·ram·a, *n.* open view in all directions; changing scene. **-ic**, *a.* **-i·cal·ly**, *adv.*

pan·sy, *n. pl.*, **-sies.** small perennial flower; *inf.* male homosexual.

pant, *v.* breathe rapidly; gasp; long for. *n.* rapid breath.

pan·ther, *n.* cougar, leopard, etc.

pan·to·mime, *n.* a play or actions without speech.

pan·try, *n. pl.*, **-tries.** room or space for food and dishes.

pa·pa·cy, *n. pl.*, **-cies.** office or authority of the pope.

pa·pal, *a.* of the pope or papacy.

pa·per, *n.* thin flexible material used to write on or wrap in; newspaper; official document. *v.* cover with paper.

pa·per·back, *n.* book with flexible paper binding.

pa·pier-mâ·ché, *n.* molding material made from paste and paper pulp.

pa·poose, *n..* N·A. Indian baby.

pap·ri·ka, *n.* mild red condiment made from certain peppers.

Pap test (smear), *n.* examination for uterine cancer.

pa·py·rus, *n. pl.*, **-rus·es, -ri.** water plant; ancient paper.

par, *n.*, *a.* average; normal.

par·a·ble, *n.* moral story.

par·a·chute, *n.* thin flexible material used to retard speed down through air. *v.*, **-chut·ed, -chut·ing.** descend or drop. **-chut·ist**, *n.*

pa·rade, *n.* organized procession. *v.*, **-rad·ed, -rad·ing.** march. *a.*

par·a·digm, *n.* model; pattern.

par·a·dise, *n.* heaven; place of perfection. **-di·si·a·cal**, *a.*

par·a·dox, *n.* contradictory statement, but may be true or false; enigma.

par·a·gon, *n.* model of perfection or excellence.

par·a·graph, *n.* subdivision of a piece of writing.

par·a·keet, *n.* small parrot.

par·a·legal, *n.* person trained to assist lawyer but not licensed to practice law.

par·al·lel, *a.* lines, planes, and curves which are equidistant at all corresponding points; analogous; similar. *v.*

pa·ral·y·sis, *n. pl.*, **-ses.** muscle dysfunction; incapacity to act or move. **par·a·lyt·ic**, *a.*, *n.* **par·a·lyze**, *v.*

par·a·med·ic, *n.* trained medical assistant; midwife, corpsman, etc.

pa·ram·e·ter, *n.* fixed limit or guidelines.

par·a·mount, *a.* superior.

par·a·mour, *n.* illicit lover.

par·a·noi·a, *n.* mental disorder with delusions. **-noid**, *n.*, *a.* suspicious.

par·a·pet, *n.* protective wall; breastwork.

par·a·pher·nal·ia, *n. sing. or pl.* personal belongings; furnishings; accessories.

par·a·phrase, *n.* restatement of words, retaining meaning.

par·a·site, *n.* animal or plant that lives on or in another.

par·a·sol, *n.* lightweight sun umbrella.

par·boil, *v.* boil partially.

par·cel, *n.* package; collection; portion; lot. *v.* distribute.

parch, *v.* roast by extreme heat; make hot; make dry.

parch·ment, *n.* sheep- or goatskin prepared as writing material; paper resembling this.

par·don, *v.* free from penalty; forgive. *n.* forgiveness. **-a·ble**, *a.* **-a·bly**, *adv.*

pare, *v.*, **pared, par·ing.** cut; shave; diminish.

par·e·gor·ic, *n.* medicine to relieve diarrhea.

par·ent, *n.* father or mother; source; cause. **pa·ren·tal**, *a.*

pa·ren·the·sis, *n. pl.*, **-ses.** an inserted explanatory comment set off by ( ); the mark or marks.

pa·ri·ah, *n.* social outcast.

par·i·mu·tu·el, *n.* system of betting at races.

par·ish, *n.* district of a diocese; a congregation. **-ion·er**, *n.*

par·i·ty, *n.* equality.

park, *n.* tract of land for public use; recreation or conservation area. *v.* leave temporarily.

par·ka, *n.* outer garment with a hood.

park·way, *n.* landscaped expressway.

par·lay, *v.*, **-layed, -lay·ing.** multiply money by reinvesting bets; increase or exploit.

par·ley, *v.*, **-leyed, -ley·ing.** confer, esp. with enemy. *n.* discussion.

par·lia·ment, *n.* (*cap*) supreme legislature of the United Kingdom; formal assembly. **-men·tar·i·an**, *n.* **-men·ta·ry**, *a.*

par·lor, par·lour, *n.* living room; specialized business place.

pa·ro·chi·al, *a.* pertaining to a parish; narrow; provincial.

par·o·dy, *n. pl.,* **-dies.** ridiculing imitation of a literary work.

pa·role, *n.* conditional early release of a prisoner; promise. **pa·roled, pa·rol·ing,** *v.*

par·ox·ysm, *n.* sudden attack.

par·quet, *n.* inlaid wood flooring. **-ry,** *n.*

par·ri·cide, *n.* murder of a parent.

par·rot, *n.* bright-colored tropical bird which imitates speech. *v.* repeat without understanding.

par·ry, *v.,* **-ried, -ry·ing.** avoid; ward off. *n. pl.,* **-ries.** verbal evasion or diversion.

par·si·mo·ni·ous, *a.* stingy.

pars·ley, *n.* edible herb.

pars·nip, *n.* edible root.

par·son, *n.* clergyman.

part, *n.* section; portion; division; function; duty; role. *v.* break; divide; separate; participate. *adv.* partially. *a.* partial.

par·take, *v.,* **-took, -tak·en, -tak·ing.** take a part in; take a portion of.

par·tial, *a.* a part only; not complete; biased. **-i·ty,** *n. pl.,* **-ties.** special liking. **-ly,** *adv.*

par·tic·i·pant, *a.* participating. *n.* one who takes part in.

par·tic·i·pate, *v.,* **-pat·ed, -pat·ing.** take a part with others; share. **-pa·tion,** *n.* **-pa·tive,** *a.*

par·ti·ci·ple, *n.* verbal adjective.

par·ti·cle, *n.* minute part, piece, or portion.

par·tic·u·lar, *a.* referring to a single thing; special; exacting. *n.* specific fact; item; *usu. pl.* details. **-ly,** *adv.*

par·tic·u·lar·i·ty, *n. pl.,* **-ties.** a detail; exactness.

part·ing, *a.* leave-taking; separation; division.

par·ti·san, *n.* biased; a guerrilla. **-ship,** *n.*

par·ti·tion, *n.* division; separation. *v.* separate; divide.

part·ly, *adv.* in some part.

part·ner, *n.* one who takes part with another; associate. **-ship,** *n.*

par·tridge, *n. pl.,* **-tridg·es, -tridge.** quaillike game bird.

part-time, *a.* working or studying less than full-time.

par·tu·ri·ent, *a.* bringing forth or about to bring forth young; of childbirth. **-ri·tion,** *n.*

par·ty, *n. pl.,* **-ties.** group united for some purpose; social gathering; one who is a part of.

par·ve·nu, *n.* one suddenly wealthy but lacking social status.

pass, *v.* go past or leave behind; go across, over, etc.; meet requirements of; surpass; enact; give approval; depart; circulate; happen. *n.* road; gap; permission; act of passing; success in a test.

pas·sage, *n.* corridor, hall, etc.; way through; a passing; lapse of time; route; portion of writing.

pas·sé, *a.* old-fashioned; dated.

pas·sen·ger, *n.* traveler on a vehicle.

pass·ing, *a.* fleeting; transitory.

pas·sion, *n.* compelling emotion or devotion; lust; rage. **-less,** *a.* **-ate,** *a.*

pas·sive, *a.* inactive; submissive.

Pass·o·ver, *n.* Jewish festival.

pass·port, *n.* document of citizen's permission to travel.

pass·word, *n.* identifying word to gain entry or to pass.

past, *a.* ended; over; bygone. *prep.* beyond. *n.* time gone by. *adv.* beyond.

pas·ta, *n.* spaghetti, macaroni, etc.

paste, *n.* adhesive; dough. *v.,* **past·ed, past·ing.** to stick.

paste·board, *n.* cardboard.

pas·tel, *n.* soft, pale color; drawing.

pas·teur·ize, *n.* bacteria destroying process. *v.,* **-ized, -iz·ing. -i·za·tion,** *n.*

pas·tille, *n.* lozenge; tablet.

pas·time, *n.* recreation; hobby.

pas·tor, *n.* Christian minister.

pas·try, *n. pl.,* **-tries.** sweet baked goods; basic dough (pie, etc.).

pas·ture, *n.* grazing ground. *v.,* **-tured, -tur·ing.** graze. **-tur·age,** *n.*

past·y, *a.,* **-i·er, -i·est.** like paste; sickly and pale; wan.

pat, *n.* light stroke; small mass. *v.,* **pat·ted, pat·ting.** touch or tap lightly. *a.* suitable; facile. *adv.* in a fit manner.

patch, *n.* piece of cloth used to mend; piece of ground; eye shield. *v.* mend. **-y,** *a.* spotty.

pate, *n.* top of the head.

pat·ent, *n.* government protection giving rights to an inventor; any document securing a right. *a.* exclusive rights; apparent; open. **-ly,** *adv.* clearly.

pa·ter·nal, *a.* pertaining to a father. **-ly,** *adv.* **-ism,** *n.*

pa·ter·ni·ty, *n.* fatherhood; origin; descent; roots.

pa·ter·nos·ter, *n.* Lord's prayer; large rosary bead.

path, *n.* footway; procedure.

pa·thet·ic, *a.* inspiring pity.

pa·thol·o·gy, *n. pl.,* **-gies.** study of the nature, causes, etc., of diseases. **path·o·log·i·cal,** *a.* **path·o·log·i·cal·ly,** *adv.* **-o·gist,** *n.*

pa·thos, *n.* quality that arouses tender emotions or feelings.

pa·tience, *n.* act of enduring with composure.

pa·tient, *a.* uncomplaining; tolerant; persevering. *n.* person under medical care. **-ly**, *adv.*

pa·ti·na, *n.* greenish oxidation crust; surface change.

pa·ti·o, *n. pl.*, **-os.** inner court; outdoor terrace.

pat·ois, *n. pl.*, **pat·ois.** dialect.

pa·tri·arch·y, *n. pl.*, **-chies.** family organization headed by a male.

pa·tri·cian, *n.* aristocrat; noble.

pat·ri·mo·ny, *n. pl.*, **-nies.** heritage; property from father.

pa·tri·ot, *n.* person who loves his country. **-ic**, *a.*

pa·trol, *v.*, **pa·trolled, pa·trol·ling.** walk around to guard. *n.* a guard(s).

pa·tron, *n.* regular client; sponsor; one who protects or supports.

pat·sy, *n.* one easily victimized, duped.

pat·ter, *v.* move quickly; speak glibly. *n.* rapid talk; light taps or steps.

pat·tern, *n.* model; form; sample. *v.* make; fashion; shape.

pat·ty, *n. pl.*, **-ties.** small pastry shell; small flat cake.

pau·ci·ty, *n.* lack of; scarcity.

paunch, *n.* abdomen; potbelly.

pau·per, *n.* very poor person; one on charity.

pause, *n.* short stop; hesitation; delay. *v.* cease action temporarily.

pave, *v.*, **paved, pav·ing.** cover or surface a road, sidewalk, etc.

pave·ment, *n.* hard, solid surface for roads, etc.

pa·vil·ion, *n.* open, movable building; large tent; connected or detached part of a main building.

paw, *n.* foot of animals having claws. *v.* scratch with the paws; *inf.* handle rudely.

pawn, *n.* security for a loan; one used to advance the purposes of another. *v.* stake; pledge.

pawn·bro·ker, *n.* one lending money on personal property.

pay, *v.*, **paid, pay·ing.** to give (money, etc.) for a debt, purchase, etc.; compensate. *n.* profit; wages.

pay·a·ble, *a.* due to be paid.

pay·ment, *n.* thing that is paid.

peace, *n.* absence or cessation of war; tranquility. **-a·ble**, *a.* **-a·bly**, *adv.* calmly. **-ful**, *a.* tranquil. **-ful·ly**, *adv.* **-ful·ness**, *n.*

pea·cock, *n. pl.*, **-cocks, -cock.** male bird with rainbow-colored tail; vain person.

pea·jack·et, *n.* short thick woolen coat worn by seamen.

peak, *n.* mountain summit; pointed top; highest point.

peak·ed, *a.* sickly appearance.

peal, *n.* loud, prolonged sound, as of a bell, thunder, etc.

pea·nut, *n.* legume with edible oily seeds; unimportant; *pl.* trifling sum.

pearl, *n.* gem produced by oysters. *v.* **-y**, *a.*

peas·ant, *n.* In Europe, Asia, small farmer or farm laborer. *a.* rural. **-ry**, *n.*

peat, *n.* decayed vegetable material from bogs. **-y**, *a.*

peb·ble, *n.* small stone. **-bly**, *a.*

pe·can, *n.* thin-shelled edible nut.

pec·ca·dil·lo, *n. pl.*, **-loes, -los.** slight offense; petty sin.

pec·cant, *a.* sinning.

peck, *n.* eight quarts; *inf.* light kiss. *v.* strike with a pointed object; nag, carp at.

pec·tin, *n.* gummy carbohydrate from fruit, used for jellies.

pec·to·ral, *a.* pertaining to the breast or chest; a fish fin.

pec·u·late, *v.* appropriate wrongfully; embezzle. **-la·tion, -la·tor**, *n.*

pe·cu·liar, *a.* unusual; odd; strange; exclusive characteristic. **-ly**, *adv.* **-li·ar·i·ty**, *n. pl.*, **-ties.**

pe·cu·ni·ar·y, *a.* monetary.

ped·a·gogue, -gog, *n.* teacher.

ped·al, *n.* lever operated by foot; treadle. *a.* of the foot.

ped·ant, *n.* person who places undue stress on details. **-dan·tic**, *a.* **-ti·cal·ly**, *adv.* **-ry**, *n.*

ped·dle, *v.*, **-dled, -dling.** travel place to place to sell; hawk. **-dler, -ler, -lar**, *n.*

ped·es·tal, *n.* base; foundation.

pe·des·tri·an, *n.* walker. *a.* moving on foot; commonplace. **-ism**, *n.*

pe·di·at·rics, *n.* medical branch dealing with children's health. **-ric**, *a.* **-a·tri·cian**, *n.*

ped·i·gree, *n.* genealogy; lineage, esp. of animals. **-greed**, *a.*

pe·dom·e·ter, *n.* instrument measuring distance walked.

peek, *v.* look quickly; glance furtively. *n.* peep.

peel, *v.* strip. *n.* rind; skin.

peen, *n.* ball-shaped hammer end.

peep, *v.* chirp; look furtively. *n.* cry of bird; brief look.

peer, *n.* equal in age, rank, etc. **-age,** *n.* **-less,** *a.* unequaled. **-less·ly,** *adv.* *v.* look closely.

peeve, *v.,* **peeved, peev·ing.** annoy; irritate. *n.* annoyance.

peev·ish, *a.* fretful; irritable.

peg, *n.* wooden pin for fastening; projecting pin.

peign·oir, *n.* negligee.

pel·i·can, *n.* water bird with expandable pouched bill.

pel·let, *n.* small round balls; bullet; small pill.

pell-mell, *adv.* headlong rush; disorderly manner. *a., n.*

pelt, *n.* untanned hide. *v.* hurl; assail verbally; strike hard.

pel·vis, *n. pl.,* **-vis·es, -ves.** bony structure that joins the lower limbs to the body. **-vic,** *a.*

pen, *n.* instrument for writing with ink; enclosure for animals. *n. inf.* penitentiary. *v.,* **penned, pen·ning.** to write.

pe·nal, *a.* of penalties; of prisons. **pe·nal·ize,** *v.,* **-ized, -iz·ing.** subject to a penalty.

pen·al·ty, *n. pl.,* **-ties.** punishment; unfortunate consequence.

pen·ance, *n.* voluntary suffering to show repentance.

pen·chant, *n.* bias; inclination.

pen·cil, *n.* writing instrument with chalk or graphite core.

pend·ant, pend·ent, *n.* hanging ornament.

pend·ing, *a.* awaiting; undecided; imminent. *prep.* during.

pen·du·lum, *n.* body suspended to swing freely to and fro.

pen·e·trate, *v.,* **-trat·ed, -trat·ing.** enter; pierce; permeate; affect deeply; understand. **-tra·tive,** *a.*

pen·e·trat·ing, *a.* piercing; intrusive; keen insight.

pen·guin, *n.* flightless, black and white bird of southern hemisphere.

pen·i·cil·lin, *n.* antibiotic grown from molds.

pen·in·su·la, *n.* land almost surrounded by water. **-lar,** *a.*

pen·i·tent, *a.* repentant; sorry. *n.* one willing to atone.

pen·i·ten·tia·ry, *n. pl.,* **-ries.** prison.

pen·nant, *n.* banner; flag.

pen·ni·less, *a.* destitute.

pen·ny, *n. pl.,* **-nies.** one cent.

pe·nol·o·gy, *n.* study of crime prevention, rehabilitation, and prisons. **-no·log·i·cal,** *a.* **-o·gist,** *n.*

pen·sion, *n.* retirement or disability allowance.

pen·sive, *a.* thoughtful; melancholic. **-ly,** *adv.* **-ness,** *n.*

pent, *a.* kept in; confined.

pen·ta·gon, *n.* five-sided figure. **-tag·o·nal,** *a.* **-tag·o·nal·ly,** *adv.*

pen·tath·lon, *n.* athletic contest with five different events.

pent·house, *n.* apartment or dwelling on the roof of a building.

pent-up, *a.* confined; shut in.

pe·num·bra, *n. pl.,* **-bras, -brae.** partial shadow between area of total eclipse and total light.

pe·nu·ri·ous, *a.* miserly; stingy.

pen·u·ry, *n.* extreme poverty.

pe·on, *n.* day laborer; exploited worker; one in servitude.

peo·ple, *n. pl.,* **-ple, -ples.** persons collectively; persons under the same government, etc.; human beings. *v.,* **-pled, pling.** populate.

pep·per, *n.* pungent spice. *v.* sprinkle; pelt; spice up.

pep·per·mint, *n.* pungent herb of the mint family.

pep·tic, *a.* of digestion.

per, *prep.* through; by means of; by; for each; *inf.* in accord with.

per·am·bu·late, *v.,* **-lat·ed, -lat·ing.** walk through, over, or around. **-la·tor,** *n.* baby carriage.

per an·num, *adv.* annually.

per·cale, *n.* woven cotton fabric.

per cap·i·ta, *adv., a.* for each person.

per·ceive, *v.,* **-ceived, -ceiv·ing.** become aware of; understand.

per·cent, per cent, *n. pl.,* **per·cent, per·cents.** proportion of every hundred. **-age,** *n.* a part or share.

per·cept, *n.* recognizable sensual impression.

per·cep·ti·ble, *a.* discernible.

per·cep·tion, *n.* insight; intuitive recognition or judgment.

perch, *n.* roost; elevated seat; edible fish. *v.* alight; sit on.

per·chance, *adv.* possibly.

per·co·late, *v.,* **-lat·ed, -lat·ing.** pass through a filter; brew coffee.

per·co·la·tor, *n.* coffeepot.

per·cus·sion, *n.* impact; musical instrument sounded by striking.

per diem, *adv., a., n.* for the day; daily expense allowance.

per·di·tion, *n.* hell; damnation.

per·emp·to·ry, *a.* dogmatic; absolute; imperative; final.

per·en·ni·al, *a.* lasting throughout the year; continuing a long time; perpetual; lasting more than two years. *n.* **-ly,** *adv.*

per·fect, *a.* faultless; exact; absolute; pure; complete. *v.* improve; refine; complete. **-·fec·tion,** *n.* flawlessness. **-ly,** *adv.*

per·fi·dy, *n.* treachery. *a.*

per·fo·rate, *v.,* **-rat·ed, -rat·ing.** make a hole by boring; pierce a row of holes.

per·force, *adv.* of necessity.

per·form, *v.* do; act; execute.

per·for·mance, *n.* entertainment; exhibition; deed; feat.

per·fume, *n.* fragrance; scent. *v.,* **-fumed, -fum·ing.** give a fragrant odor.

per·func·to·ry, *a.* careless; superficial; indifferent; apathetic.

per·haps, *adv.* maybe, possibly.

per·i·gee, *n.* orbit point nearest the earth.

per·i·he·li·on, *n. pl.,* **-a.** orbit point nearest the sun.

per·il, *n.* danger; risk; jeopardy. *v.,* **-iled or -illed, -il·ing or -il·ling.** expose to danger.

per·il·ous, *a.* full of peril.

pe·rim·e·ter, *n.* outer boundary around an area.

pe·ri·od, *n.* portion of time; punctuation mark (·).

pe·ri·od·ic, *a.* recurring.

pe·ri·od·i·cal, *n.* publication appearing at fixed intervals.

per·i·pa·tet·ic, *a.* walking about.

pe·riph·er·y, *n. pl.,* **-ies.** outer surface or boundary; surrounding area.

per·i·scope, *n.* tube that reflects objects out of direct vision.

per·ish, *v.* die; be destroyed.

per·ish·a·ble, *a.* liable to spoil. *n.*

per·i·to·ne·um, *n. pl.,* **-ums, -a.** membrane of the abdomen.

per·jure, *v.,* **-jured, -jur·ing.** commit perjury.

per·ju·ry, *n. pl.,* **-ries.** intentional lie under oath.

perk, *v.* regain vigor; vivacity.

per·ma·nent, *a.* continuing.

per·me·a·ble, *a.* allowing passage, esp. fluids.

per·me·ate, *v.,* **-at·ed, -at·ing.** spread through; saturate.

per·mis·si·ble, *a.* allowable.

per·mis·sion, *n.* formal consent.

per·mit, *v.,* **-mit·ted, -mit·ting.** allow; consent; tolerate; authorize. *n.* a license.

per·mute, *v.* alter; change.

per·ni·cious, *a.* destructive.

per·o·ra·tion, *n.* concluding portion of an oration.

per·pen·dic·u·lar, *a.* at right angles with a plane; vertical.

per·pe·trate, *v.,* **-trat·ed, -trat·ing.** commit a crime, etc.

per·pet·u·al, *a.* continuous; ceaseless. **-ly,** *adv.*

per·pet·u·ate, *v.,* **-at·ed, -at·ing.** make enduring, perpetual.

per·plex, *v.* confuse; complicate.

per·qui·site, *n.* something extra beyond salary; benefits; gratuity.

per se, *adv.* by, in, or of itself.

per·se·cute, *v.,* **-cut·ed, -cut·ing.** harass; oppress. **-cu·tion,** *n.*

per·se·vere, *v.,* **-vered, -ver·ing.** persist despite difficulties.

per·si·flage, *n.* light, flippant style of writing or talking.

per·sist, *v.* be insistent; endure.

per·sist·ent, *a.* persevering; enduring; stubborn.

per·snick·et·y, *a. inf.* fussy.

per·son, *n.* human being; an individual; self.

per·son·a·ble, *a.* pleasing in appearance and personality.

per·son·al, *a.* pertaining to a person's character, affairs, habits, etc.

per·son·al·i·ty, *n. pl.,* **-ties.** characteristics that distinguish a person, group, or nation; a person who is famous or notorious.

per·son·al·ly, *adv.* in person.

per·son·i·fy, *v.,* **-fied, -fy·ing.** represent as a person; typify. **-fi·ca·tion,** *n.*

per·son·nel, *n.* persons employed in any work. *a.*

per·spec·tive, *n.* appearance; ability to evaluate; relationship to distances.

per·spi·ca·cious, *a.* with keen judgment; discerning.

per·spic·u·ous, *a.* easily understood.

per·spi·ra·tion, *n.* sweat.

per·spire, *v.,* **-spired, -spir·ing.** sweat.

per·suade, *v.,* **-suad·ed, -suad·ing.** convince; induce by reasoning or arguing. **-sua·sion,** *n.*

pert, *a.* impudent; lively.

per·tain, *v.* relate; be appropriate; belong to.

per·ti·nent, *a.* relevant.

per·turb, *v.* agitate; alarm.

pe·ruse, *v.,* **-rused, -rus·ing.** read carefully; study.

per·vade, *v.,* **-vad·ed, -vad·ing.** pass through; permeate. **-va·sion,** *n.* **-va·sive,** *a.*

per·verse, *a.* obstinate; contrary. **per·verse·ly,** *adv.*

per·ver·sion, *n.* deviation from the normal, esp. sexual.

per·vert, *v.* misuse; corrupt; distort; debase. *n.*

per·vi·ous, *a.* permeable; open-minded.

pes·ky, *a.,* **-ki·er, -ki·est.** *inf.* annoying; troublesome.

pes·si·mism, *n.* tendency to take unfavorable view; negative outlook. **-mist,** *n.*

pest, *n.* noxious thing; nuisance.

pes·ter, *v.* annoy; irritate.

pest·i·cide, *n.* chemical used to kill vermin or weeds.

pes·ti·lence, *n.* widespread, infectious disease; harmful thing.

pes·tle, *n.* tool for grinding substances, esp. in mortar.

pet, *n.* tamed animal; favored person. *a.* favorite. *v.,* **-ted, -ting.** fondle; stroke.

pet·al, *n.* leaflike part of a flower.

pe·tite, *a.* little; demure.

pe·ti·tion, *n.* formal request; entreaty. *v.* solicit; ask.

pet·ri·fy, *v.,* **-fied, -fy·ing.** change to stone; stupefy; scare.

pe·trog·ra·phy, *n.* science of classification of rocks.

pe·tro·le·um, *n.* oily, flammable liquid; gasoline source.

pet·ti·coat, *n.* underskirt; slip.

pet·ty, *a.,* **-ti·er, -ti·est.** small-minded; trivial.

pet·u·lant, *a.* showing irritation; impatient; bad humor. **-lance, -lan·cy,** *n.*

pew, *n.* benchlike seat.

pew·ter, *n.* dull, silvery-gray alloy of tin and lead. *a.*

pe·yo·te, *n.* hallucinogen obtained from cactus.

phal·lus, *n. pl.,* **-li, -lus·es.** penis; symbol of generative power. **-lic,** *a.*

phan·tasm, *n.* apparition; ghost.

phan·ta·sy, *n. pl.,* **-sies.** fantasy.

phan·tom, *n.* apparition. *a.* spectral; illusionary.

phar·aoh, *n.* Egyptian ruler.

phar·ma·ceu·ti·cal, *a.* pertaining to pharmacy. *n.* a drug.

phar·ma·cist, *n.* druggist.

phar·ma·cy, *n. pl.,* **-cies.** drugstore; art of dispensing drugs.

phase, *n.* part of a cycle or development. *v.,* **phased, phas·ing.** synchronize.

pheas·ant, *n. pl.,* **-ant, -ants.** long-tailed game bird.

phe·no·bar·bi·tal, *n.* a sedative.

phe·nom·e·non, *n. pl.,* **-na, nons.** extraordinary thing; observable fact. **-e·nal,** *a.* **-nal·ly,** *adv.*

phi·lan·der, *v.* make love frivolously.

phi·lan·thro·py, *n. pl.,* **-pies.** to aid mankind; charitable group or activity. **-throp·ic,** *a.* **-throp·i·cal·ly,** *adv.* **-thro·pist,** *n.*

phi·lat·e·ly, *n.* study of stamps, postmarks, etc.

phil·har·mon·ic, *a.* fond of music; symphony orchestra.

phi·los·o·pher, *n.* person who studies philosophy. **phil·o·soph·i·cal,** *a.* **phi·los·o·phize,** *v.*

phi·los·o·phy, *n. pl.,* **-phies.** study of morals and character; study of principles underlying all knowledge; insight applied to life.

phlegm, *n.* thick stringy mucus; apathy; self-possession.

phleg·mat·ic, *a.* apathetic; stolid; sluggish. **-i·cal,** *a.*

pho·bi·a, *n.* abnormal, persistent fear. **-bic,** *a.*

phoe·nix, phe·nix, *n.* mythical bird, symbol of immortality.

pho·no·graph, *n.* record player. **-ic,** *a.* **-i·cal·ly,** *adv.*

pho·net·ics, *n.* system of sounds of a language.

phon·ics, *n. pl.* method of teaching reading, spelling, pronunciation by the use of phonetics.

pho·ny, pho·ney, *a.,* **-ni·er, -ni·est, -ney·er, -ney·est.** *inf.* fake, counterfeit. *n. pl.,* **-nies, -neys. -ni·ness,** *n.*

phos·pho·res·cence, *n.* light without heat. **-resce,** *v.,* **-resced, -resc·ing. -cent,** *a.* **-cent·ly,** *adv.*

pho·to·cop·y, *n.* photographic reproduction; duplication.

pho·to·e·lec·tric, *a.* pertaining to the electric effects caused by light.

pho·to·en·grav·ing, *n.* photographic process of producing a relief plate for printing.

pho·to fin·ish, *n.* close finish of a race or game.

pho·to·gen·ic, *a.* favorable qualities for photography; giving off light.

pho·to·graph, *n.* picture made by photography; snapshot. *v.* take a photograph of.

pho·tog·ra·phy, *n.* art of producing images on a surface.

pho·to·sen·si·tive, *a.* sensitive to light.

pho·to·stat, *n.* device for making facsimile copies of documents, printed matter, etc.

pho·to·syn·the·sis, *n.* formation of carbohydrates in chlorophyll-filled plant tissues exposed to light.

phrase, *n.* short expression; group of words not containing a subject or verb.

phrase·ol·o·gy, *n.* wording.

phy·lum, *n.* classification of animals and plants.

phys·ic, *n.* cathartic; remedy.

phys·i·cal, *a.* relating to the human body, the universe, natural sciences, etc.

phy·si·cian, *n.* doctor of medicine; one who heals.

phys·ics, *n.* science of matter and energy.

phys·i·og·no·my, *n.* face; external features.

phys·i·ol·o·gy, *n.* science of functions and processes of living organisms.

phy·sique, *n.* body structure and appearance.

pi·a·nis·si·mo, *a. mus.* very soft.

pi·an·ist, *n.* piano player.

pi·an·o, *n.* large musical instrument with keyboard, steel wires, and hammers.

pi·az·za, *n.* open square in a city, esp. in Italy; arcade.

pi·ca, *n.* printing type size.

pic·a·yune, *a.* petty; trivial.

pic·ca·lil·li, *n.* relish of vegetables, spices, mustard.

pic·co·lo, *n.* small flute.

pick, *v.* choose; harvest; select; pluck. *n.* choice; selection; pointed tool; best one.

pick·et, *n.* stake that is pointed; demonstrator; sentinel; striker.

pick·le, *n.* vegetable preserved in brine; marinade.

pick·pock·et, *n.* one who steals from pockets or purses.

pick·up, *n.* acceleration; small open truck.

pick·y, *a. inf.* fussy; exacting.

pic·nic, *n.* outdoor meal, party.

pic·to·ri·al, *a.* pertaining to or containing pictures; graphic.

pic·ture, *n.* painting, drawing, or other visual representation; resemblance; mental image.

pic·tur·esque, *a.* having pictorial quality; striking; charming.

pid·dle, *v.* deal in trifles; dawdle.

pie, *n.* crust filled with fruit, meat, or other filling.

pie·bald, *a.* having spots of two different colors.

piece, *n.* a distinct part of or separated from the whole; single object or entity.

pièce de ré·sis·tance, *n.* main part of a meal; principal event.

piece·meal, *adv.* bit by bit.

piece·work, *n.* work paid for by the piece when completed.

pied, *a.* variegated; piebald.

pier, *n.* wharf; dock for ships.

pierce, *v.* pass into or through; penetrate; make a hole.

pi·e·ty, *n.* religious devoutness, reverence, filial honor.

pig, *n.* hog; filthy person.

pi·geon, *n.* widely distributed bird with small head; dove; *inf.* a dupe.

pi·geon·hole, *n.* small compartment in a desk for filing.

pi·geon-toed, *a.* having the feet turned inward when walking.

pig·gy·back, *adv.* on the back or shoulders; on a railroad flatcar, as a truck.

pig·head·ed, *a.* stupidly obstinate.

pig i·ron, *n.* crude iron.

pig·ment, *n.* coloring matter.

pig·men·ta·tion, *n.* coloration of plant and animal tissue.

pig·skin, *n.* leather made from skin of a pig; *inf.* football.

pig·tail, *n.* hair in a braid.

pike, *n.* freshwater fish; turnpike; spear; spike.

pi·laf, *n.* rice dish.

pile, *n.* heavy stake driven into the ground for support; heap; carpet, etc. nap; large amount.

pil·fer, *v.* steal in small quantities.

pil·grim, *n.* traveler to sacred place; wanderer; wayfarer.

pill, *n.* medicine to be swallowed whole; tablet, capsule; disagreeable thing or person.

pil·lage, *v.* plunder; loot. *n.*

pil·lar, *n.* upright support; one who strongly supports (a cause).

pil·lo·ry, *n.* formerly, frame with holes for head and hands to punish an offender; public disgrace.

pil·low, *n.* soft support for the head during sleep; cushion.

pil·low·case, *n.* removable outer case for a pillow.

pi·lot, *n.* operator of aircraft or ships; helmsman. *v.* lead.

pi·men·to, *n.* sweet red pepper.

pimp, *n.* solicitor for prostitutes; procurer. *v.*

pim·ple, *n.* small rounded swelling of the skin; acne.

pin, *n.* piece of metal, used for fastening articles together; trifle; adornment with pin; wooden peg.

pin·a·fore, *n.* sleeveless apronlike dress.

pin·ball, *n.* electronic arcade game.

pin·cers, *n.* tool with two handles and jaws for gripping; grasping claws.

pinch, *v.* squeeze between the fingers or two hard edges; nip; cause discomfort; arrest.

n. quantity fit between thumb and forefinger.

pinch hit·ter, *n.* one who substitutes for another person.

pine, *n.* evergreen tree. *v.* **pined, pin·ing.** to long intensely; languish.

pine·ap·ple, *n.* juicy, edible tropical fruit.

pin·feath·er, *n.* beginning feather, just starting to grow.

ping, *n.* metallic ringing sound.

pin·hole, *n.* small puncture.

pin·ion, *n.* bird's wing; cogwheel. *v.* bind a person's arms.

pink·eye, *n.* contagious eye inflammation; conjunctivitis.

pin·na·cle, *n.* topmost point.

pin·point, *n.* extremely small. *v.* locate, define precisely.

pint, *n.* one-half quart; 2 cups.

pin·to, *a.* spotted; esp. a horse.

pin·worm, *n.* parasitic worm infesting intestine and rectum.

pi·o·neer, *n.* one of first who enters an area. *v.* go before.

pi·ous, *a.* religious; devout.

pipe, *n.* bowl and stem for smoking; duct or tube for conveying fluid. *v.* convey by pipes.

pipe·line, *n.* pipe used to transmit oil, gas, water, etc.; source of information.

pi·quant, *a.* agreeably pungent taste; charmingly lively.

pique, *v.,* **piqued, pi·quing.** cause resentment in; offend; provoke interest. *n.* irritated, resentful feeling.

pi·qué, *n.* durable ribbed cotton or silk fabric.

pi·rate, *n.* robber on the high seas. *v.* reproduce without authorization.

pi·rogue, *n.* canoe made from hollowing out a log.

pir·ou·ette, *n.* rapid whirling on the toes in dancing.

pis·ta·chi·o, *n.* edible green nut.

pis·til, *n.* seedbearing organ of flowering plants.

pis·tol, *n.* small firearm held and fired with one hand.

pis·ton, *n.* disk that moves back and forth receiving from or exerting pressure on a fluid.

pit, *n.* cavity in the ground; abyss; scar; stone of a fruit.

pitch, *n.* black, sticky substance from distillation of tar; asphalt; slope; zenith; sales talk; baseball throw; sound wave frequency. *v.* erect; throw; incline; buck.

pitch·er, *n.* container with spout and handle; player who throws the ball, esp. baseball.

pitch·fork, *n.* large fork used in moving hay, straw, etc.

pit·e·ous, *a.* exciting pity or sympathy.

pit·fall, *n.* hidden trap or danger.

pith, *n.* soft cellular tissue in the center of plant stems; gist; soft core.

pith·y, *a.* forceful; terse.

pit·i·a·ble, *a.* arousing pity.

pit·i·ful, *a.* arousing compassion.

pit·i·less, *a.* merciless.

pit·tance, *n.* small allowance.

pi·tu·i·tar·y gland, *n.* small endocrine gland at base of brain.

pit·y, *n.*, *v.* compassion.

piv·ot, *n.* thing upon which a related part rotates; turning point; *v.* to turn.

pix·ie, pix·y, *n.* fairy; sprite.

pix·i·lat·ed, *a.* erratic; droll.

piz·za, *n.* doughy crust overlaid with cheese, tomatoes, etc.

piz·zi·ca·to, *a. mus.* plucking the strings with the finger.

plac·a·ble, *a.* appeasable.

plac·ard, *n.* notice to be publicly displayed.

pla·cate, *v.* appease; pacify.

place, *n.* space; residence; definite position; job. *v.* **placed, plac·ing.** set; assign; finish second in a race.

pla·ce·bo, *n.* preparation of no therapeutic value given to gratify a patient or to act as a control in a test.

pla·cen·ta, *n.* organ by which the fetus receives nourishment from mother.

plac·er, *n.* deposit of sand, gravel, etc. containing gold or other mineral particles.

plac·id, *a.* quiet; tranquil.

plack·et, *n.* slit in a skirt.

pla·gia·rize, *v.* to appropriate as one's own the writing, ideas, etc. of another. **-rism,** *n.*

plague, *n.* epidemic disease with a high death rate. *v.* harass.

pla·guy, *a. inf.,* troublesome.

plaid, *n.* a fabric woven in a tartan or checkered pattern.

plain, *a.* flat; open; understandable; homely; unadorned; *n.* prairie.

plain·tiff, *n.* person who begins a lawsuit; complainant.

plain·tive, *a.* expressing sadness.

plait, *n.* fold; braid of hair.

plan, *n.* a scheme, design, or arrangement; drawing or diagram; intention. *v.* think out beforehand.

plane, *n.* carpenter's tool for smoothing boards; flat surface; level surface.

plan·et, *n.* one of the large bodies that orbit the sun, as the earth.

plan·e·tar·i·um, *n.* solar system model; building housing the device.

plan·e·tar·y, *a.* of or pertaining to a planet; terrestrial.

plan·e·toid, *n.* asteroid.

plank, *n.* broad piece of timber thicker than a board; political platform principle.

plank·ton, *n.* microscopic organisms in a body of water.

plant, *n.* organism of the vegetable kingdom, having cellulose cell walls; industrial complex. *v.* stock; cause to grow; place firmly; hide secretly.

plan·tain, *n.* weed; tropical plant in the banana family.

plan·ta·tion, *n.* large estate.

plant·er, *n.* one or machine that plants; ornamental plant container.

plaque, *n.* decorative plate; calcification on teeth.

plas·ma, *n.* liquid portion of the blood, lymph, milk, etc.

plas·ter, *n.* pasty composition that hardens on drying, used for covering walls and ceilings.

plas·ter·board, *n.* laminated wallboard of paper and gypsum.

plas·ter of Par·is, *n.* quick-setting paste used for casts and molds.

plas·tic, *a.* capable of being molded. *n.* synthetic compound that can be molded.

plate, *n.* dish from which food is eaten. *v.* cover with metal.

pla·teau, *n.* flat area of elevated land; stable period.

plat·form, *n.* flat floor raised above an adjacent level; statement of principles.

plat·ing, *n.* an outer coating of metal.

plat·i·num, *n.* valuable metal used for jewelry, etc.

plat·i·tude, *n.* dull truism.

Pla·ton·ic, *a.* love that is spiritual or friendly rather than sensual.

pla·toon, *n.* unit of a military unit; specialized squad.

plat·ter, *n.* flat serving dish.

plat·y·pus, *n.* primitive aquatic mammal with ducklike bill.

plau·dit, *n.* expression of praise.

plau·si·ble, *a.* apparently true.

play, *n.* drama; fun; looseness of movement; amusement; game move. *v.* amuse self; take part in; perform; pretend.

play·back, *n.* reproduction of sound, etc. from a recording, tape, etc.

play·bill, *n.* notice of a play; theater program.

play·boy, *n. inf.* man whose time is spent in pursuit of pleasure.

play·er, *n.* one who plays; actor; musician; gambler.

play·ful, *a.* frolicsome; humorous.

play·ground, *n.* area set apart for outside recreation.

play·house, *n.* theater; small house for children.

play·let, *n.* short drama.

play·mate, *n.* companion.

play·off, *n.* in sports, games to determine a championship.

play·thing, *n.* thing to play with.

play·wright, *n.* writer of plays.

pla·za, *n.* open public square.

plea, *n.* appeal; entreaty.

plea-bar·gain·ing, *n.* pleading guilty to a lesser charge to avoid facing a more serious one.

plead, *v.* appeal; beg; argue in support of a claim.

pleas·ant, *a.* agreeable; pleasing.

pleas·ant·ry, *n.* banter.

please, *v.* **pleased, pleas·ing.** satisfy; give pleasure.

pleas·ing, *a.* giving satisfaction.

pleas·ur·a·ble, *a.* enjoyable.

pleas·ure, *n.* delight; one's choice; amusement.

pleat, *n.* double fold of cloth.

ple·be·ian, *a.* common; vulgar.

pleb·i·scite, *n.* vote to determine the popular will.

pledge, *v.* give as security; promise; bind. *n.* solemn promise.

ple·na·ry, *a.* full in all respects of requisites.

plen·i·po·ten·ti·ar·y, *n.* person invested with full power to transact government business.

plen·i·tude, *n.* state of being full.

plen·te·ous, *a.* amply sufficient.

plen·ti·ful, *a.* abundant.

plen·ty, *n.* abundance; enough; large number.

ple·o·nasm, *n.* wordiness; redundancy; unneeded word or phrase.

pleth·o·ra, *n.* superabundance.

pleu·ri·sy, *n.* painful inflammation of the pleura (lung covering).

plex·us, *n. pl.*, **-us·es, -us.** network.

pli·a·ble, *a.* flexible; adaptable.

pli·ant, *a.* flexible; compliant.

pli·ers, *n. pl.* tool with pincers for holding or cutting.

plight, *n.* distressed or complicated situation; solemn pledge.

plink, *n.* light, sharp clinking sound. *v.*

plod, *v.* walk heavily; trudge.

plop, *v.* make sound like thing dropped in water. *n.*

plot, *n.* small area of land; incidents forming the plan of a novel, etc.; conspiracy. *v.*, **plot·ted, plot·ting.** make a plan of; scheme.

plow, *n.* implement for cutting, turning over soil; move through.

plow·share, *n.* cutting blade of a plow.

ploy, *n.* tactic; maneuver.

pluck, *v.* pick; snatch.

pluck·y, *a.* spirited; brave.

plug, *n.* object used to fill a hole; stopper.

plum·age, *n.* bird feathers.

plumb, *n.* weight hung on a line to determine the perpendicularity of walls. *a.* vertical.

plumb·er, *n.* one who installs and repairs water, gas, etc. pipes.

plumb·ing, *n.* system of pipes and ducts to convey water, waste, gas, etc.

plume, *n.* large feather of a bird.

plum·met, *n.*, *v.* to drop straight down; plunge.

plump, *v.* fall heavily. *a.* fat; pudgy. *adv.* straight down.

plun·der, *v.* rob; pillage. *n.* that which is taken by theft; booty.

plunge, *v.* immerse; penetrate quickly; dive.

plunk, *v.* strum; drop heavily.

plu·ral, *a.* more than one.

plu·ral·i·ty, *n.* majority.

plus, *a.* added to; denoting addition; positive; somewhat higher.

plush, *n.* fabric with a nap. *a. inf.* luxurious.

plu·toc·ra·cy, *n.* government by the wealthy.

plu·to·ni·um, *n.* radioactive metallic element used as nuclear fuel.

ply, *v.*, **plied, ply·ing.** wield; keep supplying; employ with diligence. *n.* single layer; bias.

ply·wood, *n.* material made of layers of wood glued together.

pneu·mat·ic, *a.* pertaining to air, gas; worked by compressed air.

pneu·mo·nia, *n.* acute inflammation of the lungs.

poach, *v.* cook (eggs, fish, etc.) in boiling water; trespass to steal game or fish; trample.

pock·et, *n.* pouchlike receptacle; cavity; small area.

pock·et·book, *n.* woman's purse.

pock·et·knife, *n. pl.*, **-knives.** small knife with blades that fold into the handle.

pock·mark, *n.* scar; pit.

pod, *n.* seed vessel containing one or more seeds; outside aircraft housing.

po·di·a·trist, *n.* one who treats disorders of the foot. **-try.** *n.* Also **chiropodist.**

po·di·um, *n. pl.*, **-a, -ums.** raised platform, esp. for music conductor.

po·em, *n.* verse composition. **po·et·ic, po·et·i·cal,** *a.* **po·et·i·cal·ly,** *adv.*

po·et, *n.* one who writes poetry; expressive artist.

po·et·ry, *n.* the art of writing poems; poetic works.

po·grom, *n.* officially instigated massacre, esp. against Jews.

poign·ant, *a.* keen; moving to the feelings; incisive; piercing. **-an·cy,** *n.* **poign·ant·ly,** *adv.*

point, *n.* end of; tip; sharp end; attribute; main idea; period; limit reached; moment; detail; suggestion; unit of scoring. *v.* direct; aim; call attention to.

point-blank, *a.* direct; plain.

point·er, *n.* indicator; hunting dog; tapered rod.

poise, *n.* equilibrium; composure; balance; carriage. *v.*, **poised, pois·ing.** hover.

poi·son, *n.* agent that injures or destroys an organism. *v.* injure with poison; corrupt. **-ous,** *a.* **-ing,** *v.*

poke, *v.*, **poked, pok·ing.** thrust; jab; push out; move slowly; pierce.

pok·er, *n.* card game; iron bar for stirring fire.

po·lar, *a.* of or near the N. or S. pole; opposite in character.

po·lar·i·ty, *n. pl.*, **-ties.** quality of possessing opposing poles.

po·lar·ize, *v.*, **-ized, -izing.** cause polarity; separate into opposing factions. **-i·za·tion,** *n.*

pole, *n.* long slender piece of wood or metal; unit of measurement; outer ends of axis.

po·lem·ic, *a.* controversial argument.

po·lice, *n.* civil force for maintaining order and enforcing law. *v.*, **-liced, -lic·ing.** control; enforce; keep clean.

pol·i·cy, *n. pl.*, **-cies.** governing principle; written contract; management.

pol·i·o·my·e·li·tis, *n.* infectious viral disease causing paralysis.

pol·ish, *v.* make smooth or lustrous; make elegant. *n.* act of rubbing; glossiness; refinement.

po·lite, *a.* considerate; courteous; refined. **-ly,** *adv.* **-ness,** *n.*

pol·i·tic, *a*. prudent; expedient.

po·lit·i·cal, *a*. pertaining to government. **-cal·ly**, *adv*.

pol·i·ti·cian, *n*. one engaged in politics.

pol·i·tics, *n*. construed as sing. or pl. science of government; political beliefs, affairs.

pol·ka, *n*. lively round dance.

poll, *n*. list of persons; opinion survey; voting at an election; *usu. pl*. voting place. *v*. to vote; register votes; interview.

pol·len, *n*. male spores (yellow dust) in flowering plants.

pol·lute, *v*., **-lut·ed**, **-lut·ing**. make unclean, impure; contaminate. **-lut·er**, *n*. **-lu·tion**, *n*.

po·lo, *n*. game played on horseback with ball and mallets.

po·lo·ni·um, *n*. radioactive element in uranium.

pol·y·chrome, *a*. having many colors.

pol·y·es·ter, *n*. synthetic fiber.

po·lyg·a·my, *n*. having more than one wife/husband at same time. **-mist**, *n*. **-mous**, *a*.

pol·y·gon, *n*. closed plane figure bounded by straight lines.

pol·y·graph, *n*. lie detector; instrument for detecting emotional reactions.

pol·y·he·dron, *n. pl*., **-drons**, **-dra**. solid bounded by plane faces.

pol·y·no·mi·al, *n*. consisting of many terms.

pol·yp, *n*. an outgrowth from mucous membrane as in the nose, rectum, etc.

pol·y·syl·la·ble, *n*. word of several syllables, esp. more than three.

pol·y·tech·nic, *n*. school of applied sciences; *a*. embracing many sciences and technical fields.

pol·y·the·ism, *n*. worship of more than one god.

pom·ace, *n*. pulp.

pome·gran·ate, *n*. edible fruit with many juicy seeds.

pom·mel, *n*. saddle knob. *v*., **-meled**, **-mel·ing**. beat with fists. Also **pum·mel**.

pomp, *n*. ostentatious display.

pom·pa·dour, *n*. hair style.

pom·pon, *n*. ball-shaped ornament. Also **pom·pom**.

pomp·ous, *a*. overbearing; ostentatious. **pom·pos·i·ty**, *n*., **-ous·ly**, *adv*. **-ous·ness**, *n*.

pon·cho, *n*. blanketlike garment with hole for head.

pond, *n*. body of still water.

pon·der, *v*. consider; think.

pon·der·ous, *a*. very heavy; dull.

pon·iard, *n*. a small dagger.

pon·tiff, *n*. the Pope; a bishop.

pon·tif·i·cal, *a*. of a pontiff.

pon·toon, *n*. float used to support; seaplane floats.

po·ny, *n. pl*., **po·nies**. small horse; any miniature.

pool, *n*. small body of water; group with common interest; gambling stakes; billiards. *v*. combine into a mutual fund.

poop, *n*. stern of a ship; *inf*. information. *v*. *inf*. exhaust.

poor, *a*. having little; deficient; feeble; needy.

pop, *n*. short, explosive sound; carbonated beverage. *v*., **popped**, **pop·ping**. make a quick sound; come or go quickly; cause (corn) to pop; protrude; *inf*. take drugs.

pop·corn, *n*. corn whose kernels pop open when heated.

Pope, *n*. head of the Roman Catholic Church. Also **pope**.

pop·eyed, *a*. having bulging eyes; amazed.

pop·lin, *n*. sturdy ribbed fabric.

pop·over, *n*. light, hollow muffin.

pop·py, *n. pl*., **-pies**. flowering plant with milky juices (opium is extracted from some species).

pop·py·cock, *n., interj. inf*. nonsense.

pop·u·lace, *n*. common people.

pop·u·lar, *a*. well-liked; suitable to the masses; widespread. **-ly**, *adv*. **-i·ty**, *n*.

pop·u·late, *v*., **-lat·ed**, **-lat·ing**. furnish with people; inhabit.

pop·u·la·tion, *n*. the total number of people, etc. in an area.

pop·u·lous, *a*. thickly settled.

por·ce·lain, *n*. hard, glazed, white, translucent ceramic.

porch, *n*. veranda; covered entrance.

por·cine, *a*. relating to swine.

por·cu·pine, *n*. rodent with sharp defensive spines.

pore, *v*., **pored**, **por·ing**. read with care; ponder. *n*. minute opening.

pork, *n*. flesh of pigs; *inf*. political favors, money, etc.

por·nog·ra·phy, *n*. erotic literature or art. **-no·graph·ic**, *a*.

po·rous, *a*. permeable by liquids, etc.; having pores.

por·poise, *n*. small whale.

por·ridge, *n*. soft boiled cereal.

port, *n*. harbor; ship opening; left side of ship; sweet red wine; haven. *v*. turn to the left; to carry.

port·a·ble, *a.* capable of being carried or moved. *n.*

por·tage, *n.* carrying boats, goods, etc. overland. *v.,* **-taged, -tag·ing.**

por·tal, *n.* imposing entrance.

por·tend, *v.* presage; forebode.

por·tent, *n.* omen. **-ten·tious,** *a.*

por·ter, *n.* one who carries (luggage, etc.); janitor; doorkeeper.

port·fo·li·o, *n. pl.,* **-os.** portable case; list of investments.

port·hole, *n.* round hole in a ship to admit light, air, etc.

por·ti·co, *n. pl.,* **-coes, -cos.** open porch, walkway with columns.

por·tion, *n.* allotment; share; dowry. *v.* divide; distribute.

port·ly, *a.,* **-li·er, -li·est.** rather stout or heavy. **-li·ness,** *n.*

por·trait, *n.* picture, likeness of a person; vivid description.

por·tray, *v.* draw or describe the likeness; enact; depict. **-al,** *n.*

pose, *v.,* **posed, pos·ing.** assume a position; falsely represent; ask, or present. *n.* attitude.

po·seur, *n.* insincere person.

posh, *a. inf.* elegant.

po·si·tion, *n.* situation; status; job; point of view. *v.* place.

pos·i·tive, *a.* sure; absolute; definite; affirmative; greater than zero; confident. *adv.*

pos·se, *n.* temporary group armed with legal authority.

pos·sess, *v.* own; have as a quality; dominate; control. **-ses·sor,** *n.*

pos·sessed, *a.* calm; cool; controlled as if by evil spirits.

pos·ses·sion, *n.* ownership; property. **-sive,** *a.*

pos·si·bil·i·ty, *n.* something that can happen; potential.

pos·si·ble, *a.* may be; may happen; feasible.

pos·si·bly, *adv.* perhaps; maybe.

post, *n.* upright support timber; place where stationed; position; mail. *v.* put up; assign; mail. *adv.*

post·age, *n.* mailing charge.

post·date, *v.* affix a future date.

post·er, *n.* large printed sheet.

pos·te·ri·or, *a.* situated behind; subsequent. *n.*

pos·ter·i·ty, *n.* all following generations.

pos·tern, *n.* back door; side entrance.

post·grad·u·ate, *a.* studies pursued after a first college degree.

post·haste, *adv.* speedily.

post·hu·mous, *a.* born, occurring, etc. after one's death.

post·mark, *n.* post office mark to cancel stamps, etc.

post me·rid·i·em, *a.* after noon. *Abbr. p·m.,* *P·M.*

post-mor·tem, *n.* autopsy. *a.* occurring after death.

post·na·tal, *a.* period immediately after birth.

post·par·tum, *a.* existing or occurring after childbirth.

post·pone, *v.,* **-poned, -pon·ing.** put off to future; defer. *n.*

post·script, *n.* something added to a letter or book.

pos·tu·late, *v.,* **-lat·ed, -lat·ing.** demand; claim; assume without proof. *n.* axiom; plain without proof.

pos·ture, *n.* body position; pose; attitude. *v.*

post·war, *a.* period after a war.

po·sy, *n. pl.,* **po·sies.** single flower; nosegay; motto.

pot, *n.* round cooking vessel; gambling stakes; *inf.* sum of money; marijuana.

po·ta·ble, *a.* suitable for drinking.

po·tas·si·um, *n.* metallic element essential to life.

po·ta·to, *n. pl.,* **-toes.** starchy, edible tuber; *inf.* **spud.**

pot·bel·ly, *n.* protuberant belly.

po·tent, *a.* powerful; effective. **-ten·cy,** *n.* **-tent·ly,** *adv.*

po·ten·tate, *n.* sovereign; one with controlling power.

po·ten·tial, *a.* possible; latent. *n.* anything possible.

po·tion, *n.* medicinal drink.

pot·luck, *n.* meal with whatever is available.

pot·pour·ri, *n.* dried sweet smelling flower petals to perfume a room; mixed collection.

pot·tage, *n.* thick soup.

pot·ter, *n.* one who makes earthenware.

pot·ter·y, *n. pl.,* **-ies.** clayware; place for, or art of making it.

pouch, *n.* small bag or sack. *v.* put into; pocket.

poul·tice, *n.* warm, pulpy dressing to relieve pain, etc.

poul·try, *n.* domestic fowls.

pounce, *n.* swoop; jump on. *v.,* **pounced, pounc·ing.** seize; swoop down on.

pound, *n.* unit of weight (16 oz.); British monetary unit; enclosure; heavy blow. *v.* strike or throb heavily.

pour, *v.* cause to flow; flow continuously. *n.* downfall.

pout, v. be sullen; sulk. n. ill-humor; sullenness.

pov·er·ty, n. being poor; scarcity; dearth.

pow·der, n. fine particles; cosmetic. v. cover with powder; pulverize. **-y,** a.

pow·er, n. capability; energy source; authority.

pow·er·ful, a. potent; mighty; prestigious. **-ful·ly,** adv.

pow·er·less, a. helpless; unable.

pox, n. disease with watery skin eruptions.

prac·ti·ca·ble, a. feasible; possible; usable. **-bil·i·ty, -ble·ness,** n. **-bly,** adv.

prac·ti·cal, a. suitable; useful; workable; utilitarian. **-i·ty,** n. **-ly,** adv.

prac·tice, v. **-ticed, -tic·ing.** pursue; apply; rehearse; do habitually. n. habit; usage; pursuit. **-ti·tion·er,** n.

prac·ticed, a. skilled; experienced.

prag·mat·ic, a. practical; factual; opinionated; officious. **-tist,** n.

prai·rie, n. treeless grassland.

praise, n. express approval; glorify. **praised, prais·ing,** v.

pra·line, n. crisp confection made of nuts and sugar.

prance, v., **pranced, pranc·ing.** move with high steps, as a horse; swagger.

prank, n., v. mischievous practical joke. **-ster,** n.

prate, v., **prat·ed, prat·ing.** talk idly; chatter.

prat·tle, v., **-tled, -tling.** talk like a child.

prawn, n. shrimplike shellfish.

pray, v. beg; entreat; implore.

prayer, n. petition; entreaty or thanks to God.

preach, v. deliver a sermon; advocate earnestly. **-er,** n.

pre·ad·o·les·cence, n. ages 9 to 12; preteen.

pre·am·ble, n. introduction; preface; preliminary event.

pre·car·i·ous, a. risky; dubious; dangerous. **-ly,** adv.

pre·cau·tion, n. forethought; safeguard. **-ar·y,** a.

pre·cede, v., **-ced·ed, -ced·ing.** go before in order, place, time, etc.

prec·e·dence, n. act or right of preceding; higher rank.

prec·e·dent, n. an example. a. previous; prior; preceding.

pre·cept, n. prescribed rule of conduct.

pre·cep·tor, n. a teacher.

pre·cinct, n. subdivision of a city; election district.

pre·ci·os·i·ty, n. fastidious refinement.

pre·cious, a. beloved; valuable.

prec·i·pice, n. steep place; cliff.

pre·cip·i·tant, a. rushing quickly and heedlessly; rash.

pre·cip·i·tate, v., **-tat·ed, -tat·ing.** hasten; cause; separate out. a. hasty; sudden and brief.

pre·cip·i·ta·tion, n. rash haste; falling down rapidly; rain, etc.

pre·cip·i·tous, a. very steep; headlong.

pre·cise, a. accurate; clearly defined; exact. **-ness,** n.

pre·ci·sion, n. exactness; relevance; accuracy.

pre·clude, v., **-clud·ed, -clud·ing.** make ineffectual; prevent. **-clu·sion,** n. **-clu·sive,** a.

pre·co·cious, a. prematurely developed. **-coc·i·ty,** n.

pre·con·ceive, v., **-ceived, -ceiv·ing.** form an idea or opinion in advance.

pre·con·di·tion, n. prerequisite.

pre·cur·sor, n. forerunner.

pred·a·to·ry, a. preying on other animals; plundering. **-tor,** n.

pre·de·cease, v. to die before.

pred·e·ces·sor, n. one who goes or has gone before; ancestor.

pre·des·ti·nate, v., **-nat·ed, -nat·ing.** divinely foreordained.

pre·des·ti·na·tion, n. fate.

pre·de·ter·mine, v. **-mined, min·ing.** determine beforehand; decide in advance.

pre·dic·a·ment, n. trying, puzzling, or embarrassing situation.

pred·i·cate, v., **-cat·ed, -cat·ing.** declare; affirm; base on. n. Gram. word or words that makes a statement about the subject.

pre·dict, v. foretell. **-a·ble,** a.

pre·dic·tion, n. forecast.

pre·di·lec·tion, n. liking for.

pre·dis·po·si·tion, n. tendency. **-pose,** v., **-posed, -pos·ing.**

pre·dom·i·nant, a. superior in power, influence, number, etc.

pre·dom·i·nate, v., **-nat·ed, -nat·ing.** be superior to; rule over.

pre·em·i·nent, a. distinguished above others. **-nence,** n.

pre·empt, v. seize beforehand; take land for public use. n. **-emp·tion,** n.

preen, v. groom; primp; adorn.

pre·fab·ri·cate, v., **-cat·ed, -cat·ing.** fabricate beforehand (usu. in sections). **-ca·tion,** n.

pref·ace, n. introduction.

pre·fer, v., **-ferred, -fer·ring.** like better; give priority to.

pref·er·a·ble, *a.* more desirable.

pref·er·ence, *n.* choice over another; favoritism.

pref·er·en·tial, *a.* indicating partiality; giving priority.

pre·ferred, *a.* having first claim; chosen by preference.

pre·fix, *v.* put before. *n.* syllable at the beginning of a word.

preg·nant, *a.* carrying a fetus; weighty idea; teeming; full. **-nan·cy,** *n. pl.,* **-cies.**

pre·hen·sile, *a.* adapted for grasping or holding.

pre·his·tor·ic, *a.* period or time before written history.

prej·u·dice, *n.* unfair or unfounded opinion; bias. *v.,* **-diced, -dic·ing.** affect with a prejudice. **-di·cial,** *a.*

prel·ate, *n.* dignitary of the church; ecclesiastic.

pre·lim·i·nar·y, *a.* introductory; preparatory. *n. pl.,* **-ies.**

prel·ude, *n.* opening piece, section, or event.

pre·ma·ture, *a.* occurring before the proper time; untimely.

pre·med·i·tate, *v.,* **-tat·ed, -tat·ing.** plan, consider beforehand.

pre·mier, *a.* chief; principal; earliest. *n.* head of a government.

pre·miere, *n.* first performance. *v.* present for the first time.

prem·ise, *v.,* **-ised, -is·ing.** set forth. *n.* proposition; *pl.* land.

pre·mi·um, *n.* incentive; reward; bonus; amount paid for insurance.

pre·mo·ni·tion, *n.* forewarning.

pre·na·tal, *a.* before birth.

pre·oc·cu·py, *v.,* **-pied, -py·ing.** engross. **-pa·tion,** *n.* **-pied,** *a.*

prep·a·ra·tion, *n.* readiness, being prepared.

pre·par·a·to·ry, *a.* introductory.

pre·pare, *v.,* **-pared, -par·ing.** make or get ready; equip.

pre·pay, *v.,* **-paid, -pay·ing.** pay for in advance. **-ment,** *n.*

pre·pon·der·ant, *a.* having superior importance, weight, number, etc. **-an·cy,** *n.* **-ant·ly,** *adv.*

prep·o·si·tion, *n.* word used to show the relationship between noun or pronoun and other words.

pre·pos·ter·ous, *a.* ridiculous.

pre·puce, *n.* foreskin of penis.

pre·req·ui·site, *a.* necessary beforehand. *n.* necessity.

pre·rog·a·tive, *n.* hereditary right; recognized right. *a.*

pres·age, *n.* foreboding.

pre·scribe, *v.,* **-scribed, -scrib·ing.** designate; ordain; order for use; direct; dictate.

pre·scrip·tion, *n.* act of dictating, etc.; medicine prescribed.

pres·ence, *n.* being present; close proximity; bearing.

pres·ent, *a.* being there; at hand; current time. *n.* now.

pre·sent, *v.* make a gift; offer formally; exhibit; put forward. **pres·ent,** *n.* gift.

pre·sent·a·ble, *a.* suitable.

pres·en·ta·tion, *n.* offering or presenting someone or something.

pres·ent·ly, *adv.* soon; shortly.

pre·serv·a·tive, *a.* tending to preserve. *n.* substance which preserves.

pre·serve, *v.,* **-served, -serv·ing.** protect; maintain. *n. usu. pl.* cooked fruit; wildlife shelter.

pre·side, *v.,* **-sid·ed, -sid·ing.** direct; occupy official position.

pres·i·dent, *n. (often cap·)* chief executive; chief officer.

press, *n.* machine for applying pressure or for printing; newspapers, periodicals; journalists; throng; urgency. *v.* compress; smoothen; hug; importune; insist.

press·ing, *a.* urgent; critical.

pres·sure, *n.* impelling or constraining force; burden of responsibility; severity; compression; exigency. *v.,* **-sured, -sur·ing.** compel.

pres·su·rize, *v.,* **-rized, -riz·ing.** maintain pressure in; increase pressure.

pres·ti·dig·i·ta·tion, *n.* the art of sleight of hand.

pres·tige, *n.* renown; influence.

pres·tig·ious, *a.* having prestige or renown.

pre·sum·a·ble, *a.* probable; acceptable as an assumption. **-bly,** *adv.*

pre·sume, *v.,* **-sumed, -sum·ing.** assume to be true; suppose; impose on.

pre·sump·tion, *n.* supposition; probability; arrogance.

pre·sump·tu·ous, *a.* unduly bold; forward.

pre·tend, *v.* make believe; claim falsely; deceive.

pre·tense, *n.* making believe; ruse; false claim.

pre·ten·sion, *n.* claim to privilege; aspiration; affectation.

pre·ten·tious, *a.* ostentatious.

pre·text, *n.* false reason.

pret·ty, *a.* attractive. *adv.* moderately; very.

pret·zel, *n.* glazed, salted knot-shaped cracker.

pre·vail, v. overcome; persuade; influence; succeed.

pre·vail·ing, a. current; prevalent; having power.

prev·a·lent, a. widely spread.

pre·var·i·cate, v. **-cated, -cating,** deviate from the truth; lie.

pre·vent, v. thwart; hinder; obviate; avert. **-a·bil·i·ty, -ven·tion,** n. **-vent·a·ble, -vent·i·ble,** a.

pre·ven·tive, a. hindering. n. that which hinders.

pre·view, n. advance showing.

pre·vi·ous, a. prior; before.

prey, n. animal seized as food; booty; victim. v. victimize; take as prey.

price, n. cost; worth. v., **priced, pric·ing.** assign a value to.

price·less, a. invaluable; expensive; rare; inf. amusing.

prick, n. puncture; a pointed thing. v. pierce slightly; sting; incite; point upward; goad.

prick·le, n. sharp, small point; a tingling sensation.

prick·ly, a. tingling; stinging; having prickles.

pride, n. feeling of one's personal worth; justly proud; best of a group; conceit; group of lions.

priest, n. clergyman.

prim, a., **-mer, -mest.** stiffly proper; decorous.

pri·ma·cy, n. pl., **-cies.** first in rank; preeminence.

pri·ma don·na, n. main female singer (opera); vain person.

pri·ma fa·cie, adv. at first view. a. evident.

pri·mal, a. original; important.

pri·ma·ri·ly, adv. mainly.

pri·ma·ry, a. earliest; first in series, order; principal; basic. n. pl., **-ries.** political caucus.

pri·mate, n. highest order of mammals including man, apes, etc.; highest prelate.

prime, a. first in rank, value, etc. n. best part, time, or period. v., **primed, prim·ing.** prepare; pour liquid into.

prime me·rid·i·an, n. 0° longitudinal reckoning point.

prim·er, n. first reader; small cap of explosive.

pri·me·val, a. of the first age.

prim·i·tive, a. of the earliest ages; simple; undeveloped. n. primitive person or thing.

pri·mor·di·al, a. first in time.

primp, v. groom; dress up.

prince, n. king's son. **prin·cess,** fem. n. **-ly,** a. noble; regal; generous.

prin·ci·pal, a. first in importance. n. chief authority; sum owed or invested; star.

prin·ci·ple, n. basic truth or law; essential quality; moral standard.

prin·ci·pled, a. having principles, esp. moral principles.

print, v., **-ed, -ing.** to mark, impress, or produce on a surface; to produce (a book, etc.); publish. n. printed matter; picture or design (on something); photographic copy. **-er,** n.

print-out, n. automatically printed material, as by a computer.

pri·or, a. before; earlier.

pri·or·i·ty, n. pl., **-ties.** precedence in date or position.

pris·on, n. penitentiary.

pris·sy, a. prim; fussy.

pris·tine, a. uncontaminated; pure.

pri·va·cy, n. seclusion; secrecy.

pri·vate, a. not public; independent; personal; confidential. n. enlisted man.

pri·va·tion, n. lacking necessities.

priv·i·lege, n. prerogative; special benefit; right.

priv·i·leged, a. having special rights or advantages.

priv·y, a. confidential; secret. n. pl., **-ies.** outdoor toilet.

prize, n. reward; something won. v. value highly.

pro, adv. in favor of; n. affirmative side or vote. a. professional.

prob·a·bil·i·ty, n. pl., **-ties.** something probable; likelihood.

prob·a·ble, a. possible; likely. **-bly,** adv.

pro·bate, n. validation of a will.

pro·ba·tion, n. suspension of sentence unless further offense; preliminary trial period.

probe, n. instrument to explore a wound; a search. v., **probed, prob·ing.** investigate; examine; search.

pro·bi·ty, n. strict honesty.

prob·lem, n. puzzling question or situation. a.

prob·lem·at·ic, a. doubtful; questionable. **-i·cal,** a.

pro·bos·cis, n. elephant's trunk; any long snout; inf. nose.

pro·ce·dure, n. method of action.

pro·ceed, v. go forward; come from; continue; advance.

pro·ceed·ing, n. action; legal step; transaction.

pro·ceeds, *n. pl.* financial return.

proc·ess, *n.* method of operations; forward movement; writ; proceedings. *v.* prepare by some method.

pro·ces·sion, *n.* formal parade.

pro·claim, *v.* announce; declare.

proc·la·ma·tion, *n.* official announcement.

pro·cliv·i·ty, *n. pl.,* **-ties.** natural disposition or tendency.

pro·cras·ti·nate, *v.,* **-nat·ed, -nat·ing.** delay; put off.

pro·cre·ate, *v.,* **-at·ed, -at·ing.** originate; beget. **-a·tion**, *n.*

proc·tor, *n.* supervisor; monitor.

pro·cure, *v.,* **-cured, -cur·ing.** obtain; secure; pimp; get.

prod, *v.,* **-ded, -ding.** poke; rouse; stir; urge.

prod·i·gal, *a.* wasteful; extravagant; bountiful. *n.* spendthrift.

pro·di·gious, *a.* extraordinary.

prod·i·gy, *n.* gifted child.

pro·duce, *v.,* **-duced, -duc·ing.** bring about; bear; manufacture; compose. *n.* product.

prod·uct, *n.* thing produced; multiplication result.

pro·duc·tion, *n.* act of producing; amount produced; an artistic work.

pro·fane, *a.* irreverent; secular. *v.,* **-faned, -fan·ing.** desecrate.

pro·fan·i·ty, *n. pl.,* **-ties.** swearing; irreverent language.

pro·fess, *v.* assert; declare.

pro·fes·sion, *n.* occupation.

pro·fes·sion·al, *a.* engaged in a profession; skillful.

pro·fes·sor, *n.* highest ranking college teacher. **-so·ri·al**, *a.*

prof·fer, *v.* tender. *n.* offer.

pro·fi·cien·cy, *n.* skill; progress.

pro·fi·cient, *a.* skilled. *n.* expert.

pro·file, *n.* outline; contour.

prof·it, *n.* benefit; advantage; return; gain. *v.*

prof·it·a·ble, *a.* beneficial.

prof·li·gate, *a.* dissolute; highly immoral. *n.* spendthrift.

pro·found, *a.* intellectually deep; complete.

pro·fun·di·ty, *n.* depth of thought; intellectualism.

pro·fuse, *a.* lavish; generous.

pro·fu·sion, *n.* great supply.

pro·gen·i·tor, *n.* forefather.

prog·e·ny, *n. pl.,* **-nies.** offspring; descendant.

prog·no·sis, *n. pl.,* **-ses.** forecast, esp. the future course of a disease.

prog·nos·ti·cate, *v.* foretell.

pro·gram, *n.* printed list of items, actors, etc.; plan; sequence of computer instructions. *v.,* **-grammed, -gram·ming,** or **-gramed, -gram·ing.** arrange; schedule.

prog·ress, *n.* moving forward; advancement. *v.* advance.

pro·gres·sive, *a.* advancing; moving forward; increasing.

pro·hib·it, *v.* forbid; enjoin; preclude. **-i·tive**, *a.*

pro·hi·bi·tion, *n.* decree forbidding anything.

proj·ect, *n.* plan; undertaking; housing complex. *v.* extend out; plan; throw forth.

pro·jec·tile, *n.* missile.

pro·jec·tion, *n.* prediction; estimate; image produced.

pro·jec·tor, *n.* device for projecting images.

pro·le·tar·i·at, *n.* working class.

pro·lif·er·ate, *v.,* **-at·ed, -at·ing.** reproduce rapidly.

pro·lif·ic, *a.* producing abundantly.

pro·logue, *n.* preface.

pro·long, *v.* lengthen; extend.

prom·e·nade, *n.* walk; formal march; square dance step.

prom·i·nent, *a.* jutting out; conspicuous; important. **-nence**, *n.*

pro·mis·cu·ous, *a.* sexually indiscriminate. **-i·ty**, *n.*

prom·ise, *n.* pledge; expectation of hope. *v.* foretoken; assurance.

prom·is·so·ry, *a.* containing a promise or assurance.

prom·on·to·ry, *n. pl.,* **-ries.** high point of land; headland.

pro·mote, *v.,* **-mot·ed, -mot·ing.** encourage; advocate; advance; help organize; wrangle.

pro·mo·tion, *n.* advancement; advertising; publicity.

prompt, *a.* quick; punctual. *v.* remind; suggest; incite.

prom·ul·gate, *v.,* **-gat·ed, -gat·ing.** make known; announce.

prone, *a.* disposed; inclined; supine; prostrate.

prong, *n.* pointed projection; fork. *v.* stab; pierce.

pro·noun, *n.* word used instead of a noun, as *he, she, it, they.*

pro·nounce, *v.,* **-nounced, -nounc·ing.** assert; articulate. **pro·nounced**, *a.* decided; clearly noticeable.

pro·nounce·ment, *n.* announcement; declaration.

proof, *n.* evidence; validity; test. *a.* impenetrable; standard strength. *v.* examine for errors; protect.

proof·read, *v.,* **-read, -read·ing.** read and correct.

prop, *n.* support; *inf.* theatrical equipment; airplane propeller.

prop·a·gan·da, *n.* information spread to promote a cause.

prop·a·gate, *v.,* **-gat·ed, -gat·ing.** breed; transmit; reproduce; originate. **-ga·tion,** *n.*

pro·pel, *v.,* **-pelled, -pel·ling.** drive forward; motivate.

pro·pel·lant, *n.* something that propels, as rocket fuel.

pro·pel·ler, *n.* rotating shaft fitted with vanes.

pro·pen·si·ty, *n. pl.,* **-ties.** tendency; inclination.

prop·er, *a.* suited; appropriate; decent; fit; becoming.

prop·er·ty, *n. pl.,* **-ties.** anything owned, esp. land.

proph·e·cy, *n. pl.,* **-cies.** prediction; foretelling.

proph·e·sy, *v.,* **-sied, -sy·ing.** predict; foretell.

proph·et, *n.* one who foretells.

pro·phy·lac·tic, *a.* preventive.

pro·phy·lax·is, *n.* preventive treatment for disease.

pro·pin·qui·ty, *n.* kinship; nearness in place or time.

pro·pi·ti·ate, *v.,* **-at·ed, -at·ing.** conciliate; appease.

pro·pi·tious, *a.* auspicious; favorably disposed.

pro·po·nent, *n.* advocate.

pro·por·tion, *n.* relative magnitude, number, etc.; ratio; balance. **-ate,** *a.*

pro·por·tion·al, *a.* of or being in proportion.

pro·pose, *v.,* **-posed, -pos·ing.** present; offer; nominate.

prop·o·si·tion, *n.* plan; scheme.

pro·pound, *v.* propose; offer.

pro·pri·e·tar·y, *a.* protected; denoting exclusive control.

pro·pri·e·tor, *n.* owner.

pro·pri·e·ty, *n. pl.,* **-ties.** being proper; conformity.

pro·pul·sion, *n.* being propelled.

pro rata, *adv.,* *a.* proportionate.

pro·sa·ic, *a.* commonplace; dull.

pro·scribe, *v.,* **-scribed, -scrib·ing.** denounce; prohibit; outlaw.

prose, *n.* ordinary speech or writing, not poetry.

pros·e·cute, *v.* pursue; enforce legally; bring suit against. **-cu·tor,** *n.*

pros·pect, *n.* outlook; survey; possibility; anticipation; potential customer. *v.* explore.

pro·spec·tive, *a.* anticipated.

pro·spec·tus, *n.* summary; outline.

pros·per, *v.* thrive; flourish.

pros·per·i·ty, *n.* wealth; success; economic well-being.

pros·per·ous, *a.* successful; flourishing; wealthy.

pros·tate, *n.* male gland at base of bladder concerned with semen production.

pros·the·sis, *n. pl.,* **-ses.** artificial device to replace body part.

pros·thet·ics, *n. pl., sing. or pl. in constr.* medical branch dealing in artificial replacements.

pros·ti·tute, *n.* whore. *v.* debase.

pros·trate, *v.,* **-trat·ed, -trat·ing.** lay flat; cast down; humble oneself; overcome. *a.* flat; prone.

pro·te·an, *a.* assuming different shapes or aspects easily.

pro·tect, *v.* guard; defend.

pro·tec·tor·ate, *n.* weaker nation protected by one stronger.

pro·té·gé, *n.* one aided by another, esp. in a career.

pro·tein, *n.* chemical compound essential to life.

pro tem, *a.* for the time being.

pro·test, *v.* object; assert. *n.* objection; complaint.

Prot·es·tant, *n.* member of a Christian church deriving from Reformation.

pro·to·col, *n.* diplomatic etiquette; treaty draft.

pro·ton, *n.* positive particle.

pro·to·plasm, *n.* living substance of all cells.

pro·to·type, *n.* original model.

pro·to·zo·an, *n.* microscopic single-celled organism.

pro·tract, *v.* extend; prolong.

pro·trac·tor, *n.* instrument for measuring angles.

pro·trude, *v.,* **-trud·ed, -trud·ing.** thrust; jut out. **-tru·sion,** *n.*

pro·tu·ber·ant, *a.* sticking out; prominent; bulging. **-ance,** *n.*

proud, *a.* self-respecting; arrogant.

prove, *v.,* **proved, proved** or **prov·en, prov·ing.** verify; test; establish the truth.

prov·erb, *n.* adage; maxim.

pro·vide, *v.,* **-vid·ed, -vid·ing.** furnish; arrange for; supply.

pro·vid·ed, *conj.* on condition that.

prov·i·dence, *n.* God's will or care; foresight.

prov·ince, *n.* division of a country; *pl.* territory at some distance from the city.

pro·vin·cial, *a.* simple; unsophisticated. *n.* naive person.

pro·vi·sion, *n.* advance preparation; a requirement; *pl.* food, supplies. *v.* to provide.

pro·vi·sion·al, *a.* temporary.

pro·voc·a·tive, *a.* stimulating; provoking. **prov·o·ca·tion,** *n.*

pro·voke, *v.*, **-voked, -vok·ing.** irritate; arouse; incense.

prow, *n.* forepart of a ship.

prow·ess, *n.* skill; courage.

prowl, *v.* roam about stealthily. **-er,** *n.*

prox·i·mate, *a.* next; near.

prox·im·i·ty, *n.* nearness in time, space, order, etc.

prox·y, *n., pl.*, **-ies.** substitute; one who acts for another.

prude, *n.* one who is overly modest, esp. in sexual matters.

pru·dence, *n.* caution; economy.

prune, *n.* dried plum. *v.*, **pruned, prun·ing.** cut off; trim with a knife; remove as superfluous.

pru·ri·ent, *a.* tending to excite lustful thoughts; lewd.

pry, *v.*, **pried, pry·ing.** raise; open; peer; snoop. *n.* lever, as a bar, etc.

psalm, *n.* sacred song; poem.

pseu·do, *a.* false; pretended.

pseu·do·nym, *n.* false name.

pshaw, *int.* exclamation of contempt, disgust.

psych·e·del·ic, *a.* hallucinatory.

psy·chi·a·try, *n.* branch of medicine dealing with mental disorders. **-trist,** *n.*

psy·chic, *a.* mental clairvoyance. *n.* a medium.

psy·cho·a·nal·y·sis, *n.* Freudian treatment of mental disorders. **-an·a·lyst,** *n.* **-an·a·lyze,** *v.*

psy·cho·gen·ic, *a.* originating in the mind.

psy·cho·log·i·cal, *a.* pertaining to or affecting the mind.

psy·chol·o·gy, *n.* science dealing with the human mind and behavior.

psy·cho·path, *n.* one exhibiting severely deranged behavior.

psy·cho·sis, *n., pl.*, **-ses.** severe mental disorder.

psy·cho·so·mat·ic, *a.* physical ailments due to emotional causes.

psy·cho·ther·a·py, *n.* treatment to correct mental disorders.

pto·maine, pto·main, *n.* food poisoning.

pu·ber·ty, *n.* period of sexual maturity; early teen years.

pu·bes·cent, *a.* reaching puberty; covered with soft hair.

pub·lic, *a.* relating to people collectively; for use of all; well-known; not private. *n.* people collectively.

pub·li·ca·tion, *n.* any printed work.

pub·lic·i·ty, *n.* spreading of information to create interest.

pub·li·cize, *v.*, **-cized, -ciz·ing.** promote; make known.

pub·lish, *v.* make generally known; disseminate; declare; print for sale.

pub·lish·er, *n.* one who publishes books, periodicals, etc.

puck, *n.* rubber hockey disk.

puck·er, *v.* gather into wrinkles; fold; constrict.

pud·ding, *n.* flavored soft food dessert.

pud·dle, *n.* small pool of liquid.

pudg·y, *a.*, **-i·er, -i·est.** fat and short; chubby.

pueb·lo, *n. pl.*, **-los.** village built of adobe; communal dwelling.

pu·er·ile, *a.* immature; childish.

puff, *v.* blow with short blasts; breathe hard and fast; smoke. *n.* short, quick blast; swelling; powder pad; fluffy mass.

pug, *n.* small bulldog; *inf.* prizefighter.

pu·gil·ism, *n.* boxing.

pug·na·cious, *a.* belligerent.

puke, *v.*, **puked, puk·ing.** vomit.

pul·chri·tude, *n.* beauty; grace.

pull, *v.* tug at; drag; draw toward; tear; attract. *n. inf.* influence.

pull·back, *n.* withdrawal.

pul·let, *n.* young hen.

pul·ley, *n.* rimmed wheel and rope for changing direction of the pull.

pull·out, *n.* leaving; withdrawal.

pul·mo·nar·y, *a.* of the lungs.

pulp, *n.* soft organic tissue; succulent part of fruit.

pul·pit, *n.* elevated stand from which the clergyman preaches.

pul·sate, *v.*, **-sat·ed, -sat·ing.** emit rhythmical impulses; throb.

pulse, *n.* rhythmic throbbing or beating, as of the heart; surge.

pul·ver·ize, *v.*, **-ized, -iz·ing.** reduce to powder; crush.

pu·ma, *n. pl.*, **-mas, -ma.** mountain lion.

pum·ice, *n.* porous lava used for smoothing and polishing.

pump, *n.* machine for circulating or raising liquid; low-cut shoe. *v.* inflate; drive; force; pour forth; question.

pum·per·nick·el, *n.* dark bread.

pump·kin, *n.* vine with edible orange gourd-like fruit.

pun, *n.* humorous play on words.

punch, *v.* pierce; poke; strike; prod. *n.* tool for piercing; blow; cold beverage.

punc·til·i·ous, *a.* exacting.

punc·tu·al, *a.* on time.

punc·tu·ate, *v.,* **-at·ed, -at·ing.** mark with punctuation; to emphasize. **-a·tion,** *n.*

punc·ture, *n.* hole. *v.,* **-tured, tur·ing.** pierce; perforate.

pun·gent, *a.* biting; caustic; acrid; clever.

pun·ish, *v.* subject to a penalty.

punk, *n. inf.* petty hoodlum.

punt, *n.* football kick; flat-bottomed boat; gamble.

pu·ny, *a.,* **-ni·er, -ni·est.** small or inferior.

pup, *n.* young dog, seal, fox.

pu·pa, *n. pl.,* **pu·pae, -pas.** quiescent stage of an insect.

pu·pil, *n.* student; circular opening in the eye's iris.

pup·pet, *n.* doll moved by hand or cords; controlled person.

pur·chase, *v.,* **-chased, -chas·ing.** acquire; buy. *n.* acquisition.

pure, *a.* unadulterated; clean; absolute; innocent.

pu·rée, *n.* thick pulp or soup.

pur·ga·tive, *a.* cathartic.

pur·ga·to·ry, *n. pl.,* **-ries.** place or state of temporary suffering.

purge, *v.,* **purged, purg·ing.** purify; cleanse.

pu·ri·fy, *v.,* **-fied, -fy·ing.** make pure; free of noxious matter.

pur·ism, *n.* insistence on rigid rules or usage.

pu·ri·tan, *n.* one excessively strict in religion and morals.

pu·ri·ty, *n.* chastity; cleanness.

purl, *v.* backward knitting stitch.

pur·loin, *v.* steal; filch.

pur·ple, *a.* red/blue blend color; royal.

pur·port, *n.* meaning; intent.

pur·pose, *n.* objective; resolution; intention; aim.

pur·pose·ly, *adv.* deliberately.

purse, *n.* handbag; prize money; pouch; finances. *v.,* **pursed, purs·ing.** pucker.

purs·er, *n.* ship's officer.

pur·su·ant, *a.* following upon.

pur·sue, *v.,* **-sued, -su·ing.** follow; chase; strive for.

pur·suit, *n.* act of pursuing; interest; career.

pu·ru·lent, *a.* secreting pus.

pur·vey, *v.* furnish; supply.

pur·view, *n.* scope of an act or bill; range of control.

pus, *n.* yellowish substance found in sores, infections.

push, *v.* exert pressure; advocate; press; shove. *n.*

push·y, *a.,* **-i·er, -i·est.** unpleasantly aggressive.

push·o·ver, *n. inf.* anyone easily deceived; dupe.

pu·sil·lan·i·mous, *a.* cowardly.

puss·y, *n. pl.,* **-ies.** a cat.

puss·y·foot, *v.* move stealthily.

pus·tule, *n.* blister; swelling.

put, *v.,* **put, put·ting.** move; place; lay; subject; assign; apply.

pu·ta·tive, *a.* supposed.

pu·tre·fac·tion, *n.* decomposition of organic matter.

pu·tre·fy, *v.,* **-fied, -fy·ing.** rot.

pu·trid, *a.* offensive; vile; foul.

putt, *n.* light golf stroke.

put·ter, *v.* dawdle; tinker. *n.* golf club.

put·ty, *n.* doughy paste used for filling cracks, etc.

puz·zle, *v.,* **-zled, -zling.** perplex; bewilder; confound; ponder. *n.* thing which tries the ingenuity.

puz·zle·ment, *n.* bewilderment.

pyg·my, pig·my, *n.* dwarfish person. *a.* very small.

py·lon, *n.* supporting tower; course marker.

py·or·rhe·a, *n.* infection of the gums and tooth sockets.

pyr·a·mid, *n.* solid structure with square base and triangular sides meeting in a point. *v.* increase by steps.

pyre, *n.* combustible funeral pile.

py·ro·ma·ni·a, *n.* compulsion to commit arson.

py·rom·e·ter, *n.* instrument which measures high temperatures.

py·ro·tech·nics, *n. pl., sing. or pl. in constr.* display of fireworks; dazzling array.

py·thon, *n.* non-poisonous snake that crushes prey.

Q

quack, *n.* duck sound; charlatan. **-ish,** *a.* **quackery,** *n.*

quad·ran·gle, *n.* figure with four sides and angles. **-gu·lar**, *a.*

quad·rant, *n.* quarter of a circle; instrument for measuring angles. **-ran·tal**, *a.*

quad·ri·lat·er·al, *a.* four sided.

quad·ri·ple·gi·a, *n.* body paralysis from the neck down.

quad·ru·ped, *n.* four-footed animal.

quad·ru·ple, *v.*, **-pled**, **pling.** make four times as great.

quad·ru·plet, *n.* one of four children born at one birth.

quaff, *v.* drink with relish.

quag·mire, *n.* bog; predicament. **-mired**, **-mir·y**, *a.*

quail, *n.* bobwhite. *v.* cower.

quaint, *a.* pleasingly old-fashioned.

quake, *v.*, **quaked**, **quak·ing.** shake; vibrate. *n.* earthquake.

qual·i·fy, *v.*, **-fied**, **-fy·ing.** make fit; restrict; license; moderate. **-i·fi·a·ble**, *a.* **-i·fi·er**, *n.*

qual·i·ty, *n. pl.*, **-ties.** characteristic; attribute; excellence.

qualm, *n.* scruple; sick feeling.

quan·da·ry, *n. pl.*, **-ries.** perplexity; predicament.

quan·ti·ty, *n. pl.*, **-ties.** amount.

quar·an·tine, *n.* isolation period to prevent spread of disease. *v.*, **-tined**, **-tin·ing.** isolate.

quark, *n.* hypothetical subatomic nuclear particle.

quar·rel, *n.* angry dispute. *v.*, **-reled**, **-rel·ing**, **-relled**, **-rel·ling.** dispute; fight.

quar·ry, *n. pl.*, **-ries.** prey; excavation pit to secure stone.

quart, *n.* two liquid pints.

quar·ter, *n.* 25 cents; one-fourth of anything; *pl.* shelter.

quar·ter·back, *n.* football signal caller. *v.* manage; lead.

quar·ter·ly, *a.* done every three months. *n. pl.*, **-lies.**

quar·tet, *n.* any set of four.

quartz, *n.* crystallized mineral.

qua·sar, *n.* distant object that emits radio waves.

quash, *v.* put down; suppress.

qua·si, *a.* resembling.

qua·ver, *v.* shake; tremble.

quay, *n.* loading wharf.

queen, *n.* female monarch; preeminent woman. **-ly**, *adv.*, *a.*

queer, *a.* strange; queasy; odd.

quell, *v.* crush; quiet; subdue.

quench, *v.* put out; satisfy; extinguish; suppress.

quer·u·lous, *a.* complaining.

que·ry, *n. pl.*, **-ries.** question. *v.*, **-ried**, **-ry·ing.** inquire.

quest, *n.* search; hunt.

ques·tion, *n.* inquiry; point of doubt; uncertainty. *v.* ask.

ques·tion·a·ble, *a.* doubtful; uncertain. **-bly**, *adv.*

ques·tion mark, *n.* symbol (?) used to indicate a question; something unknown.

ques·tion·naire, *n.* series of questions to gather information for statistical data.

queue, *n.* braided hair; line of persons or cars.

quib·ble, *n.* minor objection; cavil. *v.*, **-bled**, **-bling.**

quiche, *n.* cheese custard pie.

quick, *a.* rapid; brisk; prompt.

quick·en, *v.* hasten; animate; arouse. **-er**, *n.*

quick·sand, *n.* deep wet sand capable of engulfing objects.

quick·sil·ver, *n.* mercury.

quick-tem·pered, *a.* easily angered; irascible.

quick-wit·ted, *a.* mentally alert.

quid pro quo, *n.* something equivalent; substitute.

qui·es·cent, *a.* still; in repose; quiet. **-cence**, *n.*

qui·et, *a.* silent; still; undisturbed. *n.* rest; calm. *adv.* **-ness**, **-er**, *n.* **-etude**, *n.* repose.

qui·e·tus, *n.* release from debt; death; any killer.

quill, *n.* large bird feather; horny spine.

quilt, *n.* thick, warm bed cover. **-er**, *n.*

quince, *n.* acid yellow fruit used in making preserves.

qui·nie·la, *n.* bet where one picks the 1st and 2nd place race winners (but not the order).

qui·nine, *n.* bitter alkaloid used as a malaria remedy.

quin·tes·sence, *n.* perfect example; purest form of a thing.

quin·tu·ple, *a.* five times as many. *v.*, **-pled**, **-pling.**

quin·tu·plet, *n.* five of a kind; one of five offspring born at one time.

quip, *n.* clever remark; gibe; oddity. *v.*, **quipped**, **quip·ping. quip·ster**, *n.*

quire, *n.* $\frac{1}{20}$th of a ream.

quirk, *n.* peculiar trait or mannerism. **-y**, *a.*, **-i·er**, **-i·est.**

quit, *v.*, **quit** or **quit·ted**, **quit·ting.** leave; cease; resign.

quite, *adv.* totally; very; wholly.

quiv·er, *n.* arrow case; tremor. *v.* shake; tremble.

quix·ot·ic, *a.* impractical aims.

quiz, *n. pl.,* **quiz·zes.** brief test. *v.,* **quizzed, quiz·zing.** ask.

quiz·zi·cal, *a.* comical; odd.

quon·dam, *a.* former; sometime.

quo·rum, *n.* number of group members necessary to legally act, *usu.* a majority.

quo·ta, *n.* proportional share.

quo·ta·tion, *n.* passage quoted; current price.

quo·ta·tion mark, *n.* symbol (" ") used to indicate a quotation.

quote, *v.,* **quot·ed, quot·ing.** repeat words exactly; cite.

quo·tid·i·an, *a.* daily; ordinary.

quo·tient, *n.* answer of a division problem.

R

rab·bi, *n. pl.,* **-bis.** ordained teacher or head of a Jewish synagogue.

rab·bit, *n.* hare.

rab·ble, *n.* disorderly crowd; masses. *v.,* **-bled, -bling.** mob.

rab·id, *a.* raging; mad; infected with rabies.

rabies, *n.* infectious viral disease of mammals.

race, *n.* contest of speed; ethnic division of mankind; swift current. *v.,* **raced, rac·ing.** run rapidly; contend against.

ra·cial, *a.* pertaining to a race.

rac·ism, *n.* belief in the superiority of a particular race.

rack, *n.* something on which articles can be stored or hung; pool ball holder; instrument of torture. *v.* torture; think deeply.

rack·et, *n.* netted hoop; noisy confusion; *inf.* scheme.

rack·et·eer, *n. inf.* one engaged in dishonest ventures.

rac·on·teur, *n.* story teller.

rac·y, *a.,* **-i·er, -i·est.** spicy; spirited; slightly risqué.

ra·dar, *n.* system for determining the location of an object by microwaves.

ra·di·al, *a.* branching from a common center; like a radius.

ra·di·ance, *n.* sparkling luster.

ra·di·ant, *a.* emitting rays; shining; beaming.

ra·di·ate, *v.* emit rays; spread out from.

ra·di·a·tion, *n.* radiant energy.

ra·di·a·tor, *n.* device for heating a house or cooling an engine.

rad·i·cal, *a.* basic; thorough; extreme; fundamental; *math.* forming a root. *n.* extremist.

ra·di·o, *n. pl.,* **-os.** wireless signals sent through space; broadcast. *a.* wireless. *v.,* **-oed, -o·ing.** transmit by radio.

ra·di·o·ac·tiv·i·ty, *n.* emission of particles or rays.

ra·di·ol·o·gy, *n.* science dealing with use of x-ray energy in medicine.

rad·ish, *n.* pungent, edible root.

ra·di·um, *n.* radioactive metallic element.

ra·di·us, *n. pl.,* **-i, -us·es.** line segment from the center to the circumference of a circle.

ra·don, *n.* heavy radioactive gaseous element.

raff·ish, *a.* disreputable; vulgar.

raf·fle, *n.* lottery. *v.*

raft, *n.* float of logs fastened together; inflated float.

raft·er, *n.* parallel support timber of a roof.

rag, *n.* waste piece of cloth. *v.,* **-ged, -ging.** *inf.* tease; talk.

rage, *n.* violent anger; passion; intensity. *v.,* **raged, rag·ing.** act furiously; spread fast.

rag·ged, *a.* torn; shabby; rough.

ra·gout, *n.* stewed meat, vegetables.

rag·time, *n.* quick tempo dance music, popular 1890-1920.

rag·weed, *n.* flowering herb which causes hay fever.

raid, *n.* sudden attack, invasion. *v.* take part in a raid.

rail, *n.* bar extending from one post to another; fence; steel bar or track to guide wheels. *v.* use abusive language.

rail·ing, *n.* fence; balustrade.

rail·road, *n.* tracks on which trains run; the system; *v. inf.* rush through.

rai·ment, *n.* garments; apparel.

rain, *n.* condensed atmospheric water vapor. *v.* **rained, -ing.** to fall (like rain).

rain·bow, *n.* arc of prismatic colors. *a.* of many colors.

rain·fall, *n.* shower of rain.

raise, *v.,* **raised, rais·ing.** set upright; construct; elevate; breed; rear; increase in amount; bet. *n.* increase.

rai·sin, *n.* dried grape.

rai·son d'ê·tre, *n.* justification for existence.

rake, *n.* tool with tines; lewd man. *v.,* **raked, rak·ing.** gather together; clean; search carefully.

rak·ish, *a.* dashing; jaunty.

ral·ly, *v.,* **-lied, -ly·ing.** bring together; revive spirits; call together. *n. pl.,* **-lies.** assembly of people; quick recovery; unite.

ram, *n.* male sheep; device for battering. *v.* force; crash.

ram·ble, v., **-bled, -bling.** wander; roam; talk or write aimlessly. n.

ram·bler, n. one or that which rambles; climbing rose.

ram·bunc·tious, a. inf. unruly.

ram·e·kin, n. cheese preparation; individual baking dish.

ram·i·fi·ca·tion, n. result; branch; offshoot.

ram·i·fy, v., **-fied, -fying.** divide into branches.

ra·mose, a. having branches.

ramp, n. sloping surface; movable stairway.

ram·page, v., **-paged, -pag·ing.** act violently; storm. n. violent actions.

ram·pant, a. unrestrained.

ram·part, n. embankment.

ram·rod, n. rod to clean firearms. v. push through.

ram·shack·le, a. dilapidated.

ranch, n. large farm. **-er**, n. one who owns ranch.

ran·cid, a. bad taste or smell from spoiled fats.

ran·cor, n. ill will; enmity.

ran·dom, n. lack of purpose or intention. a. left to chance.

range, v., **ranged, rang·ing.** place in order; classify; rank; align. n. row; grazing land; distance; stove; scope.

rang·er, n. mounted policeman; park or forest warden.

rang·y, a., **-i·er, -i·est.** having long slender limbs.

rank, n. line of objects; official standing. a. flourishing growth; total; utter; foul; rancid.

ran·kle, v., **-kled, -kling.** cause resentment; irritate; inflame.

ran·sack, v. plunder; pillage.

ran·som, n. payment for the release of a person or thing.

rant, v. speak loudly, violently. n. bombastic talk.

rap, v., **rapped, rap·ping.** sharp blow; knock; inf. discuss. n. knock; criminal charge; inf. blame.

ra·pa·cious, a. avaricious; covetous; voracious.

rape, n. sexual intercourse by force; an outrageous violation. v. **raped; rap·ing.** ravish; plunder.

rap·id, a. fast; great speed.

ra·pi·er, n. long, two-edged sword.

rap·port, n. harmony; accord.

rap·proche·ment, n. reconciliation; restoration of cordial relations.

rapt, a. engrossed; enraptured.

rap·to·ri·al, a. predatory.

rap·ture, n. state of ecstasy.

rare, a., **rar·er, rar·est.** distinctive; choice; seldom seen; unusual; underdone.

rar·e·fy, v., **-fied, -fy·ing.** refine; make rare, thin, less dense.

rare·ly, adv. not often; seldom.

rar·ing, a. inf. full of eagerness.

rar·i·ty, n. pl., **-ties.** something that is rare; infrequent.

ras·cal, n. scoundrel; rogue; mischievous person.

rash, a. acting hastily, recklessly. n. skin eruption.

rash·er, n. thin slice of bacon.

rasp, v. scrape; irritate. n. coarse file; grating sound.

rasp·ber·ry, n. pl., **-ries.** small, edible red or black fruit.

rat, n. long-tailed rodent; inf. informer; contemptible one.

rate, n. valuation; estimation; price; degree. v., **rat·ed, rat·ing.** fix the value; rebuke; inf. be entitled to.

rath·er, adv. preferably; somewhat; with more reason.

rat·i·fy, v., **-fied, -fy·ing.** confirm; approve; sanction.

rat·ing, n. grading; standing.

ra·tio, n. pl., **-tios.** relation between two similar values; proportion.

ra·tion, n. fixed amount; portion; allowance; share. v. distribute; use savingly.

ra·tion·al, a. able to reason; sane; reasonable.

ra·tion·ale, n. statement of reasons; basis; explanation.

ra·tion·al·ize, v., **-ized, -iz·ing.** explain plausibly; justify.

rat·tan, n. palm stems used in wickerwork.

rat·tle, v., **-tled, -tling.** make sharp, quick clicking noises; chatter; inf. confuse. n. sound; infant's toy.

rat·tle·snake, n. poisonous snake with rattles on the tail.

rau·cous, a. noisy and rowdy.

raun·chy, a., **-i·er, -i·est.** inf. lewd; sexually vulgar.

rav·age, n. ruin. v., **-aged, -ag·ing.** pillage; devastate.

rave, v., **raved, rav·ing.** rant; speak wildly; speak enthusiastically. n. frenzy; very favorable criticism.

rav·el, v., **-eled, -el·ing.** unwind; fray; disentangle.

rav·en·ous, *a.* starved; rapacious.

ra·vine, *n.* deep gorge or gully.

rav·ing, *a.* raging; delirious.

ra·vi·o·li, *n. pl.* small dough casings containing spicy mixture.

rav·ish, *v.* rape; violate; plunder; enrapture.

rav·ish·ing, *a.* very attractive.

raw, *a.* not cooked; harsh; unrefined; coarse; green; chilly.

ray, *n.* narrow light beam; stream of particles; flat fish. *v.* radiate; emit rays.

ray·on, *n.* synthetic fiber.

raze, rase, *v.,* **razed, raz·ing, rased, ras·ing.** demolish.

ra·zor, *n.* sharp cutting implement used for shaving.

razz, *v. inf.* heckle; tease.

re, *prep.* with regard to.

reach, *v.* stretch out, as the hand; extend; project; achieve; attain; penetrate to. *n.* act of reaching; scope; distance.

re·act, *v.* act in response, as to a stimulus.

re·ac·tion, *n.* action in response to a stimulus.

re·ac·tion·ar·y, *n.* one who opposes change in policy.

re·ac·ti·vate, *v.,* **-vat·ed, -vat·ing.** to make active again.

re·ac·tor, *n.* apparatus that utilizes atomic energy.

read, *v.,* **read, read·ing.** apprehend the meaning of something written; utter aloud; peruse; interpret; indicate. *a.* well-informed.

read·er, *n.* one who reads, esp. in church; schoolbook.

read·ing, *n.* action of one who reads; literary knowledge; a given passage; data.

read·out, *n.* display of data processed by computer.

read·y, *a.,* **-i·er, -i·est.** prepared; willing; convenient; at hand. *v.,* **-ied, -y·ing.** prepare.

read·y-made, *a.* not made to order.

re·al, *a.* existing; genuine.

re·al es·tate, *n.* land and all that is a part of it; property.

re·al·ism, *n.* concern for fact; doctrine of actuality; fidelity in art and literature.

re·al·i·ty, *n. pl.,* **-ties.** totality of real things and events.

re·al·ize, *v.,* **-ized, -iz·ing.** understand fully; convert into cash; accomplish.

re·al·ly, *adv.* actually; truly.

realm, *n.* domain; sphere.

re·al·ty, *n.* real estate.

ream, *n.* bundle of paper of 480, 500, or 516 sheets. *v.* enlarge (a hole); *inf.* victimize.

re·an·i·mate, *v.,* **-mat·ed, -mat·ing.** revive; resuscitate.

reap, *v.* harvest; obtain; win.

re·ap·praise, *v.* reconsider.

rear, *v.* bring up; breed; grow; erect. *n.* buttocks; hind part.

re·ar·range, *v.,* **-ranged, -rang·ing.** put in different order or in a new way.

rea·son, *n.* justification; intelligence; understanding; sanity. *v.* discuss; think logically.

rea·son·a·ble, *a.* rational; moderate; inexpensive.

rea·son·ing, *n.* process of logical thinking.

re·as·sure, *v.,* **-sured, -sur·ing.** hearten; give confidence to.

re·bate, *v.,* **-bat·ed, -bat·ing.** return; deduct. *n.* refund.

reb·el, *n.* one who revolts. *a.* defiant; disobedient.

re·bel·lion, *n.* resistance; revolt; insurrection.

re·bel·lious, *a.* insubordinate.

re·bound, *v.* bounce back; reecho; recover. *n.* recoil.

re·buff, *n.* denial. *v.* repel; snub; check sharply.

re·buke, *v.,* **-buked, -buk·ing.** reprimand. *n.* reproof.

re·but, *v.,* **-but·ted, -but·ting.** refute; contradict; disprove.

re·but·tal, *n.* refutation.

re·cal·ci·trant, *a.* obstinate; rebellious; not complying.

re·call, *v.* order to return; call back; revoke; remember. *n.* revocation.

re·cant, *v.* disavow; retract.

re·ca·pit·u·late, *v.,* **-lat·ed, -lat·ing.** summarize; restate.

re·cap·ture, *v.,* **-tured, -tur·ing.** capture again. *n.* recovery.

re·cede, *v.,* **-ced·ed, -ced·ing.** retreat; withdraw; diminish.

re·ceipt, *n.* receiving something; paper showing something received.

re·ceive, *v.,* **-ceived, -ceiv·ing.** acquire; admit; obtain; take; welcome.

re·ceiv·er, *n.* person controlling property in a lawsuit; apparatus for receiving signals; recipient.

re·ceiv·er·ship, *n.* status of an enterprise in the hands of a receiver.

re·cent, *a.* of late origin; fresh.

re·cep·ta·cle, *n.* container.

re·cep·tion, *n.* receiving; formal ceremony; response.

re·cess, *n.* work break; indentation; cleft; pause.

re·ces·sion, *n.* withdrawal; temporary economic setback; departing procession.

rec·i·pe, *n.* instructions for preparing a food dish.

re·cip·i·ent, *n.* receiver.

re·cip·ro·cal, *a.* inversely related; opposite; mutually corresponding; mutual; moving alternately backward and forward.

re·cip·ro·cate, *v.,* **-cat·ed, -cat·ing.** give in return; interchange; retaliate; move backward and forward.

rec·i·proc·i·ty, *n.* equal trade rights; reciprocal action.

re·cit·al, *n.* program *usu.* given by a soloist; narration.

rec·i·ta·tion, *n.* reading aloud; act of enumerating.

re·cite, *v.,* **-cit·ed, -cit·ing.** relate; repeat from memory.

reck·less, *a.* rash; careless.

reck·on, *v.* compute; estimate; consider; *inf.* suppose.

reck·on·ing, *n.* computation; a settlement; estimate.

re·claim, *v.* claim again; recover in a usable form.

re·cline, *v.,* **-clined, -clin·ing.** lie or lay down or back.

re·cluse, *n.* one who lives in solitude; hermit. *a.* secluded.

rec·og·ni·tion, *n.* attention; acceptance; acknowledgment.

rec·og·nize, *v.,* **-nized, -niz·ing.** perceive; identify; acknowledge.

re·coil, *v.* spring back; shrink; flinch; quail. *n.* rebound.

re·col·lect, *v.* compose oneself; recover; recall; remember.

rec·om·mend, *v.* praise; commend; advise; urge.

rec·om·men·da·tion, *n.* favorable representation; advice.

rec·om·pense, *v.,* **-pensed, -pens·ing.** pay or repay; reward; compensate. *n.* payment; reward.

rec·on·cile, *v.,* **-ciled, -cil·ing.** resolve; adjust; settle. **-cil·a·ble,** *a.* **-cil·a·bly,** *adv.* **-cil·i·a·tion,** *n.*

rec·on·dite, *a.* hidden; obscure.

re·con·di·tion, *v.* restore.

re·con·firm, *v.* confirm again.

re·con·nais·sance, *n.* exploratory observation or survey.

re·con·noi·ter, *v.,* **-tered, -ter·ing.** make a survey of.

re·con·struct, *v.* rebuild; remodel.

re·con·struc·tion, *n.* something reconstructed.

re·cord, *v.* write down; chart; make a record.

rec·ord, *n.* written account; phonograph disc; highest achievement.

re·count, *v.* count again; enumerate; recite; narrate.

re·coup, *v.* recover; repay.

re·course, *n.* a resort for help or protection in trouble.

re·cov·er, *v.* regain after losing; recoup; restore; retrieve.

re·cov·er·y, *n. pl.,* **-ies.** regain health; retrieval; restoration.

re·cre·ant, *a.* cowardly; unfaithful; false. *n.* deserter.

re·cre·ate, *v.,* **-at·ed, -at·ing.** impart fresh vigor; refresh.

rec·re·a·tion, *n.* diversion; relaxation; amusement.

re·crim·i·nate, *v.,* **-nat·ed, -nat·ing.** accuse in return.

re·cruit, *n.* new member of a group. *v.* enlist new members.

rec·tan·gle, *n.* parallelogram with all right angles.

rec·tan·gu·lar, *a.* right-angled.

rec·ti·fy, *v.,* **-fied, -fy·ing.** set right; correct; refine. **-fi·a·ble,** *a.*

rec·ti·tude, *n.* uprightness.

rec·tor, *n.* clergyman in charge of a parish or school.

rec·tum, *n. pl.,* **-tums, -ta.** last part of the large intestine.

re·cum·bent, *a.* lying down.

re·cu·per·ate, *v.,* **-at·ed, -at·ing.** regain health, strength; recover from loss. **-a·tion,** *n.*

re·cur, *v.,* **-curred, -cur·ring.** happen again. **-rence,** *n.*

re·cy·cle, *v.* **-cy·cled, -cy·cling.** process to reuse basic raw materials.

red, *a.,* **red·der, red·dest.** color of blood; communistic. *n.* Communist.

re·deem, *v.* pay off; buy back; make amends; expiate.

re·demp·tion, *n.* repurchase; recovery; salvation.

re·de·ploy, *v.* transfer (troops, etc.) from one area or activity to another.

re·de·vel·op, *v.* develop again; rebuild, as a slum area.

red-hand·ed, *a.* caught in the act of doing something, esp. crime.

red her·ring, *n.* something to draw attention away from real issue; subterfuge.

red-hot, *a.* very hot; greatly excited; fresh; new.

red·let·ter, *a.* memorable.

re·do, *v.,* **-did, -done, -do·ing.** do over or again; redecorate.

red·o·lent, *a.* aromatic; reminiscent.

re·doubt·a·ble, *a.* formidable.

re·dress, *v.* set right; compensate. *n.* amends; correction.

re·duce, *v.,* **-duced, -duc·ing.** diminish; make less; subdue; lower in grade.

re·duc·tion, *n.* small copy; amount reduced, discounted.

re·dun·dant, *a.* superfluous; excessive; wordy. **-dance, -dan·cy,** *n.*

red·wood, *n.* sequoia; its wood.

reed, *n.* tall, slender marsh grass; musical pipe; mouthpiece of wind instruments.

reef, *n.* ledge of rocks, sand, or coral in water.

reef·er, *n.* short jacket; *inf.* marijuana cigarette.

reek, *v.* give off a strong odor. *n.* offensive smell.

reel, *n.* spool; lively dance. *v.* sway; stagger; wind a reel.

re·fec·to·ry, *n. pl.,* **-ries.** dining hall, esp. in monastery.

re·fer, *v.,* **-ferred, -fer·ring.** direct to; assign; consult. *n.*

ref·er·ee, *n.* one who decides or judges. *v.,* **-eed, -ee·ing.**

ref·er·ence, *n.* a mention; allusion; a note; information book; testimonial.

ref·er·en·dum, *n. pl.,* **-dums, -da.** submission for public vote.

ref·er·ent, *n.* something referred to.

re·fi·nance, *v.* obtain a new loan for.

re·fine, *v.,* **-fined, -fin·ing.** make fine or pure; improve; perfect.

re·fined, *a.* polished; pure.

re·fine·ment, *n.* fineness of thought, taste, language, etc.

re·fin·er·y, *n. pl.,* **-ies.** place for extracting from raw materials.

re·fit, *v.,* **-fit·ted, -fit·ting.** repair; replace equipment.

re·flect, *v.* show (image); throw back; consider seriously; meditate.

re·flec·tion, *n.* reflected rays or images; careful thought.

re·flex, *n.* reflection; movement; involuntary response to stimulus. *a.*

re·flex·ive, *a.* a verb whose subject and direct object refer to same; thing turned back on itself.

re·form, *v.* amend one's behavior; mold again. *n.* improvement.

re·form·a·to·ry, *n. pl.,* **-ries.** institution for reformation and instruction of juveniles.

re·fract, *v.* deflect light rays.

re·frac·to·ry, *a.* stubborn, obstinate; resisting heat or disease treatment.

re·frain, *v.* abstain; forbear. *n.* phrase repeated at intervals in a poem or song.

re·fresh, *v.* give new energy to; replenish; revive; make fresh.

re·fresh·ments, *n. pl.* food and/or drink; light meal.

re·frig·er·ant, *n.* cooling agent.

re·frig·er·ate, *v.,* **-at·ed, -at·ing.** keep cool; freeze.

reft, *a.* robbed of; bereft.

ref·uge, *n.* shelter; protection.

ref·u·gee, *n.* one who flees to foreign country for protection.

re·ful·gent, *a.* radiant; shining.

re·fund, *v.* give or pay back; reimburse. *n.* repayment.

re·fur·bish, *v.* redo; renovate.

re·fuse, *v.,* **-fused, -fus·ing.** deny; decline to do. **re·fus·al,** *n.* denial.

ref·use, *n.* garbage; trash.

re·fute, *v.,* **-fut·ed, -fut·ing.** disprove; show to be false.

re·gain, *v.* recover; reach again.

re·gal, *a.* royal; splendid.

re·gale, *v.,* **-galed, -gal·ing.** delight; entertain lavishly.

re·gard, *v.* look at; consider; think about; heed. *n.* reference; gaze; respect; attention.

re·gard·ful, *a.* respectful; heedful.

re·gard·ing, *prep.* concerning.

re·gard·less, *a.* having no regard. *adv. inf.* in spite of.

re·gat·ta, *n.* boat race.

re·gen·er·ate, *v.,* **-at·ed, -at·ing.** be reborn spiritually; renew a body part; recreate; reform. **-a·tion,** *n.*

re·gent, *n.* one who rules in place of a sovereign; officer in charge of education.

re·gime, *n.* system of government or administration.

reg·i·men, *n.* system of therapeutic diet, exercise, etc.

reg·i·ment, *n.* military unit. *v.* systematize; organize.

re·gion, *n.* locality; specific area.

reg·is·ter, *n.* device which records date; official record; device which regulates the passage of air; tonal range. *v.* enroll; indicate; record.

reg·is·trar, *n.* record keeper.

reg·is·tra·tion, *n.* enrollment.

re·gress, *v.* go back; return. **-gres·sion,** *n.* retrogression.

re·gret, *v.*, **-gret·ted, -gret·ting.** feel grief, sorrow. *n.* disappointment; distress; polite refusal.

reg·u·lar, *a.* normal; common; habitual; orderly; methodical. *n.* one who is loyal.

reg·u·late, *v.*, **-lat·ed, -lat·ing.** direct; manage; adjust; control.

reg·u·la·tion, *n.* prescribed rule. *a.* requirement; normal.

re·ha·bil·i·tate, *v.*, **-tat·ed, -tat·ing.** restore; train; reinstate. **-ta·tion,** *n.*

re·hash, *v.* go over again.

re·hearse, *v.*, **-hearsed, -hears·ing.** practice repeatedly; recite; tell in detail.

reign, *n.* sovereign rule; domination; influence. *v.* rule; prevail.

re·im·burse, *v.*, **-bursed, -burs·ing.** compensate; pay back; refund. **-ment,** *n.*

rein, *n. usu. pl.* strap which restrains a horse; any restraint. *v.* guide, check or halt.

re·in·car·na·tion, *n.* rebirth of a soul in a new body or in a new form.

rein·deer, *n. pl.* large deer with branching antlers.

re·in·force, *v.*, **-forced, -forc·ing.** give new force; strengthen.

re·in·state, *v.*, **-stat·ed, -stat·ing.** restore to a former state, position, etc. **-ment,** *n.*

re·it·er·ate, *v.*, **-at·ed, -at·ing.** say or do again and again. **-a·tion,** *n.*

re·ject, *v.* refuse to take; deny; cast away; discard. **-jec·tion,** *n.*

re·joice, *v.*, **-joiced, joic·ing.** feel joyful; exult.

re·join, *v.* reunite; answer.

re·join·der, *n.* retort; answer.

re·ju·ve·nate, *v.*, **-nat·ed, -nat·ing.** give new youthful vigor; refresh. **-na·tion,** *n.*

re·lapse, *v.*, **-lapsed, -laps·ing.** lapse back; backslide; worsen. *n.* recurrence of illness or bad habits.

re·late, *v.*, **-lat·ed, -lat·ing.** tell; narrate; show a connection; show sympathy.

re·lat·ed, *a.* connected; allied; connected by blood or marriage.

re·la·tion, *n.* connection between things; kinship; reference; narrative.

rel·a·tive, *a.* relevant; pertinent; comparative. *n.* related person; kin.

rel·a·tiv·i·ty, *n.* relation of one thing to another; interdependence of matter, energy, space, and time.

re·lax, *v.* slacken; make less tense; ease; allay stress.

re·lay, *v.*, **-laid, -lay·ing, -layed, -lay·ing.** transmit by stages; lay again. *n.* race; fresh supply; electric switch.

re·lease, *v.*, **-leased, -leas·ing.** set free; relinquish; let go. *n.* liberation; relief; waiver; discharge.

rel·e·gate, *v.*, **-gat·ed, -gat·ing.** assign to a position; banish.

re·lent, *v.* soften in attitude.

rel·e·vant, *a.* pertinent; germane. **-vance, -van·cy,** *n.*

re·li·a·ble, *a.* dependable; true.

re·li·ance, *n.* dependence; trust.

rel·ic, *n.* something outmoded; souvenir; old thing.

re·lief, *n.* ease from pain, duty, etc.; a relieving; aid for the needy; background projection; sharp outline.

re·lieve, *v.*, **-lieved, -liev·ing.** lessen; ease from something; release from duty.

re·li·gion, *n.* worship of God or gods; faith; system of beliefs.

re·li·gious, *a.* devout; pious.

re·lin·quish, *v.* give up; release.

rel·ish, *v.* be keenly pleased with. *n.* liking; pickled sauce.

re·luc·tance, *n.* unwillingness.

re·luc·tant, *a.* not willing.

re·ly, *v.*, **-lied, -ly·ing.** depend on; trust.

re·main, *v.* stay behind or in one place; endure.

re·main·der, *n.* thing left over; result after subtraction.

re·mand, *v.* order or send back.

re·mark, *n.* casual statement. *v.* comment; notice.

re·mark·a·ble, *a.* unusual; extraordinary; noticeable.

re·me·di·al, *a.* correction of faulty habits or knowledge; remedy.

rem·e·dy, *n. pl.*, **-dies.** something that corrects; medicine. *v.*, **-died, -dy·ing.** cure; relieve.

re·mem·ber, *v.* recall; bear in mind; recollect; commemorate.

re·mem·brance, *n.* thing recalled; keepsake; warm greetings.

re·mind, *v.* cause to remember.

rem·i·nisce, *v.*, **-nisced, -nisc·ing.** recall past incidents, events.

rem·i·nis·cence, *n.* recollection.

re·miss, *a.* lax; careless.

re·mis·sion, *n.* forgiveness; lessening of symptoms.

re·mit, *v.*, **-mit·ted**, **-mit·ting**. send payment; pardon.

re·mit·tance, *n.* payment; money.

rem·nant, *n.* fragment; trace.

re·mod·el, *v.* reconstruct; redo.

re·mon·strate, *v.*, **-strat·ed**, **-strat·ing**. plead or protest in opposition. **-strance**, *n.*

re·morse, *n.* keen, guilty anguish; self-reproach. **-ful**, *a.*

re·mote, *a.*, **-mot·er**, **-mot·est**. distant; apart; aloof.

re·mov·al, *n.* change of place or site; dismissal. **-a·ble**, *a.*

re·move, *v.*, **-moved**, **-mov·ing**. displace; cause to leave; transfer; eliminate.

re·mu·ner·ate, *v.*, **-at·ed**, **-at·ing**. pay; recompense.

ren·ais·sance, *n.* a new birth; resurrection. (*cap.*) revival of letters and art in Europe, 14th to 16th century.

rend, *v.*, **rent** or **rend·ed**, **-ing**. tear apart forcibly; distress.

ren·der, *v.* give; perform; pay back; furnish; boil down.

ren·dez·vous, *n. pl.*, **-vous**. appointment; meeting. *v.*, **-voused**, **-vous·ing**. assemble.

ren·di·tion, *n.* interpretation; performance, as of music.

ren·e·gade, *n.* one who gives up conventional or lawful behavior.

re·nege, *v.*, **-neged**, **-neg·ing**. violate a rule; fail to keep promise.

re·new, *v.* restore; resume.

re·nounce, *v.*, **-nounced**, **-nounc·ing**. give up; repudiate.

ren·o·vate, *v.*, **-vat·ed**, **-vat·ing**. renew; restore. **-va·tion**, *n.*

re·nown, *n.* fame.

rent, *n.* compensation to the owner of a property; hole or slit. *v.* lease; let.

rent·al, *n.* sum paid for rent; place rented.

re·nun·ci·a·tion, *n.* repudiation.

re·pair, *v.* restore; to go. *n.* good condition.

rep·a·ra·tion, *n.* amends; *pl.* indemnities paid.

rep·ar·tee, *n.* witty reply.

re·past, *n.* meal; food.

re·pay, *v.*, **-paid**, **-pay·ing**. pay back; refund; requital.

re·peal, *v.* revoke; annul; rescind. *n.* revocation.

re·peat, *v.* say again; recite; execute again. *n.* repetition.

re·pel, *v.*, **-pelled**, **-pel·ling**. reject; repulse; cause distaste.

re·pent, *v.* feel remorse, regret. **-ance**, *n.*

re·per·cus·sion, *n.* aftereffect or result; reverberation.

rep·er·toire, *n.* collective works.

rep·e·ti·tion, *n.* doing something again. **-tious**, *a.*

re·place, *v.*, **-placed**, **-plac·ing**. put back; supersede. **-a·ble**, *a.*

re·plen·ish, *v.* restock.

re·plete, *a.* plentifully supplied.

rep·li·ca, *n.* reproduction; copy.

re·ply, *v.*, **-plied**, **-ply·ing**. answer; respond. *n.* answer.

re·port, *v.* be agent for; typify; describe; symbolize; portray. **-sen·ta·tion**, *n.*

re·port·er, *n.* one who reports.

re·pose, *v.*, **-posed**, **-pos·ing**. place confidence in; lie or lay at rest; rest. *n.* peace; composure; rest.

re·pos·i·to·ry, *n.* storage place.

re·pos·sess, *v.* regain possession.

rep·re·hend, *v.* criticize; blame.

rep·re·hen·si·ble, *a.* censurable.

rep·re·sent, *v.* be agent for; typify; describe; symbolize; portray. **-sen·ta·tion**, *n.*

rep·re·sent·a·tive, *a.* typical; agent for. *n.* one who acts for another; typical one or thing.

re·press, *v.* subdue; restrain; curb; control. **-pres·sion**, *n.*

re·prieve, *n.* temporary relief; respite. *v.*, **-prieved**, **-priev·ing**. delay in punishment; relief from pain, etc.

rep·ri·mand, *n.* severe reproof. *v.* rebuke.

re·pris·al, *n.* retaliatory act.

re·proach, *v.* rebuke, blame. *n.* reproof; disgrace; discredit.

rep·ro·bate, *a.* depraved. *n.* depraved, corrupt person.

re·pro·duce, *v.*, **-duced**, **-duc·ing**. have offspring; produce again; copy; imitate; multiply.

re·proof, *n.* censure; rebuke.

re·prove, *v.*, **-proved**, **-prov·ing**. rebuke; censure.

rep·tile, *n.* air-breathing, scaly cold-blooded vertebrate.

re·pub·lic, *n.* a nation in which power is vested in all the people.

re·pu·di·ate, *v.*, **-at·ed**, **-at·ing**. reject; disown.

re·pug·nant, *a.* offensive.

re·pulse, *v.*, **-pulsed**, **-puls·ing**. repel; rebuff; disgust. *n.*

re·pul·sive, *a.* disgusting.

rep·u·ta·ble, *a.* respected; honorable. **-bly**, *adv.*

rep·u·ta·tion, *n.* good or bad opinion of character; fame.

re·pute, *v.,* **-put·ed, -put·ing.** regard or consider. *n.* reputation. **-put·ed·ly,** *adv.*

re·quest, *n.* petition, entreaty; demand. *v.* solicit.

re·quire, *v.,* **-quired, -quir·ing.** demand; insist on; need. **-quire·ment,** *n.* requisite.

req·ui·site, *a.* necessary. *n.* something indispensable.

req·ui·si·tion, *n.* formal request, order (for supplies, etc.). *v.* request.

re·qui·tal, *n.* adequate return for good or evil; compensation; reward.

re·scind, *v.* cancel; revoke.

res·cue, *v.,* **-cued, -cu·ing.** save from danger; reclaim. *n.*

re·search, *n.* studious investigation. *v.* investigate.

re·sect, *v.* remove part of (an organ).

re·sem·ble, *v.,* **-bled, -bling.** look like; be similar to. **-blance,** *n.* similarity.

re·sent, *v.* be indignant at.

res·er·va·tion, *n.* skepticism; saved or held for; qualification; public land set aside for special purpose.

re·serve, *v.,* **-served, -serv·ing.** set aside; hold back; retain. *n.* land set aside; something withheld for future use; reticence.

res·er·voir, *n.* place for storing, esp. a lake; extra supply.

re·side, *v.,* **-sid·ed, -sid·ing.** dwell for some time; exist. **res·i·dence,** *n.* residing place.

res·i·dent, *a.* person residing; inherent. *n.* doctor in training; one who resides in a place.

re·sid·u·al, *a.* thing left over.

res·i·due, *n.* remainder.

re·sign, *v.* give up; relinquish. **res·ig·na·tion,** *n.* **-signed,** *a.*

re·sil·ient, *a.* springing back; buoyant. **-ien·cy,** *n.*

res·in, *n.* substance from plants used in plastics, varnishes, and medicines.

re·sist, *v.* withstand; hold off; oppose. **-er,** *n.*

re·sist·ance, *n.* opposition; thing hindering motion; guerrilla force.

res·o·lute, *a.* determined.

res·o·lu·tion, *n.* determination; formal decision; solution.

re·solve, *v.,* **-solved, -solv·ing.** analyze; explain; determine. *n.* resolution.

res·o·nance, *n.* resounding quality; vibrations.

res·o·nant, *a.* resounding.

re·sort, *v.* to go to; have recourse. *n.* vacation place; recourse; refuge.

re·sound, *v.* echo; reverberate.

re·source, *n.* means of support; something available; *pl.* raw materials; assets. **-ful·ness,** *n.* having ability to cope.

re·spect, *n.* esteem; regard; honor; courtesy; reference to. *v.*

re·spect·a·ble, *a.* decent; worthy; proper; fairly large, good. **-a·bil·i·ty,** *n.*

res·pi·ra·tion, *n.* breathing; oxidation process. **-to·ry,** *a.*

res·pi·ra·tor, *n.* apparatus for artificial respiration.

re·spite, *n.* delay; reprieve.

re·splend·ent, *a.* dazzling.

re·spond, *v.* reply; react.

re·sponse, *n.* reply; reaction.

re·spon·si·bil·i·ty, *n. pl.,* **-ties.** duty; accountability.

re·spon·si·ble, *a.* accountable; trustworthy.

re·spon·sive, *a.* sensitive.

rest, *n.* sleep; relief; a support; inactivity; remainder. *v.* relax; sleep; cease activity.

res·tau·rant, *n.* place preparing and serving meals.

rest·ful, *a.* peaceful; quiet.

res·ti·tu·tion, *n.* restoration to the former state; making good.

res·tive, *a.* restless; unruly.

rest·less, *a.* uneasy; unsettled; discontented; disturbed.

re·store, *v.,* **-stored, -stor·ing.** bring back to former condition; renew. **res·to·ra·tion,** *n.*

re·strain, *v.* hold back; restrict.

re·straint, *n.* a holding back; reserve; restricting device.

re·strict, *v.* limit; confine.

re·stric·tion, *n.* restraint; limitation.

re·stric·tive, *a.* limiting.

re·sult, *v.* have as a consequence. *n.* outcome; calculated amount.

re·sume, *v.,* **-sumed, -sum·ing.** begin or take up again.

rés·u·mé, *n.* summary of employment, education, etc.

re·sur·face, *v.* **-faced, fac·ing.** provide with new surface; to come up again (in water); show up again.

re·sur·gent, *a.* rising again. **-gence,** *n.* renaissance.

res·ur·rect, *v.* restore to life; bring back into use.

re·sus·ci·tate, *v.,* **-tat·ed, -tat·ing.** revive from unconsciousness. **-ta·tion,** *n.*

re·tail, *n.* selling goods directly to the consumer. *v.* sell in small quantities to consumer.

re·tain, v. keep possession of; remember; hire.

re·tain·er, n. fee paid to secure services of lawyer, etc.

re·tal·i·ate, v., **-at·ed, -at·ing.** revenge; repay; return like for like. **-a·tion,** n.

re·tard, v. hinder. n. delay.

re·tard·ed, a. slow in development, esp. mental development.

retch, v. strain to vomit.

re·ten·tion, n. ability to retain, remember data, etc.

ret·i·cent, a. reluctant. **-cence,** n.

ret·i·cu·lar, a. netlike; intricate.

ret·i·na, n. pl., **-nas, -nae.** membrane at back of the eyeball.

ret·i·nue, n. attendants.

re·tire, v., **-tired, -tir·ing.** withdraw; retreat from action; go to bed; give up work.

re·tir·ing, a. reserved; shy.

re·tort, v. reply sharply. n. sharp or witty reply.

re·tract, v. take back; withdraw; disavow; draw in.

re·treat, n. withdrawal; safe or secluded place. v.

re·trench, v. economize; curtail; cut back. **-ment,** n.

ret·ri·bu·tion, n. requital.

re·trieve, v., **-trieved, -triev·ing.** get back; recover; rescue; restore; revive.

ret·ro·ac·tive, a. made effective as of a prior date.

ret·ro·spect, n. looking back on things past.

re·turn, v. give back; restore; reciprocate; yield; reelect; render; repay. n. that which is returned; recurrence.

re·un·ion, n. a reuniting after separation.

re·vamp, v. make over; renovate.

re·veal, v. make known; expose; display; make visible.

rev·eil·le, n. morning signal given servicemen to rise.

rev·el, v. take delight; make merry; make noise. n. wild party.

rev·e·la·tion, n. disclosure.

re·venge, v., **-venged, -veng·ing.** avenge; inflict punishment. n. retaliation.

rev·e·nue, n. income.

re·ver·ber·ate, v., **-at·ed, -at·ing.** rebound; recoil; reecho; reflect. **-a·tion,** n.

re·vere, v., **-vered, -ver·ing.** regard with profound respect; venerate. **re·vered,** a. one worthy of respect. **rev·er·ence,** n.

rev·er·end, n. worthy of reverence. (cap.) clergyman.

rev·er·ie, rev·er·y, n. pl., **-ies.** daydream.

re·verse, v., **-versed, -vers·ing.** turn in an opposite direction; turn upside down or inside out. a. opposite; contrary. n. back side; opposite side; unfavorable turn of events. **-ver·sal,** n.

re·vers·i·ble, a. having two usable sides, as a coat; capable of being reversed.

re·vert, v. go or turn back.

re·view, v. examine again; study carefully; evaluate; write reviews. n. evaluation; survey.

re·vile, v., **-viled, -vil·ing.** attack verbally, abusively.

re·vise, v., **-vised, -vis·ing.** change, correct, and amend. n. **-vi·sion,** n.

re·vi·tal·ize, -ized, iz·ing. v. restore vitality. **-i·za·tion,** n.

re·viv·al, n. restoration; religious awakening, meeting.

re·vive, v., **-vived, -viv·ing.** bring to life again; present again; gain vigor; reanimate.

re·voke, v., **-voked, -vok·ing.** annul; void; rescind.

re·volt, v. rise against; repel. n. rebellion; uprising.

rev·o·lu·tion, n. overthrow of a government; radical change; complete cycle; rotation.

rev·o·lu·tion·ar·y, a. drastic change or idea. n. pl. **-ies.**

rev·o·lu·tion·ize, v., **-ized, -iz·ing.** cause a complete change.

re·volve, v., **-volved, -volv·ing.** move in a circle; orbit; rotate; think over.

re·volv·er, n. pistol; handgun.

re·vue, n. musical show often comical or satirical.

re·vul·sion, n. aversion, disgust.

re·ward, v. remunerate; or award. n. compensation; profit.

rhap·so·dy, n. pl., **-dies.** rapturous writing; musical composition; great delight.

rhet·o·ric, n. skill in effective writing and speaking; insincere language.

rhe·tor·i·cal ques·tion, n. question asked for effect with no answer expected.

rheu·mat·ic, a. of, causing, or affected with rheumatism.

rheu·mat·ic fe·ver, n. infectious disease, usu. in children.

rheu·ma·tism, n. painful disorder of the joints.

rhine·stone, n. artificial glass gem; imitation diamond.

rhi·noc·er·os, n. pl., **-os·es, -os.** large thick-skinned mammal with horns on the snout.

rhom·bus, n. equilateral parallelogram.

rhu·barb, n. large-leaved plant having edible stalks; inf. noisy argument.

rhyme, n. word having a sound similar to another; poem. **rhymed, rhym·ing**, v.

rhythm, n. regular recurrent beat, sound, change, etc.

rib, n. curved chest bone; a cut of meat; raised ridge. v. inf. tease.

rib·ald, a. vulgar; coarse.

rib·bon, n. narrow cloth band.

rice, n. starchy grain; cereal grass. v. form into granules.

rich, a. wealthy; abundant; sweet; abounding; costly.

rich·es, n. pl. wealth; resources.

rick·ets, n. bone softening disease from lack of Vit. D.

rick·et·y, a., **-i·er, -i·est**. shaky; tottering; feeble; infirm.

ric·o·chet, n. glancing rebound.

rid, v., **rid** or **rid·ded, rid·ding**. free; dispose of.

rid·dle, n. coarse sieve; puzzling question. v., **-dled, -dling**. perforate with holes; refute.

ride, v., **rode, rid·den, rid·ing**. sit on and be borne along; sit in or on and control; travel on. n. journey; trip.

rid·er, n. passenger; item added to bill, contract, policy.

ridge, n. raised part of something; chain of hills. v., **ridged, ridg·ing**. form into ridges.

rid·i·cule, n. derision. v., **-culed, -cul·ing**. make fun of; mock.

ri·dic·u·lous, a. absurd; silly.

rife, a. prevalent; widespread.

rif·fle, n. choppy water in stream. v. thumb through; ripple; intermix.

riff·raff, n. rabble; low persons.

ri·fle, n. firearm with grooved bore. v., **-fled, -fling**. ransack and rob.

rift, n. cleft; fissure; estrangement; split.

rig, v., **rigged, rig·ging**. fit; equip; inf. dress; manipulate. n. equipment on a ship; gear.

right, a. just or good; correct; sound or normal; virtuous; true; conservative; fitting; side opposite left. n. that which is just, moral. adv. correctly. v. redress; make correct.

right·eous, a. virtuous; moral.

right·ful, a. just claim; proper.

rig·id, a. rigorous; severe; stiff; set; inflexible. **-i·ty**, n.

rig·ma·role, n. nonsense.

rig·or, n. harshness; hardship; strictness. **-ous**, a. harsh; difficult.

rig·or mor·tis, n. muscular stiffening after death.

rile, v., **riled, ril·ing**. inf. anger; irritate; roil; make muddy.

rim, n. edge or border, esp. of circular object. **rimmed, rim·ming**, v.

rime, n. hoarfrost.

ri·mose, a. having many cracks or fissures.

rind, n. skin or outer coat of fruit, cheese, bacon, etc.

ring, n. circular band; enclosure; circle; sound of a bell; group of persons. v., **rang, rung, ring·ing**. ring a bell; form a ring; resound; reverberate; signal; hem in.

ring·lead·er, n. leader of a group, esp. unlawful one.

ring·let, n. lock of hair; curl.

ring·mas·ter, n. leader of circus ring performances.

ring·side, n. any area for close viewing.

ring·worm, n. contagious skin disease caused by fungi.

rink, n. smooth area for skating.

rinse, v., **rinsed, rins·ing**. wash lightly; flush; dip. n.

ri·ot, n. vivid display; violent public disorder or show. v. participate in a public disorder. **-ous**, a.

rip, v., **ripped, rip·ping**. tear or cut apart. n. tear or split.

ri·par·i·an, a. located on the bank of a natural watercourse.

ripe, a. ready for harvest; matured; developed. **rip·en**, v.

rip·ple, v., **-pled, -pling**. form small waves; become slightly agitated. n. small wave or undulation.

rise, v., **rose, ris·en, ris·ing**. move upward; stand up; swell up; become greater; occur; ascend. v. advance; increase; extension upward; upward slope.

ris·i·ble, a. capable of laughing.

risk, n. hazard; peril. v. expose to the chance of injury or loss.

ris·qué, a. improper; off-color.

rite, n. prescribed solemn ceremonial practice. **rit·u·al**, a.

ritz·y, a., **-i·er, -i·est**. inf. smart; swank; elegant.

ri·val, n. competitor. a. competing; peer. v. strive to equal or excel.

ri·val·ry, n. pl., **-ries**. competition; act of rivaling.

riv·er, n. large, natural stream of flowing water; copious flow.

riv·et, *n.* short metal bolt. *v.* fasten firmly; engross; attract and hold.

riv·u·let, *n.* small stream; brook.

road, *n.* highway; route; course.

roam, *v.* wander. *n.*

roar, *v.* emit loud cry, as of rage; howl. *n.* loud noise or din.

roast, *v.* cook by exposure to heat; dry and parch; *inf.* ridicule. *n.* piece of meat.

rob, *v.*, **robbed, rob·bing.** seize and steal unlawfully.

robe, *n.* flowing outer garment. *v.*, **robed, rob·ing.** dress.

ro·bot, *n.* automated apparatus performing human functions. **-ics**, *n.*

ro·bust, *a.* strong; healthy.

rock, *n.* stone; person or thing supporting; *inf.* any gem. *v.* move to and fro; shake; sway; disturb.

rock·er, *n.* rocking chair.

rock·et, *n.* missile; projectile.

rock·et·ry, *n.* science of rocket flight, design, and construction.

rock·y, *a.*, **-i·er, -i·est.** having rocks; having difficulties; unsteady.

ro·co·co, *a.* ornate; elaborate.

rod, *n.* straight bar; linear measurement equal to $5\frac{1}{2}$ yards.

ro·dent, *n.* mammal with teeth adapted for nibbling or gnawing.

ro·de·o, *n. pl.*, **-os.** contest of cowboy skills; roundup.

roent·gen, *n.* unit of radiation. *a.* relating to x-rays.

rogue, *n.* rascal. **ro·guish**, *a.*

roil, *v.* make muddy; annoy.

roist·er, *v.* bluster; carouse.

role, *n.* actor's part; character portrayed; specific behavior.

roll, *v.* move by turning over; move on wheels; beat a drum; flow; pass; make level by pressing with a roller; *inf.* rob. *n.* anything rolled up; register; scroll; swaying motion; small cake of bread.

rol·lick, *v.* be gay; frolic. **-ing**, *a.* carelessly gay.

ro·ly-po·ly, *a.* short and fat.

Ro·man Cath·o·lic, *a.* member of or pertaining to the Roman Catholic Church. *n.*

ro·mance, *n.* love affair; prose narrative; love story. *v.* act romantically; make love.

Ro·man nu·mer·als, *n.* numerals based on letters of ancient Rome.

ro·man·tic, *a.* of romance; amorous; fanciful; visionary.

ro·man·ti·cism, *n.* artistic movement of early 19th century, based on imagination. **-cist**, *n.*

romp, *v.* play boisterously; win easily. *n.* frolic.

rood, *n.* cross or crucifix.

roof, *n.* upper cover of a building; top; summit. *v.*

roof·ing, *n.* material for roofs.

rook, *n.* chess piece; crow; a cheat. *v.* defraud; swindle.

rook·ie, *n. inf.* beginner; new recruit in army, etc.; novice.

room, *n.* space in building for use or occupancy; space for some specific purpose. *v.* occupy a room.

room·mate, *n.* one who occupies a room with another.

room·y, *a.*, **-i·er, -i·est.** spacious. **-i·ly**, *adv.* **-i·ness**, *n.*

roost, *n.* perch; place for resting. *v.* lodge; settle down.

roost·er, *n.* male chicken.

root, *n.* subterranean part of a plant; basal part; source; elemental form of a word or number; foundation; essence; cause of. *v.* send forth roots; be firmly fixed; implant; unearth.

rope, *n.* cord of twisted or braided fibers. **roped, rop·ing**, *v.*

ro·sa·ry, *n. pl.*, **-ries.** string of beads used in counting prayers.

rose, *n.* attractive flower; pinkish color. *a.*

ro·se·ate, *a.* rose-colored; cheerful; optimistic.

ro·sette, *n.* ornament which resembles a rose.

Rosh Ha·sha·nah, *n.* the Jewish New Year.

ros·in, *n.* resin from turpentine used in making varnish.

ros·ter, *n.* any list of names.

ros·trum, *n. pl.*, **-tra, -trums.** speaker's stage or platform.

ros·y, *a.*, **-i·er, -i·est.** rose-colored; promising; blooming.

rot, *v.*, **rot·ted, rot·ting.** decompose; become morally rotten. *n.* decay; *inf.* nonsense.

ro·tate, *v.*, **-tat·ed, -tat·ing.** revolve around an axis; alternate in succession. **-ta·tion**, *n.*

rote, *n.* mechanical repetition. **by rote**, mechanically by memory.

ro·tor, *n.* revolving part of a machine.

rot·ten, *a.* decomposed; putrid; dishonest; *inf.* disagreeable; very bad.

ro·tund, *a.* rounded; spherical; plump; full-toned voice. **-tun·di·ty**, *n.*

ro·tun·da, *n.* round domed building; large center area.

rouge, *n.* coloring cosmetic; powder used for polishing.

rough, *a.* not smooth; uneven; coarse; wild; stormy; crude; not perfected. *n.* anything rough. *v.* make rough; treat harshly. *adv.*

rough·age, *n.* coarse foods that stimulate peristalsis.

rough·neck, *n. inf.* a rowdy.

rou·lette, *n.* gambling game.

round, *a.* spherical; semicircular; plump; approximate number. *n.* anything round; period of play; ammunition; circuit. *v.* make round; make a circuit. *adv.* encircled; circularly. *prep.* about; encircling.

round·a·bout, *a.* circuitous; indirect.

round·up, *n.* driving or bringing together; summary.

rouse, *v.,* **roused, rous·ing.** stir up; awaken; excite; agitate.

rous·ing, *a.* stirring; lively.

roust, *v. inf.,* arouse (roughly).

roust·a·bout, *n.* transient worker; deckhand.

rout, *n.* disorderly flight; disastrous defeat; rabble. *v.* dig up; rummage; put to flight in disorder.

route, *n.* course taken; regular line of travel; highway; channel; *v.,* **rout·ed, rout·ing.** set the route of.

rou·tine, *n.* procedure regularly followed; habit; fixed entertainment repeated. *a.* uninspired; customary.

rove, *v.,* **roved, rov·ing.** wander.

row, *v.* propel with oars; place in a line; quarrel. *n.* trip in a rowboat; objects in a series; brawl.

row·dy, *n. pl.,* **-dies.** rough, disorderly person. *a.* **-di·er, -di·est.** disorderly.

roy·al, *a.* sovereign; imperial; noble. **-ly,** *adv.*

roy·al·ty, *n. pl.,* **-ties.** sovereignty; nobility; generosity; share of proceeds paid to the owner of a right (author, etc.).

rub, *v.,* **rubbed, rub·bing.** move over surface with pressure; grate; scour; chafe. *n.*

rub·ber, *n.* series of games; flexible waterproof elastic solid.

rub·bish, *n.* garbage; waste; debris; nonsense. **-y,** *a.*

rub·ble, *n.* broken pieces of stone, brick, etc.

ru·bel·la, *n.* German measles.

ru·be·o·la, *n.* measles.

ru·bi·cund, *a.* ruddy.

ru·bric, *n.* title of a book; first letter in distinctive type.

ru·by, *n. pl.,* **ru·bies.** deep red corundum; precious gem.

ruck·us, *n. inf.* commotion.

rud·der, *n.* device used in steering a ship or airplane.

rud·dy, *a.,* **-di·er, -di·est.** having a reddish color.

rude, *a.,* **rud·er, rud·est.** coarse; discourteous; crude; raw; simple.

ru·di·ment, *n.* a first step or stage; *usu. pl.* fundamental skills. **-men·ta·ry,** *a.*

rue, *v.,* **rued, ru·ing.** feel remorse.

rue·ful, *a.* sorrowful.

ruff, *n.* pleated collar; feathers or hair around neck of bird or mammal.

ruf·fi·an, *n.* brutal person.

ruf·fle, *v.,* **-fled, -fling.** disturb; rumple; draw into folds; irritate; shuffle. *n.* disturbance; pleated strip.

rug, *n.* floor covering·.

rug·ged, *a.* rough and uneven; rocky; irregular; stormy.

ru·in, *n.* destruction; downfall; dilapidation; damage. *v.* destroy; fall into ruins; wreck.

ru·in·a·tion, *n.* destruction.

rule, *n.* control; maxim; regulation; custom; point of law. *v.,* **ruled, rul·ing.** govern; control; manage; guide.

rul·er, *n.* one who rules; straight-edged strip used for measuring length, drawing lines.

rul·ing, *a.* prevalent; predominant. *n.* official decision.

rum, *n.* alcoholic liquor made from molasses.

rum·ble, *v.,* **-bled, -bling.** make low, rolling sound, as thunder. *n.* heavy rolling sound; *inf.* street fight.

ru·mi·nant, *a.* chewing again; reflective. *n.* cud chewing mammal, as a cow.

ru·mi·nate, *v.,* **-nated, -nating.** meditate or reflect upon. **-na·tion,** *n.*

rum·mage, *v.,* **-maged, -mag·ing.** ransack; search through. *n.* odds and ends.

rum·my, *n.* card game; *inf.* drunkard.

ru·mor, *n.* hearsay; common gossip. *v.* tell or spread gossip.

ru·mor·mon·ger, *n.* one who spreads rumors.

rump, *n.* buttocks; hindquarters; last part.

rum·ple, *v.,* **-pled, -pling.** wrinkle; ruffle; crease.

rum·pus, *n. inf.* commotion.

run, *v.,* **ran, run, run·ning.** move faster than walking; flee; regular trips; contend in a race; campaign; flow; manage; operate. *n.* act of running; trip; flow; period of continuous performance; trend; path. *a.* melted.

run·a·round, *n. inf.* series of evasive or deceptive actions.

run·a·way, *n.* one or that which runs away. *a.* escaped; uncontrolled; easily won; rising rapidly.

run·down, *n.* summary. *a.* dilapidated; debilitated.

rung, *n.* round crosspiece of ladder or chair; wheel spoke.

run-in, *n.* a quarrel; bicker.

run·ner, *n.* one who runs; smuggler; messenger; part on which something runs or slides; narrow piece of carpet or cloth.

run·ning, *a.* moving rapidly; fluid; continuous; functioning; successive. *n.* quantity run. *adv.* consecutively.

run·ny, *a.*, **-ni·er**, **-ni·est**. tending to discharge.

run-off, *n.* rainfall that drains off; final deciding contest.

run-of-the-mill, *a.* average.

runt, *n.* smallest in a litter.

run-through, *n.* rapid reading.

run·way, *n.* stream channel; landing strip; pathway.

rup·ture, *n.* hernia; a breaking apart; breach of peace.

ru·ral, *a.* pertaining to the country; bucolic; rustic.

ruse, *n.* stratagem; trick.

rush, *v.* move or go quickly, act with haste; attack suddenly. *n.* marsh plant; surge or drive; haste. *a.* with urgency.

rus·set, *n.* reddish-brown.

rust, *n.* reddish coating which forms on iron when exposed to air and moisture; plant disease. *v.* to rust; corrode.

rus·tic, *a.* of the country; rural; uncultured. *n.*

rus·tle, *v.*, **-tled**, **-tling**. make small, light rubbing sounds; *inf.* forage; steal cattle; move with energy.

rust·y, *a.*, **-i·er**, **-i·est**. covered with rust; impaired through neglect or lack of practice.

rut, *n.* track worn by use; habitual behavior; furrow. **rut·ted**, **rut·ting**. *v.*

ru·ta·ba·ga, *n.* turnip with large yellow root.

ruth·less, *a.* cruel; merciless.

rye, *n.* cereal plant, seed used for flour and whiskey.

S

Sab·bath, *n.* day of rest and religious observance. *a.*

sa·ber, *n.* cavalry sword.

sa·ble, *n.* carnivorous mammal having dark, lustrous fur; the color black. *a.*

sab·o·tage, *n.* destruction of employer's property; obstruction of a war effort; malicious subversion. *v.*, **-taged**, **-tag·ing.** destroy by sabotage.

sab·o·teur, *n.* one who engages in sabotage.

sac, *n.* pouch or cavity, often filled with fluid.

sac·cha·rin, *n.* synthetic sugar substitute.

sac·cha·rine, *a.*, *n.* overly sweet; too friendly.

sa·chet, *n.* scented packet.

sack, *n.* large, strong bag; dismissal; bed. *v.* pillage; plunder.

sac·ra·ment, *n.* solemn religious rite, as marriage, baptism, etc.; (*often cap.*) Eucharist. **-men·tal**, *a.*

sa·cred, *a.* consecrated; holy.

sac·ri·fice, *n.* offering to a deity; giving up of something cherished; loss without return. *v.* **-ficed**, **-fic·ing.** make a sacrifice of; offer. **-fi·cial**, *a.*

sac·ri·lege, *n.* violating anything sacred. **-le·gious**, *a.*

sac·ro·sanct, *a.* most holy; inviolable.

sad, *a.*, **-der**, **-dest**. sorrowful or depressed; grieving; deplorable. **-ly**, *adv.* **-ness**, *n.*

sad·den, *v.* make or become sad.

sad·dle, *v.* seat for a rider; ridge. *v.*, **-dled**, **-dling.** put a saddle upon; to load, as with a burden.

sad·ism, *n.* take sexual pleasure in cruelty; sexual perversion. **-ist**, *n.*, *a.* **sa·dis·tic**, *a.*

sa·fa·ri, *n. pl.*, **-ris**. hunting expedition, esp. in Africa; journey.

safe, *a.*, **saf·er**, **saf·est**. free from danger; unhurt; secure; reliable; involving no danger or risk. *n.* strong metal box for keeping valuables.

safe·guard, *n.* defense; device to protect from injury. *v.* guard; defend.

safe·keep·ing, *n.* act of keeping in safety; protection.

safe·ty, *n. pl.*, **-ties.** freedom from danger or risk.

sag, *v.*, **sagged**, **sag·ging.** droop, esp. in the middle; lose vigor or firmness. *n.* sagging place.

sa·ga, *n.* tale of heroic exploits; myth.

sa·ga·cious, *a.* intelligent; shrewd; discerning. **-gac·i·ty**, *n.*

sage, *a.*, **sag·er**, **sag·est**. wise; prudent. *n.* man of profound wisdom. **-ness**, *n.*

sail, *n.* cloth spread to the wind to propel a craft in water or air. *v.* move over water or in the air by wind action; glide; navigate. **-or**, *n.*

sail·boat, *n.* boat propelled by a sail or sails.

sail·plane, *n.* light glider used for soaring.

saint, *n.* canonized, holy person; patient, unselfish person. *a.* holy. **-hood,** *n.*

saint·ly, *a.,* **-li·er, -li·est.** like a saint; unusually good, kind person.

sake, *n.* purpose; benefit; end.

sa·ke, *n.* Japanese rice liquor.

sa·la·cious, *a.* lustful; lewd.

sal·ad, *n.* cold dish of vegetables, fruits, or meat, with dressing or molded.

sal·a·man·der, *n.* lizardlike, tailed, scaleless amphibian.

sa·la·mi, *n.* highly seasoned sausage.

sal·a·ry, *n. pl.,* **-ries.** compensation paid for work; wages. **-ried,** *a.*

sale, *n.* act of selling; amount sold; offering of goods at lower prices; auction.

sa·li·ent, *a.* prominent.

sa·line, *a.* salty. **-lin·i·ty,** *n.*

sa·li·va, *n.* watery fluid of the mouth. **sal·i·var·y,** *a.*

sal·low, *a.* unhealthy yellowish color or complexion.

sal·ly, *n. pl.,* **-lies.** sortie; brief outburst; a going forth; bantering remark. *v.,* **-lied, -ly·ing.** rush or go out.

salm·on, *n. pl.,* **-ons, -on.** edible game fish; pinkish color.

sa·lon, *n.* elegant drawing room; stylish shop; art gallery.

sa·loon, *n.* bar; tavern; large room for public use.

salt, *n.* sodium chloride. *a.* salty; preserved with salt; tasting of salt. *v.* season or cure with salt. **-y,** *a.,* **-i·er, -i·est.**

sa·lu·bri·ous, *a.* healthful; conducive to health; wholesome.

sal·u·tar·y, *a.* beneficial; wholesome; healthful.

sal·u·ta·tion, *n.* greeting.

sa·lute, *v.,* **-lut·ed, -lut·ing.** greet with words or a gesture of welcome, honor, etc. *n.* praise.

sal·vage, *n.* the saving of a ship or its cargo from wreck or capture; any property saved; something saved as useful. *v.,* **-vaged, -vag·ing.** save. **-vag·er,** *n.*

sal·va·tion, *n.* act of saving; deliverance from sin; redemption.

salve, *n.* healing ointment; balm. *v.,* **-salved, salv·ing.** to soothe.

sal·vo, *n. pl.,* **-vos, -voes.** multiple gunfire burst; sudden burst; tribute.

same, *a.* identical; not different; equal. *pron.* identical thing or person. *adv.* equally. **same·ness,** *n.*

sam·o·var, *n.* Russian tea urn.

sam·ple, *n.* part or portion shown as representative of the whole; specimen; instance. *v.,* **-pled, -pling.** take a sample of. **-pler,** *n.* **-pling,** *n.*

san·a·to·ri·um, *n. pl.,* **-ums, -a.** institution for the treatment of chronic disorders, as mental illness, alcoholism, etc., or for invalids. Also **san·i·tar·i·um.**

sanc·ti·fy, *v.,* **-fied, -fy·ing.** consecrate; free from sin; purify. **-fi·ca·tion,** *n.*

sanc·ti·mo·ni·ous, *a.* hypocritical pretense of sanctity.

sanc·ti·mo·ny, *n.* outward appearance of sanctity.

sanc·tion, *v.* approve authoritatively; ratify or confirm. *n.* authoritative confirmation.

sanc·ti·ty, *n. pl.,* **-ties.** holiness.

sanc·tu·ar·y, *n. pl.,* **-ies.** holy place; place of refuge.

sand, *n.* rock debris finer than gravel; *pl.* sandy desert or beach. *v.* abrade or smooth. **-er,** *n.*

san·dal, *n.* shoe, consisting of a sole only fastened to the foot by straps or thongs.

sand·blast, *n., v.* clean or engrave by a blast of sand.

sand·hog, *n.* one who works under air pressure, as in caissons, etc.

sand·stone, *n.* quartz sand cemented with other minerals.

sand·wich, *n.* two slices of bread with meat, cheese, etc. between. *v.* to place between.

sand·y, *a.,* **-i·er, -i·est.** of, like, or abounding with sand.

sane, *a.,* **san·er, san·est.** mentally sound; sensible. **-ness,** *n.*

sang·froid, *n.* composure.

san·gui·nar·y, *a.* attended with bloodshed; bloodthirsty.

san·guine, *a.* blood red; ruddy; confident; hopeful.

san·i·tar·i·an, *n.* one skilled in sanitation and public health.

san·i·tar·i·um, *n. pl.,* **-ums, -a.** sanatorium.

san·i·tar·y, *a.* clean; hygienic.

san·i·ta·tion, *n.* process of establishing sanitary conditions; removal of garbage, etc.

san·i·ty, *n.* state of being sane or sound; mental health.

sans, *prep.* without.

sap, *n.* juice of plants or trees; vitality. *v.,* **sapped, sap·ping.** destroy slowly; undermine; weaken.

sa·pi·ent, *a.* wise; sagacious.

sap·ling, n. young tree, person.

sap·phire, n. blue gem, color.

sap·py, a., **-pi·er, -pi·est**. juicy; vital; inf. silly.

sar·casm, n. ironic or scornful remarks; taunt. **-cas·tic**, a.

sar·co·ma, n. malignant tumor.

sar·coph·a·gus, n. pl., **-gi, -gus·es**. stone coffin or tomb.

sar·dine, n. pl., **-dines, dine**. small fish preserved in oil.

sar·don·ic, a. scornful; derisive; ironical; mocking; cynical.

sa·ri, sa·ree, n. pl., **sa·ris, sa·rees**. length of cloth, principal garment of a Hindu woman.

sa·rong, n. rectangular, colored cloth worn as a skirt.

sash, n. ornamental band worn over the shoulder or around the waist; window, door framework.

sa·shay, v. inf. move or glide about.

sass, n. inf. pert retort. v. talk back; speak disrespectfully.

sas·sy, a., **-si·er, -si·est**. saucy; impertinent; impudent.

Sa·tan, n. devil; adversary of God. **-ic, -i·cal**, a.

satch·el, n. small suitcase or bag, often with shoulder strap.

sate, v., **sat·ed, sat·ing**. satisfy completely; glut; satiate.

sat·el·lite, n. secondary planet or moon; subservient follower; artificial body orbiting a planet, esp. the earth; small nation dependent on larger nation.

sa·ti·ate, v., **-at·ed, -at·ing**. fill or gratify excessively; glut; gorge; cloy. **-a·tion**, n. **-e·ty**, n.

sat·in, n. fabric having a smoothness and luster on one surface. **-y**, a.

sat·ire, n. literary work using caustic wit and irony to expose folly and vice. **sa·tir·i·cal**, a.

sat·i·rize, v., **-rized, -riz·ing**. attack with satire. **-rist**, n.

sat·is·fy, v., **-fied, -fy·ing**. to fulfill what is desired, expected, or needed; please; gratify; make reparation. **-fac·tion**, n. **-fac·to·ry**, a.

sat·u·rate, v., **-rat·ed, -rat·ing**. soak or imbue to capacity. **-ra·tion**, n.

sat·u·rat·ed, a. incapable of holding more of a substance.

Sat·ur·day, n. seventh day of the week.

sat·ur·nine, a. gloomy; grave.

sa·tyr, n. myth. deity, half man, half goat; a lecher. **-ic**, a.

sauce, n. liquid, relish, dressing, or gravy; stewed fruit.

sau·cer, n. small, shallow dish for holding a cup.

sau·cy, a., **-ci·er, -ci·est**. impudent; flippant; sprightly; amusing. **-ci·ness**, n.

sauer·kraut, n. shredded, fermented cabbage.

sau·na, n. Finnish steam bath; dry heat bath.

saun·ter, v. walk leisurely; stroll. n. aimless or idle stroll.

sau·sage, n. highly seasoned, chopped meat stuffed into a casing or formed into patties.

sau·té, v., **-téed, -tée·ing**. fry quickly in a little fat.

sav·age, a. wild; untamed; fierce. n. uncivilized person; barbarian; brutal person. **-ness**, n. **-ry**, n. pl., **-ries**.

sa·van·na, n. treeless plain, esp. in or near the tropics.

sa·vant, n. person with exceptional learning.

save, v., **saved, sav·ing**. rescue; keep; economize; accumulate; redeem. conj., prep. except; but.

saving, a. that which saves or rescues; frugal; qualifying; redeeming. n. economy; cost or time reduction; pl. money saved. prep. except or save. conj. except; but.

sav·ior, n. one who saves; (cap.) Jesus Christ.

sa·voir faire, n. tact; ability to do the right thing; poise.

sa·vor, n. flavor or smell; specific quality; relish. v. have a particular taste, flavor, quality; enjoy with pleasure. **-less**, a.

sa·vor·y, a., **-i·er, -i·est**. having an agreeable flavor and odor; palatable. **-i·ness**, n.

sav·vy, v. inf. understand; comprehend.

saw, n. toothed cutting tool. v., **sawed, sawed** or **sawn, saw·ing**. cut with a saw.

saw, v. past tense of **see**.

saw-toothed, a. having teeth.

sax·o·phone, n. woodwind instrument with conical tube and finger keys.

say, v., **said, say·ing**. speak; recite; state an opinion; utter; pronounce. n. right to speak; authority. adv. about.

say·ing, n. proverb; adage.

scab, n. crust on a wound or sore; nonunion worker; plant disease. v., **scabbed, scab·bing, scab·by**, a., **-bi·er, -bi·est**.

scab·bard, n. sword sheath.

sca·brous, a. difficult; rough; salacious.

scaf·fold, n. temporary elevated platform for workers and materials. **-ing**, n.

scald, v. burn with hot liquid or steam. n. scorch mark. **scald·ing**, a.

scale, *n.* device for weighing; thin plate, as on fish; progressive series; relative degree or size; *mus.* series of tones. *v.,* **scaled, scal·ing.** remove the scales from; flake; climb; measure by a scale; make to scale. **scal·i·ness,** *n.*

sca·lene, *a.* (triangle) having three unequal sides.

scal·lion, *n.* green onion; leek.

scal·lop, *n.* edible marine bivalve mollusk with radiating ribs and wavy outer edge. *v.* ornament with scallops. **scal·lop·er,** *n.*

scalp, *n.* skin and hair on top of the skull. *v.* cut the scalp off; resell tickets at profit.

scal·pel, *n.* small, sharp surgical knife.

scal·y, *a.,* **-i·er, -i·est.** covered with scales; flaky.

scamp, *n.* rascal; imp. *v.* work carelessly.

scamp·er, *v.* run quickly or in a frolicking manner.

scan, *v.,* **scanned, scan·ning.** examine; pass the eyes over quickly; examine with an electronic or radiological device. **-ner,** *n.*

scan·dal, *n.* discreditable, offensive event, action, etc.; disgrace; malicious gossip. **-ous,** *a.*

scan·dal·ize, *v.,* **-ized, -iz·ing.** offend; outrage; shock. **-i·za·tion,** *n.*

scant, *a.* scarcely sufficient; meager, **-y,** *a.*

scape·goat, *n.* one who bears the blame for others.

scar, *n.* mark of a wound remaining after healing; dent from damage or wear. **scarred, scar·ring,** *v.*

scarce, *a.* scant; unusual; rare. **scar·ci·ty,** *n.*

scare, *v.,* **scared, scar·ing.** frighten; alarm. *n.* sudden fright.

scare·crow, *n.* an effigy set up to frighten away birds from crops.

scarf, *n. pl.,* **scarfs, scarves.** broad band of cloth worn around neck, etc.; muffler.

scar·let, *n.* bright red color. *a.*

scar·y, *a.,* **-i·er, -i·est.** causing fright or alarm.

scathe, *v.,* **scathed, scath·ing.** criticize severely.

scath·ing, *a.* bitterly severe.

scat·ter, *v.* strew; throw loosely about; disperse; rout.

scav·enge, *v.,* **-enged, -eng·ing.** remove rubbish, etc.; search out useful material from amid refuse; salvage. **-en·ger,** *n.*

scene, *n.* landscape; surroundings; locale; view; part of a play; display of strong emotion; situation.

scen·er·y, *n. pl.,* **-ies.** natural view or landscape; backdrops for theater stage.

sce·nic, *a.* of natural scenery.

scent, *n.* smell; fragrance; perfume. *v.* be suspicious of. **-ed,** *a.*

scep·ter, *n.* staff; emblem of regal power; sovereignty.

sched·ule, *n.* timetable; list of details; timed plan; agenda. *v.,* **-uled, ul·ing.** plan for a date, event, or procedure.

scheme, *n.* plan; plot; design; graphic sketch or table. *v.* plot; lay plans. **schem·er,** *n.*

schism, *n.* division; separation; disharmony. **schis·mat·ic,** *a., n.*

schiz·o·phre·ni·a, *n.* mental illness characterized by withdrawal from reality and personality disintegration· **-phren·ic,** *a., n.*

schol·ar, *n.* person eminent for learning; student. **-ly,** *a.*

schol·ar·ship, *n.* learning; erudition; aid given to a student.

scho·las·tic, *a.* of schools, scholars, or education.

school, *n.* educational institution; group of fishes. *v.* teach or educate. **-ing,** *n.*

schoon·er, *n.* sailing vessel having two or more masts.

sci·at·ic, *a.* of the hip.

sci·ence, *n.* knowledge gained by systematic study and analysis; particular branch of knowledge; expertness. **-en·tif·ic,** *a.*

sci·en·tist, *n.* person learned in science.

scim·i·tar, sim·i·tar, *n.* curved-blade saber. Also **scim·i·ter.**

scin·til·late, *v.,* **-lat·ed, -lat·ing.** emit sparks; sparkle. **-la·tion,** *n.*

sci·on, *n.* child or descendant; cutting from a plant.

scis·sors, *n. pl.* cutting implement of two blades with handles movable on a pivot.

scoff, *n.* jeer. *v.* mock; deride.

scoff·law, *n.* flagrant violator of laws.

scold, *v.* chide; find fault; berate; rail. **-ing,** *n.*

sconce, *n.* wall bracket for candle or other light.

scoop, *n.* ladlelike implement; shovellike bucket attached to excavation equipment; amount taken up. *v.* take or dip out with a scoop. **-er,** *n.*

scoot, *v. inf.* dart; go quickly.

scoot·er, *n.* child's vehicle with a board set between two wheels and with a handle; motor scooter.

scope, *n.* extent; range; aim.

scorch, *v.* burn superficially; parch and discolor. **-er,** *n.*

score, *n.* total points made in a game; grade; twenty; line made with a sharp instrument. *v.,* **scored, scor·ing.** make a game point; grade; mark with cuts; orchestrate; keep score. **-less,** *a.* **scor·er,** *n.*

scorn, *n.* contempt, *v.* treat with contempt; despise. **-er,** *n.* **-ful,** *a.*

scor·pi·on, *n.* arachnid with segmented tail bearing a poisonous sting.

scotch, *v.* cut; quash.

scot-free, *a.* unhurt or unpunished; free from blame.

scoun·drel, *n.* dishonest person; rascal; villain. **-ly,** *a.*

scour, *v.* clean or brighten by hard rubbing; purge; search; move rapidly. **-er,** *n.*

scourge, *n.* a whip; punishment; affliction. *v.,* **scourged, scourg·ing.** whip; punish; afflict.

scout, *n.* person, plane, etc. sent out to observe and bring in information. *v.* act as a scout; search; explore; spy.

scow, *n.* flat-bottomed boat.

scowl, *v.* look gloomy, angry, or threatening. *n.* a frown; threatening look. **-er,** *n.*

scrag·gy, *a.,* **-gli·er, -gli·est.** rough; uneven; unkempt.

scrag·gy, *a.,* **-gi·er, -gi·est.** rough; lean; scrawny.

scram, *v.,* **scrammed, scram·ming.** *inf.* go away quickly.

scram·ble, *v.,* **-bled, -bling.** move quickly on all fours; struggle or scuffle to get; mix together. *n.* difficult climb; struggle for possession. **-bler,** *n.*

scrap, *n.* small piece; fragment; leftover food; refuse metal. *v.,* **scrapped, scrap·ping.** discard; fight; quarrel. *n.* discarded.

scrape, *v.,* **scraped, scrap·ing.** rub so as to smooth, abrade, or remove; grate or scratch; eke out. *n.* act, noise, or result of scraping; predicament. **scrap·able,** *a.* **scrap·er,** *n.*

scrap·ple, *n.* cornmeal cooked with scraps of pork and spices.

scrap·py, *a. inf.* competitive; tough.

scratch, *v.* mark the surface of; scrape; relieve an itch; strike out; scrawl. *n.* mark. **-y,** *a.,* **-i·er, -·est.**

scrawl, *v.* write hastily, or illegibly. *n.* scribble. **-y,** *a.,* **-i·er, -i·est.**

scrawn·y, *a.,* **-i·er, -i·est.** skinny, thin, and bony. **-i·ness,** *n.*

scream, *v.* utter a piercing cry, as of pain, etc. *n.* loud shriek. **-er,** *n.*

screech, *v.* shriek. *n.* shrill noise; harsh cry. **-er,** *n.*

screen, *n.* thing to shelter, conceal, or decorate; surface on which a picture is projected; fine metal mesh. *v.* protect; conceal; sift. **-er,** *n.* **-ing,** *n.*

screw, *n.* spirally grooved metal cylinder for turning into a surface. *v.* turn or twist; contort. **-er,** *n.* **-driv·er,** *n.*

screw·y, *a.,* **-i·er, -i·est.** *inf.* crazy; eccentric.

scrib·ble, *v.,* *n.* scrawl.

scribe, *n.* one who copies; public writer; author. **scrib·al,** *a.*

scrim·mage, *n.* skirmish; football play; fracas. *v.,* **-maged, -mag·ing.** struggle.

scrimp, *v.* use great economy. **-y,** *a.* meager; skimpy.

script, *n.* handwriting; text of a play or movie.

scripture, *n.* (*cap*) Bible; passage from the Bible; sacred writings. **-tur·al,** *a.*

scroll, *n.* roll used as a writing surface.

scrooge, *n.* stingy, miserly person.

scrounge, *v. inf.* forage; pilfer.

scrub, *v.,* **scrubbed, scrub·bing.** cleanse by hard rubbing; scour; cancel. *n.* stunted tree; mongrel; unimportant person; second team.

scrub·by, *a.,* **-bi·er, -bi·est.** low growth; stunted.

scruff, *n.* back of the neck.

scruff·y, *a.,* **-i·er, -i·est.** shabby; seedy; worthless.

scrump·tious, *a. inf.* elegant.

scru·ple, *n.* doubt about doing; ethical consideration; qualm. *v.,* **-pled, -pling.** hesitate at. **-pu·lous,** *a.* careful; conscientious.

scru·ti·nize, *v.,* **-nized, -niz·ing.** observe carefully; inspect in detail. **-niz·er,** *n.* **-ny,** *n. pl.,* **-nies.**

scu·ba, *n.* underwater breathing device.

scuff, *v.* shuffle; be roughened by wear. *n.* flat-soled slipper.

scuf·fle, *v.,* **-fled, -fling.** struggle roughly; shuffle. *n.* fight.

scull, *n.* propelling oar; racing boat.

scul·lery, *n.* room for kitchen work and storage.

sculp·ture, *n.* three-dimensional art form as figures, busts, etc. *v.,* **-tured, -tur·ing.** produce a sculpture. **-tor,** *n.* **-tress,** *n. fem.*

scum, *n.* impure matter on the surface of liquids; low people. **-my,** *a.,* **-mi·er, -mi·est.**

scur·ri·lous, *a.* grossly offensive; abusive. **-ril·i·ty,** *n. pl.,* **-ties.**

scur·ry, *v.,* **-ried, -ry·ing.** move quickly; scamper; hurry.

scur·vy, *n.* disease due to lack of vitamin C. *a.,* **-vi·er, -vi·est.** despicable.

scut·tle, *n.* hatchway; coal bucket. *v.,* **-tled, -tling.** sink (a ship) by making holes in the bottom; run hastily; scurry.

scythe, *n.* mowing implement with long curving blade.

sea, *n.* great body of salt water; ocean; heavy wave or swell.

sea·board, *n.* seacoast or shore.

seal, *n. pl.,* **seals, seal.** sea mammal, having four webbed flippers. **-like,** *a.*

seal, *n.* thing which closes or secures; impression or mark which authenticates, confirms, etc. *v.* fasten securely. **-er,** *n.*

seal·ant, *n.* substance (silicone wax, glue, etc.) for closing.

seam, *n.* line formed by the junction of any two edges; thin layer of rock or ore.

sea·man, *n. pl.,* **-men.** sailor.

seam·stress, *n.* woman whose occupation is sewing.

seam·y, *a.,* **-i·er, -i·est.** sordid; degraded; squalid. **-i·ness,** *n.*

se·ance, *n.* spiritualist session.

sea·port, *n.* harbor or port accessible to seagoing ships.

sear, *v.* wither; scorch. *a.*

search, *v.* explore thoroughly; examine; probe. *n.* searching. **-a·ble,** *a.*

search·ing, *a.* keenly penetrating; investigating thoroughly.

sea·shore, *n.* land bordering the sea; seacoast.

sea·sick·ness, *n.* nausea, etc. caused by motion of the sea.

sea·son, *n.* one of the four divisions of the year; a period of time. *v.* increase the flavor of; spice up; temper. **-al,** *a.*

sea·son·a·ble, *a.* suitable to the time; propitious; opportune.

sea·son·ing, *n.* process of making fit for use; condiment.

seat, *n.* thing for sitting on; part on which anything rests; site. *v.* furnish with seats. **-er,** *n.* **-ing,** *n.*

sea·way, *n.* ocean traffic route; inland waterway (for ships).

sea·weed, *n.* marine alga, plant.

se·ba·ceous, *a.* pertaining to fat; resembling fat.

se·cede, *v.,* **-ced·ed, -ced·ing.** withdraw formally from an organization. **se·ces·sion,** *n.*

se·clude, *v.,* **-clud·ed, -clud·ing.** keep apart from; isolate. **-clud·ed,** *a.* **-clu·sion,** *n.* solitude.

sec·ond, *a.* next after the first; inferior to another; being like another. *n.* coming after the first; sixtieth part of a minute. *adv.* in the second place, rank, etc. *v.* reinforce; assist; support; advance.

sec·ond·ar·y, *a.* of second rank; subordinate; derivative.

second-class, *a.* next below the first or the best; inferior.

sec·ond-guess, *v.* use hindsight in criticizing an action, decision, etc.; outguess.

sec·ond·hand, *a.* previously owned; not new; having been used or worn. **second hand,** *n.*

sec·ond-rate, *a.* inferior; mediocre; secondclass. **-rat·er,** *n.*

se·cret, *a.* not made public; hidden; remote; secluded. *n.* something hidden; mystery. **se·cre·tive,** *a.* **se·cre·cy,** *n. pl.,* **-cies.**

sec·re·tar·y, *n. pl.,* **-ies.** office worker who carries on another's correspondence, records, etc.; (*cap.*) business or government official. **-i·al,** *a.*

se·crete, *v.,* **-cret·ed, -cret·ing.** form and release; conceal; hide. **-cre·tion,** *n.* **-cre·tive,** *a.*

sect, *n.* body of persons united by philosophical beliefs; religious denomination. **sec·tar·i·an,** *a., n.* **sec·tar·i·an·ism,** *n.*

sec·tion, *n.* separate part or division; act of cutting; slice. *v.* divide into sections. **-al,** *a., a.*

sec·tor, *n.* separate part; a distinct part. **-to·ri·al,** *a.*

sec·u·lar, *a.* worldly. *n.* layman; clergyman not bound by monastic bonds.

sec·u·lar·ize, *v.,* **-ized, -iz·ing.** change from religious to civil ownership. **-i·za·tion,** *n.*

se·cure, *a.* free from danger; safe; stable; sure; reliable; dependable. *v.,* **-cured, cur·ing.** protect; guarantee; acquire; capture; make secure. **-ment,** *n.*

se·cu·ri·ty, *n. pl.,* **-ties.** state of being secure; surety; pledge of repayment; certificate of stocks, bonds, or notes.

se·dan, *n.* enclosed car.

se·date, *a.* calm; staid; composed; dignified. **-ness,** *n.*

sed·a·tive, *a.* tending to calm, soothe, esp. to allay nervousness. *n.*

sed·en·tar·y, *a.* accustomed to sit; inactive; not migratory.

sed·i·ment, *n.* matter that settles in liquids; dregs. **-men·ta·ry,** *a.* **-men·ta·tion,** *n.*

se·di·tion, *n.* incitement to revolt against lawful authority. **-tious,** *a.*

se·duce, *v.,* **-duced, -duc·ing.** lead astray; entice; induce to have sexual intercourse.

se·duc·er, n. **-duc·tion, -duce·ment,** n. **-duc·tive,** a. tending to seduce.

sed·u·lous, a. persistent; diligent. **se·du·li·ty,** n.

see, v., **saw, seen, see·ing.** perceive by the eye; visualize; look at; understand; inspect; visit; attend; discern. n. office of a bishop. **see·a·ble,** a.

seed, n. pl., **seeds, seed.** ovule of a plant; semen; source; offspring. v. sow; take the seeds out of.

seed·ling, n. very small or young tree or plant.

seed·y, a., **-i·er, -i·est.** abounding with seeds; inf. run-down; shabby. **-i·ness,** n.

see·ing, conj. since; considering.

seek, v., **sought, seek·ing.** go in search of; look for; ask for; try; request. **-er,** n.

seem, v. appear to be; feel as if; be apparent.

seem·ing, a. apparent. n.

seem·ly, a., **-li·er, -li·est.** becoming; proper; decorous; fitting. adv. appropriately. **-li·ness,** n.

seep, v. pass gradually through; drip out; ooze. **-age,** n.

se·er, n. prophet. **-ess,** n. fem.

see·saw, n. teeter-totter; back-and-forth change.

seethe, v., **seethed, seeth·ing.** boil; steep; be agitated, as by rage.

seg·ment, n. division; distinct part; section. **-men·tar·y,** a.

seg·re·gate, v., **-gat·ed, -gat·ing.** isolate; separate; set apart. **-gat·ed,** a.

seg·re·ga·tion, n. act of separating a race, social class, etc. from a larger group or society.

seine, n. large weighted fishing net. v., **seined, sein·ing.** fish with a seine.

seis·mo·graph, n. instrument for recording the intensity of an earthquake. **-mog·ra·pher,** n.

seize, v., **seized, seiz·ing.** take hold of suddenly or forcibly; grasp; capture.

sei·zure, n. sudden attack, as a heart attack; act of seizing.

sel·dom, adv. infrequently; rarely. a. infrequent; rare.

se·lect, v. choose; pick out. a. choice; excellent; exclusive. **-ed,** a. **-lec·tor,** n. **-lec·tion,** n. **-lec·tive,** a.

self, n. pl., **selves.** one's own person; distinct identity of any person.

self-as·sur·ance, n. confidence in oneself. **-sured,** a.

self-cen·tered, a. concerned exclusively with oneself.

self-com·mand, n. self-control.

self-con·fi·dence, n. confidence in one's own powers, abilities. **-dent,** a.

self-con·scious, a. embarrassed; ill at ease. **-ness,** n.

self-con·trol, n. self-restraint of one's impulses, etc. **-trolled,** a.

self-de·fense, n. defense of oneself, one's property, reputation, etc.

self-de·ter·mi·na·tion, n. free will; people's decision as to political status. **-min·ing,** a., n.

self-ev·i·dent, a. evident without proof. **-dence,** n.

self-ex·plan·a·to·ry, a. obvious.

self-ex·pres·sion, n. expression of one's own personality, individuality.

self-gov·ern·ment, n. autonomy. **-ing,** a.

self-im·age, n. one's self-concept.

self-im·por·tance, n. arrogance. **-tant,** a.

self-in·dul·gence, n. satisfying one's own desires. **-gent,** a.

self·ish, a. excessive concern for oneself. **-ness,** n.

self·less, a. unselfish.

self-made, a. having achieved success by one's own efforts.

self-pit·y, n. pity for oneself. **-ing,** a.

self-pos·sessed, a. composed; self-assured. **-ses·sion,** n.

self-pres·er·va·tion, n. protection of oneself from injury, etc.; instinctive drive to protect oneself.

self-re·li·ance, n. dependence on one's own abilities. **-ant,** a.

self-re·spect, n. proper respect for oneself, standing, position, etc.

self-right·eous, a. smug belief in one's own virtue; overly moral. **-ness,** n.

self-serv·ice, n. serving of oneself in a store, service station, etc.

self-serv·ing, n. tending to advance oneself, often at the expense of others.

self-suf·fi·cient, a. independent of the help of others. **-cien·cy,** n.

self-will, n. willfulness; stubbornness; obstinacy. **-willed,** a.

sell, v., **sold, sell·ing.** transfer to another for money; offer for sale; dispose of by sale; be on sale; betray one's trust. **-er,** n.

se·man·tics, n. pl. study of word meanings, changes. **-tic,** a.

sem·blance, n. similarity; outward, sometimes deceptive appearance.

se·men, n. sperm-containing fluid of male animals. **sem·i·nal,** a.

se·mes·ter, *n.* one of two periods into which an academic year is divided.

sem·i·an·nu·al, *a.* occurring twice a year.

sem·i·cir·cle, *n.* half of a circle. **-cu·lar**, *a.*

sem·i·co·lon, *n.* punctuation mark (;).

sem·i·con·scious, *a.* partly conscious; not fully aware. **-ness**, *n.*

sem·i·fi·nal, *a.* next before the last in a competition. *n. often pl.* next to the last match. **-ist**, *n.*

sem·i·month·ly, *a.* twice a month.

sem·i·nar, *n.* group of students engaged in advanced study; any group meeting to present, consider, or discuss special topics, *usu.* concerned with their vocation.

sem·i·nar·y, *n. pl.*, **-nar·ies.** school for the instruction of priests, ministers, etc. **-i·an**, *n.*

sem·i·of·fi·cial, *a.* partly official.

sem·i·pre·cious, *a.* gems not as valuable as precious gems.

sem·i·pri·vate, *a.* partly private.

sem·i·pro·fes·sion·al, *a.* taking part in a sport, etc. for pay but not on a full-time basis.

sem·i·skilled, *a.* partly skilled.

Sem·i·tism, *n.* any political, economic policy pertaining to Jews.

sem·i·trop·ics, *n. pl.* somewhat tropical; subtropics. **-i·cal**, *a.*

sem·i·week·ly, *a.* occurring twice a week. *n. pl.*, **-lies.** semiweekly publication.

sen·ate, *n. (cap.)* upper body of two-body legislature; legislating body. **-a·tor**, *n.* **-a·to·ri·al**, *a.*

send, *v.*, **sent, send·ing.** cause or enable to go; cause to be conveyed; dispatch; transmit; impel; emit. **-er**, *n.*

se·nes·cent, *a.* growing old; aging.

se·nile, *a.* of old age; weakened by old age, esp. in mental faculties. **se·nil·i·ty**, *n.*

sen·ior, *a.* older or elder, *abbr. Sr.;* higher in rank; longer in service. *n.* elderly person; member of the highest class in a college or high school.

sen·ior·i·ty, *n.* state of being senior; rights based on length of service.

se·ñor, *n. pl.*, **se·ñors. gentleman. -ño·ra**, *n.* lady. **-ño·ri·ta**, *n.* young lady.

sen·sa·tion, *n.* awareness due to stimulation of bodily organism; thing that produces excited interest.

sen·sa·tion·al, *a.* pertaining to sensation; shocking; thrilling; startling; exciting. **-ism**, *n.*

sense, *n.* sight, taste, hearing, etc.; feeling or perception; sound thinking; meaning. *v.*,

sensed, sens·ing. perceive; become aware of.

sense·less, *a.* unconscious; meaningless; without reason; stupid. **-ness**, *n.*

sen·si·bil·i·ty, *n. pl.*, **-ties.** power to receive sensations, experience emotion; delicacy of feeling.

sen·si·ble, *a.* having good sense, judgment; sensitive; reasonable; aware. **-bly**, *adv.*

sen·si·tive, *a.* able to receive sensations; highly responsive; of keen sensibility; reacting excessively; touchy; easily affected. **-tiv·i·ty**, *n. pl.*, **-ties.**

sen·si·tize, *v.*, **-tized, -tiz·ing.** make sensitive.

sen·so·ry, *a.* conveying nerve (sense) impulses; afferent. Also **-ri·al.**

sen·su·al, *a.* referring to the senses; lustful; lewd. **-i·ty**, *n.* **-ly**, *adv.* **-ize**, *v.*, **-ized, -iz·ing.** make sensual.

sen·su·ous, *a.* pertaining to or appealing to the senses.

sen·tence, *n.* group of words which conveys a complete thought; court judgment; decision; penalty. *v.*, **-tenced, -tenc·ing.** pass sentence on.

sen·ten·tious, *a.* short and pithy; terse.

sen·tient, *a.* possessing powers of feeling or perception.

sen·ti·ment, *n.* combination of feelings; attitude; maudlin emotion; thought behind something. **-men·tal**, *a.*

sen·ti·men·tal·ize, *v.*, **-ized, -iz·ing.** regard or treat with sentiment.

sen·ti·nel, *n.* sentry; guard. *v.*, **-neled, -nel·ing.** watch over.

sen·try, *n. pl.*, **-tries.** a guard; person to give warning.

sep·a·rate, *v.*, **-rat·ed, -rat·ing.** divide; set apart; keep apart; sever; cease living together. *a.* disjoined; distinct. **-ra·tion**, *n.* **-ra·tist**, *n.*, *a.* **-ra·tism**, *n.*

Sep·tem·ber, *n.* ninth month.

sep·tic, *a.* infective; putrid.

sep·ul·cher, *n.* tomb; burial vault.

se·quel, *n.* something that follows; result; continuation.

se·quence, *n.* arrangement of succession; continuity; series; effect or consequence.

se·quen·tial, *a.* following in sequence; consecutive.

se·ques·ter, *v.* place apart; seclude; withdraw; confiscate. **-tered**, *a.* **-tra·ble**, *a.*

se·quoi·a, *n.* gigantic coniferous evergreen tree; redwood.

ser·aph, *n. pl.*, **-aphs, -a·phim.** angel of the highest order.

ser·e·nade, *n.* evening music, *usu.* song of a lover beneath his lady's window. *v.*, **-nad·ed, -nad·ing.** entertain with a serenade. **-nad·er,** *n.*

ser·en·dip·i·ty, *n.* making fortunate discoveries accidentally.

se·rene, *n.* calm; untroubled; *(usu. cap·)* exalted. **-ness,** *n.* **-ren·i·ty,** *n. pl.*, **-ties.**

serf, *n.* person bound in the service of a landowner; any person in servile subjection.

ser·geant, *n.* non-commissioned officer; police officer.

se·ri·al, *a.* of a series. *n.* story presented in parts. **-ist,** *n.* **-ize,** *v.*, **-ized, -iz·ing.**

se·ries, *n.* succession of items or events; sequence.

se·ri·ous, *a.* grave; in earnest; important; weighty; sober; solemn. **-ness,** *n.*

ser·mon, *n.* discourse delivered by a clergyman; serious talk. **-ize,** *v.*, **-ized, -iz·ing.** preach. **-iz·er,** *n.*

ser·ous, *a.* of serum; thin and watery.

ser·pent, *n.* snake; treacherous person. **-pen·tine,** *a.*

ser·rate, *a.* having saw-like teeth. Also **ser·rat·ed,** *v.*, **-rat·ed, -rat·ing. -ra·tion,** *n.*

se·rum, *n. pl.*, **se·rums, se·ra.** the fluid part of the blood; fluid from blood of an immunized animal.

serv·ant, *n.* person who is employed by another for domestic duties; government employee.

serve, *v.*, **served, serv·ing.** wait on; furnish or provide; go through a term of service; perform official duty; attend; aid; suffice; promote. **serv·er,** *n.* **serv·ing,** *n.*

serv·ice, *n.* act of serving others; assistance; work of public servants; armed forces; religious worship. *a.* to or for service. *v.*, **-iced, -ic·ing.** maintain or repair; provide service.

serv·ice·a·ble, *a.* useful; durable; beneficial. **-a·bil·i·ty, -a·ble·ness,** *n.*

serv·ice·man, *n. pl.*, **-men.** member of the armed forces; repairman; maintenance man.

ser·vile, *a.* subservient; abject; submissive. **-vil·i·ty, -vile·ness,** *n.*

ser·vi·tude, *n.* slavery; bondage.

ser·vo·mech·a·nism, *n.* automatic control system.

ses·a·me, *n.* herb with seeds used for oil and flavoring.

ses·sion, *n.* sitting together of a court, legislature, conference, etc.; a meeting or series of meetings.

set, *v.*, **set, set·ting.** put or place; fix; regulate; adjust; assign; mount in a setting; curl, as hair; arrange; pass below the horizon; become firm or solid. *n.* number of things belonging together; social group. *a.* fixed; determined; settled; rigid; ready.

set·back, *n.* misfortune; reversal.

set·ter, *n.* long-haired hunting dog; person who sets.

set·ting, *n.* background; environment; surroundings of anything; gem mounting.

set·tle, *v.*, **-tled, -tling.** resolve; colonize; clarify; arrange for disposition; decide; pay, satisfy, or close; quiet; sink to the bottom; bring to a conclusion. **-tler,** *n.*

set·tle·ment, *n.* village; colonization; adjustment of a claim.

set-up, *n.* system or plan of operation; arrangement of machine(s), etc.; *inf.* easy to do.

sev·en, *n., a.* one more than six. **-enth,** *a., n.*

sev·en·teen, *n., a.* one more than sixteen. **-teenth,** *a., n.*

sev·en·ty, *n., a.* seven times ten. **-ti·eth,** *a., n.*

sev·er, *v.* put or keep apart; separate; dissolve a relationship. **-ance,** *n.*

sev·er·al, *a.* more than two but not many; separate; few; respective. **-ly,** *adv.*

se·vere, *a.*, **-ver·er, -ver·est.** strict or harsh; critical; grave; stern; difficult; plain; rigorous. **-ver·i·ty,** *n. pl.*, **-ties.**

sew, *v.*, **sewed, sewn** or **sewed, sew·ing.** unite with stitches; fasten; mend. **-er,** *n.* **-ing,** *n.*

sew·age, *n.* waste matter carried off in sewers or drains.

sew·er, *n.* underground conduit which carries off drainage and excrement.

sex, *n.* males or females collectively; either of the two groups into which reproductive organisms are divided; *inf.* sexual intercourse. **-u·al,** *a.* **-u·al·i·ty,** *n.*

sex·a·ge·nar·i·an, *a.* between sixty and seventy. *n.*

sex·tant, *n.* navigators' measuring instrument.

sex·tet, *n.* any group of six.

sex·tu·plet, *n.* one of six born at the same birth.

sex·y, *a.*, **-i·er, -i·est.** erotic; sexually exciting. **-i·ness,** *n.*

shab·by, *a.*, **-bi·er, -bi·est.** much worn; ragged; dilapidated; despicable. **-bi·ness,** *n.*

shack, *n.* shanty; crude hut.

shack·le, *n.* handcuff; manacle; fetter. *v.*, **-led, -ling.** confine; inhibit. **-ler,** *n.*

shade, *n.* dimness; thing to intercept light; degree of brightness of color; small difference, *v.*, **shad·ed, shad·ing.** screen from light; produce a darkening effect. **shad·ing,** *n.* **-less,** *a.*

shad·ow, *n.* semi-dark image produced on a surface by intercepted light; a remnant; a trace; one who follows. *v.* shade; darken; follow closely. **-like,** *a.* **-y,** *a.*

shad·y, *a.*, **-i·er, -i·est.** full of shade; *inf.* disreputable. **-i·ness,** *n.*

shaft, *n.* spear or arrow; pale; beam of light; column; axle; round bar; vertical passageway. **-ing,** *n.*

shag·gy, *a.*, **-gi·er, -gi·est.** having a long, rough growth; having a rough nap; fuzzy; unkempt. **-gi·ness,** *n.*

shake, *v.*, **shook, shak·en, shak·ing.** move to and fro or up and down; agitate; tremble or vibrate; weaken; totter; clasp each other's hand; disturb. *n.* act of shaking.

shake·down, *n.* thorough search; testing of something new, as a ship; *inf.* extortion of money.

shake·up, *n.* extensive change or reorganization.

shak·y, *a.*, **-i·er, -i·est.** not firm or solid; shaking; trembling; weak; unreliable. **-i·ness,** *n.*

shale, *n.* rock of slatelike, fine-grained fragile layers.

shall, *aux. v.*, **should.** used to indicate futurity, determination, resolve, obligation, etc.

shal·lot, *n.* green onion; scallion.

shal·low, *a.* not deep; superficial. *n. often pl.* shoal. **-ness,** *n.*

sham, *n.* hoax; pretender. *a.* counterfeit; false; fake. *v.*, **shammed, sham·ming.** make false pretenses.

sha·man, *n.* tribal priest; medicine man. **-ism,** *n.* a religion.

sham·bles, *n. pl.* slaughterhouse; place of disorder, destruction, confusion.

shame, *n.* painful feeling arising from guilt; unworthiness; impropriety, etc.; disgrace. *v.*, **shamed, sham·ing.** cause to feel shame; disgrace.

shame·ful, *a.* disgraceful; scandalous; indecent. **-ly,** *adv.* **-ness,** *n.*

shame·less, *a.* having no shame; brazen; immodest. **-ly,** *adv.* **-ness,** *n.*

sham·poo, *v.*, **-pooed, -poo·ing.** wash, as the hair; cleanse, as a carpet. *n.* cleansing compound. **-er,** *n.*

shang·hai, *v.*, **-haied, -hai·ing.** cause to do by deception or force; kidnap.

shank, *n.* the leg between the knee and ankle; cut of meat.

shan·ty, *n. pl.*, **-ties.** crudely built hut. **-town,** *n.*

shape, *n.* outward form, outline, or contour of a thing; figure. *v.*, **shaped, shap·ing.** give shape to; form; mold; modify. **shaped,** *a.* **shap·er,** *n.* **-less,** *a.*

shape·ly, *a.*, **-li·er, -li·est.** well-proportioned. **-li·ness,** *n.*

shard, *n.* fragment of a brittle substance.

share, *n.* one's portion; capital stock division; part. *v.*, **shared, shar·ing.** distribute in shares; use jointly.

shark, *n.* large, ferocious, marine fish; swindler; *inf.* an expert.

sharp, *a.* having a keen edge or a fine point; clear; distinct; harsh; clever; vigilant; abrupt change; mentally acute. *adv.* in a sharp manner; exactly. *n. mus.* tone one-half step above a given tone. **-ness,** *n.*

sharp·en, *v.* make or become sharp or sharper. **-er,** *n.*

sharp·shoot·er, *n.* skilled marksman. **-ing,** *n.*

shat·ter, *v.* reduce to fragments; break into pieces suddenly; damage; demolish. **-proof,** *a.*

shave, *v.*, **shaved, shaved** or **shav·en, shav·ing.** cut hair or beard by means of a razor; cut away thin slices; graze; scrape. *n.* shaving. **shav·er,** *n.* **shav·ing,** *n.*

shawl, *n.* loose cloth covering for the shoulders or head.

she, *pron.* pronoun referring to the female in question or last mentioned.

sheaf, *n. pl.*, **sheaves.** stalks of cut grain bound together; bundle; collection. **-like,** *a.*

shear, *v.*, **sheared, sheared** or **shorn, shear·ing.** cut or clip with a sharp instrument. **shears,** *n. pl.*

sheath, *n.* case for a sword; covering membrane; close-fitting dress. **-less,** *a.*

sheathe, *v.*, **sheathed, sheath·ing.** put into a sheath; protect or conceal. **-er,** *n.*

shed, *v.*, **shed, shed·ding.** emit, as tears; throw off; drop; repel; radiate. *n.* small, low building.

sheen, *n.* radiance; luster; brightness. *v.* shine. **-y,** *a.*

sheep, *n. pl.*, **sheep.** ruminant mammal for wool, meat.

sheep·ish, *a.* embarrassed; meek; timid.

sheer, *a.* transparent; pure; absolute; extremely steep. *adv.* completely; vertically. *v.* swerve. **-ness,** *n.*

sheet, *n.* large piece of cloth bedding; piece of paper; thin piece of any material, as metal, glass. **-ing,** *n.*

sheik, sheikh, *n.* chief of an Arab tribe; title of respect.

shelf, *n. pl.,* **shelves.** material set horizontally for holding articles; reef; shoal. **shelv·ing,** *n.*

shell, *n.* hard outside covering; external framework; projectile. *v.* remove from a shell, husk; bombard. **shelled,** *a.*

shel·lac, shel·lack, *n.* lac used for making varnish. *v.,* **-lacked, -lack·ing.** cover with shellac; *inf.* beat utterly.

shell·fish, *n. pl.,* **-fish, -fish·es.** crustacean or mollusk.

shell shock, *n.* combat fatigue.

shel·ter, *n.* anything which provides cover or protection; refuge. *v.* provide shelter for; protect.

shelve, *v.,* **shelved, shelv·ing.** place on a shelf; postpone; put aside; retire.

she·nan·i·gan, *n. inf.* trickery; mischief.

shep·herd, *n.* person who tends sheep; pastor. *v.* guard like a shepherd.

sher·bet, *n.* fruit-flavored, frozen dessert.

sher·iff, *n.* chief law enforcement officer of a county.

sher·ry, *n. pl.,* **-ries.** fortified wine.

shield, *n.* defensive armor carried on the arm; protection; badge. *v.* protect from danger.

shift, *v.* change from one position to another; exchange; manage. *n.* act of shifting; period of work. **-er,** *n.*

shift·less, *a.* lazy; inefficient.

shift·y, *a.,* **-i·er, -i·est.** changing; elusive; resourceful; tricky. **-i·ly,** *adv.* **-i·ness,** *n.*

shill, *n. inf.* one acting as a decoy.

shil·ly-shal·ly, *v.,* **-lied, -ly·ing.** hesitate; vacillate.

shim, *n.* thin wedge used to fill in a space.

shim·mer, *v.* shine with a tremulous light; glimmer; sparkle; flash. *n.* glimmer. **-y,** *a.*

shin, *n.* forepart of the leg between the ankle and knee.

shin·dig, *n. slang.* dance; noisy party.

shine, *v.,* **shone** or **shined, shin·ing.** emit light; beam; glow; excel; polish. *n.* luster. **shin·ing,** *a.*

shin·gle, *n.* thin piece of wood or other material used as a roof covering; woman's haircut. *v.,* **zb·gled,** *-gling.*

shin·gles, *n. pl. constr. as sing.* painful, inflammatory viral disease.

shin·ny, *v.,* **-nied, -ny·ing.** *inf.* climb, as a pole, using shins and arms.

shin·y, *a.,* **-i·er, -i·est.** glistening; polished; glossy. **-i·ness,** *n.*

ship, *n.* large seagoing vessel; aircraft; spacecraft. *v.,* **shipped, ship·ping.** transport by ship, rail, truck, etc. **-per,** *n.*

shipment, *n.* act of shipping; goods shipped; cargo; load.

ship·shape, *a.* trim; orderly.

ship·wreck, *n.* wreck of a ship. *v.* wreck a ship; ruin; destroy.

ship·yard, *n.* place where ships are built or repaired.

shirk, *v.* avoid doing something, as work, duty, etc. *n.* one who shirks. **-er,** *n.*

shirt, *n.* garment for the upper part of the body. **-less,** *a.*

shiv·er, *v.* shake; tremble; quiver; shatter. *n.* small piece into which a brittle thing is broken. **-ing, -y,** *a.*

shoal, *n.* place where water is shallow; sand bar; school of fish. *v.* become shallow.

shock, *n.* sudden collision or blow; sudden disturbance to the mind or body; concussion; nerve reaction to electrical charge through body. *v.* experience a shock; give an electric shock to; horrify; outrage. **-er,** *n.* **-ing,** *a.*

shod·dy, *a.,* **-di·er, -di·est.** inferior; cheap; nasty; vulgar. **-di·ness,** *n.*

shoe, *n. pl.,* **shoes.** external covering for the foot; horseshoe; braking device. *v.,* **shod, shod, shoe·ing.** furnish with shoes, metal plate, etc. **sho·er,** *n.*

shoe·horn, *n.* curved device to aid in putting on shoes.

shoe·lace, *n.* shoestring.

shoot, *v.,* **shot, shoot·ing.** fire a discharge; hit with a discharge; propel; photograph; put forth; dart; project. *n.* new growth; rapid.

shoot·ing star, *n.* meteor.

shoot·out, *n.* gunfight.

shop, *n.* store; workshop; factory. *v.,* **shopped, shop·ping.** visit shops to purchase or look at goods. **-per,** *n.*

shop·keep·er, *n.* tradesman.

shop·lift, *v.* steal goods from a shop. **-ing,** *n.* **-er,** *n.*

shop·worn, *a.* soiled, etc. from having been on display.

shore, *n.* land adjacent to water. *a.* of land. **-line,** *n.*

shore, *v.,* **shored, shor·ing.** to prop up, as a wall, with a timber. *n.* propping beam.

short, *a.* insufficient; not long; less than usual; lacking; curt; brief. *adv.* abruptly. *n.* deficiency; *pl.* short pants. *v.* cheat; short circuit. **-ness,** *n.*

short·age, *n.* deficiency; lack.

short·cake, *n.* sweet dessert biscuit served with fruit.

short·change, *v.,* **-changed, -chang·ing.** cheat.

short·com·ing, *n.* deficiency; defect; imperfection.

short-cut, *n., v.,* **-cut, -cut·ting.** (use) a quicker or more direct route or method.

short·en, *v.* reduce in length or duration; curtail; abbreviate; abridge.

short·en·ing, *n.* butter, vegetable oil, or other edible fat.

short·fall, *n.* failure to meet a requirement or expectation.

short·hand, *n.* abbreviated writing.

short·hand·ed, *a.* having an insufficient number of workpeople.

short-lived, *a.* living or lasting but a short time.

short-sight·ed, *a.* near-sighted; lack of foresight. **-ness,** *n.*

short-tem·pered, *a.* quick-tempered; easily angered.

short-wind·ed, *a.* becoming easily out of breath.

shot, *n.* act of shooting; pellet; missile; an attempt; cutting remark; *inf.* injection; jigger of liquor; snapshot.

shot·gun, *n.* double-barreled shoulder weapon; football formation. *v.,* **-gunned, -gun·ning.** coerce (as with a gun).

should, *aux. v.* past form of **shall,** used to show obligation, futurity, duty, probability.

shoul·der, *n.* joint connecting the arm with the body; projecting part; space bordering a roadway. *v.* assume a burden; shove.

shout, *n.* loud cry; outburst. *v.* utter with a shout. **-er,** *n.*

shove, *v.,* **shoved, shov·ing.** push; thrust; jostle; drive forward. *n.* push. **shov·er,** *n.*

shov·el, *n.* flattened scoop with handle for digging, etc. *v.,* **-eled, -el·ing.** take up and toss or turn with a shovel; dig.

show, *v.,* **showed, shown** *or* **showed, show·ing.** cause to be seen; display; explain; teach; guide; appear. *n.* display; performance; pretense; trace. **-ing,** *n.*

show·down, *n.* confrontation.

show·er, *n.* short fall of rain; similar fall, as of tears, sparks, etc.; bath in which water is sprayed on the body. *v.* spray; sprinkle; bestow lavishly. **-y,** *a.*

show·man, *n., pl.,* **-men.** one skilled in producing a show. **-ship,** *n.*

show·off, *n.* one who makes a pretentious display of himself.

show·y, *a.,* **-i·er, -i·est.** gaudy; striking; brilliant. **-i·ness,** *n.*

shrap·nel, *n.* shell fragments.

shred, *n.* strip torn off; fragment; scrap. *v.,* **shred·ded** *or* **shred, shred·ding.** tear or cut into small pieces. **-der,** *n.*

shrew, *n.* small, nocturnal insect-eating mammal; nagging woman. **-ish,** *a.* **-like,** *a.*

shrewd, *a.* astute; sharp; clever; wily. **-ness,** *n.*

shriek, *n.* sharp, shrill cry; screech. *v.* cry in a shriek.

shrill, *a.* high-pitched and piercing; strident. **-ness,** *n.*

shrimp, *n. pl.,* **shrimps, shrimp.** small, long-tailed crustacean; *inf.* small person.

shrine, *n.* place made sacred because of significant associations; receptacle; tomb.

shrink, *v.,* **shrank** *or* **shrunk, shrunk·en, shrink·ing.** draw back; recoil; contract; huddle; cower; diminish. **-age,** *n.*

shriv·el, *v.,* **-eled, -el·ing.** shrink and wrinkle; wither.

shroud, *n.* burial cloth; thing that conceals. *v.* enshroud for burial; veil or conceal.

shrub, *n.* low, woody plant. **-ber·y,** *n. pl.,* **-ies. shrub·by,** *a.,* **-bi·er, -bi·est.**

shrug, *v.,* **shrugged, shrug·ging.** draw up the shoulders, as in expressing doubt or indifference. *n.* shrugging.

shrunk·en, *pp.* of **shrink.** contracted and atrophied.

shud·der, *v.* tremble. *n.* convulsive shiver of the body.

shuf·fle, *v.,* **-fled, -fling.** move the feet without lifting them; shift; mix; jumble together. *n.* scraping movement; evasive act. **-fler,** *n.*

shun, *v.,* **shunned, shun·ning.** keep clear of; avoid. **-ner,** *n.*

shunt, *v.* turn aside; shift; switch; sidetrack; divert.

shush, *int.* be quiet. *v.* quieten.

shut, *v.,* **shut, shut·ting.** close; confine; fasten; enclose; bar. *a.* closed.

shut-in, *n.* invalid confined to home or bed. *a.* obliged to stay in; secretive; withdrawn.

shut·ter, *n.* cover, as for a window; movable camera part.

shut·tle, *n.* device in a loom, for passing thread from one side to the other; vehicle moving to and fro along a short route. *v.,* **-tled, -tling.** move to and fro. **-like,** *a.*

shy, *a.*, **shi·er**, **shi·est**, **shy·er**, **shy·est**. bashful; timid; less than needed. *v.*, **shied**, **shy·ing**. rear in fright; recoil; fling. **shy·ness**, *n.*

shy·ster, *n. inf.* dishonest lawyer; professionally disreputable.

sib·ling, *n.* brother or sister.

sick, *a.* not healthy; upset or ill; nauseated; tired of. *n.* those who are sick. **-ness**, *n.*

sick·en, *v.* make or become sick or disgusted. **-ing**, *a.*

sick·le, *n.* curved blade for use in cutting grain or grass.

sick·ly, *a.*, **-li·er**, **-li·est**. habitually ailing; languid; weak; disgusting. **-li·ness**, *n.*

side, *n.* surface or line bounding a thing; right or left side of human body; aspect; party. *a.* being at or on one side; incidental.

side·board, *n.* piece of dining room furniture in which silver and linens are kept.

side·burns, *n. pl.* whiskers on the sides of the face.

side·kick, *n. inf.* close friend.

side·line, *n.* extra line of goods; secondary work or job; boundary line of athletic field.

side·split·ting, *a.* extremely funny or uproarious.

side·step, *v.*, **-stepped**, **-step·ping**. avoid by stepping to one side; avoid responsibility.

side·swipe, *v.* strike or scrape along the side, as a car.

side·track, *v.* shift to a side track; deflect; divert. *n.* railroad siding.

side·walk, *n.* paved pedestrian walk.

side·ward, *adv.*, *a.* lateral; toward one side. **-wards**, *adv.*

side·ways, *adv.* toward or from one side; facing to the side. *a.* obliquely; askance.

sid·ing, *n.* side railway track; material used to cover the outer wall of buildings.

si·dle, *v.*, **-dled**, **-dling**. move sideways, esp. cautiously or stealthily. *n.* sideways movement.

siege, *n.* military blockade, persistent attack.

si·er·ra, *n.* range of mountains with jagged peaks.

si·es·ta, *n.* midday nap.

sieve, *n.* utensil with meshed wire bottom. *v.*, **sieved**, **siev·ing**. sift.

sift, *v.* pass through a sieve; examine carefully; select. **-er**, *n.*

sigh, *v.* emit a long, audible breath. **-ing**, *n.*

sight, *n.* faculty of seeing; vision; view or glimpse; range of vision; spectacle. *v.* see; aim. **sighted**, *a.*

sight·less, *a.* blind; invisible.

sight·ly, *a.* pleasant to the view.

sight·see·ing, *n.* act of visiting points of general interest; tourism. **-se·er**, *n.*

sign, *v.* write one's signature; engage by written agreement; signal. *n.* indication; symbol; advertising, directions, etc., publicly displayed; omen. **-er**, *n.*

sig·nal, *n.* any device, gesture, sound to give warning or information, etc. *a.* outstanding. *v.*, **-naled**, **-nal·ing**. make a signal to; communicate. **-er**, *n.*

sig·na·ture, *n.* billboard displaying information, advertising.

sig·nif·i·cance, *n.* meaning; consequence; importance. **-cant**, *a.*

sig·ni·fi·ca·tion, *n.* meaning.

sig·ni·fy, *v.*, **-fied**, **-fy·ing**. to represent; mean; suggest; make known. **-fi·er**, *n.*

si·lage, *n.* fodder; livestock feed.

si·lence, *n.* absence of sound; secrecy. *v.*, **-lenced**, **-lenc·ing**. bring to silence; suppress. **si·lent**, *a.*

si·lenc·er, *n.* device to muffle sound of firearm shot.

sil·hou·ette, *n.* dark solid outline of a thing against a light background; profile. *v.*, **-et·ted**, **-et·ting**. show in silhouette.

silk, *n.* soft, shiny fiber from the silkworm; thread or fabric made of this; *pl.* jockey's uniform. **-en**, *a.* **-like**, *a.*

silk·worm, *n.* moth larva which produces a cocoon of silk.

silk·y, *a.*, **-i·er**, **-i·est**. of silk; soft and smooth; lustrous; smooth or insinuating. **-i·ness**, *n.*

sill, *n.* horizontal piece at the bottom of the door, window, etc.

sil·ly, *a.*, **-li·er**, **-li·est**. foolish; senseless; frivolous; absurd. **-li·ly**, *adv.* **-li·ness**, *n.*

si·lo, *n. pl.*, **si·los**. pit or cylinder for storing grain.

silt, *n.* fine earth; deposit of sediment. **-y**, *a.*, **-i·er**, **-i·est**.

sil·ver, *n.* white ductile, metallic element; coins; flatware; shade of gray. *a.* of silver. **-y**, *a.*

sil·ver-tongued, *a.* eloquent.

sil·ver·ware, *n.* articles made of or plated with silver, esp. tableware.

sim·i·an, *a.* of or like apes and monkeys. *n.* ape or monkey.

sim·i·lar, *a.* like; resembling. **-i·ty**, *n. pl.*, **-ties**.

sim·i·le, *n.* figure of speech which compares things.

si·mil·i·tude, *n.* similarity; likeness; counterpart.

sim·mer, *v.* boil gently. *n.* simmering.

sim·per, *v.* smirk. *n.* silly, affected smile. **-er,** *n.*

sim·ple, *a.,* **-pler, -plest.** easy to do; not complicated; plain; ordinary; weak in intellect. **-plic·i·ty,** *n. pl.,* **-ties.**

sim·ple·ton, *n.* weak-minded or foolish person.

sim·plex, *a.* simple; single.

sim·pli·fy, *v.,* **-fied, -fy·ing.** make simple, or easier. **-fi·ca·tion,** *n.*

sim·ply, *adv.* in a simple manner; merely; candidly; plainly.

sim·u·late, *v.,* **-lat·ed, -lat·ing.** feign; sham; counterfeit; imitate. **-la·tion,** *n.* **-la·tor,** *n.*

si·mul·cast, *v.,* **-cast** or **-cast·ed, -cast·ing.** broadcast by radio and television simultaneously.

si·mul·ta·ne·ous, *a.* occurring or done at the same time; coincident. **-i·ty,** *n.*

sin, *n.* wickedness; transgression; misdeed; fault. *v.,* **sinned, sin·ning.** commit a sin. **sin·ner,** *n.*

since, *adv.* from a past time until now. *prep.* after a time past. *conj.* after the time when; because; seeing that.

sin·cere, *a.* without deceit; honest; real; genuine. **-cer·i·ty,** *n.*

si·ne·cure, *n.* position with pay but requiring little work.

sin·ew, *n.* tendon; power; strength. *v.* strengthen. **-y,** *a.*

sin·ful, *a.* wicked. **-ly,** *adv.* **-ness,** *n.*

sing, *v.,* **sang** or **sung, sung, sing·ing.** produce musical sounds with the voice; chant; intone. *n.* singing. **sing·er,** *n.*

singe, *v.,* **singed, singe·ing.** burn slightly; scorch. *n.* slight burn.

sin·gle, *a.* being the only one; unmarried; unique; solitary; for one person. *n.* one person or thing. *v.,* **-gled, -gling.** *baseball* make a one-base hit.

sin·gle-hand·ed, *a.* done or working alone; unassisted. **-ness,** *n.*

sin·gle-mind·ed, *a.* having only one purpose or end in mind.

sin·gle-track, *a.* having a limited scope, outlook; having one track.

sin·gly, *adv.* individually; one at a time.

sing·song, *n.* regular, rhythmical sounds. *a.* monotonous rhythm or rise and fall of the voice.

sin·gu·lar, *a.* remarkable; exceptional; individual; unique. *n.* singular number; word form denoting one. **-i·ty,** *n. pl.,* **-ties.**

sin·is·ter, *a.* malevolent; evil.

sink, *v.,* **sank** or **sunk, sunk** or **sunk·en, sink·ing.** go under the surface or to the bottom, as in water; go down slowly; descend; pass into some lower state. *n.* basin or receptacle; sinkhole; cesspool. **-a·ble,** *a.* **-er,** *n.*

sin·less, *a.* guiltless; innocent.

sin·u·ous, *a.* winding; undulating; devious; indirect. **-os·i·ty,** *n.*

si·nus, *n.* skull cavity, containing air.

sip, *v.,* **sipped, sip·ping.** drink in small quantities; taste. *n.* small draft. **-per,** *n.*

si·phon, sy·phon, *n.* tube used to convey a liquid up over a side to a lower level. *v.* draw off by means of a siphon.

sir, *n.* respectful term of address used for a man.

sire, *n.* male parent of a mammal; father. *v.,* **sired, sir·ing.** beget.

si·ren, *n.* seductive, enticing woman; device producing loud sounds for warning.

sir·loin, *n.* cut of meat from upper part of a loin.

sis·sy, *n. pl.,* **-sies.** *inf.* effeminate boy or man; coward.

sis·ter, *n.* female born of the same parents as another person; nun. **-ly,** *a.*

sis·ter-in-law, *n. pl.,* **sis·ters-in-law.** husband's or wife's sister; brother's wife.

sit, *v.,* **sat, sit·ting.** rest upon the haunches; be seated or situated; perch; pose. **sit·ting,** *a.,* *n.*

sit-down, *n.* strike where workers refuse to leave their work place until an agreement is reached.

sit-in, *n.* where a protest group occupies an area in an effort to accomplish some purpose or demand.

site, *n.* place; location; scene of an event.

sit·u·ate, *v.,* **-at·ed, -at·ing.** to place; locate; position. **-u·at·ed,** *a.* **-a·tion,** *n.* condition; status.

six, *n.,* *a.* five plus one. **sixth,** *a.,* *n.*

six·teen, *n.,* *a.* fifteen plus one. **-teenth,** *a.,* *n.*

sixth sense, *n.* keen intuition.

six·ty, *n.,* *a.* six times ten. **-ti·eth,** *a.,* *n.*

siz·a·ble, size·a·ble, *a.* relatively large; considerable. **-ness,** *n.*

size, *n.* dimensions of anything; relative measure; graded measure, as of shoes, etc.; degree or amount. *v.,* **sized, siz·ing.** make, classify, or arrange by size. **sized,** *a.*

siz·zle, v., **-zled, -zling.** make a hissing sound, from heat action; seethe with rage. n. sizzling sound.

skate, n. steel runner on a shoe for gliding over ice; wheels on a shoe; marine ray with broad fins. v., **skat·ed, skat·ing.** move on skates. **skat·er,** n.

ske·dad·dle, v., **-dled, -dling.** inf. flee; run away. n. hurried departure.

skeet, n. trapshooting with clay targets.

skein, n. fixed quantity of thread or yarn in a coil.

skel·e·ton, n. bony framework of the body; supporting structure; brief outline. a. **-tal,** a.

skep·tic, n. doubter; disbeliever. **-ti·cal,** a. **-ti·cism, scep·tic, scep·ti·cism,** n.

sketch, n. rough or undetailed short literary piece; rough draft; outline. v. make a sketch.

sketch·y, a., **-i·er, -i·est.** giving rough outlines; vague; slight. **-i·ly,** adv. **-i·ness,** n.

skew·er, n. long pin of wood or metal for fastening meat while roasting. v. pierce; fasten.

ski, n. pl., **skis, ski.** long, narrow runner fastened to boots for gliding over snow; water ski. v., **skied, ski·ing.** glide on skis. **ski·er,** n. **ski·ing,** n.

skid, n. sideslip; skidway; support platform; drag; landing gear runner. v., **-ded, -ding.** slip sidewards; slide. **-der,** n.

skiff, n. small, open boat.

skill, n. ability or proficiency; a trade or craft. **skilled,** a. **-ful,** a.

skil·let, n. frying pan.

skim, v., **skimmed, skim·ming.** take matter off from the top of liquid; move quickly, lightly; glance over. n. something skimmed off. a. skimmed. **-mer,** n.

skimp, v. scrimp. **-i·ly,** adv. **-i·ness,** n. **-y,** a. meager; scanty.

skin, n. external covering of the body; epidermis; hide or pelt; outer covering. v., **skinned, skin·ning.** strip of skin; peel; cheat; defeat. **skinned,** a. **skin·ner,** n.

skin-deep, a. only as deep as the skin; superficial.

skin·flint, n. stingy one; miser.

skin·ny, a., **-ni·er, -ni·est.** too thin; emaciated; lean.

skip, v., **skipped, skip·ping.** jump, or leap lightly; caper; bound; miss or disregard. n. hop and step gait.

skip·per, n. captain of a ship; any person in charge.

skir·mish, n. minor fight in war; brief conflict or argument. **-er,** n.

skirt, n. part of a dress, etc., that hangs from the waist down; anything like a skirt; outer edge. v. evade; border.

skit, n. short comic theatrical scene or sketch.

skit·tish, a. easily frightened; lively; playful; fickle.

skul·dug·ger·y, n. dishonesty; trickery.

skulk, v. sneak; lurk. **-er,** n.

skull, n. cranium; mind.

skunk, n. small, black-and-white mammal that emits offensive odor when scared; contemptible person. v. inf. defeat thoroughly.

sky, n. pl., **skies.** atmosphere or space above the earth; firmament.

sky·jack, v. hijack an airplane.

sky·lark, v. indulge in hilarious, boisterous frolic.

sky·light, n. window facing skyward.

sky·line, n. horizon; outline of buildings, trees, etc., against the sky.

sky·rock·et, n. rocket that is shot high in the air. v. rise rapidly, as prices.

sky·scrap·er, n. very high building.

slab, n. broad, flat, thick piece or slice, as of metal, stone, meat, etc.

slack, a. loose; negligent; weak; limp; slow. n. slack condition; period of inactivity. v. make or become slack. **-ness,** n.

slack·en, v. make slack; delay; slow up; loosen.

slacks, n. pl. trousers.

slag, n. cinder; residue from ore reduction; rough lava.

slake, v., **slaked, slak·ing.** quench; satisfy; crumble; hydrate; lessen.

sla·lom, n. zigzag ski course between upright obstacles.

slam, v., **slammed, slam·ming.** shut with a loud noise; strike, hit, or criticize violently. n. impact.

slan·der, n. false statement made about another. v. malign; defame. **-er,** n.

slang, n. colloquial words and phrases; informal vocabulary; jargon. **-y,** a., **-i·er, -i·est.**

slant, v. tilt; have bias; lean. n. incline; bias. a. sloping. **-ways,** adv. **-wise,** a., adv.

slap, n. smart blow; insult; rebuff. v., **slapped, slap·ping.** strike, esp. with the open hand; insult.

slap·hap·py, a., **-pi·er, -pi·est.** inf. punchdrunk; foolish.

slap·stick, n. comedy stressing farce and horseplay.

slash, *v*. cut violently; gash; make slits in; reduce sharply; criticize. *n*. sweeping stroke.

slat, *n*. thin, narrow strip of wood or metal; lath. **-ted**, **-ting**. *v*. **-ted**, *a*.

slate, *n*. rock that splits into plates; list of candidates. *v*., **slat-ed**, **slat-ing**. cover with slates; register; set down for nomination. **slat-y**, *a*.

slat-tern, *n*. slovenly woman.

slaugh-ter, *n*. act of killing; butchering; wanton killing. *v*. kill or butcher; slay; massacre. **-er**, *n*.

slave, *n*. person owned by another; person enslaved by a habit, as drugs; drudge. *v*., **slaved**, **slav-ing**. work like a slave. **slav-er-y**, *n*.

slay, *v*., **slew**, **slain**, **slay-ing**. kill violently; murder. **-er**, *n*.

slea-zy, *a*., **-zi-er**, **-zi-est**. lacking firmness of texture; cheap; shoddy; limp. **-zi-ness**, *n*.

sled, *n*. vehicle on runners for conveying over snow. *v*., **-ded**, **-ding**. coast, ride on a sled. **-der**, *n*.

sledge, *n*. heavy hammer; sled.

sleek, *a*. smooth and glossy; slick; suave. **-ness**, *n*.

sleep, *v*., **slept**, **sleep-ing**. period of inactivity and rest. *n*. state of sleep. **-er**, *n*.

sleep-y, *a*., **-i-er**, **-i-est**. drowsy; tired; somnolent. **-i-ness**, *n*.

sleet, *n*. partly frozen rain. *v*. fall as sleet. **-y**, *a*.

sleeve, *n*. part of a garment that covers the arm. **sleeved**, *a*. **sleeve-less**, *a*.

sleigh, *n*. light vehicle on runners drawn by horses over snow.

sleight, *n*. skill; cunning.

slen-der, *a*. slim; thin; small; meager; having small force. **-ness**, *n*.

sleuth, *n*. *inf*. detective.

slice, *n*. thin, broad piece cut from something; portion; share. *v*., **sliced**, **slic-ing**. cut into slices; divide. **slic-er**, *n*.

slick, *a*. sleek; sly; slippery; glib; trite; skillful. *n*. greasy place. *v*. make slick. **-ness**, *n*.

slick-er, *n*. raincoat; *inf*. clever, deceptive person.

slide, *v*., **slid**, **slid** or **slid-den**, **slid-ing**. glide over a surface smoothly; move past stealthily; slip from or to. *n*. sliding; chute; landslide; photographic plate. **slid-er**, *n*.

slight, *a*. small; trivial; scanty; thin; slim. *v*. disregard; neglect. *n*. discourteous act. **-er**, *n*. **-ing**, *a*.

slim, *a*., **slim-mer**, **slim-mest**. slender; slight; scanty; small. *v*., **slimmed**, **slim-ming**. make thin or thinner. **slim-ness**, *n*.

slime, *n*. soft, moist earth; muck; mucus. **slim-y**, *a*., **-i-er**, **-i-est**.

sling, *n*. slingshot; device for holding up an injured limb; device for lifting objects. *v*., **slung**, **sling-ing**. fling; hurl; suspend.

slink, *v*., **slunk**, **slink-ing**. move furtively, stealthily. **-y**, *a*., **-i-er**, **-i-est**.

slip, *v*., **slipped**, **slip-ping**. move smoothly; elapse; decline; pass; lose one's foothold; get away, escape, make an error. *n*. mistake; woman's undergarment; strip of paper.

slip-per, *n*. low, light shoe.

slip-per-y, *a*., **-i-er**, **-i-est**. surface allowing anything to slip easily; tricky; unreliable. **-i-ness**, *n*.

slip-shod, *a*. slovenly; careless.

slip-up, *n*. *inf*. mistake; oversight; mischance. **slip up**, *v*.

slit, *v*., **slit**, **slit-ting**. cut lengthwise; sever. *n*. slash.

slith-er, *v*. glide along a surface, snakelike. **-y**, *a*.

sliv-er, *n*. slender piece, as of wood, metal; splinter.

slob, *n*. *inf*. untidy person; boor.

slob-ber, *v*. let saliva dribble from mouth; drool; speak in gushy way.

slo-gan, *n*. catchword or phrase; motto. **-eer**, *n*.

sloop, *n*. boat with one mast.

slop, *n*. liquid refuse; slush. *v*., **slopped**, **slop-ping**. spill.

slope, *n*. slanting surface or line. *v*., **sloped**, **slop-ing**. slant.

slop-py, *a*., **-pi-er**, **-pi-est**. slushy; splashed with liquid; *inf*. careless; slovenly. **-pi-ness**, *n*.

slot, *n*. slit; narrow opening; niche; groove; place in a series. **-ted**, **-ting**, *v*.

sloth, *n*. laziness; indolence; arboreal mammal.

slouch, *v*. sit, stand, etc., in a drooping manner. *n*. drooping manner; incompetent person. **-y**, *a*., **-i-er**, **-i-est**.

slough, *n*. marsh; swamp; mire; shed dead tissue. *v*. shed or cast off. **-y**, *a*.

slov-en-ly, *a*., **-li-er**, **-li-est**. careless; untidy; slipshod.

slow, *a*. sluggish; not fast; gradual; stupid; not hasty. *v*. delay; make slow or slower. **-ness**, *n*.

sludge, *n.* mud; ooze; sediment.

slue, *v.* veer; slide; skid.

slug, *n.* slimy animal similar to land snail; bullet; metal disk; *inf.* drink of liquor; heavy blow. *v.,* **slugged, slug·ging.** strike heavily.

slug·gish, *a.* lethargic; lazy.

sluice, *n.* artificial water passage; flood gate.

slum, *n. often pl.* squalid section of a city. *v.,* **slummed, slum·ming.** visit slums, esp. out of curiosity.

slum·ber, *v.* sleep lightly. *n.* light sleep. **-er,** *n.*

slump, *v.* fail or fall suddenly; collapse; slouch. *n.* drop; decline.

slur, *v.,* **slurred, slur·ring.** pronounce indistinctly; disparage; belittle. *n.* slurred utterance or sound; disparaging remark.

slush, *n.* soft melting snow; mire. **-i·ness,** *n.* **-y,** *a.,* **-i·er, -i·est.**

sly, *a.,* **sli·er** or **sly·er, sli·est** or **sly·est.** ingenious; furtive; wily; underhand. **-ness,** *n.*

smack, *v.* make a quick, sharp sound; slap; strike smartly; kiss loudly. *n.* smacking of the lips; sharp blow; slap; noisy kiss.

small, *a.* little; trivial; ungenerous; diminutive; petite; unimportant; lowercase; mean; humbled; minute; miniature; tiny. **-ish,** *a.,* *n.*

small-mind·ed, *a.* petty; intolerant.

small·pox, *n.* acute contagious virus disease, marked by fever and rash that leaves scars.

small-time, *a.* unimportant.

smart, *v.* have a stinging sensation; suffer from hurt feelings. *a.* keen; stinging; having quick intelligence; chic; brisk; shrewd. **-ness,** *n.* **-en,** *v.*

smash, *v.* break in pieces; flatten; crush; strike violently. *n.* smashing sound; crash; *inf.* great success. **-ing,** *a.*

smat·ter·ing, *n.* superficial knowledge; a little bit or few.

smear, *v.* rub or soil with grease, dirt, etc.; slander; spread or apply. *n.* soiled spot; stain. **-er,** *n.* **-y,** *a.,* **-i·er, -i·est.**

smell, *v.,* **smelled** or **smelt, smel·ling.** perceive the odor of; have a scent or odor. *n.* sense of perceiving with the nose; an odor; faint suggestion. **-er,** *n.* **-y,** *a.,* **-i·er, -i·est.**

smelt, *n.* small food fish. *v.* melt or reduce ore to obtain metal; to melt or fuse.

smile, *v.* express pleasure, approval, etc., by turning the corners of the mouth upward. *n.* act of smiling. **smil·er,** *n.*

smirch, *v.* stain; smudge; defame; disgrace. Also **besmirch.**

smirk, *v.* smile in an affected manner; simper. *n.*

smite, *v.,* **smoted, smit·ten** or **smit, smit·ing.** strike (something) hard; kill.

smith·er·eens, *n. pl., inf.* small pieces; bits.

smock, *n.* loose outer garment.

smog, *n.* noxious mist of smoke, fog; haze. **smog·gy,** *a.,* **-gi·er, -gi·est.**

smoke, *n.* vapor resulting from combustion. *v.,* **smoked, smok·ing.** emit smoke; puff on a pipe, etc.; cure, as meat; force out. **smok·er,** *n.*

smoke·stack, *n.* chimney.

smok·y, *a.,* **-i·er, -i·est.** giving off much smoke; containing smoke. **-i·ly,** *adv.* **-i·ness,** *n.*

smol·der, smoul·der, *v.* burn with no flame; exist in a latent state; have suppressed emotions.

smooch, *v., n. inf.* kiss; neck.

smooth, *a.* even; flat; hairless; free from lumps or roughness; pleasant; suave. *v.* make smooth; mollify; calm. *adv.* evenly. **-ness,** *n.*

smor·gas·bord, *n.* Scandinavian buffet; variety of foods.

smoth·er, *v.* stifle; suffocate; cover closely or thickly; quell; blanket; hide. **-er·y,** *a.*

smudge, *v.* **smudged, smudging.** *v.* smear; soil; become soiled. *n.* smear; stain; smoky fire.

smudge, *n.* spot; smear; smoky fire. *v.,* **smudged, smudg·ing.** smear; make indistinct. **smudg·y,** *a.,* **-i·er, -i·est.**

smug, *a.,* **-ger, -gest.** self-complacent; self-satisfied; spruce; tidy; neat. **-ness,** *n.*

smug·gle, *v.,* **-gled, -gling.** convey illegally; import or export illicitly, secretly. **-gler,** *n.*

smut, *n.* sooty matter; obscene matter; plant disease. **-ty,** *a.,* **-ti·er, -ti·est. -ti·ness,** *n.*

smutch, *n.* smudge; soot.

snack, *n.* a light meal. *v.* eat between meals.

sna·fu, *n. inf.* confusion.

snag, *n.* sharp protuberance; jagged hole or tear; obstacle. *v.,* **snagged, snag·ging.** damage by or as by a snag; impede.

snail, *n.* mollusk having a spiral shell; sluggish person. **-like,** *a.*

snake, *n.* scaly, limbless reptile. *v.,* **snaked, snak·ing.** slither. **snake·like,** *a.* **snak·i·ly,** *adv.*

snap, *v.,* **snapped, snap·ping.** break suddenly with crackling noise; to bite or snatch; speak sharply; break under stress. *n.* sharp crackling sound; fastener operating with such a sound. *a.* done suddenly. *adv.* briskly. **-per,** *n.* **-pish,** *a.*

snap·py, *a.*, **-pi·er, -pi·est.** stylish; briskly cold; quick; lively. **-pi·ness,** *n.*

snap·shot, *n.* photograph.

snare, *n.* trap; lure. *v.*, **snared, snar·ing.** catch. **snar·er,** *n.*

snarl, *v.* entangle; growl or speak angrily;*n.* sharp, angry growl; complication; entanglement. **-er,** *n.* **-y,** *a.*

snatch, *v.* seize; grasp; take suddenly; *inf.* kidnap. *n. pl.,* **-es.** snatching; bit or scrap. **-er,** *n.*

snatch·y, *a.,* **-i·er, -i·est.** spasmodic; interrupted.

snaz·zy, *a.,* **-zi·er, -zi·est.** *inf.* stylish; fancy; elegant.

sneak, *v.* act furtively or slyly; move, put or pass in a stealthy manner; slink; lurk. *n.* one who sneaks. **-er,** *n.* **-y,** *a.,***-ier, -iest.**

sneer, *v.* scoff. *n.* look of contempt. **-er,** *n.*

sneeze, *v.,* **sneezed, sneez·ing.** expel breath forcibly by involuntary spasmodic action. *n.*

snick·er, *v.* titter. *n.* suppressed, derisive laugh.

snide, *a.* malicious, nasty.

sniff, *v.* breathe through the nose in short audible inhalations; smell with sniffs. *n.*

snif·fle, *v.* **-fled, -fling.** sniff repeatedly, as from a cold. *n.* sniffling.

snip, *v.,* **snipped, snip·ping.** clip or cut with a short, quick stroke. *n.* impertinent person; fragment.

snipe, *n.* game bird. *v.,* **sniped, snip·ing.** shoot from undercover; attack a person maliciously. **snip·er,** *n.*

snit, *n. inf.* state of irritability.

snitch, *v. inf.* steal; tattle.

sniv·el, *v.* run at the nose; act or speak whiny. *n.*

snob, *n.* one who snubs those he considers his inferiors. **snob·ber·y,** *n.* **snob·bish,** *a.*

snoop, *v. inf.* pry. *n.* one who pries or meddles. **-y,** *a.* **-ier, -iest.**

snoot·y, *a.,* **-i·er, -i·est.** snobbish; disdainful. **-i·ness,** *n.*

snooze, *v.,* **snoozed, snooz·ing.** *inf.* sleep lightly. *n.*

snore, *v.,* **snored, snor·ing.** breathe noisily while asleep. *n.* snoring. **snor·er,** *n.*

snor·kel, *n.* breathing device for underwater swimmer.

snort, *v.* force the breath violently and noisily through the nose; inhale a drug. *n.*

snout, *n.* muzzle; large nose.

snow, *n.* water vapor in frozen ice crystals. *v.* fall as snow. **-flake,** *n.*

snow·ball, *n.* round mass of snow. *v.* throw snowballs; multiply; gain in size.

snow·mo·bile, *n.* automotive vehicle for travel on snow.

snow·y, *a.,* **-i·er, -i·est.** abounding in snow; white.

snub, *v.,* **snubbed, snub·bing.** treat with contempt; slight. *a.* turned up.

snuff, *v.* extinguish; snort or sniff. *n.* sniff; powdered tobacco.

snug, *a.,* **snug·ger, snug·gest.** cozy; trim; close fitting; taut; neat. *v.* **snugged, snug·ging.** make snug. **-ness,** *n.*

snug·gle, *v.,* **-gled, -gling.** nestle; cuddle; draw close. *n.*

so, *adv.* likewise; in this manner; indeed; thereupon; thus. *a.* very well. *conj.* therefore.

soak, *v.* become saturated; submerge in liquid; steep; drench; take up. **-age,** *n.*

soap, *n.* compound used for cleansing purposes. *v.* rub with soap. **-y,** *a.,* **-i·er, -i·est.**

soar, *v.* float aloft; rise higher; sail or glide. **-er,** *n.*

sob, *v.,* **sobbed, sob·bing.** weep with convulsive catches of the breath. *n.* sobbing.

so·ber, *a.* not drunk; serious; solemn; rational. *v.* make or become sober. **-ness,** *n.* **so·bri·e·ty,** *n.*

so·bri·quet, sou·bri·quet, *n.* fanciful name; nickname.

so-called, *a.* commonly named or known as.

soc·cer, *n.* variation of football in which the ball is advanced by kicking without any hand use.

so·cia·ble, *a.* companionable; affable; friendly. **-bil·i·ty,** *n.*

so·cial, *a.* of society; relating to humans living in society; friendly. *n.* gathering. **so·ci·al·i·ty,** *n.*

so·cial·ism, *n.* social system with governmental ownership of the means of production and distribution of goods. **-ist,** *n.*

so·cial·ite, *n.* person prominent in fashionable circles.

so·cial·ize, *v.,* **-ized, -iz·ing.** adopt for the uses of society; put under group control; take part in social activities. **-i·za·tion,** *n.*

so·ci·e·ty, *n.,* **-ties.** an organization; persons with same language, culture, etc.; human beings collectively. **-tal,** *a.*

so·ci·ol·o·gy, *n.* study or science of human society and its relationships. **-o·log·i·cal,** *a.* **-ol·o·gist,** *n.*

sock, *n. pl.,* **socks, sox.** short stocking. *v. inf.* strike or hit; punch. *n.* hard blow.

sock·et, *n.* hollow part for receiving and holding some part or thing.

sod, *n.* grassy surface; soil; turf. *v.*, **-ded, -ding**.

so·da, *n.* compound of sodium; soft drink.

so·dal·i·ty, *n. pl.*, **-ties**. brotherhood or fraternity.

so·da wa·ter, *n.* water charged with carbon dioxide.

sod·den, *a.* soaked; soggy; unimaginative; dull.

so·di·um, *n.* metallic element essential for life.

so·di·um bi·car·bo·nate, *n.* baking soda; alkaline salt.

so·di·um chlo·ride, *n.* salt.

sod·om·y, *n.* anal sexual intercourse, esp. between males.

so·fa, *n.* upholstered couch.

soft, *a.* not hard or stiff; easy; docile; malleable; not glaring; gentle; mild. **-ness**, *n.*

soft·en, *v.* make soft; impair the strength of; alleviate; become less hard. **-er**, *n.*

soft-heart·ed, *a.* sympathetic.

soft-spo·ken, *a.* speaking softly; suave.

soft·ware, *n.* computer programs to control operation of the machine.

sog·gy, *a.*, **-gi·er, -gi·est**. soaked; damp and heavy. **-gi·ness**, *n.*

soil, *n.* earth; ground; land or region; spot or stain. *v.* make dirty; disgrace; defile.

soi·reé, soi·rée, *n.* evening party; social gathering; reception.

so·journ, *v.* stay or live temporarily. *n.* temporary stay. **-er**, *n.*

Sol, *n.* god of the sun.

sol·ace, *n.* comfort; alleviation of grief. *v.*, **-aced, -ac·ing**. divert; allay; soothe; relieve. **-ac·er**, *n.*

so·lar, *a.* of, by, or from the sun.

so·lar·i·um, *n.* glass-enclosed room or porch; area having overhead sun lamps.

sol·der, *n.* easily melted alloy for joining metal surfaces. *v.* unite with solder; meld; join. **-er**, *n.*

sol·dier, *n.* one who serves in an army; enlisted man. *v.* serve as a soldier.

sole, *n.* undersurface of the foot, shoe; etc.; flatfish. *v.*, **soled, sol·ing**. furnish with a sole. *a.* only; being the only one; solitary. **soled**, *a.*

sol·e·cism, *n.* mistake in using language; impropriety.

sole·ly, *adv.* as the only one or ones; wholly; merely; exclusively; entirely; only.

sol·emn, *a.* grave; serious; formal; sacred.

so·lem·ni·ty, *n. pl.*, **-ties**. solemnness; ceremonial observance. *usu. pl.*

so·lic·it, *v.* request; entreat; strongly urge; invite; ask. **-i·ta·tion**, *n.* **-i·tor**, *n.*

so·lic·i·tous, *a.* anxious; careful; apprehensive; eager. **-tude**, *n.*

sol·id, *a.* not hollow; neither liquid nor gaseous; not flimsy; having three dimensions; not interrupted; compact; firm; sound. *n.* matter that has a definite shape; three-dimensional figure. **so·lid·i·ty**, *n.*

sol·i·dar·i·ty, *n. pl.*, **-ties**. unity of purpose, interests, etc.

sol·id-state, *a.* using electric or magnetic properties of solid materials.

so·lil·o·quize, *v.*, **-quized, -quiz·ing**. talk to oneself. **-quy**, *n. pl.*, **-quies**.

sol·i·taire, *n.* single gemstone; any card game played by just one person.

sol·i·tar·y, *a.* remote; single; alone; the only one or ones; lonely.

sol·i·tude, *n.* state of being alone; remoteness; isolation; seclusion.

so·lo, *n. pl.*, **solos, so·li**. musical composition for a single voice or instrument; any performance by one person. *a.* alone. *adv.* unaccompanied. *v.*, **-loed, -lo·ing**. perform a solo. **-ist**, *n.*

sol·stice, *n.* point where sun is farthest from equator; June 22nd and Dec. 22nd.

sol·u·ble, *a.* dissolvable; capable of being solved. **-bil·i·ty**, *n.*

so·lu·tion, *n.* explanation; answer; combination of dissolved substances, *usu.* in liquid.

solve, *v.*, **solved, solv·ing**. work out the correct answer to; resolve.

sol·vent, *a.* able to pay all debts; capable of dissolving. *n.* substance that dissolves other substances. **-ven·cy**, *n.*

so·mat·ic, *a.* of the body.

som·ber, *a.* dark; gloomy; melancholy; grave; depressing. **-ness**, *n.*

som·bre·ro, *n.* Mexican hat.

some, *a.* of indeterminate quantity; not specific. *pron.* unspecified number or amount. *adv.* approximately.

some·bod·y, *pron.* person unknown or unnamed. *n. pl.*, **-ies**. person of consequence or importance.

some·day, *adv.* at some unspecified time; in the future.

some·how, *adv.* in some way.

some·one, *pron.* somebody.

som·er·sault, *n.* head-over-heels revolution of the body. *v.*

some·thing, *n.* thing not determined or stated; thing of importance.

some·time, *adv.* at some indeterminate time. *a.* former.

some·times, *adv.* at times.

some·way, *adv.* somehow.

some·what, *adv.* rather; slightly.

some·where, *adv.* in, at, or to some unspecified place.

som·nam·bu·late, *v.,* **-lat·ed, -lat·ing.** walk while asleep. **-list,** *n.*

som·no·lent, *a.* sleepy; drowsy.

son, *n.* male offspring.

so·nar, *n.* apparatus to detect submerged objects by sound.

song, *n.* vocal music; ballad.

son·ic, *a.* of or affected by sound waves; of speeds approximating that of sound. **-i·cal·ly,** *adv.*

son-in-law, *n. pl.,* **sons-in-law.** husband of one's daughter.

son·net, *n.* poem of 14 lines.

so·no·rous, *a.* giving out sound; loud and full-sounding.

soon, *adv.* in the near future; before long; promptly.

soot, *n.* fine, black carbon formed by incomplete combustion. **-y,** *a.,* **-i·er, -i·est.**

soothe, *v.,* **soothed, sooth·ing.** calm; placate; alleviate; relieve; comfort. **sooth·er,** *n.* **sooth·ing,** *a.*

sooth·say·er, *n.* person who claims to foretell the future; prophet; seer. **-ing,** *n.*

sop, *n.* wet mass; thing to pacify. *v.,* **sopped, sop·ping.** soak; absorb; dip. **sop·ping,** *a.*

so·phis·ti·cate, *v.,* **-cat·ed, -cat·ing.** make less natural or simple; refine; corrupt; disillusion. *n.* sophisticated person. **-ca·tion,** *n.*

soph·ist·ry, *n. pl.,* **-ries.** specious reasoning or argumentation.

soph·o·more, *n.* student in the second year of a high school or college.

so·pran·o, *n. pl.,* **so·pran·os, so·pran·i.** highest female voice; person who sings soprano.

sor·cer·er, *n.* magician; wizard. **-ess,** *n. fem.*

sor·cer·y, *n. pl.,* **-ies.** black magic; witchcraft.

sor·did, *a.* filthy; squalid; vile; miserly; mean. **-ness,** *n.*

sore, *a.,* **sor·er, sor·est.** painful; tender; *inf.* angered; vexed. *n.* injured flesh. **-ness,** *n.*

so·ror·i·ty, *n. pl. -ties.* women's organization with chapters at colleges, universities, etc.

sor·row, *n.* grief; sadness; contrition. *v.* grieve. **-ful,** *a.*

sor·ry, *a.,* **-ri·er, -ri·est.** feeling regret, remorse; worthless; mournful; pitiful.

sort, *n.* kind; variety; class; suit; set. *v.* classify; arrange. **-a·ble,** *a.* **-er,** *n.*

so-so, *a.* indifferent; mediocre. *adv.* tolerably; passably.

souf·fle, *n.* light, fluffy baked dish, with a sauce and other ingredients.

soul, *n.* spiritual entity of humans; seat of the feelings, emotions; a person; essential element. **souled,** *a.* **soul·ful,** *a.*

sound, *n.* any audible noise, tone, or vibration; narrow channel of water. *v.* make a sound; test the depth of water; try to determine the views of. *a.* solid; healthy; flawless; logical reasoning. *adv.* deeply. **-ly,** *adv.* **-ness,** *n.*

sound·ing, *n. often pl.* act of measuring water depth. **-er,** *n. a.* sonorous.

sound·less, *a.* making no noise; silent. **-ness,** *n.*

sound·man, *n.* man in charge of sound effects.

sound·proof, *a.* resistant to sound penetration. *v.* make soundproof.

soup, *n.* liquid food with meat, fish, or vegetables added; *inf.* fog. **-y,** *a.,* **-i·er, -i·est.**

sour, *a.* sharp, acid, or tart taste; morose; wrong pitch. *v.* turn or make sour; embitter. **-ish,** *a.* **-ness,** *n.*

source, *n.* origin; cause; place to secure information.

souse, *v.,* **soused, sous·ing.** dip or steep in liquid; drench; pickle. *n. inf.* drunkard.

south, *n.* point and region opposite the north. *a.* of, in, to, or from the south. *adv.* toward, at, or from the south. **-er·ly,** *a., adv.* **-ern,** *a.* **-ward,** *a., adv.*

south·bound, *a.* going or traveling toward the south.

south·paw, *n.* any left-handed person or player.

south·ern lights, *n. pl.* aurora australis.

South Pole, *n.* southern extremity of the earth's axis.

sou·ve·nir, *n.* token of remembrance; memento; keepsake.

sov·er·eign, *a.* supreme power; free and independent; exalted; excellent; very potent. *n.* supreme ruler; monarch; body of persons with sovereign power.

sov·er·eign·ty, *n. pl.,* **-ties.** state of being sovereign; a sovereign state.

So·vi·et, *a.* of the Union of Soviet Socialist Republics. *n. pl.* the Soviet people, esp. the officials.

Soviet Russia, *n.* Union of Soviet Socialist Republics; Russian Soviet Federated Socialist Republic.

sow, v., **sowed, sown** or **sowed, sow·ing.** scatter seed for growth; disseminate; propagate; implant (ideas). **sow·er,** n.

sow, n. adult female hog.

soy, n. dark, salty Chinese sauce from soybeans.

soy·bean, n. protein-oil-rich, leguminous plant.

spa, n. mineral spring; resort.

space, n. unlimited three-dimensional expanse of the universe; any portion of this; a specific area; reserved seat or room. v., **spaced, spac·ing.** set at intervals. **-less,** a. **spac·ing,** n.

space·flight, n. flight in outer space.

space·man, n. astronaut.

space·ship, n. vehicle for travel outside of the earth's atmosphere. Also **space·craft.**

spa·cious, a. large or ample extent; roomy; extensive. **-ness,** n.

spade, n. implement for turning soil; playing card suit; black inverted heart figure with stem. v., **spad·ed, spad·ing.** dig. **spad·er,** n.

spa·ghet·ti, n. flour paste cut in long strings; pasta.

span, n. space of time; extent, or reach of anything; 9 inch unit of length, space, or distance between supports of a bridge. v., **spanned, span·ning.** measure or extend across.

span·gle, n. small, sparkling foil or plastic ornament. v., **-gled, -gling.** adorn with spangles; glitter.

spank, v. slap, esp. on the buttocks. **-er,** n. **-ing,** a., n.

spar, n. mast, yard, or boom for a sail; derrick arm or beam. v., **sparred, spar·ring.** box; bandy words.

spare, v., **spared, spar·ing.** refrain from harming; use frugally; do without; refrain from using. a., **spar·er, spar·est.** kept as an extra; lean; scanty. n. extra thing. **spare·a·ble,** a.

spare·rib, n. cut of pork ribs closely trimmed.

spar·ing, a. scanty, slight; frugal; meager.

spark, n. ignited or fiery particle; small arc; trace; flash; glowing particle. v. give off sparks; activate; incite.

spar·kle, v., **-kled, -kling.** give off sparks; glitter; be lively; glisten. n. luster. **-kler,** n.

spar·row, n. small, plainly colored bird related to the finch.

sparse, a., **spars·er, spars·est.** thinly spread or scattered; scanty. **-ness,** n.

spasm, n. involuntary muscular contraction.

spas·mod·ic, a. intermittent; temporary; transitory; impulsive.

spas·tic, a. of, or characterized by spasm. n. person who has spasms.

spat, n. petty quarrel; splash. v., **spat·ted, spat·ting.**

spat·ter, v., n. scatter in drops; splash; spot; defame.

spat·u·la, n. implement with a thin, flexible blade.

spawn, n. eggs of fishes, mollusks, etc.; large quantity. v. deposit eggs; give rise to, as rumors; originate.

spay, v. remove ovaries from a female animal.

speak, v., **spoke, spo·ken, speak·ing.** utter words; talk; make a speech; express in speech; converse. **-a·ble,** a. **-er,** n., n.

spear, n. long, shafted weapon; sharp-pointed instrument with barbs. v. pierce; thrust. **-er,** n.

spear·mint, n. common mint.

spe·cial, a. uncommon; different; unique; having a specific function; memorable; beloved; additional; exceptional. n. **-ly,** adv.

spe·cial·ize, v., **-ized, -iz·ing.** concentrate on one particular activity or subject; make specific; adapt for some special use. **-i·za·tion,** n. **-ist,** n.

spe·cial·ty, n. pl., **-ties.** particular trade, activity, study, article, or trade, etc.; special quality.

spe·cies, n. pl., **species.** distinct kind; sort; variety; particular category of animals or plants.

spe·cif·ic, a. explicit; definite; of a special or particular kind; distinct; actual. n. **spec·i·fic·i·ty,** n. **spe·cif·i·cal·ly,** adv..

spec·i·fi·ca·tion, n. act of specifying; definite statement; usu. pl. description of dimensions, materials, etc.

spec·i·fy, v., **-fied, -fy·ing.** state explicit detail; designate.

spec·i·men, n. representative of a class; example; sample.

spe·cious, a. apparently good or right but without merit. **-ness,** n.

speck, n. small spot or stain; particle; fleck. v. spot; mark.

speck·le, n. speck. v., **-led, -ling.** mark with specks.

spec·ta·cle, n. grand, unusual sight or view; object of curiosity; public show or display; pl. eyeglasses. **-cled,** a.

spec·tac·u·lar, a. unusually wonderful; lavish display or production. **-ly,** adv.

spec·ta·tor, *n.* onlooker.

spec·ter, *n.* ghost; spirit.

spec·trum, *n. pl.*, **-tra**, **-trums.** band of wave frequencies, etc.; band of colors.

spec·u·late, *v.*, **-lat·ed**, **-lat·ing.** conjecture; ponder; theorize; make risky investments. **-la·tion**, *n.* **-la·tor**, *n.* **-la·tive**, *a.*

speech, *n.* power or act of speaking; conversation; talk; public address; language or dialect. **-less**, *a.*

speed, *n.* rapidity of motion; swiftness. *v.*, **sped** or **speed·ed**, **speed·ing.** accelerate the rate of; move with speed. **-er**, *n.*

speed·om·e·ter, *n.* device for indicating vehicle speed.

speed-up, *n.* accelerate.

speed·y, *a.*, **-i·er**, **-i·est.** swift; rapid; fast. **-i·ness**, *n.*

spe·le·ol·o·gy, *n.* exploration of caves. **-lunk·er**, *n.*

spell, *v.*, **spelled** or **spelt**, **spell·ing.** form words by letters. *n.* charm; *inf.* short distance; period of time, illness, etc.; turn of duty, work.

spell·bind, *v.*, **-bound**, **-bind·ing.** fascinate; enthrall; entrance. **-er**, *n.* **spell-bound**, *a.*

spend, *v.*, **spent**, **spend·ing.** disburse or pay out; apply time, effort; squander; pass (time). **-er**, *n.*

spend·thrift, *n.* one who is wasteful, lavish.

spent, *a.* exhausted; expended.

sperm, *n.* semen; male reproductive cell.

spew, *v.* vomit; eject or send forth. Also **spue.**

sphere, *n.* globe; celestial body; field of activity or influence, etc. **spher·ic**, *a.* **sphe·ric·i·ty**, *n.*

spher·i·cal, *a.* globular.

sphinc·ter, *n.* muscles which serve to open and close a body opening.

spice, *n.* aromatic substance used for flavoring; something that gives zest or relish. *v.*, **spiced**, **spic·ing.** season.

spic·y, *a.*, **spic·i·er**, **spic·i·est.** flavored or fragrant with spices; lively; somewhat risqué.

spi·der, *n.* eight-legged, wingless arachnid. **-y**, *a.*

spiff·y, *a.*, **-i·er**, **-i·est.** *inf.* spruce; smartly dressed.

spig·ot, *n.* faucet; plug.

spike, *n.* very large nail; sharp-pointed piece or part; ear, as of grain. *v.*, **spiked**, **spik·ing.** fasten with a spike; add alcohol; impale. **spiked**, *a.*

spill, *v.*, **spilled** or **spilt**, **spill·ing.** fall or run out or over; shed, esp. blood; cause to fall; flow out accidentally. *n.* spilling. **spill·age**, *n.*

spin, *v.*, **spun**, **spin·ning.** twist fiber into thread or yarn; produce, as a cobweb; whirl; gyrate; be dizzy; twirl. *n.* spinning; rapid movement, ride, etc.

spin·ach, *n.* plant with large, edible, fleshy leaves.

spi·nal, *a.* pertaining to the spine. *n.* anesthetic injected into the spinal cord.

spin·dle, *n.* rod on which something turns. *v.*, **-dled**, **-dling.** grow long and slender.

spin·dly, *a.*, **-dli·er**, **-dli·est.** of a slender, lank form.

spine, *n.* the backbone; pointed outgrowths, as on the porcupine; thorny projection (cactus); book back; projecting ridge; *inf.* inner strength.

spine·less, *a.* having no spine; invertebrate; weak-willed; irresolute; lacking courage.

spin·et, *n.* small, upright piano; small organ.

spin·na·ker, *n.* large triangular forward racing sail.

spi·nose, **spi·nous**, *a.* spiny, thorny.

spin·ster, *n.* unmarried woman; old maid.

spin·y, *a.* **-ier**, **-iest.** having spines; abounding with obstacles. **-i·ness**, *n.*

spi·ral, *n.* helix. *a.* winding about an axis in continually advancing planes. *v.*, **-raled**, **-ral·ing.** move higher through cyclical movements. **-ly**, *adv.*

spire, *n.* slender, tapering pinnacle; upper part of a steeple. *v.*, **spired**, **spir·ing.** **spired**, *a.*

spir·it, *n.* soul; supernatural being; energy; mettle or courage; mood; attitude; *pl.* feelings; *often pl.* alcoholic liquor. *v.* carry off secretly; encourage.

spir·it·ed, *a.* animated; lively.

spir·it·less, *a.* lacking enthusiasm, energy.

spir·it·u·al, *a.* of the spirit; incorporeal; of the soul; religious; sacred. *n.* religious song. **-ly**, *adv.*

spir·it·u·al·ism, *n.* belief that the spirits of the dead communicate with the living. **-ist**, *n.*

spir·it·u·al·ize, *v.*, **-ized**, **-iz·ing.** purify from corrupting influence. **-i·za·tion**, *n.*

spit, *v.*, **spit** or **spat**, **spit·ting.** eject saliva from the mouth; sputter; utter angrily. *n.* saliva.

spit, *v.* impale on a spit. *n.* pointed rod for holding meat; shoal.

spite, *n.* malicious grudge or ill will. *v.*, **spit·ed**, **spit·ing.** show malice toward; vex; thwart. **-ful**, *a.*

spit·fire, *n.* quick-tempered person.

spit·tle, *n.* spit; saliva.

spit·toon, *n.* cuspidor.

splash, *v.* spatter, wet, or soil by dashing liquid, mud, etc.; move, flail, or strike with a splash or splashes; display prominently. *n.* patch of color; something splashed. **-y,** *a.,* **-i·er, -i·est.**

splash·down, *n.* landing at sea of a spacecraft. **splash down,** *v.*

splat, *n.* thin, flat piece of wood; wet, slapping sound.

splat·ter, *v.* splash; spatter.

splay, *v.* spread out; bevel. *a.* spread or turned outward.

spleen, *n.* ductless, glandular organ which modifies and stores blood; ill temper.

splen·did, *a.* magnificent; imposing; glorious.

splen·dor, *n.* brilliance; pomp; grandeur.

splice, *v.,* **spliced, splic·ing.** unite, as two ropes, by intertwining the strands; to connect timbers by overlapping, etc. *n.* splicing. **splic·er,** *n.*

splint, *n.* stiff material used to immobilize a fractured bone; brace.

splin·ter, *n.* sliver; faction broken away from parent group. *v.* split or break into splinters. **-y,** *a.*

split, *v.,* **split, split·ting.** separate; break apart; share; leave; burst; tear; divide. *n.* crack; rupture. *a.* divided; fractured.

splotch, *n.* spot; blotch.

splurge, *n. inf.* showing off; extravagant expenditure. *v.,* **splurged, splurg·ing.** show off; spend lavishly.

splut·ter, *v.* make slight, explosive sounds; utter excitedly, confusedly; sputter.

spoil, *v.,* **spoiled** or **spoilt, spoil·ing.** damage; destroy; impair; become unfit for use; decay; rot. *n. often pl.* booty. **-age,** *n.* **-er,** *n.*

spoke, *n.* rod which braces a wheel rim; ladder rung.

spo·ken, *a.* oral; uttered.

spokes·man, *n.* one who speaks in the behalf of another. **spokes·wom·an,** *n. fem.*

sponge, *n.* water-dwelling animal having an absorbent skeleton; any material used for absorbing. *v.,* **sponged, spong·ing.** wipe, wet, or clean with a sponge.

spong·er, *n. inf.* one who lives off of or obtains something from others undeservedly.

spon·gy, *a.,* **-gi·er, -gi·est.** resembling a sponge; absorbent; rubbery; soft and full of cavities. **-gi·ness,** *n.*

spon·sor, *n.* one who acts as surety for another; godparent; firm paying for advertising on a TV or radio program. *v.* be or act as sponsor for. **-ship,** *n.*

spon·ta·ne·ous, *a.* arising naturally; without forethought; not planned. **-i·ty,** *n.*

spoof, *n. inf.* playful joke, hoax; deception. *v.* hoax; tease.

spook, *n. inf.* ghost; unattractive person. *v.* haunt; startle. **-y,** *a.,* **-i·er, -i·est. -i·ness,** *n.*

spool, *n.* cylinder on which something is wound, as thread.

spoon, *n.* eating utensil with a small, shallow bowl and handle. *v.,* take up in a spoon. **-ful,** *n. pl.,* **-fuls.**

spoon-fed, *a.* fed with a spoon; coddled; pampered.

spoor, *n.* footprints, droppings, traces of a wild animal.

spo·rad·ic, *a.* occurring infrequently; irregular; occasional.

spore, *n.* asexual reproductive cell of algae, ferns, fungi, etc. *v.,* **spored, spor·ing.** develop spores.

sport, *n.* diversion; athletic game or pastime; recreational activity; jest. *a.* of sport. *v.* amuse oneself; play; participate; jest. **-er,** *n.* **-ful,** *a.* **spor·tive,** *a.*

sport·ing, *a.* of athletic sports; fair; sportsmanlike. **-ly,** *adv.*

sports·man, *n. pl.,* **-men.** one who engages in field sports; one who abides by a code of fair play. **-like,** *a.* **-ship,** *n.*

sport·y, *a.,* **-i·er, -i·est.** *inf.* colorful; loud; flashy. **-i·ness,** *n.*

spot, *n.* mark; blotch; stain; particular place or locality. *v.,* **-ted, -ting.** soil; to place; to see. *a.* made at random. **-less,** *a.*

spot-check, *v.* sample or examine at random.

spot·light, *n.* strong, bright light beam. *v.* focus attention on.

spot·ted, *a.* marked with spots; stained; blemished.

spot·ty, *a.,* **-ti·er, -ti·est.** spotted; uneven; irregular; sullied. **-ti·ness,** *n.*

spouse, *n.* husband or wife.

spout, *n.* nozzle; lip; projecting tube for pouring a liquid; pipe. *v.* issue in a strong jet; discharge.

sprain, *v.* wrench or twist a ligament. *n.*

sprawl, *v.* sit or lie with limbs stretched out ungracefully; write stragglingly. *n.* sprawling position; disorderly spread.

spray, *n.* mist; liquid dispersed in small particles; device for spraying; small branch of flowers. *v.* apply as a spray; send forth spray. **-er,** *n.*

spread, *v.,* **spread, -ing.** extend; distribute in a layer; disseminate; open or unfold; be

spread, *n.* covering for a bed, etc.; food spread, etc. on bread; expanse. **-er**, *n.*

spread-ea·gle, *a.* having arms and legs spread wide apart. *v.* **-ea·gled, ea·gling.**

spree, *n.* period of heavy drinking, or fun and frolic.

sprig, *n.* shoot or sprout of a plant. *v.*, **sprigged, sprig·ging.** decorate with sprigs.

spright·ly, *a.*, **-li·er, -li·est.** vivacious. *adv.* spirited. **-li·ness**, *n.*

spring, *v.*, **sprang** or **sprung, sprung, spring·ing.** leap; dart; shoot; fly back or away; move or rise suddenly; flow; emanate; originate. *n.* leap; elasticity; elastic device; recoil; flow of water from the earth; season following winter. *a.*

spring·y, *a.*, **-i·er, -i·est.** elastic; resilient; spongy; lively.

sprin·kle, *v.*, **-kled, -kling.** scatter in drops or particles; rain slightly. *n.* sprinkling; small quantity. **sprink·ler**, *n.*

sprint, *v.* run fast. *n.* short run or race at high speed. **-er**, *n.*

sprite, *n.* elf; goblin; fairy.

sprock·et, *n.* tooth shaped projection on a rim to engage with a chain.

sprout, *v.* begin growth; put forth shoots. *n.* a shoot or bud.

spruce, *a.*, **spruc·er, spruc·est.** smart; trim. *v.*, **spruced, spruc·ing.** make oneself neat and trim.

spry, *a.*, **spry·er, spry·est** or **spri·er, spri·est.** agile; nimble; active. **spry·ness**, *n.*

spue, *v.*, **spued, spu·ing.** spew.

spume, *n.* froth; foam; scum. *v.*, **spumed, spum·ing.** to froth; foam. **spum·ous, spum·y**, *a.*

spu·mo·ni, *n.* layered ice cream with nuts and fruits.

spunk, *n. inf.* courage; mettle.

spunk·y, *a.*, **-i·er, -i·est.** *inf.* spirited; courageous.

spur, *n.* pricking instrument worn on a horse rider's heel; stimulus. *v.*, **spurred, spur·ring.** goad, prick with spurs; urge; hasten; hurry.

spu·ri·ous, *a.* not legitimate or genuine; false; counterfeit.

spurn, *v.* reject with disdain; scorn. *n.* **-er**, *n.*

spurt, *n.* sudden gush (liquid); sudden burst (energy, anger, etc.). *v.* gush forth; make sudden, strong effort.

sput·ter, *v.* throw off particles explosively; speak excitedly, incoherently. *n.* sputtering. **-er**, *n.*

spu·tum, *n.* spittle; mucus.

spy, *n. pl.*, **spies.** secret agent; observer; one who obtains secret information. *v.*, **spied, spy·ing.** act as a spy; catch sight of.

spy·glass, *n.* small telescope.

squab, *n.* young nestling pigeon.

squab·ble, *v.*, **-bled, -bling.** quarrel; bicker. *n.* petty dispute. **-bler**, *n.*

squad, *n.* small unit of soldiers; small group; a team.

squad·ron, *n.* military unit; assemblage of ships.

squal·id, *a.* filthy; wretched; foul; debased; sordid. **-ness**, *n.*

squall, *v.* cry loudly; scream. *n.* loud outcry; violent burst of wind. **-er**, *n.*

squal·or, *n.* poverty; wretchedness and filth.

squan·der, *v.* spend (money, time, etc.) wastefully. **-er**, *n.*

square, *n.* four-sided plane figure having all its sides equal. *a.* of or like a square; just; satisfying; settled; old-fashioned. *adv.* at right angles. *v.*, **squared, squar·ing.** make square; multiply, as a number, by itself; harmonize; balance. **-ly**, *adv.* **-ness**, *n.*

squash, *v.* squeeze or press; crush; suppress. *n. pl.*, **-es, squash.** pulpy food plant; court game played with racquet and ball.

squash·y, *a.*, **-i·er, -i·est.** soft and moist; muddy.

squat, *v.*, **squat·ted** or **squat, -ting.** crouch down; cower; settle on land without title. *a.* short and thickset. **-ter**, *n.*

squaw, *n.* American Indian woman or wife.

squawk, *v.* utter a loud, harsh cry; *inf.* complain. *n.* shrill harsh cry. **-er**, *n.*

squeak, *v.* utter small, sharp cry; make a sharp noise; win by a narrow margin. *n.* shrill cry or noise; narrow escape. **-er**, *n.*

squeal, *n.* prolonged, shrill cry or sound. *v.* complain; protest; emit a shrill sound; *inf.* turn informer. **-er**, *n.*

squeam·ish, *a.* prudish; easily disgusted; queasy.

squee·gee, *n.* implement for wiping liquid off a surface.

squeeze, *v.*, **squeezed, squeez·ing.** compress; extract by pressure; hug; force a way through. *n.* squeezing; embrace.

squelch, *v.* squash; *inf.* crushing reply. *n.* crushed mass; crushing retort.

squid, *n. pl.*, **squids, squid.** ten-armed marine animal.

squint, *v.* look with half-closed eyes. *n.* crossed eyes; side glance. **-er,** *n.*

squirm, *v.* wriggle; writhe. **-y,** *a.*

squir·rel, *n.* bushy-tailed rodent living chiefly on nuts.

squirt, *v.* come forth or eject liquid in a jet; spurt; wet. *n.* jet of liquid.

squish, *n.* a squashing sound.

stab, *v.*, **stabbed, stab·bing.** pierce or wound with a pointed weapon. *n.* thrust; *inf.* effort.

sta·bil·i·ty, *n. pl.*, **-ties.** steadiness; steadfastness; constancy.

sta·bi·lize, *v.*, **-lized, -liz·ing.** make or keep firm or steady. **-li·za·tion,** *n.*

sta·ble, *n.* building fitted for horses and cattle; one person's racehorses. *v.*, **-bled, -bling.** lodge in a stable. *a.* firm; enduring; unvarying; constant.

stack, *n.* pile or heap; smokestack. *v.* pile; arrange one above another. **-er,** *n.*

sta·di·um, *n. pl.*, **-di·ums, -di·a.** tiered structure with spectator seats for sports games.

staff, *n. pl.*, **staves, staffs.** stick for support or combat; cudgel; supporting pole; group of people working together. *v.* provide with personnel.

stag, *n.* male deer; man unaccompanied by a woman. *a.* for men only.

stage, *n.* step or degree in a process; raised platform in a theater. *v.*, **staged, stag·ing.** present on the theatrical stage; go by stages; produce for public view. **stag·ing,** *n.*

stage·coach, *n.* coach for passengers and mail drawn by horses.

stage-struck, *a.* longing to become an actor; fascinated by the theater.

stag·ger, *v.* reel; totter; place in alternating rows, groups, or times; amaze. *n.* unsteady gait. **-er,** *n.*

stag·nant, *a.* not flowing; motionless; stale. **-nan·cy,** *n.*

stag·nate, *v.*, **-nat·ed, -nat·ing.** become foul from lack of current; become dull, inactive. **-na·tion,** *n.*

stag·y, *a.* theatrical; affected.

staid, *a.* sober; grave. **-ness,** *n.*

stain, *v.* spot; bring shame upon; blemish; discolor; color. *n.* spot; dye. **stained,** *a.*

stair, *n.* flight of steps; a single step; *pl.* stairway.

stair·case, *n.* structure of stairs; flight of stairs. **stair·way,** *n.*

stake, *n.* sharpened piece of wood; execution post; a share in an undertaking; contest prize. *v.*, **staked, stak·ing.** mark the limits of; pledge; bet; hazard.

sta·lac·tite, *n.* calcium deposit originating from the roof of a cavern.

sta·lag·mite, *n.* calcium deposit formed on the floor of a cavern.

stale, *a.*, **stal·er, stal·est.** deteriorated from age; trite. *v.*, **staled, stal·ing.** make or become stale.

stale·mate, *n.* deadlock; chess position. *v.*, **-mat·ed, -mat·ing.** bring to a standstill.

stalk, *n.* plant stem. *v.* approach stealthily; walk with stiff, or haughty strides. **-er,** *n.*

stall, *n.* compartment for an animal; market booth. *v.* come to a standstill; delay. **stalled,** *a.*

stal·lion, *n.* uncastrated male horse; stud animal.

stal·wart, *a.* robust; muscular; strong; brave. *n.* partisan.

sta·men, *n. pl.*, **sta·mens, stam·i·na.** pollen-bearing organ of a flower; filament and sac.

stam·i·na, *n.* strength; endurance; staying power.

stam·mer, *v. n.* pause or falter while speaking; stutter.

stamp, *v.* imprint; affix a stamp to; strike heavily with the sole of the foot; eliminate opposition. *n.* mark imprinted; postage stamp; die.

stam·pede, *n.* sudden rushing or headlong flight; mass movement. *v.*, **-ped·ed, -ped·ing.** cause or engage in a stampede.

stance, *n.* style of standing; posture; point of view; attitude.

stanch, *v.* stop or check the flow of, esp. blood. **staunch,** *a.* **stanch·er,** *n.*

stand, *v.*, **stood, stand·ing.** assume or be in an upright position; have a location; set upright; endure; tolerate; fight back or resist; remain unchanged. *n.* halt; position; an attitude, etc.; *usu. pl.* raised platform; small table; a rack; stall.

stan·dard, *n.* flag or emblem; established criterion or measurement. *a.* serving as a standard; typical; normal.

stan·dard·ize, *v.*, **-ized, -iz·ing.** make, conform to, regulate, or test by a standard. **-i·za·tion,** *n.*

stand·by, *n. pl.*, **-bys.** reliable supporter; substitute.

stand-in, *n.* substitute person.

stand·ing, *n.* position or status; reputation; duration. *a.* in an upright position; for continued use; erect; stagnant.

stand-off, *n.* a draw or tie; a counterbalancing effect.

stand-off·ish, *a.* aloof; cool.

stand·point, *n.* viewpoint.

stand·still, *n.* a stopping; halt.

stan·za, *n.* division of a poem or song. **-ic,** *a.*

sta·pes, *n. pl.,* **sta·pes, sta·ped·es.** innermost small bone in the middle ear of mammals.

staph·y·lo·coc·cus, *n. pl.,* **-coc·ci.** a bacterium, often infective.

sta·ple, *n.* U-shaped wire fastener; necessary item, element; principal commodity of a country. *a.* chief. *v.,* **-pled, -pling.** fasten with a staple. **sta·pler,** *n.*

star, *n.* luminous celestial object; figure with five or more points; leading performer. *v.,* **starred, star·ring.** to star in an entertainment. **-less, -like,** *a.*

star·board, *n.* right-hand side of a vessel when one looks forward. *a.* referring to starboard. *v.* turn right.

starch, *n.* white carbohydrate in or from foods; preparation to stiffen fabrics.

stare, *v.,* **stared, star·ing.** gaze fixedly; glare. *n.* fixed, steady gaze. **star·er,** *n.*

star·fish, *n. pl.,* **-fish, -fish·es.** star-shaped marine animal with five or more arms.

stark, *a.* barren; bleak; severe; blunt; complete. *adv.* completely; utterly.

star·ry, *a.,* **-ri·er, -ri·est.** of a star; marked with stars; star shaped.

star·ry-eyed, *a.* visionary.

start, *v.* set out; commence; originate; startle. *n.* twitch; beginning. **-er,** *n.*

star·tle, *v.,* **-tled, -tling.** frighten or surprise suddenly. *n.* sudden surprise or fright. **-tling,** *a.*

starve, *v.,* **starved, starv·ing.** die or suffer from lack of food; cause to die of hunger. **star·va·tion,** *n., a.*

starve·ling, *a.* impoverished.

stash, *v. inf.* hide or conceal (money, etc.) for future use.

state, *n.* a condition; frame of mind; social status; nation; one of the territorial units of the U·S. *a.* of a state; for ceremonial use. *v.,* **stat·ed, stat·ing.** set forth; assert; declare.

stat·ed, *a.* asserted; fixed.

state·ly, *a.,* **-li·er, -li·est.** dignified; majestic; imposing; slow.

state·ment, *n.* something stated; listing of amounts due.

states·man, *n. pl.,* **-men.** man skilled and prominent in government. **-ship,** *n.*

stat·ic, *a.* fixed; showing little change; at rest. *n.* electrical interference.

sta·tion, *n.* assigned position; depot; social rank; standing. *v.* assign; position.

sta·tion·ar·y, *a.* fixed, not portable; exhibiting no change.

sta·tion·er·y, *n.* paper, pens, etc.

sta·tis·tic, *n.* datum; statistical fact; estimate.

sta·tis·tics, *n. pl.* study of data; branch of mathematics dealing with numerical data. **stat·is·ti·cian,** *n.*

stat·ue, *n.* representation that is carved, molded, etc.

stat·u·esque, *a.* resembling a statue, as in grace, etc.; shapely, comely.

stat·ure, *n.* natural height of a body; growth; status.

sta·tus, *n.* relative position or rank; condition.

sta·tus quo, *n.* existing state of affairs.

stat·ute, *n.* a law.

staunch, *a.* seaworthy; firm; steadfast; faithful; sound.

stave, *n.* piece of wood forming the side of a cask; rung; rod. *v.,* **staved** or **stove, stav·ing.** break or make a hole.

stay, *v.,* **stayed** or **staid, stay·ing.** remain; wait; abide; support; stop; postpone; restrain. *n.* time in a place; support; legal deferment.

stead, *n.* place assumed by a substitute or successor.

stead·fast, sted·fast, *a.* faithful; devoted. **-ness,** *n.*

stead·y, *a.,* **-i·er, -i·est.** firm; stable; unfaltering; regular. *v.,* **-ied, -y·ing.** make or become steady. **-i·ness,** *n.*

steak, *n.* cut of beef, fish, etc.

steal, *v.,* **stole, stol·en, steal·ing.** take dishonestly; pilfer; purloin; move stealthily. *n. inf.* theft; bargain.

stealth, *n.* secret action or behavior. **-i·ly,** *adv.*

steam, *n.* heated water vapor. *v.* emit or be covered by steam. *a.* driven by steam. **-i·ness,** *n.* **-y,** *a.*

steam·roll·er, *n.* heavy machine for flattening asphalt surfaces.

steam·ship, *n.* large ocean ship powered by a steam engine.

steam shov·el, *n.* power-operated machine for digging and excavating.

steed, *n.* horse, esp. a spirited horse.

steel, *n.* various alloys of iron and carbon; made of steel. *a.* of steel; strong. *v.* make strong; harden. **-y,** *a.,* **-i·er, -i·est.** of or resembling steel.

steep, *a.* sloping sharply; precipitous; *inf.* high (price); expensive. *v.* soak; imbue. **-ness,** *n.* **-en,** *v.*

stee·ple, *n.* lofty structure above a church, *usu.* spired.

steer, *v.* guide; control; direct. *inf.* castrated bovine.

steer·age, *n.* part of a ship for passengers paying the lowest rate.

stein, *n.* a beer mug.

stel·lar, *a.* of or pertaining to stars; astral; chief; principal.

stem, *n.* plant stalk; slender part; root of a word. *v.,* **stemmed, stem·ming.** remove the stems from; be derived; make headway. **stem·less,** *a.* **stemmed,** *a.*

stench, *n.* foul odor. **-y,** *a.*

sten·cil, *n.* pierced sheet of metal, etc., for reproducing letters, etc. by applying paint, etc. *v.,* **-ciled, -cil·ing.**

ste·nog·ra·phy, *n.* shorthand; rapid writing. **-pher,** *n.*

sten·to·ri·an, *a.* very loud.

step, *n.* one movement of the foot ahead or back; grade or degree; a single action; footprint; support for the foot, as a stair. *v.,* **stepped, step·ping.** take a step; act quickly; tread.

step·broth·er, *n.* son of one's stepparent by a former marriage.

step·child, *n. pl.,* **-chil·dren.** child of one's spouse by a former marriage.

step·daugh·ter, *n.* daughter of one's spouse by a former marriage.

step·fa·ther, *n.* husband of one's remarried mother.

step·lad·der, *n.* ladder having four legs and flat steps.

step·moth·er, *n.* wife of one's remarried father.

step·par·ent, *n.* a stepfather or stepmother.

steppe, *n.* extensive plain.

stepped-up, *a. inf.* speeded up.

step·sis·ter, *n.* one's stepparent's daughter by a former marriage.

step·son, *n.* son of one's spouse by a former marriage.

step-up, *a.* increasing by stages. *n.* an increase, as in intensity, amount, etc.

ster·e·o·phon·ic, *a.* system of sound reproduction in which two channels present different sounds.

ster·e·o·type, *n.* metal printing plate; a conventional, hackneyed expression.

ster·ile, *a.* containing no germs; barren; impotent; infertile. **ste·ril·i·ty,** *n.*

ster·i·lize, *v.,* **-lized, -liz·ing.** make incapable of reproduction; free from germs. **-li·za·tion, -li·zer,** *n.*

ster·ling, *a.* of English money; of silver; having great worth.

stern, *a.* severe; harsh; austere. *n.* rear part of a ship. *adv.* **-ly,** *adv.* **-ness,** *n.*

ster·oid, *n.* sterol and hormone compound.

stet, *v.* proofreading direction meaning let it stand or remain as is.

steth·o·scope, *n.* instrument used to detect body sounds.

ste·ve·dore, *n.* person who loads or unloads ships. *v.,* **-dored, -dor·ing.** load or unload a ship.

stew, *v.* boil slowly and gently; *inf.* to worry. *n.*

stew·ard, *n.* manager; person who serves. **-ess,** *n. fem.*

stick, *n.* long, thin piece of wood; broken branch; rod. *v.,* **stuck, stick·ing.** pierce; attach; cling; stay close; adhere.

stick·ler, *n.* one who insists on exacting standards; baffling problem.

stick-up, stick·up, *n. inf.* holdup.

stick·y, *a.,* **-i·er, -i·est.** adhesive; warm and humid. **-i·ness,** *n.*

stiff, *a.* rigid; not supple; constrained; not graceful; taut; thick; not relaxed; difficult; potent. *n. inf.* corpse. **-ly,** *adv.* **-ness,** *n.* **-en,** *v.*

sti·fle, *v.,* **-fled, -fling.** suppress; suffocate. **-fler,** *n.* **-fling,** *a.*

stig·ma, *n. pl.,* **-mas, -ma·ta.** mark of disgrace; flower part.

sti·let·to, *n. pl.,* **-tos, toes.** small dagger with slender blade.

still, *a.* sedentary; calm; motionless; silent. *v.* hush; silence; allay. *n.* distilling apparatus. *adv.* continuously; nonetheless; yet. **-ness,** *n.*

still·born, *a.* dead at birth.

stilt, *n.* pillar used to support a structure; pole to elevate wearer.

stilt·ed, *a.* excessively formal.

stim·u·lant, *n.* that which stimulates vital functions or actions.

stim·u·late, *v.,* **-lat·ed, -lat·ing.** excite; arouse; animate; give an incentive. **-la·tion,** *n.*

stim·u·lus, *n. pl.,* **-li.** incitement; stimulant; incentive.

sting, *v.,* **stung, sting·ing.** prick painfully, as a bee sting; cause mental suffering; *inf.* overcharge. *n.* stinging; sharp-pointed organ of insects. **-er,** *n.*

stin·gy, *a.,* **-gi·er, -gi·est.** miserly; scanty; penurious; niggardly.

stink, *v.,* **stank** or **stunk, stunk, -ing.** emit foul odor. *n.* strong, foul odor; stench. **-y,** *a.,* **-i·er, -i·est.**

stint, *v.* limit; be frugal. *n.* specific task assigned; restraint. **-er,** *n.*

sti·pend, *n.* regular salary.

stip·u·late, *v.,* **-lat·ed, -lat·ing.** specify as a condition or requirement, as in a contract. **-la·tion,** *n.*

stir, *v.,* **stirred, stir·ring.** mix; cause to move; agitate; rouse. *n.* stirring; movement.

stir·ring, *a.* active; stimulating.

stir·rup, *n.* strap and loop hanging from a saddle for the foot.

stitch, *v.* sew. *n.* single pass of the needle in sewing, etc.; sudden, sharp pain. **-er,** *n.*

stock, *n.* transferable share of a company; goods on hand; raw materials; horses, cattle, etc.; main stem; broth; lineage; race. *v.* supply with; keep; accumulate. *a.* kept on hand; in a common place. **-brok·er,** *n.* one who trades in stocks for others.

stock·ade, *n.* barrier made with posts and stakes; enclosure. *v.,* **-ad·ed, -ad·ing.** fortify with a stockade.

stock·hold·er, *n.* holder of shares of stock in a company.

stock·ing, *n.* covering for the foot and leg; *pl.* hose.

stock mar·ket, *n.* place where stocks are bought and sold.

stock·pile, *n.* accumulation of supplies. *v.,* **-piled, pil·ing.** accumulate a supply.

stock·y, *a.,* **-i·er, -i·est.** short and stout; thickset. **-i·ness,** *n.*

stodg·y, *a.,* **-i·er, -i·est.** dull and boring; heavy; old-fashioned.

sto·ic, *n.* person unmoved by joy or pain. *a.* impassive.

stoke, *v.,* **stoked, stok·ing.** supply with fuel, as a fire; stir up; intensify. **stok·er,** *n.*

stole, *n.* hanging vestment; fur or scarf for shoulders.

stol·id, *a.* unexcitable; unemotional; impassive. **sto·lid·i·ty,** *n.*

stom·ach, *n.* principal organ of digestion. *v.* bear; digest.

stomp, *v.* stamp; tread on.

stone, *n.* rock; hard mineral matter. *v.,* **stoned, ston·ing.** hurl stones at.

stone·wall, *v.* act obstructively.

ston·y, ston·ey, *a.,* **-i·er, -i·est.** abounding in stone; like stone; unfeeling. **-i·ness,** *n.*

stooge, *n. inf.* straight man; a dupe.

stool, *n.* backless, armless seat for one person; toilet; bowel discharge.

stoop, *v.* bend forward from an erect position; deign; lower oneself. *n.* shoulder slouch; small porch.

stop, *v.,* **stopped, stop·ping.** halt; prevent; restrain; cease; tarry; stanch; sojourn. *n.* standstill; stay; plug; obstacle. **stop·page,** *n.* **stop·per,** *n.*

stop·gap, *n.* temporary or makeshift expedient; substitute.

stor·age, *n.* storing; space for stored goods.

store, *n.* a shop; supply or stock. *v.,* **stored, stor·ing.** supply; stock; accumulate. **store·house,** *n.* warehouse.

sto·ried, sto·reyed, *a.* having stories; notable history.

stork, *n.* large, tall wading bird.

storm, *n.* heavy fall of rain, snow, etc.; atmospheric outburst. *v.* blow, rain, etc., with violence; rage; to attack.

storm·y, *a.,* **-i·er, -i·est.** turbulent; tempestuous. **-i·ness,** *n.*

sto·ry, *n. pl.,* **-ries.** narrative; account of; article; floor of a building; *inf.* lie. **-ried,** *a.*

stout, *a.* fat; thickset; courageous; brave; solid; firm. **-ness,** *n.*

stout-heart·ed, *a.* courageous.

stove, *n.* apparatus, *usu.* metal, for cooking or heating.

stow, *v.* place or arrange compactly; pack. **stow·age,** *n.*

stow·a·way, *n.* one who conceals himself on a ship, etc.

strad·dle, *v.,* **-dled, -dling.** stand, walk, or sit with legs spread apart; appear to favor both sides. **-dler,** *n.*

strafe, *v.,* **strafed, straf·ing.** bomb heavily; fire upon.

strag·gle, *v.,* **-gled, -gling.** stray; wander about. **-gler,** *n.*

straight, *a.* without curve or bend, etc.; direct; honest; erect; uninterrupted. *n.* straight piece; in a straight line; directly; without delay. **-ness,** *n.*

straight·en, *v.* make or become straight; put in order. *n.*

straight·for·ward, *a.* honest; candid; go in a straight course.

straight·way, *adv.* immediately.

strain, *n.* trace; kind; lineage; stress; sprain. *v.* draw tight; stretch to the utmost; filter; strive; overexert. **-er,** *n.*

strait, *n.* narrow passage of water; *often pl.* distress; need.

strait·jack·et, *n.* jacket for restricting a violent person or prisoner; anything that restricts.

strait-laced, *a.* strict in morals or in manners; prudish.

strand, *n.* shore; fiber, wire, etc. twisted together to form rope, etc. *v.* run aground; leave helpless or isolated.

strange, *a.,* **strang·er, strang·est.** peculiar; foreign; unfamiliar; unknown; odd. **-ness,** *n.*

stran·ger, *n.* one not known; foreigner; outsider.

stran·gle, *v.,* **-gled, -gling.** choke to death; repress; suppress; die by choking. **-gler,** *n.* **-gu·la·tion,** *n.*

stran·gle-hold, *n.* anything that chokes freedom or progress.

strap, *n.* narrow strip of leather, etc., for binding or holding. *v.,* **strapped, strap·ping.** beat with a strap; constrict; bind. **strap·less,** *a.*

strap·ping, *a.* *inf.* robust; of imposing build.

strat·a·gem, *n.* clever plan to deceive or outwit; trickery.

stra·te·gic, *a.* based on strategy; essential materials for war; assigned to destroy.

strat·e·gy, *n.* *pl.,* **-gies.** science of military operations; plan of operations; use of artifice; tactics. **strat·e·gist,** *n.* **stra·te·gic,** *a.*

strat·i·fy, *v.,* **-fied, -fy·ing.** form or arrange in strata or layers. **-fi·ca·tion,** *n.*

strat·o·sphere, *n.* atmosphere beginning about six miles above the earth.

stra·tum, *n.* *pl.,* **stra·ta, stra·tums.** natural or artificial layer; social level.

straw, *n.* stalk of grain after threshing; tube used to suck up a beverage; trifle. *a.* of or like a straw.

straw·ber·ry, *n.* *pl.,* **-ries.** red, pulpy, edible fruit.

stray, *v.* wander; err; deviate. *n. a.,* occasional.

streak, *n.* long, narrow mark, stripe; a trace; a strip. **-y,** *a·ier, -iest.*

stream, *n.* flow or current of water, esp. a small river. *v.* flow in a stream; come or arrive in large numbers.

stream·er, *n.* banner; pennant.

stream·line, *v.,* **-lined, -lin·ing.** shape in a way to lessen resistance; simplify. **-lined,** *a.*

street, *n.* public way in a city, etc.

street·car, *n.* passenger car running on rails set in the street.

street·walk·er, *n.* prostitute.

strength, *n.* state or quality of being strong; effectiveness; potency; intensity. **-en,** *v.* make strong. **-en·er,** *n.*

stren·u·ous, *a.* requiring great effort or exertion.

strep·to·coc·cus, *n. pl.,* **-coc·ci.** bacteria causing infection or disease.

stress, *n.* force; strain; tension; accent; pressure; emphasis. *v.* subject to stress; emphasize. **-ful,** *a.* **-less,** *a.*

stretch, *v.* extend or draw out. *n.* act of stretching; elasticity. **-a·ble,** *a.* **-y,** *a.* **-i·ness,** *n.*

stretch·er, *n.* portable frame for carrying injured, etc.

strew, *v.,* **strewed, strewed** or **strewn, strew·ing.** scatter; disseminate; spread.

stri·a·ted, *a.* striped; grooved.

strick·en, *a.* afflicted.

strict, *a.* enforcing exactly; austere; stringent; rigid. **-ness,** *n.*

stric·ture, *n.* severe criticism; restriction; closure or narrowing.

stride, *v.,* **strode, strid·den, strid·ing.** walk with long steps; straddle. *n.* gait; long step; rapid progress; advance.

stri·dent, *a.* shrill, harsh sound.

strife, *n.* contention; fight; struggle. **-less,** *a.* **-ful,** *a.*

strike, *v.,* **struck, struck** or **strick·en, strik·ing.** hit; crash into; attack; ignite; come upon; assume an attitude; occur to (idea); cease work to enforce a demand. *n.* act of striking; work stoppage. **-less,** *a.*

strik·ing, *a.* notable; impressive; on strike. **-ly,** *adv.*

string, *n.* slender cord or thick thread; length of things on a string, in a row, etc.; set of. *v.,* **strung, strung** or **stringed, string·ing.** thread on a string; extend.

strin·gent, *a.* constricted; rigid; convincing. **-gen·cy,** *n.*

string·y, *a.,* **-i·er, -i·est.** fibrous; ropy; wiry. **-i·ness,** *n.*

strip, *v.,* **stripped, -ping.** plunder; peel; divest; undress. *n.* long, narrow piece of cloth, wood, land, etc.

stripe, *n.* narrow band of a differing nature, color, etc. from adjacent surfaces. *v.,* **striped, strip·ing.** mark with a stripe. **striped,** *a.*

strive, *v.,* **strove, striv·en, striv·ing.** make earnest effort; endeavor; fight; contend.

strobe, *n.* device producing high-speed, brilliant light flashes.

stroke, *n.* blow; recurring single movement; apoplexy. *v.,* **stroked, strok·ing.** caress.

stroll, *v.* walk leisurely; saunter. *n.* leisurely walk. **-er,** *n.*

strong, *a.* physically or mentally powerful; healthy; potent; intense. *adv.* in a firm manner.

strong·hold, *n.* fortress; strongly defended place.

strong·mind·ed, *a.* determined; resolute; having a vigorous mind.

struc·ture, *n.* thing constructed; organized plan; arrangement of parts, etc. *v.,* **-tured, -tur·ing.** form or organize; construct. **-tur·al,** *a.* **-tured,** *a.*

strug·gle, *v.,* **-gled, -gling.** contend with; strive; exert violent efforts. *n.* violent effort; fight; strife. **-gler,** *n.* **-gling,** *a.*

strum, *v.* play idly (on a stringed instrument). **-mer,** *n.*

strum·pet, *n.* prostitute.

strut, *v.,* **-ted, -ting.** walk affectedly; support with a brace. *n.* proud, pompous walk; brace.

strych·nine, *n.* bitter, poisonous alkaloid. **-nic,** *a.*

stub, *n.* short remnant (pencil, etc.); ticket end. *v.,* **stubbed, stub·bing.** strike, as the toe, against. **-by,** *a.*

stub·ble, *n.* stubs of plants; rough beard growth. **-bly,** *a.*

stub·born, *a.* obstinate; determined; persistent; inflexible. **-ness,** *n.*

stuc·co, *n. pl.,* **-coes, cos.** plaster or cement for outside of building.

stud, *n.* male animal kept for breeding; upright post or prop; ornamental fastener, nail, etc.

stu·dent, *n.* pupil; scholar; learner.

stud·ied, *a.* deliberate; learned.

stu·di·o, *n. pl.,* **-os.** working place for movie makers, photographer, radio and TV shows, or a creative person.

stu·di·ous, *a.* given to study; diligent; attentive.

stud·y, *v.,* **-ied, -y·ing.** acquire knowledge of; examine; memorize; apply one's mind. *n. pl.,* **-ies.** process of acquiring knowledge; room for study.

stuff, *v.* fill completely; cram; plug; stop up; fill with, as a cushion; eat to excess. *n.* material or matter; element; personal possessions. **-er,** *n.* **-ing,** *n.*

stuff·y, *a.,* **-i·er, -i·est.** difficult to breathe in; uninspired; dull; stodgy. **-i·ness,** *n.*

stul·ti·fy, *v.* **-fied, -fy·ing.** cause to appear absurd; make useless or futile.

stum·ble, *v.,* **-bled, -bling.** trip in walking; discover by chance; err; speak or act hesitantly. *n.* stumbling.

stump, *n.* part of (tree, leg, etc.) remaining after cutting. *v.* walk heavily; baffle. **-y,** *a.*

stun, *v.,* **stunned, stun·ning.** render unconscious; daze; astonish; surprise completely. *n.* shock.

stun·ning, *a.* striking; beautiful.

stunt, *v.* check in growth; dwarf. *n.* unusual or daring feat.

stu·pe·fy, *v.,* **-fied, -fy·ing.** dull the senses of; amaze; astound; stun. **-fac·tion,** *n.*

stu·pen·dous, *a.* of prodigious size; marvelous.

stu·pid, *a.* mentally slow; dull; dumb. **-i·ty,** *n.*

stu·por, *n.* extreme lethargy; daze.

stur·dy, *a.,* **-di·er, -di·est.** strong; resolute; firm. **-di·ness,** *n.*

stur·geon, *n. pl.,* **-geon, -geons.** edible fish valued as a source of caviar.

stut·ter, *v.,* *n.* stammer; speak spasmodically. **-er,** *n.*

sty, *n. pl.,* **sties.** pen for pigs; filthy dwelling; inflamed bump on the eyelid.

style, *n.* manner; way of writing; mode of expression; fashion. *v.,* **styled, styl·ing.** to name; cause to conform. **styl·er,** *n.*

styl·ish, *a.* very fashionable.

sty·lus, *n. pl.,* **sty·li, sty·lus·es.** writing instrument; stencil maker; needle (phonograph).

sty·mie, *v.,* **-mied, -mie·ing.** obstruct; impede; baffle.

styp·tic, *a.* astringent. *n.*

suave, *a.* gracious; smooth; polished. **-ness,** *n.* **suav·i·ty,** *n.*

sub·a·tom·ic, *a.* smaller than an atom; parts of an atom.

sub·con·scious, *a.* not fully conscious; mentally inactive. *n.* unconscious mental activity.

sub·cu·ta·ne·ous, *a.* situated or applied under the skin.

sub·di·vide, *v.,* **-vid·ed, -vid·ing.** divide again; divide land into lots. **-vi·sion,** *n.*

sub·due, *v.,* **-dued, du·ing.** gain domination; overcome; repress; soften. **-du·er,** *n.*

sub·group, *n.* subdivision of a group; subset.

sub·head, *n.* subordinate headline or title.

sub·hu·man, *a.* below human.

sub·ject, *n.* one under power; citizen; topic; theme. *a.* being under power of; liable to. *v.* subjugate; make liable to; cause to undergo. **-jec·tion,** *n.*

sub·jec·tive, *a.* within the mind; personal opinions, etc. **-tiv·i·ty,** *n.*

sub·join, *v.* add at the end.

sub·ju·gate, *v.*, **-gat·ed**, **-gat·ing.** conquer; make subservient. **-ga·tion**, *n.* **-ga·tor**, *n.*

sub·lease, *v.*, **-leased**, **-leas·ing.** sublet from another.

sub·let, *v.*, **-let**, **-let·ting.** rent from person with original lease.

sub·li·mate, *v.*, **-mat·ed**, **-mat·ing.** refine; purify; repress impulses; act in acceptable ways. **-ma·tion**, *n.*

sub·lime, *a.*, **-lim·er**, **-lim·est.** grand; exalted; noble; *inf.* excellent. **-ness**, *n.*

sub·lim·i·nal, *a.* below or beyond the conscious level.

sub·mar·gin·al, *a.* below the margin; not productive enough to develop.

sub·ma·rine, *n.* vessel which operates under water; existing beneath the sea; large sandwich.

sub·merge, *v.*, **-merged**, **-merg·ing.** place or plunge under the surface of; cover; hide. **-mer·gence**, *n.*

sub·merse, *v.*, **-mersed**, **-mers·ing.** submerge. **-mer·sion**, *n.*

sub·mis·sion, *n.* yielding to or submitting. **-sive**, *a.*

sub·mit, *v.*, **-mit·ted**, **-mit·ting.** yield; refer or present; offer; suggest.

sub·nor·mal, *a.* below or less than the normal. **-i·ty**, *n.*

sub·or·di·nate, *a.* secondary; minor; lower in rank. *n.* subordinate person. *v.*, **-nat·ed**, **-nat·ing.** place in a lower rank. **-na·tion**, *n.*

sub·orn, *v.* bribe to commit perjury; incite to evil act.

sub·poe·na, **sub·pe·na**, *n.* writ requiring appearance in court. *v.*, **-naed**, **-na·ing.** serve with a subpoena.

sub·scribe, *v.*, **-scribed**, **-scrib·ing.** contribute; support; sign; agree to pay for (magazines, etc.). **-scrib·er**, *n.* **-scrip·tion**, *n.*

sub·se·quent, *a.* following in time, place, etc., or as a result.

sub·ser·vi·ent, *a.* obsequious; servile; submissive; subordinate.

sub·side, *v.*, **-sid·ed**, **-sid·ing.** sink to a lower level; settle; diminish; abate. **-sid·ence**, *n.*

sub·sid·i·ar·y, *a.* assisting; supplementary; auxiliary. *n. pl.*, **-ar·ies.** company controlled by another company.

sub·si·dize, *v.*, **-dized**, **-diz·ing.** give financial aid. **-diz·er**, *n.*

sub·si·dy, *n. pl.*, **-dies.** financial aid; grant of money.

sub·sist, *v.* exist; continue; live.

sub·sist·ence, *n.* sustenance; livelihood; existence.

sub·son·ic, *a.* sound waves beyond lower limits of human audibility.

sub·stance, *n.* matter; essential part or meaning; firmness; material possessions.

sub·stan·dard, *a.* below standard.

sub·stan·tial, *a.* solid; strong; of real worth; real; ample.

sub·stan·ti·ate, *v.*, **-at·ed**, **-at·ing.** give substance to; verify; establish by proof. **-a·tion**, *n.*

sub·sti·tute, *v.*, **-tut·ed**, **-tut·ing.** put or act in the place of another. *n.* one or that acting for another. **-tu·tion**, *n.*

sub·struc·ture, *n.* foundation.

sub·ter·fuge, *n.* plan or trick to conceal or to escape difficulty; stratagem.

sub·ter·ra·ne·an, *a.* below the earth's surface; hidden.

sub·ti·tle, *n.* secondary title; written translation of foreign dialogue, esp. in films.

sub·tle, *a.* sly; ingenious; delicate; not direct; elusive. **-ty**, *n.*

sub·tract, *v.* take away; deduct. **-trac·tion**, *n.*

sub·urb, *n. often pl.* district or town adjacent to a city. **-ur·ban**, *a.*, *n.*

sub·vert, *v.* overthrow; corrupt. **-ver·sion**, *n.* **-ver·sive**, *a.*, *n.*

sub·way, *n.* underground electric railway; underpass.

suc·ceed, *v.* accomplish what is attempted; come after; follow; flourish; thrive.

success, *n.* favorable termination; gaining fame; wealth, etc.; person that is successful. **-ful**, *a.*

suc·ces·sion, *n.* sequence; things following one after another. **-sive**, *a.*

suc·ces·sor, *n.* person that succeeds or follows after.

suc·cinct, *a.* terse; concise.

suc·cor, *n.*, *v.* aid; help; relieve.

suc·co·tash, *n.* mixture of lima beans and corn.

suc·cu·lent, *a.* juicy; absorbing.

suc·cumb, *v.* yield; die.

such, *a.* being the same or similar to; indicated. *pron.* such a person or thing; the same as. *adv.* so; very.

suck, *v.* draw in from, or imbibe by suction. *n.* act of sucking.

suck·er, *n.* fish with thick fleshy lips; *inf.* person easily deceived.

suck·le, *v.*, **-led**, **-ling.** nurse at the breast.

suc·tion, *n.* sucking; exertion of a force to form a vacuum.

sud·den, *a.* happening quickly or unexpectedly. **-ly**, *adv.*

suds, *n. pl.* soapy water; foam; froth. **-y**, *a.*, **-i·er**, **-i·est**.

sue, *v.*, **sued**, **su·ing**. seek justice by legal means; institute legal action. **su·er**, *n.*

suede, *n.* leather or fabric finished with napped surface.

su·et, *n.* white, solid fatty animal tissue. **-y**, *a.*

suf·fer, *v.* feel pain or distress of body or mind; allow; endure. **-ance**, *n.*

suf·fice, *v.*, **-ficed**, **-fic·ing**. be sufficient or adequate.

suf·fi·cient, *a.* adequate; enough; satisfactory. **-cien·cy**, *n. pl.*, **-cies**.

suf·fix, *n.* letter or letters added to the end of a word.

suf·fo·cate, *v.*, **-cat·ed**, **-cat·ing**. choke or kill by stopping respiration; smother. **-ca·tion**, *n.*

suf·frage, *n.* right to vote.

suf·fuse, *v.*, **-fused**, **-fus·ing**. spread over; fill. **-fu·sion**, *n.*

sug·ar, *n.* sweet, white crystalline foodstuff; sucrose. *v.* sweeten; granulate. **-y**, *a.*

sug·gest, *v.* propose; put forward; arouse in the mind; imply; insinuate; hint. **-ges·tion**, *n.*

sug·ges·tive, *a.* thing that suggests; something indecent.

su·i·cide, *n.* one who intentionally takes his own life; the act; ruin by one's own action. **-ci·dal**, *a.*

suit, *n.* set of garments worn together; legal process; one of the four sets of playing cards. *v.* adapt; accommodate; please.

suit·a·ble, *a.* fitting; proper.

suit·case, *n.* valise; luggage.

suite, *n.* connected series of rooms; retinue.

suit·or, *n.* wooer; petitioner.

sul·fur, **sul·phur**, *n.* yellow nonmetallic element.

sulk, *v.* be sullen. *n.* state or fit of moodiness.

sulk·y, *a.*, **-i·er**, **-i·est**. sullenly ill-humored. *n.* two-wheeled carriage.

sul·len, *a.* showing ill humor; gloomy silence; morose; dismal; somber. **-ness**, *n.*

sul·ly, *v.*, **-lied**, **-ly·ing**. mar; soil; defile; tarnish.

sul·try, *a.*, **-tri·er**, **-tri·est**. hot, moist, and still; close; sensual.

sum, *n.* total; amount, esp. money; aggregate; the whole. *v.*, **summed**, **sum·ming**. summarize; calculate.

sum·ma·rize, *v.*, **-rized**, **-riz·ing**. make a summary of.

sum·ma·ry, *a.* concise; quickly executed. *n. pl.*, **-ries**. condensed account of.

sum·ma·tion, *n.* addition; total; sum; final speech summary.

sum·mer, *n.* season between spring and autumn. *a.* of June, July, August. **-y**, *a.*

sum·mit, *n.* highest part; top; acme; apex. **-al**, *a.*

sum·mon, *v.* order to come; convoke; muster.

sum·mons, *n. pl.*, **-es**. call by authority to appear in court; subpoena.

sump, *n.* reservoir; pit; cesspool.

sump·tu·ous, *a.* costly; luxurious; excessively lavish.

sun, *n.* star around which the earth and other planets revolve; sunshine. *v.*, **sunned**, **sun·ning**. expose to the light and heat of the sun.

sun·bathe, *v.*, **-bathed**, **-bath·ing**. bask in the sun. **-bath·er**, *n.*

sun·burn, *n.* skin inflammation due to overexposure to the sun.

sun·dae, *n.* ice cream with fruit, syrup, nuts, etc.

Sun·day, *n.* first day of the week.

sun·der, *v.* sever; part; divide.

sun·down, *n.* sunset.

sun·dries, *n. pl.* various or miscellaneous small things.

sun·dry, *a.* several; various.

sun·flow·er, *n.* tall plant with yellow-rayed flowers.

sun·glass·es, *n. pl.* eyeglasses having colored lenses.

sunk·en, *a.* submerged; hollow; recessed.

sun·lamp, *n.* electric lamp radiating ultraviolet rays.

sun·light, *n.* sunshine.

sun·lit, *a.* lighted by the sun.

sun·ny, *a.*, **-ni·er**, **-ni·est**. lighted by sunshine; cheery; merry.

sun·rise, *n.* first appearance of the sun above the horizon.

sun·screen, *n.* suntan preparation to protect skin from ultraviolet radiation.

sun·set, *n.* time when the sun sets; old age.

sun·shine, *n.* direct light of the sun. **-shin·y**, *a.*

sun·stroke, *n.* prostration, fever from excessive exposure to the sun.

su·per, *a.* surpassing others of its kind; *inf.* outstanding; superb.

su·perb, *a.* grand; splendid; excellent; elegant. **-ness**, *n.*

su·per·charge, *v.*, **-charged**, **-charg·ing**. adapt engine to develop more power; charge excessively.

su·per·cil·i·ous, *a.* disdainful; haughty; arrogant; proud.

su·per·fi·cial, *a.* lying near or on the surface; not deep; shallow; obvious; not profound.

su·per·fine, *a.* very fine; best quality; unduly elaborate.

su·per·flu·ous, *a.* being more than is needed; oversupply; extra. **-i·ty**, *n. pl.*, **-ties.**

su·per·hu·man, *a.* above what is human; divine; herculean.

su·per·im·pose, *v.*, **-posed**, **-pos·ing.** lay over something else.

su·per·in·tend, *v.* have the charge and direction of; supervise. **-ent**, *n.*

su·pe·ri·or, *a.* higher in rank, quality, etc.; excellent; upper; better. *n.* one who is superior. **-i·ty**, *n.*

su·per·la·tive, *a.* of the highest degree; eminent; exaggerated. *n.* that which is superlative.

su·per·mar·ket, *n.* large retail food store.

su·per·nat·u·ral, *a.* happenings or forces beyond the natural; divine; miraculous.

su·per·nu·mer·ar·y, *n. pl.*, **-ies.** extra person or thing. *a.* superfluous; beyond the usual number.

su·per·pow·er, *n* one of a few large, dominant nations.

su·per·sede, *v.*, **-sed·ed**, **-sed·ing.** take the place of; replace.

su·per·son·ic, *a.* reaching speeds greater than sound; of sounds above those that can be heard.

su·per·star, *n.* outstanding performer; exceptionally talented athlete.

su·per·sti·tion, *n.* belief based on ignorance; irrational belief. **-tious**, *a.*

su·per·struc·ture, *n.* structure above the base or foundation.

su·per·vise, *v.*, **-vised**, **-vis·ing.** have charge; direct. **-vi·sion**, *n.* **-vi·sor**, *n.*

su·pine, *a.* lying on the back; inactive; apathetic; listless.

sup·per, *n.* evening meal.

sup·plant, *v.* displace; replace; supersede. **-er**, *n.*

sup·ple, *a.*, **-pler**, **-plest.** easily bent; agile; pliant; flexible.

sup·ple·ment, *n.* addition to; book continuation. *v.* provide what is lacking. **-men·ta·ry**, *a.*

sup·pli·cate, *v.*, **-cat·ed**, **-cat·ing.** beg; pray; entreat; implore. **-cant**, *n.*, *a.* **-ca·tion**, *n.*

sup·ply, *v.*, **-plied**, **-ply·ing.** furnish; give; provide. *n. pl.*, **-plies.** stock or amount. **-pli·er**, *n.*

sup·port, *v.* bear; hold up; tolerate; assist; advocate; maintain; provide for. *n.* that which supports; maintenance. **-er**, *n.*

sup·por·tive, *a.* tending or intended to support; contributing to.

sup·pose, *v.*, **-posed**, **-pos·ing.** presume; assume; conjecture; imagine; expect; imply; think. **-posed**, *a.* **-po·si·tion**, *n.*

sup·pos·ing, *conj.* on the assumption that.

sup·press, *v.* put an end to; crush; subdue; check; quell; conceal. **-pres·sion**, *n.*

sup·pu·rate, *v.*, **-rat·ed**, **-rat·ing.** fester; discharge pus. **-ra·tion**, *n.*

su·pra·na·tion·al, *a.* involving more than one nation.

su·pra·ra·tio·nal, *a.* involving factors beyond reason.

su·preme, *a.* highest in power; final; utmost. **-prem·a·cy**, *n.*

sur·cease, *n.* cessation; end.

sur·charge, *n.* extra tax or charge; overcharge. *v.*, **-charged**, **-charg·ing.** add on an extra fee.

sure, *a.*, **sur·er**, **sur·est.** indisputable; certain; steadfast; reliable; inevitable; infallible. *adv.* certainly. **-ly**, *adv.* **-ness**, *n.*

sure·ty, *n. pl.*, **-ties.** security against; certainty; guarantee.

surf, *n.* swell of the sea which breaks upon a shore; foam.

sur·face, *n.* outer part or face of an object. *a.* external; superficial. *v.*, **-faced**, **-fac·ing.** come to the surface; make smooth. **-less**, *a.*

sur·feit, *n.* excessive amount; overabundance. *v.* feed or supply to excess; overindulge.

surge, *n.* large wave. *v.*, **surged**, **surg·ing.** swell; vary or flow suddenly or powerfully.

sur·geon, *n.* physician who specializes in surgery.

sur·ger·y, *n. pl.*, **-ies.** treatment by operating; operating room. **-gi·cal**, *a.*

sur·ly, *a.*, **-li·er**, **-li·est.** ill-humored and rude; sullen; irritable.

sur·mise, *n.* guess. *v.*, **-mised**, **-mis·ing.** guess; infer.

sur·mount, *v.* prevail; rise above; overcome; place above.

sur·name, *n.* last (family) name.

sur·pass, *v.* exceed; excel; go beyond; overstep. **-ing**, *a.*

sur·plus, *n.*, *a.* that which remains over; excess.

sur·prise, *n.* something unexpected. *v.*, -**prised**, -**pris·ing**. attack unexpectedly; take unawares; astonish. -**pris·ing**, *a.*

sur·re·al, *a.* of the intense, irrational reality of a dream.

sur·ren·der, *v.* yield possession or power; abandon; relinquish. *n.* giving up.

sur·rep·ti·tious, *a.* clandestine; secret; stealthy.

sur·ro·gate, *n.* substitute; court judge. *v.*, -**gat·ed**, -**gat·ing**. put in the place of another.

sur·round, *v.* encompass; encircle; enclose. -**ing**, *n.*, *a.*

sur·tax, *n.* additional tax.

sur·veil·lance, *n.* secret watch kept over a person or thing. -**lant**, *a.*, *n.*

sur·vey, *v.* scrutinize; determine the boundaries, etc., of; appraise. *n.* inspection; systematic inquiry; surveying of land; overview. -**or**, *v.*

sur·vive, *v.*, -**vived**, -**viv·ing**. outlive; remain alive; keep existing; outlast. -**viv·al**, *n.* -**vi·vor**, *n.*

sus·cep·ti·ble, *a.* readily affected; impressionable. -**bil·i·ty**, *n.*

sus·pect, *v.* mistrust; surmise; doubt; think to be guilty. *n.* one suspected, esp. of a crime. *a.*

sus·pend, *v.* hang; bar for a time; cease for a time; defer. -**pen·sion**, *a.*

sus·pense, *n.* anxiety, interest, or excitement because of uncertainty. -**ful**, *a.*

sus·pen·sion, *n.* temporary removal from office, school, etc.; cessation; deferment; state of hanging freely.

sus·pi·cion, *n.* suspecting; feeling of something wrong; slight trace. -**cious**, *a.*

sus·tain, *v.* uphold; support; maintain; suffer; endure; nourish.

sus·te·nance, *n.* that which sustains life, as food.

su·ture, *n.* fiber to sew the human body; seam. *v.* sew together; unite.

svelte, *a.* smart; slender.

swab, *n.* bit of cotton, etc., attached to a stick; mop. *v.*, -**swabbed**, **swab·bing**. clean with a swab or mop.

swag·ger, *v.* strut; brag; boast. *n.* arrogant walk; bravado; verve. -**er**, *n.*

swal·low, *v.* cause food to pass to the stomach; absorb; endure; suppress; *inf.* believe something improbable. *n.* swallowing; mouthful; a bird.

swamp, *n.* wet spongy land; bog. *v.* overwhelm; sink; inundate; flood. **swamp·y**, *a.*, -**i·er**, -**i·est**. **swamp·i·ness**, *n.*

swan, *n.* long-necked bird.

swank, *n.* ostentatious display; stylishness. -**y**, *a.*, -**i·er**, -**i·est**. stylish.

swap, *n.*, *v.*, **swapped**, **swap·ping**. *inf.* barter; trade.

swarm, *n.* colony of bees moving; great number of things or persons, esp. in motion; throng. *v.* move in great numbers; teem.

swarth·y, *a.*, -**i·er**, -**i·est**. dark-complexioned.

swash·buck·ler, *n.* swaggering soldier; adventurer. -**ling**, *a.*

swat, *v.*, -**ted**, -**ting**. hit with a sharp blow. *n.* sharp blow. -**ter**, *n.*

swatch, *n.* sample of fabric or other material; patch.

swathe, *v.*, **swathed**, **swath·ing**. bind or wrap, as with a bandage. *n.* bandage.

sway, *v.* swing to and fro; oscillate; fluctuate; incline; control. *n.* influence. -**er**, *n.*

swear, *v.*, **swore**, **sworn**, **swear·ing**. make a solemn affirmation; vow; guarantee; promise; curse. -**er**, *n.*

sweat, *v.*, **sweat** or **sweat·ed**, -**ing**. perspire; ooze; exude; condense moisture on the surface; *inf.* toil. *n.* perspiration; condensation; drudgery. -**y**, *a.*, -**i·er**, -**i·est**.

sweat·er, *n.* knitted or crocheted jacket or blouselike garment.

sweep, *v.*, **swept**, **sweep·ing**. clean (as a floor) by a broom; clear out. *n.* stroke; movement; range or compass. -**er**, *n.* -**ing**, *a.*

sweet, *a.* flavor like that of sugar; pleasing; fresh. *n. pl.* candy. -**ness**, *n.* -**en**, *v.*

sweet·heart, *n.* beloved person; lover; darling.

sweet potato, *n.* plant having orange, edible tuberous roots.

sweet-talk, *v. inf.* cajole; coax. *n.* flattery.

swell, *v.*, **swelled**, **swelled** or **swoll·en**, **swell·ing**. increase in size or volume; bulge. *n.* a bulge, expansion; surge. -**ing**, *n.*

swel·ter, *v.* suffer from oppressive heat. *n.* oppressive heat. -**ing**, *n.*

swerve, *v.*, **swerved**, **swerv·ing**. turn; deviate; turn to one side; deflect; veer. *n.*

swift, *a.* moving with great speed; rapid; quick. *n.* bird resembling the swallow.

swig, *n. inf.* great gulp. *v.*, **swigged**, **swig·ging**. drink.

swill, *n.* liquid food, esp. food refuse given to swine; garbage. *v.* guzzle; drink greedily.

swim, *v.*, **swam**, **swum**, **swim·ming**. move through water by working the hands, feet, or fins; be flooded; be dizzy. *n.* act of swimming. -**mer**, *n.*

swin·dle, *v.,* **-dled, -dling.** cheat; deceive; defraud. *n.* fraudulent scheme. **-dler,** *n.*

swine, *n. pl.,* **swine.** hog or pig; low, greedy person. **swin·ish,** *a.*

swing, *v.,* **swung, swing·ing.** move to and fro; sway; pivot. *n.* free, swaying motion; marked rhythm; hanging seat. **-ing,** *a.* **-er,** *n.*

swipe, *v.,* **swiped, swip·ing.** strike with a sweeping motion; *inf.* steal. *n.* glancing blow.

swirl, *v.* whirl in eddies. *n.* whirling motion; spiral. **-y,** *a.*

swish, *v.* move with or make a sibilant sound; rustle. *n.* hissing sound. *a.* fashionable. **-y,** *a.,* **-ier, -iest.**

switch, *n.* flexible rod, esp. for whipping; sudden change; movable railroad track; device for connecting or breaking an electric circuit. *v.* whip; divert; shift; *elect.* switch on or off.

switch·board, *n.* apparatus with connections for circuits.

swiv·el, *n.* coupling or pivot that permits parts to rotate. *v.,* **-eled, -el·ing.** turn on or as on a swivel.

swiz·zle, *v. inf.* guzzle; get drunk.

swoon, *v.* to faint. *n.* a fainting fit or spell. **-er,** *n.*

swoop, *v.* drop or descend suddenly; seize; snatch. *n.* **-er,** *n.*

sword, *n.* weapon with a long blade. **-like,** *a.*

syc·a·more, *n.* shade tree.

syc·o·phant, *n.* servile flatterer. **-phan·cy,** *n.*

syl·lab·i·cate, *v.,* **-cat·ed, -cat·ing.** syllabify. **-ca·tion,** *n.*

syl·lab·i·fy, *v.,* **-fied, -fy·ing.** divide or form into syllables. **-fi·ca·tion,** *n.*

syl·la·ble, *n.* word or part of a word uttered in a single sound. *v.,* **-bled, -bling.** **-lab·ic,** *a.*

syl·la·bus, *n. pl.,* **-bus·es, -bi.** outline of a course; summary of principal points.

syl·lo·gism, *n.* deductive method of formal argument.

sylph, *n.* graceful, young girl.

syl·van, sil·van, *a.* of or inhabiting the woods; wooded.

sym·bi·o·sis, *n.* living together of two dissimilar organisms; mutualism.

sym·bol, *n.* object which stands for an intangible quality or idea; representation. **-ic,** *a.* **-ism,** *n.* **-ize,** *v.*

sym·me·try, *n. pl.,* **-tries.** corresponding arrangement of parts on opposite sides; balance; harmony of proportion. **-met·ric,** *a.*

sym·pa·thet·ic, *a.* of, or having sympathy.

sym·pa·thy, *n. pl.,* **-thies.** agreement; understanding; compassion; commiseration. **-thize,** *v.*

sym·pho·ny, *n. pl.,* **-nies.** composition for orchestra; concert; harmony. **-phon·ic,** *a.*

sym·po·sium, *n.* discussion group.

symp·tom, *n.* indicating disease or some problem; trace. **-to·mat·ic,** *a.*

syn·a·gogue, syn·a·gog, *n.* Jewish place of worship.

syn·chro·nize, *v.,* **-nized, -niz·ing.** make to agree in time; arrange events for coexistence or coincidence.

syn·co·pate, *v.* **-pat·ed, -pat·ing.** contract, cut short.

syn·di·cate, *n.* association of persons, companies, etc.; cartel. *v.,* **-cat·ed, -cat·ing.** combine into a syndicate; sell to many for publishing. **-ca·tion,** *n.*

syn·er·gic, *a.* cooperating; reinforcing.

syn·od, *n.* ecclesiastic council; any assembly.

syn·o·nym, *n.* word that has the same or similar meaning as another. **-on·y·mous,** *a.*

syn·op·sis, *n. pl.,* **-ses.** summary; abridgment; condensation.

syn·tax, *n.* orderly system; arrangement and interrelationship of words, phrases, clauses, etc.

syn·the·sis, *n. pl.,* **-ses.** assembling of parts into a new form or complex whole.

syn·thet·ic, *a.* of, or involving synthesis; artificial; bogus. *n.*

syph·i·lis, *n.* contagious venereal disease. **-lit·ic,** *a.,* *n.*

sy·ringe, *n.* device to inject or withdraw fluids from something.

syr·up, sir·up, *n.* thick, sweet liquid; concentrated juice. **syr·up·y,** *a.*

sys·tem, *n.* ordered arrangement of facts, phenomena, etc.; orderly method, plan, etc. **-at·ic,** *a.*

sys·tem·a·tize, *v.,* **-tized, -tiz·ing.** organize methodically or according to a system. **-ti·za·tion,** *n.*

sys·to·le, *n.* rhythmic heart contraction.

T

tab, *n.* small flap; tag; appendage; bill. *v.* **tab·bed, -tab·bing.** designate.

tab·by, *a.* striped; mottled; *inf.* cat, esp. female.

tab·er·nac·le, n. place or house of worship; tent.

ta·ble, n. flat top on legs or a pillar; list arranged for reference or comparison. v. postpone discussion.

ta·ble·spoon, n. spoon equivalent to 3 teaspoons. **-ful,** n. pl., **-fuls.**

tab·let, n. pad of paper; small, flat or round piece of medicine.

ta·ble·ware, n. dishes, utensils, etc. used for dining.

tab·loid, n. small, often sensational newspaper.

ta·boo, ta·bu, a. religious or social prohibition; forbidden. n. a prohibition.

tab·u·lar, a. in a list or tabulated arrangement; having a flat surface.

tab·u·late, v. **-lated, -lating.** arrange in a table or list.

tac·it, a. unspoken; implied.

tac·i·turn, a. habitually silent.

tack, n. short, flat-headed nail; temporary loosely sewed stitch; policy of action; course of a sailing ship. v. fasten with tacks; append to; change one's course.

tack·le, n. arrangement of ropes and pulleys; equipment; act of grabbing and stopping. v. undertake to do; seize and stop; to harness (a horse).

tact, n. facility in saying and doing the right thing.

tac·tics, n. pl. maneuvering of forces; planned action.

tac·tile, a. of or having the sense of touch.

tad·pole, n. larva of frog, toad.

taf·fe·ta, n. stiff silk or synthetic lustrous fabric.

tag, n. label or strip, to identify, classify, etc.; a loose edge; children's chase game. v. **tagged, tag·ging.** label with a tag; touch.

tail, n. rear end of animal, usu. a flexible appendage; hind part of anything;inf. detective. **tails,** pl. inf. reverse of a coin. detective. v. follow closely; shadow. a. coming from behind; rearmost.

tail·gate, n. hinged plate closing back end of truck; v. drive too close behind for safety.

tai·lor, n. one who makes or repairs clothes.

tai·lor-made, a. anything right or suitable for a particular person, specific conditions, etc.; made by a tailor.

tail·spin, n. uncontrolled descent of airplane in a steep spiral path; inf. sudden mental or emotional upheaval.

taint, v. decay or infect; corrupt; disgrace; stain; blemish. n. cause or result of that which is bad.

take, v., **took, tak·en, tak·ing.** lay hold of; grasp; seize; gain or win; choose; select; subscribe to; steal; assume duties of; subtract; submit to; undertake; understand; adopt; consume; conduct or lead; travel by; accept; catch.

take-off, n. leaving the ground as in flight; starting point.

take·o·ver, n. taking over or control, as in business, a nation, etc.

tale, n. brief story, true or fictitious; gossip; a lie.

tal·ent, n. particular aptitude for; pl. person's natural abilities.

tal·is·man, n. object supposed to ward off evil and bring good luck.

talk, v. speak words; converse; discuss; gossip; confer. n. speech; conversation; report; discussion.

talk·a·tive, a. tending to talk too much; loquacious.

tall, a. above average in height; inf. exaggerated, boastful.

tal·low, n. solid animal fats.

tal·ly, n. pl., **-lies.** a reckoning, account; score of a game, v. **-lied, -ly·ing.** score on a tally; count up; to agree.

tal·on, n. claw, esp. of a bird.

tam, n. small flat cap.

ta·ma·le, n. Mexican dish of ground meat and red pepper rolled in cornmeal dough.

tam·bou·rine, n. musical instrument of stretched parchment over a hoop with metal jingles in rim.

tame, a. domesticated; submissive; docile. v. make tame or obedient; soften.

tamp, v. pack down by repeated light blows.

tam·per, v. interfere with; meddle; plot; scheme.

tam·pon, n. plug of cotton or gauze used for absorption in body.

tan, v. **-tanned, -tan·nins** convert animal hides into leather; brown by exposure to sunlight; inf. flog. n. yellowish-brown color; brown skin color.

tan·dem, adv., a. one behind the other. n. bicycle for two.

tang, n. strong taste, flavor, odor; trace or hint. **-y,** a., **-i·er, -i·est.**

tan·gent, a. touching; touching at one point only and not intersecting. n. inf. abrupt change of course.

tan·ge·rine, *n.* small shiny loose-skinned orange.

tan·gi·ble, *a.* perceptible by touch; concrete; objective.

tan·gle, *v.*, *n.* (make, become) a confused, mixed mass; enmesh; *inf.* fight.

tan·go, *n. pl.*, **-gos.** Latin-American ballroom dance. *v.*

tank, *n.* large receptacle for liquids or gases; armored combat vehicle; *inf.* jail.

tank·ard, *n.* tall, one-handled drinking vessel.

tank·er, *n.* ship, truck, etc. for transporting liquids.

tan·ta·lize, *v.* tease or torment by promising, showing something desirable. **-liz·ing**, *a.*

tan·ta·mount, *a.* equivalent.

tan·trum, *n.* fit of temper.

tap, *n.* faucet; gentle blow; plug; metal plate for shoe heel. *v.* pierce to draw fluid from; penetrate; strike gently.

tape, *n.* narrow strip for tying, fastening; long strip of plastic, paper, etc., as cassette tape. *v.* tie with tape; record on tape.

ta·per, *v.* to gradually decrease in size; diminish. *n.* slender candle.

tap·es·try, *n.* heavy, colorful, woven, patterned or pictorial textile.

tape·worm, *n.* long, flat, parasitic intestinal worm.

tap·i·o·ca, *n.* starchy foodstuff from cassava, used in puddings, etc.

ta·pir, *n.* hoglike, hoofed mammal, with flexible snout.

tap·root, *n.* main plant root.

tar, *n.* a thick, dark, viscid substance obtained from wood and coal.

ta·ran·tu·la, *n.* large, hairy venomous spider.

tar·dy, *a.* late; delayed; dilatory; slow-paced.

tar·get, *n.* mark aimed at in shooting; objective.

tar·iff, *n.* tax on imports, exports; schedule of rates.

tar·nish, *v.* lose luster; become discolored, sully; impair. *n.* discoloration; blot.

tar·pau·lin, *n.* waterproof material for covering, esp. canvas.

tar·ry, *v.*, **-ried**, **-ry·ing.** wait; linger; stay; sojourn.

tart, *a.* sour taste; caustic (remark). *n.* small, filled pastry shell.

tar·tan, *n.* plaid patterned textile.

tar·tar, *n.* yellowish, hard deposit on teeth; juice sediment.

task, *n.* work to be done; unpleasant duty; job.

task·mas·ter, *n.* one who assigns tasks.

tas·sel, *n.* bunch of loosely hanging threads or cords.

taste, *v.* perceive flavor of by taking into mouth; eat, drink a little of; experience; have a specific taste. *n.* flavor perceived; sense for perceiving; small quantity; liking; sense of what is correct, proper, beautiful.

tasty, *a.* savory; flavorful.

tat·ter, *n.* rag; torn piece; *pl.* ragged clothing. *v.* shred. **-tered**, *a.*

tat·tle, *v.* gossip; talk idly; tell secrets.

tat·too, *n. pl.*, **-toos.** marking on skin in patterns with indelible pigments. *v.*

taunt, *n.* biting remark; insult. *v.* provoke with taunts.

taupe, *n.* dark, brownish gray.

taut, *a.* stretched tight; tense.

tav·ern, *n.* inn; place where beer, liquor is sold by the drink.

taw·dry, *a.* cheap; gaudy.

taw·ny, *a.* yellowish-brown; tan.

tax, *n.* fee imposed for government support; heavy demand; burden. *v.* impose a tax or burden upon.

tax·i, *n. pl.*, **-is**, **-ies.** taxicab. *v.*, **-ied**, **-i·ing** or **-y·ing.** travel by taxicab; move along the ground under its own power.

tax·i·cab, *n.* passenger vehicle for hire.

tea, *n.* infusion of aromatic plant leaves in hot water, used as a beverage; social gathering. **tea bag**, **tea·cup**, *n.*

teach, *v.*, **taught**, **teach·ing.** give instruction to; train. **-er**, *n.*

teak, *n.* tall Asian tree with durable, hard wood.

tea·ket·tle, *n.* kettle with cover, spout, for boiling water.

teal, *n.* short-necked wild duck. *a.* shade of blue.

team, *n.* persons working or playing together; crew; animals harnessed together. **-mate**, *n.* **-work**, *n.*

team·ster, *n.* truck driver.

tea·pot, *n.* vessel with lid, spout, handle, for brewing and serving of tea.

tear, *n.* drop of salty, liquid secretion of the eye. **-y**, *a.*

tear, *v.*, **tore**, **torn**, **tear·ing.** pull apart by force; rend; lacerate; distress. *n.* act of tearing; fissure; place torn.

tease, *v.* raise a nap on; irritate; pester; torment. *n.* act of teasing; one who teases; *inf.* flirt.

tea·spoon, *n.* small spoon; $1/3$ tablespoon. **-ful**, *n. pl.*, **-fuls.**

teat, *n.* nipple.

tech·ni·cal, *a.* of a particular art, science, trade, profession, etc.

tech·ni·cal·i·ty, *n. pl.* **-ties.** technical point, distinction, or detail.

tech·ni·cian, *n.* one skilled in a particular work.

tech·nique, *n.* method of performing certain work.

tech·nol·o·gy, *n. pl.* **-gies.** sum total of technical knowledge; applied science. **-i·cal,** *a.*

te·di·ous, *a.* monotonous; boring; fatiguing. **-um,** *n.*

tee, *n.* starting place; peg from which golf ball is driven. *v.*

teem, *v.* be full to overflowing; abound.

teens, *n. pl.* age in years from 13 through 19. **teen·ag·er,** *n.* **teen·age,** *a.*

tee·ter, *v.* seesaw; move unsteadily; vacillate; waver.

teethe, *v.,* **teethed, teeth·ing.** develop teeth. **teeth·ing,** *n.*

tee·to·tal·er, *n.* one who abstains totally from alcoholic drinks.

tel·e·cast, *v.* broadcast by television. *n.* televised broadcast.

tel·e·gram, *n.* message sent by telegraph.

tel·e·graph, *v., n.* (transmit a message by) a device for sending signals long-distance over a wire. **te·leg·ra·phy,** *n.*

te·lep·a·thy, *n.* supposed communication between two minds.

tel·e·phone, *v., n.* (speak by) instrument for transmission of sound to a distant point.

tel·e·scope, *n.* tubular optical instrument for viewing distant objects. *v.* slide one into another; shorten; compress. **-scop·ic,** *a.*

tel·e·vise, *v.* transmit or receive by television.

tel·e·vi·sion, *n.* transmission of scenes through electrical and sound waves; receiver set.

tell, *v.,* **told, tell·ing.** narrate; relate; tattle; divulge; reveal; indicate; discern; command.

tell·er, *n.* bank cashier.

tell·ing, *a.* forceful; striking; effective.

tell·tale, *a.* betraying; revealing.

te·mer·i·ty, *n.* boldness; rashness.

tem·per, *v.* soften, tone down, moderate; subdue. *n.* disposition; state of mind; fit of anger.

tem·per·a·ment, *n.* disposition.

tem·per·a·men·tal, *a.* erratic.

tem·per·ance, *n.* moderation.

tem·per·ate, *a.* moderate.

tem·per·a·ture, *n.* degree or intensity of heat or cold.

tem·pest, *n.* violent wind, storm; tumult. **-pes·tu·ous,** *a.*

tem·plate, *n.* pattern used as a guide for shaping, making.

tem·ple, *n.* building for worship; region on either side of forehead.

tem·po, *n. pl.,* **-pos, pi.** speed or pace; relative speed at which music is played; rate of speed; pace.

tem·po·ral, *a.* of present time and earthly life.

tem·po·rar·y, *a.* for a limited time; impermanent. **-i·ly,** *adv.*

tem·po·rize, *v.* act to fit the occasion or to gain time.

tempt, *v.* entice to do wrong; invite. **temp·ta·tion,** *n.* **tempt·ing,** *a.* attractive.

ten, *n.* nine plus one.

ten·a·ble, *a.* capable of being held, maintained; reasonable.

te·na·cious, *a.* adhesive; stubborn; persistent; retentive. **-nac·i·ty,** *n.*

ten·ant, *n.* person who rents house, etc. for use; occupant.

tend, *v.* be disposed or inclined towards; look after.

ten·den·cy, *n.* inclination; bent.

ten·der, *a.* delicate; soft; fragile; young; kind; loving; sensitive. *n.* one who tends; offer. *v.* present or make an offer. **-ly,** *adv.*

ten·don, *n.* fibrous tissue attaching a muscle to a bone.

ten·dril, *n.* threadlike part serving to attach climbing plant.

ten·et, *n.* principle; doctrine.

ten·nis, *n.* game in which ball is hit by rackets over a net.

ten·or, *n.* general intent; highest adult male voice.

tense, *a.* taut; apprehensive; nervous. *v.* make, become tense. *n.* a verb form expressing time.

ten·sion, *n.* act of stretching; tautness; mental strain.

tent, *n.* portable canvas shelter.

ten·ta·cle, *n.* appendage on head of some animals, used for feeling, handling, grasping.

ten·ta·tive, *a.* not definite.

ten·u·ous, *a.* slight; weak.

ten·ure, *n.* act or right of holding property or a position.

te·pee, *n.* cone-shaped tent.

tep·id, *a.* lukewarm.

term, *n.* word or phrase; prescribed time period; school period; *pl.* stated conditions; agreement. *v.* name.

ter·mi·nal, *a.* end; boundary; final. *n.* terminating point; station (railway, etc.); computer instrument where data can be input or retrieved for view on a screen.

ter·mi·nate, *v.* end; complete.

ter·mi·nol·o·gy, *n.* technical terms relating to a particular subject.

ter·mi·nus, *n. pl.*, **-nus·es, -ni.** final point; end or limit.

ter·mite, *n.* wood-eating insect.

tern, *n.* small seagull.

ter·race, *n.* raised level space; usu. with sloping sides; open area with seats or plantings; balcony; patio.

ter·rain, *n.* surface features of a tract of land.

ter·rar·i·um, *n.* glass enclosure for growing small plants.

ter·res·tri·al, *a.* of the earth; worldly; mundane.

ter·ri·ble, *a.* causing great fear; dreadful; *inf.* very bad.

ter·rif·ic, *a.* terrifying; astounding; *inf.* extraordinary; excellent.

ter·ri·fy, *v.*, **-fied, -fy·ing.** fill with terror; frighten severely.

ter·ri·to·ry, *n. pl.* **-ries.** region; area under jurisdiction of a nation, state; region not yet admitted as a state or province; area assigned to a person or group.

ter·ror, *n.* great fear; person or thing that causes fear; annoying person, child.

ter·ror·ism, *n.* use of terror to intimidate, esp. by violence. **-ist,** *n.* **-ize,** *v.*

terse, *a.* short, to the point.

ter·ti·ar·y, *a.* third.

test, *n.* trial; examination. *v.* give an examination or trial.

tes·ta·ment, *n.* a will; proof; credo; *(cap)* either of two parts of the Bible.

tes·tate, *a.* having left a will.

tes·ti·cle, tes·tis, *n.* male sex gland.

tes·ti·fy, *v.* **-fied, -fy·ing.** indicate; bear witness; give evidence under oath; declare. **-mo·ny,** *n.*

tes·ti·mo·ni·al, *n.* letter or statement of recommendation; thing given in appreciation or esteem.

tes·ty, *a.* touchy; irritable.

tet·a·nus, *n.* acute, often fatal, bacterial disease.

teth·er, *n.* rope, etc. for restricting an animal; the limit of one's powers. *v.*

text, *n.* main part of a printed work; exact or original wording; subject; topic; textbook; verse of Scripture.

text·book, *n.* book used as basis of instruction; manual.

tex·tile, *a.* pertaining to weaving or woven fabrics. *n.* woven fabric; cloth.

tex·ture, *n.* characteristic arrangement, appearance, or feel of a thing.

than, *conj.* compared to; except; but; when.

thank, *v.* express gratitude.

thank·ful, *a.* grateful; appreciative.

thank·less, *a.* ungrateful; not appreciated.

thanks, *n. pl.* expression of appreciation or gratitude.

thanks·giv·ing, *n.* act of thanks; *(cap)* national U.S. holiday.

that, *pron. pl.*, **those.** the one or thing mentioned; something more remote; unspecified object; who, whom, where, or which. *a.* one or thing mentioned or remote. *conj.* used to connect clauses.

thatch, *n.* straw roofing.

thaw, *v.* to melt or dissolve; grow less cold; become less unsociable.

the, *def. art.* used before nouns when referring to a particular person, thing, or group. *adv.* by that much.

the·a·ter, *n.* structure or place for presentation of entertainment; the theatrical world as a whole; scene of events. **-at·ri·cal,** *a.*

thee, *pron.* objective case of *thou.*

theft, *n.* act of stealing; larceny.

their, *a.* possessive case of *they.* **theirs,** *pron;* **them,** *pron.* objective case of *they.*

theme, *n.* main subject or topic; composition; short essay; leading melody.

them·selves, *pron. pl.* reflexive or emphatic form of *they.*

then, *adv.* at that time; next in time, space, or order. *conj.* in that case; accordingly.

thence, *adv.* from that place or time; therefore.

thence·forth, *adv.* from that time on; thereafter. Also **thence·for·ward.**

the·ol·o·gy, *n.* study of God, religious doctrine, faith.

the·o·rem, *n.* proposition to be proved or accepted as a truth.

the·o·ry, *n.* body of fundamental principles; hypothesis; conjecture; supposition; suggested plan of action. **-ret·i·cal,** *a.* **-rize,** *v.*

ther·a·py, *n.* treatment of disease, disability by drugs, exercise, etc.

there, *adv.* in, at, to, toward, or into that place. *n.* that place, position, point.

there·af·ter, *adv.* afterward.

there·by, *adv.* by that.

there·fore, *adv., conj.* for that or this reason; consequently.

there·in, *adv.* in that place; in that respect.

there·of, *adv.* of that, this, or it; because of that (this) cause.

there·on, *adv.* on this, that, or it; thereupon; thereat.

there·up·on, *adv.* upon that; following upon; at once.

there·with, *adv.* with this, that, or it; thereupon; thereafter; immediately afterward.

ther·mal, *a.* of, caused by heat; hot or warm.

ther·mo·dy·nam·ics, *n.* physics dealing with relations of heat and other energy forms.

ther·mom·e·ter, *n.* instrument for measuring temperature.

ther·mo·nu·cle·ar, *a.* of nuclear reactions, processes, heat.

ther·mo·stat, *n.* automatic control for maintaining desired temperature.

the·sau·rus, *n.* book of synonyms and antonyms.

the·sis, *n. pl.,* **-ses.** formal proposition to be discussed and proved; dissertation.

thes·pi·an, *n.* actor or actress.

they, *pron.* people in general; persons or things mentioned.

thi·a·mine, *n.* vitamin B₁.

thick, *a.* of relatively large extent from side to side; viscous; close together; dense; *inf.* stupid; intimate. *n.* most active part. **-ly,** *adv.* **-en,** *v.* make or become thick.

thick·et, *n.* dense shrubbery.

thick-skinned, *a.* callous; insensitive.

thief, *n. pl.,* **thieves.** one who steals. **thieve,** *v.*

thigh, *n.* leg between hip and knee.

thim·ble, *n.* pitted cover worn to protect finger in sewing.

thin, *a.* **thin·ner, thin·nest.** not thick from one side to the other; lean; scant; not dense; fluid; unsubstantial. *v.* make or become thin.

thine, *pron.* possessive form of *thou.*

thing, *n.* event; deed; item; detail; idea; entity; matter of occurrence; *pl.* personal possessions.

think, *v.,* **thought, think·ing.** produce or conceive mentally; ponder; reason; meditate; expect; believe; remember.

think·ing, *a.* using the mind; intellectually active. *n.* act of using the mind; result of thought.

thin-skinned, *a.* easily offended.

third, *n., a.* next after the second; one of three equal parts.

thirst, *n.* need for fluids; any strong desire. *v.* crave; be thirsty. **-y,** *a.*

thir·teen, *a. n.* 12 plus one. **-teenth,** *a., n.*

thir·ty, *a. n.* 29 plus one. **-ti·eth,** *a., n.*

this, *a., pron. pl.,* **these.** person, place or thing that is present, near, mentioned, understood, or referred to. *adv.* to this degree; thus or so.

this·tle, *n.* prickly plant.

thith·er, *adv.* to that place; in that direction.

thong, *n.* narrow leather strip.

tho·rax, *n.* part of the body between the neck and abdomen.

thorn, *n.* sharp, rigid outgrowth from a plant stem; shrub. **-y,** *a.*

thor·ough, *a.* complete; careful; exhaustive; detailed; attentive.

thor·ough·bred, *n., a.* animal of pure breed; pedigreed.

thor·ough·fare, *n.* unobstructed road or street.

thou, *pron.* you.

though, *conj.* although; even if; yet. *adv.* however; nevertheless.

thought, *n.* act of thinking; serious consideration; reasoning; idea; deliberation.

thought·ful, *a.* meditative; mindful; heedful; considerate.

thought·less, *a.* heedless; inconsiderate; flighty; reckless.

thou·sand, *a., n.* ten times one hundred. **-sandth,** *a., n.*

thrash, *v.* thresh, as grain; beat; flog; defeat; flail or toss about violently.

thread, *n.* very fine cord; spiral part of a screw; filament. *v.* pass a thread through; make a thread.

thread·bare, *a.* worn; shabby.

threat, *n.* statement of what will be done to hurt or punish; menace.

threat·en, *v.* utter threats; be menacing; portend.

three, *a., n.* two plus one.

three-di·men·sion·al, *a.* having three dimensions; appearing to have depth, height, and width.

thresh, *v.* beat out grain from the husk.

thresh·old, *n.* doorsill; entering point; beginning.

thrice, *adv.* three times.

thrift, *n.* economical management; frugality. **-y,** *a.*

thrill, *v., n.* (cause or feel) great or tingling excitement; a tingling sensation; quiver.

thrive, *v.,* **thrived** or **throve, thrived** or **thriv·en.** prosper; flourish; increase.

throat, *n.* front part of neck; passage from nose and mouth to lungs and stomach.

throb, *v.* pulsate rhythmically.

throe, *n.* pang or pain; agonizing activity.

throm·bo·sis, *n. pl.,* **-ses.** blood clot in the heart or a blood vessel.

throne, *n.* chair or office of a sovereign (king, pope, etc.).

throng, *n., v.* multitude; crowd.

throt·tle, *v.,* **-tled, -tling.** choke; suppress. strangle. *n.* valve to control fuel or steam volume in engine.

through, thru, *prep.* from one side or end to the other; into at one place and out another; covering all parts; having reached the end of; by means of. *adv.* from one end or side to the other; completely. *a.* going or extending without interruption; finished.

through·out, *prep.* everywhere in. *adv.* in every part; at every moment.

throw, *v.,* **threw, thrown.** propel through air by a sudden arm motion; hurl; project; put on hastily; move, as a lever or switch; discard; shed. *n.*

throw·back, *n.* reversion to an earlier type or condition.

thru, *prep., adv., a.* through.

thrush, *n.* a songbird.

thrust, *v.,* **thrust, thrust·ing.** push or shove forcibly. *n.* forcible push; propelling force; stab; attack.

thud, *v.,* **-ded, -ding.** strike or fall with a dull sound. *n.* dull, heavy sound.

thug, *n.* assassin; ruffian.

thumb, *n.* short, thick, inner digit of human hand.

thump, *n.* sound of a heavy blow; a thud. *v.* strike with a thump; throb; *inf.* defeat.

thun·der, *n.* sound which follows lightning; any similar noise. *v.* to thunder.

thun·der·bolt, *n.* lightning accompanied by thunderclap.

thun·der·struck, *a.* astonished.

Thurs·day, *n.* fifth day of week.

thus, *adv.* in this, that way; to this, that degree; so; hence.

thwart, *v.* obstruct; defeat.

thyme, *n.* mint used as seasoning.

thy·roid, *n.* endocrine gland which affects growth and metabolism.

ti·ar·a, *n.* three-tiered crown; formal woman's headwear.

tib·i·a, *n.* shinbone.

tic, *n.* recurrent muscle spasm.

tick, *n.* light recurring click; checkmark; blood-sucking insect.

tick·et, *n.* card entitling holder to something; a label or tag; list of candidates; summons. *v.*

tick·le, *v.* touch or scratch to excite tingling or twitching; to please.

tick·lish, *a.* sensitive to tickling; sensitive; delicate situation.

tid·bit, *n.* delicious morsel.

tide, *n.* periodic rise and fall of the ocean; drift of events. **ti·dal,** *a.*

ti·dings, *n. pl.* news.

ti·dy, *a.* **-di·er, -di·est.** neat; orderly; *inf.* moderately large. *v.* make orderly.

tie, *v.,* **tied, ty·ing.** fasten or bind with a cord; make into a knot; restrict; unite; make the same score. *n.* a fastening; necktie; link; equality of scores in a contest.

tier, *n.* rank or row in a series placed one above another.

tiff, *n.* petty, minor quarrel.

ti·ger, *n.* large, carnivorous, black-striped jungle feline.

tight, *a.* fitting closely; not leaky; taut; miserly; packed full; impervious to fluids, gases. **-ly,** *adv.* closely. **-en,** *v.*

tights, *n. pl.* close-fitting garment worn over hips and legs.

tile, *n.* thin piece of baked clay for covering roofs, floors, etc.

till, *prep., conj.* until. *v.* cultivate the soil. *n.* money drawer.

till·age, *n.* land cultivation.

till·er, *n.* lever to turn a rudder for steering.

tilt, *v.* incline or slant; rush at or charge. *n.* act of tilting; a slant or slope; joust; quarrel.

tim·ber, *n.* wood for building; forests, trees; wooden beam.

tim·bre, *n.* distinctive quality of sound from overtones.

time, *n.* the past, present, future; duration; definite or particular moment, period; right moment; each occasion; musical beat. *v.* record the duration of; regulate, as to time. *a.* of (a certain) time.

time·less, *a.* eternal; unending.

time·ly, *a.* opportune; well-timed; appropriate.

time·piece, *n.* clock; watch.

tim·er, *n.* one who or device that measures, controls, or records time.

time·ta·ble, *n.* schedule showing arrival, departure times.

tim·id, *a.* lacking confidence; fearful; shy. **-i·ty,** *n.*

tim·or·ous, *a.* fearful; timid.

tin, *n.* malleable metallic element; tin container.

tinc·ture, *n.* medicinal solution; a tinge of color.

tin·der, *n.* dry, flammable substance for igniting fire.

tine, *n.* prong of a fork, antler.

tinge, *v., n.* (give a) faint trace of color or quality; tint.

tin·gle, *v., n.* (have a) prickly, stinging sensation.

tink·er, *v.* work unskillfully; to potter, fuss.

tin·kle, *v., n.* (produce) small, sharp, ringing sounds.

tin·sel, *n.* thin glittering strips of metal; showy, but of little worth. *a.* superficially brilliant.

tint, *v., n.* (give) a slight coloring (to); tinge.

ti·ny, *a.* very small; minute.

tip, *n.* point or extremity; top; small gift of money; helpful hint; confidential information; tap. *v.* **tipped, tip·ping.** slant; overturn; give a gratuity; strike lightly; lean.

tip·sy, *a.* **-si·er, -si·est** mildly intoxicated; shaky; unsteady.

tip·toe, *n.* the tips of the toes. *v.* to walk on tiptoe.

tip-top, *a.* at the very top; *inf.* excellent; first-rate.

ti·rade, *n.* long, violent speech.

tire, *v.* exhaust the strength; lose patience, become weary, fatigued, bored. *n.* hoop of rubber around a wheel rim. **tired,** *a.* fatigued. **tire·less,** *a.* untiring; ceaseless.

tire·some, *a.* boring; tedious.

tis·sue, *n.* thin, light cloth or paper; mass of cells forming bodily parts.

ti·tan, *n.* person having gigantic size, strength. **-ic,** *a.*

tithe, *n.* tenth part of income paid as tax or contribution to the church.

tit·il·late, *v.* excite pleasurably.

ti·tle, *n.* name of a book, play, etc.; descriptive or distinctive name; name to show rank, office, respect; legal right to privilege or possession.

tit·ter, *v.* suppressed laugh.

tit·u·lar, *a.* existing in title or name only; having a title.

to, *prep.* toward; belonging with; resulting in; until; for; causing; into; in. *adv.* toward; forward; together.

toad, *n.* tailless, warty-skinned, jumping land amphibian.

toad·stool, *n.* inedible, poisonous mushroom.

toast, *v.* brown by heat; drink to someone's health. *n.* toasted bread; sentiment to which one drinks.

toast·mas·ter, *n.* person who proposes toasts; master of ceremonies.

to·bac·co, *n.* plant whose dried leaves are prepared for smoking, chewing, or snuff.

to·bog·gan, *n.* flat-bottomed sled. *v.* to coast; descend swiftly.

to·day, to-day, *adv.* on this present day; nowadays; the present time. *n.* the present day or age.

tod·dle, *v., n.* (walk) unsteadily with short steps, as a child.

to-do, *n. inf.* a stir; fuss.

toe, *n.* one of the five digits of the foot. **-nail,** *n.*

to·ga, *n.* loose outer garment of ancient Roman citizens.

to·geth·er, *adv.* in company with; in one group or mass; in unison; in cooperation; jointly.

toil, *v.* work strenuously. *n.* hard, fatiguing work; drudgery.

toi·let, *n.* bathroom; fixture for disposing of body waste; process of bathing, dressing.

toi·let·ry, *n.* soap, cologne, etc.

to·ken, *n.* sign; indication; souvenir; metal disk used for fares, etc. *a.* nominal; partial; symbolic.

to·ken·ism, *n.* fulfilling legal obligations by nominal conformity; minimal desegregation.

tol·er·a·ble, *a.* endurable; fairly good. **-bly,** *adv.*

tol·er·ance, *n.* openmindedness; allowable deviation; act of, or capacity to endure. **-ant,** *a.*

tol·er·ate, *v.* to put up with; bear; endure; permit.

toll, *n.* tax or fee for some right, privilege, service; number or amount lost (in a disaster). *v.* ring slowly and regularly (as for the dead).

tom·a·hawk, *n.* light ax used as war weapon by Indians.

to·ma·to, *n. pl.,* **-toes.** plant with red, pulpy fruit used as a vegetable; the fruit itself.

tomb, *n.* burial place; grave.

tomb·stone, *n.* grave marker.

tome, *n.* large, scholarly book.

to·mor·row, to-mor·row, *n., adv.* day after today; the future.

ton, *n.* 2,000 pounds.

tone, *n.* vocal or musical sound; quality of any sound; pitch; style or elegance; vocal inflection; color shade; body condition. *v.* give tone to; assume a tone; blend or harmonize; strengthen. **ton·al,** *a.*

tongs, *n. pl.* instrument with hinged arms, for grasping, holding, lifting.

tongue, *n.* moving organ within mouth for masticating and tasting, speech; power or act of speech; language.

ton·ic, *n.* medicine that promotes physical well-being; whatever imparts vigor or tone·*a.* invigorating.

to·night, to-night, *adv., n.* (in or during) the present or coming night.

ton·nage, *n.* weight in tons; carrying capacity of vehicle in tons; tax per ton.

ton·sil, *n.* one of two oval organs of soft tissue on sides of throat. **-lec·to·my,** *n.*

ton·sil·li·tis, *n.* inflammation of the tonsils.

ton·sure, *n.* act of shaving a man's head.

too, *adv.* in addition; likewise; also; excessive; very.

tool, *n.* implement for work; machine; instrument. *v.* shape with a tool.

tooth, *n. pl.,* **teeth.** one of the hard, dense structures attached in a row to each jaw; toothlike projection, as on a saw. **-ache, -brush,** *n.*

tooth·some, *a.* having a pleasant taste; tasty.

top, *n.* highest or uppermost part on surface; highest in rank; crown of the head; lid; choicest part; spinning toy. *a.* highest; foremost; greatest. *v.* **topped, top·ping.** put on, as a top; be at the top of; rise above; finish; outdo.

to·paz, *n.* yellow, quartz gem.

top·coat, *n.* light overcoat.

top·ic, *n.* subject of speech or writing; theme for discussion.

top·i·cal, *a.* of matters of present or local interest.

top·most, *a.* uppermost; highest.

top·notch, *a. inf.* best; excellent.

to·pog·ra·phy, *n.* science of showing surface features of an area on maps or charts; description of physical features of a region.

top·ple, *v.* fall, top foremost; overthrow.

top·sy-tur·vy, *adv., a.* upside down; confused; disordered.

torch, *n.* portable light; device for giving off hot flame.

tor·e·a·dor, *n.* bullfighter.

tor·ment, *v., n.* (cause) extreme pain, anguish, annoyance.

tor·na·do, *n.* destructive whirling windstorm with funnel-shaped cloud; whirlwind.

tor·pe·do, *n. pl.,* **-does.** self-propelled underwater explosive device. *v.* attack with a torpedo.

tor·pid, *a.* dormant; apathetic; sluggish. **-por,** *n.*

torque, *n.* force that causes rotation.

tor·rent, *n.* rushing, turbulent stream; flood of words, etc.; heavy storm.

tor·rid, *a.* parching or burning; scorching; ardent; passionate.

tor·sion, *n.* twisting; twisted state; stress by twisting.

tor·so, *n.* trunk of human body.

torte, *n.* rich pastry cake.

tor·til·la, *n.* flat, round, coarse cornmeal cake.

tor·toise, *n.* turtle, esp. one living on land.

tor·tu·ous, *a.* turning, winding, crooked; indirect; devious.

tor·ture, *v., n.* (inflicting) severe physical or mental pain.

toss, *v.* throw, pitch, fling about; throw up or toward; move restlessly; discuss easily; mix gently. *n.*

toss·up, *n. inf.* tossing of coin to decide a question; an even chance.

tot, *n.* young child; toddler.

to·tal, *a.* entire; complete. *n.* the whole sum or amount. *v.* add up; amount to; *inf.* demolish. **-i·ty,** *n.* **-ly,** *adv.*

to·tal·i·tar·i·an, *a.* of a government exclusively controlled by one party that suppresses dissent by force.

tote, *v. inf.* carry with.

to·tem, *n.* token or emblem of a group; symbol. **-ic,** *a.*

to·tem pole, *n.* post carved and painted with totemic figures.

tot·ter, *v.* shake or waver; walk unsteadily.

touch, *v.* perceive by feeling; place hand, fingers, etc. in contact with; reach; equal; be adjacent to; affect with emotion. *n.* act of touching; sense by which a thing is perceived by contact; a trace.

touch·down, *n.* football scoring play; act of touching down, as an airplane.

tou·ché, **fencing score; congratulatory remark for witty reply.**

touch·y, *a.* sensitive; risky.

tough, *a.* strong; durable; difficult to cut or chew; difficult to do; viscous; hardy. **-en,** *v.*

tou·pee, *n.* small wig to cover bald spot; hairpiece.

tour, *n.* lengthy trip or journey; set period of service. *v.* make a trip; drive around; brief survey or circuit. **-ism, -ist,** *n.*

tour·na·ment, *n.* series of competitive sports games.

tour·ni·quet, *n.* device to stop bleeding by compression.

tou·sle, *v.* disarrange; dishevel; rumple. **-sled,** *a.*

tow, *v.* pull, drag, as by rope. *n.*

to·ward, *prep.* in the direction of; near in time; facing; for. Also **to·wards.**

tow·el, *n.* absorbent cloth or soft paper for drying, wiping.

tow·er, *n.* tall, narrow structure; place of security. *v.* rise above or high.

tow·head, *n.* person with blond hair.

town, *n.* urban center smaller than a city.

town·ship, *n.* administrative division of county with varying corporate powers.

tox·ic, *a.* poisonous.

tox·in, *n.* poison produced by bacteria.

toy, *n.* plaything; trinket; trifle. *a.* petty; small. *v.* trifle with.

trace, *n.* mark left when thing is no longer present; minute quantity. *v.* follow the tracks or trail; to follow; copy by following lines.

tra·che·a, *n.* windpipe; tube that carries air to and from lungs.

track, *n.* parallel steel rails for railroad cars; mark(s) left by something that has passed; trail or path; course of action; course for racing. *v.* follow the tracks of; make tracks or footprints on.

tract, *n.* expanse of land, water; a system of parts, organs in the body; brief treatise or pamphlet.

trac·ta·ble, *a.* easily led or controlled; docile.

trac·tion, *n.* pulling or drawing; adhesive friction on a surface.

trac·tor, *n.* self-propelled vehicle for pulling equipment.

trade, *n.* occupation, esp. skilled mechanical work; craft; commerce; buying and selling of commodities; goods; customers. *v.* buy, sell; exchange.

trade·mark, *n.* mark, wording, symbol to distinguish one product from competitors. *v.* register a trademark.

tra·di·tion, *n.* transmission of knowledge, customs, opinions, practices from generation to generation; a custom. **-al,** *a.*

tra·duce, *v.* misrepresent willfully; defame; slander.

traf·fic, *n.* movement of goods, vehicles, persons between certain points; business flow; (illegal) commerce. *v.,* **-ficked, -fick·ing.** do business, esp. illegally.

trag·e·dy, *n.* serious play with gloomy ending; any tragic or disastrous incident. **tra·ge·di·an,** *n.*

trag·ic, *a.* causing or likely to cause suffering, sorrow, or death.

trail, *v.* follow; fall or come behind; lag behind; draw or drag lightly over the ground; be losing. *n.* the track or scent indicating the passage of someone or something; a path; something trailed behind.

trail·er, *n.* vehicle pulled by car, tractor, truck; house trailer.

train, *n.* series of connected railway cars; procession; retinue; sequence; something that drags behind. *v.* discipline and instruct; make skillful, obedient, or fit; aim; direct; guide.

traipse, *v.* wander; tramp.

trait, *n.* characteristic; feature.

trai·tor, *n.* one who commits treason or betrays.

tra·jec·to·ry, *n.* path of an object moving through space, as a bullet.

tramp, *v.* walk or wander about; trample; walk heavily. *n.* vagabond; hobo; freight ship.

tram·ple, *v.* tread heavily on or over; crush.

trance, *n.* dazed, dreamlike, or sleeplike condition; stupor.

tran·quil, *a.* peaceful; quiet; calm. **-i·ty,** *n.* **-ize,** *v.* **-iz·er,** *n.*

trans·act, *v.* conduct or carry through, as business; accomplish. **-action,** *n.*

tran·scend, *v.* surpass; go beyond the limits of; exceed. **-ent,** *a.*

tran·scribe, *v.* copy from an original; make a handwritten or typed copy of; translate. **-scrip·tion,** *n.*

tran·script, *n.* something transcribed; copy of student's acamedic record.

tran·sect, *v.* cut across.

trans·fer, *v.,* **-ferred, -fer·ring.** convey from one place or person to another; move. *n.* act of transferring; ticket to change bus, train, etc.; picture moved from one surface to another. **-a·ble,** *a.* **-ence,** *n.*

trans·fix, *v.* impale; pierce through.

trans·form, *v.* change the appearance, form, condition; convert. **-for·ma·tion,** *n.*

trans·form·er, *n.* device for changing alternating current into lower or higher voltage.

trans·fuse, *v.* instill or impart; infuse; transfer blood from one to another. **-fu·sion,** *n.*

trans·gress, *v.* break or violate a law or rule; sin. **-gres·sor, gres·sion,** *n.*

tran·sient, *a.* temporary; brief; ephemeral. *n.* transitory person or thing.

tran·sis·tor, *n.* device using a semi-conductor that performs same as an electron tube.

trans·it, *n.* passing over or through; transition; conveyance; transportation.

tran·si·tion, *n.* passage from one place or condition to another; change. **-al**, *a.*

tran·si·tive, *a.* of a verb that takes a direct object.

tran·si·to·ry, *a.* fleeting; brief.

trans·late, *v.* change into another language; explain. **-la·tion**, *n.*

trans·lu·cent, *a.* allowing passage of light but not permitting clear view of any object.

trans·mis·sion, *n.* act of transmitting; device that transmits power from engine to wheels.

trans·mit, *v.*, **-mit·ted, -mit·ting.** send from one place or person to another; send out, as radio waves; convey; communicate. **-ter**, *n.*

trans·mu·ta·tion, *n.* act of transmuting; conversion of an atom of an element into the atom of a different element, as by nuclear fission, etc.

trans·mute, *v.* change in nature or form.

tran·som, *n.* small window over door or other window.

trans·par·ent, *a.* allowing clear view of objects beyond; diaphanous; obvious.

tran·spire, *v.* emit, as through the skin or lungs; happen; occur.

trans·plant, *v.* remove and plant in another place or person. *n.* act of transplanting; thing transplanted.

trans·port, *v.* carry or convey from one place to another; carry away with emotion; enrapture. *n.* vessel or vehicle for transporting. **-por·ta·tion**, *n.*

trans·pose, *v.* change the order or place of; change to different musical key.

trans·sex·u·al, *n.* person genetically of one sex but who identifies psychologically with the other sex.

trans·verse, *a.* crosswise.

trap, *n.* device that springs shut for catching game; devious plan to catch a person unawares; golf course hazard; device to collect residual material. *v.* **trapped, trap·pings. catch in a trap; ambush.**

tra·peze, *n.* swing hanging from two ropes for acrobatic stunts.

trash, *n.* garbage; refuse; worthless matter. **-y**, *a.*

trau·ma, *n.* wound; injury; severe emotional shock. **-mat·ic**, *a.*

tra·vail, *n.* hard, wearisome work; childbirth; pain, anguish.

trav·el, *v.*, **-eled** or **-elled, -el·ing** or **-el·ling.** make a journey; go from place to place; proceed, advance. *n.* act of traveling; passage to or over; *pl.* trips.

trav·erse, *v.* pass over, across, through; scrutinize; oppose. *a.* lying or being across; transverse.

trav·es·ty, *n.* grotesque imitation; distorted or absurd occurrence; burlesque.

trawl, *v.* drag a large net behind fishing boat.

tray, *n.* shallow utensil or box with raised edge.

treach·er·ous, *a.* faithless; unreliable; untrustworthy; risky. **-y**, *n.*

tread, *v.*, **trod, trod·den** or **trod, tread·ing.** step or walk on, along, in, or over; trample; crush under the feet. *n.* act, sound, or way of walking; a step; outer tire pattern.

trea·dle, *n.* foot lever or pedal, usu. to cause rotary motion.

tread·mill, *n.* mechanism rotated by walking of persons or animals; monotonous routine or unrewarding effort.

trea·son, *n.* betrayal, treachery of one's country.

treas·ure, *n.* accumulated riches; precious or valued thing, person. *v.* hoard; cherish; prize.

treas·ur·y, *n.* place where government (or private) funds are received and disbursed. **-er**, *n.*

treat, *v.* act towards in a specific manner; give medical attention; deal with in writing, speaking, etc.; pay for another's entertainment. *n.* thing that gives pleasure; act of treating.

trea·tise, *n.* formal essay.

treat·ment, *n.* manner of treating anything; medical measures to cure or correct.

trea·ty, *n.* formal agreement or compact between nations.

tre·ble, *a.* triple; of the highest musical range; soprano. *n.* high, piping sound. *v.* triple.

tree, *n.* woody perennial plant with trunk, branches, leaves.

trek, *v.*, **trekked, trek·king.** travel laboriously, slowly; travel. *n.* slow, difficult journey.

trel·lis, *n.* latticework to support vines; open-work structure.

trem·ble, *v.* shake; quiver; vibrate; quaver.

tre·men·dous, *a.* extraordinarily large, great; awe-inspiring; *inf.* marvelous.

trem·or, *n.* involuntary shaking; vibrations. **-u·lous**, *a.*

trench, *n.* ditch; furrow.

trench·ant, *a.* clear; incisive.

trend, *v.*, *n.* prevailing or probable tendency.

trep·i·da·tion, *n.* fear; anxiety.

tres·pass, *v.* go unlawfully on another's land; encroach or infringe; intrude. *n.* offense; intrusion.

tress, *n.* lock or curl of hair.

tres·tle, *n.* supporting framework for a bridge, etc.

tri·ad, *n.* group of three.

tri·al, *n.* court examination of the facts; act of testing or proving; state of being tried; hardship.

tri·an·gle, *n.* plane figure with three sides and three angles. **-gu·lar,** *a.*

tribe, *n.* group under a leader united by ancestry, etc. **trib·al,** *a.*

trib·u·la·tion, *n.* distress; misery; trial; trouble.

tri·bu·nal, *n.* court of justice.

trib·u·tar·y, *n.* stream flowing into larger stream. *a.* contributing factor.

trib·ute, *n.* payment for peace or protection; acknowledgment to show respect, thanks, etc.

trick, *n.* a deception; annoying act; joke; prank; stratagem; clever feat; cards played and won in one round. *v.* practice trickery; deceive. **-er·y,** *n.* **-y,** *a.*

trick·le, *v.* flow by drops or in a very thin stream. *n.* thin, broken flow.

tri·cy·cle, *n.* three-wheeled vehicle worked by pedals.

tried, *a.* tested; proved; trustworthy; dependable.

tri·fle, *n.* thing of little value or importance; small amount. *v.* treat lightly.

tri·fling, *a.* of slight importance; frivolous; trivial.

trig·ger, *n.* lever pressed to release a catch, spring, etc. *v.* start, set off, or release.

trig·o·nom·e·try, *n.* mathematics of the properties of triangles.

trill, *v.*, *n.* sing or play with a tremulous tone.

tril·lion, *n.* a million times a million; 1,000,000,000,000.

trim, *v.*, **trimmed, trim·ming.** make neat; clip; lop; balance; decorate. *n.* fitting condition, ornamentation; building woodwork. *a.* in good condition; orderly. **-ming,** *n.*

trin·i·ty, *n.* state of being three; triad; (*cap*) Father, Son, and Holy Spirit as one.

trin·ket, *n.* small ornament.

tri·o, *n. pl.*, **-os.** musical composition for three players; group of three.

trip, *n.* journey; a stumble; light, nimble step; mistake. *v.* **tripped, trip·ping.** to stumble; step lightly; make an error.

tripe, *n.* animal stomach used as food; *inf.* nonsense; worthless stuff.

tri·ple, *a.* threefold; three times as many. *n.* group of three. *v.* make or become triple.

tri·plet, *n.* one of three children born at one birth.

trip·li·cate, *v.* make three times. *a.* threefold.

tri·pod, *n.* three-legged frame or stand.

tri·sect, *v.* divide into three parts.

trite, *a.* commonplace; stale.

trit·u·rate, *v.* pulverize.

tri·umph, *v.*, *n.* (win) a victory. **-um·phal, -um·phant,** *a.*

tri·um·vi·rate, *n.* group of three who govern; a trio.

triv·et, *n.* three-legged metal stand for hot dishes, iron, etc.

triv·i·a, *n. pl.* insignificant matters; trifles. **-al,** *a.* **-al·i·ty,** *n. pl.* **-al·i·ty.**

tro·che, *n.* small medicated lozenge.

troll, *v.* sing in a full, hearty voice; fish with a moving lure; to roll, turn. *n.* mythical cave-dweller.

trol·ley, *n.* electric streetcar; running pulley on overhead track.

trom·bone, *n.* brass musical instrument with sliding plate.

troop, *n.* group of people; flock or herd; cavalry unit; *pl.* soldiers. *v.* move in a group.

troop·er, *n.* cavalryman; mounted policeman; *inf.* state policeman.

tro·phy, *n. pl.*, **-phies.** prize to show victory, achievement; thing taken from an enemy.

trop·ic, *n.* one of two parallels of latitude N. and S. of equator; *pl.* regions in the torrid zone. **-i·cal,** *a.*

trot, *v.* **trot·ted, trot·ting.** go at a quick, steady gait. *n.* running gait of a person; horse's gait.

trou·ba·dour, *n.* lyric poet; wandering minstrel.

trou·ble, *v.* disturb; agitate; harass; perturb; distress. *n.* difficulty; unfortunate condition; worry. **-some,** *a.*

trough, *n.* long, shallow receptacle holding water, food for animals; gutter; narrow depression.

troupe, *n.* touring band of actors, performers. **troup·er,** *n.*

trou·sers, *n. pl.* two-legged garment; pants; slacks.

trous·seau, *n.* bride's outfit, clothes, linens, etc.

trout, *n.* salmon family fresh-water food and game fish.

trow·el, *n.* small garden tool for digging; mason's tool.

tru·ant, *n.* person who neglects duties; pupil absent from school without leave. **-an·cy,** *n.*

truce, *n.* agreement to suspend hostilities; armistice.

truck, *n.* vehicle for transporting heavy loads, goods, produce, etc.; small vehicle for baggage, etc. *v.* convey by truck; drive a truck.

truc·u·lent, *a.* savage; cruel.

trudge, *v.* walk wearily.

true, *a.* correct; loyal; trusty; honest, sincere; not false; sure; real; genuine. *n.* exact fact. *adv.* accurately; truly. **tru·ly,** *adj.*

truf·fle, *n.* fleshy, edible fungus.

trump, *v.*, *n.* (take with) a high-ranking card; outdo.

trum·pet, *n.* brass musical instrument with long, curved tube and bell-shaped end.

trun·cate, *v.*-**cat·ed,** -**cat·ing** cut off a part of. *a.* ending abruptly.

trun·dle, *v.* propel by rolling (on wheels). *n.* small wheel, caster; small carriage; bed, truck with low wheels.

trunk, *n.* main stem of a tree; large packing case; automobile storage compartment; torso; main line; elephant's long snout; *pl.* men's shorts.

truss, *v.* tie, bind, or fasten; brace, support. *n.* supporting framework; hernia brace.

trust, *n.* firm belief in some quality of a person, thing; hope; confidence in; obligation; custody. *v.* have faith or confidence in; hope; rely on; believe. **-ful, -wor·thy,** *a.*

trus·tee, *n.* one entrusted with property of another.

trust·y, *a.* faithful, dependable.

truth, *n.* conformity to fact, honesty; fidelity; reality. **-ful,** *a.*

try, *v.*, **tried, try·ing** attempt to do; make an effort; test the result, effect, quality of; put a strain on; determine judicially. *n. pl.* **tries.** act of trying; trial.

try·ing, *a.* exasperating; irksome; hard to endure.

try·out, *n.* test of ability.

tryst, *n.* appointment to meet; place of meeting.

T-square, *n.* T-shaped ruler.

tub, *n.* broad, open-topped vessel; bathtub.

tu·ba, *n.* large bass instrument of bugle family.

tube, *n.* hollow, slender cylinder; collapsible round container; underground tunnel.

tu·ber, *n.* thickened portion of underground stem, as the potato.

tu·ber·cu·lo·sis, *n.* infectious disease, esp. of lungs; consumption.

tuck, *v.* wrap snugly; draw together into a fold; thrust into a small space. *n.* sewed fold in a garment.

Tues·day, *n.* third day of week.

tuft, *n.* bunch of small things tied closely or growing together with upper ends loose; clump; cluster.

tug, *v.* **tugged, tug·ging** pull with effort or strongly; drag. *n.* strong pull; tugboat.

tug·boat, *n.* small powerful boat for towing, pushing other boats or barges.

tu·i·tion, *n.* charge or payment for instruction.

tu·lip, *n.* showy cup-shaped flower grown from bulbs.

tum·ble, *v.* roll or toss about; perform acrobatics; collapse; stumble or fall over. *n.* confused heap.

tum·bler, *n.* drinking glass without stem; part of a lock or gear; acrobat.

tu·mid, *a.* swollen; inflated.

tu·mor, *n.* abnormal growth of tissue in any part of body.

tu·mult, *n.* commotion; riot; uproar. **-mul·tu·ous,** *a.*

tu·na, *n.* large ocean game and food fish.

tun·dra, *n.* treeless arctic plain.

tune, *n.* melody; correct musical pitch; agreement; concord. *v.* put into tune; adjust precisely.

tune·ful, *a.* melodious.

tung·sten, *n.* heavy, ductile, metallic element with high melting point.

tu·nic, *n.* loose, gown-like garment; blouse; uniform coat.

tun·nel, *v.*, *n.* (make) an underground passage; conduit; tube.

tur·ban, *n.* scarf wound around head; headdress.

tur·bid, *a.* muddy; dense.

tur·bine, *n.* rotary engine actuated by flow of steam, air, water against vanes.

tur·bu·lent, *a.* violently disturbed or agitated. **-lence,** *n.*

tu·reen, *n.* deep, covered dish for holding soup, etc.

turf, *n.* surface layer of grass and its roots; *inf.* territory.

tur·gid, *a.* swollen; pompous.

tur·key, *n.* large bird, usu. domesticated, eaten as food.

tur·moil, *n.* disturbance; tumult; commotion.

turn, *v.* rotate; revolve; ponder; invert; prejudice; curdle; transform; change direction; direct thought, attention toward or away from; become indifferent or hostile; change in character, appearance; deflect; divert. *n.* rotation; place in order; inclination; change in direction or position; point where change occurs; change in condition, character.

turn·a·bout, *n.* face in opposite direction; about-face in opinion, etc.

turn·a·round, *n.* time required to do a job, as maintenance, loading, etc.; space for turning around; reversal of trend, etc.

turn·coat, *n.* traitor; renegade.

tur·nip, *n.* vegetable with thick, fleshy edible root.

turn·out, *n.* quantity produced; number of persons present.

turn·o·ver, *n.* an upset; a change or revolution; money taken in and paid out; goods sold and restocked; employee replacement rate.

turn·pike, *n.* highway on which there are or were toll charges.

turn·stile, *n.* revolving gateway.

turn·ta·ble, *n.* rotating circular platform.

tur·pen·tine, *n.* oily resin.

tur·pi·tude, *n.* depravity.

tur·quoise, *n.* greenish-blue gemstone or color.

tur·ret, *n.* small tower on a building; gun enclosure.

tur·tle, *n.* reptile whose body is encased in a shell.

tusk, *n.* long projecting tooth.

tus·sle, *n., v.* scuffle; struggle.

tu·te·lage, *n.* guardianship; act of tutoring; instruction.

tu·tor, *n.* private teacher. *v.* teach. **tu·to·ri·al,** *a.*

tu·tu, *n.* short, projecting, layered skirt worn by a ballerina.

tux·e·do, *n.* suit of men's semi-formal clothing without tails.

twang, *v., n.* (make) a sharp, vibrant sound; harsh, nasal sound.

tweak, *v.* pinch and twist sharply. *n.* a twisting pinch.

tweed, *n.* twilled woolen fabric used for clothes.

tweez·ers, *n. pl.* small pincers. **tweeze,** *v.* pluck.

twelve, *n., a.* one more than 11; a dozen. **twelfth,** *a. n.*

twen·ty, *n. a.* one more than 19. **twen·ti·eth,** *a.*

twice, *adv.* two times; two times as much; doubly.

twid·dle, *v.* twirl idly; play with idly.

twig, *n.* small branch of a tree.

twi·light, *n.* dim evening light.

twill, *n.* woven cloth with parallel, diagonal lines or ribs. **twilled,** *a.*

twin, *n.* one of two born at same birth; persons or things resembling each other. *a.* one of a pair; closely alike.

twine, *n.* twisted string or cord. *v.* twist together; wrap around.

twinge, *n.* sudden, brief, darting pain; emotional pang; qualm.

twin·kle, *v.* sparkle; flicker. *n.* a gleam; wink of eye.

twirl, *v., n.* whirl; rotate.

twist, *v.* combine by winding together; coil; distort; cause to rotate; distort or confuse the meaning. *n.* act or result of twisting; curve, turn, or bend; wrench or sprain.

twitch, *v.* pull sharply; jerk. *n.* muscle spasm; sudden jerk.

twit·ter, *v., n.* (utter) series of light chirps; titter.

two, *n. a.* one plus one.

two-faced, *a.* deceitful; insincere; hypocritical.

two·fold, *a.* double. *adv.* doubly.

two-time, *v.* be unfaithful to; double-cross.

two-way, *a.* permitting vehicles to go opposite ways simultaneously; reciprocal exchanges, duties; involving two persons or groups; capable of sending and receiving.

ty·coon, *n. inf.* wealthy, important, powerful businessman.

tyke, *n. inf.* small child.

type, *n.* class or group; standard or model; metal pieces with letters, characters for printing. *v.* typewrite; determine the type of; identify.

type·writ·er, *n.* keyboard machine for producing type-like writing.

ty·phoid, *n.* serious, infectious intestinal disease.

ty·phoon, *n.* violent storm.

ty·phus, *n.* acute infectious disease with fever, rash, mental disorders, extreme prostration.

typ·i·cal, *a.* representative, or conforming to some type.

typ·i·fy, *v.* **-fied, -fy·ing** serve as an example of; represent by a type.

ty·pog·ra·phy, *n.* the arrangement, style of type, and appearance of printed matter; act of composing and printing.

tyr·an·ny, *n.pl.* **-ies.** government by absolute rule; oppressive government; despotism. **ty·rant,** *n.* **ty·ran·ni·cal,** *a.* **tyr·an·nize,** *v.*

ty·ro, *n.* novice; beginner.

U

u·biq·ui·tous, *a.* existing, or seeming to exist everywhere at once; omnipresent. **-ly,** *adv.* **-ness,** *n.*

ud·der, *n.* baggy milk gland with more than one teat.

ug·ly, *a.,* **-li·er, -li·est.** unsightly; offensive; repulsive; threatening; ill-tempered. **-li·ly,** *adv.* **-li·ness,** *n.*

u·ku·le·le, *n.* small guitar-like instrument with four strings.

ul·cer, *n.* open sore; any corrupt or evil condition.

ul·te·ri·or, *a.* secondary considerations; hidden (as motives).

ul·ti·mate, *a.* extreme; final; maximum, elementary; remote. *n.* best; most fundamental. **-ly,** *adv.*

ul·ti·ma·tum, *n. pl.,* **-tums, -ta.** final proposal, demand, offer.

ul·tra, *a.* excessive; extreme.

ul·tra·son·ic, *a.* sound wave frequencies above the limits of human audibility.

ul·tra·vi·o·let, *a.* of light rays beyond the visible spectrum.

um·ber, *n.* brown pigment.

um·bil·i·cal, *a.* referring to, situated near the navel; flexible tube that serves as conduit for air, power, etc. for astronaut, aquanaut when outside the craft; similar device to provide fuel, etc. to spacecraft before launching.

um·bra, *n. pl.,* **-bras, -brae.** area of total shadow during eclipse.

um·brage, *n.* resentment; anger; shade or shadow.

um·brel·la, *n.* portable canopy on a folding frame used for shelter from sun or rain.

um·pire, *n.* official chosen to enforce the game rules in sports; arbiter.

ump·teen, *a. inf.* very many.

un·a·bashed, *a.* not embarrassed. **-bash·ed·ly,** *adv.*

un·a·ble, *a.* not able.

un·a·bridged, *a.* comprehensive; complete.

un·ac·count·a·ble, *a.* unexplainable; odd. **-bly,** *adv.*

un·ac·cus·tomed, *a.* uncommon.

un·af·fect·ed, *a.* natural; sincere; genuine. **-ly,** *adv.*

u·nan·i·mous, *a.* showing complete accord; agreeing. **u·na·nim·i·ty,** *n.* **-ly,** *adv.*

un·ap·proach·a·ble, *a.* inaccessible; not friendly; aloof.

un·armed, *a.* without weapons; defenseless.

un·as·sum·ing, *a.* modest; not pretentious.

un·at·tached, *a.* not attached; unmarried; not connected with.

un·a·void·a·ble, *a.* inevitable.

un·a·ware, *a.* not cognizant.

un·a·wares, *adv.* unexpectedly; unwittingly.

un·bal·anced, *a.* not balanced; mentally deranged.

un·bear·a·ble, *a.* intolerable.

un·be·com·ing, *a.* unattractive; not suitable; improper.

un·be·liev·a·ble, *a.* incredible.

un·be·liev·er, *n.* skeptic.

un·bend, *v.,* **-bent** or **-bend·ed, -bend·ing.** relax; straighten.

un·bend·ing, *a.* stiff; resolute.

un·bi·ased, *a.* not prejudiced; free from bias.

un·blush·ing, *a.* shameless.

un·born, *a.* not yet born.

un·bri·dled, *a.* unrestrained; unruly; uncontrolled.

un·bro·ken, *a.* not broken or violated; uninterrupted; not tamed, surpassed, disarranged.

un·called-for, *a.* unwarranted; unnecessary; unprovoked.

un·can·ny, *a.* eerie, mysterious, weird; not natural.

un·ceas·ing, *a.* perpetual; continual. **-ly,** *adv.*

un·cer·e·mo·ni·ous, *a.* informal; abrupt; discourteous; rude.

un·cer·tain, *a.* not determined or sure; unreliable; questionable.

un·char·i·ta·ble, *a.* unforgiving; ungenerous; harsh.

un·civ·il, *a.* discourteous.

un·cle, *n.* brother of one's father or mother; husband of one's aunt.

un·clean, *a.* filthy; impure.

un·clear, *a.* clouded; indistinct.

un·com·fort·a·ble, *a.* not at ease; disquieting; uneasy.

un·com·mon, *a.* not usual; extraordinary; strange. **-ly,** *adv.* **-ness,** *n.*

un·com·mu·ni·ca·tive, *a.* nontalkative; reserved; taciturn.

un·com·pro·mis·ing, *a.* inflexible; strict; unyielding. **-mised,** *a.* **-mis·ing·ly,** *adv.*

un·con·cern, *n.* lack of anxiety; indifference. **-cerned,** *a.*

un·con·di·tion·al, *a.* absolute; without stipulations. **-ly**, *adv.*

un·con·scion·a·ble, *a.* unscrupulous; inequitable; unprincipled. **-ble·ness**, *n.* **-bly**, *adv.*

un·con·scious, *a.* not conscious or aware; unintentional.

un·con·sti·tu·tion·al, *a.* violating or contrary to the constitution.

un·con·straint, *n.* ease; abandon; spontaneity.

un·con·ven·tion·al, *a.* not ordinary; not formal.

un·count·ed, *a.* not counted; innumerable.

un·cou·ple, *v.*, **-pled**, **-pling.** unfasten; disconnect.

un·couth, *a.* lacking in manners; crude; boorish.

un·cov·er, *v.* disclose; make known; remove a cover from.

unc·tion, *n.* act of anointing; ointment; affected sincerity.

unc·tu·ous, *a.* greasy; suave; affectedly sincere. **-ly**, *adv.*

un·daunt·ed, *a.* fearless; intrepid; brave.

un·de·cid·ed, *a.* not decided or determined; irresolute.

un·de·mon·stra·tive, *a.* reserved.

un·de·ni·a·ble, *a.* indisputable.

un·de·pend·a·ble, *a.* unreliable; untrustworthy.

un·der, *prep.* beneath; below; lower than; less than; covered by; because of; subject to. *adv.* below or beneath; in a lower place, etc. *a.* lower; subordinate.

un·der·bid, *v.* bid lower than.

un·der·brush, *n.* undergrowth.

un·der·class·man, *n.* freshman or sophomore.

un·der·clothes, *n. pl.* underwear.

un·der·coat, *n.* surface-sealing compound; rustproofant.

un·der·cov·er, *a.* surreptitious; secret; engaged in spying.

un·der·cur·rent, *n.* current below the surface; hidden drift or tendency.

un·der·cut, *v.* undersell; undermine; strike ball with downward motion.

un·der·dog, *n.* predicted loser; victim of oppression.

un·der·em·ployed, *a.* employed only part-time or at low income; not employed to full extent of capabilities, education.

un·der·es·ti·mate, *v.*, **-mat·ed**, **-mat·ing.** put too low an estimate or valuation upon things or people; underrate.

un·der·foot, *adv.*, *a.* in the way.

un·der·go, *v.*, **-went**, **-gone**, **-going.** experience; endure.

un·der·grad·u·ate, *n.* student who has no degree.

un·der·ground, *a.* done or situated below ground; done in secret. *n.* thing below ground; secret group. *adv.*

un·der·hand, *a.* sly; secret; with the hand below the shoulder. *adv.* secretly; slyly.

un·der·hand·ed, *a.* secret; sly.

un·der·lie, *v.*, **-lay**, **-lain**, **-ly·ing.** be beneath; be at the basis of.

un·der·line, *v.*, **-lined**, **-lin·ing.** underscore; emphasize. *n.*

un·der·ling, *n.* one who must obey orders of others; subordinate; inferior.

un·der·ly·ing, *a.* lying under; basic; fundamental.

un·der·mine, *v.*, **-mined**, **-min·ing.** dig beneath; wear away; impair secretly.

un·der·neath, *prep.* beneath; below. *adv.* in or at a lower place. *a.* lower. *n.* underside.

un·der·pass, *n.* road, etc. that runs beneath, esp. under another road, etc.

un·der·priv·i·leged, *a.* deprived of basic rights; poor.

un·der·rate, *v.*, **-rat·ed**, **-rat·ing.** undervalue; underestimate.

un·der·score, *v.*, **-scored**, **-scor·ing.** underline; emphasize.

un·der·shoot, *v.*, **-shot**, **-shoot·ing.** shoot short of or below a target; land an airplane short of runway.

un·der·side, *n.* lower or underside of surface.

un·der·signed, *n.* person or persons who have signed their names on a document, letter, etc.

un·der·stand, *v.*, **-stood**, **-stand·ing.** comprehend; perceive the meaning or character of; believe; be sympathetic; interpret; accept. **-a·ble**, *a.* **-a·bly**, *adv.*

un·der·stand·ing, *n.* comprehension; compassion; tolerance; viewpoint; mutual agreement. *a.*

un·der·state, *v.*, **-stat·ed**, **-stat·ing.** represent as less than is the case; state in a restrained manner. **-ment**, *n.*

un·der·stood, *a.* comprehended; agreed upon; assumed; implicit.

un·der·stud·y, *v.*, **-ied**, **-y·ing.** be ready to replace. *n. pl.*, **-ies.** substitute actor.

un·der·take, *v.*, **-took**, **-tak·en**, **-tak·ing.** attempt; guarantee.

un·der·tak·er, *n.* mortician.

un·der·tak·ing, *n.* task; enterprise; guarantee; pledge.

un·der·tone, *n.* subdued tone or color; implied meaning; quality.

un·der·tow, *n.* forceful current beneath sea surface.

un·der·wear, *n.* garments worn underneath outer garments.

un·der·world, *n.* world of organized crime; Hades.

un·der·write, *v.,* **-wrote, -writ·ten, -writ·ing.** agree to; assume liability; guarantee; sign; insure.

un·do, *v.,* **-did, -done, -do·ing.** reverse, annul; release; untie; open up; destroy; disturb.

un·doubt·ed, *a.* assured; certain. **-ly,** *adv.*

un·dress, *v.* divest of clothes; strip.

un·due, *a.* improper; excessive.

un·du·late, *v.,* **-lat·ed, -lat·ing.** move in curving lines; move in waves.

un·du·ly, *adv.* excessively; improperly; unjustifiably.

un·earned, *a.* not earned by labor, skill, etc.; undeserved.

un·earth, *v.* dig up; discover.

un·earth·ly, *a.* supernatural; weird; outlandish; *inf.* absurd.

un·eas·y, *a.,* **-i·er, -i·est.** uncomfortable; disturbed; anxious; unstable. **un·ease,** *n.* **-i·ly,** *adv.* **-i·ness,** *n.*

un·em·ployed, *a.* out of work; idle. **-ploy·ment,** *n.*

un·e·qual, *a.* not equal in size, ability, etc.; insufficient; not balanced; irregular.

un·e·qualed, *a.* not equaled or matched; unrivaled.

un·e·quiv·o·cal, *a.* clear; not ambiguous; plain. **-ly,** *adv.*

un·err·ing, *a.* making no mistakes; accurate; infallible.

un·e·ven, *a.* not even, smooth, level; not straight; not fair; variable.

un·ex·pect·ed, *a.* unforeseen; not expected. **-ly,** *adv.*

un·faith·ful, *a.* disloyal; not abiding by a vow, duty, etc.

un·fa·mil·iar, *a.* not knowing well; strange. **-i·ar·i·ty,** *n.*

un·fa·vor·a·ble, *a.* adverse; not propitious.

un·fin·ished, *a.* incomplete.

un·flinch·ing, *a.* not shrinking; steadfast. **-ly,** *adv.*

un·fold, *v.* open; expand; disclose; unwrap.

un·fore·seen, *a.* unexpected.

un·for·get·ta·ble, *a.* impossible to forget; memorable. **-bly,** *adv.*

un·for·tu·nate, *a.* unlucky; disastrous. *n.* unlucky person.

un·found·ed, *a.* groundless; not established; baseless.

un·furl, *v.* unfold; open.

un·gain·ly, *a.* awkward.

un·god·ly, *a.,* **-li·er, -li·est.** godless; impious; sinful; wicked; *inf.* outrageous. **-li·ness,** *n.*

un·gra·cious, *a.* rude; offensive.

un·guard·ed, *a.* unprotected; careless; direct; without guile.

un·guent, *n.* salve; ointment.

un·hand, *v.* let go; release.

un·hap·py, *a.,* **-pi·er, -pi·est.** wretched; sad; unfortunate. **-pi·ly,** *adv.* **-pi·ness,** *n.*

un·health·y, *a.,* **-i·er, -i·est.** sickly; unwholesome; dangerous.

un·heard-of, *a.* unprecedented; unknown; outrageous.

un·ho·ly, *a.,* **-li·er, -li·est.** impious; wicked; *inf.* frightful.

u·ni·cel·lu·lar, *a.* having or consisting of one cell.

u·ni·corn, *n.* mythical horselike animal with one horn.

u·ni·form, *a.* unchanging; consistent. *n.* distinctive garb worn by members of a group. **-i·ty,** *n.*

u·ni·fy, *v.,* **-fied, -fy·ing.** cause to be one; consolidate; unite. **-fi·ca·tion,** *n.*

u·ni·lat·er·al, *a.* one-sided.

un·im·peach·a·ble, *a.* irreproachable; blameless.

un·in·hib·it·ed, *a.* heedless of convention; very informal.

un·in·ter·est·ed, *a.* indifferent.

un·ion, *n.* joining together; united; junction; coupling.

un·ion·ize, *v.,* **-ized, -iz·ing.** organize into a labor union.

u·nique, *a.* only one of its kind; exceptional. *n.*

u·ni·sex, *a. inf.* appropriate to or having characteristics of both sexes.

u·ni·son, *n.* harmony; say or sing together; same in pitch.

u·nit, *n.* fixed quantity or amount; single thing or group; whole.

u·nite, *v.,* **-nit·ed, -nit·ing.** join together; combine.

u·nit·ed, *a.* joined; combined.

u·ni·ty, *n. pl.,* **-ties.** oneness; concord; harmony.

u·ni·ver·sal, *a.* prevalent or common everywhere; involving all. **-i·ty,** *n.* **-ize,** *v.*

u·ni·verse, *n.* totality of things existing; cosmos; whole creation.

u·ni·ver·si·ty, *n. pl.,* **-ties.** institution of higher learning.
un·just, *a.* unfair. **-ly,** *adv.*
un·kempt, *a.* disheveled; rough.
un·kind, *a.* unsympathetic; harsh; cruel.
un·known, *a.* unfamiliar; not identified or recognized.
un·law·ful, *a.* illegal; not moral.
un·learn·ed, *a.* ignorant; illiterate.
un·less, *conj.* if not; except that. *prep.* except; excepting.
un·let·tered, *a.* not educated; illiterate.
un·like, *a.* different; unequal. *prep.* different from.
un·like·ly, *a.,* **-li·er, -li·est.** improbable; unpromising. *adv.*
un·lim·it·ed, *a.* not restricted; boundless; infinite.
un·load, *v.* remove the load; get rid of; dump.
un·looked-for, *a.* unexpected.
un·luck·y, *a.,* **-i·er, -i·est.** unfortunate; inauspicious.
un·man·ly, *a.* weak; cowardly.
un·mask, *v.* reveal; expose.
un·men·tion·a·ble, *a.* unfit to be noticed or talked about. *n.*
un·mer·ci·ful, *a.* cruel; pitiless; extreme; exorbitant. **-ly,** *adv.*
un·mis·tak·a·ble, *a.* obvious.
un·mit·i·gat·ed, *a.* not lessened; unmodified; absolute.
un·nat·u·ral, *a.* abnormal; perverse; strange; artificial.
un·nec·es·sary, *a.* not required.
un·or·gan·ized, *a.* not organized; without structure; not unionized.
un·par·al·leled, *a.* matchless; unsurpassed; unprecedented.
un·pleas·ant, *a.* disagreeable; objectionable. **-ness,** *n.*
un·pop·u·lar, *a.* generallly disliked, unaccepted, etc.
un·prac·ticed, *a.* not skilled; not tried; inexperienced.
un·prec·e·dent·ed, *a.* preceded by no similar case; novel.
un·prin·ci·pled, *a.* without moral principles; unscrupulous.
un·ques·tion·a·ble, *a.* certain beyond doubt; indisputable.
un·rav·el, *v.,* **-eled, -el·ing.** disentangle; solve.
un·read, *a.* uninformed; unlearned; not yet read.
un·re·al, *a.* false; imaginary.
un·rea·son·a·ble, *a.* contrary to reason; immoderate.

un·re·lent·ing, *a.* inflexible.
un·re·li·a·ble, *a.* undependable.
un·re·mit·ting, *a.* unceasing.
un·rest, *n.* uneasiness; anxiety.
un·ri·valed, *a.* having no rival.
un·roll, *v.* open; exhibit.
un·ruf·fled, *a.* calm; smooth.
un·ru·ly, *a.,* **-li·er, -li·est.** turbulent; uncontrollable. **-li·ness,** *n.*
un·sa·vor·y, *a.* disagreeable; morally offensive; tasteless.
un·scathed, *a.* unharmed.
un·scru·pu·lous, *a.* unprincipled.
un·seem·ly, *a.* indecent; unbecoming; not appropriate.
un·set·tle, *v.,* **-tled, -tling.** disrupt; upset; disturb; confuse.
un·sight·ly, *a.,* **-li·er, -li·est.** offensive to the sight; ugly.
un·skilled, *a.* untrained.
un·so·phis·ti·cat·ed, *a.* naïve; artless; simple; plain. **-ca·tion,** *n.*
un·sound, *a.* not solid; unhealthy; untrue; invalid.
un·spar·ing, *a.* merciless; liberal.
un·speak·a·ble, *a.* very bad.
un·sta·ble, *a.* not stable; shaky; unsteady; irresolute.
un·stead·y, *a.,* **-i·er, -i·est.** shaky; fickle; variable; unstable.
un·strung, *a.* nervous; upset.
un·sung, *a.* unacclaimed.
un·think·a·ble, *a.* inconceivable; impossible; not likely.
un·think·ing, *a.* lacking thought, care, or attention.
un·til, *conj.* to the degree that; before. *prep.* up to the time of; before.
un·time·ly, *a.* inopportune; premature. *adv.* before time.
un·told, *a.* not told; very great; unrevealed; vast.
un·to·ward, *a.* unfavorable; improper.
un·truth, *n.* being untrue; falsehood. **-ful,** *a.*
un·used, *a.* not or never used; unaccustomed to.
un·u·su·al, *a.* rare; uncommon.
un·ut·ter·a·ble, *a.* unspeakable.
un·veil, *v.* disclose; reveal.
un·war·rant·a·ble, *a.* not justified.
un·war·y, *a.* careless.
un·whole·some, *a.* unhealthy.
un·wield·y, *a.* bulky; awkward.
un·will·ing, *a.* reluctant; loath.
un·wit·ting, *a.* unaware; accidental; inadvertent. **-ly,** *adv.*

un·wind, *v.* **-wound, -wind·ing.** reverse; untwist; disentangle; relax.

un·wont·ed, *a.* rare; unusual; not habitual. **-ness**, *n.*

un·wor·thy, *a.* dishonorable; undeserving.

un·wrap, *v.,* **-wrapped, -wrap·ping.** open; undo; disclose.

un·yield·ing, *a.* stiff; obstinate.

up, *adv.* to, toward, in, or on a higher place; greater size or amount, etc.; in a vertical position; erect; in an activity; completely; at an end. *a.* moving or directed upward; at an end; *inf.* going on; informed. *prep.* to, toward, or at a higher point. *n.* ascent. *v.* put or take up; *inf.* increase.

up·beat, *a. inf.* lively; cheerful.

up·braid, *v.* reproach; scold.

up·bring·ing, *n.* training.

up·date, *v.,* **-dat·ed, -dat·ing.** bring up to date.

up·grade, *n.* ascending slope; increase; rise. *v.,* **-grad·ed, -grad·ing.** elevate; raise.

up·heav·al, *n.* violent change. **upheave**, *v.,* **up·heaved** or **up·hove, up·heav·ing.**

up·hill, *adv.* upward. *a.* going up against difficulties. *n.*

up·hold, *v.,* **-held, -hold·ing.** hold up; sustain; lift up; aid.

up·hol·ster, *v.* fit furniture with cushions, fabric, etc. **-y**, *n. pl.,* **-ies.**

up·keep, *n.* act or cost of keeping in good condition.

up·lift, *v.* elevate; raise.

up·on, *prep. on. adv.* on.

up·per, *a.* higher in location, rank. *n.* shoe above the sole; *inf.* stimulating drug.

up·per·cut, *n.* swinging (fist) blow directed upward.

up·per·most, *a.* highest in place, rank, etc.; foremost. *adv.* first.

up·raise, *v.* **-raised, -rais·ing.** lift up; elevate.

up·right, *a.* vertical; erect; righteous; just. *n.* thing standing erect.

up·ris·ing, *n.* rebellion; revolt.

up·roar, *n.* commotion; riot.

up·roar·i·ous, *a.* comical; loud.

up·root, *v.* eradicate; pull up.

up·set, *v.,* **-set, -set·ting.** capsize; invalidate; overturn; disturb; confuse; defeat. *n.* defeat; personal disorder. *a.* disorder.

up·shot, *n.* conclusion; outcome.

up·side, *n.* upper side or part.

up·side down, *adv.* in complete disorder; reversed in position. **up·side-down**, *a.*

up·stage, *v.,* **-staged, -stag·ing.** try to outdo.

up·stairs, *a.* of or on an upper floor. *adv.* to or on an upper story.

up·stand·ing, *a.* erect; honest; straightforward.

up·start, *n.* one who recently came into power, wealth, etc., esp. if arrogant, etc.

up·swing, *n.* increase; rise.

up-to-date, *a.* modern; including the latest data; abreast of the latest.

up·turn, *v.* turn up or over. *n.* increase; improvement.

up·ward(s), *adv.* in or toward a higher place. *a.* in a higher place.

u·ra·ni·um, *n.* metallic, radioactive element.

U·ra·nus, *n.* seventh planet.

ur·ban, *a.* characteristic of or including cities or towns.

ur·bane, *a.* sophisticated; polite; refined. **ur·ban·i·ty**, *n.*

ur·chin, *n.* roguish child.

u·re·mi·a, *n.* toxic condition due to blood in urine.

urge, *v.,* **urged, urg·ing.** drive forward; plead with; advocate; impel. *n.* strong impulse.

ur·gent, *a.* insistent; pressing; imperative. **ur·gen·cy**, *n. pl.,* **-cies. ur·gent·ly**, *adv.*

u·ri·nate, *v.,* **-nat·ed, -nat·ing.** void, pass urine. **-na·tion**, *n.*

u·rine, *n.* fluid secreted by the kidneys.

urn, *n.* large vase; vessel.

us, *pron.* objective case of *we.*

us·a·ble, use·a·ble, *a.* suitable for use. **-ab·ly**, *adv.* **-ness**, *n.*

us·age, *n.* customary, accepted, or habitual practice; custom.

use, *v.,* **used, us·ing.** put into service or practice; utilize; exploit; consume. *n.* purpose; function; employment; object; esteem; power.

used, *a.* secondhand.

use·ful, *a.* helpful; serviceable. **-ness**, *n.*

use·less, *a.* futile; worthless.

ush·er, *n.* one who conducts people to seats. *v.* escort.

u·su·al, *a.* ordinary; customary; normal. **-ly**, *adv.*

u·surp, *v.* seize unlawfully.

u·su·ry, *n. pl.,* **-ries.** charging exorbitant interest for the lending of money. **-rer**, *n.*

u·ten·sil, *n.* instrument, tool, esp. for domestic use.

u·ter·us, *n. pl.,* **-i.** womb.

u·til·i·ty, *n. pl.,* **-ties.** usefulness; a public service; fitness. **-tar·i·an**, *n.*

u·ti·lize, *v.,* **-lized, -liz·ing.** make use of. **-li·za·tion**, *n.*

ut·most, *a.* of the greatest degree; extreme. *n.* most possible.

u·to·pia, *n.* ideally perfect situation, place.

ut·ter, *a.* absolute; total. *v.* say; express. **-ance,** *n.*

ut·ter·most, *a., n.* utmost.

ux·o·ri·ous, *a.* overly fond of or submissive to one's wife.

V

va·can·cy, *n. pl.,* **-cies.** unoccupied place, space, or position. **-cant,** *a.* **-cant·ly,** *adv.*

va·cate, *v.,* **-cat·ed, -cat·ing.** make empty; leave; annul.

va·ca·tion, *n.* rest, recreation from regular work, study; holiday. *v.*

vac·cine, *n.* preparation used for inoculation to give immunity. **-ci·nate,** *v.* **-ci·na·tion,** *n.*

vac·il·late, *v.,* **-lat·ed, -lat·ing.** waver; be irresolute. **-lat·ing,** *a.* **-la·tion,** *n.*

va·cu·i·ty, *n. pl.,* **-ties.** emptiness; lack of intelligence.

vac·u·ous, *a.* empty; unintelligent.

vac·u·um, *n. pl.,* **-ums.** space devoid of matter; a void. *v. inf.* clean with a vacuum cleaner.

vag·a·bond, *a.* nomadic; wandering; vagrant. *n.*

va·ga·ry, *n. pl.,* **-ies.** wild fancy; caprice. **-i·ous,** *a.*

va·gi·na, *n.* canal leading from female, external genital orifice to uterus.

va·grant, *n.* tramp; homeless wanderer. **-gran·cy,** *n.*

vague, *a.* unclear; indefinite; obscure; indistinct. **-ness,** *n.*

vain, *a.* conceited; useless; unsuccessful. **-ly,** *adv.*

val·ance, *n.* short, decorative drapery. **-anced,** *a.*

vale, *n.* valley.

val·e·dic·to·ry, *n. pl.,* **-ries.** farewell speech. **-ri·an,** *n.*

val·en·tine, *n.* card, gift, sweetheart on St. Valentine's Day.

val·et, *n.* personal manservant; man in hotel who cleans and presses clothes.

val·iant, *a.* brave; courageous.

val·id, *a.* based on facts; legally binding. **-ly,** *adv.* **va·lid·i·ty,** *n.*

val·i·date, *v.* **-dat·ed, -dat·ing.** confirm by facts or authority; legalize. **-da·tion,** *n.*

va·lise, *n.* suitcase.

val·ley, *n. pl.,* **-leys.** land between hills or mountains; land drained by a river; depression.

val·or, *n.* marked courage; personal heroism. **-ous,** *a.*

val·u·able, *a.* having great worth; costly. *n. usu. pl.* article of value.

val·u·a·tion, *n.* appraisal; estimated value. **-al,** *a.*

val·ue, *n.* worth, merit, or importance; market price; *pl.* principles. *v.,* **-ued, -u·ing.** appraise; regard highly; prize. **-ued,** *a.*

valve, *n.* device used to regulate flow of a liquid or gas.

vamp, *n. inf.* seductive woman. *v.* repair; patch.

vam·pire, *n.* blood-sucking bat.

van, *n.* large covered truck or wagon.

van·dal, *n.* destroyer; one who willfully damages property. **-ism,** *n.,* **-ize,** *v.,* **-ized, -iz·ing.**

vane, *n.* device to show wind direction; turbine, etc. blade.

van·guard, *n.* forward part of an army; foremost position.

va·nil·la, *n.* extract from orchid pods used as flavoring.

van·ish, *v.* disappear; fade.

van·i·ty, *n. pl.,* **-ties.** excessive pride; conceit; futility; a dressing table; compact.

van·quish, *v.* defeat; conquer.

van·tage, *n.* advantage.

vap·id, *a.* insipid; flat; uninteresting. **-i·ty,** **ness,** *n.*

va·por, *n.* gaseous phase of any solid or liquid; visible mist, smoke, etc. **-ous,** *a.*

va·por·ize, *v.,* **-ized, -iz·ing.** to convert or be converted into vapor.

var·i·a·ble, *a.* changeable; not constant. *n.* thing likely to change. **-bil·i·ty, -ble·ness,** *n.*

var·i·ance, *n.* discrepancy; difference; dispute.

var·i·ant, *a.* varying; differing. *n.* thing differing in form only.

var·i·a·tion, *n.* alteration; deviation; modification.

var·i·cose, *a.* dilated; swollen.

var·ied, *a.* changed; diversified.

var·i·e·gat·ed, *a.* varied in color, with streaks and blotches; having different forms, etc.

va·ri·e·ty, *n. pl.,* **-ties.** diversity; varied assortment. **-tal,** *a.*

var·i·ous, *a.* diverse; several; separate; dissimilar; versatile.

var·nish, *n.* coating that gives smooth, glossy appearance. *v.*

var·si·ty, *n. pl.,* **-ties.** principal team that represents school.

var·y, *v.,* **-ied, -y·ing.** change; modify; diversify; differ.

vas·cu·lar, *a.* of body channels conveying fluid.

vase, *n.* flower container; urn.

vas·ec·to·my, *n. pl.*, **-mies**. removal of part of the male sperm-transferring duct.

vas·sal, *n.* serf; servile person.

vast, *a.* immense; very great.

vat, *n.* tank; tub; cistern.

vaude·ville, *n.* variety show.

vault, *v.* leap over. *n.* arched ceiling; burial chamber; storage room for valuables.

vaunt, *v.* boast. *n.* a boast. **-ing·ly**, *adv.*

veal, *n.* calf meat for food.

vec·tor, *n.* quantity having direction and magnitude; organism that transmits a disease.

veer, *v.* shift or turn; change direction. **-ing·ly**, *adv.*

veg·e·ta·ble, *n.* food plant.

veg·e·tar·i·an, *n.* one who does not eat meat. **-ism**, *n.*

veg·e·tate, *v.*, **-tat·ed**, **-tat·ing**. grow, as a plant; live passively. **-ta·tion**, *n.* **-ta·tive**, *a.*

ve·he·ment, *a.* forceful; passionate; violent. **-mence**, **-men·cy**, *n.*

ve·hi·cle, *n.* device for carrying, transporting; means of communication. **-hic·u·lar**, *a.*

veil, *n.* thin fabric worn over the head or face; anything that conceals. *v.* obscure.

vein, *n.* blood vessel to the heart; lode; channel; mood; streak or marking, as in wood. *v.* to streak. **veined**, *a.* **-ing**, *n.*

veld, **veldt**, *n.* open grassland.

vel·lum, *n.* fine parchment.

ve·loc·i·ty, *n. pl.*, **-ties**. speed.

ve·lour, **ve·lours**, *n. pl.*, **ve·lours**. soft, velvetlike fabric.

vel·vet, *n.* fabric, of silk, rayon, etc. having a short, soft pile; softness. *a.* **-y**, *a.*

vel·vet·een, *n.* fabric, usu. cotton, having a short pile in imitation of velvet. *a.*

ve·nal, *a.* corrupt. **-i·ty**, *n.*

vend, *v.* sell. **-or**, *n.*

ven·det·ta, *n.* private feud.

vend·i·ble, *a.* salable. *n.* thing for sale.

ve·neer, *n.* overlay of fine wood; superficial; ornamental facing.

ven·er·a·ble, *a.* worthy of respect, reverence. **-a·bil·i·ty**, *n.*

ven·er·ate, *v.*, **-at·ed**, **-at·ing**. revere; respect. **-a·tion**, *n.*

ve·ne·re·al, *a.* (disease) from sexual intercourse.

ven·geance, *n.* retribution.

venge·ful, *a.* vindictive.

ve·ni·al, *a.* forgivable; excusable. **-i·ty**, *n.*

ven·i·son, *n.* wild animal meat.

ven·om, *n.* poisonous secretion; malevolence. **-ous**, *a.*

ve·nous, *a.* of, pertaining to, or carried in the veins.

vent, *n.* outlet; flue. *v.*, **-ed**, **-ing**. express; discharge; expel.

ven·ti·late, *v.*, **-lat·ed**, **-lat·ing**. supply with fresh air; oxygenate; aerate; expose; utter; discuss freely. **-la·tion**, *n.*

ven·tri·cle, *n.* chamber of the heart; body cavity.

ven·tril·o·quism, *n.* art of speaking so people think the sound is coming from source other than the speaker. **-quist**, *n.*

ven·ture, *n.* chance; risk; hazard. *v.* gamble; risk. **-some**, *a.* **-tur·ous**, *a.*

Ve·nus, *n.* second planet from the sun; goddess of love, beauty.

ve·ra·cious, *a.* truthful; accurate; right. **-rac·i·ty**, *n.*

ve·ran·da, **ve·ran·dah**, *n.* open porch, usu. roofed.

verb, *n.* part of speech expressing existence, action, occurrence.

ver·bal, *a.* oral; of words; word-for-word. *n.* noun derived from a verb. **-ly**, *adv.*

ver·bal·ize, *v.*, **-ized**, **-iz·ing**. express in words; speak or write verbosely. **-i·za·tion**, *n.*

ver·ba·tim, *adv.* word for word. *a.* in the exact words.

ver·bi·age, *n.* use of too many words.

ver·bose, *a.* wordy. **-bos·i·ty**, *n.*

ver·dant, *a.* green. **-dan·cy**, *n.*

ver·dict, *n.* judgment; opinion.

ver·di·gris, *n.* green or bluish pigment found on weather exposed brass or copper.

verge, *n.* edge; brink; margin. *v.*, **verged**, **verg·ing**. border, approach; incline.

ver·i·fy, *v.*, **-fied**, **-fy·ing**. confirm; substantiate. **-fi·ca·tion**, *n.*

ver·i·si·mil·i·tude, *n.* appearance of truth; likelihood.

ver·i·ta·ble, *a.* true; genuine; real. **-bly**, *adv.*

ver·i·ty, *n. pl.*, **-ties**. truth.

ver·mi·cel·li, *n.* pasta thinner than spaghetti.

ver·mic·u·lar, *a.* wormlike.

ver·mil·ion, **ver·mil·lion**, *n.* bright red pigment. *a.*

ver·min, *n. pl.*, **ver·min**. noxious or objectionable small mammals; parasitic insects. **-ous**, *a.*

ver·mouth, *n.* white, fortified, herbed wine.

ver·nac·u·lar, *n.* local, native language; idiom; specialized vocabulary. *a.* **-ism**, *n.*

ver·nal, *a.* of spring; youthful; fresh. **-ly,** *adv.*

ver·sant, *a.* experienced; conversant.

ver·sa·tile, *a.* having many uses, talents, aptitudes. **-til·i·ty,** *n.*

verse, *n.* line of a poem; poem; Bible paragraph.

versed, *a.* experienced; skilled.

ver·sion, *n.* translation; account of; arrangement. **-al,** *a.*

ver·sus, *prep.* against.

ver·te·bra, *n. pl.,* **-brae.** any of the individual bones of the spinal column. **-bral,** *a.*

ver·te·brate, *a.* having a spinal column. *n.* vertebrate animal.

ver·tex, *n. pl.,* **-tex·es, -ti·ces.** zenith; apex; summit.

ver·ti·cal, *a.* perpendicular; upright. *n.* vertical line or plane.

ver·ti·go, *n. pl.,* **-ti·goes, -tig·i·nes.** illness causing dizziness.

verve, *n.* vigor; energy.

ver·y, *adv.* extremely; exactly. *a.,* **-i·er, -i·est.** exact; absolute; same; true; mere.

ves·i·cle, *n.* cavity; small sac; cyst or blister. **ve·sic·u·lar,** *a.*

ves·per, *n.* of or pertaining to evening.

ves·pers, *n.* religious evening service of worship.

ves·sel, *n.* ship; hollow receptacle for liquids; tube or duct.

vest, *n.* sleeveless garment. *v.* clothe; give ownership, authority.

ves·tal, *a.* chaste; virgin.

ves·ti·bule, *n.* lobby; hall.

ves·tige, *n.* trace; remnant. **-tig·i·al,** *a.*

vest·ment, *n.* clothing; robe.

vest-pock·et, *a.* smaller than usual size.

ves·try, *n. pl.,* **-tries.** church room for vestments or meetings; church administrative body.

vet·er·an, *n.* ex-member of armed forces. *a.* experienced.

vet·er·i·nar·i·an, *n.* doctor who treats animals.

vet·er·i·nar·y, *a.* pertaining to science of treating animals.

ve·to, *n.* power to refuse, prohibit, or postpone. *v.,* **-toed, -to·ing.** refuse approval.

vex, *v.* annoy; afflict; puzzle. **-a·tion,** *n.* **-a·tious,** *a.* **vexed,** *a.*

vi·a, *prep.* by way or means of.

vi·a·ble, *a.* capable of living; practicable; workable. **-bil·i·ty,** *n.* **-bly,** *adv.*

vi·a·duct, *n.* bridge, with high supports, over a valley, river, etc.

vi·al, *n.* small bottle, usu. glass.

vi·and, *n.* food; provisions.

vibes, *n. pl. inf.* vibrations.

vi·brant, *a.* resonant; vigorous; sensitive; pulsing. **vi·bran·cy,** *n.*

vi·brate, *v.,* **-brat·ed, -brat·ing.** oscillate; quiver; fluctuate. **-bra·tion,** *n.* **-bra·tor,** *n.* **-bra·to·ry,** *a.*

vic·ar, *n.* parish clergyman.

vic·ar·age, *n.* office of a vicar; vicar's residence.

vi·car·i·ous, *a.* substitute; identifying with another's experience. **-ly,** *adv.* **-ness,** *n.*

vice, *n.* evil habit; depravity.

vi·ce, *prep.* in place of.

vice pres·i·dent, *n.* officer next in rank to president. **-den·cy,** *n.*

vice ver·sa, *adv.* conversely.

vi·chys·soise, *n.* cold cream potato and leek soup.

vi·cin·i·ty, *n. pl.,* **-ties.** proximity; nearness; neighborhood.

vi·cious, *a.* depraved; evil; malicious; wicked. **-ness,** *n.*

vi·cis·si·tude, *n. usu. pl.* irregular changes or variations; alteration.

vic·tim, *n.* one hurt by an action beyond his control; dupe; sacrifice. **-ize,** *v.,* **-ized, -iz·ing.**

vic·tor, *n.* winner; conqueror. **-to·ri·ous,** *a.*

vic·to·ry, *n. pl.,* **-ries.** conquest; triumph; achievement.

vict·ual, *n. (usu. pl.)* food; provisions. *v.,* **-ualed, -ual·ing.** furnish with victuals.

vid·e·o, *a.* pertaining to television. *n.* television image.

vid·e·o·disc, *n.* disc for recording image and sound for replay on T-V.

vid·e·o·tape, *n.* recording of a T-V program on magnetic tape.

vie, *v.,* **vied, vy·ing.** attempt to excel or outdo; strive. **vi·er,** *n.*

view, *n.* something seen; sight; opinion; purpose. *v.* behold; examine; see; consider. **-er,** *n.*

view·point, *n.* opinion.

vig·il, *n.* keeping watch.

vig·i·lance, *n.* watchfulness; alertness; wakefulness. **-ant,** *a.*

vi·gnette, *n.* short word picture; sketch; decorative design.

vig·or, *n.* energy; vitality; intensity. **-ous,** *a.* **-ous·ly,** *adv.*

vile, *a.,* **vil·er, vil·est.** corrupt; offensive; mean; degraded.

vil·i·fy, *v.,* **-fied, -fy·ing.** malign; defame. **-fi·ca·tion,** *n.*

vil·la, n. sizeable country or suburban house.

vil·lage, n. small town.

vil·lain, n. scoundrel; criminal. **-ous,** a. **-y,** n. pl., **-ies.**

vim, n. vigor; energy.

vin·ci·ble, a. conquerable; surmountable. **-bil·i·ty,** n.

vin·di·cate, v., **-cat·ed, -cat·ing.** clear of suspicion; exonerate; absolve. **-ca·tion,** n. **-ca·tor,** n.

vin·dic·tive, a. vengeful; spiteful. **-ness,** n.

vine, n. climbing plant.

vin·e·gar, n. sour fermented liquid used as a condiment. **-y,** a.

vine·yard, n. area for grapevines.

vin·tage, n. grape harvest; wine of a particular region or year. a. outmoded; classic.

vint·ner, n. wine merchant.

vi·nyl, n. type of plastic.

vi·o·la, n. four-stringed instrument of violin class, but larger.

vi·o·la·ble, a. can be or is likely to be violated.

vi·o·late, v., **-lat·ed, -lat·ing.** infringe; profane; desecrate; injure; rape. **-la·tor,** n. **-la·tion,** n.

vi·o·lence, n. destructive force; intensity. **-lent,** a.

vi·o·let, n. plant with heart-shaped leaves; bluish purple color. a.

vi·o·lin, n. four-stringed musical instrument, played with a bow. **-ist,** n.

vi·o·lon·cel·lo, n. cello. **-list,** n.

vi·per, n. venomous snake.

vi·ral, a. pertaining to a virus.

vir·gin, n. female who has not had sexual intercourse. a. chaste; pure; untouched; not previously used, touched, tilled; processed, etc. **-al,** a. **-i·ty,** n.

vir·ile, a. manly; masterful; able to procreate. **vi·ril·i·ty,** n.

vir·tu·al, a. being in essence or effect but not in fact.

vir·tue, n. morality; chastity; merit.

vir·tu·os·i·ty, n. technical mastery of an art, as music.

vir·tu·o·so, n. pl., **-sos, -si.** one of special skill in fine arts. **-o·sic,** a. **-os·i·ty,** n. pl., **-ties.**

vir·tu·ous, a. upright; pure.

vir·u·lent, a. very infectious; severe; deadly; hostile.

vi·rus, n. pl., **-rus·es.** very small disease producing agents; corrupting influence.

vi·sa, n. passport endorsement allowing bearer to pass into or through a country.

vis·age, n. face; aspect.

vis·cer·a, n. pl. soft interior organs, as lungs, etc. **-al,** a.

vis·cid, a. sticky; gluelike. **-cid·i·ty,** n. **-cos·i·ty,** n.

vise, n. device with two jaws, used to hold an object firmly.

vis·i·ble, a. can be seen; perceivable; evident. **-bil·i·ty,** n.

vi·sion, n. power of seeing; foresight; anticipation; imagination.

vi·sion·ar·y, a. imaginary; speculative. n. pl., **-ies.** dreamer; seer.

vis·it, v. go to see a person, place, etc.; be a guest of; inflict upon. n. act of visiting; brief social call; official call. **-i·tant,** n. **-i·tor,** n.

vis·i·ta·tion, n. official visit.

vi·sor, n. piece projecting from a cap; glare shield.

vis·ta, n. distant view, as through an avenue, row of trees, etc.

vis·u·al, a. pertaining to sight; visible. **-ly,** adv.

vis·u·al·ize, v., **-ized, -iz·ing.** form a mental picture of. **-i·za·tion,** n.

vi·tal, a. of life; necessary to life; essential; energetic.

vi·tal·i·ty, n. pl., **-ties.** power to continue; vigor; strength.

vi·tal·ize, v., **-ized, -iz·ing.** animate; invigorate. **-i·za·tion,** n.

vi·ta·min, n. any of essential organic substances found in food.

vi·ti·ate, v., **-at·ed, -at·ing.** impair; spoil; debase; corrupt; invalidate. **-a·tion,** n.

vit·re·ous, a. like glass. **-os·i·ty,** n.

vit·ri·ol, n. glassy metallic sulfates; sulfuric acid; severe criticism; sarcasm. **-ic,** a.

vi·tu·per·ate, v., **-at·ed, -at·ing.** berate; abuse verbally. **-a·tion,** n.

vi·va·cious, a. animated; spirited; lively. **-vac·i·ty,** n. pl., **-ties.**

viv·id, a. intense; lively.

viv·i·fy, v., **-fied, -fy·ing.** animate; vitalize. **-fi·ca·tion,** n.

viv·i·sec·tion, n. cutting, dissection of a living animal.

vix·en, n. quarrelsome woman; shrew; female fox.

vo·cab·u·lar·y, n. pl., **-ies.** stock of words used or understood; list of words arranged in order with definitions.

vo·cal, a. of or for the voice. **-ize,** v., **-ized, -iz·ing.** talk freely. **-i·za·tion,** n.

vocal cords, n. pl. throat membranes that produce vocal sound.

vo·cal·ist, *n.* a singer.

vo·ca·tion, *n.* occupation; calling; work. **-al**, *a.*

vo·cif·er·ous, *a.* noisy; clamorous.

vod·ka, *n.* colorless liquor.

vogue, *n.* fashion; popularity.

voice, *n.* sound; speaking or singing, sound produced; expression; verb forms. *v.*, **voiced**, **voic·ing**. express; speak.

voiced, *a.* expressed; spoken.

voice·less, *a.* mute; silent.

void, *a.* empty; not binding; useless. *n.* vacuum. *v.* annul. **-a·ble**, *a.*

voile, *n.* fine, sheer fabric.

vol·a·tile, *a.* able to vaporize; evaporating rapidly; changeable; transient. **-til·i·ty**, *n.*

vol·ca·no, *n. pl.,* **-noes**, **-nos.** eruption on earth's surface. **-can·ic**, *a.* **-can·i·cal·ly**, *adv.*

vo·li·tion, *n.* will power; choice.

vol·ley, *n. pl.,* **-leys.** multiple discharge of many guns, bullets, etc.; return of the ball before it touches the ground. *v.*, **-leyed**, **-ley·ing.** discharge in a volley; return a ball.

volt, *n.* unit of electromotive force. **volt·age**, *n.*

vol·u·ble, *a.* talkative; fluent. **-bly**, *adv.* **-bil·i·ty**, *n.*

vol·ume, *n.* book; space occupied; quantity or amount; loudness.

vo·lu·mi·nous, *a.* having great volume or bulk; large. **-ly**, *adv.*

vol·un·tar·y, *a.* of or by free will; intentional. **-i·ly**, *adv.*

vol·un·teer, *n.* one who offers service of his own free will. *v.* offer one's service.

vo·lup·tu·ar·y, *n. pl.,* **-ies.** sensualist; lover of luxury. *a.*

vo·lup·tu·ous, *a.* caring much for the pleasure of the senses; sensuous.

vom·it, *v.* throw up; eject food; belch forth; spew. *n.*

voo·doo, *n. pl.,* **-doos.** sorcery; fetishism. **-ism**, *n.* **-ist**, *n.*

vo·ra·cious, *a.* greedy; ravenous; gluttonous. **-rac·i·ty**, *n.*

vor·tex, *n. pl.,* **-tex·es**, **-ti·ces.** whirlpool; whirlwind.

vote, *n.* formal expression of choice or opinion. *v.*, **vot·ed**, **vot·ing.** cast one's vote. **vot·er**, *n.*

vo·tive, *a.* performed or given in fulfillment of a vow.

vouch, *v.* give assurance; assert; attest; guarantee.

vouch·er, *n.* that which attests; receipt.

vouch·safe, *v.*, **-safed**, **-saf·ing.** grant; permit; deign.

vow, *n.* solemn promise; pledge; affirmation. *v.*

vow·el, *n.* relatively open speech sounds; letter representing such a sound, *a, e, i, o, u.*

voy·age, *n.* journey, esp. by sea or air. *v.*, **-aged**, **-ag·ing. voy·ag·er**, *n.*

vo·yeur, *n.* one sexually gratified by looking at sexual acts, objects. **-ism**, *n.*

vul·can·ize, *v.*, **-ized**, **-iz·ing.** heat rubber with sulfur to increase strength, etc. **-i·za·tion**, *n.*

vul·gar, *a.* coarse; offensive; obscene; the vernacular. **-ism**, *n.* **-i·ty**, *n. pl.,* **-ties. -ize**, *v.*, **-ized**, **-iz·ing.**

vul·ner·a·ble, *a.* open to attack; assailable. **-bil·i·ty**, *n.* **-bly**, *adv.*

vul·pine, *a.* of the fox; crafty.

vul·ture, *n.* large bird of prey; predatory person.

vul·va, *n. pl.,* **-vae**, **-vas.** external genitals of female.

W

wack·y, *a.*, **-i·er**, **-i·est.** *inf.* crazy; irrational.

wad, *n.* soft mass; plug; lump; *inf.* money. *v.*, **-ded**, **-ding.** press into a wad; plug; stuff.

wad·dle, *v.*, **-dled**, **-dling.** walk in short steps with a sway; totter.

wade, *v.*, **wad·ed**, **wad·ing.** walk through water, etc.; proceed laboriously. **wad·er**, *n.*

wa·fer, *n.* thin, crisp cracker.

waf·fle, *n.* crisp batter cake baked in an iron.

waft, *v.* float gently through air. *n.* slight breeze; puff.

wag, *v.*, **wagged**, **wag·ging.** move rapidly back and forth; *inf.* gossip. *n.* joker; wit.

wage, *n. often pl.* payment for services; *pl., sing. or pl. in constr.* reward. *v.*, **waged**, **wag·ing.** carry on.

wa·ger, *n.* bet. *v.* bet; gamble.

wag·on, *n.* four-wheeled vehicle; child's cart.

waif, *n.* homeless neglected child; stray animal.

wail, *v.* grieve with a mournful cry. *n.* lament; mournful sound.

waist, *n.* part of the body between the ribs and the hips; middle part of anything.

wait, *v.* stay; remain in readiness; defer; serve. *n.* delay.

wait·er, *n.* male who waits on tables; tray. **-tress**, *n. fem.*

waive, *v.*, **waived**, **waiv·ing.** relinquish; forgo; postpone.

waiv·er, *n.* written evidence of relinquishment.

wake, *v.,* waked or woke, waked, wak·ing. emerge from sleep; become aware. *n.* vigil, esp. over corpse; trail of.

wake·ful, *a.* not sleeping; alert.

wak·en, *v.* wake; awake.

walk, *v.* move or travel on foot. *n.* time or distance walked; profession.

walk·er, *n.* frame used as a support in walking.

walk·ie-talk·ie, *n.* portable two-way radiotelephone set.

walk·out, *n.* workers' strike.

walk-up, *n. inf.* building in which there is no elevator.

wall, *n.* vertical structure to enclose or divide; barrier. *v.* separate with a wall.

wal·la·by, *n. pl.,* -bies, by. small to medium-sized kangaroo.

wall·board, *n.* large rigid sheets of structural material.

wal·let, *n.* small, pocket case with compartments.

wall·flow·er, *n. inf.* person standing on sidelines at social activity.

wal·lop, *v. inf.* thrash; defeat thoroughly; trounce. *n. inf.* hard blow or impact.

wal·low, *v.* roll in mud; live self indulgently; be helpless. *n.* muddy area for wallowing.

wall·pa·per, *n.* decorative paper covering for walls.

wal·nut, *n.* nut-bearing tree.

wal·rus, *n. pl.,* -rus·es, -rus. large marine mammal.

waltz, *n.* gliding ballroom dance in $3/4$ time. *v.* dance; move quickly.

wam·pum, *n.* small beads used for jewelry or barter.

wan, *a.,* -ner, -nest. pale; feeble; dim. -ness, *n.*

wand, *n.* slender (magic) rod.

wan·der, *v.* roam; stray; err; stroll.

wan·der·lust, *n.* impulse or desire to travel; restlessness.

wane, *v.,* waned, wan·ing. diminish; decrease. *n.* decline.

wan·gle, *v.,* -gled, -gling. *inf.* obtain by devious means; manipulate; finagle.

want, *v.* need; lack; require; desire. *n.* lack; scarcity.

want·ing, *a.* lacking; deficient; missing. *prep.* lacking; minus.

wan·ton, *a.* lewd; malicious; extravagant; unprovoked. *n.* lewd person. *v.* to waste; be wanton.

war, *n.* military conflict; any conflict or struggle. **warred, war·ring.**

war·ble, *v.,* -bled, -bling. sing with trills and runs. *n.* act or sound of warbling.

ward, *v.* fend off; deflect. *n.* minor under one's care; voting district; large hospital room; prison division.

war·den, *n.* supervisor, custodian, as a game, prison warden.

ward·robe, *n.* upright cabinet for clothes; wearing apparel.

ware, *n. usu. pl.* articles for sale; pottery.

ware·house, *n.* building in which merchandise is stored.

war·fare, *n.* war; struggle.

war·head, *n.* explosive part of a bomb or missile.

warm, *a.,* -er, -est. moderate heat; sympathetic; intimate; lively; ardent. *v.* heat.

warm-heart·ed, warm·heart·ed, *a.* cordial; sympathetic.

war·mon·ger, *n.* one who favors or incites war.

warmth, *n.* gentle heat; friendliness; kindness; slight anger.

warn, *v.* caution; notify.

warn·ing, *n.* admonishment.

warp, *v.* turn or twist out of shape; distort; corrupt; deviate. *n.* twist; mental quirk; towline; lengthwise fabric threads.

war·rant, *n.* writ authorizing arrest, seizure, search; guarantee; security. *v.* authorize; justify; guarantee; attest.

war·ran·ty, *n. pl.,* -ties. guarantee of a product.

war·ren, *n.* crowded tenement; small animal pen; rabbit house.

wart, *n.* small nonmalignant projection on skin, *usu.* hard.

war·y, *a.,* -i·er, -i·est. carefully watching and guarding; shrewd; wily. -i·ly, *adv.* -i·ness, *n.*

was, past tense of the first and third person singular of the verb *to be.*

wash, *v.* cleanse with water or other liquid; flow against or over; remove by the use of water; cover with a thin coat of metal. *n.* items washed; liquid used for washing. -**cloth**, *n.*

wash·er, *n.* washing machine; flat disk used to give tightness to a joint or to prevent rubbing.

wash·ing, *n.* things washed or to be washed; material obtained after washing, as ore.

wash·out, *n.* erosion of earth by action of water; *inf.* failure.

wash·room, *n.* restroom or lavatory.

wash·y, *a.* weak; watery.

was·n't, contraction of *was not.*

wasp, *n.* winged stinging insect.

wasp·ish, *a.* irritable; bad tempered.

was·sail, *n.* drinking toast; spiced drink. *v.* carouse.

Was·ser·mann test, *n.* test for detecting syphilis.

wast·age, *n.* loss by use, waste.

waste, *v.,* **wast·ed, wast·ing.** use foolishly; fail to use; diminish gradually; devastate; squander; wear down. *n.* useless expenditure, etc.; barren region; neglect; anything left over; garbage; excrement. *a.* not used; uninhabited; left over.

waste·land, *n.* barren region.

wast·rel, *n.* spendthrift.

watch, *v.* observe closely; keep vigil or guard; wait; tend; to look or be alert for. *n.* vigil; surveillance; on guard; small timepiece; period of duty for a guard or crew.

watch·ful, *a.* attentive; alert.

watch·word, *n.* password.

wa·ter, *n.* colorless liquid covering 70 percent of earth's surface and essential element of all organisms; lake, river, ocean, etc.; body secretion, as tears, urine, etc. *v.* moisten; provide with water; dilute.

wa·ter·bed, *n.* bed whose mattress is vinyl bag filled with water.

wa·ter·col·or, *n.* paint whose pigment is mixed with water; the painting.

wa·ter·course, *n.* stream of water; channel for water.

wa·ter·cress, *n.* aqueous perennial herb used for salad.

wa·ter·fall, *n.* fall of water over a precipice.

wa·ter·fowl, *n. pl.,* **-fowls, -fowl.** swimming water bird.

wa·ter·front, *n.* land adjacent to a body of water.

wa·ter·line, *n.* line on hull of ship which shows where water level reaches; any line showing what level water has reached.

wa·ter·logged, *a.* saturated or filled with water.

wa·ter main, *n.* main pipe for carrying water.

wa·ter·mark, *n.* waterline; mark or design in paper.

wa·ter·mel·on, *n.* large edible fruit with juicy, red pulp.

wa·ter moc·ca·sin, *n.* venomous viper, found along rivers.

wa·ter·pow·er, *n.* power derived from flowing or falling water.

wa·ter·proof, *a.* watertight; impervious to water. *n.* waterproof fabric.

wa·ter·shed, *n.* region from which an area or river receives its water.

wa·ter·spout, *n.* whirling column of spray or mist; pipe for discharge of water.

wa·ter·tight, *a.* waterproof; foolproof.

wa·ter·way, *n.* channel or body of water where ships travel.

wa·ter·works, *n. pl.* city water supply system.

wa·ter·y, *a.* full of or like water; diluted; thin; vapid.

watt, *n.* unit of electric power.

watt·age, *n.* amount of power.

watt-hour, *n.* unit of energy.

wat·tle, *n.* interwoven structure; fleshy skin at throat of fowl.

wave, *n.* undulating movement on surface of water or other surface; upsurge of something, as emotion, crime, etc.; prolonged condition, as heat, illness, etc.; hair curl or curve; a waving. *v.,* **waved, wav·ing.** move freely, as a flag; signal; move up and down or back and forth.

wa·ver, *v.* flutter; hesitate; vacillate; falter. *n.* a wavering.

wav·y, *a.,* **-i·er, -i·est.** full of waves or curls.

wax, *n. pl.,* **wax·es.** bee secretion used for honeycombs; insoluble substance that burns; paraffin. *v.,* **waxed, wax·ing.** rub or polish with wax; grow in size; brighten; to become (angry, etc.). **wax·y,** *a.,* **-i·er, -i·est.**

wax·en, *a.* made of wax; pale.

wax·work, *n.* effigy in wax.

way, *n.* direction; route; path, road, etc; distance; passage; manner of acting; plan; possibility.

way·far·er, *n.* traveler.

way·lay, *v.,* **-laid, -lay·ing.** accost; intercept; ambush.

way·side, *n.* side or edge of a road. *a.* near the road side.

way·ward, *a.* willful; erratic; stubborn; disobedient.

we, *pron.* nominative pl. of *I.*

weak, *a.* not powerful; not strong; deficient; lacking; feeble; ineffectual.

weak·en, *v.* debilitate; undermine; cripple.

weak-kneed, *a.* irresolute; easily intimidated; spineless.

weak·ling, *n.* feeble or ineffectual person.

weak·ly, *a.,* **-li·er, -li·est.** feeble; sickly.

weak-mind·ed, *a.* feeble-minded; indecisive; irresolute.

weak·ness, *n.* fault; defect; feebleness; failing.

wealth, *n.* affluence; profusion; property, money, etc.

wealth·y, *a.,* **-i·er, -i·est.** rich; affluent; abounding. **-i·ness,** *n.*

wean, *v.* stop suckling; detach.

weap·on, *n.* implement of offense or defense. **-ry,** *n.*

wear, *v.* **wore, worn, wear·ing.** have on, as a garment; rub away; impair by use; exhaust. *n.* clothing; impairment from use; durability.

wear·ing, *a.* fatiguing.

wea·ri·some, *a.* tiresome; tedious; boring; irksome.

wea·ry, *a.,* **-ri·er, -ri·est.** tired; bored. *v.,* **-ried, -ry·ing.** exhaust; tire. **-ri·ness,** *n.*

wea·sel, *n. pl.,* **-sels, -sel.** small slender carnivorous mammal. *v.* be deceptive, evasive.

weath·er, *n.* atmospheric conditions, as temperature, moisture, etc. *v.* expose to the elements; survive, as a crisis.

weath·er-beat·en, *a.* worn by exposure to weather.

weath·er·man, *n.* meteorologist; forecaster.

weath·er·proof, *a.* capable of withstanding rain, snow, etc.

weave, *v.* **wove** or **weaved, wov·en** or **wove, weav·ing.** make fabric by interlacing threads; zigzag; spin (a web). *n.* style or pattern of weaving.

web, *n.* woven fabric; spider web; a network; entanglement. *v.,* **webbed, web·bing.** entangle; provide with a web.

web·bing, *n.* strong woven tape.

wed, *v.,* **wed·ded** or **wed, -ding.** marry; join closely.

we'd, contraction of *we had* or *we would.*

wed·ding, *n.* marriage ceremony; nuptials.

wedge, *n.* V-shaped piece of metal, wood, etc. for splitting, tightening, etc; facilitating action. *v.,* **wedged, wedg·ing.** split or tighten with a wedge; compress.

wed·lock, *n.* marriage.

Wednes·day, *n.* fourth day of the week.

wee, *a.,* **we·er, we·est.** very small; tiny.

weed, *n.* unwanted, unsightly plant. *v.* remove weeds or anything undesirable.

weed·y, *a.,* **-i·er, -i·est.** abounding in weeds; *inf.* lanky.

week, *n.* period of seven successive days; workweek.

week·day, *n.* any day of the week except Saturday and Sunday.

week·end, *n.* period from Friday night to Sunday night.

week·ly, *a.* happening, produced, or issued every week. *adv.* once a week.

weep, *v.,* **wept, weep·ing.** shed tears; cry; ooze.

wee·vil, *n.* small beetle, destructive to grain, cotton, etc.

weigh, *v.* determine the weight of; consider carefully.

weight, *n.* amount of heaviness; counterbalance; thing to hold something down; burden; pressure; influence. *v.* add weight to; burden with.

weight·y, *a.,* **-i·er, -i·est.** heavy; serious.

weir, *n.* dam; fence in a stream.

weird, *a.,* **-er, -est.** unearthly; odd; bizarre; uncanny.

wel·come, *a.* received gladly; pleasing. *n.* warm greeting. *v.,* **-comed, -com·ing.** greet hospitably.

weld, *v.* fuse by heating; join.

wel·fare, *n.* condition of being healthy, happy, etc; relief.

well, *n.* spring; hole or shaft to secure water, oil, etc. *v.* pour forth.

well, *adv.,* **bet·ter, best.** satisfactorily; expertly; suitably; intimately; luxuriously. *a.* suitable; in good health; cured; prosperous. *int.* exclamation of surprise, indignation.

we'll, contraction of *we will* or *we shall.*

well-be·ing, *n.* condition of happiness and good health.

well-bred, *a.* well brought up; of good stock.

well-de·fined, *a.* with sharp limits; clearly described.

well-dis·posed, *a.* favorably inclined; properly arranged.

well-done, *a.* performed skillfully or satisfactorily; well-cooked.

well-groomed, *a.* neat; tidy; well-dressed.

well-ground·ed, *a.* adequately schooled in a subject.

well-known, *a.* famous.

well-off, *a.* prosperous.

well-read, *a.* knowledgeable.

well-round·ed, *a.* balanced education or experience; having many abilities, etc.

well-thought-of, *a.* esteemed; respected.

well-timed, *a.* opportune.

well-to-do, *a.* prosperous; rich.

welt, *n.* strip to cover or strengthen a seam; raised mark on the skin.

wel·ter, *v.* wallow. *n.* turmoil.

wend, *v.* proceed.

were, past indicative plural and second person singular of *be.*

we're, contraction of *we are.*

weren't, contraction of *were not.*

were·wolf, wer·wolf, *n.* person transformed into a wolf (folklore).

west, *n.* direction the sun is at sunset. *a.* lying toward the west. *adv.* westward. **-er·ly,** *a.*

west·ern, *a.* lying toward, coming from, being in, or of the west.

west·ern·ize, *v.,* **-ized, -iz·ing.** give western characteristics to. **-i·za·tion,** *n.*

west·ward, *adv.* toward the west. *n.* westward direction.

wet, *a.,* **wet·ter, wet·test.** soaked with water; rainy; not dry. *n.* moisture. *v.,* **wet** or **wet·ted. wet·ting.** moisten; soak.

wet·back, *n. inf.* Mexican who illegally enters the U.S.

wet blan·ket, *n.* one that dampens the enthusiasm of others.

we've, contraction of *we have.*

whack, *v. inf.* strike sharply. *n. inf.* sharp blow.

whale, *n.* very large, air-breathing sea mammal. *v.,* **whaled, whal·ing.** hunt whales; *inf.* beat; thrash.

wharf, *n. pl.,* **wharves, wharfs.** docking structure for boats; pier or dock.

what, *pron.* word used in asking questions about; that or those which; whatever; something that. *a.* which or which kind of; how much; whatever. *adv.* how or how much. *int.* expression of surprise, annoyance.

what·ev·er, *pron.* anything that; no matter what; what. *a.* no matter what or which; of any amount, kind, etc.

what·not, *n.* bric-a-brac shelves.

what·so·ev·er, *pron., a.* whatever.

wheal, *n.* welt; skin elevation.

wheat, *n.* cereal grass grain.

whee·dle, *v.,* **-dled, -dling.** coax by flattery; cajole. **-dler,** *n.*

wheel, *n.* solid disk or circular rim which turns on an axis; *inf.* important person. *v.* move on wheels; revolve.

wheel·bar·row, *n.* boxlike vehicle with single wheel and handles.

wheel·chair, *n.* mobile chair on wheels for invalids.

wheeze, *v.,* **wheezed, wheez·ing.** breathe with a husky, whistling sound. **wheez·y,** *a.*

whelp, *n.* puppy; cub.

when, *adv.* at what or which time; at an earlier time. *conj.* at what time; if; after which. *pron.* what time. *n.* the time; date.

whence, *adv., conj.* from what source or place.

when·ev·er, *adv., conj.* at whatever time.

where, *adv.* in or at what place, etc; in what position; from what source. *conj.* in, at, or to what place; in or at the place in which; wherever. *n.* the place or location.

where·a·bouts, *adv.* near or at what place; about where. *n.* where located.

where·as, *conj.* since; on the contrary.

where·by, *adv., conj.* by; by which; in accordance with.

where·in, *adv.* in what way. *conj.* in which.

where·of, *adv., conj.* of which, whom, or what.

where·to, *adv.* to which, whom.

where·up·on, *adv.* whereon. *conj.* upon which or whom.

wher·ev·er, *adv., conj.* in, at, or to whatever place.

where·with·al, *n.* resources.

whet, *v.,* **-ted, -ting.** sharpen; excite; stimulate.

wheth·er, *conj.* if it be the case that; if; either.

whew, *interj.* exclamation of dismay, relief, or amazement.

whey, *n.* watery part of milk.

which, *pron.* what one; thing, etc. designated earlier. *a.* what one; whichever; one designated.

which·ev·er, *a.* no matter which. *pron.* whatever one; anyone.

whiff, *n.* puff of air, smoke, odor.

while, *n.* period of time. *conj.* although; whereas; during the time that. *v.,* **whiled, whil·ing.** cause time to pass, esp. pleasantly.

whim, *n.* capricious idea.

whim·per, *v.* plaintive, broken cry. *n.* low, broken cry.

whim·si·cal, *a.* capricious; odd; quaint. **-sy,** *n.* a whim.

whine, *v.,* **whined, whin·ing.** utter a high, plaintive sound, as in distress; complain childishly. *n.*

whin·ny, *v.,* **-nied, -ny·ing.** low, gentle cry of a horse; neigh.

whip, *v.,* **whipped** or **whipt, whip·ping.** flog; spank; drive or urge on; *inf.* defeat; beat into a froth; cast; incite; jerk suddenly. *n.* rod with a lash; frothy dessert.

whip·lash, *n.* injury to the neck.

whip·per·snap·per, *n.* pretentious, insignificant person.

whip·pet, *n.* small, fast racing dog.

whir, whirr, *v.,* **whirred, whir·ring.** fly, revolve, or vibrate with a buzzing sound. *n.*

whirl, *v.* turn or revolve rapidly; spin. *n.* swift, revolving motion; state of confusion; a try.

whirl·i·gig, *n.* something that revolves; child's spinning toy.

whirl·pool, *n.* whirling water.

whirl·wind, *n.* moving column of air; rapid activity.

whisk, *v.* move rapidly; fluff or mix with a whisk; brush lightly. *n.* wire kitchen instrument. **whisk broom,** *n.* clothes brush.

whisk·er, *n. pl.* hair on a man's face; bristly hairs near an animal's mouth.

whis·key, whis·ky, *n. pl.,* **-keys, -kies.** distilled alcoholic liquor made from grain.

whis·per, *v.* talk softly. *n.* soft sound; hint; rumor.

whist, *n.* card game.

whis·tle, *v.,* **-tled, -tling.** make a shrill sound through the lips or teeth. *n.* instrument for producing whistling sounds.

whit, *n.* small particle; bit.

white, *a.,* **whit·er, whit·est.** the color of snow; pale; blond; pure. *n.* white color.

white-col·lar, *a.* of office or professional employees.

white el·e·phant, *n.* object with much maintenance but little value.

white lie, *n.* harmless lie.

whit·en, *v.* bleach; blanch.

white·wash, *n.* mixture of lime for whitening walls; suppression of errors, defects; *inf.* defeat in which loser fails to score. *v.* cover up errors.

whith·er, *conj.* to which place.

whit·ing, *n.* powdered white chalk, edible foodfish.

whit·tle, *v.,* **-tled, -tling.** cut or shave bits from wood; wear away, down, or off.

whiz, whizz, *v.,* **whizzed, whiz·zing.** make a humming, hissing, or whirring sound; rush. *n. pl.,* **-zes.** whizzing sound; *inf.* having extraordinary ability.

who, *pron., nom.* **who,** *poss.* **whose,** *obj.* **whom.** what person; of a person; that.

who·ev·er, *pron., nom.* **who·ev·er,** *poss.* **whos·ev·er,** *obj.* **whom·ev·er.** anyone who; whatever person.

whole, *a.* well; intact; complete. *n.* entire thing; total.

whole-heart·ed, *a.* done with earnestness, energy, dedication.

whole·sale, *n.* sale of large quantities to retailers. *a.* sweeping; indiscriminate. *adv.* in bulk; extensively.

whole·some, *a.* mentally or morally good.

whole-wheat, *a.* made from the entire wheat grain.

whol·ly, *adv.* totally; only.

whom, *pron.* objective case of *who.*

whom·ev·er, *pron.* objective case of *whoever.*

whoop, *n.* loud cry, as of rage, excitement, etc. *v.* utter whoops.

whop·per, *n. inf.* big lie; something large.

whop·ping, *a.* unusually great or remarkable.

whore, *n.* prostitute.

whorl, *n.* thing having the shape, appearance of a spiral.

whose, *pron.* possessive case of *who.*

why, *adv.* for what cause, reason, or purpose; wherefore. *n. pl.,* **whys.** reason. *conj.* cause or reason for which.

wick, *n.* fabric, cord for burning in a candle or lamp.

wick·ed, *a.* evil; malicious; vile; painful.

wick·er, *n.* young, pliant twig. *a.* made of woven twigs.

wick·et, *n.* small door or gate; little window; wire arch for croquet; cricket target.

wide, *a.,* **wid·er, wid·est.** broad; extensive; of a certain width; fully open; ample. *adv.* extensively; fully open; away from the mark.

wide-a·wake, *a.* totally awake.

wide-eyed, *a.* naïve; amazed.

wid·en, *v.* broaden.

wide·spread, *a.* broadly accepted; widely prevalent.

wid·ow, *n.* woman whose husband is dead. **-hood,** *n.*

wid·ow·er, *n.* man whose wife is dead.

width, *n.* measure taken from side to side; breadth.

wield, *v.* exercise power, influence, etc; use skillfully.

wie·ner, *n.* frankfurter; hot dog.

wife, *n. pl.,* **wives.** married woman.

wig, *n.* artificial hair; toupee.

wig·gle, *v.,* **-gled, -gling.** move side to side quickly; wriggle. **-gly,** *a.*

wig·wam, *n.* American Indian hut, rounded or conical.

wild, *a.* in its natural state; uninhabited; primitive; dissolute; crazed; erratic; bizarre; unruly. *adv.* in a wild manner. *n. often pl.* wilderness.

wild·cat, *a.* financially risky; unknown gas or oil drilling territory; strike begun by workers in violation of union contract. *n. pl.,* **wildcats** or **wildcat.** medium-sized cat (lynx, etc); quick-tempered person; successful oil well.

wil·der·ness, *n.* uncultivated, uninhabited, or barren region.

wild·fire, *n.* destructive, hard to extinguish fire; something that spreads with great rapidity.

wild-goose chase, *n.* pursuit of the unattainable, unknown.

wile, *n.* cunning deception. *v.*, **wiled, wil·ing.** lure; mislead.

will, *aux. v., past* **would.** used before the infinitive to show: futurity; command; inevitability; willingness; capability.

will, *n.* conscious choice or control; determination; desire; legal declaration of a person's disposition of his estate. *v.* decide; bequeath.

will·ful, *a.* stubborn; intentional; deliberate.

will·ing, *a.* not averse; ready; voluntary; gladly done, etc.

wil·low, *n.* tree or shrub with flexible branches.

wil·low·y, *a.* tall and graceful; lithe; supple.

will·power, *n.* self-control.

wil·ly-nil·ly, *a.* happening whether willingly or not.

wilt, *v.* wither; droop; languish. *n.* plant disease.

wi·ly, *a.* sly; cunning.

win, *v.*, **won, win·ning.** gain a victory; gain by effort; succeed; persuade. *n.* success.

wince, *v.*, **winced, winc·ing.** shrink back; flinch. *n.* act of wincing.

winch, *n.* windlass; hoisting machine. *v.*

wind, *n.* moving air; breath; idle talk; *pl.* wind instruments. *v.* exhaust breath of; get scent of.

wind, *v.*, **wound, wind·ing.** coil; crank; change direction; twist; turn. *n.* turn or twist.

wind·chill fac·tor, *n.* effect of wind in reducing actual air temperature.

wind·ed, *a.* out of breath.

wind·fall, *n.* unexpected thing.

wind·ing, *n.* turning; coiling.

wind in·stru·ment, *n.* musical instrument played by breath.

wind·lass, *n.* hoisting device.

wind·mill, *n.* machine operated by the wind to produce energy.

win·dow, *n.* opening in the wall; envelope window-like opening.

win·dow·pane, *n.* pane of glass in a window.

wind·pipe, *n.* trachea.

wind·shield, *n.* front protective shield of glass in a vehicle.

wind·up, *n.* conclusion; ending.

wind·ward, *n.* direction from which the wind blows. *adv.* direction toward the wind.

wind·y, *a.*, **-i·er, -i·est.** stormy; tempestuous; verbose.

wine, *n.* fermented grape juice.

win·er·y, *n. pl.*, **-ies.** place where wine is made.

wing, *n.* one of two bird appendages adapted for flight; main supporting surface(s) of an airplane.

wink, *v.* close and open eyelid rapidly; blink; flicker; twinkle. *n.* winking; an instant.

win·ner, *n.* one who wins.

win·ning, *n.* victory; conquest; *usu. pl.* thing won. *a.* successful; winsome; attractive.

win·now, *v.* separate grain from chaff; analyze; sift.

win·some, *a.* engaging; charming; attractive.

win·ter, *n.* coldest season of the year. *a.* relating to time between fall and spring. *v.* pass the winter.

win·ter·ize, *v.*, **-ized, -iz·ing.** prepare or put in condition for winter.

win·try, *a.*, **-tri·er, -tri·est.** of or like winter; cold, bleak, cheerless.

wipe, *v.*, **wiped, wip·ing.** rub lightly; clean by rubbing lightly. *n.* act of wiping.

wire, *n.* flexible metal thread; thing made of wire; finish line of race; telegram. *v.*, **wired, wir·ing.** fasten or equip with wire.

wire·tap, *n.* concealed device connected to telephone, etc. to listen to or record messages. *v.*, **-tapped, -tap·ping.** connect or use a wiretap.

wir·y, *a.*, **-i·er, -i·est.** lean but tough and sinewy; like wire.

wis·dom, *n.* knowledge; insight; sound judgment; common sense.

wise, *a.*, **wis·er, wis·est.** having or showing insight, common sense, knowledge; shrewd; learned.

wise·acre, *n.* person who claims to know everything.

wise·crack, *n. inf.* smart, insolent remark; jest; witticism.

wish, *v.* long for; desire; invoke upon. *n.* want; mandate.

wish·ful, *a.* desirous; hopeful.

wish·y-wash·y, *a.* lacking in purpose, effectiveness, etc; diluted.

wisp, *n.* small bunch, as hay; a small bit; slight; delicate. **-y,** *a.*

wist·ful, *a.* yearning; pensive.

wit, *n.* intelligence; common sense; one who can make amusing remarks, etc; humor.

witch, *n.* one with supernatural power; hag. *v.* beguile; bewitch. **-craft,** *n.*

with, *prep.* in the company of; among; having, wearing, etc; by means of; in relation, proportion to; in the same direction, time, etc; against; in spite of.

with·draw, *v.,* **-drew, -drawn, -draw·ing.** pull or back out; remove; retract; retreat.

with·draw·al, *n.* act of withdrawing; process of overcoming drug addiction.

with·drawn, *a.* not responsive; introverted; isolated; remote.

with·er, *v.* become limp or dry; waste away; abash. **-ered,** *a.* **-er·ing,** *a.*

with·hold, *v.,* **-held, -hold·ing.** hold back; deduct; restrain; refuse to grant.

with·in, *prep.* inside of; not exceeding; not beyond. *adv.* inner part; internally.

with·out, *prep.* outside of; beyond; lacking; not having. *adv.* externally.

with·stand, *v.,* **-stood, -stand·ing.** resist; oppose; endure.

wit·less, *a.* foolish.

wit·ness, *n.* person or thing able to give evidence; testimony. *v.* perceive; give evidence; testify; give proof.

wit·ti·cism, *n.* clever remark.

wit·ting·ly, *adv.* aware; intentional.

wit·ty, *a.,* **-ti·er, -ti·est.** full of wit; cleverly humorous.

wiz·ard, *n.* magician; *inf.* skillful, clever person. **-ry,** *n.*

wiz·ened, *a.* shriveled; dried up.

wob·ble, *v.,* **-bled, -bling.** vacillate; sway unsteadily; show indecision. *n.* wavering. **bly,** *a.*

woe, *n.* grief; affliction; trouble.

woe·be·gone, *a.* sorrowful; dejected.

woe·ful, wo·ful, *a.* piteous.

wok, *n.* Chinese stir-fry cooking bowl.

wolf, *n. pl.,* **wolves.** wild carnivorous mammal; *inf.* man who pursues women. *v.* gulp down.

wom·an, *n. pl.,* **-en.** adult human female. **hood,** *n.*

wom·an·kind, *n.* all women.

womb, *n.* uterus.

wom·en's rights, *n. pl.* legal rights of women, equal to men.

won·der, *v.* be curious; marvel; speculate. *n.* surprising thing; miracle; cause of astonishment; feeling of surprise.

won·der·ful, *a.* marvelous.

won·drous, *a.* extraordinary.

wont, *a.* accustomed. *n.* habit.

won't, contraction of *will not.*

won·ton, *n.* casings of filled noodle dough used in Chinese cooking.

woo *v.,* **wood, woo·ing.** court; solicit; seek; entreat; coax.

wood, *n.* hard fibrous substance under a tree's bark; thick growth of trees.

wood·craft, *n.* skill in making anything from wood; skill in surviving in woods.

wood·cut, *n.* block of engraved wood for making prints.

wood·en, *a.* made of wood; stiff; without expression.

wood·land, *n.* land covered with trees; forest.

wood·peck·er, *n.* bird that drills holes into wood for insects.

wood·pile, *n.* stack of cut wood.

wood·wind, *n.* wind instrument.

wood·work, *n.* things made of wood; home's interior wooden fittings.

wood·y, *a.,* **-i·er, -i·est.** abounding with trees. **-i·ness,** *n.*

wool, *n.* fiber from fleece of sheep; cloth made of wool. **wool·en,** *a.*

wool·gath·er·ing, *n.* idle daydreaming; absent-mindedness.

wool·ly, wool·y, *a.,* **-li·er, -li·est.** consisting of or like wool; fuzzy; indistinct. Also **wolly.**

wooz·y, *a.,* **-i·er, -i·est.** befuddled, esp. with drink.

word, *n.* speech sound or combination of sounds; discourse; talk; command; promise. *v.* express in words; phrase.

word·ing, *n.* arrangement or style of expression; phraseology.

word·less, *a.* silent; unexpressed; mute. **ly,** *adv.*

word·y, *a.,* **-i·er, -i·est.** verbose. **-i·ly,** *adv.* **i·ness,** *n.*

work, *n.* labor; occupation; task; thing done; result; place employed. *v.* labor; be employed; operate; cause; achieve by effort.

work·a·ble, *a.* practical; feasible.

work·a·day, *a.* commonplace.

work·book, *n.* consumable textbook; manual; handbook.

worked-up, *a.* aroused; excited.

work·ing, *a.* actively employed; thing that works. *n.* act of working.

work·ing class, *n. pl.,* **class·es.** people who work for wages; proletariat. **work·ing-class,** *a.*

work·man, *n. pl.,* **-men.** manual or industrial laborer; artisan.

work·man·like, *a.* skillful.

work·out, *n.* strenuous activity; exercise.

work·shop, *n.* place one works; intensive study group.

world, *n.* the earth; area or sphere of existence; mankind; *often pl.* large quantity.

world·ly, *a.,* **-li·er, -li·est.** secular; temporal; earthly. **-li·ness,** *n.*

world-wide, *a.* extending throughout the world.

worm, *n.* long, soft-bodied invertebrate; insect larva. *v.* insinuate; grovel; purge of worms.

worm-eat-en, *a.* eaten through by worms; decayed.

worn, *a. pp.* of *wear*. exhausted; impaired by wear.

worn-out, *a.* exhausted; useless.

wor-ri-some, *a.* causing worry or anxiety.

wor-ry, *v.*, **-ried, -ry-ing.** be uneasy, anxious; fret; bother, pester. *n. pl.*, **-ries.** uneasiness; anxiety.

worse, *a.*, *compar.* of *bad* and *ill*. less favorable; in poorer health; inferior. *n.* that which is worse. *adv.* more evil; with greater severity.

wors-en, *v.* become worse.

wor-ship, *n.* religious ritual; adoration; homage; loving devotion. *v.* to worship, idolize.

worst, *a.*, *superl.* of *bad* and *ill*. bad or ill to the highest degree; least favorable; most evil, corrupt, faulty. *n.* worst condition. *adv.* to the worst degree, greatest intensity.

wor-sted, *n.* fabric made from finely twisted wool yarn.

worth, *n.* value; excellence; wealth. *a.* equal in value; deserving of. **-less,** *a.*

worth-while, *a.* of enough value to repay the effort.

wor-thy, *a.*, **-thi-er, -thi-est.** meritorious; valuable; deserving praise. **-thi-ly,** *adv.* **-thi-ness,** *n.*

would, *aux. v. past* and *pp.* of *will*. used to convey: wish; condition; futurity; determination.

would-be, *a.* desiring, professing, or intended to be.

would-n't, contraction of *would not*.

wound, *n.* injury; cut in the skin; hurt feelings. *v.* inflict a wound; hurt the feelings or pride of.

wow, *int. inf.* exclamation of pleasure, surprise. *v.* please greatly; excite.

wrack, *n.* ruin. *v.* wreck.

wraith, *n.* ghost; apparition.

wran-gle, *v.*, **-gled, -gling.** brawl; argue; herd livestock. *n.* angry dispute. **-gler,** *n.*

wrap, *v.*, **wrapped, wrap-ping.** fold around; enclose; bundle; embrace; engross. *n. pl.* outside attire; secrecy.

wrap-up, *n. inf.* summary; conclusion; final event.

wrath, *n.* violent rage; fury.

wreak, *v.* inflict or exact, as vengeance; give vent to.

wreath, *n.* band, as of flowers.

wreck, *n.* destruction; something disabled; person in poor health. *v.* cause the ruin of; damage badly; demolish. **-age,** *n.*

wreck-er, *n.* machine or person which demolishes; salvager.

wrench, *n.* violent twist; emotional shock; tool for turning pipes, nuts, or bolts. *v.* twist; turn; sprain.

wrest, *v.* twist; seize; distort the meaning of.

wres-tle, *v.*, **-tled, -tling.** contend by grappling; struggle; combat.

wretch, *n.* miserable person.

wretch-ed, *a.* miserable; despicable; dejected; very poor.

wrig-gle, *v.*, **-gled, -gling.** squirm; writhe; evade. *n.* quick twisting motion; contortion.

wring, *v.*, **wrung, wring-ing.** compress by twisting; twist violently; acquire forcibly. *n.* twisting.

wrin-kle, *n.* small crease or fold; new method. *v.*, **-kled, -kling.**

wrist, *n.* joint between the hand and arm; carpus.

writ, *n.* written court order.

write, *v.* **wrote, writ-ten, writ-ing.** to inscribe words, as on paper; to set down, describe in words by writing; communicate; produce by writing.

write-off, *n.* thing cancelled as a loss.

writ-er, *n.* author; journalist.

write-up, *n.* description; review.

writhe, *v.*, **writhed, writh-ing.** twist or distort the body. *n.*

writ-ing, *n.* written; composition; literary work.

wrong, *a.* immoral; improper; not right; inaccurate. *n.* unjust act; harm, injury. *adv.* incorrectly. *v.* treat with injustice; violate; malign.

wronged, *a.* harmed unjustly.

wroth, *a.* very angry; riled.

wrought, *a.* fashioned; formed; decorated; shaped by tools; excited.

wry, *a.*, **wri-er, wri-est.** contorted; askew; warped; ironic. **wried, wrying** *v.* twist; contort.

X-Y-Z

xan-thous, *a.* yellow.

X-chro-mo-some, *n.* female sex chromosome.

xen-o-pho-bi-a, *n.* dislike or fear of foreigners or strangers.

Xmas, *n.* Christmas.

x-ray, *n.* electromagnetic radiations used in medical diagnosis. *v.*

xy·lo·phone, *n.* percussion instrument of wooden bars struck with mallets. **-phon·ist**, *n.*

yacht, *n.* relatively small sailing or motor ship for pleasure or racing. **yacht·ing**, *n.* **yachts·man**, *n.*

yak, *n. pl.*, **yaks, yak.** large, long-haired Tibetan ox. *v. inf.* chatter; boisterous laugh.

yam, *n.* sweet potato.

yank, *v.* jerk. *n.* sharp pull.

Yan·kee, *n.* New England inhabitant; native of northern U·S. states; northern soldier in the American Civil War; U·S. native.

yap, *v.*, **yapped, yap·ping.** bark or yelp; *n. inf.* worthless talk.

yard, *n.* unit of length (3 feet); small area adjacent to a building; plot. **-age**, *n.*

yard·age, *n.* amount in yards.

yard goods, *n.* fabrics.

yard·stick, *n.* measuring stick 3 feet long; criterion.

yarn, *n.* spun fiber, as wool, etc; *inf.* story or tale.

yaw, *v.* swerve or move wildly, as a ship; deviate. *n.* deviation.

yawl, *n.* ship's small boat; small sailboat.

yawn, *v.* open mouth involuntarily with a full inhalation, as from drowsiness.

Y-chro·mo·some, *n.* male sex chromosome.

yea, *adv.* yes. *n.* yes vote.

year, *n.* 365 days; 12 months from Jan. 1 to Dec. 31. **-ly**, *a.*, *adv.*

year·ling, *n.* animal between one and two years old.

yearn, *v.* desire; long for. **-ing**, *n.*

yeast, *n.* fungus used to ferment liquor, leaven bread, etc. **-y**, *a.*, **-i·er**, **-i·est.**

yell, *v.* shout loudly; scream.

yel·low, *a.* color of butter, lemons, etc; sallow; cheap; *inf.* cowardly. **-ish**, *a.*

yel·low·jack·et, *n.* yellow-striped social wasp.

yelp, *v.* utter a sharp, shrill cry. *n.* sharp bark or cry.

yen, *n. inf.* ardent desire, urge.

yeo·man, *n. pl.*, **-men.** petty officer in the Navy; small independent farmer.

yes, *adv.* expression of consent or affirmation.

ye·shi·va, *n. pl.*, **-vas.** Jewish educational institution.

yes·man, *n. inf.* person who habitually agrees with others; esp. his superiors.

yes·ter·day, *n.* day before today; the near past.

yet, *adv.* still; in addition; besides; even; further; nevertheless. *conj.* however; but.

yew, *n.* evergreen tree, shrub.

yield, *v.* produce; give up; submit; relent; surrender. *n.* that which is produced.

yield·ing, *a.* productive; flexible; obedient; unresisting.

yip, *v.*, **yipped, yip·ping.** yelp.

yo·del, *v.*, **-deled, -del·ing.** sing by changing to and from a falsetto voice. *n.* **-er**, *n.*

yo·ga, *n.* Hindu discipline of physical and mental exercises to gain spiritual illumination.

yo·gi, *n. pl.*, **-gis.** a person who practices or teaches yoga.

yo·gurt, *n.* fermented semifluid milk product.

yoke, *n.* wooden frame to couple draft animals; a tie or bond. *v.*, **yoked, yok·ing.** unite; join.

yo·kel, *n.* country bumpkin.

yolk, *n.* yellow part of an egg.

Yom Kip·pur, *n.* Jewish Day of Atonement, marked by prayer and fasting.

yon·der, *adv.* there. *a.*

yore, *n.* time long past.

you, *pron.* person or persons addressed.

you'd, contraction of *you had* or *you would.*

you'll, contraction of *you will* or *you shall.*

young, *a.* in early period of life; new; immature; junior. *n.* youth, collectively; offspring.

young·ster, *n.* child.

your, *pron. a.* possessive of *you.* **yours**, *pron.*

your·self, *pron. pl.*, **-selves.** emphatic or reflexive form of *you.*

youth, *n. pl.*, **youth, youths.** period between childhood and adulthood; a young person; young people collectively. **-ful**, *a.*

yowl, *v.* howl; yell. *n.*

yo-yo, *n.* grooved, double-disk toy with string.

yuc·ca, *n.* tropical American plant with sword-shaped leaves.

yule, *n.* Christmas.

yule·tide, *n.* Christmas time.

yum·my, *a.*, **-mi·er**, **-mi·est.** *inf.* delicious; tasty; palatable.

za·ny, *n. pl.*, **-nies.** clown; buffoon. *a.*, **-ni·er**, **-ni·est.** absurd; silly. **-ni·ly**, *adv.* **-ni·ness**, *n.*

zap, *v. inf.* kill; clobber; overwhelm. *n.* vitality; an attack.

zeal, *n.* ardor; earnestness; fervor; spirit. **-ous**, *a.*

zeal·ot, *n.* fanatic; partisan.

zeal·ous, *a.* enthusiastic; hard-working.

ze·bra, *n. pl.*, **-bras, -bra.** wild, striped, horselike animal.

Zen, *n.* Buddhism sect.

ze·nith, *n.* point of the heavens directly overhead; highest point; acme; summit.

zeph·yr, *n.* the west wind; any gentle breeze.

zep·pe·lin, *n.* large, cigar-shaped, rigid dirigible.

ze·ro, *n. pl.,* **-ros, -roes.** symbol or number that indicates the absence of quantity; nothing; lowest point. *a.* of, at, or being zero.

ze·ro hour, *n.* starting time; crisis point.

zest, *n.* relish; enjoyment; piquancy; taste. **-y,** *a.*

zig·zag, *n.* line with short sharp turns and angles. *a., adv.* in a zigzag manner. *v.,* **-zagged, -zag·ging.** move in zigzags.

zilch, *n. inf.* zero; nothing.

zinc, *n.* bluish metallic element used in alloys, batteries.

zing, *n. inf.* sharp, high-pitched humming noise; energy; vigor.

zin·ni·a, *n.* plant with showy, long-lasting flowers.

zip, *n. inf.* hissing sound, as a bullet; *inf.* vim. *v.,* **zipped, zip·ping.** *inf.* move speedily.

zipcode, *n.* 5- or 9-digit number identifying (U·S·) postal delivery area.

zip·per, *n.* slide fastener with interlocking teeth. **zip,** *v.,* **zipped, zip·ping.**

zip·py, *a.,* **-pi·er, -pi·est.** energetic; brisk; snappy; peppy.

zith·er, *n.* stringed, musical instrument played by plucking.

zo·di·ac, *n.* imaginary circular belt of the heavens; astrological diagram of zodiac signs.

zom·bie, zom·bi, *n.* reanimated corpse; *inf.* persoon who behaves mechanically.

zone, *n.* area; subdivision; region. *v.,* **zoned, zon·ing.** divide into zones. **zon·al,** *a.*

zoo, *n. pl.,* **zoos.** collection of living animals for display.

zo·ol·o·gy, *n.* science of animals. **zo·ol·o·gist,** *n.* **zo·o·log·i·cal,** *a.*

zoom, *v.* speed sharply upward; move with loud hum or buzz; increase greatly; adjust rapidly.

zuc·chi·ni, *n. pl.,* **-ni, -nis.** green, slender summer squash.

zwie·back, *n.* dried, toasted sweet bread.

zy·gote, *n.* product of the union of a male and female gamete.

Linear Measure

Unit	U.S. equivalent
square millimeter (mm²)	0.00155 square inch
square centimeter (cm²)	0.155 square inch
centare (ca)	10.76 square feet
or square meter (m²)	
deciare (da)	11.96 square yards
aretare (a)	119.60 square yards
or square dekameter (dkm²)	
dekare (dka)	0.247 acre
hectare (ha)	2.471 acres
or square hectometer (hm²)	
square kilometer (km²)	0.386 square mile

Area

Unit	U.S. equivalent
micron (μ)	0.00003937 inch, 0.03937 mil
millimeter (mm)	0.03937 inch, 39.37 mils
centimeter (cm)	0.3937 inch
decimeter (dm)	3.937 inches
meter (m)	39.37 inches
dekameter (dkm)	10.93 yards, 32.81 feet
hectometer (hm)	109.36 yards, 328.1 feet
kilometer (km)	0.6214 mile

Capacity

Unit	U.S. equivalent dry	U.S. equivalent liquid
milliliter (ml)	0.0018 pint	0.034 fluidounce
centiliter (cl)	0.018 pint	0.338 fluidounce
deciliter (dl)	0.18 pint	3.381 fluidounces
liter (l)	0.908 quart	1.057 quarts
dekaliter (dkl)	1.14 pecks	2.643 gallons
hectoliter (hl)	2.84 bushels	26.425 gallons
kiloliter (kl)	28.38 bushels	**264.25 gallons**

Volume

Unit	U.S. equivalent
cubic millimeter (mm³)	0.000061 cubic inch, 0.016 minim
cubic centimeter (cm³ or cc)	0.061 cubic inch
cubic decimeter (dm³)	61.02 cubic inches
decistere (ds)	3.53 cubic feet
stere (s) or cubic meter (m³)	1.308 cubic yards, 35.31 cubic feet
dekastere (dks)	13.079 cubic yards
cubic dekameter (dkm³)	1,307.943 cubic yards

Mass and Weight

Unit	U.S. equivalent (*Avoirdupois weight*)
milligram (mg)	0.0154 grain
centigram (cg)	0.154 grain
decigram (dg)	1.543 grains
gram (g or gm)	0.0353 ounce, 15.43 grains
dekagram (dkg)	0.353 ounce
hectogram (hg)	3.527 ounces
kilogram (kg)	2.205 pounds
metric ton (MT or t)	1.102 tons, 2,204.6 pounds

UNIT		
		Avoirdupois
short ton		20 short hundredweight, 2000 lbs.
long ton		20 long hundredweight, 2240 lbs.
short hundredweight		100 lbs., 0.05 short tons
long hundredweight		112 lbs., 0.05 long tons
pound (lb.)		16 oz., 7000 gr.
ounce (oz.)	WEIGHT	16 drams, 437.5 gr.
pennyweight		
dram		27.343 gr., 0.0625 oz.
scruple		
grain (gr.)		0.036 drams, 0.002285 oz.
		U.S. liquid measure
bushel		
peck		
gallon		4 quarts (231 in.^{3})
quart		2 pints (57.75 in.^{3})
pint	CAPACITY	4 gills (28.875 in.^{3})
gill		4 fluidounces (7.218 in.^{3})
fluidounce		8 fluidrams (1.804 in.^{3})
fluidram		60 minims (0.225 in.^{3})
minim		1/60 fluidram (0.003759 in.^{3})
		Volume
cubic yard		27 ft.^{3}, 46,656 in.^{3}
cubic foot		1728 in.^{3}, 0.0370 yd.^{3}
cubic inch		0.00058 ft.^{3}, 0.000021 yd.^{3}
square mile		
acre		
square rod		
square yard	DIMENSION	
square foot		
square inch		
mile		
rod		
yard		
foot		
inch		

UNIT		
		Troy
short ton		
long ton		
short hundredweight		
long hundredweight	**WEIGHT**	
pound (lb.)		12 oz., 240 pennyweight, 5760 gr.
ounce (oz.)		20 pennyweight, 480 gr.
pennyweight		24 gr., 0.05 oz.
dram		
scruple		
grain (gr.)		0.042 pennyweight, 0.002083 oz.
		U.S. dry measure
bushel		4 pecks (2150.42 in.³)
peck		8 quarts (537.605 in.³)
gallon		
quart	**CAPACITY**	2 pints (67.200 in.³)
pint		½ quart (33.600 in.³)
gill		
fluidounce		
fluidram		
minim		
		Area
cubic yard		
cubic foot		
cubic inch		
square mile		640 acres, 102,400 rods²
acre		4840 yd.², 43,560 ft.²
square rod	**DIMENSION**	30.25 yd.², 0.006 acres
square yard		1296 in.², 9 ft.²
square foot		144 in.², 0.111 yd.²
square inch		0.007 ft.², 0.00077 yd.²
mile		
rod		
yard		
foot		
inch		

UNIT		
		Apothecaries'
short ton		
long ton		
short hundredweight	**WEIGHT**	
long hundredweight		
pound (lb.)		12 oz., 5760 gr.
ounce (oz.)		8 drams, 480 gr.
pennyweight		
dram		3 scruples, 60 gr.
scruple		20 gr., 0.333 drams
grain (gr.)		0.05 scruples, 0.002083 oz.
		British liquid and dry measure
bushel		4 pecks (2219.36 in.^{3})
peck		2 gallons (554.84 in.^{3})
gallon		4 quarts (277.420 in.^{3})
quart	**CAPACITY**	2 pints (69.355 in.^{3})
pint		4 gills (34.678 in.^{3})
gill		5 fluidounces (8.669 in.^{3})
fluidounce		8 fluidrams (1.7339 in.^{3})
fluidram		60 minims (0.216734 in.^{3})
minim		1/60 fluidram (0.003612 in.^{3})
		Length
cubic yard		
cubic foot		
cubic inch		
square mile		
acre		
square rod	**DIMENSION**	
square yard		
square foot		
square inch		
mile		320 rods, 1760 yd., 5280 ft.
rod		5.50 yd., 16.5 ft.
yard		3 ft., 36 in.
foot		12 in., 0.333 yd.
inch		0.083 ft., 0.027 yd.

WORD PREFIXES, SUFFIXES, AND ROOTS

Following are some of the important word prefixes used in English. The prefix is indicated in boldface type followed by the basic meaning of the prefix. Examples of the prefixes used in words are given in italic type.

ab-, a-, abs-, away from, *abduct, avert, abstain*

a-, an-, not, less, without, *agnostic, atheist, anarchy*

ad-, a-, ac-, af-, to, toward, *adhere, ascribe, accord, affirm*

ag-, al-, an-, aggressor, *allude, annex*

ap-, ar-, as-, at-, to, toward, *associate, attend*

ante-, before, *antedate, antecedent*

anti-, ant-, against, *antiseptic, antipathy, antacid*

ana-, up, through, throughout, *analysis, anatomy*

be-, by or near, *below, beside*

bene-, good, well, *benevolent, beneficial*

bi-, two, twice, *bicycle, biennial*

circum-, around, all round, *circumstance, circumvent*

com-, con-, col-, together, *combine, confound, collate*

contra-, against, *contradict, contravene*

de-, from, down away, *depart, descend, denude*

dis-, di-, apart, apart from, *distract, divert*

ex-, ef-, e-, out, out of, *export, effect, emit*

hypo-, under, beneath, *hypodermic, hypothesis*

in-, in, into, *intrude, inside, include, insight*

in-, im-, il-, ir-, un-, not, *inactive, im-press, illicit, irresistible, unreal*

inter-, between, *intermingle, interstate*

intra-, intro-, within, *intramural, introduction*

mal-, bad, *malcontent, malnourished*

mis-, wrong, *misdeed, mislead*

non-, not, *nonentity, nonconformist*

ob-, against, *object, objective*

par-, para-, beside, beyond, *paradox, parallel*

per-, through, throughout, *persist, pervade*

peri-, around, *periscope, perimeter*

post-, after, *postpone, postscript*

pre-, before, *prefer, predict*

pro-, before, forward, *prologue, promote, pronoun*

re-, back, again, *refer, report, review*

retro-, backward, *retroactive, retrogress*

se-, apart, *seduce, sedate*

semi-, half, *semicircle, semiconscious*

sub-, under, *submit, subordinate*

super-, supra-, above, over, *supernatural, suprarational*

syn-, sym-, with, *synopsis, symphony, synonym*

trans-, tra-, across, *transfer, traverse*

un-, not, reversal of action, *uncovered, untie*

uni-, single, *unity, universal*

vice-, instead of, *vice-president, vice-consul*

with-, against, back, *withdraw, withhold*

Word Suffixes

Following are some of the important word suffixes used in English. The suffix is indicated in boldface type followed by the basic meaning of the suffix. Examples of the suffixes used in words are given in italic type.

-able, -ible, -ble, capable of being, as *bearable, reversible, voluble*

-ac, -ic, pertaining to, as *cardiac, angelic*

-ac, -ic, condition or quality of, as *maniac, mechanic*

-acious, characterized by, as *pugnacious, tenacious*

-acity, quality of, as *tenacity, veracity*

-acy, having the quality of, as *accuracy, fallacy*

-age, collection of, state of being, as *garbage, marriage, storage*

-al, -el, -le, pertaining to, as *fanatical, novel, single*

-an, -ian, belonging to, one who, as *American, physician, historian*

-ance, relating to, as *reliance, distance*

-ancy, -ency, denoting state or quality, as *occupancy, dependency*

-ant, -ent, one who, as *tenant, correspondent*

-ar, -ary, ory, relating to, as *popular, dictionary, mandatory*

-ate, act, as *mandate, confiscate*

-ation, action, as *elation*, *separation*

-cle, -ule, -ling, diminutive, as *article*, *globule*, *suckling*

-cracy, rule, as democracy, autocracy

-cy, quality, as *idiocy*, *ascendency*

-dom, state of being, as *freedom*, *kingdom*

-ee, one who is acted upon, as *employee*, *trustee*

-ence, relating to, as *confidence*, *abstinence*

-er, -or, -ar, one who, as *butler*, *actor*, *scholar*

-ful, abounding in, as *grateful*, *sinful*

-fy, -efy, -ify, to make, as *deify*, *liquefy*, *solidify*

-hood, condition, as *fatherhood*, *falsehood*

-ic, pertaining to, as *historic*, *democratic*

-ice, act of, as *justice*, *police*, *practice*

-il, -ile, pertaining to, capable of being, as *civil*, *juvenile*, *mobile*

-ity, -ty, state or condition, as *sanity*, *acidity*, *safety*

-ious, full of, as *laborious*, *rebellious*

-ist, one who, as *pianist*, *machinist*

-ity, ty, state or condition, as *sanity*, *acidity*, *safety*

-ize, -yze, to make like, as *sympathize*, *analyze*

-less, without, as *careless*, *needless*, *hopeless*

-ly, manner, like, as *bodily*, *truthfully*

-ment, result, as *management*, *fragment*

-meter, measurement, as *thermometer*, *hydrometer*

-ness, state of being, as *sickness*, *happiness*

-nomy, pertaining to laws or government, distribution, arrangement, as *economy*, *harmony*, *astronomy*

-ory, place where, as *directory*, *rectory*

-ous, -ious, -eous, -uous, full of, as *dangerous*, *melodious*, *beauteous*, *strenuous*

-ose, full of, as *morose*, *verbose*

-ship, state or quality, as *friendship*, *worship*

-some, like, full of, as *gruesome*, *tiresome*

-ster, one who, person doing something, as *gangster*, *songster*

-sion, -tion, act or state of being, as *conception*, *perception*

-tude, condition, as *fortitude*, *magnitude*

-ty, ity, condition, as *clarity*, *peculiarity*, *sanity*

-ule, little, as *globule*, *granule*

-ure, act of, as *departure*, *manufacture*

-ward, direction of course, as *backward*, *forward*, *downward*

-y, full of, characterized by, as *filthy*, *icy*, *soapy*

Latin and Greek Word Roots

Following are Latin and Greek word roots which are used in English words. Word roots give the word its basic meaning, whereas prefixes or suffixes modify or change the root word. The root word is given in bold face type followed by the meaning of the root. Examples of the roots are printed in italic type. Many word roots are generally used only as prefixes or suffixes. However, as you examine the examples, you will note that many appear at the beginning, in the middle, or at the end of the English word.

aero, air, as *aerodynamics*, *aerospace*

ag, ac, to do, as *agenda*, *action*

agr, agri, agro, farm, as *agriculture*, *agronomy*

anthropo, man, as *anthropology*, *anthropoid*, *misanthrope*

aqua, water, as *aqueous*, *aquatic*

arch, rule, principle, chief, as *archbishop*, *archenemy*, *anarchy*

astra, astro, star, as *astronomy*, *astral*, *astronomical*

aud, audi, audio, hearing, as *audience*, *auditor*, *audiovisual*

auto, self, oneself, as *automatic*, *autograph*

biblio, bib, book, as *bibliophile*, *Bible*

bio, life, as *biology*, *biosphere*

cad, cas, fall, as *cadence*, *cascade*, *casual*

cant, sing, as *cantata*, *chant*

cap, cep, take, as *captive*, *accept*

capit, head, as *capital*, *capitate*

cat, cath, down, through, as *cataract*, *catheter*

ced, cess, go, yield, as *procedure*, *cession*, *antecedent*

cide, cis, kill, cut, as *suicide*, *excise*, *incision*

clud, clus, close, as *include*, *inclusion*, *preclude*

cred, believe, as *creditor*, *creditable*, *creed*

dec, ten, as *decimal*

dem, people, as *democracy*, *demagogue*

dent, tooth, as *indent*, *dental*

derm, skin, as *dermatology, taxidermist*

dic, dict, say, speak, as *diction, dictate, predicate*

duc, lead, as *induce, ductile*

equ, equal, as *equivalent, equitable, equality*

fac, fec, make, do, as *manufacture, infection*

fring, break as *infringement*

fract break as *fracture, fractious*

frater, brother, as *fraternal, fraternize*

fund, fus, pour as *refund, confuse*

gam, gamos marriage as *monogamous, bigamist, polygamous*

gen, produce as *generate, generation*

geo, earth as *geology, geometry, geography*

gastro, gast, stomach as *gastronomy, gastritis*

greg, group as *gregarious*

gress, grad walking, moving as *progress, degrade, retrograde*

gyn, woman as *gynecologist*

hemo, blood, as *hemorrhage, hemorroid*

homo, man, same as *homocide, homogeneous*

hydr, water as *dehydrate, hydralic*

idio, own, private, as *idiocy, idiosyncrasy*

iso, equal as *isothermal, isomorph*

ject, throw as *reject, project*

jud, jur, right as *judge, jury*

logy, study of as *psychology, biology*

loqu, speak as *loquacious, eloquent*

mand, order as *remand, command, demand*

manu, hand as *manuscript, manual*

mater, mother as *maternal, matricide*

meter, measure, as *thermometer, barometric*

micro, small as *microscopic, microbe*

mit, mis send as *permit, commission*

mono, mon, single, one as *monotony, monogram, monarch*

mort, death as *mortician, mortal*

nom, law as *economy, astronomy*

onym, name as *synonym, pseudonym*

pathos, feeling as *pathology, pathos*

philo, love as *philosophy, philosophical*

phobia, fear as *claustrophobia, hydrophobia*

porto, carry as *portable, export, report, transport*

pseudo, false as *pseudonym, pseudo*

psych, mind as *psychiatry, psychic, psychology*

scope, see as *telescope, microscope*

scrib, write as *inscription, description*

sec, cut as *dissect, bisect, resection*

sens, feel as *sensuous, sensitive*

sequ, follow as *sequence, inconsequent*

spec, spect, look as *specimen, inspect, spectacular*

spir, breath as *inspire, respiratory*

state, stand as *status, statutory*

ten, hold as *retention, detention*

term, end as *terminal, interminable*

typ, print as *typography, typewriter*

ven, vent, come as *prevent, convene, adventure*

vert, vers, turn as *divert, subversion, controversy*

vict, conquer as *evict, victim*

vid, vis, see as *video, visual, revise*

voc, call as *vocal, vocation*

TABLE OF SQUARES, CUBES, SQUARE ROOTS, AND CUBE ROOTS

No.	Square	Cube	Square Root	Cube Root	No.	Square	Cube	Square Root	Cube Root
1	1	1	1.000	1.000	51	2,601	132,651	7.141	3.708
2	4	8	1.414	1.260	52	2,704	140,608	7.211	3.732
3	9	27	1.732	1.442	53	2,809	148,877	7.280	3.756
4	16	64	2.000	1.587	54	2,916	157,464	7.348	3.780
5	25	125	2.236	1.710	55	3,025	166,375	7.416	3.803
6	36	216	2.449	1.817	56	3,136	175,616	7.483	3.826
7	49	343	2.646	1.913	57	3,249	185,193	7.550	3.848
8	64	512	2.828	2.000	58	3,364	195,112	7.616	3.871
9	81	729	3.000	2.080	59	3,481	205,379	7.681	3.893
10	100	1,000	3.162	2.154	60	3,600	216,000	7.746	3.915
11	121	1,331	3.317	2.224	61	3,721	226,981	7.810	3.936
12	144	1,728	3.464	2.289	62	3,844	238,328	7.874	3.958
13	169	2,197	3.606	2.351	63	3,969	250,047	7.937	3.979
14	196	2,744	3.742	2.410	64	4,096	262,144	8.000	4.000
15	225	3,375	3.873	2.466	65	4,225	274,625	8.062	4.021
16	256	4,096	4.000	2.520	66	4,356	287,496	8.124	4.041
17	289	4,913	4.123	2.571	67	4,489	300,763	8.185	4.061
18	324	5,832	4.243	2.621	68	4,624	314,432	8.246	4.082
19	361	6,859	4.359	2.668	69	4,761	328,509	8.307	4.101
20	400	8,000	4.472	2.714	70	4,900	343,000	8.367	4.121
21	441	9,261	4.583	2.759	71	5,041	357,911	8.426	4.141
22	484	10,648	4.690	2.802	72	5,184	373,248	8.485	4.160
23	529	12,167	4.796	2.844	73	5,329	389,017	8.544	4.179
24	576	13,824	4.899	2.884	74	5,476	405,224	8.602	4.198
25	625	15,625	5.000	2.924	75	5,625	421,875	8.660	4.217
26	676	17,576	5.099	2.962	76	5,776	438,976	8.718	4.236
27	729	19,683	5.196	3.000	77	5,929	456,533	8.775	4.254
28	784	21,952	5.292	3.037	78	6,084	474,552	8.832	4.273
29	841	24,389	5.385	3.072	79	6,241	493,039	8.888	4.291
30	900	27,000	5.477	3.107	80	6,400	512,000	8.944	4.309
31	961	29,791	5.568	3.141	81	6,561	531,441	9.000	4.327
32	1,024	32,768	5.657	3.175	82	6,724	551,368	9.055	4.344
33	1,089	35,937	5.745	3.208	83	6,889	571,787	9.110	4.362
34	1,156	39,304	5.831	3.240	84	7,056	592,704	9.165	4.379
35	1,225	42,875	5.916	3.271	85	7,225	614,125	9.219	4.397
36	1,296	46,656	6.000	3.302	86	7,396	636,056	9.274	4.414
37	1,369	50,653	6.083	3.332	87	7,569	658,503	9.327	4.431
38	1,444	54,872	6.164	3.362	88	7,744	681,472	9.381	4.448
39	1,521	59,319	6.245	3.391	89	7,921	704,969	9.434	4.465
40	1,600	64,000	6.325	3.420	90	8,100	729,000	9.487	4.481
41	1,681	68,921	6.403	3.448	91	8,281	753,571	9.539	4.498
42	1,764	74,088	6.481	3.476	92	8,464	778,688	9.592	4.514
43	1,849	79,507	6.557	3.503	93	8,649	804,357	9.644	4.531
44	1,936	85,184	6.633	3.530	94	8,836	830,584	9.695	4.547
45	2,025	91,125	6.708	3.557	95	9,025	857,375	9.747	4.563
46	2,116	97,336	6.782	3.583	96	9,216	884,736	9.798	4.579
47	2,209	103,823	6.856	3.609	97	9,409	912,673	9.849	4.595
48	2,304	110,592	6.928	3.634	98	9,604	941,192	9.899	4.610
49	2,401	117,649	7.000	3.659	99	9,801	970,299	9.950	4.626
50	2,500	125,000	7.071	3.684	100	10,000	1,000,000	10.000	4.642

METRICATION TABLES

Conversion to Metric Units	Conversion from Metric Units

LINEAR MEASURE (LENGTH)

To convert	Multiply by	To convert	Multiply by
inches to millimeters	25.4	millimeters to inches	0.039
inches to centimeters	2.54	centimeters to inches	0.394
feet to meters	0.305	meters to feet	3.281
yards to meters	0.914	meters to yards	1.094
miles to kilometers	1.609	kilometers to miles	0.621

SQUARE MEASURE (AREA)

To convert	Multiply by	To convert	Multiply by
sq. inches to sq. centimeters	6.452	sq. centimeters to sq. inches	0.155
sq. feet to sq. meters	0.093	sq. meters to sq. feet	10.764
sq. yards to sq. meters	0.836	sq. meters to sq. yards	1.196
acres to hectares	0.405	hectares to acres	2.471

Conversion to Metric Units	Conversion from Metric Units

CUBIC MEASURE (VOLUME)

To convert	Multiply by	To convert	Multiply by
cu. inches to cu. centimeters	16.387	cu. centimeters to cu. inches	0.061
cu. feet to cu. meters	0.028	cu. meters to cu. feet	35.315
cu. yards to cu. meters	0.765	cu. meters to cu. yards	1.308

LIQUID MEASURE (CAPACITY)

To convert	Multiply by	To convert	Multiply by
fluid ounces to liters	0.03	liters to fluid ounces	33.814
quarts to liters	0.946	liters to quarts	1.057
gallons to liters	3.785	liters to gallons	0.264
imperial gallons to liters	4.546	liters to imperial gallons	0.220

Conversion to Metric Units	Conversion from Metric Units

WEIGHTS (MASS)

To convert	Multiply by	To convert	Multiply by
ounces avoirdupois to grams	28.35	grams to ounces avoirdupois	0.035
pounds avoirdupois to kilograms	0.454	kilograms to pounds avoirdupois	2.205
tons to metric tons	0.907	metric tons to tons	1.102

TEMPERATURE

Fahrenheit thermometer		Celsius (or Centigrade) thermometer
32°F	freezing point of water	0°C
212°F	boiling point of water	100°C
98.6°F	body temperature	37°C

To find degrees Celsius, subtract 32 from degrees Fahrenheit and divide by 1.8.
To find degrees Fahrenheit, multiply degrees Celsius by 1.8 and add 32.

TABLES OF WEIGHTS AND MEASURES

Linear Measure

1 mil = 0.001 inch		=	0.0254 millimeter
1 inch = 1.000 mils		=	2.54 centimeters
12 inches = 1 foot		=	0.3048 meter
3 feet = 1 yard		=	0.9144 meter
5½ yards or 16½ feet = 1 rod (or pole or perch)		=	5.029 meters
40 rods = 1 furlong		=	201.168 meters
8 furlongs or 1,760 yards or 5,280 feet = 1 (statute) mile		=	1.6093 kilometers
3 miles = 1 (land) league		=	4.83 kilometers

Square Measure

1 square inch	=	6.452 square centimeters
144 square inches = 1 square foot	=	929.03 square centimeters
9 square feet = 1 square yard	=	0.8361 square meter
30¼ square yards = 1 square rod	=	25.292 square meters
(or square pole or square perch)		
160 square rods or 4,840 square yards or 43,560 square feet = 1 acre	=	0.4047 hectare
640 acres = 1 square mile	=	259.00 hectares or 2.590 square kilometers

Cubic Measure

1 cubic inch	=	16.387 cubic centimeters
1,728 cubic inches = 1 cubic foot	=	0.0283 cubic meter
27 cubic feet = 1 cubic yard	=	0.7646 cubic meter
(in units for cordwood, etc.)		
16 cubic feet = 1 cord foot	=	0.453 cubic meter
128 cubic feet or = 1 cord	=	3.625 cubic meters
8 cord feet		

Nautical Measure

6 feet = 1 fathom = 1.829 meters
100 fathoms = 1 cable's length (ordinary)
(In the U.S. Navy 120 fathoms or 720 feet, or 219.456 meters) = 1 cable's length
(In the British Navy, 608 feet, or 185.319 meters) = 1 cable's length
10 cable's length = 1 international nautical mile = 1.852 kilometers (exactly)
(6.076.11549 feet, by international agreement)
1 international nautical mile = 1.150779 statute miles (the length of a minute of longitude at the equator)
3 nautical miles = 1 marine league (3.45 statute miles) = 5.56 kilometers
60 nautical miles = 1 degree of a great circle of the earth = 69.047 statute miles

Dry Measure

	1 pint	=	33.60 cubic inches	=	0.5506 liter
2 pints	= 1 quart	=	67.20 cubic inches	=	1.1012 liter
8 quarts	= 1 peck	=	537.61 cubic inches	=	8.8098 liter
4 pecks	= 1 bushel	=	2,150.42 cubic inches	=	35.2390 liters

According to U.S. standards, following are the weights avoirdupois for single bushels of the specified grains: for wheat, 60 pounds; for barley, 48 pounds; for oats, 32 pounds; for rye, 56 pounds; for shelled corn, 56 pounds. Some States have specifications varying from these. The British dry quart = 1.032 U.S. dry quarts

Liquid Measure

1 gill	= 4 fluid ounces	=	7.219 cubic inches	=	0.1183 liter
	(see next table)				
4 gills	= 1 pint	=	28.875 cubic inches	=	0.4732 liter
2 pints	= 1 quart	=	57.75 cubic inches	=	0.9464 liter
4 quarts	= 1 gallon	=	231 cubic inches	=	3.7854 liters

The British imperial gallon (4 imperial quarts) = 277.42 cubic inches = 4.546 liters. The barrel in Great Britain equals 36 imperial gallons, in the United States, usually 31½ gallons.

Tables of Weights and Measures (Con't)

Apothecaries' Fluid Measure

	1 minim	= 0.0038 cubic inch	= 0.0616 milliliter
60 minims	= 1 fluid dram	= 0.2256 cubic inch	= 3.6966 milliliters
8 fluid drams	= 1 fluid ounce	= 1.8047 cubic inches	= 0.0296 liter
16 fluid ounces	= 1 pint	= 28.875 cubic inches	= 0.4732 liter

See table immediately preceeding for quart and gallon equivalents.
The British pint = 20 fluid ounces.

Circular (or Angular) Measure

60 seconds (")	= 1 minute (')
60 minutes	= 1 degree (°)
90 degrees	= 1 quadrant or 1 right angle
180 degrees	= 2 quadrants or 1 straight angle
4 quadrants or 360 degrees	= 1 circle

Avoirdupois Weight

(The grain, equal to 0.0648 gram, is the same in all three tables of weight.)

1 dram or 27.34 grains		= 1.772	grams
16 drams or 437.5 grains	= 1 ounce	= 28.3495	grams
16 ounces or 7,000 grains	= 1 pound	= 453.59	grams
100 pounds	= 1 hundredweight	= 45.36	kilograms
2,000 pounds	= 1 ton	= 907.18	kilograms

In Great Britain, 14 pounds (6.35 kilograms) = 1 stone, 112 pounds (50.80 kilograms) = 1 hundredweight, and 2,240 pounds (1,016.05 kilograms) = 1 long ton.

Troy Weight

(The grain, equal to 0.0648 gram, is the same in all three tables or weight.)

	3.086 grains	= 1 carat	= 200.00	milligrams
	24 grains	= 1 pennyweight	= 1.5552	grams
20 pennyweights or	480 grains	= 1 ounce	= 31.1035	grams
12 ounces or 5,760	grains	= 1 pound	= 373.24	grams

Apothecaries' Weight

(The grain, equal to 0.0648 gram, is the same in all three tables of weight.)

	20 grains	= 1 scruple	1.296 grams
	3 scruples	= 1 dram	3.888 grams
8 drams or 480 grains		= 1 ounce	31.1035 grams
12 ounces or 5,760 grains		= 1 pound	373.24 grams

THE METRIC SYSTEM
Linear Measure

	1 millimeter	= 0.03937	inch
10 millimeters	= 1 centimeter	= 0.3937	inch
10 centimeters	= 1 decimeter	= 3.937	inches
10 decimeters	= 1 meter	= 39.37	inches or 3.2808 feet
10 meters	= 1 decameter	= 393.7	inches
10 decameters	= 1 hectometer	= 328.08	feet
10 hectometers	= 1 kilometer	= 0.621	mile or 3,280.8 feet
10 kilometers	= 1 myriameter	= 6.21	miles

Tables of Weights and Measures (Con't)

Square Measure

	1 square millimeter =	0.00155	square inch
100 square millimeters =	1 square centimeter =	0.15499	square inch
100 square centimeters =	1 square decimeter =	15.499	square inches
100 square decimeters =	1 square meter =	1,549.9	square inches or 1.196 square yards
100 square meters =	1 square decameter =	119.6	square yards
100 square decameters =	1 square hectometer =	2.471	acres
100 square hectometers =	1 square kilometer =	0.386	square mile or 247.1 acres

Land Measure

1 square meter =	1 centiare	=	1,549.9 square inches
100 centiares =	1 are	=	119.6 square yards
100 ares =	1 hectare	=	2.471 acres
100 hectares =	1 square kilometer	=	0.386 square mile or 247.1 acres

Volume Measure

1,000 cubic millimeters =	1 cubic centimeter =	0.06102	cubic inch
1,000 cubic centimeters =	1 cubic decimeter =	61.023	cubic inches or 0.0353 cubic foot
1,000 cubic decimeters =	1 cubic meter =	35.314	cubic feet or 1.308 cubic yards

Capacity Measure

10 milliliters =	1 centiliter =	0.338	fluid ounce
10 centiliters =	1 deciliter =	3.38	fluid ounces or 0.1057 liquid quart
10 deciliters =	1 liter =	1.0567	liquid quarts or 0.9081 dry quart
10 liters =	1 decaliter =	2.64	gallons or 0.284 bushel
10 decaliters =	1 hectoliter =	26.418	gallons or 2.838 bushels
10 hectoliters =	1 kiloliter =	264.18	gallons or 35.315 cubic feet

Weights

10 milligrams =	1 centigram =	0.1543	grain or 0.000353 ounce (avdp.)
10 centigrams =	1 decigram =	1.5432	grains
10 decigrams =	1 gram =	15.432	grains or 0.035274 ounce (avdp.)
10 grams =	1 decagram =	0.3527	ounce
10 decagrams =	1 hectogram =	3.5274	ounces
10 hectograms =	1 kilogram =	2.2046	pounds
10 kilograms =	1 myriagram =	22.046	pounds
10 myriagrams =	1 quintal =	220.46	pounds
10 quintals =	1 metric ton =	2,204.6	pounds

TIME CHANGE

Business today in many industries is done on a worldwide basis. Government and military personnel, too, often must communicate with others in many foreign countries. There is often a need, then, for knowing the time in other locations or other travel itineraries. The listings on the pages which follow will enable you to quickly determine the time in other locations.

In the listing, if all of a country is in one time zone, only the name of the country is given. Where there is more than one zone, the principal cities of the country are given with their time zone.

The *Eastern Standard Time* Zone in the United States is used as a base. If you are in that zone, you only need to add or subtract the number of hours indicated after the name of the country or city whose time you are determining.

For example, if you are in New York or New Jersey or any other Eastern Time Zone area, and wish to know the time in Rome, Italy, look up *Italy*. You will find it has only one time zone indicated as +6. Simply add 6 hours to your time. In other words, if it is 12 o'clock where you are, it is 6 p.m. in Rome.

If you are not in the Eastern Standard Time Zone, follow these steps:

1. In the list, find the name of the country or city *where you are* or near.
2. Reverse the sign given for your location; e.g. change a +3 to a −3. Then add or subtract that number from the actual time where you are.
3. Find the name of the country whose time you wish to know and add or subtract the figure you arrived at in step 2 above.

For example, if you are in San Francisco and wish to know the time in Hong Kong when your time is 2 p.m.:

1. Locate San Francisco in the list.
2. Change the −3 to +3 and then add that amount to your actual time. Your time 2 p.m. plus 3 = 5 p.m.
3. Look up Hong Kong which shows +13. Add that amount to the time from step 2 above: 5 p.m. +13 = 18 or, in other words, it would be 11 a.m. in Hong Kong when the time is 2 p.m. in San Francisco.

Note: If Daylight Savings Time is in effect in your time zone, *subtract* one hour from the result you found by following the steps above. In the example above, you would subtract one hour from 6 a.m. making it 5 a.m. You would then not want to call until after 5 p.m. San Francisco time to reach someone in Hong Kong after 8 a.m.

Afghanistan +9½	Austria +6	Rio de Janeiro +2	Vancouver −3
Algeria +6	Bangladesh +11	Sao Luis +2	Winnipeg −1
Angola +6	Barbados +1	Sao Paulo +2	Central Africa
Argentina +1	Belgium +6	Bulgaria +7	Republic +6
Australia	Bolivia +1	Burma +11½	Chad +6
Adelaide +14½	Botswana +7	Burundi +7	Chile +1
Brisbane +15	Brazil	Cambodia +12	China +13
Canberra +15	Belo Horizonte +2	Cameroon +6	Columbia 0
Darwin +14½	Brasilia +2	Canada	Congo, Rep. of +6
Melbourne +15	Campo Grande +1	Montreal 0	Costa Rica −1
Perth +13	Recife +2	Ottawa 0	Cuba 0
Sydney +15	Pôrto Velho +1	Toronto 0	Cyprus +6

Czechoslovakia +6	Jordan +7	Rumania +7	United States
Dahomey +6	Kenya +8	Samoa, W. −6	Anchorage −5
Denmark +6	Korea +14	Saudia Arabia +9	Atlanta 0
Dominican Rep. 0	Kuwait +8	Senegal +5	Baltimore 0
Ecuador 0	Laos +12	Singapore + $12\frac{1}{2}$	Boston 0
Egypt +7	Lebanon +7	Somalia +8	Buffalo 0
El Salvador −1	Lesotho +7	South Africa +7	Chicago −1
Equatorial	Liberia + $5\frac{3}{4}$	Spain +6	Cincinnati 0
Guinea +6	Libya +7	Sri Lanka + $10\frac{1}{2}$	Cleveland 0
Ethiopia +8	Luxembourg +6	Sudan +7	Columbus 0
Finland +7	Malagasy Rep. +8	Sweden +6	Dallas −1
France +6	Malawi +7	Switzerland +6	Denver −2
Gabon +6	Malasia + $12\frac{1}{2}$	Syria +7	Detroit 0
Gambia +5	Maldive Is. +10	Taiwan +13	Ft. Worth −1
Germany, East +6	Mali +5	Tanzania +8	Honolulu −5
Germany, West +6	Malta +6	Thailand +12	Houston −2
Ghana +5	Mauritania +5	Togo Rep. +5	Indianapolis −1
Greece +7	Mauritius +9	Trinidad and	Kansas City −1
Greenland +2	Mexico	Tobago +1	Memphis −1
Guatemala −1	Guadalajara −1	Tunisia +6	Minneapolis −1
Guinea +5	Mexico City −1	Turkey +7	New York 0
Guyana +2	Monterey −1	Uganda +8	Los Angeles −3
Haiti 0	Mazatlán −2	USSR	Milwaukee −1
Honduras −1	Mongolian Rep. +13	Alma-Ata +11	New Orleans −1
Hong Kong +13	Morocco +5	Baku +9	Oklahoma City −1
Hungary +6	Nepal + $10\frac{1}{2}$	Gorki +9	Phoenix −2
Iceland +4	Netherlands +6	Kharkov +8	Pittsburgh 0
India + $10\frac{1}{2}$	Newfoundland + $1\frac{1}{2}$	Kiev +8	Philadelphia 0
Indonesia	New Zealand +17	Kuybyshev +9	St. Louis −1
Bandung +12	Nicaragua −1	Leningrad +8	San Antonio −1
Djakarta +12	Niger + 6	Minsk +8	San Francisco −3
Irian Jaya +14	Nigeria +6	Moscow +8	Seattle −3
Semarang +13	Nova Scotia +1	Novosibirsk +12	Washington 0
Surabaya +12	Pakistan +10	Odessa +8	Upper Volta +5
Iran + $8\frac{1}{2}$	Panama 0	Omsk +12	Uruguay +2
Iraq +8	Paraguay +1	Perm +12	Venezuela +1
Ireland +6	Peru 0	Rija +8	Vietnam +13
Italy +6	Philippines +13	Rostov +9	Yemen +8
Ivory Coast +5	Poland +6	Tashkent +11	Yugoslavia +6
Jamaica 0	Portugal +6	Vladivostok +15	Zaire
Japan +14	Rhodesia +7	Volgograd +9	Kinshasa +6
		United Kingdom +6	Lumbumbashi +7
			Zambia +7

ROMAN NUMERALS

Roman numerals are not widely used, but used often enough so you should be able to read or interpret them. Following is a table of Arabic numerals and their equivalent Roman Numerals.

Table of Roman Numerals

Arabic Numeral	Roman Numeral	Arabic Numeral	Roman Numeral
1	I	50	L
2	II	60	LX
3	III	70	LXX
4	IV	80	LXXX
5	V	90	XC
6	VI	100	C
7	VII	200	CC
8	VIII	300	CCC
9	IX	400	CD
10	X	500	D
11	XI	600	DC
12	XII	700	DCC
13	XIII	800	DCCC
14	XIV	900	CM
15	XV	1,000	M
16	XVI	4,000	$M\overline{V}$
17	XVII	5,000	$\overline{V}$
18	XVIII	10,000	$\overline{X}$
19	XIX	15,000	$\overline{XV}$
20	XX	20,000	$\overline{XX}$
30	XXX	100,000	$\overline{C}$
40	XL	1,000,000	$\overline{M}$

The following examples illustrate the use and meaning of Roman Numerals.

1. A Roman Numeral or letter preceding *a letter of greater value* subtracts from it:

$$V = 5 \qquad IV = 4$$
$$L = 50 \qquad XL = 40$$
$$C = 100 \qquad XC = 90$$

2. A letter preceding *a letter of equal or lesser value* adds to it.

$$V = 5 \qquad VI = 6$$
$$L = 50 \qquad LX = 60$$
$$C = 100 \qquad CXI = 111$$

3. You will quickly, of course, be able to remember and recognize smaller numbers.

$$XVI = 16$$
$$X (10) + VI (6) = 16$$

$$XLIV = 44$$
$$XL (40) + IV (4) = 44$$

$$XCI = 91$$
$$XC (90) + I (1) = 91$$

For larger numbers simply examine the numbers and break it down into its elements and you will readily interpret the number. You will be able to recognize the elements or parts by applying rules 1 and 2 given above or by looking at the table of Roman Numerals.

$$CDXCIII = 493$$
$$CD\ (400) + XC\ (90) + III\ (3) = 493$$

$$DCXCIX = 699$$
$$DC\ (600) + XC\ (90) + IX\ (9) = 699$$

$$MDCLXXV = 1,675$$
$$M\ (1,000) + DC\ (600) + LXX\ (70) + V\ (5) = 1,675$$

4. A bar over a Roman Numeral multiplies it by 1,000.

$$\overline{MV} = 4,000 \qquad \overline{V} = 5,000$$
$$\overline{XV} = 15,000 \qquad \overline{XX} = 20,000$$

NOTES

NOTES